THE TRAVELS OF
JOHN HECKEWELDER
IN FRONTIER AMERICA

John Heckewelder
Courtesy of the American Philosophical Society

THE TRAVELS OF
John Heckewelder
IN FRONTIER AMERICA

Edited by

PAUL A. W. WALLACE

UNIVERSITY OF PITTSBURGH PRESS

Published by the University of Pittsburgh Press, Pittsburgh, Pa.
Copyright © 1958, Paul A. W. Wallace
All rights reserved
Feffer and Simons, Inc., London
Manufactured in the United States of America
Paperback reprint 1985

No part of the journals printed in this book may be reproduced without the express permission of the Provincial Elders Conference of the Northern Province of the Moravian Church.

Originally published as *Thirty Thousand Miles with John Heckewelder*

Library of Congress Cataloging in Publication Data

Main entry under title:

Travels of John Heckewelder in frontier America.

   Reprint. Originally published: Pittsburgh, Pa.: University of Pittsburgh Press, 1958.
   Includes bibliographical references and index.
   1. United States—Description and travel—To 1783. 2. United States—Description and travel—1783–1848. 3. Indians of North America. 4. Heckewelder, John Gottlieb Ernestus, 1743–1823. I. Wallace, Paul A. W.
E163.T73   1985   917.3044   84-22085
ISBN 0-8229-5369-2 (pbk.)

To
THE RIGHT REVEREND S. H. GAPP
Archivist of the Moravian Church in America, 1948-1957

From John Heckewelder's
DEDICATION
TO
CASPAR WISTAR, M.D.
PRESIDENT OF THE AMERICAN PHILOSOPHICAL SOCIETY, ETC.

... The sure way to obtain correct ideas, and a true knowledge of the characters, customs, manners, &c., of the Indians, and to learn their history, is to dwell among them for some time, and having acquired their language, the information wished for will be obtained in the common way; that is, by paying attention to their discourses with each other on different subjects, and occasionally asking them questions; always watching for the proper opportunity, when they do not suspect your motives, and are disposed to be free and open with you. . . .

November, 1817. JOHN HECKEWELDER.

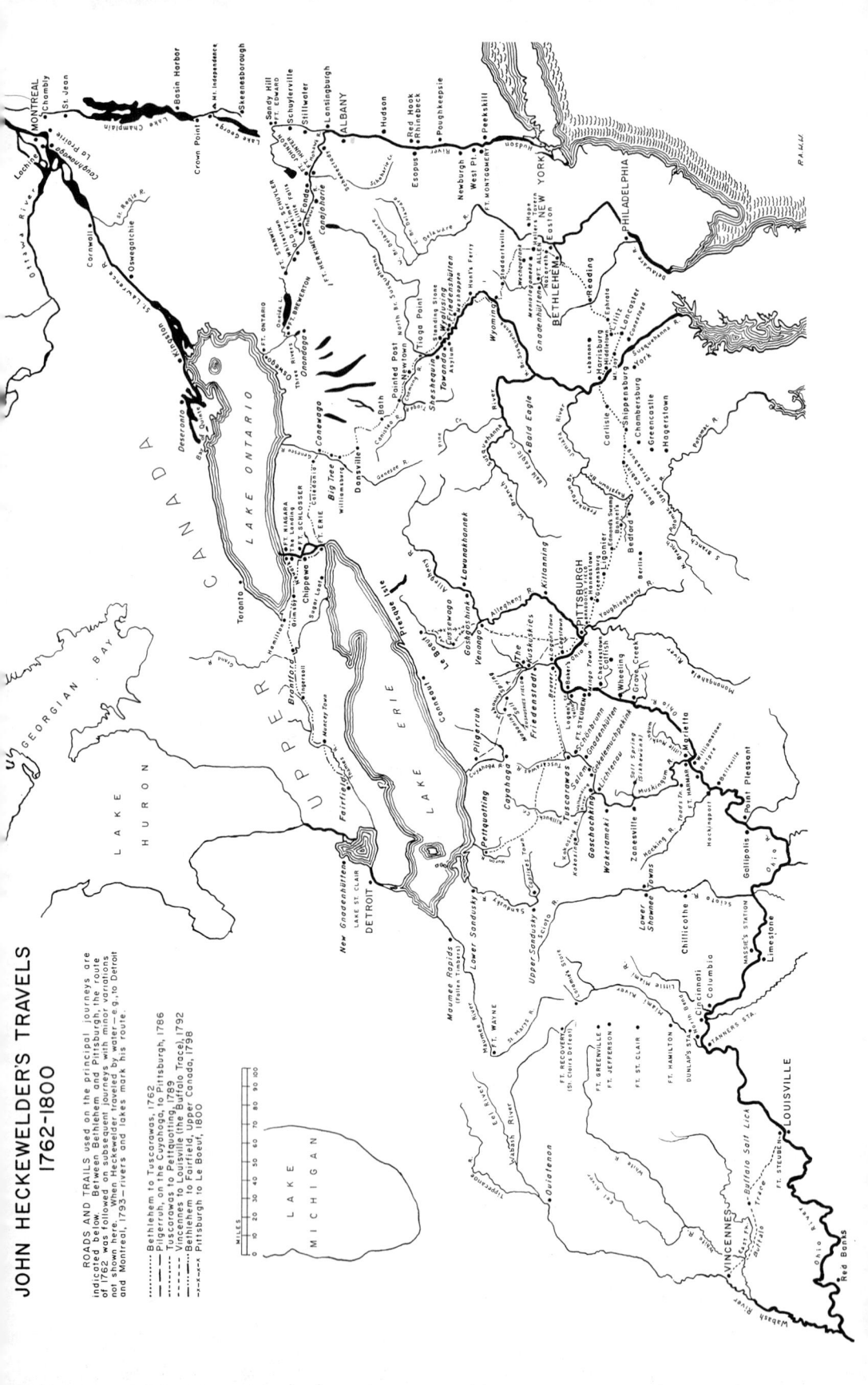

Contents

	Foreword	xi
	Introduction: The Moravians	1
I.	From Bedford, England to Bethlehem, Pennsylvania: 1743-1751	33
II.	The Muskingum in the Shadow of Pontiac's War: 1762	36
III.	The Delawares at Home: 1762	50
IV.	Shingas the Terrible: 1762	57
V.	A Black Cloud Rising: 1762	63
VI.	Philadelphia Mounts Guard: 1763-1765	69
VII.	Courier to Wyalusing: 1765-1770	85
VIII.	Glickhickan and the City of Peace: 1771-1772	93
IX.	Schönbrunn, the Beautiful Spring: 1773	101
X.	The Three Sisters	115
XI.	Logan and the Shawnee War: 1774	118
XII.	Shamans or Sorcerers: 1775	123
XIII.	Between Two Black Clouds: 1775-1777	130
XIV.	To Goschochking with a Message from Congress: 1777-1778	144
XV.	Death of Captain White Eyes: 1778	151

XVI.	Salem on the Muskingum: 1779-1780	156
XVII.	Pachgantschihilas: 1781	165
XVIII.	Enter the Half King: 1781	170
XIX.	Captivity: 1781	177
XX.	Upper Sandusky: 1781	182
XXI.	Detroit: 1781	185
XXII.	Gnadenhütten: 1782	189
XXIII.	Simon Girty: 1782	201
XXIV.	The Chippewa Country: 1782-1785	203
XXV.	Cayahaga: 1785	208
XXVI.	Return to Bethlehem: 1786	212
XXVII.	Down the Ohio to Marietta: 1788	219
XXVIII.	To Pittsburgh and Petquotting on the Huron River: 1789	234
XXIX.	To the Falls of the Ohio and Vincennes: 1792	258
XXX.	To the Indian Conference at Detroit: 1793	294
XXXI.	Gnadenhütten Revisited: 1797	334
XXXII.	To Fairfield (Moraviantown) in Upper Canada: 1798	339
XXXIII.	To French Creek: 1800	373
XXXIV.	Thirty Thousand Miles with John Heckewelder: 1754-1813	384
	Epilogue	393
	Biographical and Geographical Glossary	395
	Index	449

Foreword

John Heckewelder was one of the most active and observant American travellers in the eighteenth century. His extensive journeys through our eastern woods in the service of the Moravian Church and, at times, of the government of the United States, have been preserved for us in a number of superb travel journals. Hitherto these either have lain unseen in manuscript collections or, if published, have appeared disconnectedly, so that few readers have suspected how engrossing they are and how illuminative of our early history when read as a continuous narrative.

From 1754 to 1813 Heckewelder's adventures are interwoven with the movements of the Moravian Indian mission. Like Chaucer's Knight, "Full worthy was he in his Lordes war." The editor has had to decide whether this book was to take the form of a mission study, a biography, an ethnological treatise, or a travelogue. He has chosen the last. In consequence the reader need not expect to find here a "life and times," nor a disquisition on the amazingly modern character of early Moravian missions, with their emphasis on education and economic help. He will find, rather, the story of a man on the move, whether on foot or on horseback, in a canoe or "Kentucky boat." Outside of his travels, Heckewelder's life is presented only very briefly, while the story of the mission serves only to give the milieu in which he worked and a motive to his travels. The routine diaries he wrote of daily life in his various mission stations are not included.

Heckewelder lived among the Indians for nearly sixty years, learning their languages, sharing their activities, setting down clearly and vividly what he saw and heard. He was most at home with the "Ohio Country" Delawares and Mahicans, 1762-1813. As a reporter of Indian life during his time and in his vicinity he has no superior. He crossed the Allegheny Mountains thirty times, made a number of trips down the Ohio River from Pittsburgh, and recorded from his own observation the first great drive of white population into the West. He saw the Kentucky boats taking advantage of the seasonal floods to descend the Ohio with crowds of immigrants from the east on board, new towns springing up like mushrooms all along the banks. He saw also the Indian trails in western Pennsylvania and what is now Ohio during a time of transition when they were travelled alike by white men and brown, not seeking each other's scalp but more often in pleasant companionship.

In his pages we meet in person the possessors of legendary names, such as Daniel Boone, Ebenezer Zane, Simon Girty, and James O'Hara of Pittsburgh. Heckewelder visited Marietta, Ohio, in the year of its birth, and he described many other cities in their infancy: Cincinnati and Gallipolis, Ohio; Louisville, Kentucky; Vincennes, Indiana; Albany and Schenectady, New York; Detroit, Michigan; Pittsburgh, Carlisle, and Harrisburg, Pennsylvania.

Errors in historical judgment, which mar some parts of his *History, Manners, and Customs of the Indian Nations*, are less in evidence in the journals. In them he tells only what he saw and what he heard, which is all to the good, for Heckewelder was a better reporter than expositor.

The editor's function in presenting these travel journals to the reader has been to gather them together from various repositories, to translate those among them that were written in German (as a writer, Heckewelder was bilingual), to take certain incidents described in his published reminiscences—the History mentioned above and his *Narrative of the Mission of the United Brethren*—and to weave them into the connected story of the journals. Where there are such interweavings, they are carefully noted and the sources are given, so that the reader may know at what point he leaves the contemporary observation of the journals for the reminiscences of age. In a few places the journals have been abbreviated or summarized. Where this occurs, abundant warning is given in the text. Where several versions of a journal have been found, the editor has interwoven them (taking care that the points of transition from one to another be noted) in order to preserve the best of both.

Foreword

Most of the Indians introduced here are what today would be called "displaced persons." Not long before Heckewelder began to write, they had been uprooted from their eastern Pennsylvania homelands. Heckewelder shows them trying to reestablish themselves farther west. We may be surprised, considering this circumstance, to see how cheerful in temper and healthy in outlook most of them managed to remain. That does not mean that this is a sentimental book, nor that the Indians in these pages are devoid of the picturesque. That could hardly be, with John Heckewelder writing. He was frank and he was candid. Though he had deep affection for the Indians, he saw them with a white man's eyes.

That he was instinctively, but not obtrusively, an artist, may be seen in the play of light and shade in these journals. The scenes and the people come alive. He knew how to select detail and fix a scene sharply in the mind. We shall not soon forget the "dismal music" of his horse's hooves striking bones and skulls on Braddock's lost field; the howling of wolves at night in Edmond's Swamp; the man who was careless with the candle in the gunpowder shed; the Indian boy, Tobias, reading his book by the light of the campfire; the joy of Indian captives when, on being returned to the Wabash, they found themselves once more "in their own country and on their own soil."

Certain typographical devices have been employed for the reader's convenience. Extended quotations from Heckewelder's journals or from his printed books are set in smaller type, so that the reader may distinguish at a glance Heckewelder's original from the editor's comment. To avoid unnecessary recourse to footnotes, brief identifications of persons and places are sometimes enclosed within brackets in the text. A biographical and geographical glossary is appended.

Occasional changes have been made in punctuation and paragraphing for the sake of clarity.

Wherever possible the original manuscript journal, in John Heckewelder's hand, has been used in our text. These early journals were edited (whether by Heckewelder himself or by a colleague it is sometimes difficult to say) for circulation among the Moravian communities of the time. In consequence we now find every now and again, that someone has drawn a pen through certain words, phrases, or even whole passages. When it is apparent that such a deletion has been made merely to correct an awkward expression, the former editor's judgment is here accepted and the offending passage is omitted. When, however, the words crossed out contain additional information, they are retained here within brackets and set in italics. Sometimes a desire for closer accuracy, but more often prudence or generosity (the war fever of 1775-1783 having died down and some of the Moravians' former enemies having become their friends) motivated these changes, as, for instance, "a certain [*Simon Girty*] noted Villain."

The sources from which the journals and other narratives in these pages have been taken are as follows:

A. Twelve manuscript journals:

1. "Br. *John Heckewælders* Bericht von ihrer Reise zu Wasser von *Langundoutenünk* nach *Welhik Thuppeek* im *April* 1773." From the Archives of the Moravian Church, Bethlehem, Pa. In John Heckewelder's hand.

2. "John Heckewelders Narrative of the Indian Mission on Muskingum Captivity and Murder." From the Archives of the Moravian Church. It is not certain in whose hand the text is written, but the valuable notes in the margin appear to be in John Heckewelder's hand. In the Moravian Archives there is another version of this "Narrative," presumably a revision of this early one in preparation for the printed *Narrative* of 1820. The later (revised) version is undoubtedly in John Heckewelder's hand.

3. "Reise Diarium der Geschw^r *Joh^n.* u. *Sarah Heckewälders* mit ihrer 2jährigen Tochter *Anna Salome* von *Cayahaga R.* bis *Bethlehem* vom 9 *Oct.* bis 15 *Nov.* 1786." From the Archives of the Moravian Church. In John Heckewelder's hand.

4. "Kurze Nachricht von B. *Joh. Heckewelders* Reise nach *Musgingum,* seinem Aufenthalt daselbst und seiner zurück Reise vom 10^{tn} Sept. bis 23 Dec. 1788." From the Archives of the Moravian Church. In John Heckewelder's hand. This copy has been collated by the present editor with another version in a copyist's hand, also in the Moravian Archives.

5. "Reise beschreibung des Br. *Abraham Steiners* von seiner mit Br. *Johann Heckewelder* gethanen Reise von *Bethlehem* nach *Pettquottin* am *Huron River* ohnweit *Lake Erie* und von da wieder zurück. 1789." From the Archives of the Moravian Church. There are three copies of this in the Archives, comprising two different versions. All are in a copyist's hand.

6. "Br. *John Heckewelders* Reise *Diarium* von *Beth^m.* nach *Post Vincennes* am *Wabash* Fluss, u. von da wieder zurück. 1792." From the Archives of the Moravian Church. In John Heckewelder's hand.

7. "Journey with the Commissioners to the Indian Treaty—J.H."

Foreword

(1793). From the Historical Society of Pennsylvania, Philadelphia. In John Heckewelder's hand.

8. "Bericht von Verrichtungen an *Muskingum*—mit Anmerkungen &c." 1797. In a copyist's hand.

9. "Diary of the brethren John Heckewelder and Benjamin Mortimer, on their journey from Bethlehem in Pennsylvania to Fairfield in Upper Canada, from the 30th April to the 22^{d} May 1798." From the Archives of the Moravian Church. In Benjamin Mortimer's hand.

10. "*Diarium* von der Reise der Brr. *J. Heckewelder* und *Jacob Bush* nach *Gnadenhütten* an *Muskingum*—und von den aufenthalt und Verrichtungen derer daselbst im Dienst der Heiden-Societaet angestallen Personen. 1799." From the Archives of the Moravian Church. In John Heckewelder's hand.

11. "Eine Reise von *Pittsburg* nach Le Beauff jenseit der *French Creek* darinnen alle Wege; Gegenden; Plätze &c heraus und nach der Wahrheit beschrieben sind von J. Heckewelder" (1800). From the Archives of the Moravian Church. In John Heckewelder's hand.

12. "*John Heckewelders* Reisen zwischen 1754 und 1814." From the Archives of the Moravian Church. In John Heckewelder's hand.

B. Two printed documents:

1. Heckewelder narrative of his journey to the Muskingum with Frederick Post in 1762 and their attempt to establish a mission at the Indian town of Tuscarawas. Rev. Edward Rondthaler, *Life of John Heckewelder* (Philadelphia, 1847), pages 38-58.

2. Heckewelder's autobiography: "Memoir of the Life of Br. John Gottlieb Heckewelder, Missionary among the North American Indians. (Written by Himself.)," *Periodical Accounts*, XIII, 49-56.

C. Heckewelder's two histories:

1. *History, Manners, and Customs of The Indian Nations Who Once Inhabited Pennsylvania and the Neighboring States. By the Rev. John Heckewelder of Bethlehem Pa. New and Revised Edition, with an Introduction and Notes by the Rev. William C. Reichel, of Bethlehem, Pa.* (Philadelphia: Publication fund of The Historical Society of Pennsylvania, 1876). Printed from the 1819 edition, which was published under the auspices of the American Philosophical Society.

2. *A Narrative of the Mission of the United Brethren among the Delaware and Mohegan Indians, from Its Commencement, in the Year 1740, to the Close of the Year 1808. Comprising All the Remarkable Incidents Which Took Place at Their Missionary Stations During that Period. Interspersed with Anecdotes, Historical Facts,*

Speeches of Indians, and other interesting Matter. By John Heckewelder, Who was many years in the service of that Mission (Philadelphia, 1820).

The editor wishes to thank the Elders Conference of the Northern Province of the Moravian Church in America for making the records in their Indian Department available for study and publication, and for the generous assistance they have offered all along the way. The American Philosophical Society, of which the present editor is a Library Research Associate, has given through the Phillips Fund substantial help in this study of John Heckewelder, who was an early member of the Society. Particular thanks are due to Dr. William E. Lingelbach, librarian of the Society, under whose guidance the work was undertaken. I am much indebted also to the members and the staff of the Pennsylvania Historical and Museum Commission for supporting the work in its final stages, and particularly to Dr. S. K. Stevens, executive director, and Dr. S. W. Higginbotham, director of the Bureau of Research, Publications, and Records. Thanks are due to the Historical Society of Pennsylvania, and in particular to Dr. Richard N. Williams, *second* director, for assistance in the original search for Heckewelder manuscripts and permission to print the journal of 1793.

Since the German texts herein reproduced were often carelessly composed and written, availing themselves at times of a vocabulary and idiom no longer familiar, the editor has seen to it that every page should be translated by at least two persons, himself and one other, in the hope of avoiding the errors which, as is well known, too easily beset such undertakings as this. Particular thanks are due to Mrs. John Fliegel of the Moravian Church, whose translation of the journals, undertaken in connection with this work, has been carefully collated with the editor's. For further help of this kind, thanks are due to Miss Mari Luise Huth and Mrs. Barbara Wrightstone.

The Rev. John Fliegel's monumental Index, now approaching completion, of the Indian records in the Archives of the Moravian Church at Bethlehem, has been invaluable. I am much beholden to Mr. and Mrs. Leslie R. Gray, whose careful researches in preparation for their excellent work on the Fairfield mission, which has appeared under the title, *Wilderness Christians* (Ithaca, 1956), have in many cases run parallel with and ahead of my own. I am indebted to my colleagues on the Pennsylvania Historical and Museum Commission, especially to Mr. John Witthoft, chief curator of the Museum, Mr. Donald H. Kent,

Foreword

chief of the Division of Research and Publications, and Mr. William A. Hunter, associate state historian.

To Dr. William N. Fenton, assistant commissioner, New York State Museum; Dr. Frederick B. Tolles, director, Friends Historical Library of Swarthmore College; Dr. William A. Ritchie, New York State archaeologist; The Very Reverend Thomas Grassman, director, Mohawk-Caughnawaga Museum; and to many librarians, archivists, curators, and local historians in Pennsylvania, Ohio, West Virginia, Indiana, Kentucky, Michigan, New Jersey, Massachusetts, and Ontario, I heartily acknowledge my debt for information generously contributed.

It is impossible to acknowledge all those of the Moravian community who have helped me; the names of a few must suffice to represent them: the Right Rev. Kenneth G. Hamilton to whom I am grateful for many favors and in particular for his *John Ettwein and the Moravian Church During the Revolutionary Period* (Bethlehem, Pa., 1940), a mine of accurate information; the Rev. E. H. Swavely, curator of the Moravian Historical Society, Whitefield House, Nazareth, Pa.; and Dr. Paul Eugene Miller, who has permitted me to see the manuscript of his well-annotated "David Zeisberger's Official Diary, Fairfield, 1791-1795."

To the Right Rev. S. H. Gapp, archivist, an unusual debt is acknowledged, above all else for making possible to the editor an understanding of the qualities that for five hundred years have made Moravianism enduring and inspiring: its faith without bigotry; its scholarship, artistry, kindness, and gentleness matched with manliness and *savoir faire*.

PAUL A. W. WALLACE

Harrisburg, December 19, 1957.

A Note from the Publisher on the Paperback Edition

It has unfortunately not been possible to correct all the typographical errors that were found in the first edition of this book. Below is a list of errata that remain.

Page xv, line 12: For "angestallen" read "angestallten."
    xvi, line 18: For "*second*" read "2nd,"
    21, line 8: For "Sileian" read "Silesian."
    24, line 29: For "Next year" read "In 1736."
    24, line 31: After "recently" add "been."
    78, line 43: For "hatch" read "hatchet."
    198, line 30: For "March" read "May."
    258, line 5: For "the Retrenche River" read "La Tranche River."
    408, line 28: For "the Retrenche" read "La Tranche."
    409, line 6: For "opening sketches" read "opening stretches."
    414, line 12: For "Society for the Propagation of the Gospel "read "Society for Propagating the Gospel."
    417, line 10: Delete "Brother of Shingas and King Beaver."
    437, line 34: For "Schechschquanünk" read "Schechschiquanünk."
    446, line 4: For "Kinhaschican" read "Kinhanschican."
    Passim: For "Friedenstadt" read "Friedensstadt."

THE TRAVELS OF
JOHN HECKEWELDER
IN FRONTIER AMERICA

The Moravian Lamb—the Church emblem
From the Alphabet Book, courtesy of Ephrata Cloister

Introduction: The Moravians

Deerslayer: "Not so—not so, warrior. I'm not good enough for the Moravians."

THE *Unitas Fratrum* or Unity of the Brethren, is the oldest international Protestant church in the world.* It had its origin five hundred years ago (1457) in Bohemia and Moravia, quickly spread across Europe, established missions in every continent, and now, under the name of the Moravian Church, finds its chief home in the United States. Of this communion Luther said, "Since the time of the Apostles no church has so nearly resembled the apostolic church as the Bohemian Brethren"; and John Wesley, when asked why he was going to Herrnhut, then the headquarters of the Moravian Church, replied, "To see the place where the Christians live."

What Luther claimed for them in the sixteenth century and Wesley in the eighteenth, is still true in the twentieth. But that does not mean that the Moravians are "frozen" in the past. On the contrary, they keep up with the times. They have always been leaders in preserving the life and vigor of the Christian Church by keeping it sensitive to its environment and adaptable to the needs of a changing world.

The Moravians are not distinguished from Christians of other denominations by eccentricities of clothing or by pet doctrines. They live normal, healthy, uninhibited lives, going out into the world and sharing its tasks and its pleasures. If they differ from other Christians, it is not in matters of creed but in the fidelity with which they follow the spirit

---

* Edward Langton, *History of the Moravian Church* (London, 1956), p. 7.

of Christ as expressed in the Sermon on the Mount. They find in Him, rather than in theological doctrines invented by men to explain Him, the springs of their religion and their life.

If we know less than we should about the Moravians, it is not because they have contributed little to the world we live in. They have contributed much. As followers of John Huss, they led the Protestant Reformation a hundred years before Martin Luther. Their Bishop, John Amos Comenius, was one of the greatest leaders of modern education. By means of the *Diaspora* (Scattered Seed), they have energized and at the same time mellowed the evangelical movement in many Protestant denominations. Through John Wesley, who acknowledged his debt to them, they contributed to Methodism its strongest quality: reliance on the experience of Christ within the heart rather than on the acceptance of any dogma. In enlightened Christian mission work, all churches stand today where the Moravians stood alone two hundred years ago.

It is missionary work that constitutes their most glorious achievement; and, among their many noble undertakings in this field, none surpasses the mission to the Delaware and Mahican Indians of the United States and Canada, in which John Heckewelder spent the best years of his life.

Heckewelder was not what the public still likes to think of as the typical missionary. He was not a good preacher. He was neither a theologian nor a student of church history. He was not even very hortatory. But he loved the Indians. He lived with them, shared their interests, worked with them in the fields, in the sugar-bush, and on the river. In his travel journals he tells quite simply what he saw and heard as he moved about among them in the woods of Pennsylvania, Ohio, and Indiana. He was unconcerned about backgrounds, never discussing the significance of his work in the light of Moravian history, for he was writing for his own people, who knew as much about such things as he did.

To get the full force of his narrative, it is necessary for today's readers to know more than he tells us, especially about Moravian history. We need to understand the instinctive sympathy which their own sufferings and exile enabled Moravians to feel with the dispossessed American Indians. We must understand the deep interest these followers of Huss and Comenius took in education. Above all, we must understand the broad statesmanship—an inheritance from their former leaders in Bohemia, Moravia, Poland, and Germany—which moti-

Introduction: The Moravians

vated their missionary work among the Indians and gave it form. Without such knowledge we cannot realize how great their story is, nor understand that the tragedy of the Gnadenhütten mission, which is described in Heckewelder's pages, lay not so much in the murder of ninety Christian Indians as in the stark ending it gave to the noblest experiment in race relations this continent has yet seen.

Numerically the *Unitas Fratrum* is a small church, numbering (as of December 31, 1956) no more than 81,039 members in its five Home Provinces (Continental, Czechoslovakia, British, American North, and American South), besides 214,959 in its Foreign Missions—a total membership of 295,998. Its influence, however, throughout the Protestant world has been profound and healthy. The Methodists in England and the Evangelical United Brethren in Pennsylvania owe most to them, having been powerfully influenced by the Moravians at their inception. But the whole church world of today, insofar as it is diminishing in denominational arrogance, is putting itself in tune with the Moravians. The present ecumenical movement is accomplishing what the Moravians attempted two centuries ago.

The *sanity* of pure religion has never been better exemplified than by the *Unitas Fratrum*. Throughout their history the members of the Unity have maintained a healthy balance between piety and breadth of view, avoiding both the moral looseness and the fanaticism which at different times have disfigured organized Christianity. Piety without intolerance, purity without asceticism—such have always been the distinguishing marks of the Moravians. They have bothered little about questions of orthodoxy. Picturesque heresy trials are not to be looked for in their church annals. A Christian, they believe, is to be recognized by the evidences in his life that, through Jesus of Nazareth, he has touched the spiritual current flowing from God. They teach their children the Apostle's Creed, but they have no distinctive creed of their own. They define "faith" as knowing God and loving Him. They keep away from theological disputation. They work for peace, ecclesiastical as well as national, taking these words for their guide: "In essentials, unity; in non-essentials, liberty; in all things, charity."

The Moravian Church originated in the protest which arose throughout Europe during the Middle Ages against the abuses which had grown up in the Roman Catholic Church. Bohemian scholars studying at Oxford read the writings of John Wycliffe, "the morning star of the Reformation." Copies of these books, taken back to Bohemia by Jerome of Prague and others, about 1400, strengthened the reform movement already well advanced there among the high-spirited Bohemian people. "For one person that Wycliffe stirred in England, he stirred hundreds in Bohemia." * What gave the Bohemian movement a particularly sharp edge was its involvement in national and racial, as well as religious, antagonisms. The Slavs, who constituted the bulk of the population, resented the intrusion of Germans among them, especially so many German-speaking priests. A spirit of suspicion and intolerance, moreover, had grown up on Bohemian soil during centuries of struggle between the Roman and Greek branches of the Church. Race, religion, and nationality make an explosive mixture.

The spark that set off the explosion was provided by John Huss (c 1373-1415). The son of well-to-do peasants, he was sent to the University of Prague, where he became a bachelor of arts, 1393, bachelor of theology, 1394, and master of arts, 1396. In 1398 he began to lecture at the university, and rose rapidly, becoming dean of the philosophical faculty in 1401. He is said to have used some of Wycliffe's philosophical writings for his textbooks. It was his appointment as Rector of the Bethlehem Chapel at Prague in 1402 that drew him into his career as a church reformer and national leader. He drew great crowds, preaching in the Bohemian tongue on topics of the day. He declaimed against the presence of German armies in the land and of German priests who could not speak the language of the people. He denounced the sins of the idle rich. So far so good. But he went on to denounce the sins of the clergy, climaxing all with a denunciation of the Popes, and he was excommunicated as a heretic.

There were at that time three claiming to be Popes. Pope John XXIII, finding himself in need of money for war against the King of Naples, who had driven him from Rome, and against the two "antipopes," Gregory XII and Benedict XIII, sent agents into Bohemia in 1412 to sell remission of sins for cash. Papal pardons were auctioned off in district lots, outside the city, to the highest bidders, who then retailed them for what they could get. Inside Prague the priests conducted the sale. Wenzel Tiem and Pace de Bononia, preceded by drummers, marched through the streets advertising their wares, and proceeded to sell indulgences in the city churches. Sophisticates smiled at the cynicism of the transaction. The unlettered fumbled for their purses—for who is without sin?—until they heard a rousing call to common sense and honesty from John Huss. "God alone," he said, "can forgive sins through Christ."

---

* J. E. Hutton, *A History of the Moravian Church* (London, 1909), p. 12.

Introduction: The Moravians

The town was soon in a ferment. Students heckled the priests. Three young men, each at a different church, shouted: "Priest, thou liest. The indulgences are a fraud." For this they were seized by the authorities and beheaded on the street. The university students went wild. With Huss at their head, they carried the dismembered bodies away and buried them in the Bethlehem Chapel. Huss conducted the funeral. He found himself at the head of a national movement of protest.

Pope John XXIII (Baldassare Cossa, a lively Neapolitan who had given up the life of a corsair for the more lucrative career of a church politician and terrorist) summoned a Church Council to meet at Constance on the Rhine, ostensibly to discuss church reforms. Huss was invited to participate. He was promised a safe conduct, but on arrival at Constance he was seized and imprisoned. For months he lay in a dungeon next to a sewer. When at length he was called to trial as a heretic, he was given no opportunity to defend himself. He was accused, among other things, of having discussed Wycliffe's doctrines, protested the burning of Wycliffe's books, and attacked the papal bulls of His Holiness, John XXIII. Refusing to recant, he was, on July 6, 1415, burned at the stake. His ashes were thrown into the Rhine.

"John Huss," wrote Erasmus, "was burned, not convicted."

Avenge, O Lord, thy slaughtered saints . . .

There followed the Hussite Wars. In *The History of the Bohemian Persecution* (London, 1650), we read: "When after the death of Wensislaus in the year 1419, Sygismund took the Kingdom . . . some thousands of those that imbraced the pure Religion, gathered together to a strong mountain, ten miles from Prague, which they named Tabor, that mountaine they compassed about with a wall, and constituted a commonwealth determining to defend it by arms if need were."

We need not detail the campaigns of the Bohemian followers of John Huss, under their blind general, Ziska, who fortified Tabor, making it the center of a revolutionary effort to establish a classless society, and who taught his army of peasants how to use their wagons, slings, and clubs to break up charges of Europe's feudal chivalry and beat down the armored knights. The Pope declared crusade after crusade against these Bohemian heretics, but under Ziska they appeared to be invincible. They held off all Europe. By 1434, however, Ziska had died and the Hussites had broken up among themselves. The conservative Utraquists came to terms with the Roman Catholic Church, and in 1733 were recognized by the Pope as the national church of Bohemia. The more radical Taborites, whose high principles were marred by fanaticism, were defeated at the Battle of Lipan in 1434 and slaughtered without mercy.

Meantime Peter of Chelcic, though he was neither priest nor scholar, was carrying on the work of John Huss. In his writings he advanced principles which were to become the foundation of the *Unitas Fratrum*. He followed Huss in his zeal for church reform. But, with the brutalities of the Hussite Wars in mind, he preached love and non-violence. He attacked the union of church and state, the taking of oaths, and many Roman Catholic doctrines such as purgatory, the invocation of the saints, and the worship of the Virgin. Above all, "He looked upon Christianity rather as a life than a creed." *

Peter of Chelcic was not an organizer. It was Gregory the Patriarch who put the teachings of Huss and Peter of Chelcic into institutional form. It came about in this way. Here and there small groups of men, moderate followers of Huss and Peter of Chelcic, desired to worship together quietly and without fear of persecution. Gregory, through the mediation of John Rockycana, Archbishop-elect of Prague, received permission from King George Podiebrad for these brethren to assemble at the hamlet of Kunwald, near the castle of Lititz, on the northeast border of Bohemia. When news of this retreat spread, men gathered to it from all parts of Bohemia and Moravia: peasants, noblemen, scholars from the University of Prague, Taborites, Utraquists, Waldensians. All crossed the mountains to the secluded Valley of Kunwald to worship as brethren in the unity of the spirit.

So it came about that in 1457 or 1458 (a tradition without substantial evidence sets the date as March 1, 1457) the *Jednota Bratrska* (Unity, Communion, or Church of the Brethren—in Latin, *Unitas Fratrum* †) took form. Special meetings were held to determine on what central Christian doctrines this varied group, united only in a desire to follow Christ sincerely, could agree. How were they to com-

---

* Edmund de Schweinitz, *The History of the Church Known as The Unitas Fratrum or The Unity of the Brethren, Founded by the Followers of John Hus, the Bohemian Reformer and Martyr* (Bethlehem, Pa., 1885), p. 97.

† For discussion of *Jednota* as meaning "Church" rather than "Brotherhood" or "Unity," see Hutton, *op. cit.*, p. 70. The present name, "Moravian Church," is popular only in England and America. Its incorporated title is "The Church of the United Brethren"; its international name is "Unitas Fratrum." The reader must be careful not to confuse it with the Church of the Brethren (otherwise known as the German Baptists or "Dunkers,") nor with the United Brethren in Christ (now the Evangelical United Brethren) which took origin in Pennsylvania a little over one hundred and fifty years ago.

Introduction: The Moravians

pose their differences of opinion on matters of theology and doctrine? How, for instance, were they to regard the Lord's Supper?—a question that then tore the Christian world apart. Some of the followers of Huss accepted the Roman Catholic doctrine of transubstantiation; others preferred the Taborite view that the bread and wine were merely symbols. At an early Synod the *Unitas Fratrum* decided to accept Christ's words, "This is my body, this is my blood," without attempting to explain them.

We are reminded of the reply made by Elizabeth I of England, before her accession to the throne, when confronted with a question about transubstantiation. Her devout but fanatical sister, Mary, then the reigning queen, suspected her of a leaning toward Protestantism, and put her to the test with a question about the real presence of Christ in the bread and wine. Elizabeth replied:

> *Christ was the word that spake it;*
> *He took the bread and brake it;*
> *And what his word did make it,*
> *That I believe and take it.*

The Brethren adopted a resolution that they "should be satisfied with God's word and simply believe what it taught, avoiding all tracts [i.e., polemical works]." Experience had taught them that theological controversy is a device of the Devil to unmake Christians.

The Brethren were not long to enjoy the protection that King George Podiebrad had promised. That weak and excitable monarch, hearing a rumor that they were celebrating the Lord's Supper in unorthodox fashion, tried to crush them out of existence. Gregory the Patriarch was put to the rack. Four other leaders were burned at the stake. The Brethren at Kunwald fled into the mountains. Some lived in caves, lighting their fires only at night lest the smoke betray them.

But persecution did not destroy the Unity. It strengthened it. The sympathy which the spectacle of their undeserved punishments roused in decent people brought them new adherents; and the organization itself, hitherto very loose, was tightened to help their members protect one another.

It was at this point in their development that the use of the lot was introduced. The recent persecutions had shown them how deep was their disagreement with the Utraquist and Roman Catholic branches of the Church. At the same time they were hesitant about making a complete break with Rome—not because they feared for themselves, but because they did not wish to encourage division in the Christian Church. Not trusting their own judgment on the matter of setting up a new church, they decided to take no vote on the question of secession but to appeal to the lot, believing that God would make His will known by the operation of this medium.

There was Biblical precedent:

And they appointed two, Joseph called Barsabas, who was surnamed Justus, and Matthias.

And they prayed, and said, Thou Lord, which knowest the hearts of all men, shew whether of these two thou hast chosen,

That he may take part of this ministry and apostleship, from which Judas by transgression fell, that he might go to his own place.

And they gave forth their lots; and the lot fell upon Matthias; and he was numbered with the eleven apostles.

Acts I, 23-26 (*King James Version*)

At a Synod (held probably in 1465, though the date is uncertain), the Brethren cast lots to decide these two questions:

1. Is it God's will that we shall separate entirely from the power of the Papacy and hence from the priesthood?

2. Is it God's will that we shall institute, according to the model of the primitive Church, a ministerial order of our own? *

The lot answered both questions in the affirmative.

In years to come the lot was to assume great importance in Moravian councils, being used to settle all manner of questions. It is easy for us now to smile at it, as the Moravians do themselves, recognizing that their earlier trust in it was based on a fallacy. They no longer believe that God uses the so-called laws of chance—whether operating through dice, the roulette wheel, a flipped coin, or bits of paper—to disclose His mind to man. At the same time none of us should be too quick in condemning the Bohemian Brethren for relying on the lot. There were then, as there are still, circumstances under which a "tossup" seems the best policy.

When faced with difficult alternatives, [writes Bishop Kenneth G. Hamilton †] men often found relief by turning to it for a solution of honest perplexity. . . . Further, where marked division of opinion existed among any group, resort to the lot meant the elimination of all lingering dissatisfaction

---

* De Schweinitz, *op. cit.*, pp. 130-31.

† *John Ettwein and the Moravian Church During the Revolutionary Period* (Bethlehem, Pa., 1940), p. 74.

Introduction: The Moravians

among the minority; for, after the Saviour had spoken, no difference of opinion could persist. On the other hand, the unpredictable nature of the lot tended to restrain any single man from dominating the policies of the Church; even the most dogmatic views could be silenced by an appeal to the "government of the Saviour." And finally, any course of action which had the approval of the lot could be followed with utmost courage and confidence; men who know their acts to possess the immediate sanction of God are not easily appalled by lesser considerations.

The use of the lot in certain other categories is not, however, to be defended on the same grounds. When, during its greatest vogue in the eighteenth century, it came to be used in the matter of clerical appointment, school admissions, travel, and marriage, the dangers of the system are apparent. Conrad Weiser, travelling with Count Zinzendorf, was rightly provoked when the Count insisted on using the lot to determine a question of itinerary which could be settled by the exercise of plain common sense. To the credit of the Moravians it should be remembered that, even in the days of its greatest use, they set healthy checks upon it. When it was invoked to determine appointments to office, the names of none but highly qualified persons, well screened in advance, were submitted to it. In matters of church policy, if the decision of the lot went against the best judgment of the Brethren, the question, after a decent interval, was submitted a second time. It was not that the Brethren believed the Lord had made an error at the first casting, nor that He had since changed His mind. They supposed, rather, that dangers unsuspected by the Brethren might have been an obstacle at first, but now, having been removed, the way might be clear for the Lord's real purpose. When John Ettwein planned to visit New England in 1798, the lot forbade him.* A few days later, the man who was to have accompanied him took sick and died. Plainly the lot's interdiction had been for Ettwein's protection. Now that the danger was past, Ettwein submitted his question to the lot again, and this time he was permitted to go.

Marriage came under the jurisdiction of the lot. But it was not (except in rare, though much advertised, instances) followed blindly nor accepted irrevocably. Usually, before the question of marriage could be submitted, the young people themselves were expected to have come to an agreement. If then the lot forbade marriage, the verdict need not be accepted as final. The young people might try again later. When, on the other hand, an affirmative answer was received, the young couple's

---
* Hamilton, *Ettwein*, p. 74.

judgment was confirmed: the marriage had been made in Heaven.

The appeal to the lot was usually made with three slips of paper, on one of which was an affirmative answer, on another a negative, while the third was a blank. At Bethlehem in 1777, John Heckewelder, who was about to return to his mission station on the Muskingum River, applied to the lot for permission to marry the lady of his choice, Sara Ohneberg. He drew a blank, and returned to the Muskingum without a bride. Three years later, however, the couple were married.

To return to the Synod of 1465: The lot having authorized the Brethren to institute a ministry of their own, they proceeded to do so at the Synod of Lhota in 1467. Three ministers, Matthias, Thomas, and Elias, were chosen by lot from a group of nine nominated by ballot. An elderly Waldensian priest who attended the Synod was chosen by lot to ordain them.

There was much to draw the *Unitas Fratrum* and the Waldenses together. Like the Bohemian Brethren, the Waldenses sought to revive the simple faith of the primitive church, and to trust in the Bible rather than the priests for religious instruction. Like the Brethren, too, they had behind them a long history of persecution. Peter Waldo and his followers, the "Poor men of Lyons" (they had taken vows of poverty) were driven from this French city as heretics. Peter Waldo died in Bohemia in 1217. His followers took refuge in the Alps of southern France and northern Italy, settling in Dauphiné, Provence, Piedmont, and Lombardy. At approximately the time of John Huss's death, a colony of Waldenses came north and settled in Moravia. Finding themselves for a time unmolested here, they began to worship openly, taking part in the mass with the Utraquists. It was their claim that they had preserved the beliefs and many of the customs of the primitive church. They claimed that their episcopate preserved unbroken the Apostolic Succession.

The Bohemian Brethren were particularly interested in this last claim. Having at one time considered uniting with the Waldenses, they had looked into their episcopacy and believed it to be historically sound.*

In order to strengthen their new church, it was decided by the Synod at Lhota to appoint bishops; and in order to give these officials standing in Bohemia, it was decided also to have them consecrated in

---

* For evidence on the Apostolic Succession in the Moravian episcopacy, see: De Schweinitz, *op. cit.*, pp. 141-52; Hutton, *op. cit.*, pp. 56-57; *Report of the Committee appointed by the Archbishop of Canterbury to consider the Orders of the Unitas Fratrum or Moravians* (1906).

Introduction: The Moravians

such a way as to bring them into the Episcopal Succession. For this purpose, they sent a deputation, headed by Michael Bradacius, to the Waldensian colony in Moravia, with the request that the Waldenses consecrate a bishop for the *Unitas Fratrum*. The request was granted. Bishop Stephen of the Waldenses consecrated Michael Bradacius a bishop. Michael, on his return, consecrated Matthias.

The Moravians have never believed that the Apostolic Succession is essential to the life of the Church. It was introduced to meet a practical need of the day. But they have always been interested in history. Since the day when Bishop Stephen gave them the Episcopal Succession, thus giving them an institutional link with the early church, they have taken pride in preserving the continuity of their episcopate, even through dark days in the sixteenth century when their church was dismembered and their sole remaining bishop, John Augusta, lay for years in prison.

When word of the Moravian episcopacy reached the authorities at Prague, fresh persecutions were launched against them and against those who had assisted them. Bishop Stephen of the Waldenses was arrested and burned at the stake. The Waldenses in Moravia were dispersed, many of them ultimately joining the *Unitas*. Their accession was to have important consequences.

As these men spoke the German language, the Brethren, naturally, for their benefit, prepared German editions of their Confessions, Catechisms, and Hymn-books; and through these German editions of their works they were able, a few years later, to enter into closer contact with the Reformation in Germany. But that is not the end of the story. It was descendants of this German branch of the Church that first made their way to Herrnhut in 1722, and thus laid the foundations of the Renewed Church of the Brethren.*

Cordial relations were established also with the Waldenses of northern Italy and southern France.

When the Brethren entered again a period of relative freedom, their church grew rapidly. By the year 1500 they had some four hundred parishes in Bohemia, with a membership approaching two hundred thousand. Printing presses were established. Books of scholarship and devotion appeared. Between the years 1500 and 1510, the Brethren printed no less than fifty of the sixty works published in Bohemia. In 1505 appeared their first catechism, *Questions for the Children*, prepared by Bishop Luke, who edited also (1501) the first Protestant hymn-book.

---

* Hutton, *op. cit.*, p. 58, n.

In spasmodic bursts of sadistic fanaticism, their enemies tried to stamp out the new church. We do not wish to follow in any detail the wretched story of these persecutions, but it is impossible to understand later Moravian history without some knowledge of the oppressions they learned to expect and became tempered to withstand.

By the Edict of St. James (July 25, 1508) it was made a criminal offense to conduct the religious services of the Brethren. Their books were burned. All their parishes and revenues were taken over by the Roman Catholic or Utraquist priests. But the Brethren, already accustomed to danger and undaunted by the prospect of prison, torture, or the stake, continued to worship in secret. They received not a little satisfaction from the fatal accidents that continually befell their enemies as if by Divine judgment. One of their chief persecutors was thrown from his horse and fell on a nail, which tore out his bowels. Another was upset from a sleigh and stabbed to death by his own hunting knife. Sudden sickness took off others. It became a saying in Bohemia that, if a man was tired of life, all he had to do was start persecuting the Brethren.

When this wave of persecution at length passed on, the Unity emerged a large and flourishing church. It was governed by three bodies: the General Synod (highest authority), consisting of two houses, in one the bishops and in the other the priests; the Executive Council, consisting of the bishops and their assistants; and an Ecclesiastical Judge, who settled church disputes. The ministry consisted of bishops, priests, and acolytes or ministerial candidates. The organization of the church today has evolved out of these early forms. Today the ministry consists of bishops, presbyters, and deacons: the names have changed but the functions remain. The General Synod, which meets every six years, is still the supreme legislative authority. There is now a Unity Elders' Conference which serves as the administrative authority. Each province (e.g., American North and American South) is self-governing, by means of a Provincial Synod (consisting of all the ordained ministers along with representatives from each congregation) and a Provincial Elders' Conference, which is the governing board.

Persecution never made them bitter nor narrowed their outlook. They did not feel that theirs was the only church. In conduct the Brethren, lay as well as clerical, remained temperate, modest, and industrious. They were kind to their neighbors in sickness *and in health*, thus avoiding the stigma that attaches to some Christians who are kind only to those whom they pity. The Brethren were strict with their

Introduction: The Moravians

children, seeing to it that they had good religious instruction. If some touch of the puritanical is seen in the early Brethren's deprecation of painting and music equally with witchcraft and alchemy, at least they evinced none of the cruelty that disfigured the Puritans of a later century. In more recent years, music and painting have been their *forte*. Though it was piety rather than scholarship that determined their choice of priests, they were interested in education, and they established schools throughout the land. The concern for education that distinguishes the Moravians today (some of the best schools in the United States are under their auspices) derives from a tradition that has its roots in the University of Prague, at one time the greatest university in Europe, where John Huss taught and preached.

By the year 1517, a date which is often taken as the beginning of the Protestant Reformation because that was the year in which Luther nailed his ninety-five theses to the door of the court church in Wittenberg, the *Unitas Fratrum* was already a well-organized Protestant church with a long history and a sound tradition behind it.

Erasmus (a Roman Catholic) wrote a spirited defense of the Brethren against their detractors: "That they call themselves brethren and sisters, I can not recognize as wrong, but wish to God that this mode of address might become common among all Christians. That they have less faith in the teachers of the Church than in the Holy Scriptures, is right." *

Calvin wrote to Bishop John Augusta of the Bohemian Brethren, congratulating him on the pure doctrine, good morals, and discipline of the Unity. Melancthon approved of their "Confession of Faith." Martin Bucer wrote to Bishop Augusta, thanking him for the letter and books the bishop had sent him, adding, "Both show that God has given us one mind. . . . God preserve to you that which He has given you, and encourage us through your example." †

Luther, in his last letter to the Brethren, addressed to John Augusta and dated October 5, 1542, wrote: ". . . I admonish you in the Lord, that even as you began, so you may continue with us to the end, in the fellowship of the Spirit and of doctrine. Help us to fight, with the word and with prayer, against the gates of hell, which continually oppose the Church of God and its Head, Christ the Lord." ‡

Such fighting words did not go unremembered by the Bohemian

---
* De Schweinitz, *op. cit.*, p. 230.
† De Schweinitz, *op. cit.*, p. 258.
‡ De Schweinitz, *op. cit.*, p. 261.

Brethren when, soon after the death of Luther in 1546, fresh persecutions sprang up. The Smalkald War, first of the religious wars following the Lutheran Reformation, tore Bohemia apart. Many of her people sided with the Protestants; but her king, Ferdinand, first of the Hapsburgs to rule Bohemia, sided with his brother, the Emperor Charles V of the Holy Roman Empire. The Protestant forces were defeated at the Battle of Mühlberg in 1547. Thereupon King Ferdinand, a devout but fanatical man who had been educated in Spain, revived the scaffold and torture chamber as means of restoring his church to supremacy in Bohemia and Moravia. Such of the Brethren as lived on Royal estates were given six weeks in which to make up their minds whether to join the Roman Catholic Church or leave the country. Nearly two thousand left their homes and crossed the mountains into Poland, where, under George Israel, they founded a strong branch of the Unity.

Meanwhile under Ferdinand the Protestant nobles were being beheaded. Bishop John Augusta, imprisoned and tortured, became a symbol of courage to all persecuted Brethren. No torments could draw from him information harmful to his flock. When asked under torture where the Brethren were, he replied, "They are seeking refuge, with one accord, in impassioned prayer to God!"

Though he remained in captivity from 1548 to 1564, he continued active in the cause. Through the connivance of one of his warders, he managed to send messages to the Brethren from his cell, urging them to stand fast. From his cell also he published a volume of sermons and issued a number of hymns, some of which are still sung by the Moravians.

> *Praise God forever.*
> *Boundless in his favour,*
> *To his Church and chosen flock*
> *Founded on Christ the Rock.*

When Ferdinand became Emperor of the Holy Roman Empire and his son Maximilian II ascended the throne of Bohemia, the persecution of the Brethren was relaxed. The power of the king was waning, that of the nobles increasing, and the nobles were almost all Protestants. In 1564 Bishop Augusta was released from prison, and in 1575 Maximilian made the Brethren this promise: "I will never oppress or hinder you in the exercise of your religion; and I pledge my word in my own name and also in the name of my successors."

Introduction: The Moravians

Then came the golden age of Unity. A great part of the people of Bohemia were with them, rich and poor, nobles and tradesmen, magistrates and even soldiers. The Brethren were leaders in business and statecraft. They built hospitals and cared for the poor with funds specially set aside for their security. Above all, they advanced education. Students were sent to foreign universities. Free elementary schools were opened. Books of religious instruction were prepared and published. A school edition of the Brethren's catechism was printed in three languages, Bohemian, German, and Latin, so that the children might learn to read in their own and other languages. A rhymed *Book of Morals* was prepared from which the children learned, among other things, not to put their elbows on the table and not to speak to their elders unless spoken to. In 1616 the Brethren published a code of religious and moral regulations entitled, *Ratio disciplinae* (Account of Discipline). When persecution again closed over them and the Brethren in Bohemia and Moravia were deprived of their churches and their pastors, it was through these remembered lessons from the Catechism, the hymn-books, and the rules of the *Ratio disciplinae* that the Unity was kept alive in their minds and hearts.

During their time of prosperity, their greatest glory was in their publications. Blahoslav in 1558 published a treatise on music. In 1565 he published a Bohemian translation of the New Testament *from the Greek*. He published also a Bohemian grammar, a biography of Bishop Augusta, and a Latin history of the *Unitas Fratrum*.

Best of all, Blahoslav set in motion the preparation of the Kralitz Bible, which appeared in 1593—the "grandest monument," as it has been called, of the *Unitas Fratrum*. Earlier Czech versions had been based on the Latin Vulgate; this was translated from the original tongues. A body of Greek and Hebrew scholars, some of whom had been specially trained for the task at the Universities of Wittenberg and Basel, worked for fourteen years, producing in the end six volumes, printed in Moravia at Kralitz Castle, the residence of Baron John von Zerotin, who financed the whole project. The Kralitz Bible, like Luther's Bible in Germany and the King James Version in England, gave a standard to the language. It is still used by Protestants in Czechoslovakia.

The interests of the Brethren having now become national in scope, the Bohemian nation honored and followed them. When peril again threatened the Protestants of Bohemia, the people made the Brethren's new champion, Wenzel von Budowa, a national hero.

Budowa was in the imperial service, a member of the Emperor's Privy Council and of the Imperial Court of Appeal. He had travelled widely, spoke Turkish and Arabic, and had published a Bohemian version of the Alcoran. He was scholar, statesman, soldier, preacher. During his later years, his greatest interest lay in freeing the *Unitas Fratrum* from the curse of the Edict of St. James. Despite Maximilian's promises, the Edict had never been repealed. It made the Brethren virtually outlaws.

In 1602 the weak Emperor Rudolph revived the Edict, and informed the Diet that its terms would be enforced. Meetings of the Brethren were forbidden. Their properties were seized. In 1605 all priests, teachers, booksellers, and printers were required to sign an oath of allegiance to the ecclesiastical authorities. In response, the Protestants united, and Budowa came to their head. When in 1609 Rudolph declared Roman Catholic worship to be the only lawful one in Bohemia, Budowa went into action. With overwhelming numbers behind him, he prepared to lead the country in armed revolt. The King backed down, signing a "Letter of Majesty" that granted the Brethren full religious liberty. "No decree of any kind," ran the letter, "shall be issued either by us or our heirs and succeeding kings against the above established religious peace."

It is needless to follow the intricate political maneuverings that brought an unwilling Diet to elect Ferdinand II, a fanatical Roman Catholic, to the Bohemian throne. The protests of Budowa, who knew that Ferdinand would try to stamp out Protestantism in Bohemia as he had already done in Styria, were unheeded until too late. The Protestants fumbled. A Catholic army under Tilly, who had been trained by the Jesuits for the priesthood, had served in the Spanish army in the Netherlands, and was now Commander-in-Chief of the forces of the Catholic League, appeared before Prague. On November 8, 1620, in an action that lasted only an hour, he defeated the Protestants at the Battle of the White Mountain, three miles from the city. Thirteen days later Budowa and twenty-six other Protestant leaders who had come in on the promise of a free pardon, were beheaded and hanged in the Great Square of Prague. Their heads, stuck on poles and set up in the city, marked the end of the Old Bohemian Church.

King Ferdinand destroyed the Letter of Majesty. First the Brethren, and later all Protestants who would not join the Roman Catholic Church, were banished from Bohemia. Some were tortured, some hanged or burned at the stake. Their churches were not destroyed but

Introduction: The Moravians

"purified"—by sprinkling holy water and lashing the pulpits with whips—and committed to Roman Catholic priests. The books of the Brethren were burned by the thousands: the Kralitz Bible, Blahoslav's *History*, hymn-books, and catechisms. The schools and colleges were "reconstructed." Throughout the nation literature declined, scholarship disappeared. Private properties were seized. Soldiers (mostly foreign) ravaged the countryside, committing every atrocity. Villages were sacked, women and children slaughtered. Graves were despoiled. The remains of Ziska and Rockycana were dug up and dishonored. The work of extirpation showed a thoroughness never to be surpassed until the rise of Adolph Hitler. In a few years the population of Bohemia dropped from three million to one.

"Almighty God," wrote John Amos Comenius, who saw the village of Fulneck where he was pastor and rector of a school, sacked by Spanish troops, his own library destroyed, and his manuscripts burned—"Almighty God, what is happening? Must the whole world perish?"

But this was not the end for the *Unitas Fratrum*. Banishment turned the Unity from a national into a world-wide church. The Brethren scattered. Some escaped to Poland, some to Hungary, Prussia, Silesia, Transylvania, and in these places tried to organize again and keep the church alive. Others remained in Bohemia and Moravia, worshipping in secret and passing down from generation to generation the tradition of the Unity. In Moravia especially the "Hidden Seed" retained vitality, and flowered a century later.

Zerotin, who had sponsored the Kralitz Bible, escaped to Breslau in Silesia. But it was in Poland that the Brethren's hopes now rose highest. To Lissa in 1628 came John Amos Comenius, with his father-in-law, Bishop Cyrill. Other bishops gathered here, joined by many ministers from Bohemia and Moravia. They reorganized the Executive Council, installed their archives, set up a publications office, established parishes, and made this Polish city the new center of their church.

At Lissa the career of Comenius came into full flower. He had already, while in hiding after the sack of Fulneck, written *The Labyrinth of the World and Paradise of the Heart* (1623), a satire contrasting the worldly professors of Christianity with those who truly serve the Lord in quiet. Comenius, "the father of modern pedagogy," believed that universal education held the key to the good life for men and nations. At Lissa he wrote and published books on education that are amazingly modern in outlook, insisting as they do on happiness rather than fear as the prime motive for learning, and on things rather than words as proper objects of study. He wished to introduce politics, mechanics, and good manners into the curriculum.

In *The Great Didactic* he dealt with the methods and objectives of universal education. He planned to establish in England a university where *all* things should be taught. "The basis of the so-called pansophic studies of Komensky [Comenius]," wrote Edward Benes,* "was the principle that all created things have an interior association between them, that they are logically connected with one another, and that all of them can be accommodated in a common system of knowledge." He believed that the harmonization of knowledge is a prerequisite to the harmonization of men and nations.

Comenius' *Janua linguarum reserata* (The Gate of Languages Unlocked), published in 1631, was a Latin grammar taught by the conversation method, the rules being memorized only after the student had some grasp of vocabulary and idiom. This book, which was translated into fifteen different languages, made him famous. He advocated using pictures in teaching. His *Orbis sensualium pictus* (The World in Pictures), published at Nürnberg in 1658, was the first children's picture-book. Anticipating John Locke, he wrote, "The foundation of all learning consists in representing clearly to the senses sensible objects." He travelled in England, 1641, on invitation from parliament to advise on the reform of the English schools, and might have revolutionized English educational methods had not the outbreak of the Civil War broken off his work. He visited Sweden, 1642, on a similar mission. His fame was world-wide. Cotton Mather asserts (though the evidence is inconclusive) that at one time Comenius was invited to the presidency of Harvard College. Of all his works, the one that most directly influenced the development of the Moravian Church was, as we shall see, his revision of the *Ratio disciplinae*.†

The Peace of Westphalia, 1648, which brought an end to the Thirty Years War, had been expected by Comenius to sanction the return of his people to their homes in Bohemia and Moravia, but it did no such thing. The Brethren were completely forsaken. There was to be no return for them. Worse yet lay in store. In 1656, when Charles X of Sweden invaded Poland, the Polish army sacked and burned the town

---

* "The Place of Comenius in History as a Good European," in *The Teacher of Nations. Addresses and Essays in Commemoration of the Visit to England of the great Czech Educationalist Jan Amos Komenský 1641-1941*, ed. by Joseph Needham, F. R. S. (Cambridge, 1942), p. 4.

† *Ratio disciplinae ordinisque ecclesiastici in unitate fratrum Bohemorum*, Account of Ecclesiastical Discipline and Order in the Unitas Fratrum of Bohemia (1660).

Introduction: The Moravians

of Lissa, which the Swedes had garrisoned. Comenius' library was destroyed and his manuscripts were burned. Many of the Brethren were murdered. For miles around Lissa their properties were destroyed. It seemed as if the Unity were broken and scattered forever.

Yet Comenius had not failed. He left the revised *Ratio disciplinae* behind him to guide a resurrected church in the next century. In the dedication of that book, he made an appeal to the Church of England to take the *Unitas* under her protection. The Church of England in the next century did so, thus facilitating the reëstablishment of the Brethren's church in Pennsylvania. There is a short passage in the dedication which has since seemed to be prophetic:

> But to you, our friends, we leave and commit . . . our dear mother, the church itself. Whether God will deem her worthy to be revived in her native seats, or let her die there and resuscitate her elsewhere, in either case do you, in our stead, care for her.

The rebirth of the church of Gregory the Patriarch and John Amos Comenius makes as inspiring a story as that of its dissolution had been distressing. That the renewal came about through two Lutherans, one of them a former Roman Catholic, is a tribute to the traditional breadth of the *Unitas Fratrum*, which declined to be halted by doctrinal disputes from going straight to the heart of religion.

Christian David, whom John Wesley called "the first planter" of the renewed Moravian Church,* belonged to a type of man two world wars have made familiar to us in the twentieth century. He knew his way about the underground—the Protestant underground—of Bohemia and Moravia, and risked his life bringing religious refugees out to safety.

Christian David was born December 31, 1690, at Senftleben in Moravia. He was brought up a zealous Roman Catholic, but he had a probing, restless mind that drove him afoot through Europe on a "Research Magnificent," conversing, reading, adventuring, seeking everywhere the truth about essential things, above all about religion. He sought instruction from priests of his own faith, from Jews, from Protestants. He visited Hungary, Austria, Saxony, Silesia, Prussia. For a time he was a soldier in the Prussian army. He read the Bible, and the conviction grew upon him that the Protestants were right. Here, in the simple truths of the Gospels which his own heart seemed to authenticate, he had found what he was seeking. He joined the Lutherans

---
* Wesley's *Journal*, August, 1738.

in Berlin. Disillusioned, however, by the cold orthodoxy of the particular group in which he found himself, he moved on. At Görlitz in Silesia he met Melchior Schäfer and other pietists. Their company he found congenial. It seemed to him that they actually lived in the current that flowed from God.

Impelled to carry the news of his discovery to others, he became a preacher, putting to the service of religion the same spirit of adventure that had driven him all over Europe. He returned to his homeland in Moravia, where, as "the Bush Preacher," he stirred a revival of the Protestant worship that had secretly been maintained there. In the neighborhood of Fulneck, he visited a colony of German-speaking members of the *Unitas Fratrum*. He went to Zauchtenthal where the Zeisbergers and Heckewelders were, to Kunewalde * where the Nitschmanns were, and to Sehlen where the Jaeschkes and Neissers were. Prison and torture were still the lot of those found by the authorities to be true to the old *Unitas Fratrum*; but yet, a hundred years after the Day of Blood at Prague, the Brethren in Moravia preserved their faith. The dying words of old George Jaeschke were still vividly remembered at Sehlen when Christian David preached there.

It is true [Jaeschke had said (this was in 1707)] that our liberties are gone. . . . It may seem as though the final end of the Brethren's Church had come. But, my beloved children, you will see a great deliverance. The remnant will be saved. How, I cannot say; but something tells me that an exodus will take place; and that a refuge will be offered in a country and on a spot where you will be able, without fear, to serve the Lord according to His holy Word.†

At Sehlen, when Christian David preached from the text, "And every one that hath forsaken houses, or brethren, or sisters, or father, or mother, or wife, or children, or lands, for my name's sake, shall receive an hundredfold, and shall inherit everlasting life," the Neisser family recalled their grandfather's words about finding a place where they might worship without fear. They asked Christian David in his wanderings to look for such a place for them, and he promised to do this.

Months passed at Sehlen, and years, but still no word from Christian David. Meantime persecution in Moravia had been stepped up. Spies were everywhere, seeking out the Hidden Seed to destroy it. At last, on May 25, 1722 (a day of remembrance for the Unity), Christian David

---

* Not to be confused with Kunwald in Bohemia.
† Hutton, *op. cit.*, p. 195.

Introduction: The Moravians

returned to Sehlen. "The servant of the Lord," as David is still called by the Moravians, brought news that he had found a refuge for them. A young Lutheran Pietist, Count Zinzendorf, had consented to receive them on his estate at Berthelsdorf in Saxony. Two days later, at ten o'clock at night, ten members of the Neisser and Jaeschke families, leaving all their possessions, farms and houses, behind them forever, stole away with Christian David as a guide, and crossed the mountains by secret paths to the Sileian border. By June 8 they had arrived in Berthelsdorf.

Christian David risked his life on ten more journeys to bring out religious refugees from Moravia to Zinzendorf's estate in Saxony: among others, the Nitschmanns, the Zeisbergers, and the Heckewelders. Soon there was gathered on Count Zinzendorf's estate the nucleus of what came to be known, because of Christian David's exertions in his homeland, as the Moravian (rather than the Bohemian) Church.

Since the subsequent history of the renewed church was shaped so closely to the mind of Count Zinzendorf, we must pause here to see what sort of a man he was. Nicholas Lewis, Count Zinzendorf (1700-1760), was born at Dresden. His father, an important official at the court of Saxony, died within a few weeks of his son's birth. After his mother's remarriage the boy, at the age of four, was taken care of by his grandmother, Catherine von Gersdorf, at Gross Hennersdorf Castle. There, in the Pietist circles with which his grandmother surrounded him, his young mind was stimulated by the story of Jesus as told in the Gospels.

With all the warmth and tenderness of Zinzendorf's nature, there was a core of stubborn self-will in him which the bullying he received at school, from schoolmates and masters alike, did nothing to allay. He was neither broken nor hardened by the cruel treatment he received at Francke's school at Halle, but strengthened in self-reliance. He declined to join the boys in the vicious pastimes that flourished in the school. In protest, he and his friend, Count Frederick de Watteville, formed little religious societies. That is how the famous Order of the Grain of Mustard Seed came into being—a society with doctrines so broad that in later years it had among its members John Potter, Archbishop of Canterbury; Cardinal Noailles of the Roman Catholic Church; and General Oglethorpe, Governor of Georgia.

While he was still at school, Zinzendorf met the Danish missionary, Ziegenbalg, with some of his converts from Malabar. Inspired by what he saw, he made a convenant with De Watteville that when they were in a position to do so, they would organize missions among the forgotten peoples of the earth.

From Halle, Zinzendorf went to the University of Wittenberg to study law. Later he went abroad on the traditional Grand Tour. Travel widened his sympathies and clarified his opinions. Conversation with men of all persuasions taught him to believe that the Church of Christ transcended denominational boundaries, and included men of many sects and of different beliefs.

He began his public career as King's Councillor at Dresden, but his real interests lay elsewhere. In April, 1722, he bought the small estate of Berthelsdorf, near Hennersdorf, and set about establishing there such a "fellowship of true believers" as Luther himself had dreamed of.*

He installed John Andrew Rothe as pastor. The introductory sermon was preached by Melchior Schäfer, the Pietist clergyman who had influenced Christian David so strongly at Görlitz. Schäfer introduced Christian David to Rothe, Rothe introduced him to Zinzendorf, and Zinzendorf, when he heard of the plight of the persecuted Brethren in Moravia, offered to make a place for them on his estate.

"This," said the Neissers when the offer was reported to them at Sehlen, "is a call from the Lord."

So it came about that at Berthelsdorf, to accommodate the refugees who came in considerable numbers, trees were cut down (Christian David felling the first of them) on a hill known as the *Hutberg* or Watch Hill. Soon a small village arose which was named *Herrnhut*, the Lord's Watch. Not all the refugees who assembled there were members of the *Unitas Fratrum*. Many different denominations were represented among the approximately ninety persons already gathered there by May, 1725. Next year this group was joined by a number of Schwenkfelders from Silesia.

As Herrnhut increased in numbers, it increased in confusion, until Zinzendorf, who had been paying little attention to the colony on the Hutberg, found it necessary to intervene. In consultation with Christian David and other influential Moravians, he drew up forty-two statutes for the guidance of the community. Twelve elders were chosen, four of whom (Christian David among them) were selected by lot as "Chief Elders." Herrnhut settled back into orderly fellowship.

Up to this time Zinzendorf had not made any serious study of the *Unitas Fratrum*. But one day, July, 1727, he saw a copy of Comenius's

---
* Hutton, *op. cit.*, p. 190.

Introduction: The Moravians

Ratio disciplinae, from which he learned not only that his statutes were in harmony with the discipline of the ancient Unity, but also that the Bohemian and Moravian Brethren held a faith almost identical with his own.

I could not read the lamentations of old Comenius [he wrote] addressed to the Church of England, . . . I could not read his mournful prayer, "Turn Thou us unto Thee, O Lord, and we shall be turned; renew our days as of old," (Lament. 5:21)—without resolving there and then: I, as far as I can, will help to bring about this renewal.*

It was at Herrnhut that the beautiful custom of the Love Feast grew up, quite informally. A few persons, meeting in one another's houses to discuss the work of the church, provided a simple meal of rye bread and water. Later the custom became general, without losing its informality. White bread and tea were provided, and the Love Feast became a meeting of the whole congregation.† In the United States today, where the Love Feast is observed at congregational meetings—sometimes for special purposes, to hear a lecture, it may be, or listen to music—the pews are served by young ladies specially attired in "plain clothes" (not unlike the Quaker costume), who pass cups of coffee and "Moravian buns."

Zinzendorf instituted the system of "choirs," which was to be one of the most noticeable characteristics of the Brethren at Bethlehem in eighteenth century Pennsylvania. Members of the community were divided into ten classes or choirs, each with its own officers, services, festivals, love feasts, and special duties. There were choirs for the married

---

* *Büdingische Sammlung,* I, pp. 640-41; quoted in translation by De Schweinitz, *op. cit.,* p. 605, and Hutton, *op. cit.,* pp. 208-209.

† The origin of the Love Feast among the Moravians (it was already practised by the Pietists) is described more exactly by Bishop S. H. Gapp, Archivist, of the Northern Province of the Moravian Church in America, in a letter to the present writer dated at Bethlehem, Pennsylvania, May 30, 1956: "In 1727, August 13th, immediately after the experience which others call the 'Moravian Pentecost,' Zinzendorf noticed seven groups of the people sitting in the shade of trees, singing, praying, and conversing about their experience. As it was after meal hours, Zinzendorf sent food from his kitchen to each of the groups. It pleased them very much. In succeeding weeks Zinzendorf was gravely concerned about the danger of the extreme spiritual experience turning into fanaticism, and very sensibly determined to find some way of satisfying a natural human social craving. Then he remembered the groups around the church, eating, talking, singing— and he called it a love feast. Originally it was not a religious service in any sense—no Scripture reading, formal prayer or benediction. Often it took the form of morning or afternoon snack. In many congregations the love feasts are still very informal, except the love feast before Holy Communion. It represents human fellowship before fellowship with Christ."

people, widows, widowers, single Sisters, single Brethren, big girls, little girls, big boys, little boys, and infants. Each of the elder choirs had its own house with an elected leader. The system has long since been discarded, but today in Bethlehem the Brothers' House and the Sisters' House, built two centuries ago, are landmarks of the old order.

The choirs, love feasts, and other customs that grew up in Herrnhut owed most to Count Zinzendorf's influence. But the spirit of the renewed church and the tenor of its beliefs were derived from the ancient *Unitas*. The current flowed from John Huss, Peter of Chelcic, Gregory the Patriarch, Bishop Augusta, and Comenius, although Count Zinzendorf, overwhelming leader as he was, directed it into such channels as appealed to him.

It is, however, unprofitable to spend time here over the question, to which did the renewed Moravian Church owe most, the tradition inherited from the Bohemian Church Fathers or the Pietism of Count Zinzendorf. What drew the Moravian refugees to Zinzendorf, and the Count to them, was the recognition that in essentials they were one: they felt Christ in the heart, relied on the Bible for guidance, revived the simplicity of the early Church, avoided clerical disputes, and promoted godliness rather than denominationalism. When the Count insisted on having his own way in matters of procedure, the Brethren usually let him have it. "In essentials, unity; in non-essentials, liberty; in all things, charity."

What further drew the Count and his followers together was the threat of persecution. Zinzendorf had enemies at court, and his unorthodoxy gave them a hold on him. It was said that he harbored fanatics. Anticipating trouble in Saxony, he sent a company of Moravians to Georgia in 1734 to prepare a haven in the New World. In that same year he was ordained a Lutheran minister. Next year he sent another group of Moravians to Georgia, among whom was David Nitschmann II, who had recently consecrated the first bishop of the Renewed Church, by Bishop David Ernest Jablonsky—a bishop of the *Unitas Fratrum* now serving with the Reformed Church as pastor of the court church in Berlin. It was this second group of colonists with whom John Wesley voyaged to Georgia; and it was through observing them and conversing with them that he was brought to understand a quality in religion that was to enrich all his subsequent work.

August III of Saxony, in 1736, banished Count Zinzendorf for introducing religious novelties. Later the edict was rescinded, but in 1738 it was issued again, and Count Zinzendorf left the country.

Introduction: The Moravians

In an age of denominational chauvinism, as the early eighteenth century undoubtedly was, the double allegiance of Count Zinzendorf, to the Lutherans and to the Moravians, seemed to most people to be inexplicable on any honest grounds. He was ordained to the Lutheran ministry in 1734, and never left it. He was consecrated a bishop of the Moravian Church in 1737, and remained the great leader of that church until his death. In his own mind there was no problem. The Moravian *Diaspora*, "Scattered Seed," was a non-denominational movement. Members of the Moravian Church worked with other churches as occasion arose, accepting membership or even pastorates, as Bishop Jablonsky did in Berlin.* The object was, not to capture recruits for the Unity, but to make better Lutherans or Reformed, as the case might be. It must be understood, of course, that the Moravians were not without pride in their own denomination, and they were too well informed in history to discount the value of church organization, church discipline, and church tradition. They understood, too, the inevitable differences in doctrine that arise when men of different temperaments and backgrounds try to explain in the scientific or philosophical terms familiar to them the experience of the living Christ. They did not pretend that they agreed at all points with most Lutherans, Reformed, or what not. But they believed their distinctive message to the world was to hold fast to this central experience and not be disturbed by varying interpretations of it. That is what Peter Boehler had in mind when he said to John Wesley, "My brother, my brother, this philosophy of yours must be purged away."

Bishop J. Taylor Hamilton, in *A History of the Church Known as the Moravian Church, or the Unitas Fratrum*,† writes of the threefold calling of the Church: to foreign missions, *diaspora* work, and education. As we have seen, the third objective was fully realized in the schools instituted by the early Unity and in the writings of Comenius. The second objective was also realized in the early Church, though Zinzendorf's *ecclesiolae in ecclesia*, (churches within the Church), which he adopted from the Pietists, gave it form. The third objective, foreign missions, was Zinzendorf's particular contribution.

As we have seen, the founder of the Order of the Grain of Mustard Seed had from his school days dreamed of himself as an organizer of

---

* See John R. Weinlick, *Count Zinzendorf* (New York, 1956), p. 61: "Daniel Ernest Jablonsky, Reformed court preacher and grandson of John Amos Comenius. Jablonsky, though a Reformed clergyman, had been consecrated a Moravian Bishop in 1699, and at this time was one of the two surviving bishops of the ancient Brethren's Church.

† Bethlehem, Pa., 1900, pp. 381-82.

missions. The *Herrnhuters* (as in his day the Moravians were called) provided him with a tool for that purpose. In his large and often farsighted way, he made general arrangements for foreign work long before he had any definite plans or even a chosen field for a mission. He organized a band of Single Brethren to study medicine and geography in order to be ready for the call when it came.

In 1731, when the Count on a visit to the Danish Court met a negro slave, Antony Ulrich from the Island of St. Thomas in the West Indies, he knew the call had come. He heard Antony tell how his sister Anna, his brother Abraham, and other slaves longed to hear the Gospel. When, soon after, Antony himself came to Herrnhut, asking for help for his people, volunteers came forward. The lot was consulted. On August 21, 1732, Leonard Dober and David Nitschmann (the carpenter) left Herrnhut with bundles on their backs and a few shillings in their pockets, setting in motion the great movement of Protestant church missions.

The Moravians were not the first Protestant missionaries. But theirs was the first Protestant *church* (as distinct from the *state*, as in Denmark, and from *volunteer societies* like the Society for the Propagation of the Gospel, as in England) to carry on regular missionary work. They financed these missions themselves. The congregations discussed mission problems and circulated among themselves the letters and diaries of the missionaries.

With Leonard Dober and David Nitschmann an impulse was released that was to give this small but great-spirited church a beneficent influence throughout the world. To say that they were intent upon "saving souls," though this is true, is to invite misunderstandings. Their purpose was more nearly what we today might call a "point four program": an attempt to help backward peoples overcome their handicaps by means of a psychological and economic regeneration.

It has always been the policy of the Moravians to establish missions among the most neglected people. The Moravians were the first to conduct missions among the negro slaves. Their work in the West Indies was so successful, showing the white man that the negro was capable of civilized living, that they provided Wilberforce with his most powerful argument to convince the English Parliament that the negroes were ready for emancipation.

In 1733 Christian David set off with two companions, Matthew and Christian Stach, to establish a mission in Greenland. They set up villages and churches on the narrow strip of arable land between the

Introduction: The Moravians

glacier and the sea. There they taught the Greenlanders to cultivate gardens of cabbages, turnips, and lettuce. Other mission bases were established in Jamaica, Surinam, and South Africa—where the Calvinistic Boers believed the negroes to be "elected to damnation," and placed them in the animal kingdom with the baboons. There were Moravian missions also in Egypt among the Copts, and in Russia among the Calmucks. There were missions among the Eskimo in Labrador. The best known of all their missions, and in some ways the most fruitful despite its tragic outcome, was that among the Delaware and Mahican Indians of North America.

It was not missionary zeal, however, but the instinct of self preservation that first brought the Moravians to the New World. Once there, the Moravian colonists reached out to help their less fortunate neighbors, the negro slaves and the native Indians. The work in Georgia was soon interrupted. When war threatened with Spain and the British required all settlers, including the Moravians, to take up arms, the colony broke up. Like the Quakers, the Moravians had adopted the principle of nonviolence.* Some members of the Moravian colony returned to Europe. Others moved to Pennsylvania.

It was in the Forks of the Delaware (the territory enclosed between the confluent Lehigh and Delaware Rivers, where now stand the great industrial centers of Easton, Bethlehem, Nazareth, and Allentown) that the Moravians made their headquarters in America. In later years their American work was divided, Salem (now Winston-Salem) in North Carolina becoming headquarters of southern Moraviandom. But Bethlehem remained the center from which the mission to the Delawares was conducted.

Early in 1740 we find the first group of Pennsylvania Moravians, among whom were Melchior Zeisberger and his son David, working as carpenters at Nazareth for George Whitefield, who planned to establish here homes for insolvent debtors and a school for negroes. Subsequently the Moravians bought the tract from Whitefield. It was they who gave it the name Nazareth.

Next year five hundred acres were bought at the foot of the Lehigh Mountain, where Monocacy Creek enters the Lehigh River. Trees were cut down and a log building erected. It was in this building that Count Zinzendorf passed the night of December 24, 1741. The lowing of the cattle on the other side of the partition in this primitive dwelling

---
* Today, among the Moravians, the propriety of taking up arms in the service of one's country is left to each man's conscience.

reminded the Count of the first Christmas Eve, and he named the spot Bethelehem.

Once established in Bethlehem, the Moravian colony set itself three main objectives: missions among the Indians, *diaspora* work among the settlers of all denominations, and the establishment of schools. Of these it was the Indian mission that absorbed the greater part of their efforts. The whole economy of Bethlehem was geared to it. In order to mobilize their resources quickly and so keep a large mission force in the field, they introduced a communal system which they maintained for some twenty years—for as long, that is, as the emergency lasted.

The thought of conducting an Indian mission in the northern British colonies seems to have been inspired by something Conrad Weiser, Pennsylvania's Indian ambassador, had heard when, in 1737, he visited the Indian town of Otseninky (near modern Binghampton) on the North Branch of the Susquehanna River. It was a time of great famine. Hunters found no game in the woods. The children, as Weiser says, "looked like dead persons." The people were hopeless. "Rum will kill us," they said, "and leave the land clear for the Europeans without strife and purchase."

A prophet among them declared he had had a vision in which God denounced equally the fur trade and the rum trade, and sent this message to His Indian people:

You inquire after the cause why the game has become scarce. I will tell you. You kill it for the sake of the skins, which you give for strong liquors, and drown your senses, and kill one another, and carry on a dreadful debauchery. Therefore have I driven the wild animals out of the country, for they are mine. If you will do good, and cease from your sins, I will bring them back; if not, I will destroy you from off the earth.

The great Moravian organizer, Bishop Spangenberg, who was then in Pennsylvania, heard of this Indian prophecy and sent an account of it to Christian David, who in turn communicated it to the Brethren at Herrnhut. To them the words of the Otseninky prophet seemed to constitute another call.

Christian Henry Rauch, accordingly, was sent to the northern American colonies to see what could be done. The great story of the Moravian Indian mission began on August 16, 1740, when Rauch arrived at Shekomeko, a Mahican village in what is now northern Duchess County, New York. Here, and at the nearby towns of Wechquadnach and Pachgatgoch, he found descendants of the Mahicans, a proud people who had once measured their strength with the Iroquois, but who now were drowning in liquor the sense of frustration with which the white man's irresistible encroachment on their lands afflicted them.

It seemed to the Mahicans that their gods had deserted them. They listened at first in derision, afterwards in wonder and hope, at the story brought by Rauch of *his* God, who had come to earth and suffered on the cross a mental as well as physical anguish they could well understand; a God who had triumphed in that ordeal, who now desired their love, and who in exchange for it offered to share with them His love and something of His power. To this message they responded as the miners of England were doing to the tension-releasing sermons of John Wesley.

Never was seen such a transformation as that of the ruffianly Wassamapah (later to be known as *Tschoop*, i.e., Job) who, amazed at Rauch's courage in trusting his life to Wassamapah when he slept in his cabin, and touched by the story of Jesus, changed his life utterly. He renounced his grandmother's idol made of leather, gave up his brutal ways, and remained till death a loyal Christian. Other Mahicans, seeing the beneficent change in Wassamapah, examined the Moravian message more carefully. Those who accepted Christianity found that, although they had lost some threads of their Mahican past, they had gained confidence in themselves and a new hope.

The old way of life, of course, could never be wholly restored; but these Mahicans had found a way to keep their souls intact as they entered a new one. The Moravians taught them trades. Joshua, whom we shall meet again later, became a cooper. Finding their new converts artistic, the Brethren trained them also in letters and music. Joshua learned to play the spinet. The success of these experiments caused some of the Moravian leaders to dream of larger things. Might not the regeneration of the whole Indian race be accomplished through the leaven of a chosen few?

But the spirit of the times seemed to be against them. The populace was uneasy. Scores had not yet been settled between the English and the French in America. English-speaking settlers on the exposed colonial border suspected men of an alien tongue, who refused to take oaths or bear arms, of disloyalty. Magistrates began to put pressure on them. Laws against unauthorized preachers were passed. The Moravians, recognizing the all-too-familiar signs, decided to move.

They brought their Christian Indians to Pennsylvania, having first obtained permission from both the Pennsylvania authorities and the Iroquois, the latter claiming suzerainty over the Mahicans as well as title to most of the lands comprised in King Charles' grant to William Penn. In Pennsylvania, the Moravians hoped Penn's enlightened religious and racial policy would bring them safety.

Pennsylvania and New Jersey Delawares now joined the Mahicans, and all were settled temporarily near Bethlehem. In 1746 they were moved to a new site on Mahony Creek at its junction with the Lehigh River, where Lehighton now stands. This town, which the Moravians named Gnadenhütten, soon became an important place, properly laid out, with church and school and various industries. Its name was repeated, again and again, in the many subsequent removals of what came to be known as the "wandering Indian congregation." What happened to Gnadenhütten during the French and Indian War is told in Heckewelder's *Narrative.**

The story of the Moravian mission among the Indians is as heroic as the better-known story of the winning of the West, involving as both do a life and death struggle against the sternness of nature and the cruelty of man. Americans of Caucasian blood take pride in the story of their triumphant advance across the continent. But our victory—as it seems in these latter days when men are concerned about exploited and disinherited peoples—has gone a little sour. We cannot forget the Walking Purchase, the Cherokee Trail of Tears, the Squaw Campaign, the Battle of Wounded Knee. The Moravian story, on the other hand, leaves no bitter taste in the mouth. We may, therefore, all of us take unquestioning pride in what the Moravians did to help the Indians at Shekomeko, Gnadenhütten, Schönbrunn, and Fairfield.

Wherever the Moravians went among the Indians, they brought not only religion but also education, industry, and the arts. Their success in introducing the better elements of the white man's culture did not involve the destruction of the native *ethos*. They did not make an assault upon the Indian's personality. The Moravian purpose was to restore the morale of broken peoples, to give them enough of the white man's skills to enable them to live beside him without pauperization, in a word, to give hope to the displaced persons whom the Europeans' roaring advance across the continent had left in its wake.

---

* *Narrative of the Mission of the United Brethren Among the Delaware and Mohegan Indians, from Its Commencement, in the Year 1740, to the Close of the Year 1808* (Philadelphia, 1820).

Introduction: The Moravians

It was to this task, that of the Good Samaritan, that Moravian missions in America were dedicated.

The late Julius Cook, a Mohawk, once observed that his people had to have education if they were to survive in the modern world. "We must learn to think like white men," he said. "But we must hold fast to the best elements of our own culture. If we lose the latter we shall die inside."

The Moravians of Heckewelder's day understood the problem that Philip Cook had in mind. While of course the principal object of the mission was "to win souls for the Lamb," † the missionaries were engaged in a great work of rehabilitation. In their villages, the school accompanied the church. They introduced European tools and new methods of crop raising. Most important of all, the missionaries entered upon their work with a genuine respect for the people they had come to help. They did not try to break the Indian's spirit by reviling all his old customs. There were some differences of opinion about this policy, but on the whole it was followed.

They prudently refrained from any effort to wean [the Indian] from deeply-rooted usages and practises, as long as these were not sinful or inconsistent with Christian profession. While the converts were Christian, they continued to be Indians, following the pursuits and retaining many of the useful manners and usages which their fathers before them had engaged in. . . .*

The fact that the Moravian missionaries had, in a measure, learned to think like Indians, gave their work a quality that makes it seem so congenial to the twentieth century, in which Christianity has availed itself of the best wisdom of the sciences—in particular anthropology and psychology—to enrich the application of the Sermon on the Mount.

---

† Kenneth G. Hamilton, "Cultural Contributions of Moravian Missions Among the Indians," *Pennsylvania History*, January, 1951, pp. 1-15.

* Mabel Haller, "Early Moravian Education in Pennsylvania," *Transactions of the Moravian Historical Society*, Vol. XV (1953), p. 195.

Crayon portrait of a Delaware Indian, *Circa* 1804 by St. Mémin (1770-1852)
Courtesy of the New-York Historical Society, New York City

I

From Bedford, England, to Bethlehem, Pennsylvania: 1743-1754

LONGFELLOW in *Evangeline* speaks of the "meek" Moravians, but the epithet is misleading. There is a resilience in the Moravian Church that surprises: a gentleness, graciousness, artistry which when struck rings like iron.

The blend of piety and *élan* which, throughout its history, has gone into the metal of the *Unitas Fratrum* or Moravian Church, is exemplified in the career of John Heckewelder. He was a true scion of that persecuted but indomitable church, whose temperate doctrines stem from the teachings of the martyred John Huss, and whose energies since the early eighteenth century have been devoted very largely to foreign missions.

John Heckewelder was born in England of a Moravian family. His grandfather, George Heckewelder, and his father, David Heckewelder, had both been born in Zauchtental, Moravia, the former about 1676, the latter May 25, 1711. Recurring persecution of this ancient Protestant church drove George, with his son David, to find refuge in Saxony, where Count Zinzendorf had in 1722 offered a home to the much harried people. On his lands these religious refugees built a small village which they called Herrnhut (the Lord's Watch), and which under Count Zinzendorf's inspiration became the headquarters of the Renewed

Moravian Church. Here at Herrnhut George Heckewelder died, February 17, 1746.

Meanwhile his son David had in 1742 emigrated to England, where we pick up our story in the words of his first-born, John Gottlieb Ernst Heckewelder:

I was born March 12, 1743, at Bedford in England, where my father David Heckewelder, one of the refugees who left Moravia under the guidance of Br. Christian David, was at that period engaged in the service of the Brethren's Church. My juvenile years I spent in the Brethren's schools at Buttermere (in Essex), Smithhouse, and Fulneck. To this very day, I continue to cherish a grateful recollection of the blessed impressions made upon me on a certain prayer-day, held by Bishop John de Watteville at Fulneck, when his address created a lively desire in the hearts of his youthful audience, to serve the Lord in the Missionary field, should they attain to years of maturity. Some of my companions, with myself, actually entered into a covenant for this purpose.

In January, 1754, I travelled on foot to London, in company of the late Br. Pyrlaeus, and thence to Chelsea, my parents having received a call to America, whither I was to accompany them. The whole company, destined to sail for New-York in the Brethren's ship Irene, Capt. Garrison, amounted to forty persons, including fourteen children, of whom I was the eldest. The day previous to our departure, Count Zinzendorf conversed with the individuals belonging to our company. I was also called in, Br. Spangenberg being present, when the Count began by inquiring what progress I had made in learning, one main object of which ought to be, that I one day might be prepared for the ministry. In child-like simplicity I related my experience on the above-mentioned prayer-day, and informed him of the covenant into which several of us had entered. He then gave me his benediction, laying his hand upon my head and offering up a prayer, a circumstance which made a deep impression on my mind.

We set sail * March 12, 1754, being my eleventh birth-day, and had a very prosperous voyage; for, without encountering a single heavy gale, we crossed the Atlantic in twenty-one days, which at that time was considered as something approaching to a miracle. At New-York, we were very kindly received and hospitably entertained by our Brethren and Sisters. The majority of our party remaining there until the waggons could be sent for their conveyance to Bethlehem, I travelled on foot through New-Jersey, in company of the late Bishop David Nitschman. No bridges being erected over the watercourses at that time, my conductor, with the kindness of a father, carried me across the numerous creeks we had to pass. The whole of our company

---

* On the Moravian ship *Irene*, in a "Sea Congregation" which included Bishops Ettwein, Spangenberg, Nitschmann, and other leaders in the Moravian Church.

reached Bethlehem in safety on the 20th of April, and were cordially welcomed by the congregation at a general love-feast. In the first instance, I was placed in the children's seminary; and two years after, removed to Christiansbrunn, to follow agricultural pursuits and other useful occupations. Here, as well as at Bethlehem, I had frequent opportunities of seeing Indians who lay encamped near the latter place. The sight of these people gradually confirmed the desire and expectation cherished in my younger days, of being employed as a Missionary among them, at some future period.—*Memoir of the Life of Brother John Gottlieb Heckewelder, Missionary among the North American Indians. (Written by Himself.) Periodical Accounts, XIII, (1834), 49-56.*

※ II ※

The Muskingum in the Shadow of Pontiac's War: 1762

FROM EARLY BOYHOOD, as we have seen, John Heckewelder had wanted to be a missionary among the North American Indians. At Bethlehem, during the years of the French and Indian War, he had brief glimpses of these people, most of them fugitives, cast out by their own kin because they had adopted Christianity, and hounded by white men of the border because they were Indians. Heckewelder liked what he saw of these brave, friendly, gentle people. At last, in the year 1762, during a lull in hostilities along the Pennsylvania border, he left the trim streets and gracious architecture, the old-world, scholarly, artistic atmosphere of the little town on the Lehigh which Count Zinzendorf had named Bethlehem on Christmas Eve, 1741, and entered upon his first adventure in the Indian country.

His companion was Christian Frederick Post (*c.* 1710-1785). Young Heckewelder could have had no better guide and leader. Post was a man whom the Indians could not but admire. He possessed the three qualities which Conrad Weiser, Pennsylvania's famous Indian ambassador, had said were prerequisite to a man's success in the Indian world: integrity, devotion to the job in hand, and courage. Post had another: sympathy with and respect for the native people among whom he worked. Armed with these natural gifts and with an acquired knowledge of woodcraft, he had made two journeys into the western

The Muskingum: 1762

wilderness in 1758, carrying peace messages from the English to the Indians in the Ohio-Allegheny Valley, journeys which stripped the French at the Forks of the Ohio of their Indian allies and so prepared the way for General Forbes' bloodless entry into the ruins of Fort Duquesne.

The route described in Heckewelder's journal was in large part the one General Forbes had used in 1758. From Shippensburg, however, Post and Heckewelder took a short cut (a "mountain path" not practicable for Forbes's artillery) to Burnt Cabins over the Blue, Kittatinny, and Tuscarora Mountains. They followed Forbes through the blackness of Edmond's Swamp—formerly known as "the Shades of Death." But, as they approached Fort Pitt, they rejected Forbes' safe but roundabout road *via* the present Murrysville and took the more direct route (chosen the following year by Colonel Bouquet in his haste to relieve Fort Pitt) *via* Bushy Run near what is now Harrison City. This brought them to Fort Pitt by way of Braddock's field, thus giving Heckewelder occasion for one of his most memorable descriptions. Their journey ended at Tuscarawas on a branch of the Muskingum River, near the site of Bolivar, Ohio.

When Post first proposed to the nineteen-year-old *Schanne* (Johnny) that he come with him among the Delawares at Tuscarawas, the boy hesitated. For one thing he was—quite rightly, as it turned out—not sanguine about the outcome of this adventure. For another, he was already apprenticed to a mechanic at Bethlehem and therefore was not his own master. When, however, his release was granted by Mr. Nixon, and Bishop Spangenberg, director of the American Indian missions, encouraged him to go, Heckewelder saw his course set for him. It was clearly a "call." His apprenticeship papers were signed over to Christian Frederick Post, a precaution that was to save him from being pressed into military service.

Heckewelder set out from Bethlehem on March 8, 1762. Post, who had gone a few days earlier to Philadelphia, was to join him at Lititz.

But little preparation was necessary for the journey, and I was soon ready. On the evening before my departure from Bethlehem, the Congregation took leave of me by the singing of farewell hymns, and the next day Brother Martin Schenk and myself set out for Litiz. A deep snow had fallen, which in many places covered the fences; so that we frequently had to break our roads through the fields, and it was not until the fourth evening after our departure from Bethlehem that we arrived at Litiz. It was the 12th of March,

1762; my 20th birthday. My choir-labourer,* Brother Pezold, who was warmly attached to me, had promised to see me at Litiz, and there take leave of me. True to his word, he arrived in a few days: but he had overtasked his strength, a sudden thaw had rendered the roads almost impassable, and the sick and way-worn traveller came only to die. Before he "went home," he bade me an affectionate farewell, and gave me his last blessing.

From Litiz we pursued our journey on horseback. When we were ready to start, Post, in his enthusiastic way, began to sing. The brethren stood before the doors of their houses, and took leave of us as we travelled along the street. At Lancaster we were kindly received by the Brethren and the friends of the Congregation. The latter could not help considering the idea of going to the distant Indians merely to bring them the word of reconciliation, as a most daring adventure; still they did all in their power to render our short stay comfortable. Among them the well-known Jew, Joseph Symonds, was foremost. At the close of our first day's journey from Lancaster, we put up at Middletown for the night. The next day, after a ride of eight miles, we crossed the Susquehanna at Harris's ferry [Harrisburg]. The river had risen fearfully from the melting of immense quantities of snow; and it was with great difficulty that we could persuade the ferrymen to attempt the dangerous passage. At last we crossed in safety, after having been carried nearly a mile down the stream by the rapid current. Having been delayed so long at the ferry, we could only travel four miles farther before nightfall. The next day we arrived at Carlisle; where we remained several hours, as Post had to make arrangements for the reception of the Indians, whom he had promised the Governor to invite and accompany to this place, in order to hold a talk with the Government officers. We stopped for the night at Mount Rock, eight miles from Carlisle; and on the following day reached Shippensburg, a distance of twenty-one miles from Carlisle. Here we took leave of the white settlements; the howling wilderness being full before us. In every direction, the blackened ruins of houses and barns, and remnants of chimneys met our eyes; the sad memorials of the cruelties committed by the French and Indians, during the savage warfare of 1756, and the following years; concerning which many horrible stories were related to us by eye-witnesses. This was nothing to cheer us; but there was certainly an exhortation contained in all this, to hasten to bring the tidings of peace to the ferocious red men, for they are "to all people."

Eleven miles beyond Shippensburg, Post struck into a mountain path; it

---

* "Congregations were subdivided into separate sections, men, women, and children being gathered into homogeneous groups. Thus the Married People formed one Choir, the Widowers another, and Widows a third; Single Brethren made up another, as did the Single Sister; Older Boys, Older Girls, and Children also constituted separate Choirs. Each group was put under the care of special church workers."—Rt. Rev. Kenneth Gardiner Hamilton, *John Ettwein and the Moravian Church During the Revolutionary Period* (Bethlehem, 1940), p. 56.

The Muskingum: 1762

being shorter by several miles than the wagon road, which made the circuit of the mountain. The path was almost invisible, and the ascent was excessively steep and rocky. When we had ascended half way, Post made a halt and said: "Here let us keep our Sabbath lovefeast. It is the very day and hour in which the Congregation are assembled for a similar purpose at Bethlehem; let us sit down on this rock and sing with them." We raised our voices and sang one of our missionary hymns.

> *Ye chosen of God, who to every nation*
> *Bring tidings of his pard'ning grace,*
> *O tell us, ye heralds of blood-bought salvation,*
> *The paths on which ye run your race!*
> *Through the dark storm-night, over roaring waves,*
> *On desert rocks, in the mountain caves,*
> *In the deep dim woods where no foot hath trod,*
> *Will ye journey and rest, and go forth with God.*

During the singing of the last lines, we broke and ate a piece of bread which we had with us, in token of fellowship and love. After we had thus refreshed both soul and body, we continued our ascent.—Edward Rondthaler, *Life of John Heckewelder*, 38-41.

After a narrow escape from drowning at the Juniata Crossing and another narrow escape from recruiting officers at Fort Bedford, Heckewelder began the ascent with Frederick Post on March 30 of the Allegheny Mountain.

The snow began to fall rapidly, and had already covered the ground to the depth of three feet and a half. The cold became more intense; and we were reminded of our possible fate by a large number of carcasses of horses, which were scattered along the mountain path. However, there was nothing left to us but to push on as fast as we could. It was eleven miles to the nearest habitation; and to turn back was out of the question. Fortunately the snow ceased falling in the afternoon; otherwise we should have lost the road and perished. After a most painful ride, we managed to gain the summit of the mountain. Without halting, we began to descend, and soon found ourselves in the midst of a thick and dark forest of hemlock trees. At last, after a hard day's journey, and just as night came on, we succeeded in reaching the cabin of a hunter, whose name was Jack Miller, (also Saucy Jack,) in Edmonds's Swamp. Scarcely had we entered, when the wolves began their dismal howl, which was the hunter's night music all the year round. Jack had no stable; but our horses found tolerable pasture on a piece of land of about three acres, which had been cleared and fenced in by the hunter and his sons. The young men offered to watch our beasts, and protect them from the wolves. A bell was fastened to the neck of each horse, a few fires were kindled, the hunters took their guns, and, followed by their dogs, began their watch, while we tried to refresh ourselves by a good night's sleep. But in this we were disappointed. The howling of the wolves, the barking of the dogs, the tinkling of the bells, by means of which the young men were enabled to tell where the horses were, and more than all the continual shouting of the guard from without, to assure their father of their watchfulness, and the answering cry of the old hunter from within, drove sleep from our eyes. Still we were thankful for the safety in which we were permitted to pass the night; and the next morning we took an affectionate leave of this wild but hospitable family.

We soon reached Stony Creek; where we were very nearly brought to a perfect stand. The bed of the creek is about four rods wide, but the water had risen to a great height; the canoe had been carried off by the stream the night before, and the few settlers, together with a small garrison, were all on the other side of the creek. After many entreaties and promises on our part, a sugar trough was brought from the woods; and in this novel vessel, we were safely ferried over; but had almost lost our horses, which were saved only by the greatest exertions. Having crossed the Laurel Hill and the Chesnut Ridge, we reached Bushy Run on the 1st of April, and pushed on rapidly, in order if possible to reach Pittsburgh, distance twenty-five miles, before night. Having approached the Fort within seven or eight miles, we suddenly found ourselves on the field of Braddock's defeat. A dreadful sight was presented to our eyes. Skulls and bones of the unfortunate men slain here on the 9th of July, 1755, lay scattered all around; and the sound of our horses' hoofs continually striking against them, made dismal music, as, with the Monongahela full in view, we rode over this memorable battle-ground.

We felt as if relieved from an insupportable weight, when, on arriving at Fort Pitt, we again found ourselves in the company of the living. The only private dwelling in the neighborhood of the Fort was situated at the junction of the Allegheny and Monongahela. It was owned by two traders, Messrs. Davenport and McKinney; who received us in a very friendly and hospitable manner. Within the Fort, also, we met with kind well-wishers; and the treatment we received at the hands of the gallant commander Col. Bouquet, and all his officers, calls for my lasting gratitude. To a youth far from home and friends, engaged in an enterprize the success of which was more than doubtful, each kind word is as an angel from heaven.

Post had expected to be able to make arrangements at Fort Pitt for a supply of flour, which could easily have been brought to our new home by the travelling traders. But to our great disappointment, the magazine had been overflowed by a tremendous inundation, and no flour was to be had. Neither could any be procured from the surrounding country, as there were no farms within hundreds of miles.

On the 5th of April, we crossed the Alleghany. The heavy rain of the preceding day, had swelled the different streams in our way, so that we

The Muskingum: 1762

could travel only sixteen miles before night. We pitched our tent on a rising ground near a creek. During the night a dreadful thunder storm came on, and we were awakened by the water rushing through our tent. We immediately laid our baggage on the top of the tent, to prevent it from being washed away, and the night being perfectly dark, we heaped wood on the fire, to produce a bright blaze, that we might see our way to a safer resting place. Our companion from Pittsburgh, a Virginian, who seemed accustomed to a life of hardships, and perfectly at home in such scenes as these, led the way with lighted firebrands, and enabled us to find the most shallow places. Here we crossed while the water was running knee deep around us. By dint of great exertion, we managed to save our horses, tents and baggage. There was no time to lose. The last time we crossed from our first encampment, we could scarcely stem the flood; and in the morning the spot where our tent had been standing was covered by the deep waters. Our baggage had been completely wetted; and as we supposed that the creeks we should have to pass must have risen during the night, we resolved to remain where we were till the next morning.

The Virginian kindly offered to go out hunting and procure us food; and Post and myself spent the greater part of the day together, thanking God for his mercy, and reminding each other, that a path like ours could not be strewn with flowers. The next day we continued our journey, and found the smaller streams fordable. The Beaver river we crossed in canoes with the assistance of the Indians who lived there. They also gave us some venison and bear's fat; and one of them, White Eyes, presented us with a few chickens. Four days after, on the 11th of April, we arrived at Tuscarawas on the Muskingum, after a pilgrimage of thirty-three days. We entered our cabin singing a hymn.

The cabin which Post had built the year before [a mile and a half above the Indian town of Tuscarawas, which was just above the present Bolivar]; stood on a high bank, on the east side of the Muskingum [Tuscarawas], about four rods from the stream. No one lived near us on the same side of the river; but on the other, a mile down the stream, resided a trader, named Thomas Calhoon, a moral and religious man. Farther south was situated the Indian town called Tuscarawas; consisting of about forty wigwams. A mile still farther down the stream, a few families had settled; and eight miles above our dwelling, there was another Indian village.

The Indians, having been aware of Post's intention, had allowed him to erect his cabin. But during his absence, they had become suspicious; fearing that this missionary scheme might prove a mere pretence, in order to enable the white people to obtain a footing in the Indian country, and that in course of time a fort would be erected, and the original inhabitants of the land be driven from their territory. When they now observed Post marking out three acres of ground for a corn-field, and beginning to cut down trees, they became alarmed, and sent him word to appear before them at the council house on the following day, and meanwhile to desist from doing any further work on the premises. On his appearance before them at the time appointed, the speaker, in the name of the Council, delivered the following address.

"Brother! Last year you asked our leave to come and live with us; for the purpose of instructing us and our children; to which we consented; and now being come, we are glad to see you.

"Brother! It appears to us, that you must since have changed your mind; for instead of instructing us or our children, you are cutting down trees on our land; you have marked out a large spot of ground for a plantation, as the white people do every where; and by and by, another and another may come and do the same, and the next thing will be, that a fort will be built for the protection of these intruders; and thus our country will be claimed by the white people, and we driven further back, as has been the case ever since the white people came into this country. Say, do we not speak the truth?"

In answer to this address, Post delivered himself thus. "Brothers! What you say I told you, is true, with regard to my coming to live with you, namely for the purpose of instructing you; but it is likewise true, that an instructor must have something to live upon, otherwise he cannot do his duty. Now, not wishing to be a burden to you, so as to ask of you provision for my support, knowing that you already have families to provide for, I thought of raising my own bread; and believed that three acres of ground were little enough for that. You will recollect that I told you last year, that I was a messenger from God, and prompted by him to preach and make known his will to the Indians; that they also by faith might be saved, and become inheritors of his heavenly kingdom. Of your land I do not want a foot; neither will my raising a sufficiency of corn and vegetables on your land for me and my brother to subsist on, give me or any other person a claim to your land."

Post then retired to give the chiefs and council time to deliberate on an answer; this done, they again met, when the speaker thus addressed my companion.

"Brother! Now, as you have spoken more distinctly, we may perhaps be able to give you some advice. You say that you are come at the instigation of the great Spirit, to teach and to preach to us. So also say the priests at Detroit, whom our Father, the French, has sent among his Indian children. Well, this being the case, you, as a preacher, want no more land than those do; who are content with a garden lot, to plant vegetables and pretty flowers in, such as the French priests also have, and of which the white people are all fond.

"Brother! As you are in the same station and employ with those preachers we allude to, and as we never saw any one of those cut down trees and till the ground to get a livilihood, we are inclined to think, especially, as those men without laboring hard, yet look well, that they have to look to another

The Muskingum: 1762

source than that of hard labour for their maintenance. And we think, that if as you say, the great Spirit urges you to preach to the Indians, he will provide for you in the same manner as he provides for those priests we have seen at Detroit. We are agreed to give you a garden spot, even a larger spot of ground than those have at Detroit. It shall measure fifty steps each way; and if it suits you, you are at liberty to plant therein what you please."

To this proposal Post agreed, as there was no remedy. . . .—Rondthaler, *Heckewelder*, 42-48.

Elsewhere Heckewelder tells us that "the lot was on the following day stepped off by captain Pipe, stakes drove in at the corners, and Post told that now he might go on with his work again." *

This Captain Pipe who stepped off the bounds of their land for them, was a Delaware war chief of the Wolf tribe. The nickname, "Captain Pipe," had been given him by white men. His real name was *Koniesch-quanoheel*, Maker of Daylight. He was not well known among white men at the time Heckewelder first met him, but he was soon enough to cut a niche for himself in history. He was to take part in Pontiac's war, besiege Fort Pitt, and, in 1764, to be held as a hostage by Colonel Bouquet. During the Revolutionary War it was he who opposed Captain White Eyes, then the head chief of the Delawares and friend of the Americans. In the end, Captain Pipe swung the bulk of his nation over to the British side. Heckewelder, in good time, was to owe him both fear and gratitude, in full measure, as our narrative will show.

When Captain Pipe measured off the land, "fifty steps each way," to serve the two white men for their garden, they had reason to be uneasy. This tiny tract would be insufficient for their support.

We perceived at once the insurmountable difficulties of our situation. As was mentioned above, there was no flour to be procured at Fort Pitt. Neither was Indian corn to be had, as a famine prevailed at the time among the Indians, and every grain of maize was saved for planting. Potatoes were also very scarce. We were therefore forced to depend, partly on my expertness with the gun and fishing hook, and partly on the few vegetables that were to be found in the surrounding forest. There were wild ducks in abundance; but the river being in some places too deep to ford, and we having no canoe, I often had to wait very long, until they flew so near the bank that I could reach them when shot. The wild geese were still more difficult to get, as these seldom approach the banks, but generally keep in the middle of the river. Pheasants and squirrels are almost worthless in summer; and the larger game of the forest was rapidly shot down by the more expert Indians, whom

---

* Heckewelder, *Narrative of the Mission of the United Brethren among the Delaware and Mohegan Indians* . . . (Philadelphia, 1820), p. 64.

hunger rendered still more active. Of fish we could procure more than enough; but in the manner in which we were forced to prepare them they became tasteless and even disgusting; and besides, when used exclusively, these are not a food calculated to give strength to the body. We lived mostly on nettles; which grew abundantly in the bottoms, and of which we frequently made two meals a day. We also made use of some other vegetables and greens. Besides, we had brought along some tea and chocolate; which we drank as well as we could without milk or sugar.

Of course such a diet could have no other effect than to weaken us from day to day. Nevertheless, we were obliged to clear the space allotted us for a garden, and which was covered by thick trees. When these were removed, the ground had to be loosened with pickaxes. The wood we chopped very short, so that we could roll and drag it from the enclosure. How often, while engaged in this laborious employment without strengthening food, did I think of the pieces of bread which I had frequently seen given to the hogs; and how gladly would I have shared them!

One day some chiefs came to request my assistance for a few days in making a fence round their land. I gladly accepted the invitation, being desirous of doing any thing to secure their good will; and I did my best to be of service to them. At the same time, I was enabled to restore my health and strength; for as long as I staid with them, I could eat enough to satisfy the cravings of hunger. Thus I found myself suddenly transferred as it were to a land of plenty, and where I had opportunities to cultivate the acquaintance of the Indian youth, and to secure the favour of the tribe by my industry. During my stay with them, I received the name of "Piselatulpe," Turtle; by which I am still known among the Delawares.—Rondthaler, *Life of Heckewelder*, 48-50.

Though in time Heckewelder was to become a noted linguist, well versed in English, German, and the Unami dialect of Delaware, he at first had some difficulty with the language.

The first and most important thing for a traveller is a competent knowledge of the language of the people among whom he is. Without this knowledge it is impossible that he can acquire a correct notion of their manners and customs and of the opinions which prevail among them. There is little faith to be placed in those numerous vocabularies of the languages of distant nations which are to be found in almost every book of voyages or travels; they are generally full of the most ridiculous mistakes; at least (for I must speak only of what I know) those which relate to the Indian languages of North America. I was some years ago shown a vocabulary * of the idiom of the Indians who inhabited the banks of the Delaware, while Pennsylvania was

---

* Vocabularium Barbaro-Virgineorum, bound with an Indian translation from the Swedish of Luther's Catechism. Stockholm, 1696, duod.—Heckewelder's note.

The Muskingum: 1762

under the dominion of the Swedes, which idiom was no other than the pure Unami dialect of the Lenape, and I could hardly refrain from laughing at the numerous errors that I observed in it; for instance, the Indian word given for *hand* in fact means *finger*. This is enough to shew how carelessly those vocabularies are made, and how little their authors are acquainted with the language that they pretend to teach.

The cause of these mistakes may be easily accounted for. When pointing to a particular object you ask an Indian how it is called, he never will give you the name of the *genus*, but always that of the *species*. Thus, if you point to a tree, and ask for its name, the answer will be oak, beech, chestnut, maple, &c., as the case may be. Thus the Swedish author of the vocabulary that I have mentioned, probably happened to point to a *finger*, when he asked what was the Indian word for *hand*, and on receiving the answer, without further enquiry enriched his work with this notable specimen of Indian learning.

When I first went to reside among the Indians, I took great care to learn by heart the words *Kœcu k'delloundamen yun?* which means *What do you call this?* Whenever I found the Indians disposed to attend to my enquiries, I would point to particular objects and repeat my formulary, and the answers that they gave I immediately wrote down in a book which I kept for the purpose; at last, when I had written about half a dozen sheets, I found that I had more than a dozen names for "*tree*," as many for "*fish*," and so on with other things, and yet I had not a single generic name. What was still worse, when I pointed to something, repeating the name or one of the names by which I had been taught to call it, I was sure to excite a laugh; and when, in order to be set right, I put the question *Kœcu*, &c., I would receive for answer a new word or name which I had never heard before. This began to make me believe that everything was not as it should be, and that I was not in the right way to learn the Indian language.

It was not only in substantives or the proper names of things that I found myself almost always mistaken. Those who are not acquainted with the copiousness of the Indian languages, can hardly form an idea of the various shades and combinations of ideas that they can express. For instance, the infinitive *Mitzin* signifies *to eat*, and so does *Mohoan*. Now although the first of these words is sufficiently expressive of the act of eating something, be it what it may, yet the Indians are very attentive to expressing in one word what and how they have eaten, that is to say whether they have been eating something which needed no chewing, as pottage, mush or the like, or something that required the use of the teeth. In the latter case the proper word is *mohoan*, and in the former *guntammen*. If an Indian is asked *k'dapi mitzi?* have you eaten? he will answer *n'dapi guntammen*, or *n'dapi mohoa*, according as what he has eaten did or did not require the aid of chewing. If he has eaten of both kinds of provisions at his meal, he will then use the generic word, and say, *n'dapi mitzi*, which means generally, *I have eaten.*

These niceties of course escaped me, and what was worse, few of the words I had taken down were correctly written. Essential letters or syllables, which in the rapidity of pronunciation had escaped my ear, were almost everywhere omitted. When I tried to make use of the words which I had so carefully collected, I found I was not understood, and I was at a loss to discover the cause to which I might attribute my want of success in the earnest endeavours that I was making to acquire the Indian tongue.

At last there came an Indian, who was conversant with the English and German, and was much my friend. I hastened to lay before him my learned collection of Indian words, and was very much astonished when he advised me immediately to burn the whole, and write no more. "The first thing," said he, "that you are to do to learn our language is to get an Indian *ear*; when that is obtained, no sound, no syllable will ever escape your hearing it, and you will at the same time learn the true pronunciation and how to accent your words properly; the rest will come of itself." I found he was right. By listening to the natives, and repeating the words to myself as they spoke them, it was not many months before I ventured to converse with them, and finally understood every word they said. The Indians are very proud of a white man's endeavouring to learn their language; they help him in everything that they can, and it is not their fault if he does not succeed.

The language, then, is the first thing that a traveller ought to endeavour to acquire, at least, so as to be able to make himself understood and to understand others. Without this indispensable requisite he may write about the soil, earth and stones, describe trees and plants that grow on the surface of the land, the birds that fly in the air and the fishes that swim in the waters, but he should by no means attempt to speak of the disposition and characters of the human beings who inhabit the country, and even of their customs and manners, which it is impossible for him to be sufficiently acquainted with. And indeed, even with the advantage of the language, this knowledge is not to be acquired in a short time, so different is the impression which new objects make upon us at first sight, and that which they produce on a nearer view. I could speak the Delaware language very fluently, but I was yet far from being well acquainted with the character and manners of the Lenape.

The Indians are very ready to answer the enquiries that are made respecting the usages of their country. But they are very much disgusted with the manner which they say some white people have of asking them questions on questions, without allowing them time to give a proper answer to any one of them. They, on the contrary, never ask a second question until they have received a full answer to the first. They say of those who do otherwise, that they seem as if they wished to know a thing, yet cared not whether they knew it correctly or properly. There are some men who before the Indians have well understood the question put to them, begin to write down their answers; of these they have no good opinion, thinking that they are writing something unfavourable of them.

There are men who will relate incredible stories of the Indians, and think themselves sufficiently warranted because they have Indian authority for it. But these men ought to know that all an Indian says is not to be relied upon as truth. I do not mean to say that they are addicted to telling falsehoods, for nothing is farther from their character; but they are fond of the marvellous, and when they find a white man inclined to listen to their tales of wonder, or credulous enough to believe their superstitious notions, there are always some among them ready to entertain him with tales of that description, as it gives them an opportunity of diverting themselves in their leisure hours, by relating such fabulous stories, while they laugh at the same time at their being able to deceive a people who think themselves so superior to them in wisdom and knowledge. They are fond of trying white men who come among them, in order to see whether they can act upon them in this way with success. Travellers who cannot speak their language, and are not acquainted with their character, manners and usages, should be more particularly careful not to ask them questions that touch in any manner upon their superstitious notions, or, as they are often considered even by themselves "fabulous amusements." Nor should a stranger ever display an anxiety to witness scenes of this kind, but rather appear indifferent about them. In this manner he cannot be misled by interested persons or those who have formed a malicious design to deceive him. Whenever such a disposition appears (and it is not difficult to be discovered), questions of this kind should be reserved for another time, and asked in a proper manner before other persons, or of those who would be candid and perhaps let the enquirer into the secret.

"I have been led to consider Carver, who otherwise is deserving of credit for the greatest part of what he has written on the character of the Indians, to have been imposed upon in the story which he relates of having learned by means of a conjurer (the chief priest of the Killistenoes, as he calls him) who pretended to have had a conversation with the great Spirit, the precise time when a canoe should come, and certain traders who had been long expected to arrive.* Had Carver resided a longer time among the Indians, so as to have acquired a more intimate acquaintance with their customs,† he would have known that they have one in particular (which I understand is universal among all the tribes), which would have easily explained to him what he thought so mysterious. Whenever they go out on a journey, whether far or near, and even sometimes when they go out on hunting parties, they always fix a day, on which they either will return, or their friends at home shall hear from them. They are so particular and punctual in "making their word true," as they call it, that when they find that at the rate they are travelling, they would probably be at home a day or so sooner than the time

---

* Carver's Travels, Introduction, p. 72. Boston Edit., 1797.—Heckewelder's note.

† Carver was only 14 months in the Indian country, during which time he says he travelled near 4000 miles and visited twelve different nations of Indians.—Heckewelder's note.

appointed, they will rather lay by for that time than that their word should not be precisely made good. I have known instances when they might have arrived in very good time the day preceding that which they had appointed, but they rather chose to encamp for the night, though but a few miles distant from their home. They urge a variety of reasons for this conduct. In the first place, they are anxious not to occasion disappointment in any case when they can avoid it. They consider punctuality as an essential virtue, because, they say, much often depends upon it, particularly when they are engaged in wars. Besides, when the day of their return is certainly known, everything is prepared for their reception, and the family are ready with the best that they can provide to set before them on their arrival. If, however, unforeseen circumstances should prevent them from coming all on the same day, one, at least, or more of them, will be sure to arrive, from whom those at home will learn all that they wish to know.

On all important occasions, in which a tribe or body of Indians are concerned or interested, whether they are looking out for the return of an embassy sent to a distant nation, for messengers with an answer on some matter of consequence, for runners despatched by their spies who are watching an enemy's motions, or for traders who at stated periods every year are sure to meet them at certain places, they always take proper and efficacious measures to prevent being surprised.

The case which appears to have excited so much astonishment in Captain Carver, I believe to have been simply this. The Indians * had at the season that he speaks of failed to arrive at the trading place at the time appointed. The Indians who had assembled there for the purpose of meeting them could not be ignorant of the cause of their delay, as they had, no doubt, learned it by the return of some of their runners sent out for that purpose, who, as is their custom, probably informed them that another set of runners would be in the next day with further advices. The priest must have known all this, and the precise spot where those fresh runners were to encamp the night preceding their arrival, which is always well known and understood by means of the regular chain of communication that is kept up. These runners say to each other, pointing to the heavens: "When the sun stands there, I will be here or at such a particular spot," which they clearly designate. The information thus given is sure to reach in time the chiefs of the nation.

The manner in which this priest spoke to Captain Carver of his pretended intercourse with the great Spirit, clearly shews the deception that he was practising upon him. "The great Spirit," said he, "has not indeed told me when the persons we expect will be here, but to-morrow, soon after the sun has reached his highest point in the heavens, a canoe will arrive, and the people in that will inform us when the traders will come." The question,

---

* For *"Indians"* read *"traders."*—Heckewelder's note.

then, which he had put to the great Spirit, "when the traders would come?" was not answered, and there was no need of asking the Manitto when the *canoes* should come, for that must have been known already, and that the people in it would tell them where the traders were, and when they might be expected to arrive.—Heckewelder, *History*, 318-324.

☙ III ☙

The Delawares at Home: 1762

SOME QUESTIONS that had bothered Heckewelder when he first encountered Indians in the neighborhood of Bethlehem, found an answer at Tuscarawas.

When I was a boy between twelve and fifteen years of age, I had often heard of white people conversant with the Indians, who at that time would continually come to this place, (Bethlehem) in great numbers, even by the hundreds, that the Indians did not eat rabbits, because they thought them infected with the venereal disease, and that whoever ate of their flesh, was sure to take that disorder. Being then myself fond of catching those animals in traps, I asked questions on this subject of several Mohican Indians, who spoke the German language; but though they said nothing about the disease that rabbits were said to be infected with, yet they advised me by no means to eat of their flesh. They gave me no reason whatever to induce me to abstain from this food; but afterwards, in the year 1762, when I resided at Tuscarawas on the Muskingum, I was told by some of them, that there were some animals which Indians did not eat, and among them were the *rabbit* and the *ground-hog;* for, said they, they did not know but that they might be *related* to them!

I found also that the Indians, for a similar reason, paid great respect to the rattle-snake, whom they called their *grandfather,* and would on no account destroy him. One day, as I was walking with an elderly Indian on the banks of the Muskingum, I saw a large rattle-snake lying across the path, which I was going to kill. The Indian immediately forbade my doing so; "for," said he, "the rattle-snake is grandfather to the Indians, and is placed here on purpose to guard us, and to give us notice of impending danger by his rattle, which is the same as if he were to tell us 'look about!' Now," added

The Delawares at Home: 1762

he, "if we were to kill one of those, the others would soon know it, and the whole race would rise upon us and bite us." I observed to him that the white people were not afraid of this; for they killed all the rattle-snakes that they met with. On this he enquired whether any white man had been bitten by these animals, and of course I answered in the affirmative. "No wonder, then!" replied he, "you have to blame yourselves for that! you did as much as declaring war against them, and you will find them in *your* country, where they will not fail to make frequent incursions. They are a very dangerous enemy; take care you do not irritate them in *our* country; they and their grandchildren are on good terms, and neither will hurt the other."

These ancient notions have, however in a great measure died away with the last generation, and the Indians at present [This was written in 1817, published in 1819.] kill their grandfather the rattle-snake without ceremony, whenever they meet with him.

That the Indians, from the earliest times, considered themselves in a manner connected with certain animals, is evident from various customs still preserved among them, and from the names of those animals which they have collectively, as well as individually, assumed. It might, indeed, be supposed that those animals' names which they have given to their several tribes were mere badges of distinction, or "coats of arms" as Pyrlæus calls them; but if we pay attention to the reasons which they give for those denominations, the idea of a supposed family connexion is easily discernible. The Tortoise, or as it is commonly called, the *Turtle* tribe, among the Lenape, claims a superiority and ascendancy over the others, because their *relation*, the great Tortoise, a fabled monster, the Atlas of their mythology, bears according to their traditions this great *island* on his back, and also because he is amphibious, and can live both on land and in the water, which neither of the heads of the other tribes can do. The merits of the *Turkey*, which gives its name to the second tribe, are that he is stationary, and always remains with or about them. As to the *Wolf*, after whom the third tribe is named, he is a rambler by nature, running from one place to another in quest of his prey; yet they consider him as their benefactor, as it was by his means that the Indians got out of the interior of the earth. It was he, they believe, who by the appointment of the Great Spirit, killed the deer whom the Monsey found who first discovered the way to the surface of the earth, and which allured them to come out of their damp and dark residence. For that reason, the wolf is to be honored, and his name preserved for ever among them. Such are their traditions, as they were related to me by an old man of this tribe more than fifty years ago.—Heckewelder, *History*, 251-253.

Indian costume interested Heckewelder, and he has much to tell us of what he saw, and what he heard about it, among the Delawares on the Muskingum.

In ancient times, the dress of the Indians was made of the skins of animals and feathers. This clothing, they say, was not only warmer, but lasted much longer than any woollen goods they have since purchased of the white people. They can dress any skin, even that of the buffaloe, so that it becomes quite soft and supple, and a good buffaloe or bear skin blanket will serve them many years without wearing out. Beaver and raccoon skin blankets are also very pliant, warm and durable; they sew together as many of those skins as is necessary, carefully setting the hair or fur all the same way, so that the blanket or covering be smooth, and the rain do not penetrate, but run off. In wearing these fur blankets they are regulated by the weather; if it is cold and dry the fur is placed next the body, but in warm and wet weather, they have it outside. Some made themselves long frocks of fine fur, and the women's petticoats in the winter season were also made of them, otherwise of dressed deer skins, the same as their shirts, leggings and shoes. They say that shoes made of dressed bear skins, with the hair on and turned inside, are very warm, and in dry weather, durable. With the large rib bones of the elk and buffaloe they shaved the hair off the skins they dressed, and even now, they say that they can clean a skin as well with a well prepared rib-bone as with a knife.

The blankets made from feathers were also warm and durable. They were the work of the women, particularly of the old, who delight in such work, and indeed, in any work which shews that they are able to do their parts and be useful to society. It requires great patience, being the most tedious kind of work I have ever seen them perform, yet they do it in a most ingenious manner. The feathers, generally those of the turkey and goose, are so curiously arranged and interwoven together with thread or twine, which they prepare from the rind or bark of the wild hemp and nettle, that ingenuity and skill cannot be denied them. They show the same talent and much forethought in making their *Happis*, the bands with which they carry their bags and other burdens; they make these very strong and lasting.

The present dress of the Indians is well known to consist in blankets, plain or ruffled shirts and leggings for the men, and petticoats for the women, made of cloth, generally red, blue, or black. The wealthy adorn themselves besides with ribands or gartering of various colours, beads and silver broaches. These ornaments are arranged by the women, who, as well as the men, know how to dress themselves in style. Those of the men principally consist in the painting of themselves, their head and face principally, shaving or good clean garments, silver arm spangles and breast plates, and a belt or two of wampum hanging to their necks. The women, at the expense of their husbands or lovers, line their petticoat and blue or scarlet cloth blanket or covering with choice ribands of various colours, or with gartering, on which they fix a number of silver broaches, or small round buckles. They adorn their leggings in the same manner; their mocksens, (properly *Maxen*, or according to the English pronunciation *Moxen*), are embroidered in the neatest manner, with coloured porcupine quills, and are besides, almost entirely covered with various trinkets; they have, moreover, a number of little bells and brass thimbles fixed round their ancles, which, when they walk, make a tinkling noise, which is heard at some distance; this is intended to draw the attention of those who pass by, that they may look at and admire them.

The women make use of vermilion in painting themselves for dances, but they are very careful and circumspect in applying the paint, so that it does not offend or create suspicion in their husbands; there is a mode of painting which is left entirely to loose women and prostitutes.

As I was once resting in my travels at the house of a trader who lived at some distance from an Indian town, I went in the morning to visit an Indian acquaintance and friend of mine. I found him engaged in plucking out his beard, preparatory to painting himself for a dance which was to take place the ensuing evening. Having finished his head dress, about an hour before sunset, he came up, as he said, to see me, but I and my companions judged that he came *to be seen*. To my utter astonishment, I saw three different paintings or figures on one and the same face. He had, by his great ingenuity and judgment in laying on and shading the different colours, made his nose appear, when we stood directly in front of him, as if it were very long and narrow, with a round knob at the end, much like the upper part of a pair of tongs. On one cheek there was a red round spot, about the size of an apple, and the other was done in the same manner with black. The eye-lids, both the upper and lower ones, were reversed in the colouring. When we viewed him in profile on one side, his nose represented the beak of an eagle, with the bill rounded and brought to a point, precisely as those birds have it, though the mouth was somewhat open. The eye was astonishingly well done, and the head, upon the whole, appeared tolerably well, shewing a great deal of fierceness. When we turned round to the other side, the same nose now resembled the snout of a pike, with the mouth so open, that the teeth could be seen. He seemed much pleased with his execution, and having his looking-glass with him, he contemplated his work, seemingly with great pride and exultation. He asked me how I liked it? I answered that if he had done the work on a piece of board, bark, or anything else, I should like it very well and often look at it. But, asked he, why not so as it is? Because I cannot see the face that is hidden under these colours, so as to know who it is. Well, he replied, I must go now, and as you cannot know me to-day, I will call to-morrow morning before you leave this place. He did so, and when he came back he was washed clean again.

Thus, for a single night's *frolic*, a whole day is spent in what they call dressing, in which each strives to outdo the other.

When the men paint their thighs, legs and breast, they, generally, after laying on a thin shading coat of a darkish colour and sometimes of a whitish clay, dip their fingers' ends in black or red paint, and drawing it on with their outspread fingers, bring the streaks to a serpentine form. The garments of some of their principal actors are singular, and decorated with such a number of gewgaws and trinkets, that it is impossible to give a precise description of them. Neither are they all alike in taste, every one dressing himself according to his fancy, or the custom of the tribe to which he belongs. While the women, as I have already said, have thimbles and little bells rattling at their ancles, the men have deers' claws fixed to their braced garters or knee bands, and also to their shoes, for the same purpose; for they consider jingling and rattling as indispensably necessary to their performances in the way of dancing.

The notion formerly entertained that the Indians are beardless by nature and have no hair on their bodies, appears now to be exploded and entirely laid aside. I cannot conceive how it is possible for any person to pass three weeks only among those people, without seeing them pluck out their beards, with tweezers made expressly for that purpose. Before the Europeans came into the country, their apparatus for performing this work, consisted of a pair of muscle shells, sharpened on a gritty stone, which answered very well, being somewhat like pincers; but since they can obtain wire, of which that of brass is preferred, they make themselves tweezers, which they always carry with them in their tobacco-pouch, wherever they go, and when at leisure, they pluck out their beards or the hair above their foreheads. This they do in a very quick manner, much like the plucking of a fowl, and the oftener they pluck out their hair, the finer it grows afterwards, so that at last there appears hardly any, the whole having been rooted out. The principal reasons which they give for thus plucking out their beards and the hair next to their foreheads, are that they may have a clean skin to lay the paint on, when they dress for their festivals or dances, and to facilitate the *tattooing* themselves, a custom formerly much in use among them, especially with those who had distinguished themselves by their valour, and acquired celebrity. They say that either painting or tattooing on a hairy face or body would have a disgusting appearance.—Heckewelder, *History*, 202-205.

Tattooing, in 1762, was still practised among the Delawares at Tuscarawas.

. . . a valiant chief of that village, named *Wawundochwalend*, desirous of having another name given him, had the figure of a water-lizard engraved or tattooed on his face, above the chin, when he received the name *Twakachshawsu*, the water-lizard. The process of tattooing, which I once saw performed, is quickly done, and does not seem to give much pain. They have poplar bark in readiness burnt and reduced to a powder, the figures that are to be tattooed are marked or designed on the skin; the operator with a small stick, rather larger than a common match, to the end of which some sharp needles are fastened, quickly pricks over the whole so that blood is drawn, then a coat of this powder is laid and left on to dry. Before the whites came

The Delawares at Home: 1762

into this country, they scarified themselves for this purpose with sharp flint stones, or pricked themselves with the sharp teeth of a fish.

In the year 1742, a veteran warrior of the Lenape nation and Monsey tribe, renowned among his own people for his bravery and prowess, and equally dreaded by their enemies, joined the Christian Indians who then resided at this place [Bethlehem]. This man, who was then at an advanced age, had a most striking appearance, and could not be viewed without astonishment. Besides that his body was full of scars, where he had been struck and pierced by the arrows of the enemy, there was not a spot to be seen, on that part of it which was exposed to view, but what was tattooed over with some drawing relative to his achievements, so that the whole together struck the beholder with amazement and terror. On his whole face, neck, shoulders, arms, thighs and legs, as well as on his breast and back, were represented scenes of the various actions and engagements he had been in; in short, the whole of his history was there deposited, which was well known to those of his nation, and was such that all who heard it thought it could never be surpassed by man.* Far from murdering those who were defenceless or unarmed, his generosity, as well as his courage and skill in the art of war, was acknowledged by all. When, after his conversion, he was questioned about his warlike feats, he frankly and modestly answered, "That being now taken captive by *Jesus Christ*, it did not become him to relate the deeds he had done while in the service of the evil spirit; but that he was willing to give an account in the manner in which he had been *conquered*." At his baptism, on the 23rd of December 1742, he received the name of *Michael*, which he preserved until his death, which happened on the 23rd of July 1756. He led the life of a true Christian, and was always ready and willing to relate the history of his conversion, which I heard myself from his own mouth. His age, when he died, was supposed to be about eighty years.—Heckewelder, *History*, 206-207.

The cutting of the ears, which formerly was practised among the Indians, is now no longer so common with them. Their reasons for laying this custom aside, are that the operation is painful, not only when performed, but until the ears are perfectly healed, which takes a long time, and that they often lose that part of their ears which is separated from the solid part, by its being torn off by the bushes, or falling off when frost-bitten. I once heard of a gay Indian setting off on a severe cold morning for a neighbouring village not more than three miles distant, whose ears had been touched by the frost, and

---

* Heckewelder's *History*, p. 206, note 2 (by William C. Reichel, editor): " 'The serenity of Michael's countenance,' writes Loskiel, 'when he was laid in his coffin, contrasted strangely with the figures scarified upon his face when a warrior. These were as follows: upon the right cheek and temple, a large snake; from the under lip a pole passed over the nose, and between the eyes and the top of the forehead, ornamented at every quarter of an inch with round marks, representing scalps; upon the upper cheek, two lances crossing each other; and upon the lower jaw, the head of a will boar.' "

dropped off before he arrived at the place to which he was going. He had not even felt that he had lost them, and when told of it, he was so chagrined that he was going to destroy himself. I have seen a great many Indians with torn ears; but now the custom of cutting them is nearly if not entirely disused.—Heckewelder, *History*, 207.

An Indian loves to see his wife well clothed, which is a proof that he is fond of her; at least, it is so considered. While his wife is bartering the skins and peltry he has taken in his hunt, he will seat himself at some distance, to observe her choice, and how she and the traders agree together. When she finds an article which she thinks will suit or please her husband, she never fails to purchase it for him; she tells him that it is *her* choice, and he is never dissatisfied.

The more a man does for his wife the more he is esteemed, particularly by the women, who will say: "This man surely loves his wife." Some men at their leisure hours make bowls and ladles, which, when finished, are at their wives' disposal.

If a sick or pregnant woman longs for any article of food, be it what it may, and however difficult to be procured, the husband immediately sets out to endeavour to get it. I have known a man to go forty or fifty miles for a mess of cranberries to satisfy his wife's longing. In the year 1762 I was witness to a remarkable instance of the disposition of Indians to indulge their wives. There was a famine in the land, and a sick Indian woman expressed a great desire for a mess of Indian corn. Her husband having heard that a trader at Lower Sandusky had a little, set off on horseback for that place, one hundred miles distant, and returned with as much corn as filled the crown of his hat, for which he gave his horse in exchange, and came home on foot, bringing his saddle back with him. Squirrels, ducks, and other like delicacies, when most difficult to be obtained, are what women in the first stage of their pregnancy generally long for. The husband in every such case will go out and spare no pains nor trouble until he has procured what is wanted.—Heckewelder, *History*, 159.

IV

Shingas, the Terrible: 1762

CONCERNING HECKEWELDER'S NEIGHBOR at Tuscarawas, "King" Shingas, the people of Pennsylvania had strong but unfavorable opinions. In 1756 the following notice had appeared in the *Pennsylvania Gazette*:

SEVEN HUNDRED DOLLARS REWARD

Notice is hereby given, That the sum of *Seven Hundred Pieces of Eight* is raised by Subscription among the Inhabitants of the City of *Philadelphia*, and now offered with the Approbation of his Honour the *Governor*, as a Reward for any Person or Persons who shall bring into this City the Heads of *Shingas*, and Captain *Jacobs*, Chiefs of the Delaware Indian Nation; or Three Hundred and Fifty Pieces of Eight for each . . .*

Virginia followed suit with an offer of "AN HUNDRED PISTOLES" for the "Heads of King Shingas and Captain Jacobs . . . ; or FIFTY PISTOLES for each . . ."

After Captain Jacobs's death at Kittanning (he was killed when Colonel Armstrong's party attacked the town, September 8, 1756), King Shingas rose to eminence as the foremost Delaware warrior. Whether in peace or in war he was a man of distinction: active and resolute in battle, but at the same time magnanimous, sensitive to the point of honor, and kind to those dependent on him. After being rebuffed by Braddock on the march to Fort Duquesne, he withdrew his forces from the General's support. Observing the British disaster at the

---

* *Pennsylvania Gazette*, No. 1410, p. 2, cols. 2-3.

Monongahela, despairing of effective British aid to his people in case they should oppose the French invaders of the Allegheny Valley, and remembering how his people had been dispossessed of their lands in Pennsylvania, he decided to ally himself with the French. During the Indian war that ensued on Braddock's defeat, he scourged the frontiers of Pennsylvania and Virginia. He was the Black Douglas of that border and that time.

"Were all his war exploits on record," writes Heckewelder, "they would form an interesting document, though a shocking one. Conococheago, Big Cove, Shearman's Valley and other settlements along the frontier felt his strong arm sufficiently to know that he was a bloody warrior, cruel in his treatment, relentless in his fury. His person was small, but in point of courage, activity and savage prowess, he was said to have never been exceeded by anyone."—Bausmann, *History of Beaver County* (New York, 1904) I, 29.

Yet, from Christian Frederick Post, Heckewelder learned that Shingas, however implacable in battle, never treated a prisoner with cruelty.* He learned also, from his own observation, that this valiant warrior in his own community was considerate, generous, and capable of the warmest personal attachments.

Passing one day with him, in the summer of 1762, near by where his two prisoner boys (about twelve years of age) were amusing themselves with his own boys, and he observing me looking that way, inquired what I was looking at. On my replying that I was looking at his prisoners, he said, "when I took them they *were* such; but *they* are now *my* children, eat their victuals out of one and the *same* bowl!" which was saying as much as, that they, in all respects, were on an equal footing with *his own* children—alike dear to him.— Heckewelder, "Names of Delaware Chiefs . . . ," *Transactions of the American Philosophical Society*, New Series, IV, 396.

During that summer the death of Shingas' wife not only provided a spectacle of which the young white boy eagerly wrote a description in his notebook, but also afforded some insight into hidden parts of the great warrior's character.

His wife had fallen ill of a fever. Rejecting the help of Indian doctors (for whom Heckewelder had a deep and well-founded respect), she

---

* See Post's Journal, *Pennsylvania Archives*, 1st Series, III, 533, August 29, 1758: "This day I dined with Shingas, he told me tho' the English had set a great price on his head he never thought to revenge himself, but was always very kind to any Prisoners that were taken & brought in, & that he assured the Governor he would do all in his Power to bring about an established Peace . . .

accepted the diagnosis of local conjurors who told her she was bewitched. Under the ministrations of these "hex doctors," she died.

At the moment that she died, her death was announced through the village by women specially appointed for that purpose, who went through the streets crying, *"She is no more! she is no more!"* The place on a sudden exhibited a scene of universal mourning; cries and lamentations were heard from all quarters; it was truly the expression of the general feeling for a general loss.

The day passed in this manner amidst sorrow and desolation. The next morning, between nine and ten o'clock, two counsellors came to announce to Mr. Thomas Calhoon, the Indian trader, and myself, that we were desired to attend and assist at the funeral which was soon to take place. We, in consequence, proceeded to the house of the deceased, where we found her corpse lying in a coffin, (which had been made by Mr. Calhoon's carpenter) dressed and painted in the most superb Indian style. Her garments, all new, were set off with rows of silver broaches,* one row joining the other. Over the sleeves of her new ruffled shirt were broad silver arm-spangles from her shoulder down to her wrist, on which were bands, forming a kind of mittens, worked together of wampum, in the same manner as the belts which they use when they deliver speeches. Her long plaited hair was confined by broad bands of silver, one band joining the other, yet not of the same size, but tapering from the head downwards and running at the lower end to a point. On the neck were hanging five broad belts of wampum tied together at the ends, each of a size smaller than the other, the largest of which reached below her breast, the next largest reaching to a few inches of it, and so on, the uppermost one being the smallest. Her scarlet leggings were decorated with different coloured ribands sewed on, the outer edges being finished off with small beads also of various colours. Her mocksens were ornamented with the most striking figures, wrought on the leather with coloured porcupine quills, on the borders of which, round the ankles, were fastened a number of small round silver bells, of about the size of a musket ball. All these things, together with the vermilion paint, judiciously laid on, so as to set her off in the highest style, decorated her person in such a manner, that perhaps nothing of the kind could exceed it.

The spectators having retired, a number of articles were brought out of the house and placed in the coffin, wherever there was room to put them in, among which were a new shirt, a dressed deer skin for shoes, a pair of scissors, needles, thread, a knife, pewter basin and spoon, pint-cup, and other similar things, with a number of trinkets and other small articles which she was fond of while living. The lid was then fastened on the coffin with three straps, and three handsome round poles, five or six feet long, were laid across it, near

---

* A kind of round buckle with a tongue, which the Indians fasten to their shirts. The traders call them broaches. They are placed in rows, at the distance of about the breadth of a finger one from the other.—Heckewelder's note.

each other, and one in the middle, which were also fastened with straps cut up from a tanned elk hide; and a small bag of vermilion paint, with some flannel to lay it on, was then thrust into the coffin through the hole cut out at the head of it. This hole, the Indians say, is for the spirit of the deceased to go in and out at pleasure, until it has found the place of its future residence.

Everything being in order, the bearers of the corpse were desired to take their places. Mr. Calhoon and myself were placed at the foremost pole, two women at the middle, and two men at the pole in the rear. Several women from a house about thirty yards off, now started off, carrying large kettles, dishes, spoons, and dried elk meat in baskets, for the burial place, and the signal being given for us to move with the body, the women who acted as chief mourners made the air resound with their shrill cries. The order of the procession was as follows; first a leader or guide, from the spot where we were to the place of interment. Next followed the corpse, and close to it *Shingask*, the husband of the deceased. He was followed by the principal war-chiefs and counsellors of the nation, after whom came men of all ranks and descriptions. Then followed the women and children, and lastly two stout men carrying loads of European manufactured goods upon their backs. The chief mourners on the women's side, not having joined the ranks, took their own course to the right, at the distance of about fifteen or twenty yards from us, but always opposite to the corpse. As the corpse had to be carried by the strength of our arms to the distance of about two hundred yards, and hung low between the bearers, we had to rest several times by the way, and whenever we stopped, everybody halted until we moved on again.

Being arrived at the grave, we were told to halt, then the lid of the coffin was again taken off, and the body exposed to view. Now the whole train formed themselves into a kind of semi-lunar circle on the south side of the grave, and seated themselves on the ground. Within this circle, at the distance of about fifteen yards from the grave, a common seat was made for Mr. Calhoon and myself to sit on, while the disconsolate *Shingask* retired by himself to a spot at some distance, where he was seen weeping, with his head bowed to the ground. The female mourners seated themselves promiscuously near to each other, among some low bushes that were at the distance of from twelve to fifteen yards east of the grave.

In this situation we remained for the space of more than two hours; not a sound was heard from any quarter, though the numbers that attended were very great; nor did any person move from his seat to view the body, which had been lightly covered over with a clean white sheet. All appeared to be in profound reflection and solemn mourning. Sighs and sobs were now and then heard from the female mourners, so uttered as not to disturb the assembly; it seemed rather as if intended to keep the feeling of sorrow alive in a manner becoming the occasion. Such was the impression made on us by this long silence.

At length, at about one o'clock in the afternoon, six men stepped forward to put the lid upon the coffin, and let down the body into the grave, when suddenly three of the women mourners rushed from their seats, and forcing themselves between these men and the corpse, loudly called out to the deceased to "arise and go with them and not to forsake them." They even took hold of her arms and legs; at first it seemed as if they were caressing her, afterwards they appeared to pull with more violence, as if they intended to run away with the body, crying out all the while, "Arise, arise! Come with us! Don't leave us! Don't abandon us!" At last they retired, plucking at their garments, pulling their hair, and uttering loud cries and lamentations, with all the appearance of frantic despair. After they were seated on the ground, they continued in the same manner crying and sobbing and pulling at the grass and shrubs, as if their minds were totally bewildered and they did not know what they were doing.

As soon as these women had gone through their part of the ceremony, which took up about fifteen minutes, the six men whom they had interrupted and who had remained at the distance of about five feet from the corpse, again stepped forward and did their duty. They let down the coffin into the earth, and laid two thin poles of about four inches diameter, from which the bark had been taken off, lengthways and close together over the grave, after which they retired. Then the husband of the deceased advanced with a very slow pace, and when he came to the grave, walked over it on these poles, and proceeded forward in the same manner into an extensive adjoining prairie, which commenced at this spot.

When the widowed chief had advanced so far that he could not hear what was doing at the grave, a painted post, on which were drawn various figures, emblematic of the deceased's situation in life and of her having been the wife of a valiant warrior, was brought by two men and delivered to a third, a man of note, who placed it in such a manner that it rested on the coffin at the head of the grave, and took great care that a certain part of the drawings should be exposed to the East, or rising of the sun; then, while he held the post erect and properly situated, some women filled up the grave with hoes, and having placed dry leaves and pieces of bark over it, so that none of the fresh ground was visible, they retired, and some men, with timbers fitted beforehand for the purpose, enclosed the grave about breast-high, so as to secure it from the approach of wild beasts.

The whole work being finished, which took up about an hour's time, Mr. Calhoon and myself expected that we might be permitted to go home, as we wished to do, particularly as we saw a thundergust from the west fast approaching; but the Indians, suspecting our design, soon came forward with poles and blankets, and in a few minutes erected a shelter for us.

The storm, though of short duration, was tremendous; the water produced by the rain, flowing in streams; yet all had found means to secure themselves during its continuance, and being on prairie ground, we were out of all danger of trees being torn up or blown down upon us. Our encampment now appeared like a village, or rather like a military camp, such was the number of places of shelter that had been erected.

Fortunately, the husband of the deceased had reached the camp in good time, and now the gust being over, every one was served with victuals that had been cooked at some distance from the spot. After the repast was over, the articles of merchandise which had been brought by the two men in the rear, having been made up in parcels, were distributed among all present. No one, from the oldest to the youngest, was excepted, and every one partook of the liberal donation. This difference only was made, that those who had rendered the greatest services received the most valuable presents, and we were much pleased to see the female mourners well rewarded, as they had, indeed, a very hard task to perform. Articles of little value, such as gartering, tape, needles, beads, and the like, were given to the smaller girls; the older ones received a pair of scissors, needles and thread, and a yard or two of riband. The boys had a knife, jews-harp, awl-blades, or something of similar value. Some of the grown persons received a new suit of clothes, consisting of a blanket, shirt, breech-cloth and leggings, of the value in the whole of about eight dollars; and the women, (I mean those who had rendered essential services) a blanket, ruffled shirts, stroud and leggings, the whole worth from ten to twelve dollars. Mr. Calhoon and myself were each presented with a silk cravat and a pair of leggings. The goods contributed on this occasion, were estimated by Mr. Calhoon at two hundred dollars; the greatest part of them had, the same morning, been taken out of his store.

After we had thus remained, in a manner, under confinement, for more than six hours, the procession ended, and Mr. Calhoon and myself retired with the rest to our homes. At dusk a kettle of victuals was carried to the grave and placed upon it, and the same was done every evening for the space of three weeks, at the end of which it was supposed that the traveller had found her place of residence. During that time the lamentations of the women mourners were heard on the evenings of each day, though not so loud nor so violent as before.

I have thus described, from minutes which I took at the time, the ceremonies which take place among the Delaware Indians on the death of a person of high rank and consideration among them."—Heckewelder, *History*, 270-275.

These honours of "mourning over the corpse" are paid to all; the poor and humble, as well as the rich, great, and powerful; the difference consists only in the number of mourners, the undistinguished Indian having few besides his immediate relations and friends, and sometimes only those. Women (notwithstanding all that has been said of their supposed inferior station and of their being reduced to the rank of slaves) are not treated after their death with less respect than the men, and the greatest honours are paid to the remains of the wives of renowned warriors or veteran chiefs, particularly if they were descended themselves of a high family, which, however strange it may appear, is not an indifferent thing among the Indians, who love to honour the merit of their great men in their relatives.—*Ibid.*, 269.

V

A Black Cloud Rising: 1762

MEANWHILE EVENTS of another kind were taking shape, which were to give John Heckewelder an unpleasant glimpse of politics behind the forest curtain. Secret conferences were being held among the Indians to discuss proposals initiated by the western Senecas for war against the English. The recent British victory over the French had upset the balance of power toward which Iroquois policy had been directed since 1701 *; and the policies of the new British Commander-in-Chief in America, General Amherst, seemed to give prospect of unsatisfactory British-Indian relations.

An air of hostility, the causes of which were as yet unknown to him, oppressed young Heckewelder in this Indian community.

> Hitherto, amidst all my privations, I had still enjoyed the company of a white man; but of this comfort too I was soon to be deprived. Previously to our leaving Philadelphia, Post had promised the Governor of Pennsylvania to do his best to encourage the chiefs of the Western Delawares to come to Lancaster, in the latter part of summer, in order to hold a talk with the Government; and had also given his word to accompany them. In view of this arrangement, it had been resolved at Bethlehem by the Elders of the Congregation, that in case of Post's succeeding in this negotiation, he should not leave me in Ohio, but that we should set out together for Lancaster, and then return to our station.—Rondthaler, *Life of Heckewelder*, 50.

---

* See Anthony F. C. Wallace, "Origins of Iroquois Neutrality," *Pennsylvania History*, XXIV, No. 3 (July, 1957), pp. 223-235.

The Governor desired in particular that Shingas and his brother, King Beaver (who had supplanted "King" Shingas as head-chief of the Western Delawares *), should be brought down to the treaty. King Beaver accepted, but Shingas "positively declared that he would not go, believing that the English only wanted to murder him for the damage he had done them during the late war." †

The time when Post was to set out being near at hand, he became not a little embarassed. It was evident that if we both left the Muskingum, we should not be able to return, and in travelling to Lancaster together, would be virtually abandoning our missionary enterprize. For the Indians were already suspicious; and during our absence, designing men might easily increase their fears, and induce them to destroy our cabin and forbid our return. On the other hand, Post was unwilling to leave me alone in a strange country, surrounded by an unfriendly and savage tribe, of whose very language I was still ignorant. He laid the whole matter before me; and we at last agreed that I should remain.

In order to enable us to bring down cedar wood, for the purpose of making tubs and the like articles for the Indians, and also to procure the game that I might shoot on the river, we resolved to make a canoe. We set about the work without delay, and with the assistance of one of Mr. Calhoon's men, we succeeded in finishing one that answered our purpose very well.

To assist me in passing the time, Post left me a number of old sermons and religious books, requesting me at the same time, never to read or write in presence of the Indians, and even to conceal the books from their sight. "For otherwise," said he, "you will be in great danger. The Indians are very suspicious of those white people whom they see engaged in reading and writing, especially the latter; believing that it concerns them or their territory. They say that they have been robbed of their lands by the writing of the whites." I was therefore compelled to keep my books and papers in the garret, from a window of which I could see whether any one was approaching the cabin. Here I whiled away many an hour, far from civilization, alone with my books, my thoughts and God.—Rondthaler, *Heckewelder*, 50-51.

Scarcely had six weeks elapsed from the time of the departure of those

---

* Shingas had in 1753 been appointed head-chief (by Tanacharisson, the Half King, on behalf of the Six Nations, who claimed suzerainty over all the Delawares) to fill the place left vacant by the death of Olumapies in 1747. The Western Delawares, newly organized beyond the Allegheny Mountains, had asserted their independence, while the Susquehanna Delawares followed the lead of Teedyuscung who (since 1758) had been content to sit under the Six Nations' Tree of Peace. Many of the Western Delawares, protesting an appointment made under the authority of the Six Nations, preferred to acknowledge Shingas's brother, the Beaver (Tamaqua), as their rightful chief. The situation being thus confused, the Governor desired to treat with both brothers, Shingas and the Beaver, together.

† Heckewelder, *Narrative*, 64.

A Black Cloud Rising: 1762

who had gone on the treaty, when it became known that the French had succeeded in persuading the Indian nations, once more to try their strength against the English. And it was further added: "that a treaty at this time would be of no effect; and that even Post would not be permitted to return to this place again."—Heckewelder, *Narrative*, 64-65.

As long as I had my canoe, I could always procure a plentiful supply of provisions. The wild ducks were so numerous that I frequently brought down five or six at one shot. But by the carelessness or dishonesty of the Indian boys, who often borrowed the canoe in order to spear fish, or to pursue deer on the river by torchlight, it was lost before many days were over. I was often in great distress for food; and indeed, many a day I was entirely destitute of it. The nettles had become too large and hard; and every vegetable that grew in my garden was stolen by the passing traders. Whenever I wished to visit Mr. Calhoon, I had to wade through the Muskingum; in consequence of which I was soon attacked by fever and ague. . . .

The fever soon prostrated my strength, and the gloom of my situation increased. It would be impossible to give an adequate idea of my sufferings, both in mind and body; alone and sick, and almost famished. More than once, on returning from Mr. Calhoon's, the paroxysm of fever became so violent that I had to lie down on the path till it was over. An Indian once found me in this condition, and kindly led me to my cabin. Mr. Calhoon, a man of open hand and heart, invited me to come and stay with him; and I would gladly have accepted the kind offer, but I had promised Post to remain at the cabin, as otherwise the Indians would have stolen every thing. At last my strength failed to such a degree that I was afraid to venture upon fording the river, and was compelled to stay at home, if such a place might be called a home. . . .

Whilst I was in this miserable condition, I was once visited by an Indian of my acquaintance; and I begged him to make me a little bark canoe; in return for which I promised to give him a knife. He did so, and I soon made my first trial with it, passing down the river to visit Mr. Calhoon. He hardly recognized me, so much had hunger and fatigue changed my appearance. I was received in the most friendly manner, and food was immediately set before me. I told him of my new acquisition, and I told him that I intended to use my canoe to visit him and the Indians in the village, in order to procure some food, until I should be sufficiently recovered to hunt. "Very well;" said he, "never pass me by in your expeditions, I shall cheerfully share with you." I then preferred my first request for a knife to give the Indian as I had promised. The good-natured trader immediately told me to send the man to his store, so that he might have his choice; as he was the best Indian that he had ever known; and that I need not pay him any thing for it. I had in fact not one cent in my possession, but had permission from Post, in case of necessity, to draw upon the trader for what was absolutely necessary. At this time I was frequently reduced to such distress, that the least morsel of food, if offered, would have been acceptable. But although I could make out to live, I was unable to do any thing towards effecting the object for which I had come. Indeed, it soon became evident that our enterprize was to be a complete failure.

Post had hardly been gone three weeks, when the rumor was spread, that he never intended to return; nay more, that even were he to attempt it, he would not be allowed by the tribe to do so; that his sole purpose was to deliver the Indian country into the hands of the white people, and that this was the secret of his pretended missionary efforts. It was also reported that a war would soon break out between the English and Indians, in which the latter would be assisted by their old allies, the French. All this I had written to Post; having found means to send him the information by a Mr. Denison, from Detroit, who was travelling to Philadelphia. He returned answer, that he had already heard the unwelcome news, and that, in the pass things had come to, I could do no better than to return as speedily as possible. Gladly would I have followed his advice, but my horse was lost, or had been stolen, for upwards of three months. I was too weak to travel on foot; and Mr. Calhoon's pack-horse drivers, who had intended to set out for Pittsburg with furs, were all laid up with the fever. I was therefore under the necessity of waiting for their recovery, and in the mean time put my trust in that Lord whom I served.

Meanwhile I was twice warned by friendly Indians to leave their country; and every time I visited Tuscarawas, I saw strangers among the real inhabitants, and perceived that I was the object of their scrutiny. But I remained in happy ignorance of my dangerous situation, until, one afternoon, one of Mr. Calhoon's men called from the opposite bank of the Muskingum, requesting me to lock my door and cross the river immediately, as Mr. Calhoon wished to speak with me on business of great importance. Having wrapped up a few articles of dress in my blanket, I paddled across. As soon as I arrived at Mr. C's, he told me privately, that an Indian woman who frequently came to his store, and who made spirits [shirts], which he kept for sale, had asked him that day whether the white man who lived above, on the other side of the river, were his friend; and that, on his answering in the affirmative, she had said: "Take him away: don't let him remain one night longer in his cabin: he is in danger there."

The next morning I wished to return, to see whether any thing had taken place at the cabin, and if possible, to fetch a few necessary articles which had been left behind in the hurry of my departure. Mr. Calhoon however would not let me go, but sent two of his strongest men to see how things stood. One of them, James Smith, was a man of such uncommon strength, that the Indians considered him a Manitto, and would hardly be anxious to engage him personally. They reported that the house had been broken open during the night, and that judging from appearances there, two persons had been in. There were signs of a late fire on the hearth, and they had evidently been

A Black Cloud Rising: 1762

waiting for me. Of course my return was out of the question; the attempt would have been actual fool-hardiness. I never saw my lonely cabin again, remaining under the hospitable roof of the trader. Meanwhile, as I afterwards heard, emissaries of the Senecas and Northern Indians, were busily engaged in exciting the Delawares to take up the hatchet against the English; and soon after my departure, war broke out, and more than thirty white people of my acquaintance lost their lives.

At Mr. Calhoon's I experienced nothing but the most true-hearted friendship; and under his kind treatment I recovered from the fever.

About this time the Indian chiefs whom Post had accompanied to Lancaster, returned home; and we soon perceived that from some cause or other, their friendship had considerably cooled. One of them, however, King Beaver, remained favorably disposed; but all he could do was to give me several friendly hints to hasten my departure. Fortunately, Mr. Calhoon's men were now restored to health, and determined to set out on their journey to Pittsburgh. My kind host lent me a young horse to ride on; and in return I offered what assistance I could give his men in loading and unloading at the encampments.

We now took an affectionate leave of each other. His conduct had been that of a Christian indeed; and his kindness will be remembered by me as long as I live. He would have left the country with me; but property of great amount had been entrusted to him, and this he considered himself bound to guard as long as possible. After my return to Bethlehem, I learned through the public papers, that he and his brother, together with their servants, had been ordered by the Delaware chiefs to leave their country; as they were unable any longer to protect them. They set out for Pittsburgh; but were attacked on the road, at the Beaver river, by a party of warriors, and only two saved their lives, Mr. C. himself, who outstripped his pursuers in the race, and James Smith, who had strangled his antagonist.—Rondthaler, *Heckewelder*, 51-57.

In his intinerary, entitled, "John Heckewelder's Travels Between 1754 & 1814," the bulk of which is printed on pp. 386-91, of this volume, Heckewelder adds this further information:

Scarcely had I got away when a fierce war broke out, and the traders with whom I had stayed the last 2 months were killed, and the war grew worse and worse. Almost all the traders who were out there were killed. Of 9 white people who traded on the Muskingum & Gajahaga, & who were with me there, 7 lost their lives & the other 2 saved their lives by swimming; and among a company of men trading to Sandusky 16 out of 18 perished.

On the third day after our departure from Muskingum, we met Post and the Indian agent, Captain McKee; who were returning to the Indian country, totally ignorant of the real state of affairs. In spite of our earnest remonstrances, they insisted on proceeding, not considering the danger so imminent. They were soon undeceived on their arrival; and their lives were in danger. The agent was protected by the friendship of the chiefs; but Post, whom the Indians suspected of secret designs against them, as they were at a loss to explain his missionary movements, had to fly for his life, and was conducted to a place of safety, through a secret forest path, by one of his former fellow-travellers to Lancaster [Pittsburgh].

Having taken leave of Post, I hastened after my companions, who had proceeded in the meantime. At a distance of five miles I expected to find their tents; and seeing the smoke of an encampment curling above the trees, I rode on, but was much surprised to find myself suddenly in the midst of a war-party. The sight of the Indian captives, and of the scalping pole with its savage decorations, was not calculated to encourage me. I was however suffered to pass on; and on riding five miles farther, I found my company, by whom I was informed that I had fallen in with a party of Senecas, who had just returned from an expedition against the Cherokees.—Rondthaler, *Heckewelder*, 57-58.

Fever attacked him intermittently during the long return journey. He cured it, as he tells us, by *furious riding,* and reached Bethlehem on the evening of November 27, 1762.

Reports soon followed him of white traders murdered in the country he had left. The Delawares had joined the Ottawas, Chippewas, and Potawotamis, who, under Pontiac, were besieging Detroit. In June of 1763 they were joined by the Shawnees and Geneseo Senecas. No grass, as the Indian phrase ran, grew on the warpath. The forts at Venango, Le Boeuf, Presque Isle and Sandusky were surprised and captured. The "Scalp Cry" was heard all along the Pennsylvania border.

⚔ VI ⚔

Philadelphia Mounts Guard: 1763-1765

WE HAVE SEEN HOW in 1762 Post and Heckewelder had attempted to establish a Moravian mission in the Ohio country. It had ended in failure. The outbreak of Pontiac's War, indeed, put even the well-established eastern mission on the defensive. The annihilation of the mission and all the Christian Indians in it was only narrowly averted.

By 1765 the black cloud had rolled away. In that year John Heckewelder helped to establish a new Indian settlement at Wyalusing, above Wyoming on the North Branch of the Susquehanna. The disturbances that led to the founding of this colony, named Friedenshütten, "Abode of Peace," are best described in Heckewelder's own printed *Narrative*. What part he himself played in these events is not precisely known.

In his Introduction to this work, he acknowledges his indebtedness to George Henry Loskiel's *History of the Mission of the United Brethren among the Indians in North America* (Barby, 1789; English edition, London, 1794), "from which," as he writes, "I have in some instances copied passages." But he notes that he has supplemented Loskiel's work with important information from his own knowledge.

Certainly he did not follow displaced Indians in all their enforced migrations. But his close acquaintance with the setting and the *dramatis personae*, as well as his known employment at the time (he speaks of this in his autobiography) as a guard and messenger, give us assurance that his narrative is intimate and understanding. It is presented in full because it gives us the best understanding we can get of the racial passions which impelled the events described by Heckewelder in his Ohio journals.

The murder of "King" Teedyuscung in the Wyoming Valley set in motion a whole train of disasters. In 1753, the year before John Heckewelder arrived at Bethlehem, Teedyuscung, a Delaware Indian formerly of New Jersey but now a Moravian convert living at the mission village of Gnadenhütten on the Mahoning, at its junction with the Lehigh River, accepted the invitation of the Six Nations to come north to Wyoming (a district of which Wilkes-Barre is now the center), to assist in holding that Indian outpost for his race. During the French and Indian War, he played a dubious role, siding for a time with the western Delawares and Shawnees who rejected the advice of their Uncles, the Six Nations, and attacked the English, with whom the Six Nations were at peace. For this he was, at the Easton treaty of 1758, chastised by his Uncles, who set him aside and made peace for the Delawares over his head. On his submission, however, he was reinstated by the Six Nations as guardian of the Wyoming Valley. In that position he atoned for his earlier dereliction by loyally upholding Indian rights, under Six Nations title, in the Susquehanna Valley.

With all his faults (which were not small, as those who had seen him in his drunken orgies very well knew) there was something admirable about Teedyuscung. It took courage to stand guard at Wyoming and assert, against all pressures, the rights of his people. The Susquehanna Company, under sanction of a dubious purchase made at Albany in 1754, was determined to sell real estate at Wyoming. Teedyuscung, true to his instructions from the Six Nations, stood like a lion in the path, yielding neither to bribes nor threats of violence. His courage, however, was his death warrant. In April, 1763, he was burned to death in his cabin. At the same time all the other Indian houses at Wyoming went up in flames. The evidence is persuasive that friends of the Susquehanna Company were at the bottom of this. Certainly it seemed so to Teedyuscung's son, John, who, with a band of Delaware warriors, swept to his revenge in that valley and killed or captured every white man found in it.

The Indians of those days had no propaganda machine. They employed no press agents, as the white man did, to explain their cause to the world. When John, Teedyuscung's son, was captured and asked why he had committed this deed, known in history as the first massacre of Wyoming, we are told that he merely smiled and said nothing. The

Philadelphia Mounts Guard: 1763-1765

white populace of Pennsylvania, unaware of John's motives, unaware of the land company's intrigues which had given cause for his revenge, saw nothing in the incident but savage, motiveless ferocity. As the year drew on and bad news poured in from the West where Pontiac's War was raging, a black mood settled over the frontier. Fear and ignorance mingled in men's minds to make all Indians suspect. The frontier was working up to an Indian pogrom.

John Heckewelder had more than a taste of this border frenzy. Looking back, at a later time, on some narrow escapes he had once had, he remembered one the late fall of 1763 and

> the flight of our Indian congregation from Wechquetank [near Gilbert, fifteen miles west of Stroudsburg] to Nazareth, when a mob from the two Irish Settlements had collected to kill them. The Indians fled in haste, leaving behind their livestock, property, & all their harvested crops. The Brethren sent up a number of wagons to bring away as much as possible of the property that had been left behind, and, in addition to a small unit of troops, several Brethren were sent with each wagon as a guard. It was intended on the first day to slaughter the fattened pigs and load the wagons, and on the 2nd day to take them to Nazareth. But when we were within 2 miles of Wechquetank, an express messenger came rushing up from the Minesinks station [near Stroudsburg] with orders to the troops to be in their quarters by next morning, because it was rumored that enemy Indians were approaching in great numbers to attack. So the pigs, 20 or so of them, were simply shot—gutted, & thrown into the wagons, and as much else as they could, & before evening the wagons had gone—for one report followed another that the rabble from the settlements was about to attack us.—"John Heckewelder's Travels Between 1754—1814": Archives of the Moravian Church, Bethlehem, Pa.

We shall take the full story, from its beginning in the spring of 1763 to its climax in the barracks at Philadelphia, from John Heckewelder's printed *Narrative*.

> As yet the troubles which early in the year had begun in the western country, had not reached the eastern. The Susquehanna Indians [i.e., the Indians living on the North Branch of the Susquehanna, most of them Delaware and Shawnee] travelled as usual through the settlements of the white people without fear.—The peace which had been enjoyed for several years together, had in a manner done away animosities formerly existing against the Indians; and the Christian Indians, both at Nain [on the outskirts of Bethlehem] and Wequetank [near Gilbert] were in a prosperous state at the time, having built for themselves and their missionaries convenient dwelling houses, enlarged the chapel at the former place, and enjoyed the fruits of their agricultural labours. But in the fall of this year (1763) the scene suddenly changed.

The intelligence received of hostilities committed on the Lakes of Canada and Ohio river, caused many to entertain fears, that a repetition of the dreadful scenes of 1755, and the years following, would take place.

Such accounts were eagerly caught at by fanatics, to serve the doctrine they heretofore had held, viz: that the Indians were the Canaanites, who by God's commandment were to be destroyed; and that this not having been done by them at that time, the present war might be considered as a just punishment from God for their disobedience.

The threats of these fanatics having reached the ears of the Christian Indians at Nain and Wequetank, they joined in an humble address to the governor of Pennsylvania, testifying their abhorrence of the cruelties committed by their countrymen, and begging his excellency's protection; to which the governor replied in a most satisfactory manner.

Soldiers being raised for the defence of the country, it became necessary that the Christian Indians generally should wear a mark to distinguish them from the enemy, lest some of them, while out on business, might be taken for enemies, and be molested.

Yet the object of government in raising these troops, was not that real danger already existed, but for the purpose of making the minds of the people easy, who seemed much alarmed at the reports of murders committed by Indians, although they happened at the distance of some hundred miles, and to be prepared, in case of emergency, to protect and guard all Indians passing and repassing on their lawful business, either for the purpose of exchanging their peltries for other necessaries, or otherwise coming on business with the governor of Pennsylvania; for with all the noise of real danger, the Brethren saw as *yet* none, the Indians coming to them to trade, conducting themselves in a peaceful and becoming manner, not giving the least cause of alarm; nay, even the missionary Zeisberger, remained undisturbed, and without the least knowledge of Indian hostilities, at his post at Wyalusing on Susquehanna, preaching the gospel with great freedom and success to numbers, some of whom came from a great distance to hear him. The Brethren, however, thought proper to apprise him of the current reports, and the danger he might subject himself to by remaining there, at the same time inviting him to return to Bethlehem.

As it sometimes happens, that from a want of authority, energy, or inclination of the officer entrusted with troops, acts are committed, not only dishonourable to such officer, but also highly injurious to the inhabitants of a district, nay, often to the community at large, so also here in the *outset*, an unjust and highly criminal act—an act of murder—was committed on harmless, inoffensive Indians, by the new levies; and that under the very eye of their commander. The Indians who in *this* instance had fallen a sacrifice, were Zachary, with his wife and a young child, and another woman related to him; who all had come to a store for the purpose of exchanging their peltry for wearing apparel—not knowing at the time that the soldiers who were in the house were drinking (the storekeeper also trading in liquors). These soldiers, however, together with their officers, being in a high state of intoxication, fell upon these defenceless Indians, and murdered the whole of them.*

The soldiers, now fearing that Zachary's four brothers, who were living at Wequetank, might revenge his death, went to that place, forbidding any of those Indians to hunt, and threatening to kill every Indian they should meet with in the woods; however, by the repeated remonstrances of the missionary of this place, captain Wetterhold was at length prevailed on to desist from the measure.

Although the party had nothing to dread from the Christian Indians, yet the act he had committed (or suffered to be committed) on these harmless, peaceable Indians, was of such a nature that the *nation*, as might naturally be expected, would sooner or later take revenge. Well would it have been if the matter could have been adjusted, as thereby many lives would have been saved; but as one licentious act left unpunished generally leads to another, so here a number of people embodied themselves, and, as an armed mob, threatened that they would kill every Indian both at Wequetank and Nain, and that without even consulting the government thereon.

Situated as the Christian Indians were, they relied more on God for their preservation, than on man; yet every precaution was taken for their safety, and when they had to go out on their lawful pursuits, they were supplied with passports—yet with all this, it was considered next to a miracle, when they returned to their homes again.

After having passed nearly two months in this situation, and frequently disturbed by false alarms, the Brethren were, in the forenoon of the 8th of October, apprised that at the break of day on that morning, the house of a Mr. John Stinton [where a group of friendly Indians, returning to their distant homes from a shopping expedition to Bethlehem, had recently been robbed],† about 8 miles distant from Bethlehem, had been attacked by the savages, and himself, together with captain Wetterhold, his lieutenant, and several of the soldiers with them, either killed or mortally wounded,‡ these being lodged in that house for the night.

Dreadful did this intelligence sound in the ears of every one that heard it; but to the Brethren it was the more so, as no other Indians then lived in the parts, but the Christian Indians, at the two above mentioned places. During the day the people were continually on the alert, seeking for further information on the subject, and making report of what they had heard; at the same time proclaiming the number of hostile Indians to be very great—some saying hundreds, while others would have their numbers considered by thousands. At length it was maliciously reported, and spread throughout the neighbourhood, that the Christian Indians had been accomplices in the act,

---

* Heckewelder's *History of Indian Nations*, Chap. xliv. p. 332.—Heckewelder's note.
† See Heckewelder, *History*, 332-34.
‡ See letter from Lt. Dodge, in Wallace, *Conrad Weiser*, Philadelphia, 1945, p. 574.

and that one man in particular had been recognized by the woman of the house, and to whom she also had made oath.

The wounded, among whom were the captain and his lieutenant (both of whom however died * of their wounds) were as speedy as possible removed to Bethlehem, where every attention was paid them by the surgeon and physician of the place.

Frequent enquiries were made of the Brethren in their settlements in these parts, as to the measure they meant to take for their own safety, and on their advice the whole neighbourhood were disposed to regulate themselves; these finding that the Brethren would not quit the ground, they were also encouraged to stay.

However, insults and threats were renewed against the Indians under the care of the Brethren, in consequence of the oath which the woman before mentioned had made. The mob presenting themselves before their village at Wequetank, and threatening to murder them if they did not soon leave the place. The missionary finding that intreaties made no effect on them, it became necessary that without loss of time, this congregation should break up and retire to Nazareth for safety. The white settlers in the neighbourhood, not being of the mob party, regretted their departure, believing that while the Christian Indians continued to be their neighbours, they had nothing to dread from the enemy, but when removed they would be exposed to their attacks—(a very just observation), but the waggons had arrived, and on the eleventh day of October, the whole congregation sat [sic] out, leaving their harvest and many of their cattle behind.

The governor being informed of this sudden flight, requested that their missionary, the Rev. Bernhard Grube, would come to Philadelphia, that he might learn from him the particulars; and being convinced of the untruth of the evil reports spread against the Christian Indians, he delivered himself in a very respectful manner on the subject of the Brethren's missions among the Indians.

Whilst the party that threatened and persecuted the Christian Indians in this quarter, were fabricating additional falsehoods against them, with the view of facilitating their destruction, the savages were pouring in from the Northward, and laying waste the settlement of the New England people † at Wyoming. These incursions were alleged by the above party, as a further reason why every Indian living ought to be cut off from the face of the earth. The inhabitants of Nain, little more than a mile distant from Bethlehem, who for some time past dare not venture to that place on their lawful business, were not only obliged to keep a watch both by day and night in their

---

* It will be recollected that it was captain Wetterhold's party that murdered the harmless Indians; the same party happening to be at his house while the attack was made, and fell victims.—Heckewelder's note.

† These people were at that time considered by the Indians as intruders on their land.—Heckewelder's note.

town, but had even to place guards at their chapel doors during service, from apprehension of being surprised and murdered, while assembled for divine worship.

In this trying situation they had patiently to endure four weeks, though suffering much by the cold at nights. Every morning their joys were renewed at seeing each other again, after the fears of the night. Their hopes were, that government would commiserate their situation, and grant them protection. But alas! on the 19th day of October, one of their number (Renatus,) an harmless Indian, and son of aged and venerable parents, was unexpectedly seized, as the one sworn to have been of the murdering party, and forthwith taken to Philadelphia and imprisoned.

The government of Pennsylvania, however sensible of the innocence of these Indians, and the falsity of the reports, purposely propagated to enrage the people against them, ordered all the baptized Indians from both places to be brought to Philadelphia for protection. The Indian congregation being informed of the orders, they could not refrain from weeping, considering that they were now to part from their dearest friends and Brethren at Bethlehem; yet, resigned to the will of the Lord, and in the hope that they would be permitted the benefit of their teachers, their minds became easy. The sheriff of the county, John Jennings, esq. a gentleman of affability, and high in the esteem of those Indians, arrived by appointment to take charge of, and safely conduct them to Philadelphia; they delivered to him their arms with great composure, and on the 8th of November, after attending a farewell sermon, preached in the church at Bethlehem by the bishop, Peter Boehler, from Psalm 5th, verse 8th, "make thy way straight before my face," taking a final leave of the inhabitants of the place, they set out in waggons, accompanied by several of their missionaries and other Brethren, exclusive of those officers of government who had been appointed to protect them on the way to that place; where, after having suffered much on the journey, both by the inclemency of the weather, and from the insults and threats thrown out against them by the inhabitants of some places, who declared that hanging and burning ought to be their doom, they arrived on the 11th of the same month at Philadelphia.

Although, by order from the governor, they were to be lodged in the barracks, yet the soldiers quartered therein refused them admittance. Thus, from ten o'clock in the forenoon, to three in the afternoon, they were detained in the street.

Meanwhile a great mob had assembled around them, deriding, reviling, and charging them with all the outrages committed by the enemy, at the same time threatening to kill them on the spot; to all which they were silent, not uttering one word, but relying wholly on the providence of God, to whom alone they afterwards ascribed their preservation.

The magistrates finding that the soldiers persisted in refusing to admit them into the barracks, ordered them to proceed; and while passing through the city, not knowing where they were going, nor what would become of them, accompanied by a thousand spectators who were following in a tumultuous manner, until at length they arrived at Province Island, about six miles below the city, where they settled themselves as well as circumstances would permit, in which the missionaries assisted them, and held with them their daily meetings.

Several gentlemen in Philadelphia, especially those of the Friends, (by some called Quakers) humanely endeavoured to render their situation more agreeable. Indeed this worthy class of citizens, did on all occasions exert themselves in their behalf, both in protecting them against an infuriated mob, as also in relieving their wants. Oftentimes since, these Indians have been heard to say, that during their troubles, which lasted between one and two years, even "the sight of a Quaker made them feel happy."

The village of Christian Indians at Wequetank, was fired and burnt to the ground before its inhabitants had reached Philadelphia; while, at the same time, some incendiary in the night set fire to the oil mill in Bethlehem, which was likewise destroyed and, but for the vigilance of the inhabitants of the place, the costly waterworks,* which already were in flames, would, together with other buildings, have shared the same fate.

Towards the end of this month (November,) John Papunhank, an Indian, deservedly high in the esteem of government, on account of his peaceable and friendly disposition to the English, arrived with twenty-one Indians, all of the Delaware Nation and averse to the war, at Bethlehem, from Wyalusing on Susquehanna. They were conducted to Philadelphia, and there lodged with the Christian Indians.

Whilst the Brethren viewed with gratitude the benevolence of a humane governor, exerting himself to protect a persecuted congregation of Indians, together with such of the nation who had fled from their savage neighbours, to avoid being compelled to take up the hatchet against their brethren, the English; a party of fifty-seven white people, bearing the name of Christians, sat out from Paxton [Harrisburg], to attack and destroy a small settlement of peaceable and inoffensive Indians in Canestoga [southeast of Washington Borough], near Lancaster, where they had resided for more than a century, and whose ancestors had been among those who had welcomed William Penn on his first arrival in this country; presenting him at the time with venison, &c.—These not happening to be all at home at the time, some being scattered among their white neighbours, they murdered those they met with, to the number of fourteen persons, men, women and children; the rest learning what had befallen their friends and relations, fled, by the advice of their friendly neighbours, to Lancaster for protection, and were there placed in the gaol for safety—where however this mob party, now under the name of Paxton boys, arrived; and having broken open the door, entered, and most

---

* The first municipal water pumping system in the country, installed 1755.

cruelly murdered every one of them; although they begged on their knees that their lives might be spared, they being real friends of the English. The mob were so intoxicated with their success, that after they had finished their inhuman butchery on those truly innocent Indians, they threw their mangled bodies into the street * and with a dreadful shout, as if they had gained a great victory, threatened that the Indians on Province Island, (the Christian Indians, together with Papunhak's peaceable party,) should soon share the same fate.

Note: That there appeared to be something unaccountable in this affair, will be seen from the following extract of a letter, addressed to the writer of this narrative, by a respectable and intelligent gentleman † of Philadelphia. "There are," (says he) "few if any murders to be compared with the cruel murder committed on the Canestoga Indians in the gaol of Lancaster in 1763, by the Paxton boys, (as they were then called). From 15 to 20 Indians, as report stated, were placed there for protection. A regiment of Highlanders were at the time quartered at the barracks in the town, and yet these murderers were permitted to break open the doors of the city gaol, and commit the horrid deed. The first notice I had of this affair, was that while at my father's store, near the court house, I saw a number of people running down street towards the gaol, which enticed me and other lads to follow them. At about sixty or eighty yards from the gaol, we met from 25 to 30 men, well mounted on horses, and with rifles, tomahawks, and scalping knives, equipped for murder. I ran into the prison yard, and there, O what a horrid sight presented itself to my view!!— Near the back door of the prison, lay an old Indian and his squaw (wife) particularly well known and esteemed by the people of the town, on account of his placid and friendly conduct. His name was Will Sock; across him and his squaw lay two children, of about the age of three years, whose heads were split with the tomahawk, and their scalps all taken off. Towards the middle of the gaol yard, along the west side of the wall, lay a stout Indian, whom I particularly noticed to have been shot in the breast, his legs were chopped with the tomahawk, his hands cut off, and finally a rifle ball discharged in his mouth; so that his head was blown to atoms, and the brains were splashed against, and yet hanging to the wall, for three or four feet around. This man's hands and feet had also been chopped off with a tomahawk. In this manner lay the whole of them, men, women and children, spread about the prison yard: shot—scalped—hacked—and cut to pieces."

The governor issued a proclamation against these outrages—forbidding, under the severest penalties, any one to molest the Indians on Province Island; and offering a reward of two hundred pounds to any one who should bring the two ringleaders of the above party to justice; but it soon became evident

---

* So the public papers stated, but ought to be Prison Yard.—Heckewelder's note.
† William Henry, Esq., then an inhabitant of Lancaster.—Heckewelder's note.

that their numbers was daily increasing, and that even in Philadelphia many were in secret connection with the ring-leaders, who paid so little regard to government orders at that time, that they not only publicly walked the streets, but even presented themselves in front of the governor's house, deridingly bidding him defiance.

Every day fresh reports were raised or brought into the city, of the intentions of the rioters; and it was evident that they became daily more daring. When therefore on the 29th day of December, intelligence was brought to Philadelphia, that a large party of the Paxton boys were on their march, to fall on and murder the Christian Indians, the governor seeing no other way of protecting them, sent them some large boats, in which they were to embark and take flight. They having embarked and proceeded to Leach Island, they were there overtaken by a messenger sent to them by the governor, to inform them, that it having proved to be a false alarm, they might return; yet withal advising them to have their boats always in readiness, and that he further would furnish them with a guard.

But the government at the commencement of the year 1764 received more certain intelligence concerning the murderous intentions of the rioters, and resolved to conduct the persecuted congregation to a place of more safety, by sending them under an escort by way of New York to the English army, particularly recommending them to sir William Johnson, Indian agent for the crown of Great Britain.

These Indians were accordingly advised to hold themselves in readiness, to set out at a moment's warning; and on the 4th of January at midnight they left Province Island, and were met below the city by two gentlemen, (Lewis and Jacob Weiss) and by them conducted almost unobserved through the city, to the Brethren's chapel; where a number of Brethren and friends had met to receive them, having also provided a breakfast for them in the chapel. Here they were visited by the commissary, Mr. Fox, who was so struck at the sight of these poor emigrants, that he immediately ordered a number of blankets to be distributed among them, and waggons being provided to carry the aged, the blind, the sick, and the children, together with their baggage, they set out, accompanied by their missionaries. By this time, however, a crowd of people had assembled, so that they could scarcely proceed, by whom they were cursed and reviled in a dreadful manner, yet without receiving personal injury; however captain Robertson, with the escort of 70 Highlanders falling in, the mob dispersed. Commissary Fox, and Mr. Logan, went with them as far as Trenton, where the latter addressed them in the name of the governor, respecting the murders committed on the innocent Conestoga Indians, signifying the governor's abhorrence of these acts; at the same time delivering two belts of Wampum, which by them were to be forwarded to the Iroquois, (the Six Nations). With the one belt they were exhorted to lay down the hatch and conclude a peace—they having began the war without a cause—and with the other, the graves of their murdered relations, the

Philadelphia Mounts Guard: 1763-1765

Conestoga Indians, were to be covered, and the tears wiped from their eyes.

The speech being delivered, and the before mentioned gentlemen about to return, the Christian Indians desired that their humble thanks might be presented to the governor, for the many favours they had received during their troubles. The commissary, Mr. Epty, now took charge of them, and provided every thing needful for their convenience on the road.

In passing through New Jersey, they were frequently insulted by mob parties; however they reached Amboy in safety, where two sloops lay in readiness to carry them to New York, but at the moment they were to embark, an express arrived from the governor of that place, strictly forbidding any Indian from his setting foot on the New York territory, captain Robertson being at the same time ordered by general Gage to prevent them from proceeding,—nay, even the ferrymen were, by a severe penalty, prohibited to cross the river with them.

As Mr. Epty, who immediately despatched an express with an account of these proceedings to the governor of Pennsylvania, had to wait for further orders, the Indians were lodged in the barracks at Amboy, where they held their meetings in the usual order; and at which, frequently, a greater or less number of the white people attended, much admiring their devotion; and were so delighted with their singing, that they conceived a more favourable opinion of them—nay, one of the soldiers exclaimed, "would to God all the white people were as good Christians as these Indians."

Having received orders from the governor to return to Philadelphia, they set out with cheerfulness; their guard of Highlanders being here relieved by 170 men from gen. Gage's army, commanded by captain Schlosser,* one party led the van, and the other brought up the rear.

On their arrival at Philadelphia, January 24th, they were lodged in the barracks, where they were guarded both day and night. Nevertheless they met daily for divine service. It was, however, not long before the mob disturbed them so much, that it was found necessary to double the guard; especially as the ring leaders of the before mentioned murderers, were attempting by force to put their wicked designs into execution, pretending that having been highly offended by the proclamation lately issued by the governor, they now would not rest until all these Indians were delivered up to them.

Matters seemed drawing to a crisis. Certain information was received that large mobs were marching towards Philadelphia, where numbers were ready to join them on their arrival. The magistrates were called on to do their duty; and there appeared no other alternative, but that of repelling force by force. Eight pieces of heavy ordnance were drawn up to the barracks, and a rampart thrown up in the middle of the square. The citizens, and even many young Quakers took up arms, and repaired to the barracks to assist the soldiers in defending the poor Indians, who, in haste, had already been re-

---

* An officer deservedly esteemed by all good men, for his humanity and manly conduct, in protecting these persecuted Indians.—Heckewelder's note.

moved from the lower, into the upper part of the building; where, at midnight, the governor himself visited them, bidding them to be of good cheer, and soothing their fears by his condescending behaviour. Several persons of distinction likewise came, and showed their friendly disposition towards these Indians; even some remained in the barracks, supposing they would be no where more safe.

Intelligence having been received on the 4th of February, of the approach of the rioters, every preparation was made to receive them. The whole town was in an uproar, as the report of their guns was already heard. The soldiers became alarmed;—the eighteen pounders were discharged, which terrified the poor Indians, they never before having heard the report of such guns. The rioters however did not venture to approach, and the citizens again returned to their homes. But in the night, between the 5th and 6th, a report prevailing that the rioters were again advancing, the whole town was in motion. The church bells were rung—the streets illuminated—and the inhabitants being awakened from their sleep, were ordered to attend at the town-house, where arms and ammunition were distributed among them. Two companies of armed citizens repaired to the barracks, and, in addition, four more cannon were mounted. Thus the following day was spent in terror, and hourly expectation of the rioters. The Indians, who were sensible that these thirsted after their blood, considered themselves as devoted to slaughter; and, though they were very thankful for the spirited exertions of the government, made in their behalf, and for their defence, yet their strongest hope was placed in the Lord—they saying: "God can help us!"

At length certain information was received that the rioters, in consequence of the preparations made to receive them, had resolved to proceed no further. Some gentlemen were deputed by government, to ask them what they had to complain of; when, after much insolent behaviour, they asserted that there were several murderers among these Indians, and demanded that these should be given up. To convince them of their error, one of their ringleaders was invited to come into the barracks, and point such out; but not finding any one whom he could charge with any crime, the party gave out that the Quakers had privately taken six of the Christian Indians out of the barracks and hid them. This being investigated, and also proving false, the rioters (as they themselves declared,) relinquished their design, and marched off.

Although at first it was believed, that the only object of the rioters was the destruction of all the Indians, under the idea that they were descendants of the Canaanites, who, by God's commandment, were to be cut off from the face of the earth; it soon became evident that they aimed at nothing short of overturning the whole form of government. Their design appearing now to be; first to cause a general consternation, thereby spreading devastation and misery over the country, and then to take the reins of government into their own hands.

The Christian Indians however saw themselves delivered from their enemies, and therefore offered up praises and thanksgiving to God, that he had so graciously defeated their designs; and now people of all ranks came to see the Indians, who were literally become a spectacle to thousands. The public worship of the congregation, especially on Sundays, was attended by crowds of attentive hearers, among whom were also some of the soldiers, who were glad to hear the gospel preached again, having been deprived of this benefit for several years together.

Four single Indian women, who had lived in the single sisters' house at Bethlehem for several years, but now not considered safe in that place, were conducted to the barracks; and their serene and modest appearance caused them to be respected by all who saw them, even by the soldiery. In general, the latter deserves this good testimony, that they always treated the Christian Indians with kindness; and the friendly and wise conduct of their officers, who kept strict order among the men, cannot be sufficiently praised.

Although government provided in the best manner they could for these persecuted Indians, yet their situation was a hard trial, and very afflicting to some of them—nay, considered little short of imprisonment. The high seasoned victuals did not agree with their stomachs. They could have no bodily exercise; the men were deprived of the occupation they had been brought up to—namely, that of hunting. Their living so close together, seemed to them insupportable. These, and other privations which they had to endure, caused some of them to become low spirited, and they wished to be set at liberty.

To pave the way for a peace, they, with the consent of government, sent John Papunhank, with one of their brethren, as messengers of peace to the hostile Indians, to inform them that they were all alive and to desire them to lay down the hatchet.

Encouraged by the reply to their messenger, they addressed government to escort them safely to the frontiers, from whence they would find their way to Sir William Johnson; but as the war still continued, government would not grant the request. This refusal increased their uneasiness; nor was this all, for as the summer advanced, fevers and the small-pox broke out amongst them, which occasioned much dread and horror, so that many meditated their escape; but, by the advice and perseverance of the missionaries, who were unwearied in visiting and comforting them, their uneasiness was changed into a perfect resignation to the will of the Lord. To the sick, relief was afforded by that benevolent and humane Friend, Jacob Weiss, whom the Lord alone can reward for his great attention and labours of love.

Fifty-six of the sick were released from all misery, pain, and distress, by a most happy translation into everlasting life. Most edifying was it to all who had visited them, to see with what resignation they bore their sufferings, and their cheerfulness, in the hope of soon seeing their Saviour face to face. Their bodies were interred in a burying ground, called Pottersfield. Poor Renatus, who was in prison, on hearing of the death of his beloved father, his wife, and his child, wept most bitterly.

The time however had arrived when this afflicted man was to be delivered from his bonds. During eight months imprisonment, he spent most of his time in reading a hymn book. He had been frequently visited by the missionary, who had a particular regard for him. He was now taken from his cell, and sent to Easton under a guard, there to stand a trial for the murder of Mr. Stinton, in the Irish settlement [near Easton], whose wife swore that it was him who perpetrated the act. The missionaries of the place where he lived at that time, together with other Brethren, were summoned to attend at the trial. There were not wanting enemies to the Brethren, who wished to have the poor innocent Indian hung; every effort was made to have him condemned. The rabble became impatient to learn the verdict, that they might afterwards witness the execution of a "Moravian" Indian; however the jury brought in their verdict of *not guilty;* upon which the prisoner was immediately relieved from confinement—yet on accound of the mob, who were enraged at his liberation, he had to be kept hidden until night, when Mr. John Jones, a respectable neighbour to Bethlehem, took him to his house, and from thence had him safely conducted to Philadelphia. It appeared that the object of the adversaries had been, to cast a general odium on Indians, said to have become *Christians;* and to render the Brethren's missions among these people, suspected.

On the 4th day of July, 1764, the Christian Indians in the barracks had the joy to see and embrace their beloved Renatus; for whose deliverance they could not sufficiently express their thankfulness to God, while he, speaking out of the abundance of his heart, gave glory to the Lord, his Redeemer.

In the autumn the Indians in the barracks made another effort to procure their enlargements, and government granted passports to some to go to the Susquehanna, but the proper time had not yet arrived for all to go, as it was yet doubtful whether a peace would take place; negociations for the purpose were however continued, and the Iroquois (the Six Nations,) being at length reconciled, they caused the other nations also to lay down the hatchet.

On the 4th of December, 1764, the same day on which an account of a peace having been concluded with the hostile nations was brought to Philadelphia, a proclamation was published by government, that forthwith all hostilities should cease. The joy the Christian Indians manifested on the occasion, exceeded all description.

All troubles being at an end, the Indians were at liberty to leave the barracks, but where to go was now the great question. The directors of the society feared to advise them to re-occupy their former places, which lay within the settlements of the whites; and they themselves having witnessed the trouble and ill will brought on the Brethren, in consequence of their residing near them, determined to settle in their own country. Government being informed of their resolution, afforded them every assistance in its power to make their future situation agreeable, and themselves happy.— Mr. Fox even procured an order, by which they were to be supplied with flour until their harvest of corn should be gathered and housed. . . .

Arriving at Bethlehem they were well received, and rested for some time at Nain, their former place of abode; when every thing being arranged for the journey, a farewell sermon was preached to them by their old and much respected missionary, Grube, at which a number of the Bethlehem congregation were present; when on the 3rd of April they broke up, and in passing through Bethlehem took an affectionate leave of all the inhabitants of the place, who were assembled for that purpose.— The conductors appointed by government to escort them part of the way, were Mr. Moore, a justice of the peace; Mr. Ruchline, high sheriff; Lieutenant Huntsecker; and Mr. Epty, gentlemen whose names are here inserted with gratitude, for their attention and kindness to those Indians. Some Brethren from Bethlehem likewise accompanied them until they had passed the frontier settlements: the distance to which the waggons with the sick, infirm, and the heavy baggage, had been ordered to proceed.

Their route was through Nazareth, crossing the Blue and Broad mountains, and the great Pine and Beach swamp, direct to Wyoming, from whence the principal part of them went by water to Wyalusing, accompanied by the two missionaries, Schmick and Zeisberger. During this journey, which was very fatiguing, several departed this life, otherwise they were of good cheer, cutting a path as they travelled, and met every evening around a fire for divine service. . . ."—Heckewelder, *Narrative*, 67-93.

This path they laid off and cut as they proceeded, two, three or four miles at a time, according to the nature of the ground and the convenience of water, bringing up their baggage by making two or more trips, as they had no horses to carry it. Having arrived at the great Pine Swamp, then supposed to be about fourteen miles wide, it was found very difficult to cut a passage on account of the thickets and of the great number of fallen trees which incumbered it; they were, besides, unacquainted with that part of the country. An old Indian [revised in a footnote to read, "*several old men*"], however, took the lead, and undertook to be their guide. After a tedious march of near two weeks, attended with much labour, he brought them across the Swamp, to the large creek which borders upon it on the opposite side. There they found a very steep mountain, through which no passage could be found either above or below. Discouraged at the prospect before them, they now saw no alternative but to return the same way they had come, and take the route by Fort Allen [Weissport] to Nescopeck, and so up the Susquehannah to Wyoming, a distance of nearly one hundred miles round. In this difficulty, it fortunately struck their Missionary, Mr. Zeisberger, that a certain Indian named David, who was one of their party and had followed them all the way, was acquainted with that part of the country, and might, perhaps, be able to point out to them some better and shorter road. He soon found that he was not mistaken. David was perfectly acquainted with the country, and knew a good road through which the party might easily pass, but not having been questioned on the subject, had hitherto kept silence, and followed with the rest, though he knew all the while they were going wrong. A dialogue then took place between him and the Missionary.

Zeisb.—David! You are, I believe, acquainted with this country; perhaps you know a better road [revised to read "course"] and a shorter one than that which we are going to take.

David.—Yes, I do; there is such a road ["course"], which we may easily get through, and have a much shorter distance to travel than by that which is proposed; I am sure of it.

Zeisb.—What; David! we were all going wrong, and yet you are with us?

David.—Yes, 'tis so.

Zeisb.—And yet you said nothing, and followed with the rest as if all had been right!

David.—Yes; the guides are somewhat older than myself; they took the lead, and never asked me whether I had any knowledge of the country. If they had enquired, I would have told them.

Zeisb.—Will you *now* tell them?

David.—No, indeed; unless they ask me. It does not become an Indian to instruct his elders.

The question was then asked him at the instigation of Mr. Zeisberger, when he immediately told them that they must all return to a certain spot, six miles back, and then direct their course more to the north-east, which would bring them to a gap in the mountain, where they could pass through with great ease. They did so, and he followed them, and being now desired to take the lead, he did it, and brought them to the very spot he had described, and from thence led them all the way to Wyoming. This difficult part of the road, in the swamp, has been since called *David's path*, and the state road now passes through it.*—Heckewelder, *History*, 166-168.

---

* Note by William C. Reichel: "The road from Easton, via Ross Common and the Pocono, to Wilkes-Barré, formerly called the Wilkes-Barré turnpike."

~ VII ~

Courier to Wyalusing: 1765-1770

THE JOURNEY FROM BETHLEHEM to Wyalusing was completed in five weeks.

They next determined upon a convenient spot for a town, situate on the banks of the Susquehanna, about one mile below Wyalusing creek; where they, for the present, erected temporary huts for themselves, but for their missionaries they built a tolerable good log house, and another for a meeting-house, and the place was called Friedenshutten, (tents of peace). It was delightful to see with what cheerfulness they set to work, at clearing and fencing in ground to plant on. Provisions being very scarce, they had, in a great measure, to look for a supply from the woods; and, in addition to what the hunter would procure in the meat way, the women and children would dig wild potatoes, and various other roots and plants, to serve as substitutes both for bread and sauce.

The welfare of the congregation much depended on its internal regulations; and that subject claimed all attention. Morning and evening meetings were daily held when the weather permitted, and the Sundays were entirely devoted to solemn reflection and divine service. The sacraments were also administered at proper seasons, and every regulation necessary for keeping peace and good order, made and agreed to.

Thus situated, they were content and happy; and their numbers increasing, brightened their prospect as to the future. To promote their security, they soon, after their arrival sent a message with a string of wampum to the chief of the Cayugas, (who, as plenipotentiary of the Six Nations, claimed the lordship or right over all the lands on the Susquehanna,) to inform him of their having settled on this spot with the approbation of the governor of

Pennsylvania, and believing that this could not but meet their full approbation; but by the answer returned, this was not found to be the case. The council of Onondago had indeed welcomed them on their arrival in this country, but objected to their living where they at present resided, saying that the land they had pitched upon had been stained with blood; * they therefore would advise them to come and settle at the head of the Cayuga Lake; which answer not being pleasing to the Christian Indians, they, in return, replied after the oriental style, leaving them to guess what they meant to do. They, in fact, knew the Six Nations too well to trust to *their* word, and were not willing to be tools in their hands.† However, they afterwards thought proper to send a deputation of Christian Indians, accompanied by their missionary Zeisberger, to explain matters to the great council, by which their objections were removed, and they permitted to stay where they were, together with their teachers.

The missionary Zeisberger, who many years since had been adopted as a son in the family of a principal chief of the Onandagoes, having more influence in their councils, than the Delawares themselves, was always the first character sought for, to effect a settlement, when matters of an unfavourable nature had taken place between the two nations. In what he said they placed full confidence; and when he was absent from treaties held with the white people, they could not easily be reconciled, believing that his presence served as a check upon the interpreters, who (as the Indians were apt to say,) would suffer themselves to be bribed—especially when purchases of land were about being made from them.

Towards the end of the second year of this new settlement, the traders in liquor, both white and Indians came on with this article to exchange with the Christian Indians for their peltry; they however determined not to suffer the article to be sold in the town: these traders were ordered to depart, and never hereafter attempt to impose their liquor upon any of their people, for, if they did, their kegs would be stoved to pieces. The Indians indeed went off peaceably, saying that they never hereafter would come here with that article; while the white traders from Paxton (the very people who were of the party that were going to murder these Indians while they were in the barracks at Philadelphia,) refused to take their liquor away; saying that they had a right to sell liquor *where*, and to whom they pleased; but the Indian Brethren, to whom the police of the place was committed, remaining firm by their resolution, they at length went off.

---

* Stained with blood, meaning the blood spilt in destroying the New England Settlement at Wyoming.—Heckewelder's note.

† Here Heckewelder, always a violent partisan in Indian politics, betrays his prejudice against the Six Nations, with whom many of the Delawares at this time were at odds. The Delawares, construing in a derogatory sense the ceremonial designation of *woman* which the Six Nations applied to them (cf. Dominion Status in the British Commonwealth), seized every opportunity of asserting their *manhood*.

In other respects the settlement enjoyed perfect tranquillity during the whole time of there residence there; and increased so fast, that in 1767, their meeting-house was much too small to contain their number—wherefore they built a large and spacious church, of squared white pine timber, shingle roofed, with a neat cupola and bell on the top. And as they hoped they would be permitted to remain in this place for a great number of years, they did all their work in the best manner possible, both in building and fencing, so that at this time there were forty well built houses of squared timber, and shingle roofed, in the village; and the gardens back of them were all in good clap-board fence.

The Indians who from time to time visited this place, were of various tribes and nations: viz., Mohawks, Mahicans, Wampanos, Cayugas, Senecas, Onondagoes, Tutelas, Tuscororas, Delawares, and Nanticoks. Famine at their respective homes, together with the general report, that the Christian Indians were hospitable, and at all times had plenty of provisions—they being an industrious and agricultural people, may be considered as one cause of these frequent visits; however, as most of them had heard the gospel preached while here, it was supposed that at least some of them might have reaped a blessing. Exclusive of visitors, travellers often passed through their town, some of whom would make a halt for a few days. Thus, at one time, seventy-five Tuscorora Indians emigrating from North Carolina to join their people in the country of the Six Nations rested on their journey, and were well provided for, during their stay; while, at another time, fifty-seven Nanticoks emigrating from the sea shore of Maryland, remained three weeks with them.
—Heckewelder, *Narrative*, 94-98.

The seven prosperous and for the most part happy years spent by the Indian community at this place provided them with a memory to cling to during their many subsequent uprootings.

Friedenshutten (Wyalusing,) . . . was a favorite spot of the Christian Indians, having both natural advantages, and artificial charms. The town had been regularly laid out, and built for the greatest part of squared white pine timbers. Their chapel was an ornament to the place. Most of their garden lots were put under good palings—the fields in fine order and cultivation, with a number of fruit trees planted out in proper places.—Heckewelder, *Narrative*, 119.

It was their Shangri-La, a model for all their later villages. When the fierce winds of war and intolerance drove them farther and farther west in search of the City of Peace, the memory of Friedenshütten gave substance to their hopes as they moved from the Susquehanna to the Beaver River in Western Pennsylvania, thence to the Muskingum River in Ohio, the Huron River in Michigan, the White River in Indiana, and the Thames River in Ontario.

But Friedenshütten was never Heckewelder's home, and the years of its flourishing were certainly not the happiest in his life. Indeed, the nine years that followed his return to Bethlehem from his adventure in the Muskingum country seem to have been for him the most unsatisfactory of his career. He was at a loose end. The Indian mission work he had dreamed of as a boy was not, after all (or so it seemed at the time) to be his. His life in consequence lacked purpose and his activities a center.

How this had come about may be understood, in part at least, if we look at the changes which had occurred in Bethlehem during his nine months absence in the country of Shingas, King Beaver, Captain Pipe, and Netawatwees. Many of his friends had gone. William Nixon, the cedar-cooper to whom he had been apprenticed, had moved to New York. Bishop Spangenberg, inspirer and organizer of the Indian missions, had returned to Europe. Moreover, the whole tenor of life at Bethlehem had changed. The communal system, in which everyone contributed the fruits of his labor to the common store, drawing from the latter according to his need wherever he might be, on the mission field or in Bethlehem,—this "family economy," which had been a temporary expedient to get the young community, with its heavy missionary burdens, established, was now given up. The return to private enterprise called for readjustments, not all of which were easy.

Heckewelder found difficulty in supporting himself as a cedar-cooper. Indian missions, in which he was so much interested, were now on the defensive and seemed hardly likely to survive. No wonder the young enthusiast, deprived of the encouragement of former friends and patrons, became discouraged and disillusioned. In temperament he was nervous, spirited, impetuous. True to his English upbringing, he was a freedom-loving soul, an individualist. Sincerely religious, he was nevertheless aware of some things in the church at Bethlehem which irritated him acutely. He was impatient of the rules and regulations on which, as it seemed to him, some of the Brethren insisted too rigidly. He experienced moods of rebellion, and at times his untamed nature gave these moods expression. More than once he was seized with the impulse to leave the Brethren.

Soon after my return to Bethlehem, various circumstances induced me to form the resolution of returning to England. Accordingly I set out for New-York in the spring of 1763; but on my way was twice in danger of being pressed by recruiting officers. At one time, I escaped their search by the landlord's hiding me under a bedstead; and on another occasion, a baker's wife at Newark hid me in a closet. In process of time, I was led to trace in these circumstances, a marked display of the restraining grace of the Lord, who would not have me follow the bent of my own inclination. From Newark, I proceeded to New-York. Here I worked some time in a cooper's shop, in order to earn some money, to defray the expence of my intended voyage. Not meeting with a vessel sailing directly for England, I entered into a bargain with a Dutch captain from Surinam, intending to return to England by way of the West-Indies, where I hoped to see my parents, who had been called to labour on that station. Previous to the execution of this design, however, the Brethren's ship Irene, Captain Jacobson, arrived at New-York. The Captain being apprized of my intention, endeavoured to dissuade me from it by the most powerful arguments, representing, among other things, the danger of going with Dutch captains, many of whom were kidnappers. Moreover, he begged me in the most affectionate and pathetic terms, to consider the unhappy consequences which might result from my project, and which might affect my whole future course of life. I accordingly followed his advice, and returned to Bethlehem, after an absence of several months.—"Memoir of the Life of . . . Heckewelder. (Written by Himself)," *Periodical Accounts*, XIII, 49-56.

The date of the escapade is found in the Bethlehem Diary for May 6, 1763: *"John Heckewælder, who left the community a few weeks ago, turned up again today with fervent entreaty for readmission."* *

Here, however, I was far from happy; various occurrences tended to mar my peace, and seeing no prospect of gaining a decent livelihood, I three several times formed the resolution of abandoning my connexion with the Brethren. . . . The first time, while actually on my way, a citizen of Bethlehem, a simple, kind-hearted Brother, met me, and immediately discovered by my looks the state of my mind and the design I had in view. Though he cordially sympathized with my situation, he nevertheless strongly urged me to return, adding that circumstances might soon give a favorable turn to my affairs, and that, if I looked to our Saviour, He would not fail to help me. Overcome by his arguments, I quietly returned home.—Heckewelder's "Memoir," *Periodical Accounts*, XIII, 49-56.

During the seven years of the Friedenshütten mission, Heckewelder, stationed at Bethlehem, was not altogether denied the life of movement he so much desired. On occasion he served as a courier, traveling the Indian paths to Fort Allen, Wyoming, and Wyalusing. He had some near brushes with death.

The "Gunpowder Affair" was one of them. In the spring of 1768, he was traveling to Friedenshütten in company with four other Mora-

---

* Translated from the Bethlehem Diary (manuscript), Archives of the Moravian Church, Bethlehem, Pa.

vians, David Zeisberger, Gottlob Senseman (who were on their way to establish a permanent mission on the Allegheny at Goschgoschink), Bishop Ettwein, and John Angerman. The latter was a tenderfoot, zealous but footsore.

The only white man at Wajomick [Wyoming], a trader by the name of Ogden, entertained us hospitably, and did what he could to make our stay with him as agreeable as possible; particularly so, as the Indians, who were expected from Friedenshütten, had not yet arrived. The dwelling of this man consisted of two small buildings adjoining each other. In one his goods were stored for sale; in the other several kegs of powder were deposited. He slept in the store-room, from which a door opened into the powder-magazine; another opened into it from the outside. A change of weather threatening to come on, he prepared a couch of dry straw or hay for us in his powder magazine; requesting us, in the most friendly terms, on no account to smoke tobacco in the apartment, not only because some grains of powder might be scattered upon the floor, but because some of the kegs were opened. It being now bed-time, Mr. Ogden placed a lighted candle in his store, in such a direction as to throw sufficient light through the middle door, left open for that purpose, till we should have retired to rest. Brother Angerman, however, wished to have the candle placed nearer to him, in order to inspect and bind up his lacerated feet. The landlord and the rest of us represented to him the danger to which he would expose himself and us; but he ceased not to plead for it, promising neither to bring the candle in contact with the straw nor to blow it out, but to leave it standing on the door-sill, and then to extinguish it on the outside of the house. Mr. Ogden at last gave way to his request, and then shut the middle door. We now lay down, after having once more earnestly charged Brother Angerman to be careful with the light. We soon fell asleep, and he too was overpowered by sleep before he had extinguished the light. Next morning Brother Zeisberger awakened me, and took me alone with him into the woods. He then drew the candle out of his pocket, and imparted to me in confidence, what he would reveal to no soul besides; saying; "If, in the preceding night, we had not had an invisible watchman with us, we should all have been blown to atoms, and no soul could have known how it happened. I was fast asleep, for I was tired and in my first doze; suddenly I felt a shock, as though somebody was forcibly rousing me; I jumped up, and lo! the candle was burnt down on the one side, and just on the point of dropping in a blaze on the straw; to prevent which accident, there was but one moment left. From that instant, I could sleep no longer; for one chill after the other thrilled through my veins. Thanks be to our Lord for this extraordinary preservation of our lives."—Rondthaler, *Heckewelder*, 63-65, quoting from *The United Brethren's Missionary Intelligencer*, I, No. 10 (1824).

On another occasion, in the year 1769, being despatched on an uncommonly hot day, about harvest time, with letters to the missionaries at Friedenshütten on the Susquehanna, whilst yet eight miles distant from the town, I was so worn out by the heat, and tormented with a raging thirst, that I resolved to seek a certain spring near the path, which the Indians called the cold spring. But hardly had I tasted the water, cold as ice, when I was seized with the most violent pains, and my limbs refused to bear me any further. I expected to die here; and feared most of all that, whilst I was in this defenceless condition, I might be torn to pieces by the wild beasts. In this emergency, I prayed God to send an Indian to take charge of the letters, which were of great importance; when I recollected that one of the Brethren at Christian Spring, foreseeing the probable danger on account of the overpowering heat, had sent a phial of anodyne drops after me, when I had already left the place. A good dose of this medicine enabled me to reach Friedenshütten, after night had already set in; but it was long before I was so far restored as to be able to accompany a party of Indians to Bethlehem on horseback.—*Ibid.*

It is seldom that a man who falls asleep in the snow, exhausted by the cold, awakes to tell the tale. But John Heckewelder in his old age recalled such an adventure.

At one time while travelling on foot in a very cold night, to Gnadenhütten, beyond the Blue Mountains, my strength was so much exhausted, that I sat down on a tree which had been partially felled and was covered with snow, with the intention of merely resting my weary limbs, although a secret monitor cautioned me to beware of sleep. But the moment I sat down, I fell asleep, and should probably have never awaked more, if the tree had not suddenly given way under me, whereby I was thrown broad awake into the path. Grateful to the Lord for this providential escape, I immediately prosecuted my journey, and late that night reached Gnadenhütten.—Heckewelder, "Memoir."

It is not to be inferred from these incidents that death perpetually stalked the Indian paths. The travellers Heckewelder encountered were friendly, the Indians most of all. These people, he found, as did other eighteenth century travellers, were conspicuously generous to strangers whom they met on the trail.

Heckewelder's Indian friends made good companions. They were loyal, gay in conversion, invariably courteous. They knew how to be witty, even satirical, without causing offense.

I have heard them, for instance, compare the English and American nations to a pair of scissors [this was written after the Revolutionary War and the War of 1812], an instrument composed of two sharp edged knives exactly alike, working against each other for the same purpose, that of *cutting*. By the construction of this instrument, they said, it would appear as if in shutting, these two sharp knives would strike together and destroy each other's edges; but no such thing: they only cut *what comes between them*. And thus the English and Americans do when they go to war against one another. It is not each other that they want to destroy, but us, poor Indians, that are between them. By this means they get our land, and, when that is obtained, the scissors are closed again, and laid by for further use.—Heckewelder, *History*, 104.

Yet even among this gregarious people, as among white men, there were solitary spirits who preferred to retire from the world. On his journeys to Friedenshütten, Heckewelder saw the Indian hermit's field.

There is a spot of land at the edge of the great Pine or Beech Swamp, precisely where it is crossed by the road leading to Wyoming, which is called *the Hermit's Field*, and of which the following account is given. A short time before the white people came into Pennsylvania, a woman from some cause or other had separated herself from society, and with her young son, had taken her abode in this swamp, where she remained undiscovered until the boy grew up to manhood, procuring a livelihood by the use of the bow and arrow, in killing deer, turkeys and other animals, planting corn and vegetables, and gathering and curing nuts and berries of various kinds. When after her long seclusion she again saw Indians, she was much astonished to find them dressed in European apparel. She had become so attached to her place of abode, that she returned thither and remained there for several years. I was shewn by the Indians in the year 1765, and often afterwards, the corn hills that she had made; the ground, being a stiff clay, was not wasted or worn down, but was covered with bushes, and the traces of the labour of the female hermit were plainly discoverable.—Heckewelder, *History*, 200-201.

VIII

Glickhikan and the City of Peace: 1771-1772

ON THE BANKS of the Susquehanna, no less than in the capitals of Europe, prosperity brought its dangers. The Moravian Indians who, like their relatives in the woods, had long since adopted the use of European cloth and tools, had to buy these commodities from the traders who visited them seeking peltries. There were some taut moments, as we have already seen, when traders tried to pay for deerskins in rum and had to be sent away. At Wyoming, white men from Connecticut and Pennsylvania, quarreling over title to the Indian lands there, were launching into the disturbances which came to be known as the Pennamite Wars. From lower down the Susquehanna, near Shamokin, came the shocking news that a white man had murdered ten Indians—four men, four women, and two children.* The spectre of the land agent had risen again, whose "purchase" of Wyoming (confirmed by the murder of Teedyuscung) had set an ominous pattern for the exploitation of Indian lands. In 1768, by the Treaty of Fort Stanwix, the English wrung from the Six Nations a new Indian boundary, the eastern limits of which lay far to the west of Wyalusing. After the conclusion of this treaty, the Six Nations, as an ironical gesture of disgust at the white man's hard bargaining (so Heckewelder interpreted it †), sent the Friedenshütten Indians two Spanish dollars, their proportionate

---
* Heckewelder, *Narrative*, 98.
† *Ibid.*, 108.

share of the new purchase money which, their Uncles meant to say, came to two dollars for every five miles square of land surrendered.

The Moravian Brethren read the signs: incoming white settlers, murder of Indians, retaliation, race hysteria, massacre.

It was Glickhikan, a famous Delaware war chief, who opened the way for their escape. Glickhikan, whose name Heckewelder tells us means the stud or foremost sight on a gun barrel, was living at one of the Kuskuskies (near the present New Castle) on the Beaver River. He came into the story in this way: When David Zeisberger, in 1767 and 1768, travelled the Forbidden Path from Tioga (Athens, Pa.) on the Susquehanna to Goshgoshing on the Allegheny, establishing a mission there and later at nearby Lawunakhannek, he ran into opposition. The Senecas had not easily forgiven him for using the Forbidden Path, gateway to the Seneca country, the traversing of which by white men had been forbidden as a matter of Iroquois national policy. The Senecas, Keepers of the Western Door of the Six Nations (Iroquois), continued to admonish him. The Delaware prophet, Wangomen, came to Goshgoshing to preach against him. Zeisberger, never given to compromise, defied the Six Nations and reviled his Delaware opponent. The situation grew tense. There was in some quarters fear of violence. Talk arose in Indian governing circles of removing Zeisberger from their country. The famed Glickhikan, who had fought the English colonies in the French and Indian War, and who in Pontiac's War had come near to taking Fort Pitt, was sent to prepare the way for Zeisberger's removal.

This extraordinary man was, by all who knew him, both admired and dreaded, on account of his superior courage as a warrior—his talents in council—and his unequalled manner of delivering himself as a national orator, or speaker: he at that time being first councellor to the chief of the Wolf tribe [the Munsey Delaware], *Pakanke*, at Cascaski (Cushcushke) [in the vicinity of New Castle] on the Big Beaver.— This man, with the approbation of his chief and the council, had undertaken to go purposely to Lawunakhannek, there to dispute with, and confound the missionary Zeisberger, on the doctrine he was preaching to the Indians. Although he had thought himself armed at all points, sufficiently to withstand any white preacher's doctrine, he had the good sense not to begin the contest, but suffer the missionary to preach as usual, until he should be able to detect doctrinal errors. Having attended the preachings of Zeisberger, for that purpose, he was so struck with conviction of the truth of what he heard, and feeling the power of the precious word, that he, wherever he went, and on his return to Cushcushke, reported favourable of the missionary and his converts; which was the reason that, in the year following, they were invited to come and settle in that country.

The declaration of this much admired man, effected also a change in the minds and conduct of the chief and council of Goshgoshink; who now, instead of forbidding their people to go to hear the missionary preach, encouraged them to go, the consequence of which was, that many went, heard and believed, and joined the congregation at Lawunakhannek; while Wangomand, the Indian preacher, finding himself deserted by those who had hitherto supported him, now sought to gain the good will of those he had hitherto persecuted. (Heckewelder, *Narrative*, 109-110.)

In a short time Zeisberger, on behalf of the Christian Indians, "accepted," as Heckewelder tells us, "the friendly offer so repeatedly made to them by the chiefs of Cushcushke [Kuskusky], to come and settle on Big Beaver River."

The whole colony set out in sixteen canoes, on April 17, 1770, descended the Allegheny River to Pittsburgh, and went on down the Ohio as far as the mouth of the Beaver, which they ascended. At the Falls of the Beaver they were met by Glickhikan with a party of his men to help them carry their baggage over the mile-long portage. Twenty miles up the river from the mouth, they disembarked on the west bank and proceeded to make a settlement, which they called *Langundo-utenink* * (*Friedenstadt*, or Peace Village). The site, six miles south of New Castle, is now known as Moravia.

The chief came from Kushkushke to welcome them; but the scene was soon changed, when he saw that his first counsellor, Glikhikan, left him and joined the Christian Indians. Indeed, the loss of this man was considered a partial loss to the whole nation.

While Pakanko, the chief, and Glikhikan, were contending together on the propriety of such conduct, a black belt of wampum, which had been brought on from the great council at Gekelemukpechink [Newcomerstown] (in English, *still water*,) was laid before the chief, containing the following advice and notice; namely, "that in consideration of an epidemical disease, which had raged among them for some time, carrying off great numbers of Delawares, and believed to have been brought on them by the power of witchcraft, some of the counsellors were of the opinion, that by embracing Christianity the contagion would cease. That therefore they were unanimous, that this remedy should be resorted to; and that they hereby declared, that the word of God should be received by them; and further, that whoever should oppose the measure ought to be considered an enemy to the nation."

This resolute and sincere message, so favourable to the cause of the Brethren, silenced their adversaries; and was, in a great measure, the cause of the prosperity of the Brethren's mission from that time forward. . . .

---

* Heckewelder sometimes spells it *Langundowi-Otenink* and sometimes *Langundowi oteey*, but the other spelling is the one more commonly used by the Moravians.

The invitation given by the great council at Gekelemukpechink, extended not only to Zeisberger and the congregation settled on Beaver creek, but a deputation was also sent in the year 1771, to the Christian Indian congregations at Wyalusing and Sheshequon (Ulster), on the Susquehanna, inviting them to come on with their teachers, and settle on the Muskingum (in English, *Elk's eyes*) where they would be received as friends, and have the choice of land, on which they might live in peace and safety—and as a proof, that by sending this message, no evil was intended, they requested Zeisberger to certify their sincerity, by a letter in his own hand writing, which being done, Wangomend immediately set out with the dispatches, and having delivered the same to the Christian Indians at Friedenshutten (Wyalusing) and Sheshequon, he received the short answer; "that they thanked the chiefs on the Muskingum for their kind interposition in their behalf,* but that at present they were too heavy to rise—that when they should have lightened themselves, they would inform the chiefs and give them a decisive answer.†

Sometime after, the chief, Natawatwes repeated the invitation in a more pressing manner, in which the Wyandots (whom the Delawares call their uncles,) joined, assuring the Christian Indians that they would give them sufficient land, and never sell the ground under their feet to the white people, as the Six Nations had done to them.‡—Heckewelder, *Narrative*, 112-115.

This year, 1771, was to be the turning point of John Heckewelder's career. After the Muskingum fiasco of 1762, as we have seen, he had been restless, unsure of himself. It was Glickhikan of Kuskusky and the Delaware chiefs at Gekelemukpechink on the Muskingum who gave the right turn to Heckewelder's affairs.

With the . . . year, 1771, a new period of my life commenced; the dark clouds which had hitherto obscured my horizon were dispersed. . . . In the Spring of the said year, Br. David Zeisberger arrived at Bethlehem from Beaver Creek, and requested the Conference to send me along with him as an assisteant in the Mission. A proposal to this effect was made to me, and although I had a fair prospect of settling comfortably at Nazareth, I preferred entering on the Missionary service among the Indians, which, in those turbulent times had become a situation of peculiar danger.—Heckewelder, "Memoir."

With Zeisberger he travelled to Friedenshütten, where conferences were held with the Indians to determine whether they should remain where they were or move out of the white man's rapidly expanding

---

* Alluding to their being distressed by the Six Nations, who had sold their land to the English.
† "Too heavy," meaning they had their whole harvest of corn and vegetables on hand, it being the fall season.
‡ The reference here is to the Treaty of Fort Stanwix, 1768.

orbit. They "were unanimous in the opinion—that as these lands were sold, and the white people were becoming troublesome—often imposing liquor on them—there was no prospect of their living in undisturbed peace—that they therefore would accept the offer of the chiefs on the Muskingum, and the next spring move thither in a body." *

In September, accordingly, John Heckewelder set off as David Zeisberger's assistant for Friedenstadt on the Beaver River. Arriving there in October, he found a "handsome village" with "comfortable dwelling houses" for the Indians and "a spacious chapel of squared timber."

He made his home at Friedenstadt for less than a year. Of his experience there, little has been recorded except a few reminiscences written in his old age. One of these is of a chance encounter by means of which he learned, with some humiliation, one cause of the contempt in which Indians held most white men.

In the year 1771, while I was residing on the Big Beaver, I passed by the door of an Indian, who was a trader, and had consequently a quantity of goods in his house. He was going with his wife to Pittsburg, and they were shutting up the house, as no person remained in it during their absence. This shutting up was nothing else than putting a large hominy pounding-block, with a few sticks of wood outside against the door, so as to keep it closed. As I was looking at this man with attention while he was so employed, he addressed me in these words: "See my friend, this is an Indian lock that I am putting to my door." I answered, "Well enough; but I see you leave much property in the house, are you not afraid that those articles will be stolen while you are gone?"—"Stolen! by whom?"—"Why, by Indians, to be sure."—"No, no," replied he, "no Indian would do such a thing, and unless a white man or white people should happen to come this way, I shall find all safe on my return."—Heckewelder, *History*, 190-191.

Two Indians once saved John Heckewelder from drowning:

Crossing Beaver Creek in 1772, after heavy rains, my canoe struck upon a large log, which upset it, and plunged me into water ten or twelve feet in depth. By holding to the canoe, I kept myself above water for some time; but considering the rapidity of the torrent and the great falls a short distance below, I must inevitably have perished, if two Indian brethren, seeing my distress, had not plunged into the stream and saved me and the canoe, while one of them swimming dragged it along, and the other propelled it from behind.—Heckewelder, "Memoir."

After a winter and spring at Friedenstadt, Heckewelder found himself on the move again. His first long trip was, as he tells us, to the

---
* Heckewelder, *Narrative*, 116.

Allegheny to meet the Christian Indians moving west from Friedenshütten under conduct of the Brethren Rothe and Ettwein. From near Kittanning, Ettwein's band came overland to Friedenstadt; Rothe's group completed the journey by canoe, using the Allegheny, Ohio, and Beaver Rivers, with a portage at Beaver Falls.

A few days after the two bands had united at Friedenstadt, Heckewelder, with Ettwein and Zeisberger, led part of them over the Indian path to their final destination on the Muskingum (Tuscarawas Branch). They reached the town of Schönbrunn [near New Philadelphia] August 23, 1772

and by their Deputies inform'd the Delawar Chief Netawatwees & his Council at New Comers town of their arrival and their Intention to live as Christians in their Neighbourhood. The Chief & Council allotted unto them the Land on both Sides Muskingum River from Tuskerawy till within 3. Miles of New Comers Town and they seated themselves in that District in 2. Villages 9. Miles distant both on the East Side of the River.—Heckewelder, MS., "Captivity and Murder," p. 3: Archives of the Moravian Church, Bethlehem, Pa.

The upper town, Schönbrunn, was assigned to the Delawares; the lower town, the later-built Gnadenhütten ("on the Spot where King Beaver died, who in his last hours did admonish his People to receive the Word of God"), was assigned to the Mahicans, differences between these two peoples making it advisable for them to live apart—since it is a truth not confined to New England, where Robert Frost has given it a new currency, that "good fences make good neighbors."

As soon as they were settled they sent a Message to the Wiandots, under whom it was that the Delewares held what title they had to this land, informing them of their arrival and the Care the Delwares had taken of them which the Wiandots did much approve in their Cousins.*—*Ibid.*

Heckewelder took the trail again, October 19, for Friedenstadt, at which place he gathered a few more *émigrés* and brought them back to Schönbrunn on November 8. On still another trip over this same trail and for the same purpose (identified by him in his *History* as a journey from the Muskingum to the Big Beaver in the spring of 1773) Heckewelder observed an Indian taboo against the eating of wildcat.

Having been at one time confined two days by the overflowing of two large creeks, between which we were, we found our provisions at an end.

---

* Heckewelder MS., "Captivity and Murder," p. 7, n.: "All Indian Nations on this side of the Missisipi term the Dellawares (Grandfather) except the 5 Nations and Wyondotts who call them Cousins."

Glickhikan: 1771-1772

Every man who had a gun was called upon to turn out into the woods, and try to kill something. Their endeavours, however, were to no purpose; the day passed away, and they all, except the well-known *Popunhank*,* who had lost himself, returned to camp at night without bringing any thing of the meat kind but a wild cat, which our guide had shot. The Indians never despair, not even in the worst of times and under the severest trials; when placed in difficult situations they never use discouraging language, but always endeavour to raise their spirits and prevent them from sinking, under the hardships or dangers to which they are exposed. True to this national character, one of our old Indians immediately pronounced this wild cat to be "good, very good eating," and it was immediately ordered to be put on the spit and roasted for our supper. While this was performing, the old Indian endeavoured to divert the company by extolling in a jocular manner the country they had now got into, and where such good things were to be had; to which some one or other of the old men would reply: "all very true." At length, about nine o'clock at night, the call was given by the old cook (for so I now call him) that the meat was done and we might come in to eat. I, who had heard so much praise of this repast, being greatly pinched with hunger, had kept myself in readiness for this expected call; but seeing nobody rise, and observing much merriment through the camp, I began to suspect that something was the matter, and therefore kept my seat. The night was spent without any body attempting to eat of the wild cat, and in the morning a different call was given by one of the old men, signifying that a large kettle of tea had been made by some of the good women, who invited all to come and take their share of it. Every one obeyed this call, and I went with the rest, the jovial old cook taking the roasted wild cat with him to the mess. The scene was not only very diverting, but brought on an interesting discussion between the men on the propriety or impropriety of eating the flesh of all animals without restriction, some contending that they were all by the will of the great Creator ordained for some use, and therefore put in the power of man; and how were we to know which were intended for our nourishment and which not? The old cook had himself taken that position, adding that the hog and the bear fed on dirty things, and yet we ate their meat with a good appetite. The cat, however, notwithstanding all the arguments in its favour, remained untouched, and was taken back by the old hunter and cook to its former place at his fire.

But now, Popunhank, whom we believed to be lost, and our guide, who once more had gone out, and exerted himself in vain to kill a deer, came in together. The guide had been desired as he pursued his hunt to look for our

---

* Heckewelder, *History*, note by the editor, William C. Reichel, p. 197: A Monsey of Wyalusing, at whose persuasion the Moravian Indians settled on that stream in 1765, who became one of their number, following them to the Big Beaver and the Tuscarawas, where he died in May of 1775. Papunhank's name occurs frequently in the annals of Provincial history between 1762 and 1765.

lost companion, and had the good luck to find him at the distance of five or six miles, with a fine deer that he had killed. He lost no time in bringing him back to our camp.

The sight of these two men dragging a large deer along was truly joyful to us, as well on account of the recovery of our lost friend, as of the meat that he brought. All felt the cravings of hunger, all were delighted with the certain prospect of immediate relief, yet no boisterous or extraordinary rejoicing took place, but all called out with one voice: *Anischi! Anischi!* we are thankful. The wild cat, which yet remained untouched, was thrown out of the camp, and dismissed by the old cook with these words: "Go, cat, we do not want you at this time!"—Heckewelder, *History*, 196-198.

At Schönbrunn Heckewelder made his home for the next few years, and here a new version of Penn's "Holy Experiment" was happily maintained until 1777, "the Year in which most of the Western Nations took the Hatchet from the English to strike the Americans." *

---

* Heckewelder MS., "Captivity and Murder," 3.

⚝ IX ⚝

Schönbrunn, the Beautiful Spring: 1773

AT SCHÖNBRUNN (*Welhik-Tuppeek*, the Beautiful Spring), on what is now known as the Tuskarawas branch of the Muskingum River, near New Philadelphia, Ohio, the Indians built a town that surpassed even Friedenshütten, their former town at Wyalusing on the Susquehanna. Something of its quality may be seen today in the restoration, recently completed after careful and ingenious historical and archaeological research. Here are the Indians' log houses, neat but substantial, their gardens, the church with David Zeisberger's cabin adjoining, and the school where John Heckewelder, now in his early thirties, for a time taught the Indian children.

Heckewelder was proud of it, "the largest and handsomest town," as he describes it, "the Christian Indians had hitherto built; containing upwards of sixty dwelling houses, most of which were of squared timbers. The street, from east to west, was long, and of a proper width; from the centre, where the chapel stood, another street run off to the north. The inhabitants had, for the greatest part, become husbandmen. They had large fields under good rail fences, well pailed gardens, and fine fruit trees; besides herds of cattle, horses and hogs." *

The Moravians had cause to be pleased with Schönbrunn and of its sister town, Gnadenhütten (named in honor of the former mission town at the junction of Mahoning Creek and the Lehigh) ten miles

---
* Heckewelder, *Narrative*, 157.

down the river. These two small but vigorous plants were producing seeds which, if given time to mature, seemed capable of producing a crop of goodwill sufficient to nourish a continent.

The Delaware chiefs at Gekelemukpechink (Newcomer's Town) recognized the promise contained in this Moravian-Indian experiment. "King" Netawatwees, urged by his counselor, White Eyes, received the Moravian Indians and their teachers as "full-fledged citizens" of the Delaware nation. It was understood, however, that this Christian Indian community preserved its separate identity (like each of the component parts of the modern British Commonwealth), possessing sovereignty and the right to pursue its own way of life unmolested and unquestioned. Its individual members had the right to preach the Christian gospel of peace and goodwill wherever they would, outside as well as inside their own domain.

When Netawatwees died at Pittsburgh in 1776, his last message to his nation was in praise of the Moravians and a plea to his people to follow them. White Eyes delivered this message, holding a string of wampum in one hand and a Bible in the other, to the Great Council of the Delawares at Gekelemukpechink.

Of this Christian Indian commonwealth (dreamed of at Friedenshütten, on the verge of fulfilment at Schönbrunn and Gnadenhütten) Dr. August C. Mahr has written, "Had it not been swept away by the muddy frontier backwash of the Revolutionary War, this unequalled creation of White Eyes' superior statesmanship might have changed the entire history of the United States, if not of the world." *

John Heckewelder spent a happy winter at Schönbrunn. His experience among these friendly people, generous and devout, just in their dealings with one another and with strangers, merry in conversation, and gentle even under provocation, gave him fresh assurance that to work with them as a teacher was, as he said, in a letter to Brother Arbo, March 20, 1773, his "Call and Destination."

Writing next day to the Elders Conference at Bethlehem, he reported that he was getting along so well with the language that he could now understand almost everything that was said to him. To speak Delaware fluently, however, would take more time, because he tended to think of everything in his own language. He was at last, however, beginning to think in Indian, which kept the words fresher in his mind. He had also learned a little of the Shawnee tongue, and when Echpala-

---

* August C. Mahr, "The Conversion of Echpalawehund," *Archiv für Reformationsgeschichte*, XLIII (1952), No. 2, p. 233.

Schönbrunn: 1773

wehund (one of Netawatwees' most valued counselors) came to the mission, Heckewelder had a good teacher, for Echpalawehund was perfect in that tongue and had promised to be his tutor, and Heckewelder became proficient in the Shawnee language.

He spent the early spring in the sugar bush. In his letter to Brother Arbo, noted above, he said that he had only yesterday got back from sugar boiling. He had, he tells his friend, made 178 pounds of sugar in all, at the rate of eighteen or nineteen pounds in twenty-four hours during the height of the season. Many days he got as much as sixty or seventy pails of juice from his hundred trees. Some of the best maples yielded six or seven gallons daily. It took six gallons, he observed, of the first run of sap to produce one pound of sugar. Later in the season it took eight or nine gallons.

Even the attack of sciatica which prostrated him in the autumn of 1772, scarcely interrupted the Schönbrunn idyl, so kind were the Indians and so quickly did they find means to relieve his pain. During this siege of what he calls rheumatism, he at first suffered agony in both legs, from hip to foot. Then for several days his limbs became lifeless, without feeling. The Indians went out into the woods to collect medicinal plants. Of these they made poultices for him, which induced sweating and brought everything out in blisters. Heckewelder thought this "folk cure" might help anyone else suffering from "rheumatism." He promised to learn more about these plants, and to let his friend know what he found.

The *Materia Medica* of the Indians consists of various roots and plants known to themselves, the properties of which they are not fond of disclosing to strangers. They make considerable use of the barks of trees, such as the white and black oak, the white walnut, of which they make pills, the cherry, dogwood, maple, birch, and several others. They prepare and compound these medicines in different ways, which they keep a profound secret.—Heckewelder, *History*, p. 224.

The conversion of Echpalawehund to Christianity and the determination of that chief to join the Moravian community, though it produced political tensions at Gekelemukpechink, the Delaware capital—tensions eventuating in a compromise by which the chief was granted permission to live with the Moravians if he agreed, nevertheless, to retain his place on Netawatwees' council—was a measure of the success of Moravian statesmanship at the Beautiful Spring. Here in the wilderness which some hundreds of displaced Delawares and Shawnees (who had fled from the Ohio-Allegheny Valley after the success of

General Forbes' army at Loyalhanna and Fort Duquesne, now called home, was a Christian community which sought, not to destroy the Indian ethic, which had much of nobility in it, but to save the best of it from extinction (as Rauch had done among the Mahicans at Shecomeco) by giving it the Christian dynamic; and which sought at the same time to give the Indian the skills needed to enable him to hold his own in competition with the now numerically dominant white men. Leaders among the white people as well as the brown were being brought to see—and the success of the Schönbrunn experiment was crucial to their enlightenment in this regard—that the Moravian solution of the race problem was not only ideally good but practical. Men such as Glickhikan, Netawatwees, White Eyes, Echpalawehund (these were great names in the Indian world) were convinced of the truth of this, and their influence was wide and growing. White men, too, in government circles, though less immediately in touch with the new world dawning on the Muskingum, were interested and hopeful. Schönbrunn and Gnadenhütten were symbols of a new day in American race relations.

To this sanctuary on the Muskingum it was to be one of John Heckewelder's first tasks, and a pleasant one, to bring those of the Christian Indians who still remained at Friedenstadt on the Beaver River.

Langundo Utenink was no longer a City of Peace. Despite its propitious beginnings and the early prestige it had received through the accession of Glickhikan, Friedenstadt was unhappily situated. It was altogether too close to the Munsee settlement at Kuskusky, a town cursed with degenerates, rum-soaked debauchees and murderers, who could not be kept at a distance. The lives of the missionaries there were threatened by drunken Munsee chauvinists.

Heckewelder, writing from Schönbrunn to Brother Arbo, March 20, 1773, said that he looked forward eagerly to the journey, which he was to begin "the day after tomorrow." He would go to "Languntotening, from there to Pittsburg, then back to the former place, and from there with a Canow . . . down the Ohio and up this river [the Muskingum]." If the new country he was about to see proved interesting (there was always something of the explorer in Heckewelder), he would give his friend a description of it—landscape, animals, fish, etc. —and would perhaps send him some natural curiosity.

He went by trail to Friedenstadt. Part of the Indian community there, headed by John Rothe (who, with John Ettwein, the year before had brought the Christian Indians from Friedenshütten on the Susque-

Schönbrunn: 1773

hanna), went overland with the cattle to Schönbrunn. The remainder, under John Heckewelder, went by water: down the Beaver and the Ohio, up the Muskingum.

Heckewelder has left us a good diary of the trip:

Brother John Heckewelder's Account of Their Journey by Water from Languntoutenünk to Welhik Thuppeek in April 1773.*

April the 13th. We set out together, 22 canoes, from Languntoutenünk and by night reached the Falls. We were joined here by Shebosh, Johannes, and some other Brethren who had come by land with horses to help us carry our heaviest things round the rapids.

The 14th. These men turned back because the water was beginning to rise, and they were afraid they might be delayed in their journey overland to Welhik Thupeek.

The 15th. Many of our canoes being overloaded, it was decided to build another one here. It was arranged that the women, assisted by some of the men, should carry the things around the rapids, while several of the Brethren were sent out hunting. These latter returned to camp in the evening with 5 deer.

The 16th. The Indians found a man's head near our camp. He presumably had been killed during the last war, for his skull had been split with a hatchet. Our Indians grieved for him, because he had died an innocent victim. The rain continuing, the strongest and boldest of our Brethren made up their minds to run the rapids in the empty canoes. And so they did, though at risk of their lives. Two of them were nearly drowned; but some of our Brethren were always on hand with a canoe to help in case of emergency, and so they all got down safely, though the canoes were often half full of water.

The 17th. The canoe they had started to build the day before yesterday was now ready, so without further delay we went on down this evening to the Ohio and camped below the old French fort, some of the chimneys of which are still standing.

The 18th. Now that we were on the Ohio, we took council about how we were to proceed, and decided that, since the river was high, we would keep going until nightfall. Today we saw, here and there along the left bank, plantations belonging to white people, and at night we camped not far from the Mingo Town [Mingo Junction].

The 19th. We passed the town this morning. The Mingoes wanted to talk with us, but none of us understood their language. It was from this point,

---

* Dr. August C. Mahr has published a fully annotated edition of this journal in the *Ohio State Archaeolgical and Historical Quarterly*, Vol. 61, No. 3 (July, 1952). The present translation is a new one, but the editor acknowledges his indebtedness to Dr. Mahr's footnotes.

last year, that Brother David and his party went overland to Welhik Thuppeek.

A few miles farther on, a white man called to us and bade us come ashore and rest a while; but we did not want to lose time, and explained to him why, to which he responded, "Then I wish you good people a safe journey." We saw more houses and plantations belonging to white people at various places on the east side of the river. No sooner had we landed this evening than 6 white men appeared on the opposite bank and began to talk with me, but the river is so wide we could hardly understand each other. So with the Brethren, Anton and Boas, I crossed over to them. For the next half hour they plied us with all sorts of questions, politely enough, and chiefly about our religious beliefs and teachings. I give a few examples:

"What kind of Indians are these and where do they come from?"

Ans. "They are a Christian Indian congregation from Beaver Creek."

"Where are they going?"

"To the Muskingum."

"Are these the Moravian Indians?"

Ans. "Yes."

"Do they have a minister with them?"

Ans. "Yes. There are 2 congregations and each has its teacher."

"What is the religion of their teachers?"

"They are Brethren [Moravians]."

"Do they receive an annual stipend from the King or some recognized society?"

"No."

"Then who supports them?"

Ans. "The Brethren contribute voluntarily, each giving what he can, and their preachers are supported by these freewill offerings."

"That is praiseworthy," they said to one another. "Can their preachers talk with them in their own language?"

"Yes."

"Have any of them really been brought to believe there is a God in heaven?"

"Yes."

"Do they accept baptism?"

"Yes."

"Have these two been baptized, and what are their names?"

Ans. "They have both been baptized, and their names are Anton and Boas."

"Do they remain true to the faith after baptism?"

"They seldom leave us. Take this man Anton, for example. He has kept the faith for 20 years."

"You can see by this man's face," they said to one another, "that he is a true Christian," and they asked further, "Do they celebrate the Sabbath and keep it holy, and do no work, not even go hunting, on that day?"

Schönbrunn: 1773

Ans. "They observe the Sabbath the same as other Christian churches do."
"Which day do you regard as the Sabbath?"
Ans. "The first day of the week."
"Do they hold services on any day besides the Sabbath?"
Ans. "Yes. They have one and sometimes 2 services every day."
"It is clear enough," said they, "that these are true Christians. What do you do if one of your people misdemeans himself?"
Ans. "We rebuke him, and if that is not enough he is excluded from the congregation and sometimes even sent away."
"Do you keep school for them?"
"Yes."
"In what language?"
"In their own."
"That is right," they said.
"We think that, as long as they are not living entirely among the white people, they cannot learn their language, for many of them are too old and many are very unskilful at learning foreign languages."
Their last question was this: "Do you not do business with them, and do they not give you part of their hunting bag?"
Ans. "We have no business dealings with them, and we get nothing from them. We are content to live very simply, and as long as, from time to time, we see someone turn and become a believer, we consider ourselves well paid."
"Surely," they said, "God is with you and blesses your work. This is just what our minister, Johnes, reported of you. He told us a lot about you. He met and talked with one of your ministers (that was Brother David, whom he met at Gnadenhütten). He knows you are a true Christian community in the Indian country. We wish you success and God's blessing on your work, and may your numbers increase."
With that we parted, for night had come.

The 20th. As we were about to break camp, these same people came across the river to have a look at us and our arrangements. They commiserated with the old people on such a journey, they fondled the children, and wished us all a safe journey. I learned then that they were Baptists, one of them a gentleman from Philadelphia [Dr. James McMechan]. They sat on the bank and watched our departure. They were surprised to see how quiet all our people were.

In the afternoon, some of our party wanted to stop and hunt, because we had no meat. But we were anxious to take advantage of this fine, windless weather. When we had gone a little farther, however, and had come to a small island where, it was supposed, there must be deer, we surrounded the island in our canoes while several of the party went ashore with dogs. At once 4 deer leaped into the water. We got 3 of them.

The 21st. We started early again. The country here is very beautiful. Some of the bottom lands look like orchards. I saw many trees and plants that were unfamiliar to me, and the Indians said: "We are strangers here. The landscape, trees, and grass are all different."

Here and there we saw more houses belonging to white men, some of whom were standing on the bank. They called to us and asked, "Where are you people going?"

"Up the Muskingum to settle," I replied.

Whereupon one of them answered, "I wish it were 10 thousand times farther."

Another person standing beside him rebuked him and said: "You are wrong about these people. They are the ones our minister, Johnes, praised so highly. Don't you see how quiet and well-behaved they are? Not one of them is painted; they are just their natural selves," and they said, "We wish you a safe journey."

It is a fact that this minister could never say enough about how pleased he was with our Indians, and that is why everyone around here loves and respects us. Various people have said to me, "If war should come again, no harm would befall you."

A bear was shot today.

The 22nd. We traveled through the most delightful country of the whole trip. The Ohio, however crooked it may be elsewhere, here ran a perfectly straight course [the Long Reach], W.S.W. There were no more hills to be seen, but level bottoms on both sides. Most of the leaves were fully out, many trees and a variety of flowers were in blossom. The grass was shoe-high. We were all astonished to see such a beautiful summer prospect in this month of the year. Here on the east side of the river, a short distance inland, there is said to be a settlement of 2-300 families. They do not like to live on the river for fear of the Indians.

By noon we left the Ohio and entered the Muskingum. For a few miles above its mouth, this river is very deep and must be navigated with paddles or oars. Farther up it is not so deep, and is a little wider than the Lehigh at Bethlehem. Another bear was shot today.

The 23rd. Our beautiful landscape disappeared; the country became very hilly. The bottoms were very swampy, almost entirely grown over with beech trees.* In the evening our Brethren did a little hunting and shot another bear.

The 24th. We met an Indian acquaintance from Gekelemukpechünk, who was on his way home from a hunting trip. He had shot a buffalo ox, of which there are many hereabouts.

The 25th. We traveled till noon, when, many of our party complaining of being tired, we decided to camp beside a huge rock [near Brokaw]. Some of the Brethren immediately built a sweat oven to sweat out their fatigue;

---

* For a glimpse of travel among beech swamps, see Heckewelder's journal of 1800 to LeBoeuf, pp. 374-83.

Schönbrunn: 1773

others did a little hunting, and found some buffalo, but though they shot at them they got none.—Heckewelder's "Journey . . . to Welhik Thupeek," April, 1773.

The sweat oven is the first thing that an Indian has recourse to when he feels the least indisposed; it is the place to which the wearied traveller, hunter, or warrior looks for relief from the fatigues he has endured, the cold he has caught, or the restoration of his lost appetite.

This oven is made of different sizes, so as to accommodate from two to six persons at a time, or according to the number of men in the village, so that they may be all successively served. It is generally built on a bank or slope, one half of it within and the other above ground. It is well covered on the top with split plank and earth, and has a door in front, where the ground is level to go or rather to creep in. Here, on the outside, stones, generally of about the size of a large turnip, are heated by one or more appointed each day for that purpose. While the oven is heating, decoctions from roots or plants are prepared either by the person himself who intends to sweat, or by one of the men in the village, who boils a large kettleful for the general use, so that when the public cryer going his rounds, calls out *Pimook!* "go to sweat!" every one brings his small kettle, which is filled for him with the potion, which at the same time serves him as a medicine, promotes a profuse perspiration, and quenches his thirst. As soon as a sufficient number have come to the oven, a number of the hot stones are rolled into the middle of it, and the sweaters go in, seating themselves or rather squatting round those stones, and there they remain until the sweat ceases to flow; then they come out, throwing a blanket or two about them that they may not catch cold; in the mean while, fresh heated stones are thrown in for those who follow them. While they are in the oven, water is now and then poured on the hot stones to produce a steam, which they say, increases the heat, and gives suppleness to their limbs and joints. In rheumatic complaints, the steam is produced by a decoction of boiled roots, and the patient during the operation is well wrapped up in blankets, to keep the cold air from him, and promote perspiration at the same time.

Those sweat ovens are generally at some distance from an Indian village, where wood and water are always at hand. The best order is preserved at those places. The women have their separate oven in a different direction from that of the men, and subjected to the same rules. The men generally sweat themselves once and sometimes twice a week; the women have no fixed day for this exercise, nor do they use it as often as the men.

In the year 1784,[*] a gentleman whom I had been acquainted with at

---

[*] Heckewelder, *History*, 226, note by Reichel: "Mr. Heckewelder was in this year residing at New Gnadenhütten on the Huron (now Clinton), Michigan, where the Moravian Missionaries ministered to their converts for upwards of three years, subsequent to their compulsory evacuation of the Tuscarawas Valley."

Detroit, and who had been for a long time in an infirm state of health, came from thence to the village of the Christian Indians on the Huron river, in order to have the benefit of the sweat oven. It being in the middle of winter, when there was a deep snow on the ground, and the weather was excessively cold, I advised him to postpone his sweating to a warmer season; but he persisting in his resolution, I advised him by no means to remain in the oven longer than fifteen or at most twenty minutes. But when he once was in it, feeling himself comfortable, he remained a full hour, at the end of which he fainted, and was brought by two strong Indians to my house, in very great pain and not able to walk. He remained with me until the next day, when we took him down in his sleigh to his family at Detroit. His situation was truly deplorable; his physicians at that place gave up all hopes of his recovery, and he frequently expressed his regret that he had not followed my advice. Suddenly, however, a change took place for the better, and he not only recovered his perfect health, but became a stout corpulent man, so that he would often say, that his going into the sweat oven was the best thing he had ever done in his life for the benefit of his health. He said so to me fifteen years afterwards when I saw him in the year 1798. He had not had the least indisposition since that time. He died about the year 1814, at an advanced age.—Heckewelder, *History*, pp. 225-27.

To return to the diary of April 25, 1773: The sweat oven built by Heckewelder's Indians soothed tired muscles, but it was no defence against annoyances of another kind from without.

We had little rest that night, being much disturbed by innumerable toads, for which reason the Indians call this place, *Tsquallutene*, i.e. Town of the Toads. Toward midnight we had a violent thunderstorm with heavy rain. Some of our people took shelter under a rock near the large one. This large one is 76 feet long, 25 high, and 22 wide, all one solid rock.

The 26th and 27th. We had pretty good water and got well ahead, but, finding that our grain had got wet during the recent downpour and was beginning to sprout, we decided on *the 28th* to travel only as far as Sikhewünk and to dry the grain there. Accompanied by a few of the Brethren I went about 10 miles up this creek to see the famous salt spring [at present Chandlersville]. It is on a sandbank, and has a copious flow but no visible outlet. It is thought it must rise and disappear through underground channels. When it has been emptied, it quickly fills up again. We saw here various contraptions for boiling salt. At the mouth of this creek there is a fine mount of stone coal, lying there like a brick wall, not mixed with earth or other stones such as I have seen on the Ohio. The length of the wall was 500 ells.

From this point on the country is different from what I have previously been describing. Fine bottoms appeared again, good land, and the farther we proceeded the more attractive it became. And the river here took a change of course, raising our hopes to be soon with our Brethren, for before this, we had seemed to be getting farther and farther away.

The 29th. We had 3 bad rapids * to negotiate, and we had a lot of trouble drawing our canoes up.

The 30th. By noon we came to the Shawano Town [Waketameki, near Dresden] which Brother David had visited last fall. Some of our Brethren went ashore, but they found only a few people at home. By these they were kindly received; most of the inhabitants have moved away. We passed another town and then made camp. We had some bad stretches again today, and most of our people were feeling done out.

May 1st. At noon we stopped again at a Shawano town. The inhabitants mingled freely with our people and were very friendly. During our stay, I visited a white man who lives here with a white wife. She had been a prisoner and can speak nothing but Shawano. We went on and were hospitably received at another town inhabited by Dellawares and Monsys. They gave us their best entertainment and saw to it that everyone had all he could eat. They would have been glad if we had spent the night with them, but we did not want to lose any time, and so went on a few miles farther.

The 2nd. Again we had a lot of wading to do, hauling the canoes up the rapids and over the shallow places. We were met by an Indian Brother from Gnadenhütten, who gave us considerable help.

The 3rd. We passed several more towns, at some of which we stopped. The inhabitants were friendly. In the afternoon we passed Gekelemukpechünk, and camped at the upper end of town. I counted 106 people watching us as we went by. They hailed us with their customary shout of joy. We were not, however, able to return their greeting in the same manner. No sooner had we landed than we received visitors, some of whom brought food for the hungry.

Meanwhile I went with a few of the Brethren to visit Chief Netawatwees. He himself and those with him were very kind to us, and the thought came to me as we took our leave of him, "Some day you, too, will be the Savior's."

Then I went with one of the Brethren to see Killbuck, who, among other things, asked the Brother who was with me, "Does this man really love the Indians?"

"Yes," replied my companion, "not only he but all the Brethren who live among us. They don't have to live in this humble way. I myself have seen how comfortably they live at Bethlehem, but because they love the Indians and want to acquaint them with the Savior, they are content with a simple mode of life and rejoice when Indians are brought to the Savior. They ask and desire nothing more of us than that."

"Well, well," replied he, "now I know."

The 4th. In the morning we had many visitors again, and our Brethren

---

* The falls of the Muskingum, at what is now Duncan Falls, below Zanesville.

got in many a good word about the Savior. Then we set off again. We were glad to meet a few Brethren from Gnadenhütten and Welhik Thuppeek who had come out to help us. We were pretty well worn out. In the afternoon we reached Gnadenhütten, where everybody had been looking forward to our arrival and had been busy preparing food to refresh the tired and hungry. 3 families stopped off here to make their homes, while *on the 5th* the rest of us arrived safe and sound at Welhik Thuppeek, where we were received with all the kindness and hospitality possible.—"John Heckewelder's Account of Their Journey by Water from Languntoutenünk to Welhik Thuppeek in April 1773," Archives of the Moravian Church. Translated from the German.

It is fitting to close this narrative of a canoe trip up the Muskingum, in which we have seen so many instances of Indian hospitality, with Heckewelder's more extended remarks on this trait of Indian character, and his attempt to explain its origin.

The Indian considers himself as a being created by an all-powerful, wise, and benevolent Mannitto; all that he possesses, all that he enjoys, he looks upon as given to him or allotted for his use by the Great Spirit who gave him life; he therefore believes it to be his duty to adore and worship his Creator and benefactor; to acknowledge with gratitude his past favours, thank him for present blessings, and solicit the continuation of his good will. (An old Indian told me about fifty years ago, that when he was young, he still followed the custom of his father and ancestors, in climbing upon a high mountain or pinnacle, to thank the Great Spirit for all the benefits before bestowed, and to pray for a continuance of his favour; that they were sure their prayers were heard, and acceptable to the Great Spirit, although he did not himself appear to them.—Heckewelder's note.)

The Indian also believes, that he is highly favoured by his Maker, not only in having been created different in shape and in mental and bodily powers from other animals, but in being enabled to control and master them all, even those of an enormous size and of the most ferocious kinds; and therefore, when he worships his Creator in his way, he does not omit in his supplications to pray that he may be endowed with courage to fight and conquer his enemies, among whom he includes all savage beasts; and when he has performed some heroic act, he will not forget to acknowledge it as a mark of divine favour, by making a sacrifice to the great and good Mannitto, or by publicly announcing that his success was entirely owing to the courage given him by the all-powerful Spirit. Thus habitual devotion to the great First Cause, and a strong feeling of gratitude for the benefits which he confers, is one of the prominent traits which characterise the mind of the untutored Indian.

Not satisfied with paying this first of duties to the Lord of all, in the best manner they are able, the Indians also endeavour to fulfil the views which they suppose he had in creating the world. They think that he made the earth and all that it contains for the common good of mankind; when he stocked the country that he gave them with plenty of game, it was not for the benefit of a few, but of all. Everything was given in common to the sons of men.—Heckewelder, *History*, pp. 100-101.

The Indians Heckewelder knew were not communists. They enjoyed private possessions and they abhorred tyranny of any kind, whether exercised by a single autocrat or a well-meaning but all-managing government. By their social attitudes they cut the ground from under any such arguments as we hear today from those who preach the class war. With the Indians there could be no privileged or underprivileged classes, for so strong was each individual's sense of brotherhood with those around him, that, without the least compulsion, he shared his private possessions with anyone who had need of them—and did it, moreover, without the slightest condescension. The Indians were instinctively generous. They loved their neighbors too sincerely to dispense what we today call "charity."

They give and are hospitable to all, without exception, and will always share with each other and often with the stranger, even to their last morsel. They rather would lie down themselves on an empty stomach, than have it laid to their charge that they had neglected their duty, by not satisfying the wants of the stranger, the sick or the needy. The stranger has a claim to their hospitality, partly on account of his being at a distance from his family and friends, and partly because he has honoured them by his visit, and ought to leave them with a good impression upon his mind; the sick and the poor because they have a right to be helped out of the common stock: for if the meat they have been served with, was taken from the woods, it was common to all before the hunter took it; if corn or vegetables, it had grown out of the common ground, yet not by the power of man, but by that of the Great Spirit. Besides, on the principle, that all are descended from one parent, they look upon themselves as but one great family, who therefore ought at all times and on all occasions, to be serviceable and kind to each other, and by that means make themselves acceptable to the head of the universal family, the great and good Mannitto. Let me be permitted to illustrate this by an example.

Some travelling Indians having in the year 1777, put their horses over night to pasture in my little meadow at Gnadenhütten on the Muskingum, I called on them in the morning to learn why they had done so. I endeavoured to make them sensible of the injury they had done me, especially as I intended to mow the meadow in a day or two. Having finished my complaint, one of them replied: "My friend, it seems you lay claim to the grass my horses have eaten, because you had enclosed it with a fence: now tell me, who caused the grass to grow? Can *you* make the grass grow? I think not, and no body can except the great Mannitto. He it is who causes it to grow both for my horses and for yours! See, friend! the grass which grows out of the earth is common to all; the game in the woods is common to all. Say, did you never eat venison and bear's meat?"—"Yes, very often."—"Well, and did you ever hear me or any other Indian complain about that? No; then be not disturbed at my horses having eaten only once, of what you call *your* grass, though the grass my horses did eat, in like manner as the meat you did eat, was given to the Indians by the Great Spirit. Besides, if you will but consider, you will find that my horses did not eat *all* your grass. For friendship's sake, however, I shall never put my horses in your meadow again."—Heckewelder, *History*, 101-102.

X

The Three Sisters

THE HOSPITALITY shown to Heckewelder and his party at the towns along the Muskingum River was not at all exceptional in the Indian country. Refreshment for travelers was a courtesy an Indian housewife allowed herself neither to forget nor to stint, even if it meant she and her family had to postpone or even forego their own prepared meal.

The food provided on such occasions was not the crude fare we might suppose. The staple of Indian diet was the Three Sisters, corn, beans, and squash, with the fruits of the chase thrown in as entrees. Of these, corn, the elder sister, was the most vital. Corn was to the Indian what rice is to the people of East Asia, the basis of nearly every meal. But it was prepared in so many different ways, with such a variety of meat, fish, and vegetables to season it, and with such nice attention to the art of cooking, not forgetting the proper selection of wood for the fire, and the change from one fuel to another according as the dish being prepared called for a slow, quick, hot, or medium fire —that it makes one's mouth water to hear it spoken of.

Heckewelder, from his experience on the Muskingum, had every opportunity of appreciating the artistry that went into the concoction of good Indian dishes, from corn soup with bear's meat in it (or the flesh of deer, raccoon, turkey), to corn bread spiced with chestnuts and maple sugar.

The principal food of the Indians consists of the game which they take or kill in the woods, the fish out of the waters, and the maize, potatoes, beans, pumpkins, squashes, cucumbers, melons, and occasionally cabbages and turnips, which they raise in their fields; they make use also of various roots of plants, fruits, nuts, and berries out of the woods, by way of relish or as a seasoning to their victuals, sometimes also from necessity.

They commonly make two meals every day, which, they say, is enough. If any one should feel hungry between meal-times, there is generally something in the house ready for him.

The hunter prefers going out with his gun on an empty stomach; he says, that hunger stimulates him to exertion by reminding him continually of his wants, whereas a full stomach makes a hunter easy, careless, and lazy, ever thinking of his home and losing his time to no purpose. With all their industry, nevertheless, and notwithstanding this strong stimulant, many a day passes over their heads that they have not met with any kind of game, nor consequently tasted a morsel of victuals; still they go on with their chase, in hopes of being able to carry some provisions home, and do not give up the pursuit until it is so dark that they can see no longer.

The morning and evening, they say, are the precious hours for the hunter. They lose nothing by sleeping in the middle of the day, that is to say, between ten o'clock in the morning and four in the afternoon, except in dark, cloudy, and rainy weather, when the whole day is nearly equally good for hunting. Therefore the hunter, who happens to have no meat in the house, will be off and in the woods before daylight, and strive to be in again for breakfast with a deer, turkey, goose, bear, or raccoon, or some other game then in season. Meanwhile, his wife has pounded her corn, now boiling on the fire, and baked her bread, which gives them a good breakfast. If, however, the husband is not returned by ten o'clock in the forenoon, the family take their meal by themselves, and his share is put aside for him when he comes home.

The Indians have a number of manners of preparing their corn. They make an excellent pottage of it, by boiling it with fresh or dried meat (the latter pounded), dried pumpkins, dry beans, and chestnuts. They sometimes sweeten it with sugar or molasses from the sugar-maple tree. Another very good dish is prepared by boiling with their corn or maize, the washed kernels of the shell-bark or hickory nut. They pound the nuts in a block or mortar, pouring a little warm water on them, and gradually a little more as they become dry, until, at last, there is a sufficient quantity of water, so that by stirring up the pounded nuts the broken shells separate from the liquor, which from the pounded kernels assumes the appearance of milk. This being put into the kettle and mixed with the pottage gives it a rich and agreeable flavour. If the broken shells do not all freely separate by swimming on the top or sinking to the bottom, the liquor is strained through a clean cloth, before it is put into the kettle.

They also prepare a variety of dishes from the pumpkin, the squash, and the green French or kidney beans; they are very particular in their choice of pumpkins and squashes, and in their manner of cooking them. The women say that the less water is put to them, the better dish they make, and that it would be still better if they were stewed without any water, merely in the steam of the sap which they contain. They cover up the pots in which they cook them with large leaves of the pumpkin vine, cabbages, or other leaves of the larger kind. They make an excellent preserve from the cranberry and crab-apple, to which, after it has been well stewed, they add a proper quantity of sugar or molasses.

Their bread is of two kinds; one made up of green corn while in the milk, and another of the same grain when fully ripe and quite dry. This last is pounded as fine as possible, then sifted and kneaded into dough, and afterwards made up into cakes of six inches in diameter and about an inch in thickness, rounded off on the edge. In baking these cakes, they are extremely particular; the ashes must be clean and hot, and if possible come out of good dry oak barks, which they say gives a brisk and durable heat. In the dough of this kind of bread, they frequently mix boiled pumpkins, green or dried, dry beans, or well pared chestnuts, boiled in the same manner, dried venison well pounded, whortleberries, green or dry, but not boiled, sugar and other palatable ingredients. For the other kind of bread, the green corn is either pounded or mashed, is put in broad green corn blades, generally filled in with a ladle, well wrapped up, and baked in the ashes, like the other. They consider this as a very delicate morsel, but to me it is too sweet.

Their *Psindamócan* or *Tassmanáne*, as they call it, is the most nourishing and durable food made out of the Indian corn. The blue sweetish kind is the grain which they prefer for that purpose. They parch it in clean hot ashes, until it bursts, it is then sifted and cleaned, and pounded in a mortar into a kind of flour, and when they wish to make it very good, they mix some sugar with it. When wanted for use, they take about a table spoonful of this flour in their mouths, then stooping to the river or brook, drink water to it. If, however, they have a cup or other small vessel at hand, they put the flour in it and mix it with water, in the proportion of one table spoonful to a pint. At their camps they will put a small quantity in a kettle with water and let boil down, and they will have a thick pottage. With this food, the traveller and warrior will set out on long journeys and expeditions, and as a little of it will serve them for a day, they have not a heavy load of provisions to carry. Persons who are unacquainted with this diet ought to be careful not to take too much at a time, and not to suffer themselves to be tempted too far by its flavour; more than one or two spoonfuls at most at any one time or at one meal is dangerous; for it is apt to swell in the stomach or bowels, as when heated over a fire.

Their meat they either boil, roast, or broil. Their roasting is done by running a wooden spit through the meat, sharpened at each end, which they place near the fire, and occasionally turn. They broil on clean coals, drawn off from the fire for that purpose. They often laugh at the white hunters, for baking their bread in dirty ashes, and being alike careless of cleanliness when they broil their meat. They are fond of dried venison, pounded in a mortar and dipped in bear's oil.—Heckewelder, *History*, 193-196.

⚹ XI ⚹

Logan and the Shawnee War: 1774

WHILE HECKEWELDER was still living at Friedenstadt on the Beaver River, he met the famous Iroquois warrior, *Logan,* who was then camping near the mouth of Beaver Creek.

Logan was the second son of Shikellemus, a celebrated chief of the Cayuga nation. . . . About the year 1772, Logan was introduced to me, by an Indian friend, . . . as a friend to the white people. In the course of conversation, I thought him a man of superior talents than Indians generally were. The subject turning on vice and immorality, he confessed his too great share of this, especially his fondness for liquor. He exclaimed against the white people for imposing liquors upon the Indians; he otherwise admired their ingenuity; spoke of gentlemen, but observed the Indians unfortunately had but few of these as their neighbors, &c. He spoke of his friendship to the white people, wished always to be a neighbor to them, intended to settle on the Ohio, below Big Beaver; was (to the best of my recollection) then encamped at the mouth of this river, (Beaver), urged me to pay him a visit, &c. *Note.*— I was then living at the Moravian town on this river, in the neighborhood of Cuscuskee. In April, 1773, while on my passage down the Ohio for Muskingum, I called at Logan's settlement, where I received every civility I could expect from such of the family as were at home.—Heckewelder, quoted in *The American Pioneer,* Vol. I, page 22.

The year 1774 was a year of trial to the Indian congregations, on account of a war which broke out between the people of Virginia, and the Senecas and Shawanos tribes of Indians; in which, as it became well known, the white people were the aggressors.— Of these latter, a number were settled on choice spots of land, on the south side of the river Ohio, while the Indians dwelt on the north side, then their territory. The sale of the lands, below the Conhawa [Kanawha] river, had opened a wide field for speculation. The whole country on the Ohio river, had already drawn the attention of many persons from the neighbouring provinces; who generally forming themselves into parties, would rove through the country in search of land, either to settle on, or for speculation; and some, careless of watching over their conduct, or destitute of both honour and humanity, would join a rabble (a class of people generally met with on the frontiers) who maintained, that to kill an Indian, was the same as killing a bear or a buffalo, and would fire on Indians that came across them by the way;—nay, more, would decoy such as lived across the river, to come over, for the purpose of joining them in hilarity; and when these complied, they fell on them and murdered them. Unfortunately, some of the murdered were of the family of Logan, noted man among the Indians.—Heckewelder, *Narrative*, 130-131.

Indian reports concerning Logan, after the death of his family, ran to this; that he exerted himself during the Shawanese war, (then so called) to take all the revenge he could, declaring he had lost all confidence in the white people. At the time of the negotiation, he declared his reluctance in laying down the hatchet, not having (in his opinion) yet taken ample satisfaction; yet, for the sake of the nation, he would do it.—*American Pioneer*, Vol. I, pp. 22-23.

No passage in Indian literature is better known or more worthy of remembrance than *Logan's Lament*, which, spoken to Simon Girty for the ears of Lord Dunmore, governor of Virginia, found its way in this version into Thomas Jefferson's *Notes on Virginia*:

I appeal to any white man to say, if ever he entered Logan's cabin hungry, and he gave him not meat; if ever he came cold and naked, and he cloathed him not. During the course of the last long and bloody war Logan remained idle in his cabin an advocate for peace. Such was my love for the whites, that my countrymen pointed as they passed, and said, "Logan is the friend of white men." I had even thought to have lived with you, but for the injuries of one man. Colonel Cresap,* the last spring, in cold blood, and unprovoked, murdered all the relations of Logan, not sparing even my women and children.† There runs not a drop of my blood in the veins of any living creature. This called on me for revenge. I have sought it: I have killed many. I have glutted my vengeance: for my country I rejoice at the beams of peace. But do not harbour a thought that mine is the joy of fear. Logan never felt fear. Logan

---

* Actually Daniel Greathouse's men, who are said to have killed thirteen members of Logan's family.

† For a fuller description of this incident, in which Logan's mother, sister, and brother were killed, see Harry E. Swanger, "The Logans, Sons of Shikellamy," *Northumberland County Historical Proceedings*, XVII (1949), 21-23.

will not turn on his heel to save his life. Who is there to mourn for Logan?—Not one!—*Writings of Thomas Jefferson* (N.Y., 1894), III, 156-157.

His expressions, from time to time, denoted a deep melancholy. Life (said he) had become a torment to him: he knew no more what pleasure was: he thought it had been better if he had never existed, &c. &c. Report further states, that he became in some measure delirious, declared he would kill himself, went to Detroit, drank very freely, and did not seem to care what he did, and what became of himself. In this condition he left Detroit, and on his way between that place and Miami was murdered. In October, 1781, (while as prisoner on my way to Detroit), I was shown the spot where this should have happened.—*American Pioneer*, Vol. I, page 23.

The murder of Logan's family and other acts like it lighted a fire in these woods which was not quenched for many years. No Indian felt safe in the proximity of white men.

It is indiscribable, how enraged the relations of the murdered became, on seeing such abominable acts committed without cause, and even by some white men who had always pretended to be their friends. The cries of the relations of the sufferers soon reached the ears of the respective nations to whom they belonged, and who quickly resolved to take revenge on the long knives (so they called the people of Virginia); for (said they,) "they are a barbarous people." Some however, considering the difficulty of meeting the perpetrators, proposed killing every white man then in their country, until they should believe themselves amply revenged for the valuable lives lost by the long knife men (Virginians). Nothing could equal the rage of the Senecas, in particular; and it was impossible to foresee where the matter would end. Parties after parties came on—the missionaries had to keep within their houses—the enraged Indians insisted that every able man should do his utmost to take revenge. They kept on the look out for traders, to kill them, but these had already generally fled the country, while some were taken under protection by friendly Shawanese Indians, who afterwards conducted them safely to Pittsburg. These good people however, oh! shameful to relate! were, on their return, waylaid, by some of those white vagabonds—fired upon, and one man * shot in the breast; in which situation he, with his wounds bleeding, fortunately reached Shonbrun, where it was dressed, and all possible attention paid him.—Heckewelder, *Narrative*, 131-132.

This last incident deserves the fuller handling that Heckewelder gives it in his *History*, he himself having known this man.

I once knew a noted Shawano, who having, out of friendship, conducted several white traders in safety to Pittsburgh, while they were sought for by

---

* See Heckewelder's *History of Indian Nations*, page 223 [229]—Heckewelder's note.

Logan and the Shawnee War: 1774

other Indians who wanted to revenge on them the murders committed by white men of some of their people, was on his return fired at by some white villains, who had waylaid him for that purpose, and shot in the breast. This man, when I saw him, had already travelled eighty miles, with a wound from which blood and a kind of watery froth issued every time he breathed. Yet he told me he was sure of being cured, if he could only reach *Waketemeki*, a place fifty miles distant, where there were several eminent Indian surgeons. To me and others who examined the wound, it appeared incurable; nevertheless, he reached the place and was perfectly cured. I saw him at Detroit ten years afterwards; he was in sound health and grown to be a corpulent man. Nine years after this I dined with him at the same place.—Heckewelder, *History*, 229-230.

Heckewelder had great respect for the better class of Indian doctors.

... I must say that their practice in general succeeds pretty well. I have myself been benefited and cured by taking their emetics and their medicines in fevers, and by being sweated after their manner while labouring under a stubborn rheumatism. I have also known many, both whites and Indians, who have with the same success resorted to Indian physicians while labouring under diseases. The wives of Missionaries, in every instance in which they had to apply to the female physicians, for the cure of complaints peculiar to their sex, experienced good results from their abilities. They are also well skilled in curing wounds and bruises. I once for two days and two nights, suffered the most excruciating pain from a felon or whitlow on one of my fingers, which deprived me entirely of sleep. I had recourse to an Indian woman, who in less than half an hour relieved me entirely by the simple application of a poultice made of the root of the common blue violet.

Indeed, it is in the cure of external wounds that they particularly excel. Not only their professional men and women, but every warrior is more or less acquainted with the healing properties of roots and plants, which is, in a manner, indispensable to them, as they are so often in danger of being wounded in their engagements with the enemy. Hence this branch of knowledge is carried to a great degree of perfection among them. I firmly believe that there is no wound, unless it should be absolutely mortal, or beyond the skill of our own good practitioners, which an Indian surgeon (I mean the best of them) will not succeed in healing.—Heckewelder, *History*, 229.

War fever, during that year, 1774, kept Schönbrunn and Gnadenhütten in suspense from spring to fall. The embittered Shawnees were close at hand on the south, and the Senecas not very far away to the north and east. Rumors oppressed the mission settlements with all the terrifying urgency of nightmares. One rumor was to the effect that the Shawnees, a thousand strong, were marching against the mission towns to put to death all who would not join them against the Long Knives. Another had it that the Virginians were marching against them. Two families did give way before these rumors and fled to the Shawnee towns for refuge. The rest of the congregation remained steadfast, however, trusting to Divine protection in their own villages of the Beautiful Spring and Tents of Grace.

The rumors just mentioned proved false, but dangers of another kind soon confronted them in actuality. Bands of warriors repeatedly marched through Schönbrunn and Gnadenhütten, returning with prisoners and scalps. The more bitter among these fighting men threatened destruction to the Moravian Indians as traitors to their race because they refused to join in punishing the Long Knives for their atrocities.

In the end the armies of Lord Dunmore, governor of Virginia, marched into the Indian country (with strict orders not to molest the Christian Indians nor to pass through their towns *), and defeated the Shawnees, taking some of their chiefs as hostages, and compelling the release of white prisoners. When peace was established, the Christian Indians set aside November 8 as a day of thanksgiving.

---

* George Henry Loskiel, *History of the Mission of the United Brethren Among the Indians in North America* (London, 1794), III, 97.

⚔ XII ⚔

Shamans or Sorcerers: 1775

THE "SHOT HEARD ROUND THE WORLD" had but faint repercussions beyond the Ohio. It was to be many months after Concord before the "scalp halloo" turned what had been the friendly shelter of the forest into a place of desolation and terror.

On the Muskingum the closing weeks of 1774 and the year 1775 were a time of peace. The only journeys, at this time, which Heckewelder mentions in his itinerary are "to the Mahoning, to Sickheunck [Chandlersville, Muskingum County, Ohio], and Langundoutenünk in search of stolen horses."

We may occupy ourselves, during this quiet interval in Heckewelder's career, with a discussion of some of the customs he observed among the Indians of the Delaware and related tribes who lived near the mission towns. In general he praises the Indian, and cautions against the popular stereotype of him as a treacherous, cruel, and soulless savage.

Among the qualities Heckewelder most admired in his brown brethren was their capacity for friendship.

Those who believe that no faith is to be placed in the friendship of an Indian are egregiously mistaken, and know very little of the true character of those men of nature. They are, it is true, revengeful to their enemies, to those who wilfully do them an injury, who insult, abuse, or treat them with contempt. It may be said, indeed, that the passion of revenge is so strong in them that it knows no bounds. This does not, however, proceed from a bad or malicious disposition, but from the violence of natural feelings unchecked by social institutions, and unsubdued by the force of revealed religion. The ten-der and generous passions operate not less powerfully on them than those of an opposite character, and they are as warm and sincere in their friendship, as vindictive in their enmities. Nay, I will venture to assert that there are those among them who on an emergency would lay down their lives for a friend: I could fill many pages with examples of Indian friendship and fidelity, not only to each other, but to men of other nations and of a different colour than themselves. How often, when wars were impending between them and the whites, have they not forewarned those among our frontier settlers whom they thought well disposed towards them, that dangerous times were at hand, and advised them to provide for their own safety, regardless of the jealousy which such conduct might excite among their own people? How often did they not even guard and escort them through the most dangerous places until they had reached a secure spot? How often did they not find means to keep an enemy from striking a stroke, as they call it, that is to say from proceeding to the sudden indiscriminate murder of the frontier whites, until their friends or those whom they considered as such were out of all danger?

These facts are familiar to every one who has lived among Indians or in their neighbourhood, and I believe it will be difficult to find a single case in which they betrayed a real friend or abandoned him in the hour of danger, when it was in their power to extricate or relieve him. The word "Friend" to the ear of an Indian does not convey the same vague and almost indefinite meaning that it does with us; it is not a mere complimentary or social expression, but implies a resolute determination to stand by the person so distinguished on all occasions, and a threat to those who might attempt to molest him; the mere looking at two persons who are known or declared friends, is sufficient to deter any one from offering insult to either. When an Indian believes that he has reason to suspect a man of evil designs against his friend, he has only to say emphatically: "This is *my friend*, and if any one tries to hurt him, I will do to him *what is in my mind*." It is as much as to say that he will stand in his defence at the hazard of his own life. This language is well understood by the Indians, who know that they would have to combat with a spirited warrior, were they to attempt any thing against his friend. By this means much bloodshed is prevented; for it is sufficiently known that an Indian never proffers his friendship in vain. Many white men, and myself among others, have experienced the benefit of their powerful as well as generous protection.—Heckewelder, *History*, 277-278.

It is not true, as some have supposed, that an Indian's friendship must be purchased by presents, and that it lasts only so long as gifts continue to be lavished upon them. Their attachments, on the contrary, are perfectly disinterested. I admit that they receive with pleasure a present from a friend's hand. They consider presents as marks of the giver's good disposition towards them. They cannot, in their opinion, proceed from an enemy, and he who befriends them, they think must love them. Obligations to them are not

Shamans or Sorcerers: 1775

burdensome, they love to acknowledge them, and whatever may be their faults, ingratitude is not among the number.

Indeed, the friendship of an Indian is easily acquired, provided it is sought in good faith. But whoever chooses to obtain it must be sure to treat them on a footing of perfect equality. They are very jealous of the whites, who they think affect to consider themselves as beings of a superior nature and too often treat them with rude undeserved contempt. This they seldom forgive, while on the other hand, they feel flattered when a white man does not disdain to treat them as children of the same Creator. Both reason and humanity concur in teaching us this conduct, but I am sorry to say that reason and humanity are in such cases too little attended to.—Heckewelder, *History*, p. 281.

. . . the American Indian has one weak side which sinks him down to the level of the most fearful and timid being, a childish apprehension of an occult and unknown power, which, unless he can summon sufficient fortitude to conquer it, changes at once the hero into a coward.—Heckewelder, *History*, p. 239.

Sorcerers, it was believed, made use of a mysterious "deadening substance" (cf. the "death ray" of current science fiction) which they discharged invisibly through the air against their victims. Only professional "doctors" or jugglers, it was believed, could avert these supernatural weapons.

I call these men *Doctors*, because it is the name given them by their countrymen who have borrowed it from our language,* and they are themselves very fond of this pompous title. They are a set of professional impostors, who, availing themselves of the superstitious prejudices of the people, acquire the name and reputation of men of superior knowledge, and possessed of supernatural powers. As the Indians in general believe in witchcraft, and ascribe, as I have already said, to the arts of sorcerers many of the disorders with which they are afflicted in the regular course of nature, this class of men has risen among them, who pretend to be skilled in a certain occult science, by means of which they are able not only to cure natural diseases, but to counteract or destroy the enchantments of wizards or witches, and expel evil spirits.

These men are physicians, like the others of whom I have spoken, and like them are acquainted with the properties and virtues of plants, barks, roots, and other remedies. They differ from them only by their pretensions to a superior knowledge, and by the impudence with which they impose upon the credulous. I am sorry that truth obliges me to confess, that in their profession they rank above the honest practitioners. They pretend that there are dis-

---

* Heckewelder, *History*, 231, note 1: "They call them *Doctols;* because the Indians cannot pronounce the letter R. The Minsi or Monseys call them 'Mĕdéu,' which signifies 'conjuror.'"

orders which cannot be cured by the ordinary remedies, and to the treatment of which the talents of common physicians are inadequate. They say that when a complaint has been brought on by witchcraft, more powerful remedies must be applied, and measures must be taken to defeat the designs of the person who bewitched the unfortunate patient. This can only be done by removing or destroying the deleterious or deadening substance which has been conveyed into them, or, if it is an evil spirit, to confine or expel him, or banish him to a distant region from whence he may never return.

When the juggler has succeeded in persuading his patient that his disorder is such that no common physician has it in his power to relieve, he will next endeavour to convince him of the necessity of making him *very strong*, which means, giving him *a large fee*, which he will say, is justly due to a man who, like himself, is able to perform such difficult things. If the patient who applies, is rich, the *Doctor* will never fail, whatever the complaint may be, to ascribe it to the powers of witchcraft, and recommend himself as the only person capable of giving relief in such a hard and complicated case. The poor patient, therefore, if he will have the benefit of the great man's advice and assistance, must immediately give him his *honorarium*, which is commonly either a fine horse, or a good rifle-gun, a considerable quantity of wampum, or goods to a handsome amount. When this fee is well secured, and not before, the Doctor prepares for the hard task that he has undertaken, with as much apparent labour as if he was about to remove a mountain. He casts his eyes all round him to attract notice, puts on grave and important looks, appears wrapt in thought and meditation and enjoys for a while the admiration of the spectators. At last he begins his operation. Attired in a frightful dress, he approaches his patient, with a variety of contortions and gestures, and performs by his side and over him all the antic tricks that his imagination can suggest. He breathes on him, blows in his mouth, and squirts some medicines which he has prepared in his face, mouth and nose; he rattles his gourd filled with dry beans or pebbles, pulls out and handles about a variety of sticks and bundles in which he appears to be seeking for the proper remedy, all which is accompanied with the most horrid gesticulations, by which he endeavours, as he says, to frighten the spirit or the disorder away, and continues in this manner until he is quite exhausted and out of breath, when he retires to wait the issue.

The visits of the juggler are, if the patient requires it, repeated from time to time; not, however, without his giving a fresh fee previous to each visit. This continues until the property of the patient is entirely exhausted, or until he resolves upon calling in another doctor, with whom feeing must begin anew in the same manner that it did with his predecessor.

When at length the art of the juggling tribe has after repeated trials proved ineffectual, the patient is declared *incurable*. The doctors will say, that he applied to them too late, that he did not exactly follow their prescriptions, or sometimes, that he was bewitched by one of the greatest masters of

Shamans or Sorcerers: 1775

the science, and that unless a professor can be found possessed of superior knowledge, he is doomed to die or linger in pain beyond the power of relief.

Thus these jugglers carry on their deceit, and enrich themselves at the expense of the credulous and foolish. I have known instances in which they declared a patient perfectly cured and out of all danger, who nevertheless died of his disorder a very few days afterwards, although his doctors affirmed that the evil spirit or the effects of witchcraft were entirely removed from him; on the other hand, I have seen cases in which the patient recovered after being pronounced incurable and condemned to die. In those cases, however, he had had the good sense to apply to some of the honest physicians of one or the other sex, who had relieved him by a successful application of their medicines.

The jugglers' dress, when in the exercise of their functions, exhibits a most frightful sight. I had no idea of the importance of these men, until by accident I met with one, habited in his full costume. As I was once walking through the street of a large Indian village on the Muskingum, with the chief *Gelemend*, whom we call *Kill-buck*, one of those monsters suddenly came out of the house next to me, at whose sight I was so frightened, that I flew immediately to the other side of the chief, who observing my agitation and the quick strides I made, asked me what was the matter, and what I thought it was that I saw before me.

"By its outward appearance," answered I, "I would think it a bear, or some such ferocious animal, what is *inside* I do not know, but rather judge it to be the *Evil Spirit*."

My friend Kill-buck smiled, and replied, "O! no, no; don't believe that! it is a man you well know, it is our *Doctor*."

"A Doctor!" said I; "what! a human being to transform himself so as to be taken for a bear walking on his hind legs, and with horns on his head? You will not, surely, deceive me; if it is not a bear, it must be some other ferocious animal that I have never seen before."

The juggler within the dress hearing what passed between us, began to act over some of his curious pranks, probably intending to divert me, as he saw I was looking at him with great amazement, not unmixed with fear; but the more he went on with his performance, the more I was at a loss to decide, whether he was a human being or a bear; for he imitated that animal in the greatest perfection, walking upright on his hind legs as I had often seen it do. At last I renewed my questions to the chief, and begged him seriously to tell me what that figure was, and he assured me that although outside it had the appearance of a bear, yet inside there was a man, and that it was our doctor going to visit one of his patients who was bewitched. . . .

The dress this juggler had on, consisted of an entire garment or outside covering, made of one or more bear skins, as black as jet, so well fitted and sewed together, that the man was not in any place to be perceived. The whole head of the bear, including the mouth, nose, teeth, ears, &c., appeared the same as when the animal was living; so did the legs with long claws; to this were added a huge pair of horns on the head, and behind a large bushy tail, moving as he walked, as though it were on springs; but for these accompaniments, the man, walking on all fours, might have been taken for a bear of an extraordinary size. Underneath, where his hands were, holes had been cut, though not visible to the eye, being covered with long hair, through which he held and managed his implements, and he saw through two holes set with glass. The whole was a great curiosity, but not to be looked at by everybody.

There are jugglers of another kind, in general old men and women, who although not classed among doctors or physicians, yet get their living by pretending to supernatural knowledge. Some pretend that they can bring down rain in dry weather when wanted, others prepare ingredients, which they sell to bad hunters, that they may have good luck, and others make philters or love potions for such married persons as either do not, or think they cannot love each other.

When one of these jugglers is applied to to bring down rain in a dry season, he must in the first instance receive a fee. This fee is made up by the women, who, as cultivators of the land are supposed to be most interested, but the men will slily slip something in their hands in aid of their collection, which consists of wampum beads, tobacco, silver broaches, and a dressed deer skin to make shoes of. If the juggler does not succeed in his experiment, he never is in want of an excuse; either the winds are in opposition to one another, the dry wind or air is too powerful for the moist or south wind, or he has not been made *strong enough* (that is, sufficiently paid,) to compel the north to give way to the south from whence the rain is to come, or lastly, he wants time to invoke the great Spirit to aid him on the important occasion.

In the summer of the year 1799, a most uncommon drouth happened in the Muskingum country, so that every thing growing, even the grass and the leaves of the trees, appeared perishing; an old man named *Chenos*, who was born on the river Delaware, was applied to by the women to bring down rain, and was well feed for the purpose. Having failed in his first attempt, he was feed a second time, and it happened that one morning, when my business obliged me to pass by the place where he was at work, as I knew him very well, I asked him at once what he was doing?

"I am hired," said he, "to do a very hard day's work."

Q. And, pray, what work?

A. Why, to bring down rain from the sky.

Q. Who hired you to do that?

A. The women of the village; don't you see how much rain is wanted, and that the corn and every thing else is perishing?

Q. But can you make it rain?

A. I can, and you shall be convinced of it this very day.

He had, by this time, encompassed a square of about five feet each way,

Shamans or Sorcerers: 1775

with stakes and barks so that it might resemble a pig pen of about three feet in height, and now, with his face uplifted and turned towards the north, he muttered something, then closely shutting up with bark the opening which had been left on the north side, he turned in the same manner, still muttering some words, towards the south, as if invoking some superior being, and having cut through the bark on the southwest corner, so as to make an opening of two feet, he said, "now we shall have rain enough!"

Hearing down the river the sound of setting poles striking against a canoe, he enquired of me what it was.

I told him it was our Indians going up the river to make a bush net for fishing.

"Send them home again!" said he, "tell them that this will not be a fit day for fishing!"

I told him to let them come on and speak to them himself, if he pleased. He did so, and as soon as they came near him, he told them that they must by no means think of fishing that day, for there should come a heavy rain which would wet them all through.

"No matter, Father!" answered they in a jocular manner, "give us only rain and we will cheerfully bear the soaking."

They then passed on, and I proceeded to *Goschachking* [Coshocton], the village to which I was going. I mentioned the circumstance to the chief of the place, and told him that I thought it impossible that we should have rain while the sky was so clear as it then was and had been for near five weeks together, without its being previously announced by some signs or change in the atmosphere. But the chief answered: "*Chenos* knows very well what he is about; he can at any time predict what the weather will be; he takes his observations morning and evening from the river or something in it." On my return from this place after three o'clock in the afternoon, the sky still continued the same until about four o'clock, when all at once the horizon became overcast, and without any thunder or wind it began to rain, and continued so for several hours together, until the ground became thoroughly soaked.

I am of the opinion that this man, like others whom I have known, was a strict observer of the weather, and that his prediction that day was made in consequence of his having observed some signs in the sky or in the water, which his experience had taught him to be the forerunners of rain; yet the credulous multitude did not fail to ascribe it to his supernatural power.

The ingredients for a bad hunter, to make him have good luck, are tied up in a bit of cloth, and must be worn near his skin while he is hunting. The preparations intended to create love between man and wife, are to be slily conveyed to the frigid party by means of his victuals or drink.—Heckewelder, *History*, 231-238.

XIII

Between Two Black Clouds: 1775-1777

WHEN THE REVOLUTIONARY WAR broke out, and the people of the Thirteen Fires separated from their Great Father across the sea, both sides in the conflict at first advised the Indian nations to "sit still." This was a family quarrel, they said, which it behoved the Indian to take as little notice of as possible.

Disputes having arisen between Great Britain and her North American colonies, and a congress being chosen by the latter, it appointed commissioners, to convene the northern and western nations at Pittsburg, for the purpose of explaining the nature of the dispute to them,—and giving them their advice. As none of the missionaries were present at the meetings, which were held in October and November, the following was the report made by the chiefs, on their return to their respective nations, viz.: That the commissioners, after first having informed them that disputes had arisen between the king of England and the people of this country—and that their quarrelling with each other could not affect them in any wise, provided they did not interfere and take a part in it; they next proceeded to state the cause from whence the dispute had originated, calling the same a family dispute, a quarrel between a parent and his child, which they described as follows: "Suppose a father had a little son whom he loved and indulged while young, but growing up to be a youth, began to think of having some help from him; and making up a small pack, he bid him carry it for him. The boy cheerfully takes this pack up, following his father with it. The father finding the boy willing and obedient, continues in this way; and as the boy grows stronger, so the father makes the pack in proportion larger—yet as long as the boy is able to carry the pack, he does so without grumbling. At length, however, the boy having arrived at manhood, while the father is making up the pack for him, in comes a person of an evil disposition, and learning who was to be the carrier of the pack, advises the father to make it heavier, for surely the son is able to carry a large pack. The father listening rather to the bad adviser, than consulting his own judgment, and the feelings of tenderness, follows the advice of the hard hearted adviser, and makes up a heavy load for his son to carry. The son, now grown up, examining the weight of the load he is to carry, addresses the parent in these words: 'Dear father, this pack is too heavy for me to carry, do pray lighten it; I am willing to do what I can, but am unable to carry *this* load.' The father's heart having by this time bacame [*sic*] hardened —and the bad adviser calling to him, whip him if he disobeys, and refuses to carry the pack, now in a peremptory tone orders his son to take up the pack and carry it off, or he will whip him; and already takes up a stick to beat him. 'So!' says the son, 'am I to be served thus, for not doing what I am unable to do! Well, if entreaties avail nothing with you, father—and it is to be decided by blows, whether or not I am able to carry a pack so heavy, then I have no other choice left me, but that of resisting your unreasonable demand, by my strength; and thus, by striking each other, learn who is the strongest.' " Such (Indian reports stated,) was the parable given them for the purpose of explaining the nature of the dispute.—Heckewelder, *Narrative*, 136-38.

The Delawares in the vicinity of the Moravian settlements for some months preserved a strict neutrality. But the natural factionalism of Indian communities, being intensified by war pressures from outside, caused serious divisions in their councils and in the end brought declarations on behalf of one side or the other in the great contest. Captain White Eyes declared openly for the Americans, while Captain Pipe and Newalike declared for the British. Captain Pipe had had some provocation. In the "Squaw Campaign" of 1778 his brother (a friend to the United States) had been killed and his mother wounded.*

But for a time both parties kept quiet, balancing prudence against the sense of grievance: White Eyes' grievance against the pro-British Senecas who called his people "women," and Captain Pipe against the Long Knives who had killed his brother. An American agent invited Captain White Eyes and all peaceable Indians to come to Pittsburgh and put themselves under the protection of Congress. But White Eyes, with all the good will in the world toward the Americans and with a respect for their government, could not forget what the Paxton Boys (in defiance

---
* "Recollections of Samuel Murphy," *Frontier Defense on the Upper Ohio, 1777-1778* (Madison, Wis., 1912), pp. 218-219.

of government) had done to the poor Indians at Conestoga and what they had tried to do again at Philadelphia. He and his party decided to remain in their own towns. Captain Pipe, recognizing that despite this rebuff to Congress White Eyes' followers were strongly pro-American, decided for his own safety to withdraw from the council.

The Moravian leaders and their Indian communities at Schönbrunn and Gnadenhütten decided likewise that it was safer to remain in their settlements on the Muskingum than to accept the offer of protection from those who, with all the good will in the world, might not in the end prove able to provide protection.

Recognizing how precarious was their situation between "two black clouds drawing towards each other," the Brethren on the Muskingum laid down the strictest rules to guide their conduct.

The line of conduct the Christian Indians and their missionaries were to follow, during the contest, was plainly marked out to them, viz: They were subjected to the resolutions and decrees of those who had invited them to come into their country, with the promise of protection from their side: these alone had power over them;—and these had formerly declared, that they would keep the peace at all hazards. Added to this, an impression had for many years rested on the minds of the national assistants, that for Indian converts to join in wars, would infallibly bring them back into heathenism; That God having given the commandment to his people, "Thou shalt not kill;" it must be a great sin for such, unto whom this commandment was given, to murder men. Such was the argument and impression on the minds of the national assistants and Christian Indians; and they were determined to put out of their fellowships, any, and every person, who should join in wars, and not permit such to make a home with them.

The Delaware chiefs, having at this time in their possession documents and vouchers, both in writing and strings and belts of wampum, of all transactions that had passed between their ancestors and the government of Pennsylvania, from the time William Penn first arrived in the country, down to the present time; had hitherto been in the habit of meeting, at least once in every year, for the purpose of refreshing their missionaries [memories?] on the subject by hearing the contents; as also, that of instructing one or more promising young men to learn by heart such valuable documents, that they might not be lost to future generations. In assembling for this purpose, they chose to be by themselves in the woods, at a convenient spot, where no person could interrupt them; and when any written documents were produced, they would request one or other of the missionaries to attend, to read and interpret them —which service the missionaries always considered as their duty, and as an acknowledgment for their indulgence in favouring the cause of the mission. Now when, with the times, a change had taken place in the appointment of

Between Two Black Clouds: 1775-1777

officers, with whom of course the chiefs would have intercourse—they not being acquainted with the hieroglyphical manner the Indians expressed themselves, could not without assistance understand the contents of their speeches; wherefore a missionary was called upon, and requested to explain, in writing, the meaning of these dark, yet withal not unmeaning, expressions, for to send on to such officers or agents, with the figurative speech. The enemies of peace being informed of those services, believed they had cause to charge the missionaries as being accessary in keeping the Delaware nation from joining in the war against the American people, or, in other words, that they were acting contrary to the British interest; although it was doing no more than what any person in their situation would consider his duty to do, nay it was an act which they could not avoid performing.—Heckewelder, *Narrative*, 151-53.

Neutrality is at all times and for all persons difficult. For John Heckewelder it was impossible. Though he abominated the Paxton Boys and all their kind, his sympathies from the start were with the Americans, and he was not a man to deny his feelings expression. When British agents appeared in the woods—Elliot, McKee, Girty—soliciting the active intervention of the Indians on the British side, Heckewelder's naturally combative disposition found sanction in his avowed peace principles for the step he now took. In order to prevent the disturbers of the peace, as he saw it, from carrying out their designs, he became an unofficial American agent, reporting enemy movements to the authorities at Pittsburgh. During 1780 and 1781 he sent repeated messages, by trusted Indian runners, describing the numbers and direction of war parties headed east against the settlements. General Edward Hand, in a formal statement written February 14, 1800,* expressed his indebtedness to the Moravians on the Muskingum for regularly furnishing him "with early and authentic intelligence of the intended movements of such of the hostile tribes of Indians as were in their vicinity," such information enabling him, as he said, "to counteract them by open force and almost always to give the settlers such timely notice of a blow meditated against them as to put it in their power to make effectual arrangements for their own security." He added that, "In 1778 the United States were indebted to the active and patriotic zeal of Mr. John Heckewelder, who I firmly believe prevented the immediate commencement of hostilities between the United States and the collective forces of the Shawanese & Delware nations...." Colonel Brodhead wrote, January 14, 1799: "I do certify that I have been acquainted with the Reverend John Heckewelder

---

* Archives of the Moravian Church, Bethlehem, Pa. Microfilm, American Philosophical Society.

since the year 1778. That he resided on or near Muskingum River as Missionary from the United Brethren to the Delawares & other tribes of Indians during my command in the Western Department and discovered a decided and firm attachment to the cause of the United States giving me every possible information or intelligence of the enemies parties approaching our Settlements or posts, by which many of them were defeated & destroyed." *

A peace lover but no pacifist, Heckewelder found exhilaration in this work. He took satisfaction not merely in stopping the effusion of blood on the border, but also in thwarting the aggressors and contriving that the hatchet, once lifted, should descend on the head of those wielding it.

Killbuck (Gelelemond), whom Heckewelder had met in 1773 on the Muskingum, was one of Heckewelder's messengers, and a good fighter in his own right. Indeed, he was so active that it was rumored a certain Mr. Baby, famous in Canadian annals, had undertaken to have Killbuck liquidated. Killbuck, for his part, laid plans to turn the tables and capture Baby. But his plans miscarried. "Since my last letter to you," wrote Heckewelder to Brodhead, February 26, 1781, "I found it was an impossibility for Killbuck to lay hold of Bawbee in this part of the Country, for had he offered to have touched him, he probably would have lost his life." †

In Killbuck's letter you will find the true state of the people of Coochocking [Coshocton]. I could never learn what they were properly about, for they kept their matters very Secret; now it is almost publicly known that they are about no good business, and have been very busy in trying to deceive you this long time. . . .

I indeed believe that the greatest part will be upon you in a few days; . . . they have arranged themselves into three parties and if I am right one party is gone off already, but I hope they will receive what they deserve.—*Ibid.*

From "Coochocking March 30th 1780," he wrote:

We have heard nothing at all this whole winter what the Enemy are about, the snow being so deep, & the weather so continually cold has, I suppose, prevented this; but this day I am informed that three young fellows, two Delawares & one Wyandott, have turned back from a body of warriors consisting of twenty-six men. They inform that five or six Companies of warriors have gone out: two parties of Wyandotts towards Beaver Creek, & the others down this River. The Half King, it appears, is at the head of one

---

* Archives of the Moravian Church. Microfilm, American Philosophical Society.
† Harvard College Library.

of the parties, & Neeshaws (a Mohicon) heads a party of Muncies & Delawares. It is also reported here this day, that the Shawnese & others are gone to fight with the Army at the *Big Bone Lick* [Bigbone, Kentucky]; likewise that the Wabash Indians are all gone to war.—*Pennsylvania Archives*, First Series, VIII, 152.

By direct intervention, Heckewelder was the means of saving individual lives, as, for instance, that of a gentleman who became well enough known a little later as General O'Hara, one of Pittsburgh's most enterprising promoters.

The northern warriors being continually on the watch, for such white people who might venture out to the Delaware towns, it was dangerous for any one to attempt such a thing. Yet it so happened, that Mr. James O'Hara, who had come out to Shonbrun on business, was found out by some of these warriors, eleven of whom were coming on to seize him; but halting on their way, at an Indian cabin, nine miles distant, where the man and his sons, were equally friends to the Americans, the old man discovering their intentions, privately sent off in the night one of his sons to the writer of this narrative, with the following verbal message: "My friend! see that our white friend, now at your village, be taken from thence this night, and conducted to a place of safety, in the settlement of the white people; and do not neglect to act up to my message. Hear my son farther on the subject!"— The son giving the best assurance, that at break of day the party would be here, for the purpose of taking, and perhaps murdering Mr. O'Harra, he was informed of it, and forthwith conducted by Anthony * a smart and trusty Indian, through the woods to the Ohio river, [at Wheeling, avoiding the more direct route to Pittsburgh], and there taken across by white people, living on the opposite shore. The young man, who had, agreeable to his father's instructions, immediately returned home, after delivering the message to me, seeing them sometime after midnight preparing to set off, for the purpose of executing their design, questioned them as to their intentions and finding that the supposition had been correct, he replied, "your errand will fail, for the white man you are after, is no more there, but has returned to Pittsburg. On being assured of this, they bent their course another way.—Heckewelder, *Narrative*, pp. 155-56.

This is not the last time we shall meet Anthony (Anton, Welochalent) in the Heckewelder story, and it is well that we should know more about him. A son of Joseph Peepee ("Jo Pipi" of the Moravian diaries) and his wife, Hannah, Anton had at one time lived on the Susquehanna at Sheshequin. He was baptized at Friedenshütten on May 19, 1771,

---

* This Anthony, is the same man noticed in Heckewelder's Account of the Indian Nations, chapter XX, bearing then the name of Luke Holland.—Heckewelder's note.

and his wife, Juliana, was baptized a few weeks later. They moved with their family to the Muskingum where, at the time of O'Hara's escape, Anton was living with his wife and children. According to the Schönbrunn Diary (written by Heckewelder and now preserved in the Moravian Archives), it was on April 4, 1777 that Anton undertook to guide Mr. O'Hara through the woods to Wheeling, taking that roundabout way to Pittsburgh because the direct path by way of Beaver Creek was "blocked."

It was a complaint of white settlers in the vicinity of Pittsburgh (who knew nothing of Heckewelder's secret assistance to the American cause) that Schönbrunn and Gnadenhütten, being on an Indian warpath, were in a position to give aid and comfort to the enemy, and did in fact supply the enemy with food. It is true, as Heckewelder tells us, that war parties did sometimes pass that way on expeditions against the settlements, and that they did expect to be fed. It was useless to deny such a request. The warriors would have taken the food, anyway, and so serious a breach of Indian etiquette among a people accustomed to give generous entertainment to travellers would have brought immediate reprisals upon the community. Heckewelder, perforce, contented himself with reporting the visits of these unwelcome people to the commandant at Pittsburgh. He regarded the food he gave them as a small price to pay for the safety of the settlers.

For the most part the warriors were well behaved. The Half King of the Wyandots (from whom—though the Wyandots themselves were wards of the Six Nations—the Delawares had received permission to occupy this country) took steps to see that his warriors should not molest the Moravians.

From the time that the half king had declared the Brethren as a useful people among his cousins, the Delawares, and had assured them of his protection, he had kept a watchful eye over them; and although himself and his nation were intent on fighting against the American people, yet they avoided as much as possible coming near the settlements of the Christian Indians, he frequently inquiring of them how his people conducted themselves, when passing that way.

Providing food for so many warriors at a time, was a very disagreeable business for the inhabitants of Lichtenau,* yet it could not be avoided, especially with the more northern Indians, who were both noisy and mischievous, if not served with food. Upon the whole, the quickest way to get rid of all

---

* Lichtenau was another Moravian Indian settlement, founded 1776, "Two and a half miles below Goschachgünk, on the eastern side of the Muskingum."—De Schweinitz, *Life and Times of David Zeisberger* (Philadelphia, 1870), p. 433.

warriors, is to give them a meals victuals, which is all they want, and to refuse them this would be folly, as then they would shoot cattle, and destroy the corn in the fields.

The missionaries and Christian Indians were not without fears, that ill disposed persons on the American side might construe such acts, (unavoidable as they were,) as furnishing the warriors with provision for carrying on the war expeditions against them; nor were they mistaken in the supposition, as by some, the Christian Indians had been branded with the name of enemies to the American people, on that very account. The subjoined facts, however will, it is hoped, exonerate the Christian Indians of charges of this kind.

First. It is a settled point with Indian *warriors*, that where begging or asking for provisions, is not complied with, or refused to them, they may make free to take; and where they do take, they destroy purposely, because the person who refuses to give them the provisions, appears in *their* eyes devoid of hospitality, and consequently devoid of feeling: an *inhuman* being.

Secondly. No Indian warrior encumbers himself with provisions, on going out against the enemy, or to war: a few quarts of parched corn, finely pounded, with a little sugar mixed therewith, will serve an Indian for many days, and this is always prepared for them at home, previous to their setting out; and knowing that wherever they are, they can get meat with their guns, they take but little along with them.

Thirdly. Warriors are not always permitted to satisfy their appetites, nor even to eat every kind of food. They have to regulate themselves by a prescription given them by their captain, who has either received it from an old veteran, or from a conjurer; even sometimes fasting is recommended; and much (they say) depends on their success in living up to the directions prescribed them.

Fourthly. It is always supposed by them, that when they arrive in the settlements of the white people, they will find provision, so as to satisfy their wants.

Now, what is the demand of the warrior on arriving at an Indian town on his way? Nothing but a meals victuals, if he should make a halt, which however is seldom the case, and never, except he has some particular business, or a speech to deliver to the inhabitants of the place he has arrived at. A few ears of Indian corn, a pumpkin, or a few squashes given him, not only prevents his doing mischief, as shooting down cattle and the like, but what is of greater consequence, that it gives you the liberty of feeding their half starved prisoners, when on the return; nay more, your hospitality to them, is, in the eye of the warrior, of such consequence, that at the supplication of the women, prisoners have not only been protected against insults and blows, but have sometimes even been liberated, and again restored to their connexions.— Heckewelder, *Narrative*, 162-164.

When small war parties passed by, they always caused more disturbance than large bodies. The former being insolent, and bent on mischief, if not immediately served with a dish of victuals, would cut down corn as they passed the fields, and shoot hogs by the way. Large bodies, on the other hand, would conduct themselves in a becoming manner, and keep good order, never making a halt in a village, but would stop at some distance, sending one of their number in to inform the inhabitants, that such a number of their friends, going to war (or returning, as the case was,) had stopped at such a place to refresh themselves, hoping that, perhaps these might find it convenient to spare them a meals victuals;—adding, that they need not be afraid; that even a chicken of their's should not be hurt, &c.— Such a body (for instance,) of ninety six in number, all chosen warriors, from the Wyandot towns in the vicinity of Detroit, and headed by the greatest war chief of the nation, being on their way to make a stroke on the American people, on the south side of the Ohio river, having made a halt within a quarter of a mile of Lichtenau [below Coshocton], he sent one of his captains into the village with the following message:

"*Cousin!* I am on my way to war, with a great body of men, but you need not be uneasy, as you have nothing to fear from us. My motive for coming this way is to shake hands, both with you and your teachers, and to say something to you; for this purpose we have made a halt some distance from your village, while we wish to learn if it will be agreeable to you, for some of us to go into your village for the purpose above stated—and if you have a meals victuals to spare, my men will be thankful for it."

Glickhican, (by baptism named Isaac—the same person of whom frequent mention is made in this narrative) being an old and particular friend of this great war captain; immediately ordered victuals to be prepared and taken to the camp; while he himself went out to conduct the veteran chief into the town. He soon returned with him and fifteen of his captains, whom, according to their desire, he brought to the missionaries' dwelling. The scene, of the advance of these heroes, was indeed awful, but not dreadful, as might be supposed,—they moved on with a grave and regular pace, as though they were going to enter a chapel; all following the example of their chief, they shook hands with each of the missionaries while pronouncing the words, "Father! I thank the great spirit that he has preserved our lives for a happy meeting on this day!"— Being next taken by the national assistants to the schoolhouse, where they were served with victuals, the head chief addressed himself to the following effect:

"*Cousin!* although until now, I have never come to see you, I am no stranger to you. I knew that you had invited teachers to come among you, for the purpose of instructing you in good things, of all which I highly approve.

"*Cousin!* I love your teachers, the same as you do. It is happy for us, that such good men as your teachers and our teachers * have come among us, to

---

* These Wyandots are instructed by a Roman Catholic priest, live together, and have a chapel in their village.—Heckewelder's note.

instruct us in that which is good. Both your teachers and our teachers possess the large book, in which the will and commandments of God are written. We also have a house in which we meet for prayers.

"*Cousin!* you may perhaps be astonished at hearing such words proceed from my lips, while at the same time you cannot but observe, that I am going on a warlike errand! but listen to me what I say! Unpleasant as it is to me, to approach you in the manner you see me; yet it is for your good and safety. You! Cousins, and your teachers, have many enemies. Frequent councils have been held, tending to your destruction.— I have often thought of you—often wished that I could see you. I have this time purposely taken my course this way to show my warriors where you dwelt, that not only they may not be led into a mistake respecting you, but also warn others from disturbing, or molesting my good cousins, the Christian Indians, and their teachers.

"*Cousin!* continue always in the same way you now are, and you will fare well. Do not join in any disputes, nor in wars, and the great spirit above will protect you against all the plots of your adversaries."

The war chief having finished his address, Isaac Glickhican rose, and in behalf of the Christian Indians, returned the following answer:

"*Uncle!* You are welcome with us.— Your words proceed not from the lips only, but from the heart; therefore they are precious.

"*Uncle!* You applaud our living together for the purpose of being instructed in that which is good, and in laying aside that which is bad—in not having any thing to do with the disputes of others, nor with wars.

"*Uncle!* You love us, and since this is the case the great spirit has directed your course this way that you might see *us*, and we *you*.

"*Uncle!* You say you have a teacher, the same as we have, and that he likewise tells you what is good and what is bad; and who, like our teachers, is in possession of the large book, wherein the commandments of God are written.— I doubt, uncle, whether it be the *same* book from which our teachers instruct *us*.— In the book which these have, God commands in one place: '*Thou shalt not kill.*'— And in another place, he says: '*Love your enemies.*'— nay, even '*pray for them!*'— Can it then be supposed, that God who created man, should not be offended, when these destroy each other.

"*Uncle!* at that time, when we were accomplices together,* each of us strove to outdo the other, in murdering human beings; but then we knew no better.— No body then told us that it was a sin to kill, and that to kill man was forbidden by the creator of men.

"*Uncle!* you and I were friends, when we both were young, and have remained such to this day, when we both are old. Let us do alike, and put away from us what is bad, and forbidden by God. I mean the killing of God's creatures!" (man).

The war chief having returned to his camp for nearly an hour, now

---

* Alluding to the wars between the English and French.—Heckewelder's note.

again returned, having but a single young man with him, and requesting an audience of a few of the national assistants, of which Isaac Glickhican was to be one, he addressed himself to them thus:

"*My cousin*,* I have given your words a due consideration, and now will open my heart to you.

"*Cousin!* You have spoken the truth, in saying that God, who created man, cannot be pleased when these kill one another. So the teacher who instructs me, likewise says.

"*Cousin!* I myself am averse to war—to the killing of mankind, and had declined receiving the hatchet hitherto, although my father, (as he calls himself) threatened me, that if I did not receive the hatchet of him, for to kill the American people who were his enemies, he would withhold from me, every necessary article both in the clothing way, and for supporting myself and family with meat and provision. He said that he would cause me to suffer from my obstinacy.

"*Cousin!* Place yourself in my situation, living at the very door † of my father's house. When, however, I found that my father would compel me to receive the hatchet, when he told me to kill *all* the '*long knives*' (Americans) I should meet with, I said to him: '*Father! only men in arms, not women and children!*' to which, however, he replied: '*all! all!—kill all!!*'

"*Cousin!* Think not that I am now on my way to do what my father bid me do, no indeed not! I will tell you how I will act. I will march my men within half a day's journey of the Ohio river, and from thence send a select party off to take *one* prisoner, which prisoner shall be taken to my father, with the charge that he be not hurt, and with this I will return him his hatchet again, which he had forced upon me.

"*Cousin!* Not a life shall be lost by my party, and in *ten* days you shall see me here again, if the great spirit spares my life so long.

"*Cousin!* Were I to follow my own inclinations, I should forthwith return home from here, without even going any further, but on your account I must proceed and do something, lest you be charged by my father with having dissuaded me from doing that which he bid me to do, and he become enraged against you. No! no! you shall not suffer on my account. I act for myself.

"*Cousin!* I place the words I have spoken unto you deep under ground; ‡ and on my return shall say more to you."

After taking a farewell, this chief with his young man returned to the camp, which was broke up, and they proceeded on their expedition without a shout, or the least noise, and returning in ten days precisely, with a prisoner, encamped for about an hour on the former spot, where they all, at his request,

---

* Speeches are always addressed in the singular number.—Heckewelder's note.

† Meaning, so near to him, that I am dependant on him, he observing all my acts.—Heckewelder's note.

‡ Under ground; the meaning is, to keep what he said a profound secret—not to divulge it.—Heckewelder's note.

Between Two Black Clouds: 1775-1777

with his prisoner, were fed; meanwhile, the chief with his young man, visited the missionaries for a few moments, and afterwards had a conversation with his old friend, Isaac Glickhican, mentioning a time when he would be here again to see him, but never any more would he approach the place with implements of war in his hands.—Heckewelder, *Narrative*, 185-192.

At one time, in this spring, [1778] a party of Shawanos were discovered resting with their prisoners (an old man and two youths,) at a spring about two miles distant from Lichtenau. The women of the town immediately collected provision, went and fed the poor half starved creatures, and being particularly moved with compassion for the old man, they made an attempt to ransom him, but in this instance did not succeed, being told that his destination had already been fixed on. However Providence decreed otherwise, for after some time, when they were on Sciota, deliberating on the time and manner of putting him to death, a prisoner girl, who had over heard them, took a bridle to him bidding him to hasten to a certain spot in the woods, where he would meet with horses, one of which he should mount and ride off. The man did so, and although discovered and pursued, he escaped, and was accidentally found by two boys in the woods, eight miles from Lichtenau, ten days after he had first started. The boys who found him, reported the man as no longer able to walk, and his horse quite worn down. Of course this man was brought in by the hospitable and sympathising Christian Indians, well taken care of, and after having gained sufficient strength, taken to Pittsburg. On his being brought to the missionaries' house, he fell on his knees, exclaiming: "Merciful God! be praised that thou hast brought me, a wretched creature, to a Christian people! If it be thy will that I shall die in this place, be it so, I am happy and contented!"

While this poor man was on his flight, and quite lost in the woods, he accidentally had fell in with a Delaware Indian, who in hunting, having caught a large fish, which he had just roasted for himself, he immediately gave it to this half starved white man to eat, and besides, took him some miles distance through the woods, to put him on the path, the man being lost.—Heckewelder, *Narrative*, 167-68.

During the early years of the war, Schönbrunn, the Beautiful Spring, had enjoyed comparative quiet, but by 1777 its situation became intolerable.

Within a fortnight of Heckewelder's rescue of James O'Hara, the rumor came "that large parties were on their way to murder the missionaries." * These latter removed, accordingly, one night to Gnadenhütten. Next morning, however, Heckewelder returned to Schönbrunn, where he found a party of Indians, headed by "the Monsey chief, *Newalike*, from Sandusky, pressing those of his tribe to leave the place,

---

* Heckewelder, *Narrative*, 156.

and save themselves, since 'all living there would soon be murdered, if they remained in the parts. . . .' " *

Heckewelder "thought it his duty," as he tells us, "to inform the senior missionary, Zeisberger, at Lichtenau, thirty miles distant, of the mischief that was intended by the Monsey chief, and others from Sandusky."

The missionary, without delay having come on, and finding matters worse than he had expected, made known in a public meeting, that the place would be evacuated; inviting, at the same time, all such as had a desire to cleave to the Lord, and rely on his help, to get ready to follow their teachers: a last discourse was delivered, and concluded by a fervent prayer. Next the chapel was pulled down, that it might not be made use of for heathenish purposes; and the congregation left the place the same day. Heckewelder, *Narrative*, 157.

They gave it as their chief reason: that they were apprehensive of Danger from the Americans if we continued to Stay longer there; but it was rather thought, that they only wanted us to join them, & go to the English side. However, Captⁿ White Eyes † with the Delaware Councill who were determined for Peace, took these our Circumstances into Consideration, & concluded it to be best for the Upper Town (viz. Shoenbrunn) to move imediately to a little village [Lichtenau] which had begun shortly before within 1½ Mile of Goschachking, the latter place being the Residence of the main Part of the Delaware Nation, & Councill, the Councill fire having of late been kindled there anew.

There was at this Time a very fine Prospect of these Nations remaining peaceable. At a Treaty which had been held with them in the beginning of the Revolution at Pittsburg, [marginal note: Col? Walker, Geo: Clymer being Comissioners] they [*had been*] were made sensible, from whence the dispute between the 2 Countrys arose, but at the same Time, they were desired [*by the Comissioners attending at said Treaty,*] in a most pressing Manner not to take notice at all of these Disputes, but to be quiet, follow hunting & husbandry & remain friends with both Sides.

And to convince them of the Misery they would bring upon themselves & their Children if they acted otherwise, & took up Arms against either Side, they were asked: "Whether they could expect Mercy from a People against whom they had fought in order to destroy them, but who had now [*nearly*] fairly overcome them"—

They desired them in a pathetic Manner to consider & consult the best of themselves & Children; but were at the Same Time threatened with the Loss of their Country, in case they would act as Foes. Happy would it have

---

* Heckewelder, *Narrative*, 156-57.

† So called from the whiteness of his Eyes by the White People. His proper Ind. Name being Ogúethagéchton.—Heckewelder's note.

been for this Nation, if a certain Gentleman (M!· Geo. Morgan) * who had been ab! this Time appointed Agent etc. could have remained in that Stage untill the Close of the War. This Gentleman was much beloved & admired by the Indians for the addresses he continually made to them to remain Peaceable, yea he had their Confidence to Such a Degree, that they honoured him with a Name † which one of their Chiefs bore ab! 100 Years ago, who was known by every one, as a good & Peaceable Man. [*Indeed I as a Witness must acknowledge that*] this Gentleman in every Speech that he sent out, requested the Indians to be Strong in [*that*] which was good. They had Liberty at all Times to trade where they chose, yea they were told that the Americans for the present could not Supply them with Necessaries, that they therefore would have to go to the English for Such Things, but that they Should never suffer themselves to be bribed, or deceived by either Side to strike the other— For the Side they would Strike, would then be imediately their avowed Enemies.—"Captivity and Murder," 3-6.

---

* The Author of this Narrative who lived many Years in the Ind!! Country as a Missionary from the B!!! found sufficient Reason to acknowledge the Abilities of this Gentleman with regard to Ind!! affairs.—Marginal note in MS.

† Tamanend.—Heckewelder's note.

XIV

To Goschochking with a Message from Congress: 1777-1778

IN THE YEAR 1777, while the Revolutionary war was raging, and several Indian tribes had enlisted on the British side, and were spreading murder and devastation along our unprotected frontier, I rather rashly determined to take a journey into the country on a visit to my friends. Captain White Eyes, the Indian hero, whose character I have already described, resided at that time at the distance of seventeen miles from the place where I lived. Hearing of my determination, he immediately hurried up to me, with his friend Captain Wingenund (whom I shall presently have occasion further to mention), and some of his young men, for the purpose of escorting me to Pittsburg, saying, "that he would not suffer me to go, while the Sandusky warriors were out on war excursions, without a proper escort and *himself* at my side." He insisted on accompanying me and we set out together. One day, as we were proceeding along, our spies discovered a suspicious track. White Eyes, who was riding before me, enquired whether I felt afraid? I answered that while he was with me, I entertained no fear. On this he immediately replied, "You are right; for until I am laid prostrate at your feet, no one shall hurt you." "And even not then," added Wingenund, who was riding behind me; "before this happens, I must be also overcome, and lay by the side of our friend Koguethagechton." I believed them, and I believe at this day that these great men were sincere, and that if they had been put to the test, they would have shewn it, as did another Indian friend by whom my life was saved in the spring of the year 1781. From behind a log in the bushes where he was concealed, he espied a hostile Indian at the very moment he was levelling his piece at me. Quick as lightning he jumped between us, and exposed his person to the musket shot just about to be fired, when fortunately the aggressor desisted, from fear of hitting the Indian whose body thus effectually protected me, at the imminent risk of his own life. Captain White Eyes, in the year 1774, saved in the same manner the life of David Duncan, the peace-messenger, whom he was escorting. He rushed, regardless of his own life, up to an inimical Shawanese, who was aiming at our ambassador from behind a bush, and forced him to desist.—Heckewelder, *History*, pp. 279-80.

In the early summer of 1777, Heckewelder returned to Bethlehem, arriving there on the evening of June 9. It was his hope to marry the lady of his choice, Sara Ohneberg, and take her with him to the Muskingum; but the lot, to which these plans were submitted, declined to endorse them. The minutes of the Provincial Helpers' Conference for August 9, 1777, which may be found in Bishop Kenneth G. Hamilton's *John Ettwein and the Moravian Church During the Revolutionary Period* (Bethlehem, 1940), page 76, unfold the whole strange drama:

Brother Heckwaelder's written statement concerning his return and his plans for marriage was read to the satisfaction of conference. But since various doubts were expressed because of the uncertainties of the present time and the board could reach no decision as to what would be best under present circumstances, it was decided to submit the case to the Saviour in the form of the following lots:

1. The Saviour approves our taking steps to have Brother Heckwaelder marry now and return this fall.
2. The Saviour approves Brother Heckewaelder returning as a bachelor again for this time.
3. A blank lot.

The blank lot was drawn. Thereupon the following question was submitted: Does the blank lot indicate that we should not reach a decision in this matter for the present? Two lots were submitted and the negative drawn. Therefore, the case must lie over undcided, until after the festival of the Single Brethren, or until circumstances require its reconsideration.

During his brief stay in the east, he was ordained a deacon at Lititz in Lancaster County by the hand of Bishop Matthew Hehl. This was early in 1778.* In March of that year he set out again, in company with Brother Shebosh, for Pittsburgh and the Muskingum. His arrival at a moment when the Delawares were on the point of declaring war against the Americans, gives occasion for one of his vividest descriptions of the Indian scene.

---
* Heckewelder, "Memoir," *Periodical Accounts*, XIII, 49-56.

It so happened that the Brethren in Bethlehem, towards the latter end of February, of this year (1778), feeling an uncommon anxiety for the fate of the missionaries and Christian Indians on Muskingum, they not having received a letter, or obtained any account of them for the last six months, they applied to the writer of this narrative, who in the last summer had come to Bethlehem on a visit, to proceed to Pittsburg for the purpose; and if, when there, it was believed to be practicable and safe, even to repair to his post at Lichtenau, to which he readily agreed: brother John Shabosh, who had been prevented from returning to his family at Gnadenhütten, since August last, would cheerfully accompany him.

Some circumstances at that time in making it necessary for us to be furnished with a passport from the highest authority, we waited on the president of congress, Henry Laurens, esq. and also on the secretary of war, Horatio Gates, who at that time were at Yorktown, Pennsylvania, both which gentlemen spoke very highly of the laudable undertaking the Brethren were engaged in, of propagating the gospel among the Indians, for the purpose of bringing them to embrace Christianity and become a civilized people; assuring us, that nothing should be wanting on their part in lending aid, whenever in their power, towards such a good work, and in granting us protection when required; adding, "that it had been the wish of congress, from the beginning of the war between Great Britain and the colonies, that the Indian nations could be brought to see it their interest to remain neutral during the contest, and not join either side, as the only way for them to escape being censured and hurt by either, and finally become a happy people, and united with the white Christians."

Being supplied with a passport to Pittsburg, we pursued our journey, meeting with no difficulties by the way, to that place, except the sight of so many deserted houses along the glades, on the doors of which was written, either with chalk or coal, "good people, avoid this road, for the Indians are out murdering us;" and again, as we drew nearer to Pittsburg, the unfavourable account of the elopement of M'Kee, Elliot, Girty, and others, from the latter place to the Indian country, for the purpose of instigating the Indians to murder, as was generally expected. Indeed the gloomy countenances of all men, women and children, that we passed, bespoke fear—nay, some families even spoke of leaving their farms and moving off.

Far greater was the consternation of the people at Pittsburg, and especially that of the commandant of the place, col. Edward Hand, and col. John Gibson; on whom all eyes were fixed with regard to future safety. Of those men who had eloped but a few days since, the worst might reasonably be expected: their disaffection to the United States—their disposition to act hostile—the influence they would have over the minds, at least of many of the poor Indians, and the means they would have at command for the purpose of enforcing their evil designs, might be calculated on with certainty. In vain had the commandant sought for a trusty runner, to carry out pacific speeches to the peaceable Delawares: the risk of going out at a time when it was known that the war parties were out, and probably every path beset by them, being thought too great. Even the above named gentlemen, with many others of the place, however anxious they were that something might be done to prevent the Delawares from being deceived, would not venture to advise us to go at this time; declaring that if we should go, and escape, it must be considered a miracle.

However, the matter appearing to us of the greatest importance, we had given it a due consideration during the night; the result of which was, that in our view it appeared clear, that the preservation of the Delaware nation, and the existence of our mission, depended on the nation being at peace, and that a contrary course would tend to the total ruin of the whole mission; —that were we at this time to neglect, or withdraw ourselves from performing a service, nay a duty, in exposing the vile intentions of a depraved set of beings, whose evil designs were but too well known, we must become accountable to God. Therefore, with entire reliance on the strong hand of Providence, we determined to go at the hazard of our lives, or at least make the attempt.

Accordingly in the morning we made our resolution known to cols. Hand and Gibson, whose best wishes for our success, we were assured of; and leaving our baggage behind, and turning a deaf ear to all entreaties of well meaning friends, who considered us as lost, if we went, we crossed the Alleghany river, and on the third day, at eleven o'clock at night, reached Gnadenhutten,* after having at several times narrowly escaped falling in with war parties; and indeed, in one instance, while encamped on the Big Beaver, near the mouth, where a party of warriors on that night were murdering people on Rackoon creek, not many miles distant from where we were, though at that time not known to us. We had travelled day and night, only leaving our horses time to feed; crossed the Big Beaver, which overflowed its banks, on a raft we had made of poles, other large creeks on the way we swam with our horses, and never attempted to kindle a fire, apprehensive of being discovered by the warriors smelling the smoke.

When arrived within a few miles of Gnadenhutten, we distinctly heard the beat of a drum, and on drawing near, the war song sung to the beat of the drum, all which being in the direction the town lay, we naturally concluded that the Christian Indians must have moved off, wherefore we proceeded with caution, lest we should fall into the warrior's hands. However, the people being yet there, informed us that those warriors we had heard, were Wyandots from Sandusky, who arrived that evening, and were encamped on the Bluff, two miles below the town, on the opposite side of the river, and who probably would the next morning, travel along the path we had just come.

---

* This was on April 5, according to the Bethlehem Diary of May 14, 1778.

Fatigued as we were, after our journey, and without one hour of sound sleep, I was now requested by the inhabitants of the place, men and women, not to delay any time, but to proceed on to Goschochking (near thirty miles distant,) where all was bustle and confusion, and many preparing to go off to fight the American people, in consequence of the advice given them by those deserters, before named, who had told them, that the American people were embodying themselves at this time, for the purpose of killing every Indian they should meet with, be such, friend or foe, and further we were told, that captain White Eyes had been threatened to be killed if he persisted in vindicating the character of the American people; many believing the stories told them by M'Kee and his associates, and had in consequence already shaved their heads, ready to lay the plume * on, and turn out to war, as soon as the ten days which White Eyes had desired them to wait should be expired, and to-morrow being the ninth day, and no message having yet arrived from their friends at Pittsburg, they now were preparing to go—and further, that this place, Gnadenhutten, was now breaking up for its inhabitants to join the congregation at Lichtenau, those deserters having assured them, that they were not a day safe from an attack by the Americans, while they remained here.

Finding the matter so *very* pressing, and even not admitting of a day's delay, I consented, that after a few hours rest and sleep, and furnished with a trusty companion and fresh horse, I would proceed on, when between three and four o'clock in the morning, the national assistant, John Martin, having called on me for the purpose, we set out, swimming our horses across the Muskingum river, and taking a circuit through the woods in order to avoid the encampment of the war party which was close to our path. Arriving by ten o'clock in the forenoon within sight of the town, a few yells were given by a person who had discovered us, intended to notify the inhabitants, that a white man was coming, and which immediately drew the whole body of Indians into the street; but although I saluted them in passing them, not a single person returned the compliment, which, as my conductor observed, was no good omen. Even captain White Eyes, and the other chiefs, who always had befriended me, now stepped back when I reached out my hand to them, which strange conduct however did not dismay me, as I observed among the crowd some men well known to me as spies of captain Pipe's, watching the actions of these peace chiefs, wherefore I was satisfied that the act of refusing me the hand, had been done from policy, and not from any ill will towards my person. Indeed in looking around, I thought I could read joy in the countenances of many of them, in seeing me among them at so

---

* This plume distinguishes the warrior, and is only laid on when he is going out to war, *that* tuft of hair on their heads, termed the scalp, being daubed over with tallow, the *white* plume from the head of the eagle, is stuck on, they say that this confers the courage of that bird on them. *Long* feathers are only made use of as an ornament.—Heckewelder's note.

critical a juncture, when they, but a few days before had been told by those deserters, that nothing short of their total destruction, had been resolved upon by the "long knives" (the Virginians, or *new* American people). Yet as no one would reach out his hand to me, I inquired into the cause, when captain White Eyes boldly stepping forward, replied; "that by what had been told them by those men (M'Kee and party) they no longer had a single friend among the American people; if therefore this be so, they must consider *every* white man who came to them from that side, as an enemy, who only came to them to deceive them, and put them off their guard for the purpose of giving the enemy an opportunity of taking them by surprise." I replied, that the imputation was unfounded, and that, were I not their friend, they never would have seen me here. "Then, (continued captain White Eyes) you will tell us the truth with regard to what I state to you!"—assuring him of this, he in a strong tone asked me: "are the American armies all cut to pieces by the English troops? Is general Washington killed? Is there no more a congress, and have the English hung some of them, and taken the remainder to England to hang them there? Is the whole country beyond the mountains in the possession of the English; and are the few thousand Americans who have escaped them, now embodying themselves on this side of the mountains for the purpose of killing all the Indians in this country, even our women and children? Now do not deceive us, but speak the truth" (added he); "is this all true what I have said to you?" I declared before the whole assembly, that not one word of what he had just now told me was true, and holding out to him, as I had done before, the friendly speeches sent by me for them, which he however as yet refused to accept, I thought by the countenances of most of the by standers, that I could perceive that the moment bid fair for their listening at least to the contents of those speeches, and accidentally catching the eye of the drummer, I called to him to beat the drum for the Assembly to meet for the purpose of hearing what their American Brethren had to say to them! A general smile having taken place, White Eyes thought the favourable moment arrived to put the question, and having addressed the assembly in these words: "shall we my friends and relatives listen once more to those who call us their brethren?" which question being loudly and as with one voice answered in the affirmative, the drum was beat, and the whole body quickly repairing to the spacious council house; the speeches, all of which were of the most pacific nature were read and interpreted to them, when captain White Eyes rose, and in an elaborate address to the assembly, took particular notice of the good disposition of the American people towards the Indians, observing, that they had never as yet, called on them to fight the English, knowing that wars were destructive to nations, that those had from the beginning of the war, to the present time always advised them (the Indians) to remain quiet, and not take up the hatchet against either side. A newspaper, containing the capitulation of general Burgoyne's army, being found enclosed in the packet, Captain White Eyes once more rose up, and holding this paper unfolded with both his hands, so that all could have a view of it, said "see my friends and relatives, this document containeth great events, not the song of a bird, but the truth!"—then stepping up to me, he gave me his hand, saying: "you are welcome with us Brother;" when every one present, followed his example; after which I proceeded with my conductor John Martin to Lichtenau, where, to the inexpressible joy of the venerable missionary Zeisberger, and his congregation, we related what had taken place, while they on the other hand assured us, that nothing could have at that time come more seasonable to save the nation, and with it the mission, from utter destruction, than our arrival.

Captain White Eyes, although now relieved from all anxiety respecting his nation, could not overlook the imposition practised upon them by M'Kee and his associates. He therefore, on the next day, dispatched runners to the Shawanese towns on the Sciota, where these imposters were gone with the following message: viz. Grand children! ye Shawanese! some days ago a flock of birds, that had come on from the east, lit at Goschochking, imposing a song of their's upon us, which song had nigh proved our ruin!— Should these birds, which on leaving us, took their flight towards Sciota, endeavour to impose a song on you likewise, do not listen to them, for they lie!"

The mortification, however, which captain Pipe felt in being again so sadly disappointed, was such as might be expected from so ambitious a man. His spies, which during this critical time, he had kept at Goschochking for the purpose of watching every act of the peaceable chiefs, had brought him the doleful news, that all that White Eyes had predicted, had been verified.

The inhabitants of Gnadenhutten having now also joined the congregation at Lichtenau, as that of Shonbrun had done the preceding year, and many of the young people of the Monsey tribe, whom the Monsey chief had last spring persuaded to go off with him to a place of safety, having also since returned, the town increased to a considerable size, and the chapel was necessarily enlarged. And as one tribe of the Shawanos on Sciota, continued to be averse to the war, these, at the invitation of the chiefs of Goshochking also came on and settled near them; from whence their chief, an amiable young man, frequently visited the missionaries at Lichtenau.—Heckewelder, *Narrative*, pp. 173-83.

XV

Death of Captain White Eyes: 1778

For four years Captain White Eyes kept the Delawares in line with American policy. At a meeting held in Pittsburgh, 1775, he had "boldly declared to a select body of Senecas," as Heckewelder tells us,* "that his Indians would never join any nation or power, for the purpose of destroying a people who were born on the same soil with them." Three years later White Eyes' policy was confirmed and strengthened at Fort Pitt, September 17, 1778, during a conference in which he, Captain John Killbuck, Junior, and Captain Pipe represented the Delawares. It was then agreed that, in case of war, the Delawares were to assist the United States. "The Delawares," we read, "were guaranteed their territorial rights so long as they remained friendly to the United States, and finally, the agreement was made that in the future an Indian state might be established, which state would be entitled to representation in Congress." †

From this position, it was just one step further to the actual participation of the Delawares in the war on behalf of the United States. That step was soon taken by White Eyes' party. Captain White Eyes, finding himself compelled, as Heckewelder tells us, to take sides, declared for the Americans and joined General Lachlan McIntosh's command, accepting a colonel's commission.‡

But the sands were running out. Captain White Eyes fell victim to the white man's most dreaded disease. In November, 1778, while pre-

---
* Heckewelder, *History*, p. 69.
† August C. Mahr, *Federal Indian Relations, 1774-1788*, pp. 72-73.
‡ Joseph H. Bausman, *History of Beaver County*, I, 31.

paring to accompany General McIntosh's army against the British Indians at Sandusky, he took the smallpox and died.*

The death of this great and useful man, was severely lamented by, and a great loss to the nation; and although his ambitious and political opponent, captain Pipe, with an air of prophecy, uttered: "that the great spirit had probably put him out of the way that the nation might be saved:" it was not so considered by the faithful part. His death was according to Indian custom, made known to all the surrounding nations, even at some hundred miles distance, who all in due time condoled the nation on the loss. The person on whom, by lineal descent, the station of head chief † of the nation devolved, being yet young in years, the surviving chiefs *Gelelemend*, (alias *Killbuck*) *Machingwe Pushis*, (alias *large Cat*) and *Tetepachksi*, officiated in his stead, the two former of which kept up a lively correspondence with Colonel Broadhead, the then commandant, and their agent, col. George Morgan, on measures tending to preserve the peace; and notwithstanding captain Pipe's intrigues to decieve them, and his threats and persecutions to bring them over to his political creed, they withstood him with firmness.—Heckewelder, *Narrative*, 193.

As the tribes and nations connected and in league with the Delaware nation, had already sent condoling speeches to these on the death of their late chief Netawatwees.‡ ("*Nettowhatways*") § In like manner the Cherokee nation for one, had also by deputation come on, for the purpose of condoling the nation on the death of their chief *Coquehagechton*, (alias captain White Eyes.) The deputation, consisting of fourteen men, of whom two were princi-

---

* Heckewelder, *Narrative*, pp. 192-93, says it was "while accompanying general M'Intosh's army to Tuscorawas, where a fort was to be built for the protection of the peaceable Indians, and frontier settlers . . ." In a note he adds: "The fort was built and called Fort Laurens." William C. Reichel's note in Heckewelder's *History*, p. 69, says that he "died at Fort Laurens, on the Tuscarawas . . . before the projected expedition, which was aimed at the Sandusky towns, moved." Frank Huntington, in Hodge's *Handbook of the American Indians*, p. 944, says that he died "at Pittsburgh." The Lichtenau Diary, Nov. 20, 1778, says that he died "not far from Pittsburg."

† This young chief, fell a victim under Williamson, at the time the peaceable Indians, near Pittsburg, were attacked in their camp by this party, (1781).—Heckewelder's note.

‡ Who died in the year 1776.—Heckewelder's note.

§ The writer of col. Bouquet's expedition against the Ohio Indians, in 1764. Printed in Philadelphia, and reprinted in London, in 1766, was sadly mistaken, when he asserts, at page 23, "that the col. had deposed *Nettowhatways*, the chief of the Turtle tribe," and that he had "caused that tribe to choose another chief in his stead." This "deposed" chief, held his high station after being "deposed," as before, until his death in the fall of the year 1776, during which period of time, the writer of this narrative knew him personally, and to be the same person here spoken of. See also Loskiel's History of the mission, part I. Page 132-137, and throughout the work to page 117 in chapter III.—Heckewelder's note.

pal chiefs, were accompanied from their country to Goschochking, by a nephew of the late captain White Eye's, who, soon after the commencement of the American revolution had been, by the Delaware chiefs, dispatched thither for the purpose of using his endeavours, in keeping that nation at peace.— When this deputation had arrived within three miles of Goshochking, and within one mile of Lichtenau, they made a halt for the purpose of having the customary ceremony performed on them, which being done by one of the councellors, from the village, who by an address and with a string of wampum, drew the thorns and briars out of their legs and feet, healed the sores and bruises they had received by hitting against logs; wiped the dust and sweat off of their bodies; and cleansed their eyes and ears so that they might both see and hear well; and finally, they anointed all their joints, that their limbs might again become supple.* They were then served with victuals brought from Lichtenau, and they continued there the remainde[r] of that day.

On the next morning, two of the councellors from Goschochking, deputed for the purpose, informed the missionary and the national assistants at Lichtenau, that by order of their chiefs, they were to conduct the Cherokee deputation into their village, from whence, they expected that we would join in the procession to Goschochking, and there attend the condoling ceremonies; all which being agreed to, these soon brought them on, one leading them in front, and the other bringing up the rear.

Arriving within about two hundred yards of the town, and in sight of it (all marching Indian file) they fired off their pieces, which compliment was instantly returned by the young men of the town, drawn up for the purpose; then raising a melancholy song, they continued singing, until they had reached the long house, purposely built for their reception; yet not without first having lodged their arms against some trees they had passed, at a small distance from the town. Being seated on benches, prepared for the purpose— (the deputies on the opposite side) a dead silence prevailed for about half an hour and all present cast their eyes on the ground; at length one of these chiefs, named the Crow, rose, and with an air of sorrow, and in a low voice, with his eyes cast up to heaven, spoke to the following effect: viz.

"One morning, after having arisen from my sleep, and according to my custom, I stepped out at the door to see what weather we had, I observed at one place in the horizon a dark cloud projecting above the trees; and looking steadfastly for its movement or disappearance, found myself mistaken, since it neither disappeared, nor moved from the spot, as other clouds do. Seeing the same cloud successively every morning, and that always in the same place, I began to think what could be the cause of this singular phenomenon; at length it struck me, that as the cloud was lying in the direction that my grandfather dwelt, something might be the matter with him, which caused

---

* All which ceremonies are performed figuratively.—Heckewelder's note.

him grief. Anxious to satisfy myself, I resolved to go to my grandfather, and see if any thing was the matter with him. I accordingly went, steering a course in the direction I had observed the cloud to be.— I arrived at my grandfather's, whom I found quite disconsolate, hanging his head, and the tears running down his cheeks!— Casting my eyes around in the hopes of discovering the cause of his grief, I observed yonder, a dwelling closed up, and from which no smoke * appeared to ascend! looking in another direction, I discovered an elevated spot of fresh earth † on which nothing was seen growing and here I found the cause of my grandfather's grief. No wonder he is so grieved!— No wonder he is weeping and sobing with his eyes cast towards the ground!— Even I cannot help weeping with my grandfather, seeing in what a situation he is!— I cannot proceed for grief!"

Here, after having seated himself for about twenty minutes, and as though deeply afflicted; he again rose, and receiving from the principle chief who was seated by his side, a large string of wampum, said: "Grandfather! lift up your head and hear what your grandchildren have to say to you!— These having discovered the cause of your grief, it shall be done away! See grandfather! I level the ground on yonder spot of yellow earth ‡ and put leaves and brush thereon to make it invisible!— I also sow seeds on that spot, so that both grass and trees may grow thereon!" (here handing the string to the Delaware chiefs in succession) and taking up another, he continued: "Grandfather! the seed which I had sown has already taken root; nay, the grass has already covered the ground and the trees are growing!" (handing this string likewise to the Delaware chief, and taking up a third string of wampum), he added: "Now my grandfther! the cause of your grief being removed, let me dry up your tears! I wipe them from your eyes!— I place your body, which by the weight of grief and a heavy heart is leaning to one side, in its proper posture! Your eyes shall be henceforth clear, and your ears open as formerly! The work is now finished!" Handing this string likewise to the Delaware chief, he now stepped forward to where the chief and his councellors were seated, and having first shaken hands with these, he next shook hands with all present, the whole embassy following his example. This being done, and all again seated as before, the Delaware chief Gelelemend, (alias Killbuck) replied:

"Grand children! you did not come here in vain! You have performed a good work, in which the great spirit has assisted you! Your grandfather § makes you welcome with him!"

The meeting ‖ then broke up for the day, and as they intended paying a visit to the commandant at Pittsburg, they produced the certificates and passports they had been furnished with, (by officers stationed near them) to

---

* Meaning no person occupying the house.—Heckewelder's note.
† The Grave.—Heckewelder's note.
‡ The Grave.—Heckewelder's note.
§ The Indian speeches are delivered in the singular number.—Heckewelder's note.
‖ The whole ceremony, took up nearly three hours.—Heckewelder's note.

Death of Captain White Eyes: 1778

learn, whether these would be sufficient to recommend them, as being at peace with the United States; all which being confirmed, their minds were at ease.

On the day following, the chiefs of both nations entered on business relating to their national concerns, and finally made a covenant, not to join in the war, but to maintain the peace, while others of the Cherokee party, together with the two women who had accompanied them to this place, exchanged sundry articles they had manufactured in their country, such as neat and curiously made tobacco pipe bowls, small baskets made of cane, &c. for articles of equal value made by their grandfather the Delawares.

It was pleasing to see so much respect paid to the memory of the departed chief of the nation— Indeed, all the surrounding nations appeared to have been sensible of his worth; while living, he often encouraged his people to adopt the way of living by agriculture, and finally become civilized. His ideas were, that unless the Indians changed their mode of living they would in time dwindle to nothing, and to encourage them towards such a change, he told them to take the example of the Christian Indians, who by their industry, had everything they could wish for, and never suffered from want.
—Heckewelder, *Narrative*, 197-203.

XVI

Salem on the Muskingum: 1779-1780

AFTER THE DEATH of Captain White Eyes, the situation on the Muskingum rapidly grew tense. The winter was quiet enough, but it was followed by a year of storm.

The winter season, during Indians wars, being the only quiet and agreeable time in their country, as the warriors, from a fear of being traced by their enemies, when snow is on the ground, prefer remaining at home; the Christian Indian congregation, enjoyed perfect rest, being in no manner incommodated by them, nor even seeing any of them. The meetings therefore, could be attended without disturbance, or interruption, and the schools being put under proper regulations, added to the happiness of the parents, and made it delightful to hear the voices of so many classes of old and young, raised in praises to the Lord, when assembled for that purpose.

It had, however, during the winter of 1778-79, been taken into consideration, whether this large congregation could, with propriety, be advised to remain together at this place [Lichtenau, about two miles below Coshocton on the Muskingum] for another year; and, whether it would be proper at this present time, to advise, or even suffer such, as wished to return to their former settlements, so to do: with regard to the first point, it was evident, that the inhabitants were too much crowded and confined, and possessing a large stock in horses, horned cattle and hogs, they could not find sufficient pasture, without going to a great distance, in consequence of which, many were lost, and with regard to the other suggestion, it was observed, that the warriors from Sandusky, having within the last twelve months, made their principal war path, pass through all the Delaware towns, commencing at Gokhosing (the *habitation of Owls*) and ending with Lichtenau (the whole a distance of between thirty and forty miles) it might be expected that at one time or an other, the Americans, being in pursuit of warriors, who had committed murders on the south side of the Ohio, might, by following the traces of them along the path, be led straightway into Lichtenau, and fall upon the Christian Indians, believing them to have been the aggressors. Upon the whole, it was believed best, not to detain any one who wished to return to his former place of abode; moreover, it was believed, that very few, if any warriors continued to pass through these forsaken towns, especially that of Gnadenhutten; as every house, hut and stable, together with all the fencing and palings, were in the same situation as at the time the place was evacuated last year. Finally, it was agreed, that the former inhabitants of Gnadenhutten should return to that place, with as many of the former inhabitants of Shonbrun, as might choose to return thither, to build a new town on a convenient spot, the old one being entirely destroyed.

Accordingly, in April, 1779, the missionary Zeisberger set out with a number of families, for the last mentioned place; while the missionary Edwards, returned with his congregation to Gnadenhutten, all in good spirits, travelling by land and by water to their favourite spots, believing themselves already relieved from many inconveniences and troubles, caused by the warriors.

It fell to the lot of the writer of this narrative to remain at Lichtenau, with the remainder of the congregation somewhat longer, and he concluded to remain as long as it might be advisable, without running any serious risk. Thus, there were once more three missionary establishments on the river Muskingum, the nearest of which was about thirty, and the most remote (Shonbrun), about forty miles from Lichtenau.

During the whole of the first two years, there was not a single instance of warriors passing through Gnadenhutten or Shonbrun, or their being otherwise incommoded by that class of people. They lived as peaceably and contentedly together, as if they were the only people in the country; building houses, clearing and improving their lands, and meeting daily for divine service.— Yet, on one account, the inhabitants of Gnadenhutten were sufferers, and became somewhat alarmed. Namely: the frontier people of Virginia, living on the Ohio below Wheeling, had for a long time, and indeed, ever since the Christian Indians first settled at that place, been in the habit of stealing the Indians' horses from the licks * within a few miles of the place; and now, on learning that the Christian Indians were again returned to their settlement, they renewed this practice. Yet this was borne by the sufferers with patience, in hopes, that after a general peace should take place, these horses might be, through the influence of their agent, or by the civil

---

* To these licks, (as they are called) which contain water of a saltish or brackish nature, both horses and horn cattle resort during the summer months.

authority, recovered, in which hopes, however, they were sadly mistaken, as the sequel will shew.

At Lichtenau, the inhabitants were, with the commencement of the spring of 1779, again incommoded, by the northern warriors, frequently passing and repassing near, and sometimes through their village.— Nay, they became more insolent and mischievous.—Heckewelder, *Narrative*, pp. 194-97.

News being brought to Goschochking, that the governor of Detroit, who a short time before had gone with troops to Port Vincennes, and was there, together with his officers, taken prisoner by an American army under general Clarke, and by him taken to Virginia. The peaceable Indians, and the missionaries, entertained a hope that the threats, so repeatedly circulated through the country, and attributed to this governor, would forthwith be at an end. They however found themselves mistaken, as it now became more evident, that much had been laid to the charge of this gentleman, of which he probably had no knowledge, but which had been the work of M'Kee, Elliot and Girty. These three men, whose hostility to the United States appeared to be unbounded, were continually plotting the destruction of the Christian Indians' settlements, as the only means of drawing the Delaware nation, and with these, the Christian Indians, into the war. The missionaries, in particular, were as a thorn in their eyes, being not only considered as the cause, that, the Delaware nation would not join in the war; but they also mistrusted them of informing the American government, of the part *they* were acting in the Indian country.

At the very time that the governor was a prisoner of general Clarke, a plot was laid at Sandusky, to take off the missionary Zeisberger;—or to bring in his scalp; and Simon Girty had engaged to lead the party on for the purpose. Fortunately, there lived at the time at Upper Sandusky a trader, by the name of Alexander M'Cormick, well known to the missionaries for many years past, as a friend and admirer of missions among the Indians, who on learning the intention of this party, found means to inform the writer of this, who lived at Lichtenau, of the plot, and at which place, as it had happened, this very missionary at the time, had come on a visit from Shonbrun, which the spies of the hostile party discovering; they, to ensure his capture, waylaid the path on which Zeisberger must return. Two spirited Indian brethren of whom Isaac Glickhican was one, were selected to conduct the missionary home by way of Gnadenhutten; with direction, however, to strengthen the guard at that place, should it be thought necessary; they left Lichtenau, when having scarcely proceeded nine miles on the journey, all of a sudden the hostile party, consisting of eight Mingoes (of the Six Nations) and Simon Girty, the person who was to point out to them the object they were come for, appeared before them on the path. At this critical moment and while Girty was uttering to the captain of the gang the words! "this is the very man we are come for; now act agreeable to the promise you have made!"

two young Delawares, on their return from a hunt, accidentally, and very fortunately, struck from out of the woods, exactly on the path where these were standing, and concluding from the words spoken by Girty, as also by the appearance of the party, that something bad was intended against the missionary; they boldly stepped forward, with their arms in readiness, to defend him, at the risk of their own lives; which the captain observing, and justly concluding that the two other Delawares who accompanied the missionary, would join these against them, were they to make the attempt; he, by a signal prudently given, declined laying hands on him. The two young Delawares, seeing all safe, reported on their arrival at Goschochking, what had transpired, adding: that although they were none of the believing (Christian) Indians, yet they felt themselves interested in saving the life of such a good man as this teacher was; even at the risk of perishing themselves in the conflict.—Heckewelder, *Narrative*, 203-206.

The Christian Indians at Lichtenau soon found their proximity to the Delaware capital of Goschochking all but intolerable. Since the death of White Eyes, Captain Pipe's followers, who had always been restless, became bold and reckless. In the outskirts of Goschochking, they murdered an American soldier, and fired on another returning from Lichtenau. Seeing these things and understanding what they portended, a band of Shawnees in the neighborhood broke up and returned to the main body of their people on the Scioto.* It became known at Lichtenau, as Heckewelder tells us, that the Sandusky warriors allied with the British were now beginning to make a halt at Captain Pipe's settlements.†

Clearly it was necessary for the Christian Indians to move to a less critical neighborhood. Out of this necessity was born the village of Salem [a mile and a half southwest of Port Washington].

Every preparation having been made during the winter, to leave the place early in the spring, the congregation met on the morning of the 3d [30th] day of March (1780), once more to unite in thanks and praises to the Lord, for all the blessing received from him, during the five years this place had been occupied by them, (the Christian Indians,) after which the chapel being pulled down, that it might not be applied to heathenish purposes; they set out by land and water, and having proceeded upwards of twenty miles up the river, and to within six miles of Gnadenhutten, they built a town, which they called Salem; and the Brethren of the two towns above, (namely, Gnadenhutten and Shonbrun) offering their services, in helping to build the chapel, they worked together, with uncommon cheerfulness and industry,

---
* *Narrative*, 208.
† *Narrative*, 209.

so that on the 22d of May, the same was consecrated by the worthy senior missionary, Zeisberger, and the next day the communicants partook of the holy sacrament, for the first time, at this place. Baptism was also administered on the 28th, and it appeared as if new life had been bestowed on the three congregations generally.

The building was forty feet by thirty-six, handsomely put up, of hewed or squared timbers, with a cupola and bell, and all the dwelling houses were raised and completed by December. The peaceable Indians from Goschochking and its neighbourhood, who had frequented the meetings at Lichtenau, would occasionally come from thence to hear the gospel preached, notwithstanding the distance was more than twenty miles.—Heckewelder, *Narrative*, 209-10.

Here we may pause for a last quiet moment, before entering on the narrative which John Heckewelder entitled "Captivity and Murder," while he describes for us certain incidents, illuminating to the student of Indian character, which came under his observation at this time.

The Indians are proud but not vain; they consider vanity as degrading and unworthy the character of a man. The hunter never boasts of his skill or strength, nor the warrior of his prowess. It is not right, they say, that one should value himself too much for an action which another may perform as well as himself, and when a man extols his own deeds, it seems as if he doubted his own capability to do the like again when he pleased. Therefore, they prefer in all cases to let their actions speak for themselves. The skins and peltry which the hunter brings home, the deer's horns on the roof of his cabin, the horses, furniture and other property that he possesses, his apparel and that of his family, the visits with which he is honored by the first and best men among his nation; all these things show what he is and what he has done, and with this he rests satisfied.

So with the warrior; it is enough for him that he is known to be a man of spirit and courage by the scalps and prisoners that he brings home; he never is seen going about boasting of his war-like exploits, and when questioned on the subject, he makes his answer as short as possible. Even when he is entering a town with his prisoners and scalps, he does not stare about to see whether the people are looking at him, but walks his usual steady pace and marches straight forward without appearing to see any body. When at some of their particular festivals, every warrior is called upon to relate his feats of arms, they make it a point to be as brief as possible, leaving it to those who have done but little, to swell their actions into importance, and give themselves credit for what they have done. I cannot illustrate this subject better than by a few anecdotes.

In the year 1779, two war chiefs, the one a young man of the Shawano tribe, and the other an old warrior of the Wyandots, living near Detroit,

Salem on the Muskingum: 1779-1780

much celebrated for his great actions, but who during the whole of the Revolutionary war, could not be persuaded to take the field against the Americans, met accidentally at my house on Muskingum, where they had separately come to pay me a friendly visit. The Shawano (whose nation, by the bye, are noted for much talk,) entered upon the subject of war, and with much earnestness in words and gestures, related the actions he had been engaged in, showing at the same time on his arm the mark of a bullet wound. During all this time, the Wyandot, smoking his pipe, listened with great attention and apparent surprise; and having afterwards to answer, according to custom, by relating what he had done, he laid down his pipe, and deliberately drawing off his clothes, except the breech-cloth, rose up and said: "I have been in upwards of twenty engagements with the enemy and fought with the French against the English; I have warred against the southern nations, and my body shows that I have been struck and wounded by nine balls. These two wounds I received at the same moment, from two Cherokees, who, seeing me fall, rested their guns against a tree, and ran up with their tomahawks to dispatch me, and take off my scalp. With the aid of the Great Spirit I jumped up, just at the moment when they were about to give me the stroke. I struck them and they both fell at my feet. I took their scalps and returned home." Thus this grave and respectable veteran gave a lesson to the young Shawano, which, if he well understood, he, no doubt, ever after remembered; for in a few words, and in less than five minutes, he showed him at once the contrast between great actions briefly and modestly told, and every day occurences related and dwelt on with pompous minuteness. This contrast, indeed, was particularly striking, the more so as the modest warrior did not seem to enjoy his triumph, nor to be even conscious of the accession to his fame which must result from the publicity of the account which he had given. As both parties spoke the Shawano language, I well understood every thing they said, and I paid the most particular attention to their discourse, which was of itself sufficiently interesting.

This passion of the Indians, which I have called *pride*, but which might, perhaps, be better denominated *high-mindedness*, is generally combined with a great sense of honour, and not seldom produces actions of the most heroic kind. I am now going to relate an instance of this honourable pride, which I have also witnessed. An Indian of the Lenape nation, who was considered as a very dangerous person, and was much dreaded on that account, had publicly declared that as soon as another Indian, who was then gone to Sandusky, should return from thence, he would certainly kill him. This dangerous Indian called in one day at my house on the Muskingum to ask me for some tobacco. While this unwelcome guest was smoking his pipe by my fire, behold! the other Indian whom he had threatened to kill, and who at that moment had just arrived, also entered the house. I was much frightened, as I feared the bad Indian would take that opportunity to carry his threat into execution, and that my house would be made the scene of a horrid murder. I walked to the door, in order not to witness a crime that I could not prevent, when to my great astonishment I heard the Indian whom I thought in danger, address the other in these words: "Uncle, you have threatened to kill me— you have declared that you would do it the first time we should meet. Now I am here, and we are together. Am I to take it for granted that you are in earnest, and that you are really determined to take my life as you have declared? Am I now to consider you as my avowed enemy, and in order to secure my own life against your murderous designs, to be the first to strike you and embrue my hands in your blood?— I will not, I cannot do it. Your heart is bad, it is true, but still you appear to be a generous foe, for you gave me notice of what you intended to do; you have put me on my guard, and did not attempt to assassinate me by surprise; I, therefore, will spare you until you lift up your arm to strike, and then, uncle, it will be seen which of us shall fall!" The murderer was thunderstruck, and without replying a word, slunk off and left the house.

The anecdote with which I am going to conclude this chapter, will display an act of heroism produced by this elevation of mind which I have called *pride*, which, perhaps, may have been equalled, but, I dare say, was hardly ever surpassed. In the spring of the year 1782, the war chief of the Wyandots of Lower Sandusky sent a white prisoner (a young man whom he had taken at Fort M'Intosh) as a present to another chief, who was called the *Half-king* of Upper Sandusky,* for the purpose of being adopted into his family, in the place of one of his sons, who had been killed the preceding year, while at war with the people on the Ohio. The prisoner arrived, and was presented to the Half-king's wife, but she refused to receive him, which, according to the Indian rule, was, in fact, a sentence of death. The young man was, therefore, taken away, for the purpose of being tortured and burnt on the pile. While the dreadful preparations were making near the village, the unhappy victim being already tied to the stake, and the Indians arriving from all quarters to join in the cruel act or to witness it, two English traders, Messrs. *Arundel* and *Robbins* (I delight in making this honourable mention

---

* The Wyandot village of Upper Sandusky was three miles in a south-easterly direction from the site of the present town of Upper Sandusky, the county seat of Wyandot County, Ohio. Lower Sandusky, a trading post and Wyandot town, was situated at the head of navigation on the Sandusky. Fremont, the county-seat of Sandusky County, marks its site. Here the Moravian missionaries and their families were most hospitably entertained by Arundel and Robbins for upwards of three weeks, while awaiting the arrival of boats from Detroit, on which they were to be taken as prisoners of war to that post. It was through British influence that the Mission on the Muskingum had been overthrown in the early autumn of 1781, and that its seat was transferred to the Sandusky. Fort McIntosh stood on the present town of Beaver, Beaver County, Pennsylvania. It was erected in October of 1778 by General McIntosh, then in command of the Western Department.—Note by William C. Reichel, in Heckewelder's *History*, p. 173.

of their names), shocked at the idea of the cruelties which were about to be perpetrated, and moved by feelings of pity and humanity, resolved to unite their exertions to endeavour to save the prisoner's life by offering a ransom to the war chief, which he, however refused, because, said he, it was an established rule among them, that when a prisoner who had been given as a present, was refused adoption, he was irrevocably doomed to the stake, and it was not in the power of any one to save his life. Besides, added he, the numerous war captains who were on the spot, had it in charge to see the sentence carried into execution. The two generous Englishmen, however, were not discouraged, and determined to try a last effort. They well knew what effects the high-minded pride of an Indian was capable of producing, and to this strong and noble passion they directed their attacks: "But," said they, in reply to the answer which the chief had made them, "among all those chiefs whom you have mentioned, there is none who equals you in greatness; you are considered not only as the greatest and bravest, but as the best man in the nation." "Do you really believe what you say?" said at once the Indian, looking them full in the face. "Indeed, we do." Then without saying another word, he blackened himself, and taking his knife and tomahawk in his hand, made his way through the crowd to the unhappy victim, crying out with a loud voice: "What have you to do with *my* prisoner?" and at once cutting the cords with which he was tied, took him to his house which was near Mr. Arundel's, whence he was forthwith secured and carried off by safe hands to Detroit, whence the commandant, being informed of the transaction, sent him by water to Niagara, where he was soon afterwards liberated. The Indians who witnessed this act, said that it was truly heroic; they were so confounded by the unexpected conduct of this chief, and by his manly and resolute appearance, that they had not time to reflect upon what they should do, and before their astonishment was well over, the prisoner was out of their reach.—Heckewelder, *History*, 170-74.

At Lichtenau Heckewelder had been making good progress. In a letter dated March 3, 1780, to the Elders' Conference at Bethlehem, he rejoiced that the Indians of the congregation had such confidence in him that they visited him both day and night in his house and told him their problems. He reported that he was doing well with the language. He could understand now what was spoken to him in the Delaware tongue as well as he understood German. He was less proficient in speaking, but got along well enough. The Indians, when they were with him, never thought of using any language but their own.

But Lichtenau was no longer a good place for a mission town. The Wyandots and Mingos (western Iroquois) had made it the starting point of a new war path directed against the settlements on the Ohio. On March 28, accordingly, the inhabitants of Lichtenau began their removal to a new site farther up the valley, six miles from Gnadenhütten. The new village was to be called Salem. It was on the left bank of the Tuscarawas on a beautiful plain where a Delaware village had formerly stood, but from which the inhabitants had been removed by order of the Delaware Council to make way for the Moravians. On March 30 the last service was held in Lichtenau. The bulk of the Lichtenau Indians left the village a few days later, and on April 8 they held their first service in the new town.

This was a stirring spring and summer for John Heckewelder. On June 19 his house at Salem was completed, and he prepared it for his bride; for the "lot" no longer stood between him and Sara Ohneberg, and she was already on her way from Bethlehem to be united with him. She reached Schönbrunn on July 1. Next day Heckewelder, with a crowd of Indians from Salem, hastened over to welcome her. He returned to Salem on the 3rd; she followed him there a day later. With her came a large gathering of missionaries and Indians from the neighboring Christian villages to see Brother Bernard Adam Grube celebrate the Fourth of July by joining John Heckewelder and Sara Ohneberg * in holy matrimony. "I love her," wrote Heckewelder to Nathanael Seidel, August 9-10. The world seemed very good to him. "Oh how happy I am and all of us who have come here from Licthtenau," runs the letter, "to live in a place where we are not so disturbed by the world. As far as the outside world is concerned, we are now at peace, one almost forgets that there is a war."

---

* She is sometimes referred to as Susan and sometimes as Sarah. It is "Sara" in Zeisberger's "Catalogue," "Sarah" in *Alte Herrnhuter Familien*, pp. 48-49, but "Susanna" in the Bethlehem Church Register, *Tom* III, p. 229. It is "Sara" in the printed German edition (1826) of Heckewelder's "Memoir" or autobiography, but "Susan" in the English edition (1834) of the same.

The Bethlehem Church Register and the "Memoir" agree that the marriage took place at Lititz. They are undoubtedly mistaken. Other authorities—Zeisberger's "Catalogue," the Salem Diary, Heckewelder's letters—agree that it took place at Salem. A note in the Salem Diary of July 4 says, "Brother John Heckewelder and Sister Sara Ohneberg were united in Holy Matrimony by Brother Grube in a public service." The Bethlehem Church Register (II, 229) informs us that Sister "Susanna" was the daughter of George and Susanna Ohneberg, that she was born at Nazareth March 27, 1746, and that she died June 20, 1815.

※ XVII ※

Pachgantschihilas: 1781

JOHN HECKEWELDER, as we have already seen, kept the American authorities at Pittsburg informed of the movements of hostile Indians. But the enemy, too, had an intelligence service, and they took a dim view of these Moravian activities. The plot to kidnap Zeisberger, who was head of the Moravian settlements on the Muskingum, having failed, a movement took form to remove the Moravians as a body, white men and Indians alike, from their observation post on the Muskingum.

In the spring of 1781, Heckewelder had occasion to supply Colonel Brodhead (encamped with a body of troops a few miles below Salem) with provisions. Brodhead had come to destroy the Delaware capital of Goschachgunk, which he did, April 19. Heckewelder then had the shock of learning that the militia were with difficulty restrained by the Colonel from destroying the Moravian settlements. A few days later, on May 6, a party of warriors under Pachgantschihilas, "the head war chief of the Delaware Nation," * appeared at the Muskingum settlements and next day assembled the leading Moravian Indians at the village of Gnadenhütten for a parley.

Pachgantshihilas invited them to remove themselves to another place where they would be under his protection. He cited the Conestoga murders and the more recent atrocities

committed by the long knives (Virginians) on many of our relations, who lived peaceable neighbours to them on the Ohio! Did they not kill them without the least provocation?— Are they, do you think better now than

---
* Heckewelder, *Narrative*, p. 216.

they were then?— No, indeed not, and many days are not elapsed since you had a number of these very men near your doors, who panted to kill you, but fortunately were prevented from so doing by the *great Sun*, who, at that time, had by the great spirit been ordained to protect you! *

"Friends and relatives! you love that which is good, and wish to live in peace with all mankind, and at a place where you may not be disturbed whilst praying!— You are very right in this; and I do not reproach you in having made the choice!— But, my friends and relatives! does the place you at present are settled at, answer this purpose!— Do you not live in the very road the contending parties pass over when they go to fight each other!— Have you not discovered the footsteps of the long knives, almost within sight of your towns, and seen the smoke † rising from their camps! Should not this be sufficient warning to you; and lead you to consult your own safety! We have long since turned our faces towards your habitations, in the expectation of seeing you come from where you now are, to us where you would be out of danger; but you were so engaged in praying, that you did not discover our anxiety for your sakes!

"Friends and relatives!— Now listen to me and hear what I have to say to you.— I am myself come to bid you rise and go with me to a secure place! Do not my friends, covet the land you now hold under cultivation. I will conduct you to a country ‡ equally good, where your fields shall yield you abundant crops; and where your cattle shall find sufficient pasture; where there is plenty of game; where your women and children, together with yourselves, will live in peace and safety; where no long knife shall ever molest you!— Nay! I will live between you and them, and not even suffer them to frighten you!— There, you can worship your God without fear!— Here, where you are, you cannot do this!— Think on what I have now said to you, and believe, that if you stay where you now are, one day or the other, the long knives, will in their usual way, speak fine words to you, and at the same time murder you!" §—Heckewelder's *Narrative*, 217-219.

The Moravian Indians replied that they trusted the Long Knives, who sprang from the same soil as themselves and against whom "they, (the Christian Indians) had never committed a single hostile act . . ." ‖ They regretted that Pachgantschihilas had gone on the warpath, and declared that, as for themselves, "they lived very happy at their pres-

---

* The "great sun," is the name the Indians had given to col. Daniel Broadhead.—Heckewelder's note.

† Meaning the Militia camps, when col. Broadhead was out.—Heckewelder's note.

‡ The Miami country.—Heckewelder's note.

§ See Heckewelder's Historical account of the Indian Nations, chap. III.—Heckewelder's note.

‖ Heckewelder, *Narrative*, 220.

ent settlement and were at present much too heavy * to think of rising and going with him."

Pachgantschihilas declared that the right of choice was theirs. He accordingly departed. But first he paid a visit to Salem, in company with all his warriors, to see his old friend John Heckewelder, whom he had met at "Tuskorowas" nineteen years before. Isaac Glickhican, Heckewelder's "Helper" at that place, did the honors.

The gallant and generous Pachgantschihilas, having promised to leave the Moravian settlements in peace, was not feared. It was doubted that the Wyandot Half-King, Pomoacan, who had formerly invited them to that country, would now use force to remove them. But they were not sure about Captain Pipe. They knew he was a man of ability and understanding. They knew he was for the most part friendly. But they knew also that he could be ruthless. He was in touch with the British agents Elliot, McKee, and Simon Girty.

The weeks following Pachgantschihilas' visit were made anxious for the Moravians by rumors of intended violence and by instances of actual assault against the missionaries.

At Shonbrun, the missionary Senseman, who had gone into the field for some greens, was providentially saved, by two Brethren, coming up at the instant he was about being seized by an Indian enemy.— At Gnadenhutten the missionaries Edwards and Young, were near being shot by a white man, while they were planting potatoes in the field; and their lives were only saved by the captain of the war party, whom this white man had joined.† The writer of this narrative, was at two different times waylaid, while returning from Gnadenhutten to Salem; at one time by an Indian laying behind a log ‡ by the way side, and who had already levelled his piece at him, and the other time from the same Indian who lay concealed in the top of a tree, near the path he was to pass. Both times he was preserved by Christian Indians, providentially coming to his relief. Even an attempt was made by the same Indian to break into his house and murder him, but he was timely discovered by the people without, and prevented from carrying his designs into execution. This Indian was the same person of whom notice has already been taken as having received his education in Virginia—and was also the same person from whom the Christian Indians in March preceding had purchased the prisoner, whom they set at liberty. On being closely questioned by the national assistants respecting his attempt to take the life of their teacher, he replied:

---

* "Too heavy," means too much property, provisions, &c. on hand—immoveable property.—Heckewelder's note. *Narrative*, 220.

† See Heckewelder's Historical Account of the Indian Nations, chap. XLIV, page 339.—Heckewelder's note.

‡ Chapter XXXVIII, page 275 [279].—Heckewelder's note.

"that on his arrival at Sandusky, *without* the prisoner he had taken, he was upbraided, and called the Salem white man's slave, whom *he* must obey, the same, as he had so often told them, that the negroes in Virginia must obey their white masters—and that by and bye this Salem whiteman, would whip him also, if he did not obey his commands.— That the demand made on him for the prisoner, had been by the orders given by this white teacher, and therefore, if he did not wish to be considered by them, as a slave of that man, he must go back and take him, or his scalp, in place of the prisoner he had lost through him, &c. The Christian Indians perceiving the error the man, laboured under, thought proper to state the case to him correctly, by means of a speech, to which a string of wampum as a voucher, was annexed; which, with some presents in addition, served to prove that the purchasing of his prisoner by them, had been *their* own voluntary act, and done without the assistance or interference of their teacher.— At another time a dark looking Monsey, was on the point of shooting me, but luckily prevented by another Indian springing in between us; being questioned as to his designs against me, he replied, that, the Monseys had lost their fine country * by fraud † committed on them by people whose skin was of the colour of mine, and he, therefore, was an avowed enemy to all who had a white skin.—Heckewelder, *Narrative*, 226-28.

It was even reported that the Six Nations (who claimed title to the land on which the Moravians were settled, and who had assigned it to the Wyandots, who in turn had assigned it to the Delawares) had in council presented the Christian Indians on the Muskingum to the Chippewas and Ottawas "to make broth of."

How this threat must have affected Heckewelder, who had an almost superstitious belief in Six Nations malevolence (a belief which he imparted to Fenimore Cooper,‡ who knew nothing about the Indians at first hand) may readily be imagined.

There were so many of these escapes, each by so narrow a margin and with such well-timed intervention, that we are left wondering whether, after all, the assaults themselves may not have been staged for the purpose, not of killing the missionaries, but of frightening them away. Certainly it was not the policy of the Brititsh nor of the Indians to injure the Moravians. But it *was* their policy to have the Brethren removed—if possible without violence—from their present advantageous observation post. The Indian has always had a strong sense of humor.

---

* The Minisink, together with their settlements in the forks.—Heckewelder's note.
† Alluding to the long walk in the year 1737.—Heckewelder's note.
‡ See Wallace, "John Heckewelder's Indians and the Fenimore Cooper Tradition," *Proceedings of the American Philosophical Society*, Vol. 96, No. 4 (August, 1952), pp. 496 ff.

Pachgantschihilas: 1781

Was he indulging this faculty for a political end when, on raising his gun sights to a Moravian missionary, he allowed his aim so opportunely to be diverted and himself so easily persuaded to let his victim live?

Be that as it may, the Moravians were not easily frightened. They remained at their posts, with the result that the British in the end were constrained to use stronger measures to remove them.

On the afternoon of the 10th of August, the half king with an hundred and forty armed men suddenly appeared before the town of Salem, with British colours flying, and having formed for themselves a large camp, the colours were set in the centre, where Captain Elliot, with the half king, and Mr. M'Cormick, (the flag bearer,) had their tents fixed.—Heckewelder, *Narrative*, 232.

XVIII

Enter the Half King: 1781

FROM THIS POINT ON, we shall rely, not on Heckewelder's printed *Narrative*, but on his contemporary manuscript, "Captivity and Murder," written some forty years earlier. The manuscript is more detailed and exact than the printed account. In the former, his captors are "Indians," many of them mentioned by name. In the printed *Narrative*, they have become "savages," no doubt in compliance with the popular taste of a later time. It will be recalled that there was a magnanimity exhibited towards their enemies by the principal participants in the Revolution. The brooding jingoism of literary convention was a later development.

Certain words and passages which appeared in the original manuscript but have there been crossed out, are here enclosed within brackets and italicized.

The advent of the Wyandot Half King, Pomoacan or Sweet House, was made in the grand style.

. . . the 10th day of August at 3 in the afternoon they arrived in the following Manner. The half King with his Men from Upper Sandusky. Abraham Evan with the Wyondotts from Lower Sandusky— The Wyondotts from Detroit—Mingoes— The two Shawano Captains known by the Name of the Snakes [John and Thomas]— The Captains Pipe, and Wingenund with their Men from Upper Sandusky—Mathew Elliot (titled Captn Elliot) Allex$_{dr}$ Mc Cormick with 6 other English and French as their Attendants, besides Monsy's, Delawares and Mohicans with some Chibbaways, from different places. They endeavoured to make a grand Appearance being chiefly

Enter the Half King: 1781

mounted in a Warlike Manner on Horseback, one Man bearing an English Flag, riding in the middle, which they afterwards constantly kept flying at their Camp. The first job they did on their Arrival at Salem was as their custom is, a beggarly Speech for some Tobacco to smoke. They visited John Heckewelder, Missionary of this Place and pretended great friendship towards him. They afterwards made an introductory Speech to Us in general, and according to Custom brightened our Eyes, cleaned our Ears and sat our Hearts torights, that we might see, hear and understand well, what they had to say to Us. They received an Answer to this in the common Manner— They were waited upon with Victuals according to the custom of Ind.^{s} but were desired to behave orderly, and keep their young Men from hollowing and running after the Women &c—to which they readily agreed. In the Evening Mathew Elliot pay'd me a Visit, and tho he pretended to know nothing of all what they were come here for, would frequently break out in hypocritical Lamentations. The next Day they set off for Gnadenhütten, and for several Days after there arrived other Company's to join them, some of which were to the Number of 40, so that there were at least near 300 together. They encamped on the green on the Top of the Bank of the River, Mathew Elliot being in the midst of them.

The half King made a Speech to the following Effect. That they were to come to see their Cousins the Christian Indians— That they loved them— That they should be exceedingly Sorry if any thing bad should happen to them, that they were well convinced that their Cousins sought after nothing else but to please God—that they knew nothing about War—that they wished allways to live in Peace, and that Peace was a very good thing—that it was true their Cousins knew every thing that was good, and were ignorant to what was bad. Yet it would be good for them likewise to know something which their Oncle seeth, who knew both what was good and bad, and had now to tell them, further that your Oncle seeth two very black Clouds, that they were blowing towards one another and you are right in the middle between them. Two mighty Gods with their Mouth wide open are in these, and when they meet together while you are here, they will swallow you up. Cousins you will attend to what your Uncle says. I lift you up from where you are now, and set you down on a good place near Sandusky where the Sky is clear, there you will find every thing prepared for you, and nothing to disturb you in worshipping God, according as you are used to do &c— This Speech caused much Concern with Us for in the first place none of Us had any inclination ever to leave these places, which were so well improved, & where we had our support and then we saw, that we should be intirely ruined if we was to move away from the towns, especially at this time of the year. We consulted one another on the Matter, & gave them the following Answer: That we had well consider'd what we had been told—that it was true we sought nothing but what was good—& that we might please God—for this reason we chose to live by ourselves, where we might not be disturbed by those who loved evil—that we had allways been sorry whenever we had seen our Countrymen to go or come from murdering—as we had a good Conscience we had no Reason to think, the 2 Gods with the black Clouds would hurt Us—that we even had not seen these Clouds, but on the other hand saw it quite light about us—we never could expect to live so quiet & peaceable, where they would settle Us, & we thought it imposing upon Us to leave a place where we had every thing plenty & move into the wilderness where we should find nothing, & as it was now allready the beginning of the fall, the Winter was at hand, if we obey your demand we should infallibly all perish— But that we would desire our Uncle to leave us time to consider of the Matter untill Spring, when we would return an answer—

With this our Answer they seemed to be very well satisfied, & many of Us believed the Matter intirely over; but a certain person in the Indian Country who was a Wellwisher to the Br^{ns} Mission, had found Means to acquaint one of the Missionaries of the whole that was carrying on against them & that some English of whom Matth. Elliot was one, were determined to destroy Us one way or the other, & for this Reason the latter was gone allong with the Warriors. Indeed we found it the Case, for after we had been at home a few days, we were suddenly called together again, & a Speech of a more severe Nature deliv^d to Us, in which we were warned to move off as soon as possible, for they said at times that the Mingoes, & then again at other times—the Chipewas & Tawas would fall upon Us & destroy Us all— That it was impossible for Us to escape all, one or the other certainly would be upon Us, & if even the Nations would let us alone, the Virginians would not—for we had seen but the other day, how they killed their friends at Goschachking.* The same they would also do with us one day or other—they speak good to you with their Lips, but not from their hearts— Since they now rec^d no satisfactory Answer in their Opinion, & we did not immediately agree to their Demands they began to be hostile, first to dance & sing the War Song, then killed our fowls & hogs & Cattle sent parties to War—committed thefts &c.

By this time we saw plainly what was approaching & that we either would forcibly be taken off, or killed & therefore only wished that all our good friends & particularly our Brr^n in Bethl^m might know what was become of Us, for which reason we privately sent 2 Messengers off to Pittsburg, who were to return immediately.

The Warriors hav^g some intelligence of it, followed & waylaid them, when on their return they [*ran up &*] took them prisoners & searched them diligently even to taking off their Cloths, but finding no Letters, took their horses & rifles from them & let them go home.—"John Heckewaelders Narrative of the Indian Mission on Muskingum: Captivity & Murder," pp. 16-21.

---

* The Expedition against Goschachking in the Spring had caused that a Number of the friendly Indians turned to the other side.—Note in the margin of Heckewelder's Ms.

Enter the Half King: 1781

It must be doubted whether the Indian messengers actually reached Pittsburgh as Heckewelder thought, for in the Bethlehem Diary of September 27 we read that a garbled version of the incident had reached the Brethren there, by a very round-about route:

From Philadelphia we received a Copy of a Letter from a good friend in *Pittsburg* written to a Brother in *Yorktown*, to this effect: That an Indian woman had brought the following news to *Fort McIntosh*: That a body of about 400 *Warriors* had surrounded our Indian *Towns* on the Muskingum, made all our Indian men and women prisoners, bound the white Brethren hand and foot, and removed them (presumably to Detroit) and at the time this Indian woman escaped, had destroyed their corn and killed their cattle.

We resume the narrative in "Captivity and Murder":

Elliot, who had been very busy ever since he came here first, yet endeavoured privately [*now*] to put it into the Heads of the Warriors that these Messengers had been sent, to bring the Virginians upon them (the Warriors) and it was agreed upon, that each of these Messengers should have a seperate Examination.

This being done & nothing at all found to condemn them, they became quiet again; but it appeared that for all there was some Uneasiness among Some of them & especially Elliot, who kept continually his Sword in Hand.— They councelled Day after Day—some were for putting to Death at once, all those of us who were not willing to go with them both Whites & Indians; Others grew angry at the Proposal, and threatened such as would molest their Relations:—again on the other hand they were afraid of us, having heard by the by that some of our young Men should have said, that if ever they saw any body offer to touch their Ministers, they would immediately dispatch such— It appeared that this Elliot had likewise a dread of such of our own People.

They enquired diligently of all Warriors & Prisoners that came in, whether the Americans were not coming to the Assistance of the Christian Indians, or to fall upon them.— Fear encreasing.— Men & Women who were to carry off the Plunder arrived.— Elliot impatient to See the Matter done— They assembled to consult, & which was to be the last Time. They then sent for the Ministers to meet with their elderly Men (Helpers) once more, to hear what they had to Say to them yet. The Day appointed for meeting was the 2^d of Septr when in the Morning as John Heckewelder Minister of Salem Congregation was getting on his Horse a white Man (belonging to the Party) wispered in his Ears that before to morrow Night we would all be prisoners. In the Evening of that Day we had the same Account by an Indian, who wished we could be brought off privately in this Night, but this not only being impracticable, we being seperately at 3 Places, our Women incapable of travelling by Night, 2 of them having, likewise small Children, the Mother of one brot to Bed but 4 Days ago, & the Warriors continually watching us.—

Besides all this we looked upon it as our Duty to abide by our Congregations as well in Time of Danger, as Peace. We were satisfied as to that, to live & to dye with them, having laboured a great many years in gathering what we had, & knowing the only Comfort left to our poor Indians would be—in remaining with them.

The conference to which the missionaries and elders had been summoned was at Gnadenhütten. There Heckewelder presented himself on September 2.

On the 3^d Day of September at 8 in the morning we were at prayers in the Church according to our daily Custom. M^r McKormick * who was a friend to us (& could in no ways avoid going along with Elliot for fear of being treated as a Rebel, & loosing all his property which lay in the Woods) was present—and gave us by the by a Hint of what would be done.— At 11 o Clock our Helpers were called together, the Matter of our removal hitherto proposed by the Chiefs not being agreed to, it was now according to Custom put into the Hands of the Captains † who made a very rash Speech to us, & accused us of having been Friends to the Virginians during all the War, and by Intelligence given to them been the Cause of [*many of their lives saved*] saving the Lives of many Virginians, & loss of Lives on their Side.

They insisted now for the last Time that we might get ready & go off with them, & demanded a positive Answer.

Even to this the 3^d Time they were ready to let us remain here, & said in general Councill, that they really found no Comfort in destroying the Christian Indians; they being an honest, upright People, having no Delight in any bad Thing, but on the contrary wishing well to every body, & being Friends to their Enemies, it would be well if every body was like them. They had indeed given full Proof [*that they were*] but a few Days before that they were averse towards the Task which had been given them; for they shott down the Flag which had been stuck up at Elliotts Camp—& threw it into the Fire, as a means of discouraging the English.

But Elliot seeing the Matter so long delayed—altho' feeling trouble & Fear, yet not tired, endeavoured for this last Time to do his utmost. He ordered the Councell together, and demanded of them to know immediately, whether they would obey their Fathers Ordres or not.—he told them, that they had been fighting the Virginians ‡ this long Time, & consequently the latter had become their Enemies, & they had no Quarters to expect from that

---

* He was a Trader, and friend to our Mission.—Note in margin of MS.

† It is a custom with the Indians, that wherever force is to be exerted, the Capt^{ns} take the Command.—Note in margin of MS.

‡ It is to be observed that altho the Ind^s know the difference between every State, and have a particular Name for each, they in this War thro all in a lump, and say (when they mean the Americans in gen^l) the Big Knifes (Virginians).—Note in margin of MS.

Enter the Half King: 1781

side: Then he asked them if they wished for more Enemies, & how they could expect to have their Father (the English) for Friends, when they would not obey him— He threatened them with having his Horses fetched in immediately & Setting off for [*the*] Detroit to acquaint their Father of the Matter, and assured them that they would not only loose all Favour with their Father, but be looked upon as Enemies.— With these Words he walked off to the Woods.— The Indians fearing the Fire on both Sides at length agreed—& at 3 o Clock in the Afternoon, while we were walking together back of the Garden— The Wyondotts suddenly rushed in among us took us by the Hand & went with us Prisoners * to the Camp, which was ab.^{t} 100 Yards distant, giving the Death Halloa for each of us Seperately.—

["It is difficult to describe," Heckewelder wrote elsewhere, "the impression which the *scalp-yell* . . . makes on a person who hears it for the first time."—*History*, p. 217.]

Here we Stood in the Midst of them, not knowing what would be done with us.

Every Man in the Camp flew to his Gun, & those whose piece had been discharged loaded them instantly. Several Wyondotts came up to us, & strip'd us of our best Cloaths examining our Pocketts—taking from us Sleeve buttons & buckles—& 4 Watches. A very dark looking Munsy step'd up to us after we had been strip'd & took one after the other by the Hair, shook us by the Head; saying: quavang'omelen n Ishu. That is: I salute you my Friends; another Delaware (Sam! Grey by Name) seeing this, scolded at him & bid him get away immediately; saying I think these People do not deserve such treatment—what are you ab.^{t}—

M.^{r} McCormick who had not expected that they would have been so quick about it as they were, ran up to us, & led us to his Tent, there he lent us Cloaths & blanketts to throw ab.^{t} us, it being a cool Evening.— We enquired for Mr Elliot, but were answered that he was not to be found.

At last Abraham Cuhn with others of the Wyandotts came up— They took 2 of us to one Camp & 2 to another, where we were ordered to Sit down & here we was kept under Guard. While those with us were buisy in stripping us of what was worth any thing the Ministers House was crouded with others who robbed the same. Whatever they had no Use to make of, they destroyed; for Instance: They ripped open the Bedds, & emptied the Feathers in the Streets—

---

* When Warriors fetch in Prisoners or Scalps they give notice by a Halloo, so that it may be known by the People in the Village what success they met with, before they appear. At their entrance the Prisoners are ordered to run to the War-Post, and clap their Hands to it. The Towns People run after them endeavouring to knock them down, which they may do before they reach the Post, but afterwards dare not touch them.

They ran with us to a certain spot in the Camp, and altho several Villians endeavoured to strike us with their Tomhacks, we escaped, but the Scalp Halloo was called over Us the same as by others.—Note in margin of MS.

Coffee they emptied in the Street likewise, to get the Bags. In Short, there was nothing left in the House, that was worth any thing. But even all this was not the worst of the Matter; the Ministers who were now Prisoners, had left their Wives & Children at home, & we had observed, that the Moment we were brought into the Camp, a Number of Warriors got on Horseback, some went off for Salem & others for Shoenbrunn, who had all kinds of War Instruments with them, galloping & Shouting all along. Here we felt something, which words cannot express—

Night approaching with Rain & it being cool, we suffered for want of something to cover us, altho' it was impossible for any one to Sleep, being impatient to hear what had become of our Families and the others of our Colleagues, we had left behind, the one living at Salem,* the other at Shoenbrunn.† At length We heard the Scalp Halloo both up & down the River; it lasted continually for a full Hour before the first arrived.

About Midnight Michael Jung from Salem was brought into the Camp.

The Warriors had rushed on to the House where they found the Door bolted—they demanded Entrance imediately but as Mich! Young did not comply with their Demand, they split the Door & broke into the House. A Wyondott made a Stroke with his Tomahawk at Mich! Young—but Ab.r Cuhn who observed it, averted the Stroke.

They took him, My ‡ Wife & Child (the latter out of the Cradle) Prisoners, but upon the Supplication of many Women belonging to us, who promised faithfully to take the Woman and Child to them in the Morning, they were left with them. They robbed the House of every Thing, did the same with the Bedds as they had done at Gnadenhütten, & rode of with Mich.l Young.— About half an Hour after the Arrival of these that Party which had been at Shoenbrunn arrived likewise.

These had Robbed the 2 Houses of David Zeisberger & George Youngman under Pretence of saving every thing for them, from the greedy Hands of others; taking Geo. Youngman with his Wife the Wifes of Zeisberger & Gottlob Senseman (the latter being brought to bed 4 Days before) Prisoners. They put them into a Canoe & bro.t them in the Dark Rainy Night ab.t 15 Miles down a dangerous piece of the River. The Death Halloo being given at their Arrival. Mean while this happened the first Party (namely those from Salem) had been looking over their Spoil, & after Sharing it with those who had remained at the Camp to guard us, they lay down to Sleep. One Wyondott Man,§ who had not been along and had just now rec.d his Share, got up & gave me his Share back again, the others tho' seeing it, seemed to take no Notice of it.—Heckewelder, "Captivity & Murder," 22-29.

---

* Michael Young—Note in MS.
† Geo: Youngman—Note in MS.
‡ J.no Heckewelders Wife & Child.—Note in MS.
§ A Young Man belonging to the Village at the French Church opposite Detroit.—Note in margin of MS.

XIX

Captivity: 1781

IT WAS DURING Heckewelder's first night of captivity, September 3, 4 —the night when he heard the "death hallo" coming from Salem, where he had left his wife and baby Polly (Johanna Maria, born April 6)—that an Indian girl of Gnadenhütten earned her place among the heroines of the Revolution.

Towards the Morning of the 4.th a young Woman,* who having been an Eye Wittness of the Treatment we met with, by the Warriors, & having shed a Torrent of Tears on the Occasion resolved within herself to set off immediately & acquaint the Commanding Officer Col. Broadhead at Pittsburgh of the whole.—

This Young Woman, tho having her Mother and Relations living with us at Salem never told a single Soul what she was about, but knowing that Capt Pipe had an exceeding good Horse on which she could rely, She caught it in the Woods & made off: & altho She was closely pursued, never could be overtaken.

This causing great Uneasiness in the Camp— Capt Pipe called all the Warriors together, & accused us in a most severe Manner of having sent this Woman off to call the Americans to our Assistance. It was immediately con-

---

* A relative to one of the Indian Helpers [Glickhican], who in remorse & Sorrow for her wicked Ways among the Indians had obtained Leave to dwell among the Christian Indians. She had been a Notorious Whore formerly, but of late struck within her self and begged so long for leave to Live in the Congregation, promising to reform that We agreed to make a trial with her.—Note in the MS.

cluded that Isaac * who not only was a near Relation to the Woman, but being one of the chief Helpers belonging to the Congregations, should be taken Prisoner & strictly examined about the Cause. Accordingly a Capt with ab.^{t} twelve Men were sent to Salem as the place of his Residence who surrounded, took & tied him, and brought him up to Gnadenhütten in the Camp.

When Isaac observed them fearfull ab.^{t} taking him, he encouraged them saying:

There was a Time in which I never could have suffered any Body to take me Prisoner: in that Time I lived a Heathen Life, & knew nothing of the true God, but since thro' the Grace of God I have been converted unto him, I suffer every thing willingly for his Sake.

He was examined before the Half King & set at Liberty again, as being innocent in the Matter. A Letter which had been written to Dav.^{d} Zeisberger, a good many Years ago by Commissioners sent by Government to treat with the Ind.^{s} at Pittsburg, inviting him to attend at Said Treaty with some of the principle of our Indians, being found among others of his papers, the same was produced by Abraham Kuhn, & D. Zeis.^{r} accused of carrying on a correspondence with the Americans; but the Contents being afterwards examined, and the Date showing that the Letter had been wrote some Time before the beginning of the War, this was put aside again.

We having aplied to the Delaware Capt.^{ns} to return us the Cloathing they had taken from us, not being able to bear the Cold— Captn Pipe made a Speech to his People for the Purpose, who readily agreed to this Demand, but as the most as also the best of our Things were in the Hands of the Wyondotts; we were told that they would by no means return any thing, & threatened: that if we would say any thing more ab.^{t} it, they would know what to do with Us—meaning they would dispatch us. Abraham Kuhn with some of his Men, had in the mean time paid my House at Salem a second Visit, expecting to find something yet belonging to me. I had a Number a Bee Hives, a Quantity of Tobacco, & an excellent Garden out of which they took what they wanted, destroying the Remainder.—

The Indian Women of Gnadenhutten bo.^{t} at their own Cost (Expence) Sundry of our Cloathes from the Wyondotts, & chearfully brought them to us again.—

David Zeisberger & John Heckewelder was Served up a Meal on a Table dressed by the Warriors in a decent Manner, & with Napkins taken from us, which were afterwards laid asside again. Some of our White Woemen now Prisoners, were obliged to make Shirts for the Warriors out of the Linnen taken from them the Day before.

---

* Isaac [Glickhican] who had been formerly a Remarkable & principle Man among them, was enveyed and hated to such a degree since he had become Converted unto Our Saviour, that every Word he spoke was a Sting on them. They also knew that he understood their Tricks and was able to defeat them.—Note in MS.

Captivity: 1781

A [*Wyondott known by the name of Snip* * *who*] had William Edwards & Senseman [*Gnadnhüttⁿ Missionaries*] Prisoners in his Camp, suspecting the Latter [*being a . . . young Man*] might endeavour to make his Escape, was buisy in making a P.^r of Stocks to put him in but he (Senseman) assuring him that he never would attempt anything of the kind, more over as his Wife & little Child was with him, he quit this buissiness.

In the Evening several Parties of Warriors came in, & War Dances were kept during the greatest Part of the Night.

About 10 or 11 o Clock at Night a Report was spread in the Camp: That the Wifes of the Missionaries had deserted and were gone off to Pittsburg: I was sudden awakened by Abr.^m Kuhn who demanded of me to account for it. I assured him, that there could be no truth in the matter, and that whosoever must have spread the Report must be a Liar. Kuhn insisted on my going with him to where our Women was to sleep, which I readily did, knowing that 2 lay in one House & 2 in the other. He was so particular, that after shoing him with a Light where 2 Women lay in Bed together, he would not be satisfied without hearing each of them speak to me for fear of Deceit. Thus ended this troublesome Day and Night. In the Morning on the 5th the Warriors having assembled agreeable to Orders, and both Prisoners and Scalps being brought in the Evening before an open Councel was held, in which was reported: that the Prisoners an old Man and Boy had been examined whether they knew if the Ministers had sent to Fort Pitt for Assistance or not, and the Boy had declared that he had heard they had done the like; consequently a charge was laid against Us. Now since they had 2 Prisoners and a Scalp, the Scalp or Death hollow according to custom was repeated at different Times by a Delaware Chippewa and Tawa Man. They made all the Game of the poor old Man they ever could and let him stand stark naked among them for some Time to have their Diversion &c. Elliot who had on the Day we were taken Prisoners dispatched a Messenger to acquaint Cap.^{tn} McKee at the Shawano Town, that the Business was compleated, and we the Missionaries Prisoners, now appeared again. He pretended before Us to be sorry for what had happened, and gave us a caution that we had not done right in being so stubborn in the beginning. We ought to have agreed imediately which if we had done, We would have not been taken neither robbed in such a manner. To this we might have given him a suitable Answer, had it been the proper Time for it, and tho he pretended to show Compassion in seeing Us deprived of many Necessaries, he would never endeavour to try to get or release any thing for Us, tho indeed in his Power, but got several valuable Articles which he kept for himself. On the 6th a War party came in again without having done any Mischief. A Ottawa Man who had a suit of Cloths belonging to us dressed in the same, and mounting a Horse rode up

---

* Snip (a Mingo) a Notorious Villian and Murderer of whom both White People & Ind^s are afraid.—Note in MS.

and down in the Camp, which, (he cutting a very odd figure) created much laughter among the whole.*

Marcus One of our principle Helpers who had taken much pains to release us from Captivity had had the pleasure in the Afternoon of this Day to hear the Chiefs Pipe and Winginund declare to us, that if we would submit and willingly go with them to Sandusky, we should have the privilege of being with our Indians on the Way; to be taken care off, and assisted by them, and that for this Purpose we should order all our Indians in the 3 Towns to get ready imediately, for that in a Day or 2 we must alltogether leave these Towns. We having no other choice, readily agreed to this, and became thereby at Liberty in some Measure, after which I imediately applied to Cap.^{tn} Pipe for Leave to go to Salem in order to get every thing ready for the Journey, and as Elliot was likewise ready to go to that place, I got Permission to go with him. The half King had likewise enquired of John Bull (a Man belonging to our Society and many Years since lawfully married to an Ind.^{n} Woman) whether he was willing to go along or not, and being answered in the Affirmative, was likewise ordered to get ready. The Village stunk now so of the dead Carcasses of Hogs which had been shot down by the Warriors for Diversion, that it began to become very disagreeable to abide therein any longer. On our Arrival at Salem every Soul belonging to the Village ran up to me. They embraced me weeping and rejoicing. Elliot hardly able to bear seeing this stept aside with these words, "I never believed that your people loved you so much." Even the little Children took me by the Hand, and would hardly suffer me to be out of their Sight. The Sisters provided Tea and Victuals, and we comforted one another. The next day being the 8th Dav. Zeisberger with his Colleagues their Wifes and Children with a Number of our Indians arrived by Water likewise at Salem, the remainder following by Land. from Shönbrun also arrived the greatest part by Water and Land. All the Warriors, the half King and a Number of Wyondotts axepted, who were gone to Schönbrunn, to look for plunder and afterwards set Fire to the Town, came and encamped round about the Place. The greatest part of the horn Cattle and Horses belonging to the 3 Towns as also the Warriors Horses which were a great many in Number, were turned in a large Corn field ripe for the Harvest. It was indeed a very melancholy Prospect, both to see so much Labour lost, as also the Destruction of so much food, for at a moderate calculation there could be no less than between 4 and 5000 bushels of Corn in the fields, besides what lay in the Houses. In short it is

---

* This incident is more fully treated in Heckewelder's *Narrative*, p. 272, where he tells of "the addresses paid us by a jovial, and probably harmless Ottawa Indian, who, having obtained of the Wyandott warriors, sufficient of our clothes, to dress himself like a white man; and placing a white night cap on his head, being mounted on a horse, would ride through the camps, nodding to us every time he passed; caused much amusement through the camp, and in some measure, to us also."

not in the Power of any of us to compute our Loss precisely for even in that of Hogs there were some hundreds left behind with young Cattle and poultry which the Warriors soon destroyed.—Heckewelder, "Captivity and Murder," pages 29-37.

⚔ XX ⚔

Upper Sandusky: 1781

WE LEARN from David Zeisberger's journal that the prisoners were taken by way of Coshocton, up the Walhonding and Kokosing Rivers, past the Indian town of Gokhosing (Habitation of Owls) to the Sandusky River. From Heckewelder's journal, we learn more of their adventures on the way:

We had now to provide for a long tedious Journey and were badly off for want of Horses, every one coveting the Use of his own, and 2 of ours being taken from Us, however Our Indians prepared a very large Canoe for our Use, and took what little we had to carry on their own Horses or Backs. At lenght after having according to our Custom been at prayer in the Church on Sunday, orders were given the next Day, namely Monday the 9th for marching, and we had to bid farewell to our Peacefull Habitations. On this Journey to Upper Sandusky we had many fatalities, Elliot with his gang kept Company with us for several Days, untill we came to where the Road turned off for the Shawano Towns; Indeed he had lived this long Time (but especially since our Captivity) in continual Fear, for which Reason he kept his Sword constantly in hand. The half King with his Men had by this Time come up with us, and encamped in the Front, leaving Pipe and Wingenund in the Rear. A very high fresh unexpectedly took 2 of our Canoes off, which was of great Loss to us: on the other Hand 3 of our young Men seeing the 2 Horses which had been taken from us, at the Wyondott Camp, took the Resolution, and took them with the Saddles, which likewise belonged to Us away from them. They lent us 2 of their own Horses to ride on, and kept these in their Care, for Fear if they were with us, they might be taken away again. A party of Warriors went of to War from this place, among which were 2 of the half Kings Sons, which (namely the latter) never after returned

Upper Sandusky: 1781

again. In the following Days we were hurried on very much, even so that a Wyondott gave Michel Jung a Stroke on his Back ordering him to push on. We had in the whole a very disagreeable Journey, untill at last we arrived on the 1st October at the old Upper Sandusky Town, where we were left entirely by all the Warriors to shift for ourselves. It being the Fall of the Year and hard frosty Nights, we imediately began to build small Houses, not knowing at the same time what we should live upon in the course of the Winter. Some Days after our Arrival the half King made a Speech to us to the following purpose: That we were now in his Dominions, and must obey him both in going to War with him, and other Respects. This was far from the fair Promises he had made us in the Beginning when tempting us at our Towns, and we now plainly saw, that the Devil was about to destroy us. however we were not entirely discouraged. Mean while we were building our Houses, Elliot who as related above, after leaving Us for the Shawanoe Towns, had gone from thence to Detroit, and whatever his Bussness might have been there. he now produced a Speech to the Delaw. Chiefs from Major De Poyster, Comandant of that place, in which we all (namely the Missionaries) were ordered to come imediately and bring some of our principal Men with Us. Wingenund delivered the Message to us, with Orders to be ready, and meet Cap^{tn} Pipe at an appointed place, and from thence to be under his Direction. Alltho now late in the Season, and the Prospect of a fatuiging Journey, we had no other Choice than to go, but concluded that 2 of us should remain at home with our Wifes, untill we would further know what would be done with us. Accordingly David Zeisberger, John Heckewelder, Gottlob Senseman and William Edwards set of with 4 of our Helpers about the beginning of Novr for Detroit, and George Youngman and Michael Joung remained at home with the Congregation.

On the Way to the Tawa River (otherwise called Miami) we overtook a great many Delawares bound for Detroit and at last Cap^{tn} Pipe who lay waiting for us. We were scarcely arrived at this Place when a Messenger came Gallopping on with the hallow of Fear * after alighting he cominicated that Mr Bull with his family and others with him who had gone down to Muskingum to fetch up some Corn, were taken prisoners by the Virginians, and most certainly put to Death by this Time. This News being afterwards confirmed by other Messengers, with an addition: that the Virginians were marching on for Sandusky, and might by this time have finished the whole of the Moravians at that place, was a great Discouragement to Us on this

---

* Whenever there is Danger in any Place the Ind^s send off a Runner to all Villages in the Country round about. This Runner gives the Hollow of Fear, or Sound of Danger as he runs allong and before he enters the Village the People, Men Women and Children are Assembled to hear the News. Is there present Danger they run off altogether, or take the Women and Children to the Woods in the first place. The Runner keeps on to the Next Village, or if he be to much fatigued another must go in his stead.—Note in MS.

Journey. Whilest we were encamped together, and daily Indians arriving to receive presents from the English (there being a Vessel loaded with Goods arrived in the River for that Purpose) Cap^{tn} Pipe with the others had some Rum conveyed to them, and they soon fell a Quarreling and fighting among themselves. In this disagreeable Situation we were for a few Days, expecting Pipe to get sober that we might go on, for indeed we were much concerned about our families at home, not having had sufficient to leave them for to live upon untill our return. Suffering thus for Trouble Fear and impatience, who should make his Appearance but Elliot again. Here he was come to distribute the Goods among the Indians, and it was expected that at least 5 or 600 would assemble within a few Days. Pipe not leaving off drinking, and Liquor plenty, we applied to Elliot for Leave to go on, which he granted Us, then afterwards requesting a Pass, he likewise promised it to us, but could not fullfil his Promise, since he could not write. However we went on with our Indians and arrived at Detroit.—Heckewelder, "Captivity and Murder," 37-41.

⚔ XXI ⚔

Detroit: 1781

IN THE VIVID PASSAGE that follows from Heckewelder's journal, "Captivity and Murder," we find the missionaries on trial before the British Commandant at Detroit, Major De Peyster. It is Captain Pipe who steals the show. That chivalrous, though at times ruthless, warrior carried all through the war an admiration for the Moravians and what they were doing for his people, though he opposed them politically. He is usually remembered today as the chief who refused to intercede on Colonel Crawford's behalf when the latter was about to be put to death by torture. He refused because he believed Colonel Crawford had brought his militia out to Upper Sandusky in order to liquidate what remained of the Moravian Indians after Colonel Williamson's exploit at Gnadenhütten. Pipe should be remembered, rather, for his part in bringing about the release of the Moravians from the charge of treason. Introduced as the chief complainant against Heckewelder and his fellow missionaries, Captain Pipe gave witness instead for the defense.

The centry at the west Gate of the Town would at first sight not let us pass in, it being a Custom at Detroit, that in War times no White Person whatsoever be suffered to enter the Gate of the Town, except a Pass, Indian or Indians with him, but an Officer seeing Indians with us ordered him to let us go on. We passed on to the East end Gate, near which the Governors House is, and informed the Command^t through a Serj^t of our Arrival. We had to wait about a quarter of an Hour untill Mr Baby * Commissary for

---
* He spells his Name Baby, but is pronounced as Bawbee.—Heckewelder's note.

whom the Comand.^t had sent came. Major De Poyster the Comandant charged us of being detrimental to Government, and threatened in some Measure of sending Us down in the Country, but after a closer Examination, and finding chearfull to all the Accusations laid against Us, he informed us, that we should be lodged in a private House, and wait the Arrival of Cap.^{tn} Pipe, who was expected in a few Days. Accordingly Mr Bawbee (otherwise Baby) conducted us to the House of Mr Tybout * where we were entertained well. Here we had the privilege of walking about the City, but as we wished for a speedy Examination or Trial, we begun to be impatient, especially as the Winter was near at hand. While we were thus in a Manner confined (at least to the Town) several Officers of Rank visited us. Others, Gentlemen of the place, wished to converse with us but durst not venture for Fear of Suspition. We longed to send a petition to the Major, but applying to Mr Baby for Paper, Pen and Ink, it was refused Us. we were obliged to rest easy. At lenght Cap.^{tn} Pipe with his Councellors arrived. They walked Up the Street to the Government House with their Scalps hollowing the Death Hallow, and the next Day were ordered to meet in Councill.

In the Councill House were on the one Side the Delawares seated, and on the other Mingoes and different Nations, in the Middle a Table and Secretary, by the side of the Table, Major De Poyster and Mr Baby on Chairs, next to them Officers and Gentlemen, and behind these Interpreters and Servants, and we the Missionaries on a bench by ourselves opposite the Table. The Councill was opened with a few words by the Major, to which the Delaware Chief Pipe made a long Speech, at the close of which he gave the Major a bunch of Scalps † tied to a Stick, which were set by in a Corner. A Mingo Man made a like Speech and gave the Major 3 Scalps tied to a Stick, which were also sat in the Corner. The next was an Introductory Speech concerning us, followed by a Report brought in, and Accusations against us. The Major had been informed this 3 years past that We were People who either had no proper home, or were appointed and sent out by Congress to oppose Government in their Proceedings against the States. That we had been the Cause of many of the Enemies Lifes saved, and those of theirs the Indians lost, and that it appeared to be without Doubt, that we had corresponded with the Americans throughout this War, &c. The Major demanded of us to know in what Manner, and how long we had resided among the Indians, and being answered, that We were sent by the Bishops of our Church to preach the Gospel to the Indians, and had this 30 Years past been successful therein.

He then demanded to know, wether Congress paid any Attention to Us or had made us promises of any kind, to which he was answered: That Congress wished that all the Indians in the Woods might be converted and civilized,

---

* Mr. Bawbee took us to the house of a private French family, which consisted of Mr Tybout and wife (both elderly people,) and having no children.—*Narrative,* 289-90.

† 7 Scalps.—Note in MS.

and had given the same encouragement for that Purpose to us, as had been given formerly by Government. Several other Questions being asked and satisfactory Answers given, the Question was put to Captain Pipe and his Councellors (they being in the Character of Complainants) wether really the Blame was to be laid upon the Moravian Teachers, or not. Pipe, waiting some time in vain for his Speaker to answer, rose and defended us to his utmost; saying that he (meaning the Delaware Councel) was alone to be blamed— That We the Missionaries lived among them and must submit to their Demands. Then said Major De Peyster, they are declared innocent by yourselves, and you have no Reason to find Fault with them on this Account any more. Then turning to us he said, Gentlemen! You have ever since I have comanded this Post been continually accused of acting the Part of Enemies to Government. I never knew who you were or where you come from, but finding that nothing would serve but to remove you from your Settlements, I at lenght gave Orders to the purpose, but my Orders have been exeeded. He demanded of the Delawares to know, wether they were agreed that we should live longer among them, and Cap^{tn} Pipe told him we might, etc. Then turning again to us said. I for my Part have no Objection to your going out again, and I will not only furnish you with a Pass, but also give herewith Orders to Mr Bawbee to give you some Cloathing and Necessaries, imagining by what I have heard you must be greatly in Want.—

He further added, You will always do well not to trouble Yourselves abt. the War. War is my Buissiness, for I am a Warrior, etc.

The Councill broke up, & Mr Bawbee with the Assistance of 2 interpreters gave us sufficient of clothing etc. & we were preparing to set off the next day.

But 6 of our Horses which had been put in the Care of a Frenchman, & which one or the other of us had seen daily, were now missing & never afterwards accounted for.

A Gentleman from Sandusky lent us 2 of his Horses to help us home, & Government lent us 3 more, but the latter were of but little Service to us, they being all foundred.

In the Course of the Discourse we informed the Major, that some of our Watches, which had been taken from us, when we were taken Prisoners, were seen with a Merchant.

The Major enquired where they were & ordered them to be brought immediately, & after finding them to be ours, & that they had been purchased with Rum, gave us the Watches, and ordered Mr Bawbee to pay the Mercht the Rum back again. He also ordered us a Barrel of Pork & another of Flower.

A Merchant in the place had bot of the Indians which robbed us a Velvett Jacket; & another at Sandusky a Velvett P^r of Breeches, which they gave us freely on our Arrival. Our Indian Helpers had likewise received from Government some Cloathing & Provision.

We now took leave of our Friends & set out for Sandusky where we arrived on the 22ᵈ of Novʳ to the great Joy of the whole Congregation. During our being from home, it had been frequently reported to our People, that we would never return again. That some of us were Imprisoned at Detroit—& again that we were put on Board a Vessel & Sent down in the Country. Indeed this had been the Wish of our Enemies, & the Indians in general were surprised to see us return again, & did not know what to think of the Matter: For sensible as they were of the wrong they had done us, & of Robbing us, they either wished not to see us any more, for fear we might make them account for it, or dreaded we might one Time or other have the Advantage, of paying them a Compliment in the same Manner: tho' it was far from us to seek Revenge or the like.

In our Absence a Number of our poor Indians * had ventured to Muskingum, & fetched Corn for their starving Families at home, notwithstanding (as above mentioned) some had been taken Prisoners by the Americans, & carried off.

The Sufferings at home now encreased daily, for they had Spent all they had about them in buying Corn of the Wild Indians paying generally for 2 or 3 Quarts a Dollar.

However they resolved to build a Meeting House, for hitherto they had Prayers in the open Air.

No Sooner had the other Indians seen us busy abᵗ that Buissiness, than they began to throw out Threats against us, declaring, that Churches Should not be seen, nor Prayers heard among us any longer.

The cold Weather becoming more & more pinching, & frequently Snow falling, our Cattle which had been overdrove from the Towns, & not used to the Food of this Country (this being nothing but barren plains round about) began to fail, & Shortly after to dye, so that in the Course of the Winter about 140 head of Cattle both big & little were lost.

2 Indian Captⁿˢ who had been along at taking us, had Shortly before been talking together abᵗ us, & were overheard saying to one another in a mock manner:

"These are the People who lived so well a while ago, & had every thing plenty: Now they have nothing, & creep about looking for Food, as we are used to do."—"Captivity and Murder," 41-47.

---

* Jⁿᵒ Bull with his Son in Law and Daughter with several more were the Prissoners.
—Note in the MS.

❦ XXII ❦

Gnadenhütten: 1782

NECESSITY PRESSING US DAYLY, the Meeting House being finished, the Christmass & New Year holy Days over, such as were able, concluded to take their Families into the Neighbourhood of their former Towns on Muskingum, from thence to fetch Corn, both for the Support of their Families, as also to bury at a Distance in the Woods, meanwhile the others that remained with us at home lived chiefly upon the dead Cattle, laying in the Street & about the Houses. Whilst the former were on their Way towards the Towns; and determined (according as we had desired them) to encamp at a good Distance in the Woods for fear of a Party of Militia, they unexpectedly met those who had been taken Prisoners in the Fall, & who gave them all the Encouragement they could to go straightway to the Towns & abide in their Houses, for that the Americans had behaved in every Respect to them as Friends.

Confidently relying on this, & sensible of a good Conscience, they determined so to do, & without any Manner of Fear & Uneasiness took possession of their Houses, being industrious in gathering their Corn. Yea, by some of them who had left their Families at home, & were come in with Corn for them, we learned to our Satisfaction, that they frequently assembled, & were exhorted by the Helpers to Steadiness as well in Times of Trouble & Tribulation, as in Peace. That they lived in Harmony, & Love together, & were obedient to their Helpers.

That they also had gathered a Sufficient Quantity of Corn for their Ministers & had pitched upon a Day for Setting off home again, where they intended to assist one another by the Way. While they were there resting secure & enjoying the Fruit of their Labour, there arrived 4 Young Men, Warriors from the Settlement with Prisoners & Scalps which gave them great uneasiness. These Warriors had encamped in the Woods above the Town, & were offering the plunder they had taken for Sale. But as it had always been a Rule with us: not to purchase any Thing from Warriors on any Account, it being not only unjust, but an Encouragement for them to follow the Buissiness more closely, but refused taking any Thing, & even if it was to be bestowed to them. They moreover desired the Warriors to leave their Settlement, for that they never were easy when People of that kind were about them.

On the 4th or 5th of March the Warriors told one of our People: That they had the greatest Reason to expect a Party of Virginians here Shortly, for that they (the Warriors) had been over the Ohio, robbed the House of a Gentleman (named Wallis or Wallace) & taken his Wife & Child Prisoners: That after crossing the Ohio to this Side they had murdered the Woman & Child [& *stuck the latter on a Stake which was run up from between its Leggs until the Neck, with its belly to the Indian Country & its Face towards the Settlement over the River*], & that they believed undoubtedly to be followed, within a Short Time. That they now would push off immediately, & hoped they would do the Same. The Prisoner who afterwards found means to make his Escape, had warned them to the same Purpose giving it as his Opinion that out of regard for Such a Person as Mr Wallace was, the whole Country would rise if he called upon them, & that he most probably would do.

This Shocking Acc^t brought on a general Consternation, accompanied with Fear. Some were for going off imediately & leaving every Thing behind, but others thought best, for to advise every body in the 3 Towns to get ready within a Day or two, & go off in one Body.

They accordingly assembled to hear & speak with one another. They were much troubled about what they had heard these 4 Warriors had done, & found reason to believe, that these Murderers might be pursued, yet it appeared to some to be a Matter without Doubt. But examining Christianity (& as the Indians in general believe that all white People, whosoever and wheresoever they were, are Christians, because they have the Word & Comandments of God in Writing (meaning the Bible of which they in the present Times have some knowledge) looked on Murder as a great Sin, the Same as *they* now did, since *they* were converted unto our Saviour: & recollecting that if there even were bad People among the Whites, the worse would be governed by the better Sort, etc.—etc. Thereby all Fear disappeared.

However the Time being at Hand for their departure, & they having brought in a great Part of their Household Goods etc—they of a Sudden were apprised by a Number of Militia coming down on both Sides of the River towards Gnadenhütten surrounding both the Village on the East Side, & the Corn field on the West.

They (the Indians) were at that time much scattered, some in & ab^t the Village, & others in the Corn field, filling their Bags with Corn, & bundling up their Goods.

Jacob, Mr Bulls Son in Law, (who had been one of those that were taken in the Fall, & on whose mind the good treatment they met with throughout their Captivity had a good impression,) was the first Man who saw them coming, as he was tying up a Load above the Village by the sweat House; As they were passing by, some on Horseback & others on foot between him & the River not 50 Yards distant, he observed that he knew some of them to be those who had been at the taking of them in the Fall, & he was just ready to salute them, when they fired at one of our People on the bank that was buisy there.

The Indian, tho mortally wounded, jumped into a Canoe that was under the Bank, & crossed the River where he died.

Jacob now seeing plainly, that the case was not as he first expected, took off to the Woods, & So great was his Consternation that he kept himself hid for a Day & Night. Meanwhile these Men had taken every Soul on both Sides of the River Prisoners, or rather, the Indians had on the friendly intreatment they gave them (telling them, they were not come to hurt, but to protect them from their Enemys, for they knew them to be their Friends, & took pity on them since their late Misfortune, would Show them every Mark of Friendship, & use them as well, as they had those, that had been taken in the Fall if they would willingly surrender & go with them) joyfully ran up to them.

They enquired of the Indians into every particular of their Bussiness, & learning; that they had many Things of their own yet hid in the Woods, which they could not take along, & which they feared would be found out by the Wild Indians: they desired [*them*] to go with them, & show them wherever they had any thing burried or hid, as they would assist them in carrying every thing along so that they might loose nothing. Thus without the least apprehension of Danger they agreed to everything, & became as familiar towards one another, as if they were old acquaintances.

John Martin a Helper with his Son, who had been over the Hill burying Corn all the while this happened, was at first surprised when he came to the Cornfield & found the Tracks of so many shod Horses, meeting not a Single Indian here about: but following the Tracks towards the Town, & taking at a Distance a View of the same, he observed to his Satisfaction that the Indians were up & down the Streets together with the white People, & as he thought quite merry together. He sent his Son across the River to the Village, whilst he would go down the River to Salem, & acquaint the Brethren & Sisters there of what had passed.

He gave it, by the Prospect he had, as his Opinion, That their Friends (meaning the Americans) were come out of Love & Friendship, to take them under their Protection & Care, that they undoubtedly had considered the miserable state & poverty they were brought to by being Friends to the Americans, & that God had ordained it so that they should not perish in Sandusky, where they probably must if they were to stay there.

Israel, generally known by the Name of the Straight armed Man (one of his Arms being straight & stiff) who had been a true & steady friend to the Americans thro' the Course of the War he being a Chief much beloved by his Tribe for his Wisdom & Steadiness for Peace, produced a Number of Belts & Strings of Wampum, which he had received from Time to Time of divers Agents & Commanding Officers, all tending to Friendship & Unity between the States & the peaceable Delaware part of the Indians.

In short there was no doubt left, but that they would be received as Friends by any Number or Body of Men whatsoever from that Quarter, & being in a suffering Condition thro' the Destruction of their Towns, they quickly came to the Resolution to go with such their Friends, as would come for them. (meaning the Americans) It might be that God had prepared a Way & place for them, where they could enjoy Peace, & live undisturbed, & concluded that when they arrived at such a Place, the Brethren in Bethlehem would soon send them Teachers (Ministers).

Being quite agreed on this head, they sent John Martin, Adam & Henry off to Gnadenhütten, to inform the People there of their Resolution. It had happened that shortly before 2 Men, near Relations to a very loving & kind Family, (the Father of which was Jonas one of our principle Helpers,) had come to the Assistance of this Family, with an Intention to join the Congregation. There was likewise a young Woman, a Daughter of Nathaniel Davis, who had been sent away from the Congregation some time ago, on Account of committing Adultery [& *Fornication*]. These 3 were desired by the Helpers to go off imediately as not belonging unto them.

But on the Supplication of the former, earnestly requesting them to receive them as such, who wished to be instructed in the Gospel that they also might be converted to God their Saviour, & giving sufficient proofs, that they never had joined in the present War, were at length permitted to abide with them, as also the Woman who wept & begged for forgiveness, promising never to do the like any more.

She even expressed herself to these Words.

"That she would abide by her Brethren & Sisters if she knew beforehand that they were all to be killed, rather than live among the Heathen Indians." However severall who were uneasy about their poor old Parents at home, knowing they must be in a starving Condition resolved to sett of imediately.

In the Afternoon Adam & Henry returned with a Number of those Whites from Gnadenhütten: for having acquainted them there, that they were willing & ready to go with them wherever they intend to take them they (the Whites) desired them to Show them the place & People the belonged to. On their Arrival, they were welcomed & victuals brought up to them.

They pretended Friendship, as they had done at Gnadenhütten, & then hurried the Indians to get ready & go with them.

When they left the Village they (the Whites) sat Fire to the Houses,

Gnadenhütten: 1782

giving it as the Reason, that the Warriors might not harbour there. On the Way to Gnadenhütten Samuel Moore a well bred Jersey Indian who read the Bible, & was a principal Helper, as also the Interpreter to that Congregation: Christian, another Helper & Steward to the Church, & Tobias an old venerable Man & likewise a Helper, who all 3 spoke very good English, were satisfied in answering Questions touching Religion, & explaining Scripture Texts to such of the white People, who appeared to be religious. And it had even been acknowledged by some of the latter, that the Indians not only perfectly understood the Scripture, but indeed were without doubt good Christians.

Unto others who were inquisitive as to politicks, Israel & Isaac (the latter a Helper & Steward) answered them, every Question in a most satisfactory manner, & they became fully acquainted with these Christian Indians in every Respect. Now as there were some big Boys among them, these were playing all the Way with some of the White Lads, so that, without Doubt there would be no Apprehension of any Danger. They at length arrived at Gnadenhütten, where they in crossing the River to the Village saw the Canow bloddy, & several bloddy Tracks of a wounded Person, not knowing yet any thing of the Man that had been shot and cross'd the River. After they had them all at the Village and had in full view the Plunder they might be Master of, if these Indians could be condemned, and put to Death, they consulted seriously how to perform it. They had before taken care to get Possession of all Rifles, Hatchets, Axes &c—yea of every Thing belonging to these poor Creatures, promising the Delivery of every thing again on their Arrival at the place they intended to take them to. Thus having them in their full Power, they began to accuse them of the following Crimes, namely, that they were Warriors and had been to War against them—that they had harboured the Warriors, and found them in Provision when going and returning from War— That it was manifest that there were a number of Horses with them taken from the Settlements, for the Horses were branded with Letters, of which Indians knew nothing— That there were many Cloths, Childrens Caps, Tea-Kettles, Potts, cups & saucers ect. Saws, Axes, Chissels, Pewter Basons Porrengers &c—which were all such Things as were only made use of by White People and not by Indians. The poor Creatures gave proof enough of their Innocence, and declared that they had not been at War, neither harboured the Warriors, and that what little some had got of them going or coming from War, was far from being called furnishing, that if they had refused giving them on demand something to eat, they (the Warriors) would have took it by force, killed their Cattle, and destroyed every thing before them. That by giving the Warriors now and then a little, they got Liberty to visit and satisfy the poor hungry and starved Prisoners when passing by. That they oftentimes had persuaded partys of Warriors to turn back again when going out. That they had (to speak the Truth) furnished Col! Broadhead with provision when he was in want, and called upon them, for which they were envied by all the bad Indians, and that they never thought otherwise than that every person belonging to the States, knew them to be their true friends. All these proofs of Innocence would not sattisfy them. They held a Councill of the Manner in which they should be put to Death, wherein it appeared, that the Major part were much against hurting them. It is indeed reported that they were not only declared Innocent by many, but recomended to the Protection and Charity of all as good and true Christians, and when the condemning Party had positively declared that they must Dye, they (the former) wrung their Hands, and called God to wittness that they were not guilty of the Blood of these innocent creatures. But greediness for Plunder either overballanced Humanity, or perhaps they never must have been possesed of the latter. They had gone in to see the Indians, which they had shut up in Houses, and Two of them stroking down the Hair of Abraham, who wore his Hair very long said, what a pretty head of Hair he had, and what a fine Scalp they could get off of his Head. then looking about said to one another, is it not evident that there are many Warriors among them, having their Hair cut short and head shaved *— They certainly must die imediately. The Indians hearing and understanding these Words, and finding, that nothing would satisfy them, but putting them to Death, they told them: That they were willing to dye, tho innocent, that God knew their Innocence, that they, when they were first converted unto Jesus Christ and baptised, had made a covenant to live for him, and according to his Will Word & Pleasure as long as they lived in this World—that they were sensible they had not always fullfilled their Promise for which they were sorry, and would beg a Days time for the purpose of praying and preparing for Death, and being answered that a few Hours should be granted to them for this Purpose, they fell on their Knees praying and singing Hymns. The above mentioned Abraham had in particular acknowledged his backwardness in fullfilling the Promise he had made in holy Baptism, but was fully assured that our Saviour had forgiven him all, and he was quite ready to dye. Exhorting one another to Steadiness, and finding some of their Adversaries impatient to begin upon them, they told them, that they were now all ready, and had comitted their Souls unto God, who had given them the Assurance, that they should be with him for ever.

At hearing the first time that they should be put to Death, 2 young Lads Anton and Paulus † (or Paul) endeavored to make their Escape, but were shot down under the Bank of the River below the Village.

Now they met together once more to conclude on the Manner in which they were to be put to Death. some were for setting the Houses they were shut up in on fire, and burning them alive, but to this they could not all

---

* All must tend to condemn them, even here that some of them had their Heads shaved, altho it is known that this is a custom with the Ind? in which no harm is. —Note in MS.

† John Martins 2 Sons.—Note in MS.

agree, some thinking this too Barbarous, and others declared themselves of having a just right to revenge, did not think it tormenting enough.

One Man * being something more forward than the others, who had suffered during the War, and lost Children or Friends, picked up a Wooden Mall † behind the Houses saying that this apeared to have been made for the Purpose, and according to their own Accounts given of this Affair, this Man killed 14 in one heat before he quit it, others dispatching the Remainder in like Manner, and taking off their Scalps. It is something very remarkable, that out of each the separate Houses, namely the Men being shut up by themselves, and the Women, one Soul made his escape who were also able to give an Account of the whole. In that of the Men had been Thomas a boy of about 14 or 15 years of Age, he had been knocked down and scalped with the rest, but after recovering again (tho not knowing the Time he had laid senseless) observed all laying dead and scalped about him exept Abel a Man who had recovered his Senses again & was looking about him, and Thomas thinking within himself (perceiving it beginning to be dusk) how he might perhaps make his Escape lay quite still the same as being dead, and there presently coming in a Man to view the dead Bodies, who perceiving Abel endeavoring to get up, gave him several severe blows, which put an End to his Trouble and Live. He then after this Man had disapeared, crept nearer to the Door, and observing nobody at hand got out and behind the House where he hid himself, and night being come on ran off. The other who made his Escape from the House the Women were in, was a Boy of about the same Age as the other. This House had a large Cellar underneath, and seeing they had began in Earnest to kill them, having made a Beginning, with Judith a very loving old Widow, he found Means to get a board up and dropt down into the Cellar, being there a while and another following him, the Blood began to run a Stream down between the Blank upon them. He had observed a small Window or Air Hole at the back of the Cellar Wall, at which he attempted and got out with much Difficulty, and hid himself in the Haselnut bushes at the back of the House till dark when he also ran off. He had observed that his Companion in the Cellar had also endeavour'd to get out, but being something bulkier than he was obliged to give it up. Now after they boasted and rejoiced with one another on being so successfull they sat fire to the Houses, and the dead Bodies were burned. Whether now or before, they had gone up and surrounded the Upper Town Schoenbrunn, I am not certain, but that they had been there with the same design is evident, as may be seen by the following: It has been said in the beginning that the Missionaries had been ordered to Detroit, that some had been there and returned with a Pass from the Comandant to

---

* said to have been a German.—Note in MS.

† Probably the cooper's mallet used in his trade by Joshua. He himself was not among those at Gnadenhütten, but his two young daughters were. See DeCost Smith, *Martyrs of the Oblong and Little Nine* (Caldwell, Idaho, 1943), p. 225.

live with their Indians at Sandusky. With this, certain Whites in the Woods were not Satisfied, and is needless to mention their Names so often they being allready manifest: however it is to be observed that a certain S[imon] G[irty a] noted Villain had sent a Letter to Detroit, as a Speech from the half King, and in the name of the Wyondotts, wherein he accuses the Moravian Teachers as keeping a continual Correspondence with the Americans insomuch that they receive Letters every 10 Days from Pittsburgh. To these Accusations were added: a Number of Threats—when G[irty] (who was neither able to read nor to write) had applied to a Merchant * at Sandusky to write the Letter or Speech for him informing him of the Contents, was asked: whether the Case was realy such as he was desired to write, he was answered, it was no Matter wether it was truth or not, they wanted the Ministers out of the Way. The Man being a Gentleman refused to write any thing of the kind, for which Reason he aplied to another. On the first Day of March in the Evening we received a Message from the said G[irty] for all the Moravian Ministers to attend tomorrow Morning at Mr Mc Cormicks House near the Wyondotts Village [Upper Sandusky], which was about 8 or 9 Miles from where we lived, to hear a Letter read concerning Us from Major De Poyster Comandant at Detroit. We concluded that 2 of us was sufficient to go there, and accordingly Dav. Zeisberger and John Heckewelder with a few of their principle Indians went to hear the Letter. G[irty] with the half King and Captains being arrived, G[irty] produced the Speech, telling us we might read it ourselves. The Contents were, that Complaints having been brought against Us by the Wyondotts, he the Comandant ordered S[imon] G[irty], or if he could not himself, to appoint a proper Person, to bring the Moravian Teachers with their Families into Detr^t And that in case they should want help, he desired the half King to assist them. There being a Bunch of black Wampum given to the latter part of the Speech, G[irty] explained to us in such a Manner that if we did not agree to the Demand or Speech we would fall a prey to the Wyondotts again.

We therefore only begged for so much time to send a Messenger to our people on Muskingum informing them, that we were now to be entirely separated from them, but wished to see them before our Departure, as also to assist us with Horses to Lower Sandusky, at which Place we were to be in 15 Days hence. This being agreed to, we sent Stephan on the 3^d of March at Day break off for the Towns where he arived on the 6th namely at the upper Town Schoenbrunn but being very much fatuiged 2 Brethren were sent with the Message to Gnadenhütten and Salem. When these had come within a Mile of Gnadenhütten they were surprised to find Joseph Bull old Mr Bulls Son dead, and allover blody by the Way Side, and on examining his Body found that he was murdered. They saw a Number of Tracks of shod Horses, from which they concluded that White People not only must have committed

---

* M^r O[ediah] R[obbins].—Note in MS.

Gnadenhütten: 1782

the Murder, but also most probably must have killed the People at Gnadenhütten. Thus concluding, and Fear surrounding them, they buried the dead Body, and hurried back again, where they informed the Brethren & Sisters of what they had seen, and thereby put all those that were there to flight. It had been in the Evening when they set out to the Woods, taking their Course Northeastward to the Hills, they were upon their Legs all Night and some with their Children on their Backs. Consulting one another, they agreed to cross the River to the west side before break of Day, that they might be upon their Way home. having out of Fear gone a different Course, they were much disappointed in their Intention, for they had gone so far back, that they did not reach the plain untill Day break. To cross the open Plain at the Distance of at least 1½ Miles was a great Risk, and to the River they must get to Cross. They encouraged one another, that God could blind the Eyes of their Enemys, so that they might not see them and trusting in his Protection they went on.

At this Time in the Night, when they resolved to go to the River, they had sent off a few Men to fetch up a Canoe they had lying below at the Town, the River not being fordable any where above. It was very lucky for these, that they were not seen by the Whites, for before they had their Canoe any considerable Distance, they observed the Village surrounded on all Sides by People on Horseback, and had they only took a rout up the River, they must have seen all our People crossing the Plains, of which the Consequence most probably would have been the same as at Gnadenhütten. But after finding Nobody they took every thing they found worth any thing, and retourned to Gnadenhütten. And the Indians crossed the River and went on through the Woods for Sandusky, on which Journey a poor Child was Starved [*for want of Nourishment*]. The Militia having in those parts no further Oportunity of murdering innocent People, and no Stomach to engage with Warriors set off home with their Horses and Plunder they had taken, and afterwards falling upon the Peaceable Indians on the North Side of the Allegheny River opposite Pittsburgh killed several of those. Time passing away with Us in Sandusky, and none of our Indians coming in, we knew not what to think, having as yet not heard a Word of all that had happened at the Towns on Muskingum, at length a Young Man that had come that Way brought the bad News: *

That the Americans had been out at the Towns, and had either taken all the Christian Indians Prisoners, or had Killed them, which of the Two he was not certain. We would by no Means belive the Report, still expecting our

---

* In another manuscript Heckewelder expands this detail: ". . . the alarm yell was sounded at a distance, in the direction the path went to that place (Muskingum), and drawing nigher, the Yell was so distinctly heard, & performed in such *quick* succession, that no doubt was left on any Person's mind, but that we should hear some bad news; & which proved to be but too true; for on the arrival of this runner, who was a Sandusky Warrior, returning from the Ohio Settlements, he had heard by the way . . ."

Indians was coming or at least some of them. But all our hopes was in vain. Mr. Francis Levellie, a Frenchman who had now the Charge of us, hurried us to get ready, and in this Condition we left upper Sandusky. Those of our poor Indians at home wept bitterly at seeing us and them parted. They even followed us for Miles weeping, and some helped us along quite to Lower Sandusky.—Heckewelder, "Captivity and Murder," 47-66.

There had died that day, March 8, 1782, at Gnadenhütten, ninety Christian Indians, according to Moravian count: fifty-six adults—a large proportion of them women—and thirty-four children. Many of these were persons we have met in the course of this narrative. Of particular concern to us as we follow the Heckewelder story are these:

Isaac (Glickhikan) and his wife, Anna Benigna. Glickhikan, it will be recalled, had been Packanke's chief counsellor, whose awakening to the significance of the Christian message in the little world both chiefs were trying to pull into some sort of decency and order made a great stir in the Delaware nation, and brought about the invitation to the Moravians to set up towns in the western woods where the Christian way might be demonstrated.

Petrus (Echpalawehund), another prominent chief, who had been permitted by Netawatwees to live among the Christians at Gnadenhütten on condition that he retain his position on the Grand Council of the Delawares and attend its meetings when summoned.

Israel (Welapachtschiechen, *alias* Captain Johnny), principal chief of the Turkey Tribe of the Delawares, who had been baptised at Lichtenau in 1777.

Old Abraham (surnamed "The Mohicon"), who had joined the Moravians thirty-three years before at Gnadenhütten on the Mahoning. In 1774 he had been Heckewelder's companion on a journey from the Muskingum to Bethlehem.

Tobias who, on March 3, 1781, had saved Heckewelder's life (see pages 144-45) from hostile warriors.

It is easy to pity the dead, but it was not only those whose lives were lost at Gnadenhütten who have claim upon our sympathy. What happened to some of those who escaped the massacre was in some ways more terrible, as the case of Anton will show. Anton (Welochalent), it will be remembered, was the man who had saved James O'Hara from the enemy warriors who were searching for him. Anton was a sensitive man and a beautiful character. In the early spring of 1782 he had come with three generations of his family—his father and mother (Jo Peepee and Hannah), his brother Jonas, his wife Juliana, and his children—to see what food they could find, after suffering a winter of near-starvation at Upper Sandusky, in the burnt cornfields of the deserted Muskingum towns. On March 6, two days before the massacre, he left the family, in safety as he thought, and set off on a journey to Pittsburgh. When he learned that, during his absence, his mother, his brother, his wife, and his three children—Elisabeth, Joseph, and Marcus—had been killed, a fury mounted in him that took him out to the war trail and held him there until the mad urge to avenge himself had been exhausted. When he awoke from this bad dream, he was a broken man, never again to know peace of mind. After the first rage had died out of him, he tried to bring himself to a mood of reconciliation, in the thought of returning to the quiet Moravian community where his heart really lay. But the wound was too deep. He never found himself thereafter, lost between two worlds: that of the Indian, which he had long since renounced; and that of the white man, which he could no longer trust. John Heckewelder had a dramatic meeting with him in 1789, as we shall see, and heard him confess his dilemma. Among the Moravian records there is a reference to him as late as 1790, in which he appears sick, paralyzed, and alienated from the Christian community.

General Washington, when he heard of the Gnadenhütten atrocities, sent instructions to troops on the western border that henceforth no man was to allow himself to be taken alive. The thing that Washington feared happened not long afterward when Colonel David Williamson marched out once more with the militia (though by five votes of the men he had lost seniority to Colonel William Crawford, who thus became head of the force), this time to Upper Sandusky. It is strongly suspected that the object of the expedition was to complete the work begun at Gnadenhütten by finishing off the Moravian Indians at Captives Town. The men brought coils of rope with them to pack the plunder and secure the captured horses,* a great haul of both furs and horses having been made without cost at Gnadenhütten. When the troops arrived, however, they found, not the non-combatants they had expected, but a well-organized, well-motivated body of warriors under Captain Pipe. The militia were defeated and fled. Colonel Williamson by a peculiar irony escaped. So it was that Colonel Crawford, who was captured, made atonement by torture for Williamson's crime.

In the public park at Gnadenhütten, Ohio, there is a mound covering

---

* DeCost Smith, *op. cit.*, p. 241.

the remains of the Indians who died there. Nearby is a stone shaft with this inscription:

HERE
TRIUMPHED IN DEATH
NINETY
CHRISTIAN INDIANS
MARCH 8, 1782.

Responsible Indian leaders outside the mission found their worst fears realized. Pachgantschihilas at the parley in May, after warning the Gnadenhütten Indians against raids by the Long Knives, had said, "If you pass safely through this war, and I see you all alive at the end of it, I will regret not having joined your mission." * But such generous hopes were not destroyed. His regrets were of another complexion.

Within the mission, confidence was never fully restored. Many of the Christian Indians, disillusioned, left the community as Anton did. Others remained to share the further vicissitudes of what came to be known as the "Wandering Congregation." The mission struggled on. Individual Indians benefitted. But any hope that the Moravians' experiment, by the example of their happy towns and the influence of Christian chiefs in Indian councils, might bring a solution of the whole problem of Indian-white relations on this continent, perished with Isaac Glickhikan at Gnadenhütten.

---

* Edmund de Schweinitz, *Life and Times of David Zeisberger* (Philadelphia, 1870), p. 484.

XXIII

Simon Girty: 1782

G[irty] who had Charged Mr. Levellie to push on with us untill Detroit, and not to spare us in the least, had gone off to War. But Mr. Levellie having more of Humanity within him than the other, took all possible Care of us, yea lent Dav. Zeisberger his own Horse to ride on, saying he had no Pleasure in Riding, being young, when seing an old Gentleman walking a foot. Under much Difficulty and many Hardships, the Roads being very wet, and the Creeks high, we at lenght arrived at Sandusky, and were received by the Two Gentlemn. Traders Robbins and Arrundle in a very friendly Manner. Having lodged us in their Houses, they proposed to Mr. Levellie to recommend us in a Letter to Major De Peyster &c. and to request of him to send a Boat out for us to go in. Mr. Levellie readily agreed, Arrundle wrote the Letter, which was sent off imediately by Express. and these Gentlemen in the mean Time not only treated us with civility, but provided for us in every Respect. While we were thus waiting an Answer, some of our Brethren and Sisters from Upper Sandusky came to see us, and wished to go with us wheresoever we went, but we not being able to give them any Encouragement, on Account of not knowing ourselves, what would become of us, were obliged to part with one another with Grief, and what gave us the most pain was, that now we was informed that 96 of our Brethren Sisters and Children were actually murdered at Gnadenhütten by the Militia. Thus troubled and concerned beyond expression and jet hardly able to belive the shoking Reports, tho the truth. G[irty] arrived from War, and finding that we were yet in Sandusky, threw out the most shocking Threats against us, that perhaps ever were heard, declaring that he would not leave the House before he had split the Heads of the Moravian Ministers assunder with his Tomhawk. He then fell a quarreling with Mr. Levellie, for sending a Letter to the Comandant concerning Us, and requesting him to sent a Boat out to fetch Us in. He, G[irty] had ordered him, to drive Us in by Land, or to take M.ʳ Arrundles Boat, and let us shift for ourselves, saying We were not Ministers but — — We ought to be entirely out of the World &c. He then struck M.ʳ Levellie for not obeying his Orders, but the former being full as able as he returned the Blow. To which a general fight ensued in which G[irty] fell short. Night approaching and some Liquor being brought he fell a drinking, M.ʳ Arrundle having a Watchfull Eye over him that he might not hurt us. The next Day 2 Boats arrived from Detroit for the purpose of fetching Us in, and being manned with Rangers, a Serjant Rough produced a Letter to M.ʳ Arrundle and Levellie from Major De Poyster, the Contents of which were as follows. That he had sent some Time ago a Letter to S[imon] G[irty] to bring the Moravian Ministers in to Detroit, finding them in Danger of their Lives where they were.— That he had desired G[irty], either to come in with them himself, or to appoint a proper Person for the Purpose— That his Orders were that they should not be robbed or ill treated by any Body whatsoever, and that, should [the] it contrary have been the Case, he would make such Person or Persons account for it— That he desired M.ʳ Arrundle to inform him, if any Person he knew, that had disregarded his Orders— That he had aproved of the proposal of sending out Boats— That he expected that the Traders at Sandusky had behaved friendly, and been kind to them (the Ministers) since their first Arrival at that Place, and that he had given a written Instruction to Serjant Rough how to behave to Us on the Voyage &c. Now G[irty] hearing the Letter read, and finding that it was not only out of his Power to hurt us, but that he had Reason to believe he would be called to an Account for his Behaviour towards Us, turned Sides, but We embarked, and after a tedious Voyage of 8 Days arrived on the 20th Day of Aprill at Detroit.—"Captivity & Murder," 66-69.

XXIV

The Chippewa Country: 1782-1785

WE WERE LODGED in a New Room in the Citadell, and a Centry put before the Door, untill further Orders. But the Major visiting us, and enquiring how soon we should be ready to go on Board down in the Country, and finding that we were not at all disposed to any thing of the kind, having declared: that we were sent among the Indians to preach the Gospel of Salvation unto them— That we had been successfull, and had a Number of Indians professing true Christianity— That we never should have forsaken them, had we not been taken away by force, and that if we must go down into the Country, it would be much against our Will, and that in this Case all our Labour would be lost, and the poor forsaken Indians ruined.

He took to heart what he had heard of Us, and did not leave us without Hopes, that we might be with our Indians again. He also imediately ordered the Centry off and gave us Liberty of walking in and about the City. In the mean time we were visited by friends, among whom was an Officer by the Name of Fry, a Gentleman who was very intimate with the Major. Now since the latter had heard our Sentiments, and found we were in Earnest not to forsake our Indians without we were forced to it, he enquired of Us where our Indians at present were, and being informed, that they had moved somewhere near the Shawanoe Towns, he gave us Liberty to go there and live with them again, promising Us his Protection, and offering us a strong Guard to convey us there. But at this present Time we not only thought the task rather to difficult and dangerous, but impracticable, for firstly, the Indians had drove Us out of the Country, secondly we had worse Enemies of White People in the Indian Country, than of Indians, and thirdly the Shawanoe Towns were the worst place of all we could go to, for those Indians are continually at War. readily acknowledging the truth of this, he next proposed to apoint a place, where we could live undisturbed with our Indians, for which purpose he would sent an invitation to them, wishing that some of us would go to them with the Message ourselves. But being informed that it would answer full as well, if he would sent a proper Person with the Message to invite our Indians in the Neighbourhood of Detroit, and for some of the Heads (Helpers) to come in imediately to hear what he had to propose to them, it was agreed, and he sent a Speech both by a Frenchman, and Shawanoe Man to our Indians for the Purpose. But Elliot at the Shawanoe Towns getting Wind of the Message, demanded the Letter of the Frenchman pretending to read it to our Indians himself, and as he had the Indian under Command, who had the strings of Wampum he got him to discharge his Message according to *his* mind.

However some of our Indians had got the true Meaning of the Speech, both by the Frenchman himself as also by Indians who had been at Detroit, and unto whom we had communicated it, so that in the Middle of the Summer a few Families arrived.

The Proposal by the Major had been: That all our Indians should come in imediately, and with his Assistance settle and plant Corn on Goose-Isle (Island) [Grosse Isle] or opposite on the west Side of the River, but a Gentleman thoroughly acquainted with the Way and Life of Indians, looking on the Island to be to much of a thicket for Indians to clear ground on, and the other place right in the Warriors Path to and from Detroit, proposed the River Huron above Detroit, as being not only quite out of the Way of the Warriors, but also a good Soil. On the 20th of July David Zeisberger, Jungmanns, Edwards and Michel Young set out with near 20 Indians Men Women and Children for the new Settlement [New Gnadenhütten, near Mt. Clemens, Michigan]. The Major had not only supplied us with Provision, Axes, Saws, and other necesary Tools and Articles, but had lent us his own Boat for the Voyage. Being Strangers to the Country, we applied to Mr Riddle and his Brother in Law, Prisoners, who had recognoitered the Country, and John Heckewelder went along with them to assist in bringing the Boat back. We arrived on the 22^d at the high banck, and pitched upon this Place for our abode, to which Heckewelders and Sensemans with their 2 small Children joined the Month following. In this place Life became to be agreeable again, for since a twelf month we were either in Danger, Fear, or Uneasiness of Mind. We had made a Beginning—the spot we build upon, on the top of the Bank was level and open, but round about an entire Wilderness. The winter being moderate was greatly in our Favour towards clearing of Lands. In the Spring following a good many more of our Indians arrived, so that we were now about 100 in Number, who all drew Provision, we put in a Crop of Corn, but it did not get to its proper Perfection on Account of early Frosts in the Fall. Altho the Preliminaries of Peace apeared in the Month of May and June, it was believed by few of the Citizens that it would be the Case, but John Bull and John Weygand having arrived from Pensylvania soon

The Chippewa Country: 1782-1785

after, confirmed it to be so. Major De Poyster who had while we were in Detroit given sufficient Proof of his Friendship towards Us, and assisted us in every Respect as far as lay in his Power, continued to supply us with Provision till the beginning of Nov.^br.

He also gave the Missionaries 2 Cows and 3 Horses for a beginning, and paid great Attention to our Mission. He also begged of Us, not to lay the ill treatment we had experienced to his Charge, nor to blame him with our late Misfortune, but as he knew, that we had many Ennemies, it was his Duty to send for and take us under his Protection. He showed a Delight in serving us, & said, he knew it was well applied & this gave him full Satisfaction. In Spring 84 he departed for Niagara, previous to which he recommended Us to his Successor Governor Hay, & wished us Health and Prosperity. Thus we parted with our praiseworthy Benefactor, praying to God, to reward him for all the Good we had received from him, since it was not in our Power to do it ourselves & he embarked for Niagara as Commandant of that port. The new Governor, [*whom we had waited upon*] received us in a very polite Manner. He informed us that Governor Hamilton & He had been examined by Government at Home, on account of the very ill Treatment we met with caused by some of the Brittish with a Number of Indians— He said their conduct had been censured and our Captivity had made a great Stir at Home— That Governor Hamilton (when Comandant of this Place) never had paid any Regard to any Reports concerning Us whatsoever— But thus the Righteous must submit to the fate of War as well as the Wicked. That also one of our Bishops in England, had made Application to Sir John Johnson, the Governor, and himself, and that Government had given a particular Charge to Comandants, Agents &c. in the Indian Country, and at Posts, not only to prevent for the future such Proceedings, but to protect Us in Our Spiritual Function. He assured Us that he would serve Us as far as lay in his Power, and that if any Body should offer to disturb Us, we might only apply to him— Believing ourselves thus in a State of certainty, we made some new additions to Houses, and as we stood in need of a proper House of Worship, but being not able to purchase some Necessaries, as Boards, Nails, Glass, Hinges &c. not having as yet recovered our late Calamity, we wished to apply to some particular friends (Citizens of Detroit) by way of Subscription, for their Assistance. And having informed some of the latter of our Intention, they adviced Us, to acquaint the Governor of the Matter and let him sign the Subscription Paper. That they then would supply us with every thing we stood in Want of, yea that they took great Delight in contributing to such a purpose.

Accordingly the Governor was waited on, and tho he approved of the whole, it did not suit him to sign the Paper; he being a Man very much interested in Lands &c. We being thus disappointed, and finding that the Chibaways [Chippewas] were impatient on seeing Us remain here so long after the Peace, they having been desired by Major De Poyster only to let us live here untill a Peace should be established, it being a remote Place and out of the Way of the Warriors. We thought it expedient to look out for another Place, where We with our Indian Congregation might live contentedly and undisturbed. The Lands on Muskingum on which We had lived so many years comfortably, came imediately to our Remambrance, and a Resolve of Congress (granting the Christian Indians—otherwise called Moravians—their formerly improved Lands, namely, the Villages Schönbrunn, Gnadenhütten, and Salem, appearing in public) confirmed our Resolution. We aquanted the Governor in a proper Manner of this, but he did not thinck it a proper Time for Us to return into the Indian Country, aprehending Disturbances anew. We therefore remained here jet one whole Year, concluding to leave the place as soon as possible, yet not certain whether Government would admit of it, and we heard from Time to Time by the French that the Chibaways were getting quite impatient to see us gone. that the chief Reason was, because our Indians killed their Game. That where we lived had been a place where many Families had got their living—and that they had threatened to kill some of our Indians, if we continued here. The English Merchants wished Us to remain allways here, having experienced that through our Industry the price of Product had fallen greatly. They gave it as their opinion, that this was a Reason why the French wanted us gone, and added to it, our Religion differing from their (the Roman). The Chibbaway Chiefs had at length paid us a Visit with an Intention to speak with us, but Mr Tucker Interpreter for the Crown refusing to attend in the Character of Interpreter, (it being a great Crime in and about this place to treat with or interpret for Indians whatsoever and whosoever without orders from the Indian Agent, moreover no Councill is to be held exept at Detroit, or other proper places appointed) We had no other Satisfaction than seeing and suplying them with some Corn, which they greatly stood in Need of.

Governor Hay had departed this Life in the Course of the Summer, and William Ancrum Major of the Kings Troops of this Port was appointed at interim in his Stead. Mr Askin one of the principal Merch^{ts} of this Place, and with whom we by this Time became fully aquainted served Us in many Respects, and agreed to purchase our whole Crop of Corn in the Fall if we intended to leave the Place, he also made us Hopes of taking us across the Lake in his Vessel to Gajahaga; but we still being advised by the Comandant and Agent, rather to wait untill Spring we sattisfied ourselves with passing the Winter here once more, in the Course of which the Major with 2 other Officers and Mr Askin visited us, and after taking a vew of the improvements made by Us, resolved to make Us a reasonable Reward for our Industry, moreover as we had represented unto him, that ill designing People flattered themselves, that they would be able to reap the Fruit of our Labour, without making us the smallest Recompense.

We prepared for our Journey, and on the 20th of Aprill left the Huron River, sailing in Canoes through Lake St. Clair to Detroit. Here the Comand^t and Mr Askin behaved to Us with every mark of Esteem, and hav-

The Chippewa Country: 1782-1785

ing got the 2 Sloops Beaver and Michilimakinac in readiness We embarked on the 28th for Gajahaga [Cleveland], provision being given by the former to Us on our Voyage.

Both these Gentlemen deserve much Praise, and our Prayer will allways be to God to bless them. The Gentleman & Merchants in the Town took likewise Leave of Us in a very friendly Manner, declaring themselves sorry in seeing such good honest People leave them &c. and wishing us happiness and Prosperity evermore.—"Captivity & Murder," 69-79.

XXV

Cayahaga: 1785

THE CAPTAINS OF THESE vessels, calculated on a voyage of but a few days to Cayahaga [Cuyahoga] river, where we were to be landed, provided the wind was favourable, and the channel of the river as open as it had been the last season. Dropping down the Detroit river, we anchored in the afternoon at the mouth, for the night; and being early next morning under way, we reached the Bass islands, by dusk, where we anchored. Here however, we had by high, and for the greater part, contrary winds and storms, to lay too, for four successive weeks; shifting our anchorage, according to the wind, and when very stormy, we ran into Hope's cove, or put in the bay [Put-in-Bay]. An attempt was at one time made, to get into the Cayahaga, but found impracticable, at least for the Beaver, she drawing more water than the Mackinaw, which was a small flat bottomed vessel. It was also evident, from the breakers at the mouth of the river, that the sand from the blowing winds, which came from the opposite shore, had in a great measure lodged itself in the channel, and there being no other place, within a great distance where the vessel could anchor with safety, we again returned to our former station.

Seeing no prospect of coming to our journeys end in this way: it was resolved that the Mackinaw should take all our baggagge, and a few of our people to Cayahaga, and we be landed by the vessel's boats on the main shore opposite to these Islands, from whence we would take our chance, in getting along. Being landed at Rocky point, the Indians caught in the space of about two hours, upwards of five hundred white fish, that had retired during the high blowing wind, between Rocky island and the shore, where the water was about two feet deep. The fish lay so crowded together, that they were easily taken, by a kind of scoop net, made of a piece of linen, fixed between a pole with a wide spreading fork. Some even made use of the shirt from their

Cayahaga: 1785

backs, tying up the collar and the sleeves, while the shirt tail was fastened to a hoop, made of a piece of grape vine; when, by dipping, or drawing it under the fish, they would seldom fail of taking several at a time; and as quick as the fish were taken to shore, the women cleansed and dryed them on scaffolds, over fires, made for the purpose.

We afterwards made several canoes of the bark of large Elm trees, which enabled some to proceed by water, (whilst others travelled by land,) for the mouth of the Cayahaga river, where the Mackinaw was to await our arrival. Those by land, found the journey very fatiguing, having to cross many gullies, rivulets, creeks, rivers, and swampy grounds; they not having a single horse to help them along; whilst those by water, (with whom the writer of this narrative, with his family were,) could frequently pass on under an easy sail. Having arrived after several days sailing, at the rocky shore, which commences about eight or nine miles west of the mouth of the Cayahaga river; we, in consequence of the frequent warnings given us at Detroit, not to risk running with canoes, along these rocks, as, if overtaken by a storm or high wind, blowing from the opposite shore of the lake, we would be in an instant dashed to pieces against the rocks; we made a stop for the rest of the day, that we might leisurely consider, on the best and safest way of proceeding on the morrow.

By the time we had unloaded and secured our canoes, by drawing them on the land, a number of Chippewas, in their fine large birch bark canoes, (who likewise were going to the Cayahaga;) came up; they seeing, that we lacked courage in venturing to proceed along this wall of rocks; endeavoured to persuade us to reload our canoes, and go in company with them to the mouth of that river, saying, they would pray to the great spirit, both for themselves, and for us, that we might safely pass this dangerous place; which one of them having done, by casting his eyes upwards, and making a short prayer, he next took his tobacco pouch up, when, having taken a hand full of Glecanecan (Indian tobacco,) out of it, he cast his eyes around from the north to the south, while he was imploring the manitto (spirit) who governs the winds, to prevent any storms from gathering or coming upon them, until they were out of danger; he threw the tobacco into the air. Then taking another handful he said, "and thou, manitto of the waters, (spirit or God of the waters) deign that those do not become turbulent and swallow us up; or dash us against this wall of rocks!" and having strewed this tobacco on the water: "now, (said he) there is no more danger!" finding however, that we were not inclined to accompany them, they set sail, and went on.

In little more than an hour after these Chippewas left us, a most tremendous thunder gust came on from the north west, which obliged us on the land, quickly to shift our quarters from where we were, to an open place, where no falling trees could reach us; as they were blown down in every direction; some being torn up by the roots; while others were broken off near the tops. This rock wall, which we judged to be between thirty and forty feet higher than the level of the water—and on which we got by an easy ascent at its western extremity, trembled by the force with which the dashing waves or swells ran against it, which came rolling over a sea of at least forty miles in breadth, the water at every dash, flying high above the wall. Dreadful indeed was the fore part of the night, and not an eye was closed by sleep; but it having become calm on the land, after the storm had abated, the swells on the lake also decreased—and a light southerly wind blowing about three o'clock in the morning, assisted in turning the swells in a direction from the shore where we were. We had during that night held several consultations, as to the manner of proceeding to the Cayahaga river where the vessel lay, waiting our arrival. The Indians reported it impossible for women with small children, to travel the distance by land. The wind at break of day was as favourable as could be wished for—a gentle side wind blowing from the land and rocky shore. The canoe men full of courage, and being trusty hands, impatiently waited for the word to be given for loading the canoes and setting off. This being done at day light, we embarked, and running under an easy sail, first some distance into the lake, in order to have sea room, to run either way in case of an unfavourable wind rising; we took our course for the mouth of the river, far enough from the land to be out of danger; yet near enough to have a full view of this natural phenomenon, the length of which is said to be eight or nine miles: which distance we made, in one hour and thirty-five minutes. There appeared to be in this wall, several different strata of stone, and these of various colours; all which lying horizontal, and so nearly parrallel, that they in some places, greatly resembled the work of art. The wind continuing to increase, at the time we were opposite to the east end of this wall, and the breakers running out into the lake to a great distance, from the mouth of the Cayahaga river; we thought it safest to run in to shore at this place, from which the land was low and level for the last mile to the river. The captain of the Mackinaw, who, with his glass, had viewed our movements with great anxiety, fearing we might attempt to make the river through the breakers, when we infallibly must have been wrecked and sunk, our canoe being but small and too heavy laden; rejoiced in seeing us run into shore at that place. He told us, that the Chippewas the day before, had fortunately, reached the rivers mouth, before the storm came on.

We now began to unload the vessel, although the land travellers, (who were the greatest body,) were not yet arrived; which being finished, we commenced making canoes out of large chestnut trees; and when the land travellers arrived, they joined us in the labour with a cheerfulness not to be described. But the season being already too far advanced, to think of planting corn on our arrival at the Muskingum, it being this day the 18th of June, we resolved to select a place on this river, where we might plant some corn and vegetables, and found a suitable situation within about a dozen miles from the lake, where it appeared there formerly was an Indian cornfield. Stopping here with our canoes, we chose the east side of the river, for our encampment, and there built temporary huts; while on the opposite side we prepared the ground for planting. It is indiscribable, how happy these poor Indians felt, on being released from so long a confinement, and again walking on their native soil: for with all Indians, to live upon the land of strangers, or land belonging to another nation or tribe than their own, it is next to being in confinement. They now cheerfully went to work, meeting daily for divine service, the same as they had done on the whole journey, whether on board the vessel, or on the land; and always in the open air.—Heckewelder, *Narrative*, 368-74.

XXVI

Return to Bethlehem: 1786

IT WAS AT PILGERRUH, the mission town which the Indian congregation established on the Cayahaga in the spring of 1786, that Thomas died, the boy who had been scalped at Gnadenhütten. Since that day of agony on the Muskingum, he had suffered from fits ("rheumatism in the head," it was called *). It is supposed that it was in one of these fits that he fell out of his canoe and, though a good swimmer, was drowned. His body was found in shallow water.

In the fall of that same year, 1786, John Heckewelder left the mission because of his wife's health. There was another baby coming, and the fear of an Indian war which beset the border county was not healthy for one in her condition. Heckewelder returned with his family to Bethlehem. Heckewelder's daughter, Polly (Johanna Maria), had already returned to Bethlehem the year before. But his second daughter, two-year-old Anna Salome (born August 13, 1784, at New Gnadenhütten in the Chippewa country), was still with her parents.

When they left Cayahaga on Monday, October 9, 1786, the party consisted of himself, his wife, little Anna Salome, and a large company besides.

Travel Diary of John and Sarah Heckewälder with Their 2-year-old Daughter Anna Salome from Cayahaga River to Bethlehem Oct. 9 to Nov. 15, 1786.†

---

* Edward Rondthaler, *Life of John Heckewelder* (Philadelphia, 1847), p. 108.
† Translated from the German.

Return to Bethlehem: 1786

A few white people from Detroit and the Shawano Towns begged to go in our company. John Leath, too, was with us. He had formerly lived with us at Salem, but in consequence of the break-up of our community on the Muskingum had become separated from us for the sake of his wife, who was a prisoner. He unceasingly asked for permission to live with us. He was told that I would speak of it to the Brethren in Bethlehem, and he would soon receive a reply. We came this day about 8 miles.

On the 10th Adolph, whom Br. David had sent with us as far as the first camp to see how we got along, returned. I sent back with him a hearty greeting to dear David and all the rest. We were all 3 miserable travellers. I was suffering rheumatic pains, my wife was in the seventh month of her pregnancy, and our child was ill of a fever; but we depended upon our dear Lord who could help us under all circumstances. At 3 o'clock we camped by a small run, but we found afterwards the water had such a bad taste we simply could not drink it. Our Indians, who had shot 2 deer, were well provided.

The 11th at noon we met some Sandusky traders bringing cattle from the States. They told us: that they had found the man who had lived for a long time at the Salt Spring [near Niles] dead & scalped & they had buried him. Our Indians were much distressed, as the man had only recently been very kind to them. We came today to the old Mahony. But at night when we were about to turn in we heard a very frightened cry from someone in the distance. The Indians knew at once it was a white man, and thought he must be in trouble. But when he turned up half an hour or so later we found he was in a great fright over the news that he too had got from the traders. He had made up his mind to catch us up because we were a strong party. Our company now consisted, in addition to our own people, white and brown, of a large family of peaceable Indians and 5 white people. John Cook, the father of this Indian family, talked seriously to me about various things and seemed worried about us. I told him what he was to do in case of trouble. All the same, I assured him that for the time being I had no apprehensions. But I had to talk sternly to the white people with us, who had been saying what short work they would make of any warriors they met, and I had to be tough and lay down rules which they had to obey or else go off by themselves. They promised to control themselves.

On the 12th another deer was shot. We camped this evening about 6 miles this side of the Big Mahony.

Early on the 13th Br. Stephanus while driving in the horses was so badly poisoned by a spider that he gave us to understand he would certainly die. In a very few minutes his eyes were swollen shut, and his whole body was covered with big red spots. He pointed to his heart, and as he assured us afterwards, he felt as if it were under a heavy weight or in a press. The aforementioned John Cook, who had himself experienced this twice before, prescribed a drink of powder, tobacco and rotten leaves mixed together, and had him rubbed with this as well. At once he began to vomit, and after an hour we observed some improvement in him. While we were anxiously awaiting the outcome, I heard several amazing instances of the same. At last the Brother gave us to understand that he felt better, and at 10 o'clock he told us to set off. We put him on a horse and left this place. At 12 noon we were in Sich heunk (or Salt Spring) where we sadly and with some trepidation fixed up the murdered man's grave and made an invoice of his belongings. His brains and blood were on the floor, and from the footprints and other signs the Indians with us were able to explain to us how it happened as clearly and vividly as if they themselves had been present. But we all felt uneasy here. We hurried away and camped that night 8 miles this side of the place on Beaver Creek.

Early in the morning of the 14th we heard several shots. Our Indians were worried because they knew that 3 large war parties had gone in the direction of Beaver Creek. I tried to reassure them. At 9 o'clock an Indian from Pittsburgh met us, who had undertaken to bring seventy or so horses to Gajahaga for the Trading Company. He gave us news both good and bad, and among other things said the Cherokees were beginning to turn up around Pittsb. and had stolen some horses there. I should under the circumstances have advised the badly-frightened packers whom we met soon after, but I had good reason for not doing so. I introduced them, however, to the other white people with us, some of whom had fled from the Shawano Towns. These gave the packers a brief digest of the news, and they left us in fear and confusion. In the evening we put up our tents about 4 miles this side of Cascaskung [near Newcastle].

At 9 o'clock on the 15th we passed Languntoutenink and camped at night on a large branch of Beaver Creek. Today two more deer and several wild geese were shot.

Early on the 16th Jacob shot another deer and some wild turkies. At noon we met Br. Michael, who was on his way back from Pittsb., whither he had escorted 2 white people. They had been the first to see the man who was murdered, and afterwards they had run day and night until they reached that place. Michael was so exhausted that he could hardly walk. We asked him to give our warm greetings to our dear Brethren, white and brown. In the afternoon my wife had the misfortune to fall from her horse. But no harm came of it. We thought best to let our horses rest a little, so we camped at the first run.

On the 17th our way, like yesterday, was hilly. Jacob shot a deer. We came today to within 9 miles of Pittsb.

On the 18th we set off early, and towards noon reached the Allegheny at Mr. Robinson's where we found lodging. As the races were on during the next three days, it was almost impossible to get a word with anyone in town. Meanwhile we visited our good friends the Bousmans and Heymachers across the Monongahella. The old man, father of the last-named, told me much about the Brethren in former days, about Count Zinzendorf, and asked particularly after Br. Spangenberg whom he held in high esteem. We had much useful conversation. . . .

During his six-day stay in Pittsburgh, Heckewelder met many people, among them Mr. Weber, pastor of the Reformed Church, and Colonel Gibson, who had been Commandant at Fort Pitt, 1781-1782.

On the 23rd Col. Gibson informed me that he had found a man who would be pleased to help us with horses as far as Carlisle, and he offered to lend my wife a side saddle. I thanked him for his trouble. This afternoon I wrote a letter to Br. David.

Early on the 24th the man who was to accompany us appeared. I sent off our dear Indian Brethren, took leave of my friends in the town, and then we set off on our further journey. There was a man from Detroit in our company who had seen and talked with Br. David [Zeisberger] on the far side of Gayahaga. David had told him that he was getting stronger every day. I thanked the Lord for this good news.

In the evening at 8 o'clock we came to Thomas King's, 18 miles. Here we had a very unquiet lodging. The people of the neighborhood were all come drunk from a *vendue*. They picked quarrel after quarrel and had one fight after another, and because they disturbed us in our corner and our guide objected to it, they ended by pitching into him and he got a bloody head for his pains. Two others had their hands torn to pieces, the blood running down all over them. As this sort of thing went on all night until morning, and we could not get a moment's sleep, I decided to give the landlord a rebuke, and did it with this addition: that I would warn everone I met to avoid his establishment. We got away at last from the wretched place, and at noon entered a well-ordered house to get a little rest. The landlady (a German) complained to me with great embarrassment how badly off they were with their preacher (Weber), a man who did nothing but stir up quarrels among the people, particularly between the Reformed and Lutherans. On election day he went to Vendues, got drunk, received a large salary, and in the end accomplished nothing but lead his people into the mire where he left them sitting. She sorely wished a real pastor would come into the neighborhood. In the evening we stopped at John Bonnet's, Jun., decent folk, and we passed a quiet night.

By noon of the 26th we reached the foot of Lorrel [Laurel] hill. Here I had occasion to give a certain Mr. Patton news of our journey down. The people of the house (Germans) told me that they had once heard one of our Brethren, Melchior Schmidt by name, preach, and his sermon was remembered to this day. They wished sincerely they could have a man like that in this neighborhood. We spent the night at the Widow Baron's. She also vividly remembered Br. Schmidt's preaching.

The 27th. We stopped at a house where there were some nice people to inquire the way. By evening we had reached the foot of Allegheny Mountain on this side, but to our regret the house was so full of people travelling to Pittsburgh that we had but little prospect of a quiet night. The landlord, however, who had had some acquaintance with the Brethren, took pains to see that my wife and child got a corner where they could lie on the floor; and though I and a good many others had to do without sleep, as we had to sit or stand all night long, the house was quiet and orderly enough.

The 28th. One of our horses was missing, but we were provided with another one until the lost horse could be found and sent after us. We came at night to John Bonnet's, Sen. Our guide, who was a strict Presbyterian, informed me that we must not travel on the morrow (Sunday), which was entirely agreeable to our landlord. He gave us his own room, and seemed very much pleased to be entertaining Brethren. . . .

Like the German landlady on the 25th, their host here enjoyed a gossip about the neighborhood preachers, complaining especially about the quarrelling between the Lutherans and Reformed. He brought out a copy of Welling's *Everlasting Gospel* and other religious books, and wanted Heckewelder's opinion of them. He expressed a hope that Heckewelder might bring more books if he ever came back this way.

A man of this locality named George Eis offered to give me a plot of land if I would instruct his brother-in-law's child in Christianity. A woman traveller told us how unfortunate she was. She said she was well known among the Brethren in Grace-Hill (Ireland). While she was with her parents, she lived only a step from that place. Her father had kept a large inn, his name was Graham, and they had often put up members of the Brethren, also Count Donaw. Her parents used to send her over there when distinguished people came to visit the place, and she knew almost all the unmarried Sisters, and had received permission to enter the Sister-House. Her father, however, was actively opposed; and finally her brother, who had gone to America a few years before, had sent for her. She was now married, but in poor circumstances, and was very sorry that she had not followed the advice of the Brethren. Today I despatched a note by one of the travellers to Br. Klingsohr.

The 30th it rained all day, so that we had to remain here. The day was passed in pleasant discourse, and as I hope not without profit to the company.

We were up early on the 31st. The Juniata, which had risen a good deal, would not suffer us to cross without a wetting. In the evening we came to the Crossing.

November 1st. We put Sideling Hill behind us and came in the evening to Mr. Jenneson's at "the burning Cabbins" [Burnt Cabins]. Capt. Bird visited us in our lodging. He reminded me that he had entertained Frid.

Return to Bethlehem: 1786

Post and me 24 years before, and spoke very lovingly of Bethlehem, which he had visited a few years back.

Early on the 2nd my horse stumbled in a bad swamp. The child was thrown out of my arms and the horse jumped over it. We thanked the dear Lord for His gracious protection. Then we climbed the last 3 mountains, which together constitute the Blue Mountain, and came in the evening to Shippensburg.

On the 3rd we reached Carlisle. I searched the town for a wagon to take us to Lancaster or Lititz, and I found a man who promised to do this, but afterwards, as I realized to my embarrassment, he was only making a fool of us because (as he put it at one point) he had doubts about getting his money. Meanwhile a German named Dui turned up who knew the Brethren in Lititz and who was willing to take us there. As I had no more cash I had to find a friend who would help us. This I soon found in the person of General Buttler, who not only provided what I needed without asking for its return, but offered his services to our mission in every way. He invited us to Sunday dinner, tomorrow, and expressly wished that we should feel . . . [indecipherable] and at home with him and his wife. They loved the Brethren and had visited Lititz. I also called on General Ervin, who had been elected to Congress. This gentleman assured me that he was very much interested in the success of our mission, and he promised that if I knew of any way in which Congress could help the missionaries, I should let him know about it or give him instructions, and he would attend to it at once himself. I thanked him for this offer of assistance.

Sunday the 5th. I went with my host, Mr. Greber, to the Lutheran Church where I heard Pastor Schaefer preach on the Gospel for the day.*

I was particularly impressed when he entreated his listeners earnestly and with tears in his eyes to let the Divine Spirit show them what poor, sinful creatures they were, and then beg the Saviour's mercy and forgiveness for their sins. Afterwards we went to General Butler's. After dinner he took me to call on certain friends and then showed me everything noteworthy in and around the town. Among other things he took me to the Cave which is a mile from the town. We went in some 50 paces under this natural vault. The entrance is about 10 or 12 feet wide, and the cave is said to go some 20 or 30 rods into the mountain, though it twists about. We got home by sundown, but had to have supper with General Butler first. During our absence Mrs. Butler and my wife had much pleasant conversation, and they called to mind the hospitality and kindness they had received at Lititz when the Brethren and Sisters visited there. As we were leaving he asked us to visit him every day as long as we were here. We would always be welcome at his table. During the 3 days of our stay here, many friends called on us

---

* Lutheran pastors receive from their synod a prescribed outline from which to choose a certain biblical text for the sermon each specified Sunday and religious holiday.

in our lodging, and we were invited to return the calls. Among other visitors was a surveyor named Bohannan, who had come to know our Indians and their teachers when they were living at Friedenshütten and Schoshéquanünk. He asked us to spend a day with him. He loved and honored the Brethren for the pains they took & the hardships they suffered to bring the Christian faith to the poor Indians. He mentioned Br. Rothe as a man whose only aim was to show the Indians the way to salvation, etc.

At last at noon on the 8th, after enjoying a great deal of kindness here, and after taking leave of General Butler, whom I had often visited during these days, and especially of our kind host, the man I mentioned drove us off in his wagon at dusk. We slept that night at his house 5 miles from town.

On the evening of the 9th we came to Hummels Town, where we met people who knew Bethlehem and Lititz and had passed that way only a few days before. It was good to hear the names of the Brethren whom they knew, and to have news of them.

On the 10th we had a particularly bad road, the wagon kept getting stuck in the mud, and we had to go on foot over the worst places. Late at night we came to the New Furnace. I did not like the people here. They stole a bag of fodder from our driver. I found a corner for my wife and child in the mill belonging to a German, but I had to sleep in the wagon.

At noon on the 11th we at last had the unspeakable joy, after a long and difficult journey, of reaching to our beloved Lititz. We were warmly welcomed by everyone.

We were refreshed and strengthened both in body and in soul during the next 2 days, particularly on the 13th Nov. We are indeed grateful to the Klingsohrs and their dear co-workers for the kindness they showed us.

On the 14th, after a warm leave-taking, we set off again, and arrived in the evening of the 15th in our beloved Bethlehem.

Five days later a man passing through from Pittsburgh told John Heckewelder that it now seemed certain the dreaded Indian war was about to break out.

XXVII

Down the Ohio to Marietta: 1788

AFTER TWO QUIET YEARS in Bethlehem, Heckewelder set out again for the Indian country. His purpose was to see what arrangements could be made for surveying the lands which had been set aside by Congress, in an ordinance of 1785, for the Moravians at their old towns on the Muskingum. The difficulty was not in finding men who could make the survey, but in persuading the Indians to allow it to be made. The Indians were not averse to having Moravians in their midst, but it was a question whether they would admit the right of Congress to make this grant of lands when the ownership was still in dispute.

The treaty for which General St. Clair was preparing had originally been set for the Falls of the Muskingum, but an attack by hostile Indians on the stores he had been assembling there led St. Clair to change the place of meeting to Fort Harmar at the mouth of the Muskingum. This change was unwelcome to many of the Indians, particularly to Joseph Brant, the ablest and most influential man among them. When the treaty assembled—without Joseph Brant—it was found that the Indian representation was so meager as to be of dubious validity. Nevertheless St. Clair went ahead and at the close of the treaty claimed to have received from the Indians confirmation of earlier treaties and land cessions. The Indians, it was soon learned, regarded the whole thing as a fraud.

Timothy Pickering, in a note written about this treaty two or three years later, observed that the Indians denied "that their nations were fully represented at the treaty of Fort Harmar. Mr. Heckewelder does not find among the grants the name of even one great chief. Of all the names only 4 are known to Mr. Heckewelder as principal chiefs. Of the Delawares in particular but one tribe of the three appears to have been represented—and that the most inconsiderable Pipe was the only *chief* the other three but counsellors. The Delawares under Buckongejelas [Pachgantschihilas] constituted two-thirds of the nation—not one of whom was present. But one of the three principal Ottawa chiefs was present. But two of the Putiwatima principal chiefs. No Shawanoe. But one of the principal Chippewa chiefs." *

Meanwhile the Ohio Company of Associates, organized in 1786 at Boston by a group of New Englanders, had contracted for 1,500,000 acres at the confluence of the Ohio and Muskingum, and General Rufus Putnam, in April, 1788, had brought the first body of settlers and was laying out the town of Marietta.

The journey to Fort Harmar by way of Pittsburgh was opened dramatically for John Heckewelder by a meeting with Colonel David Williamson, the officer responsible for the Gnadenhütten massacre.

A Short Account of Br. Joh. Heckewelders Journey to the Muskingum, his Sojourn there and his Return, from Sept. 10 to Dec. 23, 1788.†

Sept. 10 1788. Today I set out on my journey to Muskingum after receiving the blessing of the congregation in Bethlehem for the work to which I had been commissioned, and on the 12th at Lititz I was joined by the single-Brother Matth. Blickensdörfer as my travelling-companion, and so we continued our journey. Between Yorktown [York] and the Susquehanna we met a man who asked us if we intended going into the backwoods, and whether we were out looking for land. We replied that we wanted to see the country. He said if we went to Muskingum we could see our yellow neighbours gathering for a treaty. I asked him if by any chance he was from that part of the country. He answered, from Catfish [Washington] in Washington County. Might I ask his name? He said: My name is Williamson. I suspected at once that this was the notorious Col. Williamson who had seized our Indians on the Muskingum. I asked him further whether he had ever been beyond the Ohio and whether the land there was really as good as it was said to be. He said it was much too good for its present inhabitants. Question: Had he ever been on the Muskingum? I had heard that the New Englanders had bought a large tract of land there from Congress, and that many were already settled on it, and I wondered if the land was any good?

---

* Quoted from MS. in Pickering Papers (Massachusetts Historical Society) by Fred Waldo Shipman in "The Indian Council of 1793: A Clash of Policies" (M. A. thesis, Clark University), p. 44, n. 42.

† Translated from the German.

He gave a deep sigh, said he had been all over that country and knew the Muskingum up to its headwaters, then bade us farewell and rode off. We heard next day on our journey that he was indeed the man I had suspected him to be. He was going to Lancaster on business connected with his office as a sheriff. Many a curse was sent after him by those who knew who he was.

The *13th*. We left Yorktown and came on the *14th* to Chamberstown [Chambersburg] where we breakfasted with a man named Reymer. This man has a great love for the Moravians. His parents used to belong to the Yorktown congregation, and he himself had gone to the Moravian school. . . .

The *15th*. We had a very bad road all the way to Sideling Hill. From there, however, as we had a beautiful (to everybody's surprise) new road up hill and down again, we recovered our spirits. Late in the evening we came to Snake Spring [about three and a half miles east of Bedford], so called because in former days hungry traders had eaten snakes there. Early on the *16th* we came to Bedford, and delivered to the well-known May a letter from his parents in Germany. This day we reached our friend John Bonnet's [at the "forks of the road" four miles west of Bedford]. No sooner had he seen me than he ran to get the *Idea Fidei*, which I had given him a year and a half ago. He said he had never had a better book in his hands than this; it was the pure truth, and no one, of what religion soever he be, could reject it without rejecting the Bible itself. His wife agreed with him and said, Yes, I spend many hours with this book, and both said they had often read it from cover to cover, and as time went on it became the more precious to them. We rested here the whole day, and our horses refreshed themselves on the beautiful meadows, of which this man owns an unbroken 110 acres.

The *17th*. After all our good entertainment this man would take no pay, but said, the Brethren on their travels should always have a day of rest with him and come and go as they pleased free of charge. We thanked him heartily, and climbed Allegheny Mountain, which made us perspire freely before we reached the top. From here the road became bad again, because the bottoms were muddy and on the mountain the swamps were knee deep, especially in Edmunds Swamp, where we were hardly able to get through. At length, however, we came to Squire Wells [Jennertown] 11 miles this side of Ligonier, where we found good quarters.

On the *18th* we crossed Laurel Hill and several streams that empty into the Ohio, and spent the night in Hannahstown 35 miles this side of Pitsburg. A new town by the name of Greensborough [Greensburg] was started in this neighbourhood 2 years ago, and it is hoped this will become the County Town for Westmoreland.

On the *19th* we came through Bushy Run (the place where Col. Bouquet in the year 1763 defeated the Indians) and reached Pittsburg in the evening. I at once sought out Mr. Hutchins the Geographer and showed him the Congressional Ordinance (which seemed agreeable enough to him). He assured me that he would do what he could in the matter, but regretted that no Indians had as yet come to the treaty. And bad news came that the Indian nations on the Tawa River were still in council and that little good was to be expected to come out of it.

The *20th*. An express came from Fort Harmer [Marietta, Ohio] with news that the Indians had attacked the troops of Congress on the Wabash River, killed 8 and wounded 10, which caused fresh apprehension.

The *22nd*. I had breakfast with Gen. Gibson, and afterwards visited some friends and acquaintances. I also made inquiries about how we were to proceed from here; to go by land seemed impossible, because from Wiling [Wheeling] on there is no proper road, and there are wide creeks too deep to cross on horseback. Meanwhile Mr. Hutchins had bought a boat for £15 & had it repaired. He invited me to go along with him, which I was very glad to do. I visited Col. Butler, who told me a number of things from a letter of Br. David Zeisberger to his Br. Gen. Butler. Two weeks ago some of our Indian brethren had been here and they had picked up the things which had been sent from Bethlehem to Pittsburg for Petquotting [near Milan, Ohio]. It grieved me to hear the news that one of the local printers named Boyd had recently hanged himself in desperation and that last winter John Monture an Indian had been secretly killed by Mingoes while out hunting, for I had known them both well. From Post St. Vincent [Vincennes] there came today a large French boat loaded with peltry, and next day one from Muskingum.

The *23rd*. Several friends expressed their pleasure over the tract of land that had been given to our Indians, and hoped that our Indians might soon settle on it again. Today 2 more large boats arrived, one from Fort Harmer & the other from Venango. With the first came Lieut. Ernst who will for the time being be the officer in command here, and with the other Major Doughty, both good friends of the Brethren. Some Delawares whom we knew, among whom was Benjamin, Nath. Davis's son, came from Sandusky. I sent a letter by the latter to David Zeisberger. The best news to me was that his parents are with the Brethren again and he himself is thinking of going back to them.

The *24th*. I crossed the Monongahella to Mr. Baasmann's. At noon I dined with Mr. Hutchins. In the afternoon I crossed the Allegheny River & on the island at Mr. Robbin's at a spot I knew dug up the lobilea root which does not grow anywhere else in this neighbourhood.

The *25th*. This was the day of our departure. We left Pittsburg with Mr. Hutchins, his servant & 2 soldiers as oarsmen, at 3 o'clock in the afternoon. We had not gone far before we came into shallow water, which is not unusual at this season of the year, and often had a good deal of trouble to get our boat along. In the evening we came to a cabin, but, as there was neither lodging nor anything else to be looked for here, we decided to go on 3 miles farther where there was said to be a roomy house & a good kitchen.

To Marietta, Ohio: 1788

But night overtook us so suddenly that we were unable to find the channels through the rapids & were in the end forced to spend the night on the round stones that lay along the bank like a pavement. We managed, though with some difficulty, to light a fire, broke off some branches over which we spread our canvas, and so got a dry resting place. Though the round stones seemed to get harder as time went on, Mr. Hutchins reminded us of one advantage we enjoyed: Here we were not bothered by the fleas and bedbugs of the lodging houses.

The *26th*. We started out under a heavy fog, passed Logstown [Legionville, near Ambridge] & before the morning was over made for a house on the south side of the Ohio, and there had breakfast, which we were much in need of. Here on top of the bank stands a very sturdy and magnificent elm, the circumference of which 2 feet above the ground is 33 feet, the diameter being consequently 11 feet. Much else we saw along these pleasant shores that filled us with astonishment. At noon we passed Big Beaver Creek and saw the site of Fort McIntosh [Beaver, Pennsylvania] which now is deserted. In its place a military post has been established on Big Beaver Creek. By 3 o'clock we were at the Pensylvania Line, which has been neatly hewn out to a width of 90 feet all the way from the Virginia Line in the south to Lake Erie in the north. The pleasant prospect of this line on both sides of the Ohio, which one can see stretching so far back into the country, especially since the land rises as it recedes from the Ohio, is enough to satisfy curiosity. But when you add that it just so happens that the south line cuts into the mouth of a large stream (called Mill Creek) and on the north side is opposite the mouth of another large stream (named the Little Beaver), it is really astonishing. The Ohio here is 480 yards wide. Towards evening we saw 3 deer on the river bank stepping towards us. Our soldier shot at them but missed. We spent the night on some rich land below Baker's Fort.

The *27th*. Early in the morning our hunters had the same luck with the wild geese they had had yesterday with the deer. We passed the deserted Fort Steuben then came to the present military post [Steubenville], which is on the north side of the Ohio, and stopped at a Col. Brown's house, where we had breakfast. These people are respectable and well-to-do. Going on, we saw 2 deer behind us swimming across the Ohio. By noon we were at Mingo Bottom [Mingo Junction], which is said to be the largest and most beautiful stretch of bottom land on the Ohio for 100 miles around. Here Mr. Hutchins showed me a hill on which stands a healthy well-grown white oak, which is 21 feet in circumference and 7 feet in diameter. At 1 o'clock we camped at the mouth of Buffaloe Creek, Mr. Hutchins having business with a McMahan, Esq., a few miles from here. Besides, he had left all his instruments & baggage here 2 years ago. I accompanied him there, but as the man was not home, we returned to our tent.

The *28th*. In the morning Mr. McMahan came to us & was very friendly.

He is said to be a Methodist & a fine man & is assemblyman for this county. At noon came Major Doughty and Seylers with their boats from Pittsburg. We left Buffaloe Creek & at 2 o'clock passed another military post, on the north side of the Ohio. (N.B. These posts were established this summer on account of the hostile Indians and because more than 50 people in one year have been killed in this county). By 4 o'clock we were at Wiling. The fort here stands on a bank that is about 40 feet high. It survived all attacks during the war although the enemy was often many in number & the garrison inside few. The land on which Wiling stands belongs to a worthy man named Zeeney [Zane], a justice. Opposite the fort is an island which is 3 miles long & ¾ wide, which belongs to this same man and has some fine plantations on it. At the lower end of the high bank and towards the lower end of the island are two large rivers almost opposite each other on the south and on the north side of the Ohio, both named Wiling (i.e, at the head).

The *29th*. We had rain all day. There were no more houses to be seen, and the oarsmen wanted to go on because they were already wet through, so we stayed on the water all day long, Mr. Hutchins & myself under a covering, the oarsmen in the open. Being wet to the skin, they wanted to go on all night because they thought it would be impossible to make a fire. We pointed out to them, however, the danger of travelling in the dark night, and so they were persuaded to land. Of course everything was full of water, the wood, the ground, the high reeds, but Mr. Hutchins and I managed to get a fire going, with the very considerable help of the lining which he tore out of his coat. Now we were all very happy at being able to dry our clothes again, and looked forward to a good drink of chocolate, but unfortunately the kettle tipped over just when it was ready to be taken off the fire.

Here the Ohio is 500 yards wide.

The *30th*. The weather was fine. We started early and came to the *long Reach* or Stretch, where the Ohio runs a perfectly straight course for 16½ miles. In this stretch there are 6 beautiful round islands and for the most part a charming countryside which from there on down the river becomes more and more attractive, especially the last 12 miles to the Muskingum, where there is good flat land on both sides of the Ohio and not a hill in sight. At 1 o'clock we passed the Little Musgingum & soon came to the upper end of the 3 mile long island, which reaches to within half a mile of the mouth of the Musgingum & on which there are several plantations. Past 2 o'clock we landed at the mouth by Fort Harmer. Mr. Hutchins and I soon reported to the Governor and Gen Harmer and dined afterwards in the former's tent, where we had various refreshments. I presented my letters to these gentlemen, who were very friendly. We soon learned that for the time being there could be no surveying, since the Governor had forbidden all such work until after the treaty in order to forestall any Indian complaints at the treaty. However, I was led to hope that it be undertaken in a few weeks and everything looked promising.

To Marietta, Ohio: 1788

We had thought at first of building a cabin on the east side of the Musgingum, but when we mentioned it the New Englanders would not permit it; instead I was lodged with Gen. Putnam & Blickensdörfer with Major White who is the commissary of the company here. At noon we dined with Gen. Harmer. The table was very well provided.

The *2nd* [October]. Major Doughty invited me for lunch. He was for many years a neighbour of the late Br. van Vleck in New York and through association with him has come to love the Moravians. I visited some Delaware Indians I knew, who told me much about the Christians at Petquotting. By the Indian, Moses, I sent a letter to David Zeisberger. The Governor and I discussed the present condition of the Indians. The Congressional ordinance pleased everyone to whom I showed it, & some expressed themselves like Mr. Hutchins, who said he was as happy about it as if he himself were personally concerned. The Governor wanted to have the land surveyed as soon as possible. I thought meantime of going with some Indians to Petquotting, but the Governor advised against it.

Sun. the *5th*. I went with the local inhabitants to their regular meeting. They have no minister at present but they come together to sing, pray, and listen to a discourse.

The *7th*. Some Indians visited me and told me that if better times and peace were here, they too would become believers. One of them, whose father *Paulus* died 30 years ago in Gnadenthal [near Nazareth] gave me the best hope.

The *9th*. I was with the Indians at *Campus Martius* & afterwards I had a look at the town-site and some of the outlying lots which are good for pasture.

The *10th*. A Seneca Indian who had been badly beaten up by some drunk people was thrown into the water and drowned. The chiefs went to the Governor to reassure him about the matter and said the incident was not important, he was a person of no consequence, and the nation could well spare him.* To my joy I received a letter today from Bethlehem from my brother. I visited the Governor who expressed his anxiety over the fact that his messengers to the Indians had failed to return and his fear for their lives. At midnight an alarm gun at the fort was fired. The guard in *Campus Martius* replied with a shot. The purpose was only to test whether everything was ready in case of an Indian attack. A soldier died though he had been ill

---

* This phrase has been misunderstood. It does not imply a sneer at the "common man." The Seneca chiefs were trying to avoid making an international incident out of the murder, and used a form of words which the Indians understood to mean just that. Compare the words reported by Heckewelder with those written July 21, 1774, by the famous Logan, who took many scalps in Dunmore's War in revenge for the slaying of his family on Yellow Creek: "Captain Cresap, What did you kill my people on Yellow creek for? The white people killed my kin, at Conestoga, a great while ago; and *I thought nothing of that*. But you killed my kin again, on Yellow Creek, and took my Cousin prisoner. Then I thought I must kill too . . ." See *American Pioneer*, I, No. 1, pp. 22-23.

for only an hour. A soldier from Fort Hockkochging brought meat for sale from a buffaloe that weighed 800 lbs.

The *13th*. I visited an Indian named Johanan. This Indian had been baptized in Bethlehem. He talked to me again as he had often done at Lichtenau about returning to the Faith, and assured me that he knew many more Indians who wanted to accept the Faith. The Governor today expressed himself very favorably about our Indian mission & wished to see a settlement of the Brethren at the Indian towns on the Musgingum. He would help all he could & let our Indians have right & justice & protect them as much as he could. A good government has now been established here and it would steadily improve and become more secure. It would also be necessary, if we should live on the Muskingum, that some of the Brethren there be appointed magistrates, so that the Indians might get an idea of the purpose of such institutions and that there should be some authority among them to restrain the evil. He was happy about the Congressional ordinance. The whole tract of land where our settlements were would come into our hands. Gen. Buttler whom I visited said the same & in case the land could not be surveyed we could move in on it anyway because the land was ours. The Brethren were entitled to every encouragement, they were quiet & useful inhabitants of the country and the only ones who could make Christians of the Indians. He admired what he had seen of their work, and how real devils had been made into good Christians. It was inexcusable that the Brethren and their Indians had been so pushed arround & persecuted, but he hoped God would bring an end to their troubles. In the evening some boats arrived, as happens nearly every day, on their way down the Ohio for Kentuke, & after they had reported to the police officer the number of persons and cattle, they went on. No boat passes here without making such a report to the proper official. At noon I dined with Capt. Ziegler who told me about the fine institutions of the Brethren at different places where he had been, especially at Sarepta [on the Volga River, Russia]. A courtmartial was held here today to try a soldier who while drunk had attempted to kill a sick Indian with a tomahawk. Fortunately he had been prevented by another Indian. When the Chiefs learned that the soldier was to get 100 lashes for it, they all asked the Governor to pardon him, and did not desist until they heard that he had been acquitted, and then the soldier had to thank them.

At the *Campus Martius* I was visited by the Monsy Chief Mannittohaliechk, whom the white men call Snake. He lives on the Allegheny above Goschgoschink [near West Hickory], where there are still more than 100 of his nation. He wished that the Indians might live & work like the white men, but he said the old Indians were against it.

Today at the request of the Seneca chiefs the plug in the rum barrel was hammered in tight, i.e., no more rum was to be sold to the Indians because the Indians drink away their deerskins & the clothes off their backs. Today I saw 3 Chippeways put in irons. 2 of the prisoners escaped a little while

To Marietta, Ohio: 1788

ago. While I was dining with the Governor, the first part of the dinner conversation was about the Turtle and how it carried up the island (the earth) out of the depths of the sea on its back and out of it made this land for the Indians, and because the turtle can live both in the water and on land, the greatest chief of all nations must be of this lineage. After dinner one of the chiefs asked that the rum plug be loosened a little, i.e., that he might have a bottle of rum. The Governor, however, said that as all the chiefs jointly had driven in the bung, it was stuck so fast they would all find it a job to pull it out again. The Cornplanter, Halftown & other Seneca chiefs expressed the wish that they might have teachers. An Oneida, however, said: If you are looking for a preacher, you had better choose a better one than we have because ours preaches what he does not practice. An old Seneca from Niagara rose and said: he did not need a teacher, because he was already too old to learn anything new. Such people had better keep away. This afternoon in company with Jake Nicolson and Capt. Kingsbury I visited the Indians who were encamped for 1½ miles along the Musgingum.

The *17th*. There came a rumor that a large body of Indians was on the march 10 miles from here, but it was not known whether they came as friends or as enemies. Orders were given to get ready for defense. It was found, however, to be a misunderstanding: it was only some messengers who had been sent out and were now returning. From them it was learned that the nations still at the Tawa River had held a council & were divided, Brand with his people being for war & others for peace. The peace party had shaken the tomhak over Brand's head, i.e., threatened him.

The *18th*. I went with Major Sarjant to Virgin Bottom, a mile up the Muskingum on this side. The 8 acre lots in this beautiful large bottom are very high in price. Indeed, 100 dollars in cash has already been offered for such lots. From Limestone [Maysville, Kentucky] came a large canoe with 10 barrels of Jensang roots. Another boat arrived with the same roots in the service of Judge Symmons.

The *25th*. A large boat arrived with people and cattle from New England.

The *27th*. I called on the judges. From Kentucke came Col. Boone one of the first settlers there (he has twice been captured by Indians) with 10,000 pounds of Jensing. He is taking it first to Wilihg, fetching another like quantity which he has in Limestone, and plans to take it all to Philadelphia. At Fort Harmer I met Nathanael Davis's son Solomon and the son of Louise and Jacob, 2 of our baptised children who after the murder of our Brethren on the Muskingum fled with their parents & now are grown up. They seemed to be rather indifferent to what I had to say to them.

The *29th*. The last Indian messenger arrived, who had been sent to get a definite report on the council held by the nations on the Tawa River. He brings advance news of the conclusion of this long council in which the nations have been very much divided, reporting that in the end the 6 Nations had decided to go to the treaty at the Musgingum. The Indian Quisohachkin told me that Capt. Pipe had told him that 4,000 Indians had assembled at the Tawa River (there were, however, only 2,000) & one was lucky to get a bite to eat each day because provisions were very scarce.

The 31st. A catfish was brought to market here which was 3 feet 7 inches long & weighed 54 pounds. The number of squirrels around here is so large that hardly a day passes but one or two hundred are killed. Since fall many 1000 have been killed on the Ohio alone, in swimming across. Their course is from south to north.

Nov. 1. Capt. Hutchins with his guard in 3 boats returned from Scioto. The continued rainy weather has greatly hindered his work. I spoke with him about the surveying of our land on the Musgingum & because Major Sargant who is one of the contractors of the Ohio Purchase and the Secretary of the Court here has said he would be glad to undertake this work, he has now been appointed and authorized to do it.

The 4th. I went with Major Sargant across to Virginia & since he was looking for a huntsman and had other business to attend to, I occupied myself looking at the beautiful landscape. The view of the Musgingum, Fort Harmer, *Campus Martius*, and the other buildings is particularly pleasing. Today 6 large boats passed, bound for Kentuke, on which there were 195 people, over 100 horses, and other livestock. In the Virginia Bottom I found a fine healthy white oak tree which (three feet from the ground) was 19 feet in circumference and 6 feet 4 inches in diameter.

The 6th. I went to Fort Harmer to speak with the Govr before my departure. He, however, objected and told me not to start before there was further news from the Indians. There were good grounds for his objections, and I had nothing to say against them. So it was decided to let the survey wait.

The 7th. The messengers arrived at last: Mr. Wilson, Ranckins & Loveless with some 20 Mohawks & a few Delawares. Among them was Capt. David, a high chief of the 6 Nations & a Mohawk by birth. He and Col. Brand's son who was also with the party are distinguished-looking & very modest persons, & both speak English well. From Mr. Wilson, with whom I had only a few minutes conversation, I learned that it was fortunate for us that we had not gone out to survey the land, and he told me, moreover, that the land which Congress had given to our Indians would be regarded by the wild Indians no other than as if it had been given to white people, & therefore they would resist the survey until they acknowledged that the land had been surrendered. An Indian, Stephanus, who had once been baptized by the Brethren & whose grandparents the Salomons had died in the barracks in Philadelphia, was glad to see me.

The 9th. John Cook's son came to see me. He had arrived a few days ago with a company of Indians. He told me that he had left Petquotting (where his parents live) 9 days ago—that all our Brethren there were well & and that he himself had tried to be a Christian but had found he was not

To Marietta, Ohio: 1788

able to, etc. Finally he revealed to me in confidence the Indian mind and intent: not to come to a treaty here but to insist on the Falls, and finally not to yield one foot of land west of the Musgingum, but only the land from Fort Mackintosh to the Muskingum & on up this river to the Fork above Tuscorawa.

The *10th*. The chiefs who had arrived here several days ago and who had insisted that the treaty be held at the Falls, received their answer from the Governor, that the fire which he had kindled last spring at the Falls had been entirely extinguished through the attack on his troops, and that he had no alternative but to hold the treaty here. No harm should come to the Indians even if he and they did not agree. They should not be held up here but go home again in safety as he himself wanted to do. For he was appointed by Congress only to talk with them & to listen to their complaints & if possible clear up what had been bothering them & satisfy them. If he did not succeed in that, he should have to report so to Congress. John Cook's son talked with me again told me he had lived for 2 months in Petquotting, and all that time he had tried to become a Christian. Indeed, he had learned 2 verses, which he recited to me, but that had not made him any better & he doubted if he could ever be a Christian. He believed Satan had too much power over him. I told him in reply, if he really wished to believe in the Saviour, Satan could not stop him; but you must be deeply in earnest and pray for His help, otherwise you cannot be helped. He replied, yes, I believe that, you have spoken the truth, for that is what they told me also at Petquotting. Well then, do it, I said. At that he began to cry bitterly.

The *11th*. We had the first snow. Next day the weather was fine again. The Ohio had risen 15 feet since yesterday and the Musgingum 9, so that the Kentucke boats went by with great speed. At this time there came also 4 Germans from Winchester in Virginia to look over the land, and they liked it so well they bought several 1500 acre lots at 400 dollars apiece. An Indian whom the Brethren had baptized Johannes (*alias* John Doughty) turned up here, but his only desire (as with all the others) was for strong drink. It is sad to see so many of those who have been baptized by us living in sin and shame.

Nov. 13th. We remembered this day of grace & blessing in the congregation & wished we could be with them. Our prayer meanwhile was to Him that he might impart to us a blessing because through His grace we belonged to His people.

The *14th*. Since the day before yesterday the Ohio has risen 23 feet and so has the Musgingum. The Kentucke boats these days pass almost every hour.

The *16th*. I was delighted to hear that 4 Ind. Brethren had arrived from Petquotting. I looked them up at once, & found Stephanus & Tobias on the other side of the Musgingum, and soon also Samuel & Thomas came down on a raft. These Brethren had started out after the great council on the Tawa [Maumee] River had broken up, leaving after the treaty, & had been sent here as delegates with a speech. They had been 15 days on the way and were much exhausted by all the rain and high water. I took them right at once to Gen. Buttler, to whom they had a letter to deliver from Br. David. They had something to eat, and I showed them a place near the *Campus Martius* where they could put up comfortably. I had them tell me how things had been with them, outwardly as well as inwardly, and learned by this that our dear old Br. Schebosch had gone to the Saviour.

The *17th*. 5 boats bound for Kentucke went by, one of which had 45 horses & 8 head of cattle on board.

The *18th*. I went to the Governor and told him what I had heard from our Indian Brethren, and what they knew of the nations' intentions. He was very sorry for our poor Indians, that they had so long been pushed around without rest, and he could see no end to it.

The *20th*. Many more boats bound for Kentucke arrived. With them came a certain Doct. Jones, a Baptist minister. He at once offered to preach here on Sunday. He was offered a lodging where I was staying. This man, who has decidedly peculiar principles, bothered me often with his questions and discourse. It was not long before the people got tired of his sermons, and so he left this place again after a few weeks.

The *21st*. The Indian Brother Samuel Nanticock dictated to me a letter for Br. Ettwein. All in all I had pleasant conversations with our Indian Brethren. In the evening the messengers, Mr. Wilson & Lovelass arrived from the camp of the savages on Licking Creek, with a letter from Joseph Brandt to the Governor here. The nations seem agreed to cede to the States the land from the mouth of the Musgingum to its headwaters and on the east side to Vanango [Franklin, Pennsylvania]. A gentleman (Doct. Brown) who had attended Sunday service at Bethlehem on the 26th of October, told a large gathering how greatly this had impressed him, and that he had felt something then which he could not describe & he could not restrain his tears. I called on the Governor, who is still sick with Podagra, and asked him to arrange for some clothing for our poor Indians, which he agreed to do.

The *23rd*. Our 4 Indian Brethren, with whom I have had many a pleasant conversation these last days, set off again for Petquotting & took the direct road by way of Salem so as not to encounter the Indians coming to the Treaty. Again Mr. Wilson was sent with a letter from the Governor to the Indians on Licking Branch.

The *29th*. I called on the Judges, & when the conversation got around to the Brethren's settlement on the Musgingum, they said they wanted to make things as easy and bearable as possible for the Brethren. As there is no hope for the time being that the land on the Musgingum can be surveyed, I looked about for an opportunity to get away from here by water.

Dec. 2nd. I helped Gen. Putnam lay out a large tree nursery., to which I gave the seed on condition I have a share in it when the Brethren started a settlement on the Musgingum. I called on the Governor and told him I

To Marietta, Ohio: 1788

was leaving. He discussed many things with me. He intended to write fully to Br. Ettwein, but had such violent Podagra pains he could not do it.

The 3rd. I took leave of the friends and acquaintances of the Brethren, & when I proposed to pay my landlord for my 9 weeks stay here, he replied that the Directors of the Ohio Company had instructed him not to take any pay from me (they would reimburse him). I felt that they liked me & would have been glad if I had stayed there until the land could be surveyed. I also felt obliged to thank these gentlemen in writing, to which I soon received a friendly answer. Today and during the night 13 Kentucke boats passed.

The 4th. I took leave of the Governor & Gen. Harmer & recommended that when the treaty was held, they should bring up our Indians' affairs, which they promised faithfully to do. I crossed the Ohio to the Virginia side where our boat lay. We got away before nightfall & and camped opposite the mouth of the Little Musgingum.

The 5th. During almost the entire day we saw flocks of wild turkies on the banks of the Ohio. Our hunters shot more than we could use.

The 6th. We met the Virginia Commissioners at work laying out a road to the Musgingum and on to Limestone and Kentuke. The many wild turkies on the banks delayed us considerably, our hunters shot many but took only the best. The rest they left lying.

The 7th. We were much incommoded by the drift ice coming down from far to the north.

The 8th. We passed Grave Creek [Moundsville] where some remarkable old fortifications are to be seen, of which the singular is a mound 70 feet high. This creek gets its name from the fact that there are Indian graves here, where one finds many hundreds of bones in one grave. In the afternoon we came to the first settlements & in the evening we at last reached Wiling [Wheeling]. As our boat went no farther, we were obliged to look around for horses, for it was impossible to continue on foot because of the streams and swamps. It was with great difficulty we got any horses and then we had to pay a very high price for them.

The 9th. We took leave of Mr Zeener [Zane] Esqr, who had lodged us free of cost, and travelled up Wiling Creek which is twice as wide as the Monakosy at Bethlehem. We had to cross it 30 times. The country hereabouts is very mountainous but very rich. We reached Catfish [Washington] and lodged with a Mr Wilson. This town of Washington in Washington County consists of 150 well-built houses, mostly 2 stories high, has a fine stone Court House & belongs to Pennsylvania. Here we had to get other horses, but without saddles. However, a certain Capt. Hughes who knows Bethlehem & expressed his great love for the Brethren, offered me his saddle, and so we continued our journey to Pittsburg. After we had travelled 8 miles we came to a handsome stone church. Yesterday we had seen pulpits and burial places by the roadside. By noon we reached Bühler's, who is a friend of our country congregations. A traveller from Buffaloe Creek came to us, with whom I got to talking about the Moravian Indians. He said his brother had been present when they were taken prisoner but he had had nothing to do with the massacre. I asked him if he believed the murderers could escape the wrath of God. To that he would say neither yes nor no, but brought up a number of accusations he had heard against these Indians. I asked him whether these charges were true & whether the Indians were the kind of people the murderers accused them of being. Oh no, he said. Most of the men on their return testified (but not publicly) that, from what they had seen of them and heard about them they must have been good Christians. And those who thought so had had no part in the massacre. Question: How comes it that not all of the men could see this? He said, I do not know. I answered, They could not see it because they were heathen themselves. Yes, said he, they have disgraced their country and it would have been better for all of us if this had never happened. I said, Yes, still better would it have been for the perpetrators if they had not committed this deed, and I expressed the wish that they might feel remorse for it & beseech God day & night for mercy that their souls might yet be saved and escape their deserved punishment in hell. At this the man's reserve broke and he said that man is by nature the worst creature in the world. I took the opportunity to go further into the matter. He listened with great attention. At last he asked who I was & when I told him he was shocked and replied, "That is just what I thought." I asked him what he thought about my words. He replied that I had spoken the truth. "Well, then, remember it and you will get good out of it." He replied: "Yes, that I will, and if you ever come back to these parts again, please be sure to visit my house." We came in the evening to the Monogahella Ferry and were taken over to Pittsburg. I was glad to be out of that dreadful country in which dwell the murderers who killed our Indian Sisters and Brethren.

The *11th*. I called on Mr Hutchins, he would have liked to see our land surveyed, but he understood well enough that it could not have been done without the greatest danger. He wished it could be done in the coming month of March, if I would come back. Col. Morgan, a true friend of the Brethren, who has been commissioned by Congress, at the desire of the Spanish Court, to start a town and settlement [New Madrid] with people from this area, on the west side of the Mississippi at the mouth of the Ohio, sent for me and told me he wanted to make an offer to the Brethren to settle there—not as a mere compliment but out of love & affection for the Brethren. He believed that the Brethren regarded him as a friend. He has long wished to serve the Brethren in one way or another, and now he seemed to have the opportunity. He wanted to write to Br. Ettwein about it. He asked me to send his greeting to the elders of the congregation & especially Br. Ettwein, Schweiniz & Birkby. The missionaries he hoped himself to visit in May or June on his return through the Indian lands. Capt. Hutchins who was present agreed in everything & he too sent greetings to the Br. & gave further assur-

To Marietta, Ohio: 1788

ance that he would not rest until our land was surveyed & that he was as anxious to get this thing done for the Br. as if he had a personal interest in it. They both said that, by the terms of the Congressional ordinance we were safe enough, but it would be a greater satisfaction when everything was settled and the deed was in our hands. Mr. Morgan spoke to me about the milliron & bolting cloth which Congress had given to the Indians at the beginning of the war, about which he wanted me to write to Mr. Anderson in Virginia in whose hand it is; which I did, & Mr. Morgan added a few lines. After I had taken leave of these gentlemen & other good friends (especially of the commanding officer, Ernst, a friend of Br. Bömpers in Bethlehem), we set out from Pittsburg on the *12th* and came on the *14th* to Lady Sinclair's near Ligonier, for whom I had a letter from the Governor. She is a High German and would gladly have had us stay for a day. In Carlisle I delivered another letter to Gen. Buttler's Lady, from her husband. She was also kind to us.

The *20th*. We reached our beloved Lititz, where we enjoyed Holy Communion with the congregation.

The *23rd*. I arrived in my dear Bethlehem again. With bad roads, a great deal of rain, high water, and drift ice in the rivers, especially in the Susquehanna, we have had a very difficult journey, but, thanks to our Saviour, we have come through safely.

❊ XXVIII ❊

To Pittsburgh and Pettquotting on the Huron River: 1789

IN THE SPRING of 1789 John Heckewelder travelled west again, this time in company with Abraham Steiner, to see once more about surveying the lands Congress had set aside for the Moravian Indians on the Muskingum. The journal, which gives an intimate picture of the unsettled Indian border during the years following the Revolution, was kept by Steiner, but it comes so close to Heckewelder's experience and so clearly betrays his influence that it belongs in this collection.

In the Moravian Archives at Bethlehem there are several versions of the journal. The one printed here has the fullest detail.

Abraham Steiner's Account of his Journey with Johann Heckewelder from Bethlehem to Pettquotting on the Huron River near Lake Erie, and Return. 1789.*

April 17th. We left Bethlehem and came in the evening by way of Emmaus to Shafers, 5 miles this side of Reading, where we had a very noisy evening; for some young gentlemen recently out from Hungary, who wanted to turn America upside down, had fault to find with everything and thought themselves very wise. They had been sent by a gentleman in Philadelphia to establish a potash factory beyond the Blue Mountains. These young men were quite sure there was no one else in America who understood potash. We left them alone with their wisdom, not feeling the need of it.

The 18th. Beyond Reading and on our way through Adamstown and

---
* Translated from the German.

To Pittsburgh and Pettquotting: 1789

Reamstown we enjoyed a pleasant conversation about the wanderings of our Brethren in former days through the country to which we are now going. Blessed were those days when everyone tended his cornfields and orchards, was at peace with his neighbor, and set the lost traveller right or welcomed him in peace to a hospitable meal in his cabin. At noon we passed Ephrata. The buildings are getting old and going to pieces. It is a pity they are only of wood, which does not last. They could be a visible monument to preserve the history of our predecessors here. In the afternoon we came to Lititz, where we rested——

On the 19th, and then, ——.

On the 20th, resumed our journey. Today we passed through Manheim where the glass-works are deserted and silent. Farther on we came to Donnegal [Mt. Joy], where we stopped a while at Abr. Friedrich's, from there to Elizabethtown, a wretched little place, and came to Middletown, a few miles this side of the Susquehanna Ferry. Middletown lies less than a mile north of the Susquehanna. It has a long street running E. N. E. and W. S. W. with a few small cross-streets, about 150 houses, and a middling-sized Lutheran church. There is a fine view from here of the Susquehanna, and the neighborhood is beautiful, fertile and pleasing. This place once had a large trade up the Susquehanna, but since the rise of Harrisburg, most of the trade has gone there and there is little left at Middletown. From here to the Blue Mountains the soil is rich and good and very fertile. Here the locust trees begin to appear, in fields and woods, and everywhere you see them until 60 or 70 miles beyond Pittsburg. From here to Carlisle many big wagons are seen on the road bringing their produce to market. From Middletown we went 6 miles farther up the Susquehanna to Forres Ferry [just below Steelton] through rich lands where locust and papaw abound. This ferry is run by 2 Germans; they are brothers and live on opposite sides of the river, about 200 rods above Chambers's Ferry. We were taken across here. The river is here a good mile wide, and the passage, which skirts the lower side of an island, offers a fine view up the river to Harrisburg, but we could see little because of the rain. On the other side of the river at the ferry is a good inn where we spent the night. A few days ago they had begun to catch shad fish. We put them to good use here ourselves.

The 21st. Half a mile beyond the ferry we came to Yellow Breeches Creek which, though sometimes a wild and dangerous stream, we were able to ride across without difficulty. 5 miles from Carlisle we saw a Presbyterian pulpit in the woods. These pulpits are built on a tree in the woods where people camp. A flight of three or four steps lead up to the pulpit, over which a small roof is built. At 1 o'clock in the afternoon we came to Carlisle, 16 miles from the ferry. We had a fine view of the place as we approached. This beautiful little town lies on an open plain. East of the town there are 5 long two-story buildings, each about 100 feet in length, built of brick, besides several smaller buildings, and an arsenal built of rough stone. During the war these buildings were put up by the States for workingmen attached to the army; they are, however, no longer maintained, and are now occupied only by Dr. Nesbitt, President of the local college, and a few young theological students. The town has about 350 handsome and for the most part two-story houses, most of which are built of handsome blue limestone, with which this vicinity abounds. The Courthouse is not large, but handsome, the prison small, and the market good. There are 3 churches, and the inhabitants, half of whom are German and half English, are mostly Presbyterians, Roman Catholics, German Lutherans and Reformed. The Methodists, too, have a meeting place here. There is a college here [Dickinson] but not in very good condition, and also two English schools; business is good, and there are many stores. There is a good printing press, and almost all trades are carried on here, in particular the making of nails and good beer. The surrounding country, especially in the direction of Yorktown and the Susquehanna, is rich and beautiful. It is only towards the Blue Mountains, which can be seen in the distance, that it is not so good. A mile north of the town is an underground cave. We should have liked to see General Butler and Mr. Alexander, but neither of them was at home. We came this evening to Semple's, 7 miles from Carlisle, where we spent the night. There is a big spring here which immediately forms a large creek. It gushes out of an opening the mouth of which is 2 feet in diameter, and is surrounded with other smaller springs which flow out of a little hill. The water is clear and fresh, coming from limestone ground, and is noticeably warmer in the large spring than in the smaller ones. There are said to be more such springs in this neighborhood.

On the 22nd we rode 14 miles through dry land where there are no springs, to Shippensburg, where we had breakfast. Shippensburg is a long town, and has only two cross streets where there are some houses. It has 103 houses, mostly well-built, of wood or stone, and 6 new houses under construction. In the town and all around it, as at Carlisle, there is plenty of the best blue limestone. Good beer is brewed here, the last on this road. We saw several acquaintances here. We saw also our first packhorses. They put packs on them which they have to carry * over the mountains. The drivers do not set off before 8 or 9 o'clock in the morning, but they drive all day till late in the evening. There are often 40 or 50 horses together. From here it is 10 miles to the foot of the Blue Mountain, where a German innkeeper lives named Kiefer. From this point on we had mountains to climb. There are 3 high ones here, one right after the other, which they call the Blue Mountains. A few years ago there was only a path over them, but now there is as good a road as can be expected on such mountains. The tops of these 3 mountains are not wide. No sooner are you up than you start down again. The road has been cut to a good width out of the mountain-side, & on the lower side, most of the

---

* Here the version (in the Archives of the Moravian Church at Bethlehem) which we have been following breaks off. We continue with another version from the same library.

way, there is a wall, sometimes pretty high, and every 20 rods there is a place for wagons to pass. On the first mountain the road up and down is neither stony nor steep. Between the first and second mountain there is a mile-wide valley [Horse Valley] through which a creek [Conodoguinet] runs north, and there are plantations and mills. Here lives Mr. Skinner [three and a half miles east of Fannettsburg], who constructed this road. The second mountain is somewhat higher & the road, especially on the far side, is steeper & more stony, but on the west side it loops about so much that one can get down without danger. Between this and the third mountain is a valley several miles wide through which Canagotshik [Conococheague] Creeks flows south. It is called Path Valley. The many plantations here are very beautiful and productive, with large old orchards attached to them. A little to the south is an iron foundry. The third mountain is rather stony, but otherwise not so bad. Among the rocks is a house whose inhabitants have neither a garden nor the least bit of field. They make their living solely by selling whiskey to travellers. There are many pines in the mountains, also oaks, and there are locust trees in the valleys. In the evening we came to Jemisson's, an inn 10 miles over the mountains from Kiefer's. Here we found a nice German, a tobacco manufacturer, who was about to move to Berlin [Somerset County, Pennsylvania] with his family. He told us that in this new 2-year-old town, which lies in the Glades, there are 20 houses all occupied by Germans. There are 60 lots reserved in it for Lutheran churches and schools. There are now 2 ministers in this locality. The Reformed is named Steg,* the Lutheran, Spangenberg. According to the regulations there, the houses must all be built to the same size, that is two stories high, & the log houses must all be built of hewn logs. The Germans are much on the move. You find them everywhere, as far as Pittsburg & beyond. From here on, every house and shack on the road is an inn, some of them as good as can be found in the most thickly settled districts. There are many others, however, where nothing is to be had but what you carry with you.

The 23rd. We passed the place where Fort Littleton formerly stood. It is now a fine plantation & a very good inn. It lies between the Blue Mountains and Sidelinghill. Now the soil becomes poorer. There are many small hills, with bigger ones seen in the distance. The soil has more gravel and there is a lot of pitch pine. 13 miles from our last night's lodging we came to the foot of Sideling Hill, a pretty high mountain. Half way up the mountain is a house where we had breakfast. The road up & down this mountain has only recently been laid out & constructed. It has been relocated a little to the north of the old road, and is so good that when you are up you hardly realize you are on such a mountain. One approaches it by a long gradual slope, rising steadily, so that when one reaches the mountain proper one is already pretty high. The road up is constructed the same way as on the Blue Mountains,

---

* John Michael Steg was the Lutheran pastor, Spangenberg the Reformed.

so that if you do not have a load you can ride up and down at a good speed. The mountain is not very broad on top, & the road along the mountain is quite clear of stones. Formerly Sideling Hill was much dreaded by travellers because of the rough steep road and the huge rocks on it. But here you can see what an efficient government can do in such a case. There is something peculiar about the country round here. When you are on top of one mountain you see another and sometimes several more ahead of you. On the far side of Sideling Hill are pine woods. The soil does not appear to be particularly fertile, but it is better than it seems. Pine, hickory, locust & oak, grow together here. The scenery here is very romantic. There used to be very good hunting in these mountains and there are still many deer. 11 miles from the house on Sideling Hill we came to the Juniata, at a place called the Crossing, on a branch of the Juniata known as the Raystown Branch. The road approaching it goes over and through the mountains and, for the last stretch down the river, between 2 mountains in a glen which is full of flat stones and through which runs a little stream.* We ferried over the Juniata because the river was too high for fording. The road then follows a ridge; one has the Juniata on both sides. 2 miles from the Crossing the river is only a good stone's throw from the road on either side. On the north side of the road the bank is very high and steep, & the road runs close to the edge. Once, it is said, a man went over here with a wagon & 4 horses, & nothing has been heard of him since. The Juniata runs a very crooked course. At first it seems to flow gently, but because of the many obstructions among the mountains it becomes violent and at last quite wild and tears its way through the mountains. From here to Bedford it is never far from the south side of the road. A few miles from the neck of the Juniata, we crossed Bloody Run [Everett], a clear stream. There are many plum thickets on its banks and for several miles farther till you come to Wills Mountain [Tussey Mountain], which is also called Great Warriors Mountain on the maps. The Juniata flows through this mountain, cutting it in two. The road runs along beside the Juniata and is perfectly level. The mountain on the other side of the river is high and well-wooded; on this side it is not so high, & the rocks overhang the road. At night we came to Snakespring, 11 miles from the Crossing, and stopped at Diefenbach's, a German Innkeeper's. While we were on the road it rained fairly hard, but once we were inside the house there came a downpour with thunder & lightning. Snakespring is said to have received its name from the Indian traders, who used to have a trading post here. Once a lot of them got together here and had a celebration, during which they killed a snake, fried it in the fire & ate it, & afterwards called the place Snakespring.

On the 24th we set off for Bedford, which lies 5 miles beyond Snakespring. A few miles this side of Bedford we crossed Denning's [Dunning] Creek, not far from where it enters the Juniata. There is a bridge over this

---

* Steiner and Heckewelder took the new road, now followed by the Lincoln Highway.

creek, but as the water had risen so high we had to ride through deep water on either side before we could reach the bridge. Both creeks here are the same size, & up Denning's Creek, where there is good land and a beautiful countryside, it is said to be very well settled. A quarter of a mile before you reach Bedford you cross the Juniata again by another bridge. On this side of the town, between it & the Juniata, lives Mr. May, a hatter, who once lived in Bethlehem. We called at his place. He invited us in for breakfast and fed our horses. The Juniata flows past Bedford on the north side of the town, so we had to cross it again farther on. As there is no bridge at that place and the water had risen very high, we had to go back and cross the bridge [at Bedford] and make a detour round [the north-east side of] the Juniata. Mr. May rode with us to show us the way. On the way he inquired about several of the Brethren, and expressed the wish that the Moravians might settle in this area: he would like to join them again. Our detour took us 4 miles through woods, swamp, and deep water. Here and higher up there are very nice bottom lands and many meadows by the Juniata, but elsewhere it is very hilly. By noon we reached our friend Bonnet's, 4 miles beyond Bedford, where we stayed till next morning & were well looked after. Brother Heckewelder made him a very welcome present, the first part of the Greenland History. They also have the *Idea Fidei Fratrum*, & his wife, who is awakened, reads in it every day and, as she says, often finds comfort in it. Her husband seldom reads spiritual books except those dealing with the Universal Restoration. This, indeed, is his favorite subject, & his conversation revolves around that and political news. If you agree with him in everything, you will have him for a friend and get good service. It would be well if there were a Moravian settlement here. The situation is excellent & very convenient for business. On an elevation, with level ground, it is suitable for a settlement; the building land is good, & field and wood furnish an abundance of pasture in summer for cattle. Below on your left flows the Juniata, where the loveliest meadows, the best grass and rich soil are found. Here & on the adjoining plantation there are more than 200 acres of cleared pasture-land, and more can be cleared. Mr. Bonnet makes several 100 pounds a year from passing travellers for hay and pasturage, and some of his neighbors do almost as well. Here the great road to Pittsburg divides into two main roads, the one called the Pennsylvania Road [by way of Ligonier], the other the Glades Road [by way of Berlin], which come together again 12 miles this side of Pittsburg.

On the 25th we had a good road for 5 miles farther till we came to Anderson's at the foot of the famous Allegheny Mountain. This is not, of course, the actual mountain. You continue to ascend for several more miles. The mountain is higher than it appears to be, for it rests, as it were, on other mountains on which you are already standing when you really see it. Several miles beyond Anderson's is Ryan's [Lyon's] Inn, which is still some distance from the mountain proper. This innkeeper has a sign, the Black Lion, which is the only inn sign between Bedford & Pittsburg. There was nothing to be had here except a little whiskey, & no oats for the horses. We kept right on climbing till we reached the real mountain. Here a brook comes down off the mountain and across the road. From this brook to the top of the mountain is about a mile. A strong wind was blowing as we climbed, and it was still blowing hard while we were on top. The road up the mountain is rather stony, & all along the lower half small springs come out of the mountain on the left and run down the road. It is not particularly steep, and you can get up if you climb slowly and don't mind tired legs. Left of the road, all down the side of the mountain, the soil is very rich & this is called the "Garden Spot." It produces tall weeds, & all kinds of timber and shrubs are found here growing together. There are cherry, walnut, locust, sassafras, mulberry, ash, chestnut, hickory, elm, maple, beech, oak, aspen, etc. On the right hand side a beautiful little brook goes tumbling down. On the far side of the brook the mountain rises rather higher and the soil is poorer. Here are Spruce, white & pitch pine, cedar & boxwood. It is flat on top of the mountain, and it continues like that with some little variations to Laurel Hill, so that it may be said that Laurel Hill stands on Allegheny Mountain. The soil on the mountain top is mostly a black, rich loam, but it is cold; the grain often freezes, but grass grows in abundance. It is fairly well settled, and although there are not many plantations to be seen along the way, the people are already complaining that their neighbors are too close to them. In many places the road is rather stony; it is like a morass when it rains and pretty bad in spots. At Stadler's, a tolerable inn on the mountain 11 miles from Anderson's, the road used to veer to the right through Edmond's Swamp; but as this swamp is so very bad the road now bears more to the left, to Stony Creek, which is 9 miles from Stadler's. The way there is rather stony, and at a small run, in which there are many trout, passes through a small pine swamp. As this creek [Stony Creek] was so very high, we had to make a detour up the creek to where it is divided into four branches. Each of these branches being a wild, rushing, stony creek, we had trouble enough in getting across. 1½ miles from this last creek, we got back on the main road, & since it was already late, & for a good stretch down the road there was not another house, we turned left off the road for half a mile to Michael Zimmerman's, a German, and spent the night there. The accommodation was good, and the price was reasonable. The man himself, his wife & servants are nice, quiet people. He conducted morning and evening prayers, which we attended. There is a good settlement here, mostly Germans, 18 miles from Berlin. There is a school here, too. The soil is good & rich, & there is plenty of grass, but it is cold here, & the people cannot grow fruit trees, not even apples. It froze hard tonight & ——

On the 26th we could not get warm all day. We crossed Laurel Hill today, which is 12 miles from Stony Creek, and has a very good road. Poor as the soil is on Laurel Hill with nothing to be seen but stones and a wretched gravel, there are locust trees growing everywhere. It is remarkable that here as elsewhere locust & pine grow together in the same soil. The road over Laurel

Hill is full of large & small flat stones, but on the east side it is good. On the west side it is much steeper and descends farther, but it is not nearly so bad as it used to be when it ran a little more to the north. Halfway down the west side is a small, clear spring beside the road. The summit of the mountain is fairly level, but not particularly broad. 9 miles beyond the east side of the mountain is Ligonier. There is scarcely a sign to be seen of the fort; there is nothing there now but a good plantation. All the land round here belongs to Governor St. Clair, whose family lives 7 miles farther on, a little north of the road. Now the mountains had come to an end and we were in the western part of the country. There was still Chestnut Ridge ahead, which from a distance looks like a mountain, but when you come up to it, it is so small & insignificant that compared with the mountains it seems no more than a small hill. 2 miles from Ligonier we crossed Two Mile Run, & 2 miles farther on crossed Four Mile Run, both of which are considerable streams. While we were at the latter, it began to snow, & it kept on snowing until evening when the snow was 2 inches deep. Thunder & lightning accompanied the snow & it was intensely cold. On the Allegheny 4 inches of snow are said to have fallen. 9 miles from Ligonier, at the 9 Mile Run, we spent the night with a German named Ried, who keeps a good inn and lives on Gov. St. Clair's land. This is rather broken country, but it has a good rich soil. Mr. Hufnagel & 2 other gentlemen from Greensburg also spent the night here. The former said a great many nice things about our Indian mission, condemned in the strongest terms the murder of the Indians on the Muskingum, & was angry because the ringleaders had not been punished.

On the 27th we went on to Greensburg, 11 miles from here. The morning was very cold, and the snow did not melt in the shade until the afternoon, when it became warmer. The road was very muddy & bad, the soil a black, sticky loam. Consequently we were unable to reach Greensburg before 12 o'clock. We had lunch there with a German innkeeper Simon Trum, who had formerly lived back of Christiansbrunn. Greensburg is 2 years old, has 30 handsome, trimmed log houses. The Courthouse is a wooden building & serves also as church. The town lies on a pleasant hill, where several springs gush out. East and west are streams and swamps. There is an English school there, and a German one nearby. The country is good, the soil rich, but in some parts rather cold. Many Germans live in this neighborhood, many of whom used to live in Northampton County. A man named Steinmez told us that his neighbors, who have driven cattle to Detroit, praise the Moravian Indians & say there are no better Christians than they. In this vicinity, which is called the German Settlement, the Indians committed many murders during the last war. We went on another 8 miles through beautiful country to a German by the name of Waldhauer, who would not let us go on. So we spent the night with him & rested well. The people around here are mostly Germans. The land in this vicinity is good, very grassy, & the trees are tall and most of them of the same girth. The timber grows straight for about 70 feet, but it rots sooner than in other places, because it grows so fast, and the same is true with the straw. A lot of people from this area are moving to the Missury. They are having particular trouble with rascals who owe them money, slip quietly off to the Youghiogany, where boats are always ready to pull out, and go down from there by way of the Mononghahela & Ohio to the Mississippi.

On the 28th we rode 12 miles through good country to Turtle Creek. It is another 12 from here to Pittsburg. It is broken country but the soil is good. By 2 o'clock in the afternoon we had the quiet Allegheny on our right hand and Pittsburg ahead of us. The view is charming. We reached Pittsburg by 3 o'clock & immediately heard that Capt. Hutchins, the Geographer General, had died 2 hours before. We stopped at a private house, Mr. Handlyn's, an honest man with a German wife and keeps a respectable house. We got a small room for ourselves and stayed there as long as we were in Pittsburg. General Gibson told us that his boat would leave in the morning for Kentucky & would stop at Marietta. We wanted to go along. But then one person advised us for it and another against it, until Br. Heckewelder found Mr. Isaac Williams, who lives in Sandusky and only recently has come from there. He said he had been sent with a "speech" from all the nations to Gov. St. Clair, which, however, as the Governor was not at home, he would take back again. This was the gist of the message: that the Indians will not allow the land which had been ceded at the last treaty to be surveyed, and no forts are to be built on it, and, more particularly, they have made up their minds to kill all surveyors who go out. He added that the Indians say they were forced to the last Treaty. They neglected their fall hunting because of it; it lasted until winter, & they became poor, naked, & hungry. This drove them to accept certain terms in hopes of getting some food and clothing, but as they found themselves for the most part cheated, they merely laughed at the Treaty when they returned from it, and did not honor it at all. The Indians have decided to make an attack on the New England settlement on the Muskingum. They were resolved to fight for their land, and then if they lost it they would lose it like men. At this time there were many Indians on the Muskingum who were there only to keep watch. If we now surveyed the tract for the Moravian Indians on the Muskingum, it might cause trouble, & if soldiers were present it would be all the worse, & what would 20 or 30 soldiers be for the Indians lying in wait for them in the woods. Mr. Connelly from Detroit was present & confirmed this. They entreated us under no circumstances to survey the land, it would certainly cause trouble. They advised us, instead, to go to our Brethren at Petquotting, where we could best inform ourselves about the matter. Not knowing what to do, we decided to stay here for a few days. All honest people here are sorry for the poor Indians, who lose their land without getting anything for it. They say the Treaty cost a lot, and most of the Indians got nothing. Some who were to have got something thought it was not even worth while to put out their hands for it, it was so small.

The 29th. In the morning we went outside the town to look at the fort.

To Pittsburgh and Pettquotting: 1789

The town has not more than 150 houses, most of them poor wooden structures. The location is beyond compare, on beautiful flats at the junction of the Allegheny & Mononghahela, which seem pretty much alike in size, and each is wider than the Delaware at Easton; they form hereafter the Ohio. To the south is the Monongahela. Beyond it is a hill where much coal is being mined. To the west is the Allegheny. Beyond it are rich bottoms & good *high land*. To the north is a plain several miles long but narrow, extending up along the Allegheny. To the east is a long hill, where much good standstone is being quarried. Beautiful though the situation is, the town itself is wretched. Disorder reigns in the streets, and business is only middling because there is no money in circulation. The best trade is in hides and peltry. There are quite a few craftsmen. They get good pay. The church is for everybody, but the Presbyterians have the greatest influence. [*The College (Academy) has now only 6 students.*] Peltries are sent to Philadelphia & Baltimore. Thence most goods come in great wagons from Lancaster & Carlisle & from there they go on by water and by pack horse. The Allegheny is a clear, still, deep stream, & has good sandy banks which are fairly high. The Monongahela is more muddy and turbulent & has high banks which not infrequently cave in. At the confluence of the 2 streams lies Killbuck's Island. The surrounding country is rather hilly & well settled on this side of the Allegheny and the far side of the Mononghahela, & is particularly rich in coal and good sandstone. There is also iron ore, & 30 miles up the Mononghahela they are building an iron foundry. The Fort at the junction of the two rivers is very much dilapidated. There is no garrison there. Some good, decent people live here. In the afternoon there was the funeral of Capt. Hutchins. At the request of General Gibson Br. Heckewelder conducted it, according to the rites of the Church of England. Capt. Hutchins was 60 years old. His landlord says that during his illness he talked much about his unworthiness & his trust in the atonement of Jesus for the sins of all mankind & for himself. The cemetery on the N. E. side of the town by the church is for everybody. They lie there all higgledy-piggledy. The place as a whole is not fenced in, but there is a fence around many of the individual graves and sometimes 2 or 3 together. Everything is cross-cross.

On the 30th we were invited to breakfast with Mr. Nicholson, an "Interpreter of Indian languages," who advised us to survey our land, & would not hear of any danger. Afterwards in company with some Germans we took a plesant walk on the far side of the Allegheny. A mile up the other side is a very small creek where a sawmill is being built. Here we were handsomely entertained, in country style, by Mr. Wisthof, who is in business with Mr. O'Hara, and who had known of our coming. The Allegheny bottoms here are very rich & are already selling for 5£ an acre. Farther back from the water are hills which have large plains on top. Then there are narrow valleys, then more hills, and so on. It is still uninhabited on this side, & except for 3 plantations nothing but woods. We also saw the site of the new town on the other side of Pittsburg, over against the upper end of the old town, a beautiful spot on high flats. A wild cherry tree on the bank of the Allegheny was 18 feet in circumference. There are plenty of them & of walnut trees, & many are being burned or used for fences. One begins to see honey locusts here, & from this point west they grow beside all streams & in all bottoms. We had a ride afterwards in a small boat down the Allegheny and across the Mononghahela, and in the evening returned to Pittsburg.

May 1st. Mr. Wilson, who had come from Washington yesterday, brought us the certain news that the Indians on Dunker Creek had killed several white people and stolen some horses. He advised against surveying the land at this time, and so did almost everyone. So we prepared to go to Petquotting.

The 3rd. As Br. Heckewelder could not make up his mind about it, he brought his letters for Pettquotting to Mr. Williams at his camp 3 miles from here on the other side of the Allegheny. He advised us to go with him. We at once decided to do so, got our horses & luggage, and returned to camp again before dark.

Early on the 4th another man and a woman arrived who wanted to travel in our company. Br. Heckewelder & Mr. Williams were both sick today. The latter brewed a potion of laurel wood which tasted all right but seemed to do little good. After taking an emetic, Br. Heckewelder ———

On the 5th got well again, and so did Mr. Williams a few days later. Several visiting neighbours told us so much about Indians stealing horses that we became worried about our own. Several Indians were camping near Pittsburg, among them Mamasu, an arch-thief and murderer. He was, as everybody supposed, busy stealing horses. He had said he wanted to kill one more man because he had to round out his measure; he had killed only 9 and it should be 10. We had a pleasant time looking over the hills and bottoms in this neighbourhood where we now had to stay from the 3rd to the 8th. Every day we saw boats going down to Kentucky, Sioto, Miami, Missisippi, & Missoury. Horses can stand in them on both sides with their heads towards the water, & in the middle there is a gangway. These boats look like a rectangular chest, quite flat on the bottom. We heard that the Indians had stolen 6 horses in Wheeling, & had killed a New England officer.

The 8th. On towards noon we set off. There were six persons: besides us two, there was Isaac Williams, our guide; Geo. Folk (a son of Wm. Folk who used to live in Bethlehem), the Indians took him & his sister prisoner during the last war, & he still lives in Sandusky; David Hill, & Mrs. Girdi, wife of the brother of the bad Girdi among the Indians. We went straight over hills & across narrow valleys, and came at night to Logtown [Logstown, near present Ambridge] & camped on this side.

Early on the 9th we came through Logtown. Where old Logtown stood there are many plums & large wild apples & beneath them good tame [cultivated] grass. The place is 18 miles from Pittsburg, & seems well situated for a town. One sees here and there the remains of Indian houses & graves, the lat-

To Pittsburgh and Pettquotting: 1789

ter are round, from 60 to more than 100 feet in circumference, & still from 5 to 10 feet high, like a little round hill. We also saw wild turkeys here. After we had ridden 2 miles down along the Ohio, through beautiful bottoms & lowlands, we came to Crowstown [Conway], where there was formerly another Indian town, the fields of which are now full of thickets & old 16-feet-high weeds.

From here we turned away from the Ohio on a good dry path over the mountains, really only hills, which are intersected by narrow valleys in which there are usually good springs. Big Beaver Creek, 9 miles from Crowstown, was too high to ford, so we went 3 miles higher up to the falls. Lieut. Spear, commandant of the blockhouse here, & his 17 soldiers were very friendly, and he invited us to lunch. Meanwhile our horses grazed on the pleasant bottom across the stream. The soldiers brought our things over in canoes, & we went on for another 4 miles.

On the 10th it rained. We met a number of Indians who were going with skins to Beaver Creek, where General Gibson had directed them to come for trading because many of them were afraid to go to Pittsburg. After them came Anton (Wellochalent), formerly one of the Brethren, but he had reverted. He had just now shot a bear. He gave us a ham from it. We let our party go on ahead. Br. Heckewelder reminded him of the grace he had once experienced. He replied that he had never intended to leave the Moravians, but, when his whole family was murdered, that not only grieved him but also so infuriated him that he resolved to go to war, & he had been weak enough to do so. Now he had avenged himself & had no longer any hatred of the white people. He often thought of going back to the Moravians, but believed he was too wicked. Br. Heckewelder said: "The thought of returning to the congregation comes from the Saviour, he has taken hold of you & will not easily let you go. He will forgive you everything if you turn to him." Anton said: "You speak words of comfort to me. I will soon return." And so we parted. Anton was once a very good man. He did much for the white people, saved their lives, & during the war brought them himself to safety, often at risk of his life. He had a good wife & lovely, promising children. These were all killed in the great massacre on the Muskingum. 12 miles farther on we came to Little Beaver Creek. The water was high & it was difficult to ford. 1½ miles on this side of it is the straight-carved Pennsylvania Line, 2 rods wide. 6 miles from the first branch is another branch of the Beaver to cross.

On the 11th we went 9 miles farther to the 3rd branch of the Beaver, & then 4 miles up along it through pleasant bottoms where we rested a little. An Indian who was camping a short distance below us came to us, talked with Br. Heckewelder, and gave us a deer ham. From here we crossed the creek and went on another 7 miles. It was cold during the night & froze.

The 12th. In the morning 2 young Delaware Indians came to our camp. The father of one of them was a brother-in-law of the woman who was travelling with us. They were friendly & confirmed the report of the horse-stealing at Wheeling. The Delawares are said to have delivered a Speech to these Mingoes, to get them to mend their ways, but to no effect, & the Delawares are said to have gone quietly off because they saw it was no use. These same Mingoes are said to have stolen 11 horses from Mr. Ludlow, a surveyor, & then returned. On the way we saw the grave of an Indian who, at sugar-making in the spring, ate so much sugar that his stomach swelled and he died. In the afternoon we came to Tuscarawi Creek, 20 miles this side of Tuscarawi. 15 miles this side of Tuscarawi are the two Tuscarawi Plains, the soil of which is a mixture of sand, brown gravel, & lime, & grows centaury, honeysuckle, & other herbs, upland willows, & small oaks which are different from the "ground oaks" of other plains.

On the morning of the 13th we were only 15 miles from the 3 towns on the Muskingum, where the Brethren formerly lived, but we could not go to see them. This was on Tuscarawi Creek. From a distance we saw the place where Fort Lawrence [Laurens, at Tuscarawas (Bolivar)] once stood. We stopped at noon on the Muskingum, 1½ miles above Tuscarawi, where Post & Heckewelder had once lived. We could still see very well where the house and cellar had been, and also the corn hills. The Muskingum, a quiet, beautiful, delightful stream, might be about 20 rods wide here. We could see the fish swimming down the current. They were very restless and rippled the surface of the water. That meant that a storm was brewing. The sky was clear and bright, but when we set out again we heard thunder in the distance. A few miles farther on, while we were crossing a plain, a violent storm hit us with thunder, wind, & rain. The rain beat so on our faces that we could not see what was happening, & in the woods many trees were blown down. The horses did not want to go on, but we drove them until suddenly they all turned and stood stockstill with their hindquarters to the rain & could not be budged till the worst was over. From here we came into wooded country. We could see, beyond the Muskingum, a hill where rich copper ore is supposed to be. At 6 o'clock in the evening, knowing we could not get much wetter, we rode through the Muskingum, carrying our luggage on our shoulders. Williams, who forded it on foot, got in up to his neck. Afterwards we made a fire, though with some difficulty, dried ourselves, and spent the night there.

On the 14th we started off across the plains, where the deer went before us, then got into some wet, warm valleys & up on to fertile hills. In the valleys the wild or horse-chestnuts were in full leaf and blooming. In the afternoon we crossed Sugar Creek at a beautiful rich bottom, where there were many rattlesnakes, & camped a little farther on, on a little hill beside a small run.

On the 15th we had to stay in camp because it rained almost the whole day, and often so hard that at times we were drenched even in our tents.

On the 16th we travelled mostly through flat, wet country with small hillocks, and came at noon into a bottom that seemed to get more and more beautiful as we went on, & at 11 o'clock we came to Killbuck's Creek, which

To Pittsburgh and Pettquotting: 1789

flows into White Woman's [Walhonding] Creek. The country hereabouts looks in places like a flower garden, & in places like an old orchard where here & there a tree has been taken out. The creek was too high. 3 of our company crossed on a tree which lay 2 feet under water. They took a lot of trouble cutting down a good-sized tree, but it sank deeper under the water than the first one. We had to be content to stay here until the water should have gone down.

On the 17th the water in the middle of the creek was still 6 inches over the tree trunk, but we swam our horses across the creek & carried our luggage over on the tree. During the morning we came to a saltlick, where out of 12 deer we shot one. From now on the country was low & in places marshy. At noon we crossed a branch of White Woman's Creek, swam our horses over & carried our belongings across on a log. Farther on, the foremost of our party was about to ride across an open, marshy flat we had just come to, overgrown with reeds, when his horse sank in up to his back & was with difficulty hauled out. We drove the horses across as best we could, & waded after them. We heard the rattlesnakes rattling in the old grass, but we had to go across. During the afternoon we found wild turkey nests by the wayside. We took the eggs & cooked them later for supper. In the evening we put up our tents at a creek where there was a beautiful meadow bottom, & crab-apple trees stood 30 feet high, standing apart as if in an old orchard.

The 18th. Mr. Williams had to stay here for a few days. He wanted us to stay, too. But we did not know the way, & might have found ourselves among Indians whose speech we none of us could understand. After much debate he consented to let Folk go on with us. So we & Mrs. Girdi went on, & made longer day's journeys. In the afternoon we came through Helltown [on a branch of the Walhonding], an abandoned town but a very beautiful site, which had once been inhabited by wicked Mingoes, & was a rendezvous of thieves & murderers. Hitherto all the streams we crossed had flowed towards the Ohio, but from here on they flowed into Lake Erie.

On the 19th there was a cold rain, and we could not get warm. The whole country through which we were passing was wet. During the morning we crossed Blackwater, one part of the outflow from a small lake. This branch flows directly into Lake Erie, while the other flows into Sandusky Creek. Farther on we caught a small yellow bird, not much bigger than a humming bird. We built a roof for it against the rain and set it under it. A little farther on we came to the place where the Indians during the late war camped overnight with Mr. Folk's sister and other prisoners. Here was a peeled tree, on which they had painted a wolf carrying a pole with 5 scalps, & behind it 3 boys & 3 girls holding hands. The wolf means that the captain was of the Wolf Clan, the scalps that 5 whites had been killed, & the boys & girls that so many prisoners of both sexes had been taken. We crossed 2 branches of the Huron River, the stream on which our Brethren are living.

On the 20th we came to the road that turns off to Pettquotting, but nobody knew exactly how far it was to Pettquotting. We found it was still about 20 miles. We took leave of Mr. Folk & Mrs. Girdi, who had shown us much kindness. They went on to Sandusky & we to Pettquotting. We had already gone so far in the direction of Sandusky that we had to turn back towards the east again. We soon came to a plain where, except for a few trees standing by themselves, nothing but grass was to be seen. We met 2 Indians, who gave us directions about our road. The plains were becoming wetter and more extensive, broken only by an occasional long narrow strip of oak trees, the hollow ones being full of bees. Now and again we saw single large sandstones, and small round, stony hills, where innumerable crawfish live & make holes in the ground. Everywhere little round hillocks had been thrown up. Otherwise the whole region was as flat as a board. The horses walked on hard ground for miles, up to their knees in water, & under the water white violets grew. So we came on Simon & his wife, who were on their way from Sandusky to Pettquotting, & here were wading through the water. They directed us on our way. We had the immense plain on our left, & on our right the Huron River's high bank on which we rode in water, and we could see that the low bottom on the other side of the river was quite dry. But that is the way it is at the lake. The high land is wet & the bottom lands often dry. 5 miles from Pettquotting we came into woods again and broken country. Better than a mile from the town was a peeled tree, on which, was written with charcoal in Delaware the whole verse, "The Saviour's blood & righteousness." This made us a good road sign. At last we saw the town before us. On a hill, at the fence of the nearest plantation, we called to the Indians working in the field. As soon as they recognized us, they dropped their hoes & ran to meet us. Several who were on the other side of the stream hurried across, & everybody welcomed us, accompanied us across the field to the river, & then over into the town, which we reached about 3 o'clock. Here we were welcomed by the Zeisbergers & the Edwards & Jung, & the Indian Brethren & Sisters swarmed about us until evening. It was an amazing sight to see a crowd of people who had once been heathen & are now true Christians & lovers of Jesus & his flock. The place is named Pettquotting after a high round hill, 5 miles from here. The town [New Salem, two miles from Milan] is set on a hill which is washed by the Huron River on the west, & has a deep, narrow valley on the east. The hill is fairly dry, but so narrow that not more than two rows of houses can stand on it, and these have only very small gardens or none at all. Towards the south the hill becomes a large, wet plain. Every cellar on this high, wet place has to have a drain. The schoolhouse is beautiful, with fireplaces on both sides, & a nice fence across the front. Not far from it, on the other side of the street, is the church. It is roomy, bark-covered, without board flooring & without windows, with 2 doors, good benches including some for the children, & candlesticks & candles. The bell hangs outside on a forked tree with a tiny roof built over it. The buildings in town are rather irregular & small, but most of them are well-built & all give protection against rain &

cold. There are, however, no glass windows here, only a few paper ones. Those who have any glass save it. The graveyard is near the town, to the southeast. When a grave is dug in the wet season, it stands full of water. But there is no better place. It is 3½ miles by land to Lake Erie northeast of here, and 5½ miles by water down the river. Huron River is here about 12 rods wide, 30 feet deep. It is also called Bald Eagle Creek from a large eagle's nest found at the rivermouth. This is the only drinking water. In summer, when it is quiet, the water is stagnant & bad. When the winds blow in from the lake, the lake water comes up the river to above the town, & this is the best drinking water. The bottoms down river are for the most part wet; up river they are dry & rich, with not many swamps. They produce everything in abundance when not too wet. All the high land is too wet. Trees of all the usual kinds grow here. Sugar trees, ginseng, & deer are scarce in this vicinity. They trap many raccoons and also beaver & otter here. There are bears, too, and many bees in the woods. There are plenty of fish in the river, especially very large catfish, and at times there are many geese & ducks. The Indians have horses, cattle, chickens, & many pigs. They can live well if they plant enough.

On Ascension Day, the 21st, we had only 2 services as it was rainy. We consulted the Brethren about our problem. They were against our surveying the land on the Muskingum at this time, but they wanted the opinion and advice of some of the Assistants. During the spring there had been a great uproar among some of the bad Indians at the thought of the Christians now moving to the Muskingum. They had settled down, but if the land were now surveyed they would be in an uproar again and might ruin the whole congregation. If someone were connected with the business whom they knew to be a former teacher, it would be so much the worse. We should not tell the Indians why we were here, for fear it might get to the ears of the bad Indians. West of here live wicked bands among whom are utterly godless whites & Indians. They are always in a stir, and are said to live in a pitiful condition. Br. David was very busy this week preparing his address for Holy Communion.

After breakfast on the 22nd we went out to see the plantations. Everywhere men, women, & children were busy planting & clearing. It is amazing what the people have accomplished here. The fields are bottom lands at the river bends, 2 miles up and one down. They plant Indian corn, beans, tobacco, & all kinds of garden stuff. They usually go out to work after the morning service, between 8 & 9 o'clock, & stay out the whole day until evening. Before morning devotions the women as a rule pound corn & bake bread. Morning prayers are well attended. All services are conducted in English. The assistants Samuel & Wilhelm are the interpreters. The latter speaks English very well. Between the men's side and the women's, husband and wife sit next to each other [across the aisle], & so do brothers and sisters among the children. The old people sit along the wall, the sacristans by the door. When a child sleeps or is disorderly, the sacristan gets up, shakes it, sets it straight, & turns its head to the preacher. The woman sacristan does the same on her side. The singing has something pleasing about it.

The 23rd. We had Communion in the evening. All communicants came afterwards to Br. David's room. The Brethren all kissed one another, the Sisters did the same among themselves, & Brethren & Sisters shook hands with one another in mutual fellowship. It is a great thing to see a congregation drawn from raw heathendom fully enjoying the reward & bounties of Jesus, & loving one another like true Christians.

On the 25th a conference was held with Samuel & Wilhelm. Much as they wished to see our affair succeed & to help us themselves, they were nevertheless of opinion we should drop the matter for the time being. Their reasons were exactly the same as those the white Brethren had advanced. They thought that, since the Indians did not want the Christians to go to the Muskingum and supposed they would have to as soon as the land was surveyed, all who had relatives at this place would take them away and very likely some wicked band would come and take the rest away. They said: "You cannot conceive how closely they watch us, and they are worse than you imagine. They are determined that no surveyor shall set foot on that land. Perhaps the matter will be cleared up after the Council meets at Deep River near Detroit, where Brant is expected." We discussed the matter further during the week, and came to the conclusion: "God forbid! It were better the land were never surveyed than that the least harm should befall the mission. The land should rather be sacrificed for the mission than the mission for the land."

On the 26th we went by water with Br. Edwards to within ½ a mile of the lake, where several Frenchmen live. 1 mile from that place live some Chippewas, who have a little land cleared for planting. Other Indian houses are made of round logs in a longish rectangle. But these Indians plant a circle of poles in the ground in such a way that they come together at the top, leaving an opening in the centre. The poles are covered from top to bottom with reed mats, and fastened with bast. This is a house, & when they move they take the mats with them and soon make a new house. Their canoes, which are all made of bark [bast], are the best on the lake. A little below is a town where Chippewas & Delawares live. A little farther on we visited the Frenchmen. Two of them are "Factors" for merchants in Detroit, & trade all kinds of goods for skins. We called on one of them, who is named Squirrel by the Indians. He told us a lot about the great famine in Detroit, Niagara, & Canada. The lakes are said to be 7 feet higher than usual, & at Detroit hardly anything can be planted because of the floods. This, in view of the present famine, makes a fearsome prospect for the future. Even on the Brethren's fields the moisture makes it impossible to cultivate as much land as they did only last year. Everybody agrees that the water in the lake rises for 7 years & recedes for another 7 years. But it rises only 18 inches, so that the present high water is something abnormal. We walked over to the lake. It was still & smooth, as there was little wind, and we could see the islands in the distance. The water tastes good & is sweet. When we came back, Squirrel was doing business with some Chippewas, & his wife entertained us with wheat bread, boiled hen's eggs, and tea, & he with a pipe of tobacco. We took our leave & went home in the canoe. The Chippewas who live here by the lake & on the other side are well-behaved & good neighbours to the Brethren. There are always some in town. They smoke tobacco & eat there. It is only a pity that none of the Brethren understands their language. This has many words a good deal like those of the Delaware language, and they are very willing to teach their language to anyone.

On the 28th, when we went out with Josua to see two old Indian forts, he showed us his hunting cabin. One fort is 5 miles from the town & about 80 rods from the Huron, on a flat-topped hill. It consists of one earthen rampart in a complete circle and another in a half circle, with 2 ditches corresponding in which water lies in patches, and an entrance 5 feet wide. Inside the circle the ground is very level, but there are no traces of buildings. The second fort lies a little better than 2 miles farther on, & about 100 rods from the Huron. It is much like the first, but it has another wall & moat running in a wide circle which encloses the others. In the space inside the inner rampart there is a round elevation & beside it a raised "Quadrat." Both forts are overgrown with bushes & trees. Starting about 5 feet outside the first fort are several regular rows of graves, but farther away they become irregular. There are 32 of these. They are 60, 70, & more, feet in circumference, some circular, some oval, & 3 or 4 feet high. Two miles farther off there are more of them, & it is the same at the second fort. It is a curious fact that the graves at each fort always lie on the side towards the other fort. It looks as if two enemies had lain there, and in an attack or sally many people had been killed & were buried on the spot. Many of the Indians believe that they will some day turn into groundhogs, because many of these creatures have their burrows in the graves.

The 29th & 30th. Until noon it was so hot that our thin clothing was wet through with perspiration; but suddenly the wind changed, & it became so cold that it froze during the night. On towards evening there was the funeral of young Brother Benjamin, who had died the night before of consumption. For the coffin, Josua first had to split the boards from a tree, & at 4 o'clock in the afternoon he & 3 other Brethren had a nicely trimmed coffin ready. The body, in a white robe with red ribbons, was displayed in front of the church, &, after an address by Br. David, it was carried to God's Acre on a bier. The Brethren & after them the Sisters followed it, two by two. The mother & relatives of the deceased were also present, & behaved as Christians should. There were some Chippewas present. They were very reverent.

The 31st was Pentecost, which the Indians observe as an important day.

There was a baptism of 3 Brethren and 1 Sister. Two of those baptized were sons of William Henry, who formerly was known as Killbuck or Gelelemind. One of them had lived 4 years at Princeton, & had attended the college there. The persons baptized were dressed in white & wore blue gowns over their garments because it was cool. Reed mats were spread before them. After an address by Br. David, the sacristans hauled water in 4 buckets with a tin basin in each. The men & women Assistants removed their gowns, & after a prayer by Br. David they were baptized in Jesus's death, & after they had worshipped they were led into Br. David's house & had dry clothes put on them. When it was all over, all the Brethren kissed the newly baptized Brethren, & the Sisters kissed the newly baptized Sister. The Brethren shook hands with the Sister, & the Sisters shook hands with the Brethren. Everyone was happy to see new partakers in the blessedness they themselves enjoyed. Things go very well, on the whole, among the young people here. A great longing fires them to surrender themselves to Him who gave His life for them. An Indian is an independent person who is not inclined to seek advice nor to change his mind to please anyone. It is a tremendous thing when such a one decides to surrender himself to Jesus, and still more so when it is a young Indian who is just as independent & who in addition has to fight the temptations of the world. Towards evening there was a lovefeast for the whole congregation. The church was crowded. There were some Chippewas present, who had come because they had heard that today was Sunday. At the lovefeast everything went off very well. Br. David told the Indians about the congregations at Bethlehem & other places, & assured them they were remembered by them. It was a happy day for the Indian congregation. I should mention with what eagerness the Indians go to school to learn reading, writing, & hymns. Br. David conducts shool here by himself, in various classes, from morning till night. School stops only during the busiest planting & harvesting seasons. Men, women, & children attend it. At other times you see, here & there, a little group in a corner, learning reading and hymns from one another. You may hear them in the evening singing hymns in their houses until late at night.

On the 1st of June, from morning till noon, there were Indians with us saying good-bye. When we left at 2 o'clock, they assembled once more and went through it all over again. The whole hill, from the houses on down, was covered with people following us with their eyes as long as they could. Brs. David, Edwards & Jung, & some Indian Brethren, accompanied us for a short distance. After taking a cordial leave of them, we continued on our way. A few Indians accompanied us for several miles. We had to take our way again through the woods. Our company consisted of: Samuel, one of the first Assistants, an upright man; Stephan, another Assistant, a quiet though also at times a lively man; Thomas, a poor man who has a loving heart & thinks not of himself; William Henry, a former Delaware chief, otherwise known as Gelelemind, an able man who does not put himself above the other

To Pittsburgh and Pettquotting: 1789

Brethren; Tobias, a young, quiet, obliging man (when his father & relatives were murdered on the Muskingum, he was imprisoned with the others who were slain, but he escaped). In addition to those, we had with us: Andreas, who for the time being is separated from the congregation & lives a few miles away—but there is hope he will find himself again; and also 3 boys & a woman with a child. She would like to live in the congregation, & so went along to Pittsburg to find her husband. There was also with us a Mr. Robins, a trader who had formerly lived in Sandusky & had done many favours to the Brethren Edwards & Jung in their captivity. Now he was impoverished & received from these Brethren full return for his kindness. He wanted to start a little business again, and among other things bring a couple of kegs of whiskey to Sanduskey. Samuel, however, refused him any help if that was what he intended to do, & gave him such a lecture that he gave up the idea. By night time we had come 12 miles to Paint Creek [Vermilion River], where a lot of red paint is to be found.

On the 2nd the Indians got our horses very early, as they did every morning afterwards. We came through rather wet land today, where many beeches & large white oaks grow. We crossed Blackwater, which looks reddish, & the waters of Tuscarawi Creek, & ——

On the 3rd reached Cayahaga Old Town [near Akron], formerly a large Indian town, on a hill with 2 good springs. The place is still clear & grown over with tame grass. There are good bottoms along the river & large clear fields. Here we met Mr. Smith of Detroit, who was coming from Pittsburg, and also several families who were moving to Pittsburg. He had bought flour in Pittsburg, & sent it up the Allegheny from there to Venango & on to Presque Isle, to be brought from the latter place by water to Detroit, as the usual route, normally considered the safest, is now rendered unsafe because of the war parties. William Henry heard from the Indians who were with Mr. Smith that a party of Mingoes had gone again to the Muskingum bent on mischief. We crossed the Cayahaga & went 2 miles farther through beautiful open country to a small run. During the night we heard the roar of the Falls of the Cayahaga and the howling of the wolves. We also heard the "Whipperwill" & our nightingale again, which we had heard every night during our journey west as far as Killbuck's Creek, but not since then. The latter bird is a small one that came to us among the trees every night at 9 o'clock, & sang so sweetly, often until dawn, that we called it the American Nightingale.

The 4th. In the forenoon our path led between the Cayahaga & a small lake, which were hardly 20 rods apart. Afterwards we crossed the Cayahaga again, at a place where there is a high rock in the middle of the stream, called the "Standing Stone." The base is like a pillar, broad at the bottom, then a ledge, then it gets quite thin as though it had been planed off; it widens again at the top, & has 3 small white pines standing on it. The rocks on the bank are mostly of the same sort. At noon we rested on a high bank.

Here was a peeled tree on which some great warrior during the last war had inscribed his exploits with charcoal & redstone. We got the Indians to interpret it for us. On one side 7 muskets had been painted, one on top of the other. This means that 7 warriors had gone to war from there. On the other side was a turkey to indicate that their leader was of the turkey tribe. Beside it were 8 thick diagonal lines one above another. This means that the chief had gone out on so many raids. In the lowest line were 4 arrows, in the 2nd two, in the 7th two. This means, each time the arrows were shown, that as many of them had been killed as there were arrows through the line. The first & seventh lines each had another arrow, which, however, did not go through the line. These indicate as many wounded as there are arrows. The 6th & 7th lines were connected at the ends with a mark. This means that the warrior after he had been out 6 times turned back from here & went out the 7th time without going home. Besides it lay 6 men one on top of another with their feet higher than their heads. This means that his party had killed so many white people. In the afternoon we passed through old Mahony, & at night came to the Big Beaver Creek [Mahoning River], where we camped at a spot called the Big Mahony, both delightful places. Here was the biggest "Lick" we had seen on the journey. 12 well-trodden deer paths led into it, & in the lick was one deer track after another. An Indian named Wehnas who was camping here with his son and his belongings told us that the day before yesterday 3 painted warriors had been here. They had carefully examined the road where it goes through the lick, presumably to see if packhorses with flour had passed that way. He had called to them, on which they disappeared. Because Samuel had seen a strange Indian dog in the woods, it was supposed that a party was camping up the Beaver. As a precaution our horses were brought into camp during the night, and Mr. Robins stuck his big knife into the ground beside him where he slept, but we were undisturbed.

On the 5th our hunters went out early, but they could get no deer. While they were away, deer came quite close to our camp, & Tobias shot one. So we all had a good meal. From this place Wechnas & his boy with his peltries came along with us. In Pittsburg he was strongly suspected of having killed a white man a year ago. Andreas & a boy left us to get meat from somewhere round here where they had stored it last year. We crossed the Beaver [Mahoning Creek] & stopped at noon at the Saltsprings. The spring proper has a good salt, & the water tasted quite salty. The stones around it have a fine white salt on them. Immediately after the war a company had planned to carry on a salt-boiling business here. When it collapsed, however, everything was left where it was. Many of the kettles were carried off by other people. 33 are still here, each holding 24 gallons, & some are broken, some are sound. Some of the buildings are still there. Towards evening we crossed the Beaver again.

Early on the 6th William Henry shot a deer, & Thomas shot five today.

At one place our path went between the Beaver and some high rocks, where there are said to be many large rattlesnakes. But we saw only one by the path. At noon we crossed the Pennsylvania Line, & 4 miles beyond, Kaskaskies field [in the vicinity of Edinburg, near New Castle], which is level and beautiful, covered with tame grass. All told we saw a great number of places on the Beaver where old Indian towns had stood, & where the loveliest & best bottoms are. But now they all have their *Herren* [i.e., white proprietors]. Towards evening we passed the old Languntuotenink. We crossed the field that the Brethren had once planted. It is still quite clear, & last winter it was flooded. Across the creek you can still see where the town stood. We camped a few miles farther down the creek.

On the 7th we had to stay in camp because Br. Heckewelder's horse was lame. Wechnas's boy caught "Pickerells," as large as a small shad, which tasted like trout. Tobias had brought along his book & some written verses, which he often read at night by the fire. Today he got the boys together & gave them lessons in reading. Among other things he recited verses to them, which they repeated until they knew them by heart. Samuel was busy singing hymns, & Tobias tanned 2 hides.

On the 8th we went over hill and dale, some distance away from Beaver Creek, & after a few miles met 2 traders who were taking bacon & salt to Pettquotting & beyond. One of them offered Samuel a dollar a day if he would turn back with them, but he declined. There were 2 Indians with them who had shot a bear the evening before & now had cooked & fried bear-meat on the fire. We were given a good portion of it to eat. Every member of our party received also a piece of bread & a portion of salt & sugar. The latter is put into the water, and by that means bad water is improved. Farther on we crossed Slippery Rock Creek, & approaching the Ganaquenising [Connoquenessing] got into a muddy swamp. There were some Indians at the creek. The woman who was with us found her husband sleeping with the brandy cask beside him. So she stayed here. Across the creek our way led through difficult broken country. In the evening we came to a cold plain, where the white oaks are only now beginning to put out leaves, although other places were in full leaf.

On the 9th we forded Muddy Run, crossed some plains, & then came to the best high land we had seen on our whole journey. At 5 o'clock we reached the Allegheny, & before dark were again in Pittsburg, ———

Where we stayed the 10th & 11th. We could do little business here. The people in whom we were chiefly interested were busy listening to the inquiry then being conducted in the church by 6 pastors from the neighbourhood into the dispute between the Presbyterian congregation and their pastor. Messrs. Morrison & Connelly told us they thanked God they had returned safely. They had gone in the spring to the mouth of the Cayahaga with flour, & thought themselves fortunate not to have known at the time the danger they were in. Had the war parties that were lying in wait not missed them, they would have been at their mercy. Everybody, by the way, advised us to take the advice of our Brethren & not survey the land at this time. We said good-bye to the Indian Brethren & our hosts, & ——

On the 12th left Pittsburg, went up the Allegheny 9 miles to Justice Irish, where we had some business, & from him round to Myers' Tavern, 12 miles from Pittsburg. The country today was all hill and valley, but with good soil & tall timber.

On the 13th we proceeded 10½ miles to Bushy Run, & from there 10 miles more to Hannas Town. This place consists of 20 wretched houses, all windowless, in a fertile but by no means beautiful region. We spent the night 10 miles farther on at Pecks Tavern.

On the 14th we passed Ligonier & Laurel Hill, & came at night to Websters [near Stoyestown] on Stony Creek, where there is a really good inn. Mr. Webster had that very day found a new way across Stony Creek, which is said to be much better than the present one.

On the 15th we came down off the Allegheny Mountain, & at noon reached Bonnets. Our friend Bonnet was not at home, but his wife was very friendly, gave us the best of entertainment, & free of charge.

On the 16th we crossed the Juniata 3 miles above Bedford, where they were busy building a bridge. Then we came through Bedford, where there are 40 houses, most of them well-built & some of them handsome. The place is on a hill, with a fine court house standing on the south side of the town. There is no lack of business here. The surrounding country is all mountainous, but the soil is fertile. We slept at Martin's at the Crossing.

On the 17th we crossed Sideling Hill & the 3 Blue Mountains to Kiefers.

The 18th. We came through Shippensburg to Carlisle. Here we were on a very different countryside from what we had recently been seeing. The finest fruit was forming, the meadows were full of grass, the gardens smiling.

Early on the 19th Br. Heckewelder visited Mr. Alexander, & talked with him about the surveying on the Muskingum. Towards evening we crossed the Susquehannah to Harrisburg, where we stayed with a German innkeeper named Kapp. Mr. John Henry called on us at once, & we enjoyed his company. He & Mr. Kapp wished a Moravian were living here. Harrisburg has a pleasant situation beside the Susquehanna on an extensive plain. It is only 4 years old, & already has 200 good houses & all the up-river traffic. Public buildings are the market & the prison. A court house is under construction & people are talking about churches. Good beer is brewed here, & there is a printing press. A New-Englander who had invented a machine for making nails without fire & consequently much cheaper, died here of smallpox two weeks ago. The inhabitants of this town & the beautiful country around it are part German, part English.

On the 20th we passed through Hummelstown, which has 20 houses, & through Millerstown [Annville], which has 35 houses, to Lebanon.

We stayed here the 21st, & ——

On the 22nd attended the funeral of the departed Brother Lorenz Bage. From here we went by way of Meyerstown & Wummelsdorf [Womelsdorf] to Heidelberg. After visiting the Sensemans, ——
On the 23rd we rode on, & ——
On the 24th, [June] arrived in Bethlehem.

XXIX

To the Falls of the Ohio and Vincennes: 1792

NOT LONG AFTER Heckewelder's visit to Pettquotting, Indian unrest drove the Brethren away from the town there, which had been christened New Salem. David Zeisberger led them to a refuge in what was then the wilderness of Upper Canada. On the banks of the Retrenche River (now the Thames), Zeisberger established the town of Fairfield in 1792. He could not know that, in another twenty years, his town in this secluded spot would again find itself in the path of armies and become the site of the Battle of the Thames, or, as it is called in Canada, the Battle of Moraviantown.

Meanwhile John Heckewelder, though no longer attached to the mission, continued to travel in the cause of peace between white men and Indians. Sometimes he went as an emissary of his church, sometimes as an adviser to the government of the United States. Two such journeys undertaken on behalf of the States to Indian Treaties, the one in 1792 to the Wabash, the other in 1793 to Detroit, have provided us with what are in some ways the best of all his travel journals.

To see these two journals in perspective, we must remember that immediately after the close of the Revolutionary War the United States, encouraging the flow of population into the west, busied itself with extinguishing Indian title to the land. In few quarters, official or unofficial, was there any sympathy with the Indian who was thus perforce losing his homeland, and there was almost no understanding of his motives and *mores*. The United States, conducting such treaties as those at Fort Stanwix in 1784 and Fort McIntosh in 1785, ignored the Indian code and dealt (conclusively, as they believed at the time) with groups of Indians of uncertain authority. Peace did not ensue from these "peace treaties." The Indians did not recognize them. They continued to oppose—sometimes with violence, as Heckewelder has shown us in his Fort Harmar Journal of 1788—encroachment upon territories which they did not admit having ceded.

To punish the Indians the United States sent military expeditions into the west against them. Harmar burned villages and corn, but his army suffered piecemeal defeat, and when it retired it left the country open to such Indian attacks as that on the Ohio Company settlement at Big Bottom. In June, 1791, General Scott, burning Indian towns and (on orders) capturing women and children as a demonstration of power, did little more than consolidate the tribes against the United States. General Wilkinson, who was sent out in August of that year against the Indians on the Wabash—particularly the Weas, a branch of the Miami—took more women and children prisoners. When, on November 4, 1791, General St. Clair was overwhelmingly defeated in the Wabash country, the bankruptcy of American Indian policy became apparent.

Next year the government took a more conciliatory course. Brigadier General Rufus Putnam was sent out to make peace with the western nations. He was acocmpanied by John Heckewelder, whose presence was a guarantee to the Indians of Putnam's good intentions. At Post Vincennes a treaty was held with the Wabash Indians—Weas and others—at the conclusion of which peace was declared. It was hoped in United States military circles that this treaty, by detaching the Indians who attended it from the Miamis farther west, would prevent completion of the Indian federation which was so greatly apprehended.

*Brother John Heckewelder's Travel Diary from Bethlehem to Post Vincennes on the Wabash River, and Return. 1792.**

The government had for some time been endeavoring to make known to the hostile Indian Nations on the northwest side of the Ohio that it had no desire to wage a bloody war with them, but was ready and willing to make

---

* The present translation has been made from copies of the journal preserved in the Archives of the Moravian Church, Bethlehem, Pennsylvania. A version of the journal, printed at Halle in 1797 and translated by Miss Clara Frueauff, was published in the *Pennsylvania Magazine of History and Biography*, Vols. XI and XII (1887-1888). To this translation the present editor acknowledges his debt in much of the phrasing and for much of the information in the notes. At the same time it should be understood that the present rendering includes a great deal of material not found in the earlier one and that many corrections have been made.

peace with them and in all matters treat them with justice and humanity. With this purpose in view, peace messengers were sent to them over 4 different routes, the government confidently believing that the Indians would consent to negotiations and would designate a place for a treaty. General Putnam was commissioned to go out and hold a treaty or treaties with them or as many nations as were peacefully inclined. He needed an assistant, and I was chosen. I received by special messenger a letter from the Secretary of War, dated May 18, 1792. I laid this paper before the Elders of the congregation, and, with their consent and best wishes, I left Bethlehem, May 26th.

On the 27th I spent the night at the Peters in Hebron, and in his company visited some of the Brethren in Lebanon, as well as Mr. Robbert Hare of Philadelphia who had just arrived.

In Carlisle on the 29th I visited Major Alexander, Mrs. Buttler, and other friends, and spent the night in Shippenstown.

On the 30th at the foot of the Blue Mountain, where 4 years ago there was but a single farmhouse, I saw to my surprise a pretty little town of over 30 well-built 2 story houses, called Strasburg. Here I was joined by a travelling companion whom I did not like the look of and whom I secretly believed to be a sharper. Before night fell I was glad enough, however, to have his company, because after a while we met 2 and farther on 3 deserters carrying big clubs. I had frequently been warned against such people, particularly in Carlisle, where they had wished to furnish me with pistols, which, however, I did not accept.

I spent the night of the 31st at the house of my good friend Bonnet, 4 miles beyond Bedford. From this place I travelled to Pittsburg in company with several gentlemen from Hagerstown & Green-Castle, arriving there June 3rd. The people between Laurel-hill and Pittsburg had heard a report that about 100 Indians were on this side of the Allegheny River, & we heard of little else but flight, indeed, many believed that not even Carlisle was safe from the Indians. Here in Pittsburg, however, the people were more courageous, especially as a scouting party, composed partly of regular troops and partly of Indians of the Seneca nation, under the command of Lieutenant Jeffers, had brought in 2 Indian scalps and several prisoners. Gen. Putnam had arrived here the day before me. He at once read his instructions to me privately and acquainted me with everything concerning the peace to be concluded with the Indians. We agreed to set free the Indian prisoners who had been brought here and through them to send a "Speech" to the enemy Indians. This was sent to the peaceful Monsy Chief & to Cornplanter, for them to forward. We were grieved to see afterwards in the newspapers that these Indian messengers, of whom Capt. Snake was one, were killed by the hostile Indians after they had delivered their message. I could visit only a few of my friends at this place because I felt very much indisposed. The journey across the mountains in the great heat, together with drinking so much

To Vincennes: 1792

water, had brought on a bilious fever. However, through the remedies applied by the physician here, I was myself again in a few days, so that we were able to continue our journey by ——

The 8th, overland through Washington County in Pennsylvania & Ohio County in Virginia to Buffaloe Creek. We spent the night in Washington, the county town of the former county. It consists of about 60 large well-built houses, and has a fine Court House and prison, both of stone. I called on the prothonotary and a few other acquaintances, & was invited to supper by Mr. van Sweringen, Esq. The good man spoke about the massacre of our Indians, threw his hands together over his head & said: "I have heard from the lips of the murderers themselves that they killed them while they were praying, singing, and kissing" & he was not surprised that our expeditions against the Indians proved a failure, because great blood-guilt lay upon the land and must be atoned for.

We set off early on the 9th & came in the evening to the mouth of Buffaloe Creek in Ohio County, Virginia. A new town, consisting of about 20 well-built houses, was started here four years ago. It is engaged in quite an extensive trade down the Ohio, and is called Charlestown [Wellsburg]. The building-lots, which are ¾ acre in size, sell for from 7 shillings 6 pence to 10 shillings, but there is a yearly groundrent to be paid. Our land journey was now at an end. Our horses were entrusted to a rich farmer of the neighborhood for forage, &—

On the 10th, in company with three gentlemen from Marietta, we continued our journey in a barge which had been brought here for our use by a detachment of soldiers from Pittsburg. At 10 o'clock in the morning we put in at Wheeling for breakfast, where another new town had been started, & many lots sold. Mr. Ebenezer Zenes [Zane], the owner of the land, sells the lots which also are ¾ acre, for from 25 to 50 dollars a lot, but without groundrent. While we were here Mr. McMahan (now a major in the 2nd Legion) returned from a "Scout" in the Indian country. He gave me a very circumstantial description of our towns on the Muskingum, & told me he had found the rendezvous of three hostile nations between Gnadenhütten and Schönbrun, opposite the mouth of Gekelemukpechink [Stillwater] Creek. Three tall painted war-posts had been erected there, and there were 3 large, distinct encampments. In the evening we came to Martin's Station [New Martinsville, West Virginia], where 13 large dogs were kept as a protection against the Indians.

On the 11th we started off again early, & in the afternoon saw 2 enemy Indians on the river bank, but they soon made off. At Marietta, which we reached in the evening, 6 cannon shots were fired in the General's honor. A week before, a man had been killed and scalped near the fort & another with him had been shot through the shoulder. Although several shots had been fired at the Indian while he was engaged in his scalping, he paid no attention until he had lifted the scalp.

In his sermon on the 15th the pastor mentioned the Brethren's missions to the heathen, particularly among the Indians of this country, & included them in his prayers.

Having learned that we were not to leave at once, I employed my time in visiting my good friends, & examining the new "improvements." I discovered that as the Indian war had been going on ever since the founding of this settlement, the inhabitants had never been able to carry out their plans, and lived in three different fortifications, situated on the points on both sides of the Muskingum, & at Camp Martius ¾ mile up the Muskingum. The present population in these 3 places numbers between 2 & 300. In addition a guard of soldiers of 60 men, in command of a captain & lieutenant, is divided between these places for protection, & 2 scouts or bushrangers are engaged by the government at 5 shillings per day. Many dwellings, some of them handsome, have been erected on the eastern point, but the householders do not own the lot on which they have built. The houses rent annually at from 50 to 70 dollars. There are 9 stores here and 3 inns. Two mills belong to the place, one of which is worked by oxen, & the other is built on boats and stands in the water. There is also a large distillery, belonging to a gentleman from Rhode Island, & near it is a small Spirits, & Cordial Distillery. At Campus Martius there is a fine well, lined with bricks, between 70 and 80 feet deep. Many thousand beautiful fruit trees and white mulberries are found on the lots and through the country, and also a few vineyards and vegetable gardens have been planted. Almost every inhabitant has bee hives, and some have a lot of them. The cleared land amounts to between 6 & 700 acres. Notwithstanding all the disturbances of war, they have cultivated a great deal of Indian corn, & have sold to the Contractor, this year alone 10,000 bushels at 2 shillings 6 pence a bushel. A great many pigs are raised, so that over 4,000 lbs. of bacon have been delivered to the commissary. Horses are scarcely ever seen, because the Indians steal them from the inhabitants as soon as they get them, and so all labor is done with oxen. There are quite a few good farms near here, and also a grist- and saw-mill, but no one dares occupy them because of the Indians. Besides this settlement, there is a New England settlement at Wolf's Creek 15 miles higher up the Muskingum, which also has a fine grist- and saw-mill, in which latter boards 36 inches wide are sawed. Here, too, the inhabitants, numbering between 50 & 60, live in fortifications. Another settlement [Belpre] lying 12 or 15 miles down the Ohio, & containing about 80 inhabitants, is also divided into three different enclosures, and has a small "commando" of troops and bushrangers to guard it, as have the inhabitants on Wolf's Creek. What militates most against the prosperity of all these New England settlements is their preposterous method of dividing the land, a method which has been used from the start, but by which the pioneer has not the least advantage over the man who stays behind in New England. The former may have lived for 5 years in constant privation and danger from Indians, many indeed have sacrificed their lives, and yet in spite of all this, not one has succeeded in having a piece of land surveyed for him and getting a deed for it, even though he paid for it in cash six years before.

There are these further difficulties: 1. The treasurer of the Ohio Company, [Richard] Platt, failed in New York, causing the company to lose thereby 80,000 dollars. 2. The fixed sum of money which was decided upon at the time of the purchase of the land, and which was to be paid in instalments on certain days, either to Congress or the treasurer, is far from being paid. Congress has, therefore, in its last session resolved that the Ohio Company shall not receive the amount of land for which they contracted, but only so much as the money already paid will cover, in consideration of the price agreed on. The consequence of this will be that all the honest but poor people who have paid their agents in full for their shares in the land will be the losers. The agents have speculated with part of the money, and used the rest for other purposes. The loss on every share, or in every 1,500 acres, amounts to 350 acres.

On the 17th General Tupper, who died the day before, was buried. In consideration of the 4 different offices or appointments he held, first, as a general in the service of the United States in the late war; 2. as member of the Order of the Cincinati; 3. as a director of the Ohio Company; & 4. as a Master among the Freemasons,—great honor was shown him at the funeral. I shall describe what seemed most noteworthy to me. After a detachment of soldiers had arrived with drum and fife from the point here at the Campus Martius, and all the Freemasons had assembled, the latter entered the deceased's house where the remains lay. They stayed for about half an hour, during which time a guard had been posted at the doors of the house. When they came out, they were furnished with tools according to their different degrees. They wore leather aprons, skilfully embroidered with red, blue or green ribbons around the edge, and bearing the design of a square and compass in the centre. A few wore only a clean white apron. Two men with drawn swords posted themselves on both sides of the door through which the body was to be taken, and when at last it was brought out and placed in the Square, the Masons gathered round it, and those with swords stood between it and the people so that no one could draw too near. There was a lid with hinges at the head of the coffin which was opened. On the coffin were laid: 1. an open Bible with square and compass; 2. a costly sword in a black sheath, lined with red velvet; 3. four black boxes, about 10 inches square; 4. a pocket book; & 5. green bushes or asparagus greens. On the 4 boxes, 2 at the head and 2 at the feet, his 4 commissions were laid. On each side of the coffin stood a Mason holding a well-turned column of walnut wood in his hand & at the foot another with a measuring lathe about 10 feet long. Others stood in other places holding wooden hammers. Some of the masons wore red, others blue, ribbons fastened at the breast, & 2 stood with long, round, beautifully carved wands in their hands, to which a blue silk ribbon was tied at the top. Two others held finely carved candlesticks, two and a half feet long, containing white wax candles, at least 2 inches in diameter. All these arrangements having been completed, the clergyman, who is also a Mason, having stepped to the coffin offered a prayer, of which, however, I could understand but little as he spoke in a very low tone. A very mournful dirge was then sung, and the order of the procession called out. Then the coffin was closed, & every Mason broke off a little branch of the greens which lay upon it, & stuck it in his coat. The Bible with the square and compass, the pocket book, the 4 black boxes with the papers resting on them, & the sword, all were now carefully raised and carried in both hands by as many men as were necessary, and the coffin, which had been covered with a large white cloth, was taken up. The soldiers, who had stood during the whole of the ceremony with fixed bayonets in a double file which extended all the way from the gates, were now stationed, in part, by a non-commissioned officer as a guard where the procession passed. After the rest of the soldiers had been put through certain exercises by their officer, the drums were muffled & covered with a black cloth, & at a given signal they marched off, while a funeral march was played. Behind them marched those of the Masons who for the time being had nothing to attend to, hand in hand and 2 and 2. They were followed by those carrying hammers, measuring lathes, the 2 round wands, columns, etc., and finally came the pastor, & behind him a man carrying the open Bible in both hands, & then 4 other men, each carrying a black box. The coffin now followed, the Master Mason walking beside it, and the mourners behind him. As they neared the grave, which according to the deceased's directions was on one of his own city lots, the soldiers who stood in double file moved up to the grave, went through a number of evolutions, and retired again. Then the Masons drew near the grave, and after a certain signal knelt down around it. The pastor then said: Lord! now lettest thou thy servant depart in peace, etc. He pronounced several passages from the Scriptures appropriate to the servants of God, & closed with the words: After labor sweet is rest. The Masons then rose and threw their green branches on the coffin, and the grave was immediately filled. The guards at the different stations were now relieved, and all returned in the former order, the Masons reassembling in the deceased's house for the closing exercises.

On the 19th I went to Williamsburg in Virginia, a town situated directly opposite the mouth of the Muskingum on the other side of the Ohio, to visit Mr. Williams.

The 22nd. In the evening two large armed boats and two canoes arrived from Fort Washington with more than 100 men in them, & early the next morning proceeded on their way to Pittsburg. Passengers in these boats were Col. Hodgen, former Quartermaster, & Gen. [James] Wilkinson's Lady with her 3 sons, whom she was taking to Philadelphia to school.

The 24th. The Freemasons celebrated this day (St. John's Day) in their fashion. They held several private meetings, and had a public dinner [Mittag-

To Vincennes: 1792

Essen] in an arbor, to which I was invited along with other guests. The Master explained to the guests the significance of the large wax candles which had been lighted. He said they were not placed there because we could not see without them, but because of the Scripture injunction, Let your light shine before men.

26th June. In the morning Gen. Putnam and I at last proceeded on our journey down the Ohio. In our vessel, manned by nine men, there were several gentlemen, passengers to Gallipolis. We landed at Belleprée [Belpre], visited friends, and saw the fine new "improvements." This settlement consists, as mentioned before, of 3 stations or fortifications, about 1½ miles distant from one another, situated on a bluff of the Ohio about 60 feet high. The upper one (named Stone's Station) lies directly above the Little Kanhawa, where there is a small settlement of Virginians. Here there is a matchless island [Blennerhasset's Island] in the Ohio, four miles long. The land in this neighbourhood is uncommonly fertile, & the people as well as their cattle show plainly that they are living in a goodly land. We spent the night with Major [Nathan] Goodale at the lower station.

Soon after we had started on the morning of the 27th and had passed a settlement destroyed by the Indians (it belonged to those mentioned before), we saw a new raft, and immediately thereafter 2 hostile Indians who, however, concealed themselves in the tall, dry weeds. At 5 o'clock we passed the great Hochhocking, & at 6 o'clock we stopped at Belleville, a settlement in Virginia, where we had breakfast. At midday we passed many abandoned improvements. In the evening at 9 o'clock we reached the Great Kanhawa, or New River. This is the spot where Col. Lewis in 1774 had a hot encounter with the Shawanese, in which the latter were totally defeated. For this the government of Virginia gave him a gift of 9,000 acres, where for the past 7 years he has been laying out a town, which now consists of 30 houses, named Point Pleasant. It is very beautifully situated on a high bank. The Kanhawa, which is about as wide as the Lecha [Lehigh], flows past the lower part of the town, and then empties into the Ohio. About 15 miles up this river is a spring which burns as soon as fire is put to it.* It was discovered by a Virginia hunter, who spent the night nearby. When he went at night with a lighted torch to get a drink, a spark fell into the water. The spring at once burst into flames. This so frightened the hunter that he moved his camp. The spring is now visited by many gentlemen travelling down the Ohio, and they tell me that, when it has been set on fire, it usually burns for about ¾ hour. It does not burn down to the ground, but only on the surface of the

---

* Closer identification of the spring, "about 15 miles up this river," does not seem possible. There were several "burning springs" in the Kanawha Valley, but since they were merely seepages of natural gas and sensitive to disturbances of terrain caused by railroads and highways, some were of short duration. We do not know the precise location of even the most famous of them: twenty-five miles below the Falls of the Kanawha on land once owned by George Washington.

water which lies below the burning stuff. Near this place a man who had been scalped and tomahawked by Indians was found in the water a few days ago. We rode on this evening to the French settlement of Gallipolis, situated on the north side of the Ohio between 3 & 4 miles from the Kanhawa. Here we spent the whole of the following day visiting the skilled mechanics and the beautiful improvements & gardens laid out in European style. The most interesting shops of the former are those: 1. of the goldsmith and watchmaker, who showed us such skilled work on watches, compasses & sun-dials as I had never seen before; 2. of the sculptor & stone mason. The latter had 2 finished mantels, most artistically carved. Gen. Putnam bought one on the spot for 12 guineas; the other was intended for a rich Dutch gentleman of this vicinity, who has built a 2 story house here 50 feet in length. The upper part of a third mantel was lying there, ordered by a Spanish gentleman in New Orleans, which, because of the fine workmanship on it was to cost 20 or 22 guineas. 3. The glassworker seemed to be a born artist. He made us a thermometer, a barometer, a glass tobacco pipe, a small bottle with a stopper which held only about a thimble full, and a number of other works of art. He also manufactures costly medicines, *aqua fortis* [nitric acid], etc., & as we were on a journey and in daily need of light & fire, he presented us with a glass full of a dry material which burns as soon as a match is applied. This, he told us, was manufactured from bones. I must say this in addition about these fine gardens, that there are in them the most beautiful flowers, artichokes, and almond trees; and, besides the gardens, there are many fine vineyards, & a few small rice fields. At a distance of about 100 paces from the Ohio is a "Mound" (a round hill) which probably was constructed by the same former inhabitants of this land who made all the strange & mysterious fortifications & works to be found in this country. This mound is about 30 feet high, has now been made into a beautiful pleasure garden, with a pretty summer-house on the flat top. The town of Gallipolis consists of 150 dwellings. The inhabitants number between 3 & 400. A detachment of regular troops of from 50 to 60 men is stationed here for their protection. In addition to these, a few Virginia scouts, or bushrangers, are kept and paid by the government. The militia also serve for pay. The Chikemage [Chicamauga] Creek flows back of the town and below it empties into the Ohio. Fine keelboats are manufactured in this town. Our vessel is one of them. At noon we dined with the most prominent French gentlemen of the place, at the house of the judge and doctor, Mr. Petit. Among the officers who were there as guests there was one by the name of Demler, who told me that he was a friend of the Eisenhart family, & to the best of his knowledge had relatives in Bethlehem.

The 29th, early in the morning, a new bark canoe drifted by along the bank, evidence that Indians had come back from the war beyond the Ohio and must be in this neighborhood. We started from here at 5 o'clock in the morning, at 9 o'clock passed the Little Gyondott, & at 1 o'clock the Big

To Vincennes: 1792

Gyondott, 2 rivers which empty into the Ohio on the Virginia side. Wild turkeys and deer were seen in great numbers on the banks of the Ohio. At 4:30 in the afternoon we passed the Big Sandy, a beautiful river emptying into the Ohio from the south, and forming the boundary between Virginia and Kentucky. Here we found frequent traces of buffaloes along the riverbank. We let our boats drift the whole night on the river, not without a guard, however, for now we had to pass what, because of the Indian warriors, was the most dangerous place, the Sciota. For some years past many Kentucky boats passing here have been attacked and seized by these warriors, the Indians having provided themselves with boats for this purpose, which they kept in the Sciota River & from there made their attacks by means of them. It is said that in the past 2 years two hundred and fifty people have either lost their lives at this place or been taken captive. We were fortunate enough to have a dense fog during the whole night & until 9 o'clock the next morning, so that when the fog cleared we found ourselves 8 miles below the Sciota River. The whole stretch of land on both sides of the Ohio, yesterday and today, was very pleasing to the eye. It was dotted with many round hills, and the chestnut trees and which stood on them, now happening to be in blossom, made the landscape still more lovely. At 3 in the afternoon we discovered a Kentucky boat drawn up at such a place that we concluded it must have been captured by Indians some time ago. Soon after we came to the 3 Sandy Islands (another Indian passage to Kentucky), where we met some white scouts (bushrangers) who were out reconnoitering. By about 4 o'clock we were at Mercer's Station [Massie's Station, now Manchester] on the north side of the Ohio, where there are about 30 families in a fort. Here there is an island in the Ohio [Manchester Island] 2 miles long, almost entirely covered with Indian corn. From this point on all the way to Limestone we met Kentuckians, on land or the river, who had gone out either to hunt or fish, or for some other business. When we reached Limestone [Maysville] at 6 o'clock in the evening, where we had supper, we observed the class of people here and their mode of life with astonishment. This place is in a manner the entrance to Kentucky, where most boats (or all boats not going to the Falls of the Ohio) land, unload, & continue overland on their journey to the more inhabited parts and towns like Washington, Lexington, etc. The inhabitants of this town live in idleness and poverty, & for support depend upon what they can lay hold of from travellers to whom they occasionally lend assistance when in difficulty. I counted 56 large millstones lying around on the banks ready to be taken away by the owners. The town stands on a bank 70 feet high (south side of the Ohio). In a well, 150 yards from the Ohio, a stout and healthy pine tree was found at a depth of 20 feet. At 9 o'clock in the evening we left this place and let our boat drift down with the current through the night. A slight contrary wind blowing, however, and the current not being strong, we made only 12 miles during the night, and came to a Station in Kentucky, where we breakfasted. The whole stretch from Limestone down for 20 miles is inhabited on the south side by Kentuckians. At 8 o'clock we arrived at the 10 Mile Reach, so called because the Ohio flows a straight course of 10 miles, with flat, low banks on both sides, and it actually looks as if this were its mouth. In the evening at 5 o'clock we landed at the town of Columbia, & took up our quarters with Major Steitz [Benjamin Stites]. This man, who is from Jersey, has purchased a tract of 20,-000 acres from Judge Symnes, and has laid out a town upon it [above Cincinnati]. The lots, which are half an acre in size, are sold for 7 shillings 6 pence each, & those situated outside the town, belonging to it, 5 acres in size, come to 7 shillings 6 pence an acre. The town is situated on the Little Miami & Ohio. On the former there is a ship-mill. There are many well-built houses, & the town is finely situated and is growing. The present number of inhabitants is over 1,100. They have 2 Baptist ministers, Smith & Clark. Judge Goforth, whom we visited, also lives here. The only disadvantage of this place is, that part of the land is inundated by high water. Most of the land was formerly covered with walnut and locust trees. Two military stations have been established several miles behind the town for protection of the settlement.

On July 2, after breakfast we left Columbia & reached the town of Cincinati, where Fort Washington is situated. Gen. Putnam was greeted on his arrival with a salute of 9 cannon. Lodgings were assigned to me with Gen. Putnam in Fort Washington, but I declined & went to a landlord in the town by the name of Martin (formerly from Sussex County in Jersey). After having rested a little, Gen. Putnam & I visited the 56 Indian women & children prisoners under strong guard in the stockade, from the Eel River & Wawiachteno Nations. They had been brought in as captives a year ago by Generals [Charles] Scott and [James] Wilkinson from Kentucky. Putnam told them they would soon be released, & that in a few days he would rejoice their hearts, for which they expressed their gratitude. About 1 o'clock in the afternoon, Gen. Wilkinson, the Commandant, arrived here. A week ago he had visited the forts as far as Jefferson, with a detachment of Kentucky militia. He brought the sad intelligence that about 100 warriors, on the day before his arrival, had surprised a guard of 14 men, placed there to watch a band of workmen, & either killed or captured all of them. This report stirred anxiety about the lives of the peace messengers who had been sent out. When we consider that this unhappy day was *the* day set by Gen. Putnam in his message to the enemy Indians for the meeting at Fort Jefferson, and when we consider also that (as we afterwards learned with certainty) that the message had been delivered correctly and in good time, we had to conclude that this expedition was directed against us, and that their purpose was to answer us with a tomahawk in our heads. General Putnam's instructions were to go directly to Fort Jefferson and there await the return and report of the messengers, especially the commissioned Mahicander Indian, Capt. Hendricks. He decided, however, to depart from his instructions and wait

To Vincennes: 1792

until he knew for a certainty how the peace messengers had fared.

On the 3rd Messrs. Vanderburgh, Vigo & Beard arrived here from Post St. Vincennes. With them came 5 men and one woman from the Wawiachteno Nation under guard, to visit their captives friends & help to bring them away, as they had been instructed to do. This fact was made known to the captives that night, the guard within the stockade was withdrawn, & the gate opened, but for the safety of the prisoners a guard was maintained outside. It was touching to see the meeting of relatives, the joy and tears that ensued. The gentlemen from St. Vincent brought this news: that the Indians of that neighborhood had reported that the 3 peace messengers, Trueman, Freeman & Hardin * had certainly been murdered by hostile Indians, and that their Speeches and Belts had afterwards been seen in the Indian towns.

On the 4th of July, the anniversary of the independence of the United States, 15 cannon shots were fired in the morning at 6 o'clock, and 15 again at noon while the assembled officers were dining, and 15 more in the evening to end the day. All salutes were fired from a 6 pounder. Judge Symnes had come to attend this celebration from North Bend, 15 miles down the Ohio, where he has a settlement.

On the 5th and 6th I spent my time taking walks and viewing the town. The well-known Col. Mentges [Menzies], Inspector of Troops in the service of the United States, & Lawyer Smith, visited me in turn. The town of Cincinati was laid out by Judge Symnes. He was formerly judge in Jersey, and is now a judge in the Western Territory, northwest of the River Ohio. A few years ago he purchased from Congress the whole tract of land between the Big and Little Miami, as far as the Ohio River, about 30 miles north and upstream along both these rivers. The place where this town has been laid out and partly built, is a plain along the Ohio about 2 miles long, and extending northward about 7 miles along the road. The town is in a manner divided into two parts, as a 2nd bank is 40 perches from the real bank of the Ohio. Each of these banks is 40 feet high, & the straight line is very pleasing to the eye. Below this second bank is what is known as the lower town; the upper town is, however, connected with the lower town. At present there are 354 lots, surveyed, purchased, and improved. With each town lot, which is half an acre in size, goes a four-acre out-of-town lot. The price of the lots at first was from 4 to 8 dollars per lot, and for the outlots 20 shillings an acre. The rush is, however, at present so great, that lots are being sold at second hand for from 30 to 60 dollars. More than 200 houses have been put up. They are well built, painted red, and many of them are two stories high. They command a rent of from 50 to 60 dollars a year. In the centre of the upper town are 2 public Squares, the one intended for a court house, etc., and the other for a church. On the latter a handsome church is being built

---

* They were released from captivity after the defeat of the Indians by General Wayne at Fallen Timbers.—*Pennsylvania Magazine*, Vol. 12, p. 40.

and is already under roof. The streets of the town are everywhere 4 perches wide. All the lots that have been surveyed are enclosed with good post fences; and Indian corn, wheat, oats, barley, millet, potatoes, & turnips are cultivated in them. Eight roads have been opened from east to west, and 6 from south to north, without obstruction and pleasant to walk in, running in one direction for ¾ mile and in the other for half a mile. At the east end of town, and on the second terrace is Fort Washington, built like the Campus Martius in Marietta. The roof and palisade in front are painted red. Near the fort are some very fine large gardens, laid out in vegetables and beautiful flowers, with tastefully built summer-houses, the most prominent of these belonging to Gen. Wilkinson and Doctor [Richard] Allison. Just below Fort Washington on the Ohio Bank is a sort of square formed by long, low buildings, where the mechanics in the service of the United States army work, and where there are storehouses. The inhabitants of this town number over 900, not counting the garrison and those attached to it. The garrison has no fixed number, but at present consists of about 200 men. The town has its judges and holds regular courts. The military want to run things, but the town insists upon its rights under the constitution, & in consequence there are frequent quarrels. The town is overrun with merchants and overstocked with goods. There are more than 30 stores here, so that one injures another. There are plenty of idlers here, and, from what respectable persons say, they are a bunch of Sodomites. Yet it is hoped that this place, like others on the north side of the Ohio, may in time, & perhaps soon, be purged of such people, for experience teaches that as soon as they become subject to the law they leave for Kentucky which lies just across the Ohio, and if they are stopped there they push on to the farthest frontiers on the Clinch or Columbia River, or as far down as Orleans. Here I met the well-known Weisser, who last year had been conscripted, had participated in the Nov. 4 expedition, and been wounded there. He was scared when he heard I was from Bethlehem, behaved like a penitent sinner, & wept to me that no sin he had committed lay so heavily upon his conscience and pained him so much as this, that he had deceived and betrayed the congregation of God. He said also that from that time on he had had no more success in the world, but had to support himself in laborious ways, with much uneasiness of heart. I said nothing to him but: "He who can see into the heart, whom no one can deceive, the same is God, a righteous judge." He replied, "That is what I now deeply feel." He spoke to me on another occasion, & begged me to take a letter to Bethlehem asking for pardon, but his behavior was such that I could not have anything more to do with him. Although from the description you might think this town consisted principally of evil doers, nevertheless a pastor resides here. The present one belongs to the Presbyterian Church. And I was really surprised to find so many, & in part so attentive, listeners in the Sunday services. A thing that adds to the beauty of the town of Cincinati, and also to its profit, is the fact that, just opposite, on the south side of the Ohio, a beautiful river, the Licking Branch, about

To Vincennes: 1792

2 thirds as wide as the Lecha, enters the Ohio. A town has been laid out there, called Newport. From the mouth of this river, which flows out of a rich and inhabited country, a straight road leads to the capital city of Lexington. It is expected that in future a lively traffice from that place to this, & from here down the Ohio & Missisipi will be carried on. At present there are 2 ferries here, one of which belongs to a German by name of Pickel, a former inhabitant of the vicinity of Bethel, who (so he says) diligently frequented the Brethren's meetings during the time of Till's, Reizenbach's, Hübner's & Schlägel's ministry. This Pickel told me that, when he was moving down here with some other Germans from the Monongahella in a boat on the way to New Spain, he was called a heretic, & they sought to take his life, but he managed to escape. From Pastor Mau in Harretsburg (Kentucky) 60 miles from here, I received almost daily tidings. He is highly spoken of, serves 2 congregations composed chiefly of Germans, & preaches in both English and German.

On the 7th at 9 o'clock 2 men, a woman, & a big boy, who had gone from here in a canoe to Columbia, were attacked by Indians about 1½ miles from here, & one man was killed and scalped, the other shot through the shoulder, & the boy was taken prisoner. The woman, who fell into the water from fright, was carried down some distance by the current, and finally came safely ashore. She brought the news here. The militia was immediately sent out. They brought in the wounded man & the body of the dead man. They at once cut out the ball, & the wound was declared not dangerous. The head of the other man has been smashed to pieces.

Sunday the 8th, in the morning the resident pastor preached, & in the afternoon a Baptist minister from Columbia.

On the 9th, the rain which had fallen yesterday and the day before caused the Ohio to rise 11 feet. The high water enabled several heavily laden Kentucky boats from Pittsburg to reach here. As they passed the Sciota, a number of Indians fired on them. The Indians had already got into their canoes to capture the boats, when 3 other boats that were a little behind & well armed, fired their guns on seeing this; whereupon the Indians had to drop their plans for the time being. One of the boats had received 12 shots, but no one was injured.

On the 12th William Wells arrived here from Louisville. This Wells was a boy 12 years old when, on his way to school in Kentucky 8 years ago, he was captured by the Eel River Wawiachtenos, & afterwards adopted into the family of the chief of that nation, where he learned the language, and became a good hunter and useful man among them. He took part in the engagement on the 4th of November. He gives good, thorough, & reliable accounts of all that has happened there, & has made known where the Indians' cannon were buried. His adopted father, Gawiahätte (i.e., Hedgehog), having given him freedom to go where he pleased, even to visit his brothers in Kentucky, he went first to Post-Vincent, where he found an opportunity to visit his brothers in the vicinity of Loisville. Gen Putnam being in need of an interpreter, there being no one here who could speak with the prisoners, he sent for him, & took him into the service of the United States. Here he found the rest of his adopted relatives, his mother and sisters, who when they met shed many tears.

Early on the 14th came an express from Fort Jefferson with the news that 2 soldiers, one of whom had served in Gen. Harmer's campaign, & the other of whom had been taken prisoner by the Indians on the 4th November last while he was some distance out of town hoeing corn, had laid plans together to escape, & had succeeded. They were brought in ——

On the morning of the 15th with an escort of light cavalry, and then cross-examined by a judge in the presence of Gen. Wilkinson and Putnam & put under oath to tell nothing but the truth. They hâd both been taken prisoner by the Pottawattami Nation, & one of them, a German by name of Schäfer, could speak the language fairly well. According to their report, the nations would entertain no peace propositions until they saw that all forts and settlements on this side of the Ohio had been abandoned and removed. Moreover, the 2 peace messengers Trueman and Freeman had certainly been killed, for the Indians had shown them their scalps, clothes, speeches, & belts, saying, "Thus will we in future treat all peace messengers & deserters." Of Col. Hardin they knew nothing more than that they had been told he and his companions had been killed. They gave further information about all the parties that had started out this summer, & they said that Simon Girty had been there in person at the last attack on Fort Jefferson, which had been made by more than 100 Indians. Altogether the reports were found to be reliable, & agreed with what we had already learned. News came today from Fort Jefferson that a party of Indians last night, a particularly dark night, had set loose and driven away all the cattle which had been penned up under the palisades of the fort, and that Indians were seen every day. From Columbia came news tonight that about 30 Indians had been there & had taken 3 persons captive. A strong party of cavalry was sent in pursuit of them. They followed their traces for 40 miles, but the Indians had entered a swamp, and the horses could proceed no farther.

On the morning of the 16th the Wawiachteno chief, who was one of those I have mentioned as having lately come from Post Vincennes, died suddenly.

At his funeral on the 17th, by order of Generals Putnam & Wilkinson, all military honors were shown him, & 3 vollies were fired over his grave. Most of the Indians followed the corpse, one of them carrying a white flag on a long pole, which he afterwards planted at the head of the grave. The procession marched in proper order, accompanied by the most prominent gentlemen of the place. The drum, draped in black, beat the funeral march. He was given a resting-place in the churchyard. It was thought this might have a good effect upon his relatives and his Nation in general. But malicious persons dug up the body during the following night, dragged it down the road, &

stood it upright. They also tore down the flag and flagpole, & threw them into a mudhole. Next morning the generals had the body quickly buried again, and set up the flag. The government secretary, Winthrop Sargent, issued a proclamation offering 100 dollars for the discovery of the perpetrators. Next night the flag and the proclamation were torn down & mutilated, but the body was left alone. Once again a flag was raised, & a guard posted nearby, and nothing further happened.

On the 19th the chief of the Indians here made a speech to General Putnam about the release of the prisoners. He wished Putnam would accompany them personally to the Wabash, & believed if he did this he would find opportunity of announcing to the Indians there the peaceful intentions of the United States. He added that, if they were obliged to remain here much longer, they would surely all die, and if they must die, they would rather die in *their own* country than be buried here on foreign soil. Putnam replied that he had set the date for their departure 30 days hence.

On Sunday the 22nd a soldier who had mutinied received judgment and punishment on the parade ground. He had to run the gauntlet, have his head shaved, have a collar fastened round his neck, and in this manner be drummed out of the fort and out of town. Some time before this he had been tied to the wheelbarrow in Philadelphia. At noon young Mr. Steitz arrived from Columbia with news that 4 Indians had been seen near Columbia, and that the militia were hunting them.

On the 24th, at the invitation of a Kentucky gentleman, I crossed the Ohio to visit him. Fort Washington & Cincinati offer a very pleasant prospect from this side of the river.

On the 28th Gen. Wilkinson, with an escort of light cavalry, went to his favorite place, Fort Hamilton.

On the 29th the Presbyterian pastor spoke with fervor on the importance of conversion. Among other things he said this: "That it was no matter of speculation: the choice was free to all, to accept grace without price & without merit, and so be saved, or remain unsaved & so be eternally lost."

On the 4th & 5th of August the Ohio rose so rapidly that by the latter evening it had risen 12 feet. Mr. Clark a Baptist minister from Columbia preached twice today in this church. He described the natural man in his sin and nakedness, showed how necessary it is that he be converted, & pointed out the path he must follow. He extoled God's compassion, & directed all sinners to Jesus the crucified one. He also spoke of the fruits of conversion whereby a regenerate person could be recognized. He told the story of his own conversion, & how *he* had sought and found grace. He spoke harshly against those who treated these matters idly and frivolously, and gave them a dreadful, burning picture of hell fire. Speaking of the Indian war, he said among other things: "God has put us in this situation as punishment for our sins. To this end he employs even the heathen, & as long as we fail to turn and be converted this chastisement will continue." He cited Nov. 4th as an example &

told how under the old dispensation God had made use of the heathen to punish his chosen people when they had fallen into unbelief, disobedience, & idoltary, and so forth. He went on to say that he believed we too were a scourge to the heathen, because they do not seek after God but serve the devil. He hoped, however, that a time might come when all the heathen nations of this country would seek the only true God & crucified Savior, obey & serve him. As we were coming out of the church, I heard some gentlemen say to one another: "That man should have been hauled down from the pulpit and thrown out. He would make everything a sin for us, & he keeps harping on Jesus Christ who was only a carpenter. Had he spoken about God's omnipotence, thrown in something about good morals, such, for instance, as how men should behave to one another, we would have listened to him, & his sermon would have passed; but there was nothing in what he had to say. He is just a disturber of the peace, a firebrand," and so on.

On the 6th some people who were going from Columbia to Dunlap's Station on horseback were attacked by about 15 Indians. One of them was killed and another wounded.

On the 10th a company of 60 men under Capt. Peters arrived. They are to escort the Indian prisoners on their journey to the Wabash.

On the 11th 4 large boats with military supplies arrived from Pittsburg.

The 12th. After church I went to dine with a gentleman in Kentucky.

On the 13th the Indians attacked three different places. At Fort St. Clair they shot a soldier through the hat. At Dunlap's Station they wounded 3 persons, one of whom died, & at Fort Hamilton they stole 17 horses. The owners of these, however, who are members of the Kentucky militia and in the service of the United States, set out after them, killed one, & brought back their horses.

On the 14th Gen. Wilkinson returned from Fort Hamilton, where he is having a handsome house built, and where he will in future take up his residence. According to all descriptions, the country thereabouts is very beautiful, there being large meadows on which over 2,000 tons of hay are said to have been cut this year. The Big Miami, which flows by the fort, is said to be full of fish.

The 16th. All the Indians, who have now been prisoners here for over a year & who (as the mustering officer informed me), have cost the United States 60,000 dollars, set off at last for Post Vincennes with an escort of 4 large boats and a guard of 60 men, besides their interpreter, Wells.

On the 18th Gen. Putnam & I followed them in our barge. Capt. Collins & Doctor Boyd accompanied us to Louisville as passengers. The former had gone in 1786 with Brethren from Bethlehem to St. Croix, but has now settled in Kentucky. The latter, just come from training under Gen. Hand in Lancaster, has accepted an army commission. In our company also was one of the gentlemen I mentioned before (Henry Vanderburgh) from Post Vincennes, who wishes to return there with us. Seven miles below Cincinati we

To Vincennes: 1792

passed a small settlement on the north side of the Ohio (called the South Bend), situated on land belonging to Judge Symnes. Eight miles farther on we stopped at North Bend, where there is a small town & a large settlement, belonging to this same gentleman, who lives here. It is really surprising to see how people have settled & cultivated this land, which 5 years ago was a wilderness. There are between 3 & 400 inhabitants in this neighborhood, part of whom live in town and part in the country on their plantations. The most singular circumstance is that they have had no hostile visits from the Indians for the past 2 years, and from the first beginning of this settlement have had only one such raid, in which 3 people lost their lives—who, however, according to the testimony of the inhabitants, deserved what they got because, when they came to visit and trade, they stole the Indians' horses. Judge Symnes, who is looked upon as a father by the people here, has by his treatment of the Indians, who at first used to come here often, gained their love and friendship, which is a better protection for this place than a regiment of soldiers would be. Symnes told me an Indian interpretation of the coat-of-arms of the United States, that is, the eagle, etc. Three years ago a considerable number of Shawanos & Delawares came here to trade. The Judge took the chiefs to his house, entertained them hospitably, & gave them presents. During their visit many things were discussed, & among others Symnes showed them the coat-of-arms of the United States, which he carefully explained. "Well," said a Shawano captain, "let me give *my* interpretation. Perhaps, according to the picture, it will come closer to the truth than yours. You tell me," said he, "that every power has its own coat-of-arms & that this is a good and useful thing. You have told me much about the peaceful intentions of the United States towards the Indians, & show me this picture as evidence! If the United States were such lovers of peace as you describe them to be, they would have chosen for their coat-of-arms something more appropriate as an expression of it. There are, for instance, many agreeable and harmless birds. There is the dove, which would not harm the smallest creature— But what is the eagle? He is the largest of all birds! He is the enemy of all birds. He is proud, because he is conscious of his size & strength! On a tree, as well as in flight, he shows his pride, & looks down in scorn upon all the birds. His head, his eyes, his beak & his long crooked talons declare his strength & hostility! Now this bird, which is terrible enough in itself, you have depicted as even more dreadful and frightful. You have not only put one of the instruments of war, a bundle of arrows, into one of his hands (claws), & rods in the other, but have painted him in the most fearful guise, & in posture of attack upon his prey. Now tell me," he continued, "have I not spoken the truth?" Symnes had to agree with his exposition, but with this qualification, that only the enemies of the United States were frightened by the eagle's posture. Friends, on the contrary, could look upon it as a sign of protection, & that all the Indians who were friends of the United States enjoyed this protection, etc.

It is remarkable how at this place the beautiful Miami River, which empties into the Ohio 6 miles below, after extraordinary windings of some 15 miles, comes finally at this point to within ¾ mile of the Ohio. The two Walkers who 2 years ago murdered the peaceful Senneca Indians on Pint Creek are still living here. At 2 o'clock in the afternoon we passed the Great Miami, on the banks of which were great numbers of wild turkeys and geese. We went on 2 miles farther to Tanner's Station [opposite Lawrenceburg] in Kentucky (south side of the Ohio), where we bought butter & watermelons. We saw deer, bear, & wildfowl feeding along the banks of the Ohio. During the night we let our boat drift with the current.

On Sunday the 19th, at 6 different times we saw herds of buffalo grazing on the shore. We put Capt. Collins ashore, who, although he shot one, was not able to follow it farther because of fresh Indian tracks. Towards evening, however, 16 buffaloes with 3 buffalo calves appeared. Our hunter shot a very fat young cow, weighing between 4 & 500 lbs. Now we had a good supply of meat, & could look upon the rest of the game with indifferent eyes. During the night we again allowed ourselves to drift with the current.

The 20th. Very early in the morning buffaloes & deer appeared again. By 10 o'clock we had reached 18 Mile Island, that is, only 18 miles from Louisville. We passed also the 12 Mile Island, & afterwards the 6 Mile Island, all thickly overgrown with the so-called Carolina reed, which covers many of the swamps in this region. From this last island on, the Kentucky side is thickly settled. In the afternoon about 3 o'clock we stopped at Fort Steuben [Jeffersonville, Indiana] (north side of the Ohio), where the Indians, with their guard of 60 men, had arrived the night before. In honor of the General, 9 cannon shots were fired on our arrival, & the commandant of this fort, Capt. Doyle, was very kind to me, and inquired about his relatives in Lancaster & Nazareth, the Hopson and Jac. Krug families. We all slept in camp under canvas on the banks of the Ohio, surrounded by sentries.

The 21st. In the morning Capt. Peters made the necessary preparations to take our 4 vessels over the Falls of the Ohio. After all our baggage had been conveyed, first across the Ohio (which is very wide here) and then by wagon 2½ miles to a place below the falls, they tried to bring the 2 empty Kentucky boats & the 2 barges over the falls, with pilots who have to be paid a guinea a trip. As the water was very low & the channel narrow, it was exceedingly difficult, & 3 of our boats grounded. Only one got down today. Every effort was made to float the grounded boats, but without success today, & the poor fellows who were on board had to pass the night there, wet as they were. The greatest misfortune of all was that one of these boats, which was 40 feet long & 16 feet wide & had cost 40 dollars, broke up and sank during the night with two sick Indian women & 2 soldiers on board, but they saved themselves on the roof of the boat. The commandant of this place, who is an honest, good man, was busy before daybreak helping the distressed. He sent a number of his strongest soldiers with a quantity of ropes from a schooner lying here, by means of which, on towards noon, they managed to accomplish their purpose, and brought the last two barges safely down below the falls. The 4 persons on the stranded boat were brought safe to land with all their effects. The poor Indians who had had to see and suffer all these difficulties and dangers, and who were now in a place where Kentucky fury raged against Indians, wept aloud. Their interpreter having gone ashore to visit his brother, I comforted them as best I could, & brought them on this unlucky evening back to the shelter of the guns of the fort. Here they were out of danger, & Capt. Doyle took the best possible care of them until at last next day they were taken to Gen. Putnam's headquarters on the other side of the Ohio, below the falls, where they seemed to be quite at ease. The commissary's 3 large boats loaded with provisions for us & for the troops at Post Vincent came safe and unharmed through the rapids, so that everything could now be organized and we all had room. There being various matters to attend to here, & Putnam's barge having lost a rudder coming over the falls, we were obliged to remain here for a few days. During this time, with Capt. Doyle & Lieut. Clark I carefully examined the falls from all quarters. After passing through 650 miles (from Pittsburg here) of nice quiet water, now to come suddenly upon such a turbulent stretch, was strange and astonishing. The falls are remarkable for having 3 separate channels, each unlike the others. The channel on the south side consists of many steps of smooth & pointed rocks; the middle one shoots down more like a milldam; while the one on the north side is a raging rapid full of big rocks. Troublesome and dangerous though it is now to run them when the water is low, one can get through easily and without the slightest danger when the water is high. The actual falls consist of a layer or bed of smooth rocks, high in some spots and low in others. In the rapids at low water, great dry, rocky banks may be seen on which everything that lodges is caught and petrified. Walnuts, hickorynuts, acorns & their shells, branches, deer & buffalo horns, roots, buffalo & goose manure, fish skeletons, snails, crayfish claws, etc., are frequently seen lying on the flat rocks; but if you try to pick them up, you find them immovable and petrified. Near the falls on both sides of the river are beautiful Lombardy poplars, which are here called the Cotton Tree. Below the falls in deep water great quantities of rockfish are caught. In summer the falls feed thousands of wild geese, & also the people's pigs, which always find dead fish and such things here. The surrounding country is beautiful and level. Although the banks rise to a height of from 60 to 70 feet, they are not steep. On the north side, at the upper end of the falls, is Fort Steuben, in which 60 men are quartered. On the same side at the lower end of the rapids is Clarksville, a little town on General Clark's land, who received from the State of Virginia a grant of 150,000 acres of land here for his former services against the Indians. On the south side of the Ohio, and nearly opposite the falls, lies the town of Louisville on a fine high plateau that extends many miles into the country and is very thickly settled. In the town there are about 150 houses, all except 2 of which are built of unfinished wood. Of these two one is built of brick and the other of limestone, 2 stories high and neatly finished. The land on which the town stands belongs to Mr. John Campbell (our former host at Pittsburg), who has a beautiful country seat not far from here. A French gentleman by the name of Lakesang lives here. He has a handsome residence, a very fine garden, and a nursery of 10,000 young trees, most of them grafted or inoculated. I was several times invited by this gentleman to dinner. Indeed, he offered me a room in his house for as long as I stayed here; but I could not accept his invitation. I found 3 former Muskingum traders, one of whom, (Henry Reed) lives in comfortable circumstances, & has 5 stores at different places in the country. He insisted on my putting up at his house. But I stayed with my companions, who were all encamped in tents below the falls, where I was free to visit friends and acquaintances as I felt inclined during the day. The town of Louisville vies with Lexington to be chosen the capital of Kentucky, and three weeks from now it is to be viewed by a commission appointed for that purpose. From here 2 great highways lead to the rest of the Kentucky towns. The one disadvantage of this place is that the thick fogs which in the autumn rise from the falls and cover the town, produce fever, and this interferes with the town's growth. The visit which the Indian warriors paid to this vicinity during our stay here, carrying off negroes & horses, caused us much uneasiness regarding the safety of our Indians. However, everything came out all right.

At last on Sunday, the 26th we were able to continue our journey. There were now 140 of us altogether, distributed in 4 Kentucky boats, 3 barges, and several canoes. In our barge was Mr. Henry Vandeburgh, a merchant and Judge of Probate Court from Post Vincennes. We had not gone far before we saw game of many kinds. But what delights the traveller most here are the majestic Lombardy poplars growing on the banks of the Ohio, under whose shade the buffaloes hide from the summer heat.

The 27th. Our hunters shot 2 bears and a deer, and ——

On the 28th they shot a fat buffalo cow which weighed 436 lbs. Today 2 more bears were shot and some turkeys.

On the 29th another buffalo, a deer, & 2 bears were shot.

On the 30th we saw almost continuously herds of buffaloes grazing on the banks. Interpreter Wells shot a fat cow, & I a calf weighing 134 lbs., the meat of which was found to be very juicy. One of our Indians shot a cow and a calf, both fat and good. We had now reached a country where there are no more hills to be seen, but everything is flat and level, & the Carolina reed grows as thick as hemp.

Early on the 31st, as we were passing with our boats and several canoes down one side of a very long, narrow island, 2 large herds of buffalo, frightened by the boats passing on the other side, plunged right in front of us into the water. We did not shoot, having enough to do to keep out of their way, for when they are in flight they do not see what is before them, but run down

To Vincennes: 1792

everything in their way. In the evening we passed Green River, at the mouth of which lies an island 6 miles long.

On Sept. 1, at 6 o'clock in the morning, we stopped at the Red Banks [Henderson], a settlement in Kentucky of about 30 families. This place, which lies 20 miles below Green River, is settled almost entirely by Jerseymen. A certain Michal Sprenkel, from near Yorktown, inquired about various Brethren at that place. Another, Friedrich Belcher, said that he had attended the Brethren's school there. And a Dane inquired about his countryman, Just Jansen in Bethlehem. On this spot, which lies very high and has a rich, sandy soil, I saw the largest and best developed sassafras trees. Some houses of hewn logs are built entirely of this wood. Indeed, one of the inhabitants, Mr. Day, showed me 9 beams, 9 inches by 6, which he had cut from one log, & he would have liked to show me a standing sassafras tree, almost 4 feet [in diameter] above the butt, if the high wet weeds had not prevented my going in. The people who live here are almost all good huntsmen, & last year shot a great many deer and caught many beaver. Here I also saw the first Pakan Tree. We travelled 8 miles farther today, and camped at a very beautiful island.

Sunday, Sept. 2. We overtook some people from Louisville who had 4 buffaloes in their boat. The Commissary (who was with us) bought the meat for 2 pence a lb., & we received our share of it. We passed the 9 Mile Island, & encamped at night under a high bank about a mile below the mouth of the Wabash.

Early on the 3rd we saw through our spyglass some white people on the island that lies at the mouth of the Wabash [Wabash Island], & afterwards found that the troops sent for our assistance & protection by Major Hamtramick at Post Vincennes had arrived. When we joined them, we began to make the necessary arrangements for our further journey. The Kentucky boats which, because the journey now is up the Wabash against the current, could be of no further service, were destroyed, & a fortification built on the point of land, in which the commissary could store his provisions, with a guard of 25 men, until such time as they could be gradually removed. After this had been done, the 6 large *Perogues* which had been brought down by the French inhabitants from Vincennes, were loaded & sent ahead with them; & then our vessels were repaired & finally loaded. General Putnam, who was particularly well pleased with this country, & especially the beautiful Wabash River, which is here not much smaller than the Ohio, observed how proudly it empties into the Ohio. In the meantime he had a sumptuous meal prepared, & a table & benches made of boards set up, where he, the 3 officers Peters, Prior & Armstrong, the commissary Mr. Poor, Mr. Vandeburgh, & I dined together. The meal was good, & consisted of buffalo, bear, deer & pork, a turkey, 2 ducks, a pike, & turtle soup, besides various vegetables. There were good beverages as well. But the "music" of the many paroquets (a small kind of parrot) was too loud & not attuned to my ears. I remembered here that I was nearly 1,300 miles from Bethlehem, & had still farther to go.

At last in the afternoon of the 4th we entered the Wabash. The Indians, who were now once more on their own land and soil, became quite cheerful. We had made about 8 miles this evening when we put up for the night.

On the 5th everything went very well. We were pleased with both the water and the landscape.

But on the 6th I felt very unwell. I thought if I could go ashore & get into a sweat I should feel better. But after I had tried this for several hours, I could go no farther, and was obliged to lie down on the bank till a boat came and took me aboard. I ran a high fever this evening, which so prostrated me for the next 4 days that for the time being I was scarcely conscious. Lieutenant Prior, who had studied medicine and was the Company's doctor, diagnosed my illness as a bilious fever, and prescribed the necessary medicine, so that I improved so much I could sit up a little during the day; yet there remained a lingering fever, & the heavy perspiration I had at night, with terrible headaches so exhausted me that I had bare life but neither strength nor spirit.

I was still in this condition when, on the afternoon of the 12th, we arrived at Post Vincennes. Mr. Vandeburgh at once took me off the boat and to his house, where I had the best attention. But I did not recover entirely until the following month, after I had proceeded several days journey from this place. In the meantime the Indians, who had been invited here for a treaty (some of whom had already arrived), when they saw from the banks their captive friends approaching, fired off their guns for joy and afterwards sang songs of rejoicing in their own peculiar melodies.

These prisoners, after a speech from Gen. Putnam on the 13th, were returned to their own people, and all rejoiced together. From now on until the 22nd, Indians were arriving almost every day for the treaty. Because of their continual drinking, however, Gen. Putnam found it necessary to issue a proclamation, in which he strictly forbade the inhabitants to give or sell liquor to the Indians during the treaty.

On the 19th, 110 head of cattle arrived. They had been driven here from Kentucky for use at the treaty and for the garrison here. Capt. Doyle from Fort Steuben with 30 men escorted the drovers.

The 20th. I rode out with several gentlemen partly for the sake of my health and partly in order to see the surrounding country.

Post Vincennes, or Saint Vincent as some call it here, was laid out in 1725 by a French lieutenant of that name. The site on which this town is built deserves to have been in the hands of a more sensible architect. He had a fancy, as it appears, for a multitude of streets, and these only 25 feet wide. Every two lots, each containing about a third of an acre, make up a block, so that the owner of any lot can look out of his windows on to three streets. He introduced some laws that are no less foolish. One of them is that the inhabi-

To Vincennes: 1792

tants must keep their cattle fenced during the summer, and that in a common field; the field outside this fence is to be unenclosed and to lie fallow. Even today this law has to be observed, though it is an annoyance to most of the present American inhabitants. They are working hard to have the law repealed, and they have already presented a petition to Congress. The town has grown very much since 1743. Most of its inhabitants came from Canada. As early as 1770, 300 houses had been erected & it already had 1,500 inhabitants. But as their chief interest was in the fur trade they paid little attention to agriculture, & lived very much like Indians. They had a church & a priest, but they preferred the billiard table to his masses. After a while they stopped supporting him, so he left them & went to the Mississippi. And that is where all those who have any religion left in them go every year or so for confession, absolution, and the Holy Communion, and they take their children along for the same purpose. They think nothing of making a journey by water of 300 miles there and 300 miles back, for they can always get plenty of meat and fish on the way. Things have changed in many ways since the United States has had control here, which dates from the year 1778 when General Clarke captured the place, and took the Lieutenant Governor of Upper Canada and other officers prisoners and brought them to Williamsburg in Virginia as war prisoners. Since the peace between England and the United States, a great number of citizens of the latter have moved in here and a great change has taken place. Near the French town here there used to be a large Indian town of the Wawiachteno Nation. They lived together for 50 years in friendship & peace. But now the troubles began. There were continual murders, now on the one side and now on the other, till at last the Indians grew tired of it, broke up the town, & moved 5 miles away. The chiefs of this nation were tireless in their efforts to restore peace and harmony, but a scoundrel from Kentucky, Hardin by name, secretly gathered some 150 Kentuckians & without warning fell upon these peaceful Indians, who at that time were camping within a mile of Post Vincent, & murdered them all. The commanding officer, Major Hamtramick [Hamtramck], having had timely warning of what these evil men were up to, sent to them immediately, representing the enormity of what they planned to do. He received answer that if he made the least movement to prevent it he would meet the same fate. When news spread of this affair, many hundreds of warriors assembled in 1791 and demanded of the French inhabitants that they surrender all Virginians (that is what they call those who belong to the United States) so that they might avenge themselves on them. The French tried to set them right, and at last came to an agreement. They collected and gave to them a present, and the Indians gave over their design. The resentment, however, has not yet subsided, & the Indians all declare that wherever the Virginians go they stir up trouble, & bring on a war, and in this the French agree with them. Trade, which as I said before is the Frenchmen's real occupation, was now almost completely destroyed. The Indians had lost all confidence, and seldom came here. They went to the British and Spaniards. The French were not accustomed to work, and could not be taught how. When from necessity they wished to plant corn, there were few or none to look after it. And so in the end, when harvest time came, there was little or nothing. The government has been obliged to help meet their needs for 2 years past with contributions. It is possible for men to become so careless and lazy that in the midst of a fruitful country, with abundant provisions, they may yet starve, because they are too lazy to reach out and help themselves. The Americans at this place, numbering about 30 families, live very well. Their fields are richly laden, their vegetable gardens in the best of condition, & they dress in cotton and linen, both of which they raise. On the other hand there is hardly *one* Frenchman in 5 who dresses decently. If you know the Indian costume, you know theirs. Their gardens are the same, full of weeds instead of vegetables; & if it were not for the fine large appletrees which grow on their lots, you might wonder why they fenced them in at all. Their cattle are starving, & all around them are good meadow lands on which they could raise every year hundreds, yes thousands, of tons of hay. In short, anyone who starves here could not support himself anywhere in the world, & hardly deserves to live. I cannot leave this place without adding this: that all who have seen it praise it in the highest terms (referring, in particular to the country and the river). The entire country is flat. The soil is black sand. The Wabash is as clear as the Manakasy, full of fish, & navigable for 600 miles from its mouth. About $1\frac{1}{4}$ miles from the town are several nice round hills which the people here call the Sugar Loaves. Seen from them, the town & fort (Fort Knox) offer a very pleasing prospect. Besides the town & fort, which stand on the east side of the Wabash, there is a little village on the west side, & these are the real farmers among the French. The French buildings are all one-story; & instead of laying the boards horizontally, they are set upright on the frame to which they are nailed. They have few beams in their houses, but instead thicker and heavier floor-boards. Of collar beams they know nothing, but in place of them put up massive rafters. Their chimneys are usually of wood & mortar. To build anything of stone here is very expensive, because no stones can be got within 5 miles; indeed not a single stone is to be seen on this land. Wages are high, & everything very dear.— There is another small settlement 5 miles south-east of here, on a small stream called De shae, inhabited entirely by people from the United States. Some of the prairies or plains in this part of the country are several days journey in extent, buffaloes graze on them in great herds, & they are hunted in the autumn by the Indians.

Sunday, Sept. 23rd. The Indians begged to get the treaty started because they wanted to be off on their fall hunting. They were promised it would begin tomorrow, and that every morning at 10 o'clock a cannon would be fired off as a signal.

So it was that, on the 24th, the treaty was opened by a speech from Gen. Putnam. He assured the assembled nations—the Eel Creek Wiachtenows from the headwaters of the Wabash; the Wiachtenows from lower down the Wabash; the Piankishaws between the Wabash & the Illinois; the Potawattamos from Lake Michigan & St. Josephs; the Kikapoos from Cahokia; the Kaskaskias & Musquetons from Kaskaskias—that the United States desired to live at peace with all the Indians, and to that end an opportunity was now given these nations to discuss with the United States all that had happened, to clear the path, and to make a fresh start. An answer was promised for the following day.

On the 25th the assembled nations, through a speaker whom they had agreed on for this purpose, presented their reply. They presented Gen. Putnam with 2 large peace-pipes & a beautiful large belt of wampum, with the request that he accept these as a token of peace & give them to Gen. Washington in order that he, too, might smoke this pipe. Afterwards the chiefs of these nations rose, one after the other, & spoke with strings of wampum. The substance of their discourse was that the white people should not take away their land, but remain on the other side of the Ohio, & accept this river as the boundary line. There being, however, some obscurity in their speeches, they were ——

On the 26th, in a speech by Gen. Putnam, earnestly requested to explain themselves more clearly, which they did in the afternoon meeting. They expressed the wish that they & the white people might never live too close to each other because there were very bad people on both sides. They wanted, and begged for, trade with us, and requested that Congress might not take away from the French who lived here the land their fathers had given them in former times.

On the 27th the articles of peace were read to the nations assembled in council, & after they were signed by 31 chiefs of these nations, peace was declared by the General in a speech, and the requisite 7 belts of wampum were presented to the head chiefs of the nations. In conclusion 8 cannon shots were fired, the first by the General himself and the others by the chiefs who had received the belts. They were also given 4 large oxen, bread & brandy for a feast. Before these festivities were over, however, 2 of them had lost their lives, killed in drunken brawls.

On the 28th Gen. Putnam, who had not been feeling well for some days, took to his bed. He had the same bilious fever that I had had on the way up, & was so ill for several days that we doubted his recovery. Many were ill with this fever, and some died.

The 29th September. All the Indians, rejoicing in the peace, held a dance in the town hall. Each Nation was distinctively painted, and all vied with one another to look as shocking and hideous as possible. They first paraded through all the streets in town with drums and songs, & then went to the town hall, and told all their war exploits in song and story. The figures and motions they went through at this dance, their distorted and horrible faces, the war weapons they brandished, striking fence-posts, benches, etc.—the dried deer hooves that rattled round their legs, the green garlands round their necks and round their bodies which were unclothed save for a few wretched rags, presented such a sight as I am unable to describe. But it was all conducted properly, after their own fashion.

On the 30th we began to distribute the presents among them, & continued that for the next few days.

October 4th. Gen. Putnam's fever broke, & we hoped he would soon recover. As he had promised to take several chiefs to Philadelphia, he wished them to get started on their journey, and I was to take them as far as Marietta, where I was to remain until he arrived. Another party of chiefs was despatched at the same time with messages to the enemy Indians. The interpreter, Wells, was to go with them.

Oct. 5th. In the afternoon the chiefs, 16 in number, with their wives, started on their journey to Philadelphia. In their company were Lieut. Prior, who was in charge, myself, 2 Kentucky pilots [guides] & 2 soldiers with the provisions on packhorses, altogether 23 souls. As we passed Fort Knox, 7 cannon shots were fired. The journey was overland to the Falls of the Ohio [by the Buffalo Trace]. We camped this evening at a run 5 miles from Vincennes.

The 6th. We travelled all day through a fine rich level country, & the pleasant odor of quantities of ripe persimmons made the day very agreeable. Towards evening we crossed the beautiful White River, which is as wide as the Lecha at Bethlehem. It is a branch of the Wabash, into which it empties about 14 miles below Post Vincennes. Our Kentucky hunters today shot 6 wild turkeys.

The 7th. We travelled up along the eastern branch of the White River for a good 12 miles, & then our path led us off into a wilderness where we could hardly get through the grapevines and bushes. Our guides today shot a very large old buffalo, estimated as weighing 800 lbs. I saw here in the evening a new dish prepared from the intestines of the buffalo. Both Prior and I had a taste of it. I saw at once it was not for *my* stomach.

On the 8th we marched all day again through a wildernes, & over steep disagreeable mountains. Today 2 lean bears were shot. We camped at a run, but it was almost dried up.

On the morning of the 9th we reached the so-called Buffalo Salt Lick [French Lick, Indiana], where (as people say) 500 buffalo may sometimes be seen at one time, especially during the months of June, July, & August. The salt place, several acres in extent, is so much trodden down & grubbed up that not a blade of grass can grow, & the *busch* for some distance round has been eaten bare. On the ground are many buffalo sculls & the skeletons of these animals, which had either been shot from time to time or been killed by themselves. At the Lick were many hundred paroquets (a small species of parrot) which made a terrible noise. There were also flocks of wild pigeons, & thousands of small black gnats, which look like fleas & which attacked me so viciously, so that I could not bring myself to taste the water, but as soon as we got through rode off into the woods. A great many buffalo paths lead out from here, & we had the misfortune to take one of these instead of the right one. When, however, our guides, who were not with us at the time, returned, they led us back on to the right path and then went ahead again to hunt. After we had gone about 5 miles, a herd of buffaloes came directly towards us, as if they meant to run us down. We fired into them, killed one, & wounded another. We took all the meat of the former, which was very fat, with us on our horses. The Indians would have liked to stay here till all was eaten, but we could not consent. In the evening we came to a water-hole where we spent the night. Some of the Indians ate so much they were sick, & we had to carry their bundles on our horses next day.

Today, the 10th, we had a terrible road again, and in 19 miles found water only once. A lean bear was shot today.

The 11th. During the night, about 2 o'clock in the morning, we were suddenly overtaken by a thunderstorm. We had neither cabin nor roof, & the night was very dark. The rain poured down on us like a torrent, & little streams flowed under us. Not one of us had a dry stitch. We were now still 18 miles from Fort Steuben, & in a territory through which the Miami warriors pass on their way to Kentucky & where the Kentuckians often pursue them. We had cause enough for anxiety. If the warriors had recently been committing ravages in Kentucky, & were now pursued, our Indians would have to pay for it. So Mr. Prior spoke with them & the guides, & ordered a forced march. We had gone scarcely half a mile when another thundergust struck us. It lasted so long that at 1 o'clock in the afternoon, when we reached Clarksville, & I dismounted from my horse, the water oozed out of the tops of my boots, although I wore 2 greatcoats, one over the other, and had tried to protect myself as well as possible. At this place I saw the well-known Indian murderers, Daniel Owen & Robbin George (now Capt. George) who had once stolen some of our horses on the Muskingum. From here we had still 3 miles to go to Fort Steuben, & had to make it through the rain. As soon as we reached there, the Indians said: "Give us a good dose of brandy, or we shall be sick." They got it from the officer in charge, drank themselves full, and kept on drinking all the next day. This life was unendurable to me & as I knew Capt. Doyle's mind on the subject, I talked seriously about it to Prior, & represented to him how he would lose his Indians by death, one after another, if he went on in this way. At first he took this amiss, & wanted to know if I was to give him orders about his Indians & issue regulations to him. I replied: that these Indians had been sent for by Congress for their own good and that of the country, and since he had been put in charge of them it was only reasonable to expect that he would behave like a sensible man. He could now bring himself either credit or disgrace, and either help or harm his country. He acknowledged this, but during the following days he went on as before, so I had to talk to him even more seriously. I told him positively that, if he continued like this, I would not travel with him another step and would lay complaint against him in the proper place. This frightened him. He begged my pardon and promised he would follow my advice in every particular, & he kept this promise all the rest of the journey. I spent the remainder of the time with my good friend Capt. Doyle, & visited the French gentleman, Mr. Lakesang, in Louisville. In the garrison almost everybody was ill with the fever, which usually shows itself here in the fall.

On the 16th the canoes in which we were to travel from here to Fort Washington were brought up over the falls and repaired. During this time some Kentucky gentlemen came over to call on us. The worthy Mr. Sebastian, a lawyer from Kentucky, who wished to go with us to Cincinati also appeared.

At last, on the 17th, we resumed our journey up the Ohio. The cannon of the fort announced our departure, & the Indians in a speech thanked Commandant Doyle for his kind behavior to them. In starting off we found ourselves in real difficulty, however, because there was not room enough in the 3 canoes, & there were no more to be had. The Indians chiefs looked upon themselves as the great & wise men of their nations, and considered they had nothing to do but sit in their canoes, eat, & drink, & smoke tobacco. The 15 soldiers we had with us under command of Ensign Lang, were to act as guards and paddle the canoes. We went along on this way for a few hours, in continual danger of drowning as the canoes shipped water. Prior did not know what to do—the soldiers swore at the Indians & there was talk of going back. "Now," I said to Prior, "there will be an end to this trouble if you will do as I tell you!" He said he would, and I gave him this advice: That he, I, the 3 interpreters, & Ensign Lang should continue our journey by land, each taking a gun with him. The steersmen in the canoes were ordered not to approach the shore. And so it was. Mr. Sebastian, who saw what we were driving at, came ashore with us. We had gone scarcely half a mile when a wildcat came within range. We shot at her but missed. In a bay farther on, we shot 4 turkeys & wounded a young bear. The Indians, seeing this, wanted to land the canoes. But, when the soldiers refused, 7 of the Indians jumped out of the canoes into the water and waded ashore. They took our guns from us & said hunting was their business & they would attend to it, & we could stay in the canoes. Our object was thus accomplished, & we had a pleasant journey.

The 18th. The Indians who had gone ashore shot 5 bears & several turkeys. At the 18 Mile Island we met Kentucky hunters who had 2 large canoes loaded with buffalo meat, bear meat, & venison. They advised us not to leave our Indians alone on shore, because there were at this time many Kentucky hunters scattered about in the woods who might harm them. It was decided that from now on 1 or 2 of their interpreters should go with them, to which they all agreed.

On the 19th 5 more fat bears & a deer were shot.

To Vincennes: 1792

On the 20th we passed the Kentucky River at 9 o'clock in the morning. Today two more bears and some turkeys were shot.

Sunday the 21st, in the afternoon a herd of buffaloes was seen and one of them was shot. In the evening we camped at Big Bone Lick Creek [Big Bone Creek], & about 2 miles from the Lick, where the big bones and teeth are found.

Several times on the 22nd we met people who were going to and from this Lick, where large salt works have been built. Late at night we reached Tanner's Station. This Tanner, a Baptist minister, has fortified himself here on his own beautiful, rich land, and has a rotating sergeant's guard for his protection.

Early on the 23rd we passed the Great Miami, & rested for the day with Judge Symnes (at North Bend). We might have reached Cincinati today, but the inhabitants of this place had given the Indians so much whisky to drink that they could hardly stand and still less walk.

In consequence we did not reach there until 1 o'clock in the afternoon of the 24th. The Indians were saluted with 15 cannon shots from Fort Washington.

On the 26th Gen. Wilkinson arrived from Fort Hamilton with 4 officers as prisoners under a guard of more than 100 Kentucky militiamen on horseback. In the evening a "malefactor" was hanged. He and another man, both of them drunk, had vowed to murder the first man they should meet. A few minutes later they were caught in the act. They were imprisoned & finally brought to trial. One of them was acquitted by the jury & the other condemned. The saddest thing about it was that this young man could by no means be brought to reflection. Under the gallows, however, he ascribed his misfortune to the fact that he had always associated with evil companions, & he warned the rest of his comrades.

Oct. 27. Col. Winthrop Sargent (Secretary of the Western Territory) gave the Indians a noon dinner to which he invited Gen. Wilkinson, other gentlemen, & myself. He gave the Indians good advice & instructions on how they were to behave on their journey to Philadelphia, & begged them, in their own interest, to stop drinking, etc.

The following Sunday, the 28th, Gen. Wilkinson did the same at the fort. At this meal the healths of the President, Gen. Knox, Putnam, etc., and of each of the chiefs present was drunk, & at the announcement of each chief's name a cannon was fired. During the meal an Indian chief rose and, in the name of all the chiefs present, addressed Gen. Wilkinson about the preparations for war which he observed here, and especially about the numerous packhorses & soldiers he had seen day after day taking the road towards that part of the country where their wives and children were. This raised the question in his mind whether these latter might not suffer harm during his absence, etc. Then Gen. Wilkinson rose and, in a friendly speech, gave assurance that the friends and relations left behind should suffer no harm in their absence.

Nevertheless he told them quite plainly that the United States still had many enemies—that he was a soldier and served the States and must obey them; that his first endeavors must be to pursue the enemies of the United States until they acknowledged their error and were brought to make peace. He said further: "See, my brown brethren from the Wabash! See how we are seated at this big table! There is no difference between us and you! You have lately made peace with us! and today you sit among us, & eat with us from one dish," and so on. The Indians rose, shook hands with Gen. Wilkinson & all the officers and gentlemen present, about 30 of them. Each Nation separately expressed its thanks for his satisfactory statement, & for the dinner, and said that after this they would feel perfectly at ease in their minds. I must just add that Gen. Wilkinson had so arranged the seating that whites and Indians were interspersed. Throughout the dinner there was great cordiality on both sides.

During the night of the 30th, one of the Wawiachteno chiefs died. He had been suffering from pleurisy ever since our arrival here.

At his funeral on the 31st, at which all the officers and gentlemen of the city were present, they fired in platoons 3 times over his grave, and each time the salute was answered by a cannonshot from the fort. After the coffin had been lowered, the Indians present, following their custom, threw each a handful of earth on the coffin, & the onlookers followed their example. In the coffin they had put the dead man's gun, powder-horn & bullets, tobacco and tobacco-pipe, several pairs of shoes & leather to mend them, a tin cup, knife, tomhock, etc., etc., besides provisions & a small bottle of whisky, for him to use on the journey and in the new country. At the head of the grave a long pole stripped of bark was put up with a white flag suspended from it.

Nov. 1. Towards evening we set off from here in a large boat & 2 very big canoes. Thirteen cannon shots were fired, and about 9 o'clock we arrived at Columbia. Prior (who had now received a captain's commission) and I stayed at Major Steitz's, & were invited next day to Major Gunno's for breakfast.

On the evening of the 2nd, we camped at a nice bottom on the north side (or, as they say around here) on the Federal side of the Ohio.

On the 3rd we met two canoes going to Fort Washington with a load of buffalo, deer, and bear meat. We made about 20 miles today, & spent the night on the Kentucky side near a settlement, where we were visited by honest, unpretending people until midnight.

All day Sunday, the 4th, we passed settlements on the Kentucky side. The citizens of the new town of Charlestown were particularly friendly toward us, but when we came to the town of Limestone the case was just the opposite, & it really looked as if the Indians (and perhaps we who were with them) would find their graves here. Several 100 men had collected here on the riverbank, of whom a good third were on horseback, threatening what they would do. Just at this juncture 16 Kentucky boats passed on to the other side of us, with 400 troops on board, who rained curses on us, strong and plentiful.

To Vincennes: 1792

Fortunately for us, Major Rudolph, commander of the light cavalry, was on the shore. He tried to quieten the people, & advised Prior to get away as soon as possible. This we did, & pushed on until late at night. As we did not know what might happen, & whether they might not follow us & attack us during the night, Prior set up his quarters in a suitable position on the north side of the Ohio. He put out good pickets, instructing them how to act in any emergency. The Indians, understanding the situation, slept little, but everything turned out all right, & we were able ——

On the 5th to continue our journey. We made good progress, & by evening reached the settlement of the Virginia gentleman, Colonel Graham. We were much pleased to meet so brave and kind a gentleman, whose people, about 30 in number, all imitate their master's example. All were kind to us, & gave our Indians various presents. This gentleman, with whom Prior & I took supper, owns an unusually attractive tract of land 6 miles square, on which he is making a settlement.

The 6th. In the evening we camped again on Kentucky soil.

The 7th. At 11 o'clock in the morning we reached the Sciota, where we landed and examined the country. The tall Lombardy poplars on the banks are a magnificent sight, looking as if they had been planted. Our Indians discovered no evidence of warriors having been here for a long time past. We went on till evening, and camped opposite Tyger Creek. Here our Indians soon discovered, hidden in the bushes, a raft on which they said 3 or 4 warriors had gone the day before yesterday, presumably to raid the settlements.

On the 8th our canoes attacked a very large bear that was swimming across. When someone struck at it with a paddle, it seized the paddle in its mouth and started to swim away with it. He had to give it back, however, and himself into the bargain.

Early on the 9th, as we were starting out, another bear was seen swimming across. It was surrounded & shot. At noon we passed the Big Sandy, which forms the boundary between Kentucky & Virginia. We spent the night below Guyondot.

Early on the 10th we met hunters from Canhawa. Midday, at 1 o'clock, we arrived in a drenching rain at Gallipolis, where to our surprise towards evening, one of these same hunters was brought in as a corpse. Soon after we had left them, he had gone off with his comrades after a herd of buffaloes. The gun of one of them had gone off accidentally and killed him on the spot. The unfortunate man gave himself up at once to the authorities to await his fate. Seeing, however, what grief & pain he suffered at the death of his good friend, they comforted him instead of imprisoning him. I felt great pity for the condition of the poor people of Gallipolis. These, in brief, are the circumstances: A certain gentleman in New York (Duer), who with other gentlemen had made "contract" with Congress for the land on the Sciota, sent an agent to France to see if a number of people could be found disposed to settle here or at least buy some of the land. For this purpose a pamphlet was printed, in which the land was touted far above its true value. The pamphlet was distributed among the people by the agent and the land offered for sale. These poor people, & many more, came out & bought the land for 20 shillings an acre, & had to give notes for the balance they owed. In this manner many hundreds came to settle on their land. Meanwhile Duer's application was rejected and his agent disappeared with the money. Duer thought he could count on the land which he had in the Ohio Company, & sent these people there. After they had settled there, Duer failed, & the Ohio Company to whom he owed large sums seized his interest in these lands; and so in the end these people were defrauded. The Ohio Company has indeed informed them (or rather let them understand) that, if they applied to them, they might be allowed under certain conditions to live there. But they do not want any of these companies to lead them by the nose any longer, and intend to appeal directly to Congress.

On the evening of the 12th we reached Point Pleasant, & spent the night in Col. Lewis's house. He showed us much kindness. As Capt. Prior has his father living here, the Indians wished to greet him formally as is their custom, and they gave him the name, Wawiachteno.

At last, on the 13th, we left Kanhawa again, & camped about 8 miles above this place on the Virginia side.

On the 14th we met 2 Kentucky boats like those we had passed in such numbers these last few days, the water having risen considerably. We also met hunters, from whom we bought 3 deer, & pitched camp on a beautiful island.

On the 15th & 16th we met many more boats with families bound for Kentucky, Post Vincent, New-Madrid or *Lans le gress* [on the Mississippi, below St. Louis].

On the 17th we arrived at Belleprée near Goodal's Station, & as I was now here among the New Englanders, who knew me and wanted to hear all the news, we had to stop. Indeed, we could hardly get away from them before evening. We made our camp in the woods.

On Sunday the 18th we reached Marietta in heavy rain. Everybody, instead of attending the divine service for which they had assembled, came running to meet us, partly because they wanted to hear the news, and partly to see the Indians. The Indians were lodged in a vacant house, & Prior & I in McIntosh's Tavern.

The 20th. The citizens invited the chiefs to dinner at noon at the Campus Martius. Capt. Hascall, the Commandant, accompanied them thither with the music of pipes & drums. As they entered the gates, they were saluted with 3 cannon shots, whereupon they were presented to Gen. Putnam's family, & then conducted to the table, where, in company with the principal inhabitants of this place, they enjoyed, in sobriety, a well-prepared meal. The Indians paid many compliments to the pastor, who sat at the head of the table &

asked a blessing. They requested him to ask God to preserve them from the smallpox (for they are very much afraid of this desease). At the conclusion of the meal, they gave thanks for food and drink, & expressed the wish that the table might always be as it was today, in other words, that this place might never know want. They said: "May God give man food; else he would have none." They invited the distiller to visit their country, promising him plenty of business. At last the party broke up. They went back to the Point well pleased.

On the 21st I took leave of my travelling companions. I should have preferred to continue with them, but I had agreed with Gen. Putnam at Post Vincennes to wait for him here, and this I explained to them. They liked me, and could not easily understand why I should stay behind. They said they would weep for me for days, but I promised I would soon follow them. Capt. Hascall gave them a last meal, and at its conclusion after they had expressed their thanks they embarked. As they pushed off, they were given a salute from 2 cannon which had been stationed on the high bank for that purpose. Seven shots were fired in their honor, they being of 7 nations. They answered with their guns. As they left, they said, "Now one more shot for our friend Wapanachki" (for so they called me), & this was given, too.

On the morning of the 22nd an amusing, witty poem was found on the well-post, containing a description of the dinner given the Indians here the day before yesterday. The heavy & continuing rain had caused the Ohio & Muskingum to rise considerably. In consequence a great many Kentucky boats passed.

On the 26th the Ohio, which during these last few days had risen 15 feet, began to go down again, & as so many boats had been waiting for this (the fall flood, as they call it here), they made use of it now. It has been estimated that between the 18th & 28th of this month over 100 of these boats passed, with at least 2,000 souls and several 100 horses in them. One such boat which put in here had 54 children on board.

On the 28th we heard that Capt. Prior with the Indians had been seen 40 miles from here. The high water had forced him to lay by for several days.

Sunday, Dec. 2. The flight of wild pigeons was quite indescribable. The bottom lands were covered with them. The inhabitants (with few exceptions) forgot it was Sunday, & instead of going to church, went out pigeon shooting.

On the 3rd we heard that Capt. Prior had arrived safely with the Indians at Pittsburg, & that they had been very kindly received.

On the 6th a canoe arrived from Fort Washington, but of Gen. Putnam they had no news, which puzzled us.

On the 8th the Ohio was high again, & many boats passed.

On the 10th one of the scouts here shot 8 buffaloes in this vicinity, and brought the meat in during the next few days. He made about 80 dollars out of it.

Between the 11th and the 18th many more boats passed. It was on the 18th that Gen. Putnam at last arrived, much to our delight. He had had a 2nd attack of illness on the Ohio, for which reason he had been obliged to remain at the Falls for 3 weeks.

On the 23rd we learned from a newspaper that the hostile Indians had at last decided to hold a treaty [i.e., peace conference]. During the Christmas holidays there was no divine service here, & I must say that I felt quite disgusted with these pious but wooden Christians.

On the 27th the Freemasons celebrated St. John's Day [St. John Evangelist] in their usual fashion.

On New Year's Night, January 1, 1793, there was shooting in every nook and corner. How often I wished myself then in Bethlehem!

On the 6th various large boats from Pittsburg came here to load corn for Fort Washington, and ——

On the 8th several others arrived, & after being loaded they set off for their destination. But the ice, coming down in quantities out of the Allegheny, closed in on them about 40 miles below this place, & destroyed 5 of the boats, with 2,500 bushels of corn. The loss to the public was £75 for the boats, £362. 10/ for the corn, total, £437. 10/.

The 12th. The long desired day of our departure came at last. We got off about 11 o'clock in the morning. In our company were the 2 gentlemen, Rome & Van den Benden, deputies who had been despatched with a remonstrance & petition from the inhabitants of Gallipolis to Congress.

On the 16th we passed Wheeling & came at night to Charleston on Buffalo Creek. Here we sent our boat back, & had our horses, which we had left in the spring with a farmer of this neighborhood, brought in. Major MacMahon, whose home is only a few miles from here, though he is now with a rifle company attached to Gen. Wayne's main army, had just arrived on a visit to his family; & because he had lately been with scouts (as often happens in summer and autumn) at our ruined towns on the Muskingum, & well knew I would like to hear about them, he gave me the following news: That this fall in Gnadenhütten he had eaten the largest and best apples he had ever tasted— That the peach trees at the 3 towns were extraordinarily full of peaches, but that the bears had got after them and had broken almost all the branches— That Gnadenhütten was almost unrecognizable, the town site and all the cleared land around it being thickly overgrown with honey locust. In like manner the beautiful "prairies" ("plains" or grassy places) are covered with closely tangled thickets, clear evidence that these open "prairies" are the result of forest fires. On his last expedition, he had found an encampment of 4 Indians near Gōkósing, far up the Walhanding (otherwise known as White Woman's Creek). He attacked them, killed 2 of them, & wounded another (who had a very white skin, handsome-looking) severely. This man set up a screaming, but he and the uninjured one of the 4 plunged over the high bank into the Walhanding & swam across. The night, which was very dark, enabled them to escape. Meanwhile the scouting party got the stolen horses, their weapons, & everything they had. They fled naked except for such rags as Indians wear.

On the 17th we spent the night at Charles Wells', a Virginia assemblyman. The boundary line between Virginia & Pennsylvania goes by his house.

The night of the 18th we spent not far from Cannonsburgh, in Washington County, where there is an academy for young gentlemen, & ——

On the evening of the 19th we reached Pittsburg. Here on the following day I visited several friends & acquaintances, among them Mr. James Henry (son of the late Brother William Henry of Lancaster), who works here at the watchmaker's trade. He has an "attachment" to the Brethren, and I had pleasure in seeing him.

On the 21st we left Pittsburg, and spent the night at Turtle Creek, where a certain Capt. MacIntire also arrived. When we became acquainted, he told me a lot about the Brethren's Garden in the East Indies, where he had been in the year 1786. He seems to have been quite intimate with some of the Brethren there. He had received presents from them, & had given some in return. He knew also that in the matter of the Nicobar mission nothing had as yet been done. He said that the Brethren's Garden had last year yielded revenue of some 200 guineas.

On the 27th we reached Carlisle, where I visited acquaintances again, & especially Mr. Alexander, who (if anything ever comes of this) is to survey our land on the Muskingum.

On the 29th I took leave of Gen. Putnam, & went by way of Litiz to Bethlehem, where I arrived on the 31st.

The treaty was laid before the Senate, February 13, 1793, but failed to be ratified. Senators did not like its vague terms, nor the Indian insistence that the Ohio be forever the boundary between them and the United States.

What came of the proposed Muskingum survey will be seen in Heckewelder's 1797 journal.

⚜ XXX ⚜

To the Indian Conference at Detroit: 1793

IN THE FALL of 1792, at a council held by Indians of various tribes at the junction of the Auglaize and Maumee Rivers (where General Anthony Wayne a few months later was to build Fort Defiance), an invitation was extended to the Americans to attend a peace conference the following spring at Lower Sandusky. The United States government accepted the invitation; but, understanding the three-way cold war the Indians, British, and Americans were then waging in the woods, they accepted with so little hope of a peaceful outcome that they permitted General Anthony Wayne to advance at the same time with a large army into the Indian country.

When the American Commissioners were appointed, Secretary of War Knox recommended that John Heckewelder accompany them to the treaty, which in the end was held at Detroit. It was believed that his presence, as on the Wabash in 1792, would have a conciliating effect, and in particular would serve to offset the suspicions roused among the Indians by Anthony Wayne's maneuverings in the neighborhood.

We present here in full the English language manuscript preserved in the Historical Society of Pennsylvania:

> *Journey with the Commissioners to the Indian Treaty—J. H.**

Agreeable to the request of the President of the United States (signifyed to me by a Letter from the Secretary of War) to accompany the Commis-

---

* The journal is in English. For further information about this journey, see the Pickering MSS. at the Massachusetts Historical Society, and the following published journals:

sioners to Sandusky, & to assist them in bringing about a Peace with the hostile Indian Nations on Principles of Justice & humanity— And with the full Approbation of the Directors of the Brethⁿ. Society in Bethlehem—

I sat out Ap.^r 8.th 1793 for Philadelphia, to join the Commissioners there assembled for the purpose; & when in the course of the following Days, all Necessary preparations were made towards this Business, & the Journey— The Quakers having resolved that a Deputation from among themselves should be appointed to attend at this Treaty, in order to use their endeavours likewise in bringing about a Peace: the following Persons voluntarily agreed to attend, Vizt: John Parish, William Savory & John Elliot from the City of Philadelphia: Jacob Lindley from Chester County; & Joseph Moore & William Hartshorn from Jersey.

Accordingly on the 27th day of Ap.^r Genl Lincoln from the State of Massachusetts (first Commissioner) & myself with several other Gentlemen (passengers for N. York) set out in the Stage for that place, in order to proceed from thence by Water to the place of our destination; & the 2 other Commissioners, Beverly Randolph from Virginia, & Coll.^l Timothy Pickering Post Master General from Philadelphia, resolved to take the Road thro' Northumberland direct to Niagara, by Land. The Quakers divided themselves in both Parties.

The heavy Rains which fell at this time made Travelling extremely difficult insomuch so, that instead of arriving at NYork this day, we did not reach that place untill the afternoon of the 29th. At Brunswick the Horses in the Stage with which we were to go, took fright, running with great fury down the Street for the River, but accidentally hitting against a Pump near the same, where the Stage was stop'd (but broke to pieces) the 2 fore Horses tore loose, & could not be taken untill they had crossed the Bridge at the Landing; whereas one of the hindmost Horses, into whose body the Tounge [Tongue] of the Wagon had run was so much Wounded, that it was supposed must Die. At New York I took Lodging in Fair Street at B.^r & Sister Birkby's, untill the rest of the Company, & the Baggage should arrive, which was to be sent in the Stage Boat from Philadelphia by way of Burlington & Amboy to this place; But the heavy Rain with a North Easterly Storm had also detained them, & made the passage very difficult, so that they did not arrive untill the 3^d of May at Night. Meanwhile Gen. Lincoln with the Secretary Mr Charles Storer had set out for Albany, his Buisness calling him speedily thither, & I had resolved to stay for the rest of the Comp.^y & Baggage. All being arrived & ready, the three Quakers Willm Savory, Jacob Lindley & Willm Hartshorne, & following gentlemen Doct.^r Willm McCoskry from Carlisle, Capt.ⁿ Scott, Commissary, Robert Hilary a young Gentleman from England & myself all for the Indian Treaty; & several other Way Passengers

---

Gen. Benjamin Lincoln, *Collections of the Massachusetts Historical Society*, Third Series, V, 109-176; Jacob Lindley, The Friends Miscellany, II, 49-156; Joseph Moore, The Friends Miscellany, VI, 289-343; William Savory, *The Friends Library*, I, 327-368.

embarked on the 4th in the afternoon on board the Sloop Shenectady, Capt<u>n</u> Abraham Lansing for Albany, & sailed with a fair Wind that evening some Miles up the North River, when the Wind Dying away, we cast Anchor. But a NorthEast Storm arriving about Midnight, we thought it best to run into port again; moreover as we saw the sloop Genl Schyler, which sat out with us drove on Shore. I once more Visited B^r & Sister Birkby, & at evening returned to the Vessel again, where soon after running out with the Tide, & a light Breeze we made 18 Miles that Night; but, a head Wind springing up that Morning, we were obliged to cast Anchor between a Craggy range of Mountains, full of Cliffs, which continue for many Miles in length, & appear very Romantic, moreover as many of these Rocks lay Perpendicular & are several 100 feet high, & some projecting bejond others. At 3 O Clock we took advantage of the Tide again, & soon came in view of a Number of Excellent Farms on the East Side. At 6 we passed Tapan Bay on the West Side, & Tarry Town on the East Side, about 30 Miles from NYork, & at 7 we passed Picks. Kill [Peekskill]. The River from hence is much narrower, but lined with surprising high Rocks & Mountains on its sides. In the Morning we passed Fort Montgomery on the West Side, & at 10 O Clock Fort Putnam & Fort Clinton at West Point 60 Miles from NYork, & both on the same side. Fort Clinton lieth on the Point which runneth out into the River, & which is here very Narrow, & Fort Putnam lieth on an Eminence about 600 Y^{ds} back, & hath a full command on the River both above & below the Point. besides these, there are a Number of small Fortification & Breastworks situate on top, & Rocks on both sides of the River. Another place of such consequence would perhaps not easily be found on so large & Navigable a River as this is; for the Country on both sides appears to be nothing but Rocks, & these thrown or hove down upon each other in the most confused State immaginable, forming in the whole Hills & Dales, yet the principle spotts & eminences are placed to advantage, & require but little improvement. Here are yet a Number of Cannon &^{c} of which an Officer & some Troops have the care of. At 12 OClock we passed Pollipas [Polopels] Island, an Island round & high, but consisting chiefly of Rocks. from hence the Country has a more favourable appearance, there being Farms in many places on the Banks & Ridges. At 1 OClock we passed New Windsor, & soon after Newbery [Newburgh], both small Towns on the West Side, & Fish Kill on the East Side of the River. At 4 OC. we passed Pogepsie [Poughkeepsie], a pretty little Town on the East Side, & situate on a Hill, in which are 60 good dwelling Houses, besides a Court-House. This Town is 80 miles from NYork, & just half way to Albany.

At 6 we passed Esopus [Kingston] on the West, & Rheinbeck & Red-hook on the East Side. Just below the latter place & next the River is Mr Reads Seat, on which 2 large elegant brick Buildings are, at the distance of about 100 Y^{ds} from each other, & upon the whole the Situation here delightful, tho in the Vicinity broken & Craggy. At 9 in the Evening we passed Hudson, a new rising Town on the East Side, & containing about 150 Houses. A fair Wind which had sprung up at 12 oClock at Noon, & which continued to blow fresh since, brought us up after Midnight to Albany before which place we Anchored.

Albany was to my surprise a larger Town than I expected, containing about 700 private buildings, 6 Churches, a Court House & Prison. From the latter, which is situate on an Eminence above the Town, there is a most beautiful Prospect of the Country around, & the River both up & down for many Miles, with the Shipping on the same. Also a full view of the Town of Terry [Troy] at 6 Miles distance up the River, & Lansingburgh 3 Miles beyond this. Likewise the hill on which Gen. Burgoyne laid down his Arms after surrendering to the American Army at Saratoga close by & no more than 30 Miles distance from this place.

There are in this Town many Elegant Brick-houses, built since the War. The Seats of both Gen. Schyler & M^r. Ranselær distinguish themselves by their elegant Situations. The former lying Southward of the Town, & the latter (whoom they call the Patroon) (Lord of the Manor) having his Seat at the North East, with a very Beautiful Orchard on the same, which seems otherwise to be generally neglected at this place, very few fruit Trees being there & thereabouts. M^r. Abraham Lansing conducted me thro the place, visiting some of his friends by the Way, & I having Letters from some of the Misses at the Boarding School at Beth^m. to their Parents at this place, was very Welcome at their Houses. The 3 Quakers & I dined at the above mentioned Gentlemans, & I took lodging at Captn. Lansings. The principle Articles of Trade in this Country, is Flowers, Pot & Pearl Ash, Peas, Boards & Scantling; all which is raised & Manufactured on the North & Mohawk Rivers, & transported to NYork &^{c}. so as that Place & the adjacent Country & Towns are supplied from Pogepsie with Lime for Building &^{c}. The People of Albany & the Country around are principally Low Dutch, or Descendants from the same. In their Manners they seem to be rather reserved, & attentive to their own Interest. Before the American War, they were deeply engaged in the Indian Trade, Niagara & Detroit being supplied with the Necessary Trading Articles from NYork, thro this Channel, but now those places are supplied from lower Canada, & there remains nothing more of this Branch in their hands, except a Trade with their Neighbors the Oneidas, Mohicans & Onondagos; & a few others.

May 9th. We sat out in a light Stage, & some Waggons for Shenectady, to which place Genl. Lincoln & the Sec^{tary}. Storer had gone on the preceeding Evening. This whole Country from Albany to this place, a distance of 16 Miles, makes but a dreary appearance, being barren & Sandy Soil, covered chiefly with Aspin, Water Birch & Pine bushes. But Shenectady & the country on the Mohawk River makes up this deficiency, & is striking to the Eye.

This place which is situate on the Banks of the Beautiful Mohawk, consists of between 3 and 400 Houses, 3 Churches, & an Academy; & is surrounded with excellent Meadows & Oarchards. The River is Navigable with Boats from hence upwards to Fort Stanwix, a distance of 96 Miles, & thro a rich & fertile Country; but from hence downwards to its confluence with the North River, a distance of 17 Miles, it is very Rapid, ending within 1½ mile of its Mouth, with a Fall of 73 feet. The Inhabitants of this place (seemingly generally pretty Industrious) are likewise chiefly Low Dutch, & appear pretty Sociable. They keep up a Number of light Waggons to transport the Produce brought down the River to this place, to Albany, to which place they go & return the same day. The 8 new boats made here for the purpose of transporting our Baggage, & for our Use to Niagara being loaded we sat off at 3 in the Afternoon, with 30 hands from hence to work the Boats.

After passing 3 Miles up the River we called at a House, where 4 grown up Persons; Children of one Family, were perfect Idiots ever since their Youth & the Mother of the Family *since*. They were indeed true Objects of Compassion. At Evening we took lodging at Mr Maybees 6 Miles from Schenectady, having passed this way thro a delightful Country, close Settled, & lined with Beautiful Oarchards.

On the morning of the 10th we sat out with a fair Wind, sailing the Whole Day thro similar Lands & Settlements, among which were 2 Elegant Seats, formerly belonging to Sir Willm Johnson. At 4 in the Afternoon we put up at a House on Shohary [at Fort Hunter] (a large branch of this River). Here is a Stone Church built in the time of Queen Anne for the Mohocks, then, & untill the beginning of the late American War, Inhabiting this Country. A Fort also was built here in the French War, for the defense & Protection of the White Inhabitants & friendly Indians of this Country, which was called Fort Hunter, & is yet extant. Surely the Mohocks must have lived here formerly very comfortable, there being extensive Flatts of level, Rich Land for Planting, & the Country in general promising, & abounding with Game. Even the Neighbourhood both above & below them, which were settled there upwards of 50 Years before they left this place, were (as I am informed) very kind to them, & they lived in a good Understanding with each other. But moving off with Sir John Johnson to Canada, they turned inveterate Enemies to these their former friends & Neighbours; & accompanied by Buttler, Brandt & others of the same description, they frequently stole in upon the Settlements & most inhumanly butchered all they could catch or come accross. The last Seat of Sir William Johnson (called Johnsons Hall) lieth 7 Miles from this place a due NW. course. It is now a rising County Town, with a Court-house & other Publick Buildings thereon, & called Johnstown, 20 Miles from Shenectady.

May 11th we sat out early in the Morning, & Breakfasted at Mr Fundays, 5 Miles from the former place, & 4 Miles from Johnstown. Here are great

To Detroit: 1793

Potash Works (a Buissness carried on very briskly in this Country. The relation which M.̱ Funday gave Us of the Incursions made by the Indians in these parts, during the late War, were truly Shocking. At 10 oClock we passed the Narrows,* or a Chain of high Rocks, lying on both sides of the River, in which many Denns of Rattle-Snakes are; also a remarkable Cove. On the Side of a large Smooth Rock, fronting the River, is the picture of a Canoe painted with Vermilion & 7 Indians therein, which (as we are told) were a party of Canada Indians, who had come down many Years ago with a design of to fall upon the Mohocks, but these discovering them in Season, waylayed them as they were passing this place, & cut them off to a Man. In remembrance of this, & according to their custom, the conquerors come yearly down to renew this painting † which is executed tolerably well. At 11 OClock we passed Canejoharre, & soon after Cachnawaga.‡ from hence there is a large Road to Cooperstown 14 Miles distant. At 12 oClock we stop'd & dined at Fry's who are Germans. In the Afternoon we passed a Number of fine Buildings & Farms, Churches & Stores, & put up at 5 in the Evening at John Christ.ṉ Nellis Esq.̱ who informed us; that there were within 7 Miles Square, 6 Churches here. From this place it is no more than 15 Miles to the head Waters of Susquehannah, & only a Days Ride to the Delaware Navigation. The Oarchards of this Country make a fine Aspect; but a strange Custom prevails among the Farmers Vizt. that of leaving all the Shell Bark Hickory on the Land in order to gather the Nutts for Market. So that many fields on account of the Number of these; resemble Oarchards at a distance. The Cattle of this Country were generally poor, & but few of them, for the most Farmers are set upon raising Wheat, which they can sell from 5 to 6/ a Bush. on the Spot. Many of the Farmers of this Country sell upwards of 1000 Bush. of Wheat per Annum. They have alltogether the Skippel [skipple] in use here, 4 of which makes 3 Bushels. Vegetation was here much in the same State, as we left it in Philad.ᵃ which proves that the Season is 2 Weeks later then there.

Sunday May 12 we sat out at 7 OClock in the Morning, & soon after passed Fort Hendricks on the South Side, & Canada Creek on the West Side, & arrived at 2 in the Afternoon at the little Falls of the Mohock. Here is a carrying place of 1 Mile, over which we had to Transport our Baggage in Waggons. These Falls are admirable, the River being cram'd up between the

---

* [Also known as "the Noses," being a spot where two hills known as the Big Nose (or Anthony's Nose) and the Little Nose, constrict the Mohawk Valley.]

† According to the Very Reverend Thomas Grassman of the Mohawk-Caughnawaga Museum, Fonda, N. Y., Heckewelder is in error here. The Indian painting was near Amsterdam, some seventeen miles to the east. Jacob Lindley, who was with Heckewelder's party, notes in his journal that this rock painting was seen on May 10, not May 11.

‡ General Benjamin Lincoln correctly places Caughnawaga near present Fonda. See his journal, May 11, 1793: "Stopped, at the distance of five miles [from Fort Hunter], at a placed called Cachnawaga, a settlement which has been made nearly eighty years [by white people]."

Mountains in some places in a very narrow Compass, & full of Rapids & Rocks. The whole fall of the Water in this distance is 39 feet 2 Inches. Every preparation is now made by the NYork Canal Comp.y to cut a Canal thro, & 300 hands are ready to set about to Work at it. A M.r Fredrick Augustus de Lang, a native of Saxony, (but late an Officer) has the Management of this Bussiness here— A remarkable Bridge of 276 feet in length is accross this River nearly about the middle of the Falls— This place also affoards a great plenty of Pike & large Trout— A M.r Porteus who own's this Land, has erected a Number of Buildings on the same, as Grist, Saw & Fulling-Mill with a Diehouse, Store & Tavern &.c & much Buissness is done here.

May 13.th at 1 in the Afternoon we left this place, & arrived at Evening at Fort Herkimer, on the German Flatts. Thee People of this Country, tho the Soil is exceeding Rich, & settled ever Since the Year 1722, & that by Germans, are by no means Wealthy; & they themselves give this account, Vizt. That they do not attend to Labour as they ought to do— That they do not manure their Lands, but keep them in use Year after Year— That they are to apt to spend what they earn in Taverns &.c That tho a Man of Credit applied to all his Neighbours to lend him 12 or 15 £ cash, it were not in one mans Power to produce that Sum— That on the other hand, the New England Settlers, but of late Years residents of this Country, become daily more Wealthy &.c The Farms of these German Settlers, consisting of 100 Acres each, were granted them by the Crown of Great Brittain. They are however not conveniently situated, being no more than 40 Rod in front, & the remainder in depth, so as to make up that Compliment— On the South Side of the River is a large Stone Church, & near this a large Stone dwelling House, both of which, with additional Block-houses, served to shelter the Inhabitants against the dreadful Incursions made upon them in the last War, by their disaffected Neighbours in combination with the Indians.

On the opposite side of the River is a little Town called Harkimer, in which a Court-House is. From this place it is said to be no more than 6½ Miles to the head of Susquehannah.

May 14.th we passed the whole day thro a fine Settlement, the greatest part of which improved since the Year 1784. At Evening we put up at M.r John Posts at Fort Schyler [Utica], where a Number of scattered, but well built Houses are, & the spot intended for a Town. Here is also a well constructed Arch Bridge of 140 feet in length & 20 in breadth across the River, all of which is Wood. The River from hence upwards being on account of the Dry Season rather Shallow, & upon the whole very Winding, some of us set out on the 15.th on Horseback for Fort Stanwix [Rome], 16 Miles by Land. At Whites-Town 4 Miles from this, we took View of M.r Kains Potash Works. This Gentleman in partnership with 6 others of his Brothers, carry on this Buissness very extensively on this River, besides having a Number of Stores & Merchant Mills at different stations. He told Us, that he expected to make at least 1,000 Barrels of Pearl Ash (near 143 Ton, at 7 Barrels to the Ton) this Season. Each Barrel fetching him the Sum of from 9 to 10 £.

Judge White Proprietor of a Town laid out here, where some good houses are built, sells His Town Lotts of an Acre at 40 £. He visited us at Mr Breezes, where we halted some time, in order to make some enquiries respecting this Country, where also the Revd Mr Kirkland, who living but 9 Miles from here, having heard of our arrival visited Us, & afterwards rode with Us several Miles.

After riding about 7 Miles, we passed that Spot where the hard Battle [Oriskany] was fought last War between a great Body of Indians & Gen! Harkimer, in which the latter was mortally Wounded. The Sculls & Bones of the Slain are to be seen in abundance. From hence passing as before through a heavy Timbered Country, consisting chiefly of Beech, Sugar-Maple &^{c} we at length arrived about the Middle of the Afternoon at Fort Stanwix, that remarkable Fortification built in the French War, & which held out so well against a very large Body of Whites & Indians, Buttler at their head; but is now quite demolished. Here is the end of Navigation up the Mohock, from whence Boats, Baggage &^{c} are carried on Waggons, about 1½ Miles accross into Wood Creek. But the Canal Comp.^{y} of this State, likewise intend cutting a Canal accross here next Season, which will be of great advantage to Travellers & Settlers; This particular Spot of Ground, containing 1300 Acres, 400 of which is cleared, & about ⅓ of this Meadows, is the Property of a Mr Linch in NYork, & who has let it out to the present Tennant (a New England Man) at £300 a Year, & for 16 Years. A new City is also laid out here, & Workmen are arriving to make a beginning. Baron de Steuben also owns a Tract of Land of 30,000 Acres in this Neighbourhood, & is settling People thereon as fast as possible. Upon the whole this is a promising part of the Country, the Land being Rich & level, abounding with Sugar Maple &^{c} & the Produce easily Transported either to NYork or Canada, by Water. The common Wood Land in these parts, sell at 4 Dollars an Acre, & some particular spotts will fetch more. Vegetation seemed on this side the little Falls to be more forward, than below them; But this Morning May 16th a white frost was on the Ground, & even in some places Ice.

May 17th early in the morning we left this place for Wood Creek, to which place Mr Barnard had Transported our Boats & Baggage the preceeding Day. Altho this Creek is here no larger than Christ^s Brunn Run, yet by Means of a Dam, the Boats are supplied with a sufficiency of Water, untill they reach Canada Creek, 6 Miles by Land, & 10 by Water. In this route we passed the spot were formerly Fort Bull stood, & where in the year 1759 [1756] a most cruel Slaughter was made by the French & Indians on the British Troops, in which Col! Bull also perished. At the above mentioned Creek we stop'd to dine, & caught a number of fine Fish, principally Trout. Strange as it appears, yet it is asserted as a fact: that between Canada Creek mentioned on the 12th & the Creek of the same Name we passed this Day, never a Rattle Snake has been seen; whereas without this Compass they are in Number. This Afternoon we passed through a Spot of Land of 20 Miles Square, reserved by the Oneidas to themselves; & encamped at Evening on a high spot of Ground, but thinly covered with White Oak Timber.

May 18th sat out after 4 in the Morning, Stop'd & Breakfasted at 7, continuing afterwards our Route down the Creek, & fishing by the Way. The Country on both Sides is chiefly Timbered with Linden, Sugar Elm, White Walnut & Shell bark Hickory. At 3 in the Afternoon we arrived at Fish Creek, which unites here with Wood Creek at the upper end of the Oneida Lake. We were now rid of a Creek, the difficulty of Navigating which, is at present very great, on account of the abundance of Timber lying therein, much of which was purposely cut into it last War, both by the British & Americans, in order to prevent the passage of either. At the Oneida Lake we were visited by the Revd Mr Kirkland, & several of the Oneidas Captns & Chieffs, who after partaking of some refreshments with Us, & delivering Salutary Speeches to Genl Lincoln, returned to their respective homes again. At Evening we attempted crossing this Lake, which is 30 Miles in length, & 8 or 10 in breadth, & arrived in the Morning of the 19th on the Spot where formerly Fort Bennington Stood, & where some Familys of White People were settled. Here were some Onondago & Cachnawaga Indians for the sake of Fishing; who informed us that it was no more than 8 Miles to the Onondago Town. After Breakfast we sailed down a beautiful River, full as wide as Leheigh by Bethm & stop'd to dine at 3 in the Afternoon at Mr Isaac Van Vlecks (Cousin to the late Henry Van Vleck Mercht at N York) who resideth here on a choise Spot of Ground, which place is called the 3 Rivers on account of the Rivers from the Onondagos, Cayuga & Seneca Lakes meeting here. Here we also found a Number of the Onondago's for the sake of Fishing. In passing from hence downwards, we caught a Number of Oswego Bass (a kind of Rock Fish) & saw the contrivances of the Onondagos for catching Eels, & arrived at 6 in the Evening at the Oswego Falls, where again meeting with Onondago Indians, who had caught a Number of Salmon Trout, from 10 to 15 lb a piece, we were supplied with this excellent Fish, which abounds so much in these Lakes & Rivers. We encamped on the Bank of the River at the Falls, where we had to draw our Boats & Baggage 30 Yards across a point of Land below the first Pitch, or main Fall of the Water. The Indians were May 20th early again under the Falls, catching the Salmon, & brought soon 2 very large ones on Shore. We could sometimes see these Fish jumping high above Water, & trying to get above the Fall, but failing in the attempt. This Fall is occasioned by a smooth Rock which lieth across the River from which the Water falleth 8 feet perpendicular on other Rocks of the same Nature, & from thence continues to fall gradually from one Shelve to the other for the distance of ¾ of a Mile, which occasions a Rough rapid Current. The River is here about 500 feet wide, & confined withing high Banks on both sides.

To Detroit: 1793

The State of NYork to whom the Soil belongeth, have reserved here that profitable spot, considered as a Carrying place, & on which formerly a British Fort stood. Adjoining this Tract (which only consists of 40 Acres) Mr. Henry Tenbrook, Mercht. of NYork owns a Tract of Land of about 1,500 Acres, & a Number of other Gentlemen from this State, own more or less Lands in this Neighbourhood, on which a Number of Familys are already settled, & others coming in daily.

At 10 in the forenoon we left the Falls, & had generally a strong current & in part dangerous Rappids, untill Oswego 12 Miles from the above place, where we arrived at Noon. The British Commandant, Captn. Wickham, was very polite, & invited us to Dine with him. It is however strange that on the ground of the United States, & here, within the State of NYork; the Brittish keep up a Garrison— While we were here several Boats loaded with Merchandize from Montreal for Detroit arrived, which as we were informed is as Cheap a Way, & sometimes cheaper than to send the Goods &c. by Vessels.

At 5 in the Afternoon we left Oswego, pursuing our Route by Water thro Lake Ontario to Niagara, & a Breeze springing up in our Favour, carried us into little Sorres [Sodus], 15 Miles from Oswego.

May 21. we sat out at 8 in the morning without any Wind, but being soon after relieved from the Oars by a good Breeze, we passed big Sores [Sodus], the Wind however dying away again we could not proceed as we had wished for, to which may be added the mutinious disposition of some of the Boatmen, who had ever since we had left Shenectady, been noisy & troublesome, & were now determined to have more Wages, or conduct so that the Journey might be prolonged. Their Complaints running entirely against their employer, who had remained at home, but was making out of each Man 1/6 per Day, nothing could well be done with them; however Genl. Lincoln found means to make their Minds easy again. We had passed in the course of this Day a Number of high Clay banks, the Land on which as we supposed, but poor. In the Evening we put in Apple Tree harbour, about 45 Miles fm Oswego.

May 22 we could not think of setting out from hence, untill a Storm which had set on last Night should in some Degree abate, & which was not before 4 in the Afternoon, when we attempted to row against the Wind, made 7 Miles with great difficulty, & encamped on a Beach, where a Boat also arrived from Niagara which remained with Us that Night.

May 23d we sat our early in the Morning with a favourable Wind; passed at 9 Thirundigat [Irondequoit]; at 10 the Chinesee [Genesee] River, where a Trading House is on the Lake, & at 12 oClock we put into Bradocks Bay to Dine. Here the Country is pleasant, & we viewed a spot of ground on which a Town is laid out. At 2 oC. we passed sandy Creek-harbour, out of which a Boat with Settlers from the Chinesee Country joined Compy. being also bound to Niagara. At 8 in the Evening we put into Oak Oarchard Harbour [by Point Breeze], having sailed since morning near 60 Miles; here is also a pretty Point of Land on which an Ind.ⁿ Burrying Ground is.

May 24. we sat out in the Morning with a fair Wind & soon after passed Johnsons Creek at 5 Miles distance; but the Wind rising about Noon too high for Boats, we were obliged to look out for a Harbour, which we found in the 18 Mile Creek, & remained there that Day.

May 25 at 1 oClock in the Morning we left this place & at 5 arrived at Niagara Fort, where after refreshing ourselves, we crossed the River about ¾ of a Mile wide, & took lodging on the opposite side, in the new Town [Newark], where we were visited the next Day by Gov.ʳ Simcoe & other Gentlemen. The Commissioners had agreeable to Invitation of the Gov.ʳ took lodging at his house in Navy Hall, about a Mile higher up the River.

May 27. The Quakers, Doctor, Commissary & myself set out with our Boats & Baggage for the Landing [Queenston] 7 Miles higher up the River, where we encamped in an Oarchard under Tents. Here the Gov.ʳ & Commissioners visited Us, & I had an Opportunity of conversing with the former on our Ind.ⁿ Congregation on the River La Trenche [Thames], who as well this time as the preceeding day signified much sattisfaction with respect to them & their Mission, & said they were settled on an excellent spot of Land, & had plenty of good Butter & Milk, but were otherwise very Poor, especially the Indians, but that this was no Wonder, for they had been driven about so often; however he hoped they would now do well, for they were settled on good Land, & might remain there as long as they pleased— He said he knew Mess.ʳˢ Senseman & Young, & expected the former here in a few Days &.ᶜ I informed him that I had a few Necessaries for the Missionaries, & as the Treaty was delayed, I intended visiting them, to which he promised me his passport.

May 28ᵗʰ we were visited at our Camp by many People of this Neighbourhood, some of which were very sensible, that they had changed better for worse, in comeing from the United-States to these parts.

May 29.ᵗʰ The Quakers & myself went in a Boat to Navy-Hall, in order to consult the Commissioners on our intended Voyage to Detroit, which met with their Aprobation; & Doct.ʳ M.ᶜ Caskry who wished to accompany Us on this Route, made in like manner application next Day, & returned at evening with the necessary Passports, accordingly

May 30.ᵗʰ the Doct.ʳ & I sat out in the Morning on Horseback for Fort Erie, in order to engage a Passage with one of Vessels now lying at that place for Detroit. After ascending the Hill at the Landing, we travelled over a level & pretty dry Country, well covered with White & black Oak Timber, & a Number of Farms. The Thundering sound of the Falls, which we had heared so distinctly at Fort Niagara, 16 Miles distance, increased as we approached them. Here, after refreshing ourselves at a House within several 100 Yᵈˢ distance of the same, we descended the Hill on which we had Travelled, to the Rock connected with the one, over which the Water falls; & viewed with surprise, the dreadful Element (bidding as it were defiance to any obstruction thrown in its way) pitching over a Precipice 137 feet into the Deep, & there roaring & boiling with great Vehemence—from hence we rode to Chippuwa 2 miles higher up, which is the upper end of the Carrying place; & from thence we had a most intolerable Road, thro' mires & broken Bridges for 12 Miles, when Night coming on we put up at Mr Wenternutes Tavern, where we had very good Accomodation. In the course of this Day we had met Mr Willm Wilson from Pitsburg on his Way to the Commissioners, & engaged as an Interpreter at the ensuing Treaty.

June 1st we sat out from our Lodging for Fort Erie, 5 Miles higher up, & Breakfasted on Board the Sloop Dunmore, Captⁿ Ford, with whom we had engaged a Passage to Detroit; & then returned to our lodging again. A Tuscorora Chief who visited Us, told me how the Nations had meditated the Destruction of the Christian Indian Congregation while at Petquottink 2 Years ago— That they sent them Speeches to move into *their* Neighbourhood on Miami, where they not only might exercise their Religion, but would also be out of Danger of the Virginians falling upon them, & Murdering them, as they had done on Muskingum &^c But this (said he) was far from what they meant, for they were determined, whenever they had them among themselves: they would put to Death their Missionaries, & compel the Indian B^{rn} to go to War with them. That however this Congregation had paid no regard to their deceitful Speeches, but on the other hand bent their course to Detroit, & were now setled on River La Trenche on good Land, & entirely out of their way, & he wished them well &^c

Sunday June 2^d We kept close to our Quarters all Day, where we were visited by a Number of People of this Neighberhood, who gave us a concise Discription of this Country. We found these to be principally of 2 Classes 1) such who had been disaffected to their Country last War, & had either joined the British, or turned out with the Indians against the United States; or 2dly of that roving disposition, that they cannot find themselves a home. Several Persons from the latter place, who had been guilty of Forgery, Murder &^c had also come over here, & taken the Oath of Alegiance to the King, in hopes of finding Protection; among whom was Peter Nagel of Northampton County, Pennsylv^a Some Families who had been deluded with false Representations of this Country, & the benefits they would derive by living under a generous British Government; now fret, & pass away their time unhappy, & wish themselves back in the United States again, but have not the means of executing this, their all being spent. Numbers of Indians, chiefly of the Mohock & Massesagues Tribes, are continually hovering up & down this River in quest of a Dram.

June 3^d the Docter took a Ride to the Landing, to learn what kept the Quakers back, & to hurry them on, the Captⁿ having already received Orders to Sail, & only waited for a fair Wind; & I walked up to Fort Erie, where I had some Conversation with Capt^s Ford, & Harra, of the Vessels, &

Captn Platt of the Troops, on a Peace with the Indians, which seemed to be the wish of these Gentlemen. At Evening we returned to our Lodging, & Mr Wilson with Cornplanter & Big Tree arrived also, having met the Quakers & Baggage by the way.

June 4th being the 7th Day since it first began to Rain, the Sky became clear again, & now we could plainly see the Misty Vapours rising at the Falls 15 Miles distance, the roaring Sound of which, we had by this time become accustomed to. This being the Day appointed for the Militia to Muster; above 100 Persons were assembled by 11 OClock at this Tavern, among whom were Quakers, Dunkers, Menonists &^{c} & some from the sugar Loaf (round-hill) a distance of 30 Miles. On enquiry whether the latter were not exempt from Military Duty; we were informed that as yet no Act had been passed in their favour, but probably would next Session; but that the present Meeting was rather to learn the Number of each Family; what cleared Lands they had; what number of Horses; Horn Cattle; Sheep, Hogs &^{c}. Our Company being now together, we sat out after Dinner for Fort Erie.

As the above mentioned places Fort Niagara, the Landing, Chippuwa & Fort Erie are places of Consequence, I shall give a Short Discription of each of them first; & then take a view of that remarkable Cataract, the Falls of Niagara.

1) Niagara Fort (in the United States Territory) is situate on a Point, at the entrance of the Niagara River into Lake Ontario. The spot for a Fortification is high & commanding; the Works to all appearance strong & admirable. The Prospect from the North side into the Lake & down the same for a great distance & from the West side across the River (which is ¾ of a Mile wide) where on a high level Bank a New Town (called New Ark) is building; & the View of Navy-Hall on the same side about a Mile higher up the River, & where the Governor at present resides: is delightful. Between the Fort & the River there are a Number of private Buildings, chiefly Traders, who being under cover of this Fort, claim Protection. Inside the Fort, & fronting the Lake is a large stone House, built by the French, when they were in possession of the Country & this place. All shipping & Boats going out of the River into the Lake, or coming up the same for the Landing, must pass by this place. The Landing which is 8 Miles up the River from this, is the extent of Navigation below the Falls. Here is a very large Stone Store House with Iron Doors, Window Shutters, (or rather Port-hole Shutters) & covered entirely with plate Iron; where all Goods, Amunition &^{c} is secured, untill further Transported in Waggons over the carrying place to Chippuwa, nearly 10 Miles distance. There are also a Number of other Store-houses & Buildings below the Hill, & several 100 of the Queens Rangers encamped just above these, who also guard the Publick Stores; but of these the Flux & a Billeous Fever took off these 3 Weeks past near 80, & the remainder in order to save themselves, moved to the top of the Hill, where several private houses & Stores are. At Chippuwa 2 Miles above the Falls, there are large Store Houses

To Detroit: 1793

again, & Troops stationed as a guard. Here the row Boats recieve the Goods, & carry them 17 Miles up a strong Current to Fort Erie, where if there be no Vessel ready to recieve them, they are stored up in Buildings erected for the purpose, a third time, & here are also a Number of Troops in Garrison. Formerly Vessels used to go down as far as Fort Schlosser on the South Side, & opposite Chippuwa, but the risk was to great, & indeed it is here at Fort Erie oftentimes with difficulty that Vessels Anchor safe, for the whole bed of the River here, & from hence downwards, is a smooth Limestone Rock.

The Cataract, or Falls of Niagara which is the cause of many inconveniences, & vast Expence as already observed; is truly astonishing to evry one that beholdeth it. In my Power it is not to give that lively & just Discription, which it deserveth— But perhaps in addition to my Observations, my friend Jacob Lindley (a Quaker Preacher) his account (as I coppied it from his Journal) may serve to make up this Defect, which is as follows Vizt.

"The 30th of 5th Month; 5th of the Week, Joseph Moore, John Elliot & myself, went to visit that Phenomenon in Nature, the great Falls of Niagara, whose Thunder for several Days had reached mine Ears. When I approached this Tremendous Cataract, it truly appeared amazing, & with the Voice of Thunder, Smoke, & dashing Waves, did loudly proclaim the terrible Majesty of its infinitely sublime Architect. When we came to the Margin of the River below the Falls, we descended on the almost Perpendicular Bank by several Windings from one Rock to another; & with the aid of several Indian Ladders, at length reached the surface of the Water, after near I suppose at least 150 feet below the summit, where the irregular Position of Multitudes of huge Rocks, which no doubt had tumbled from their antient Seats on the sides of the Banks, made our Progress up, (towards the Pitch) rough & difficult, amongst which we found Log's, pieces of Canows, wrecked in abundance, 12 or 15 feet above the present level of the Water, also, Ducks, Loons, Cormorants, Catfish, Pickerel, &^{c} & various kinds of Fish & Water Fowl, which had been killed by the Violent Dashing, and weight of the Columns of Water, tumbling over a Precipice, not less than 130 feet perpendicular, which appeared strange that they should be destroyed by the Element which gave them Existence. The Rocks & Stones are mostly excellent Limestone, as are the stones in the Banks for 6 or 7 Miles below, where from every appearance I think it not absurd to suppose the Falls once were, but has worn up to the present Barrier where the River makes a bend, & the Water is divided by an Island, the 2 thirds of the Water, or more pass on the North side of the Island. I think it not impossible that the Lands adjoining derive considerable advantage to Vegetation, from the Misty Vapours which arise, & are exhaled to the Clouds, or blown by the Varying Winds on the Neighbouring Farms, some of which are exceeding fertile, abounding with Grass & Grain— After spending an hour or two, & almost lost in Admiration, we ascended again by the Way we went down, & coming on wet, we rode 8 Miles down to the Landing."

In addition to the above I must add, that below the Falls, & for many Miles, the Water seems to remain in a state of Confusion; for tho' it is thrown in a Channel between 2 high Rocky Mountains, & so conducted to the Landing; yet it continues boisterous, contracting Numbers of Whirlpools & eddys, & these continually changing their positions, which makes crossing difficult & dangerous, yea in many places impracticable. As the current from Lake Erie approaches the Falls, the succion increases, untill arriving at the distance of about a Mile, whence it falls in short pitches roaring & foaming, untill at length it divides at an high steep Rocky Island, one third of the Water passing on the South side, & two thirds on the North, & then with the greatest Violence immaginable pitches down into the Deep, where it boils up again, foams, & throws its Vapours up to an amazing heigth, which may in a clear Day be seen at the distance of 20 Miles & upwards; & appears like a thick Smoke. The Rock over which this Water falls, contains 2 principle Angles; & appears to be solid, smooth & Perpendicular. The upper falls measure 57 feet; the main Pitch 137 feet. The Spectators are very much divided in Opinion with respect to the Falls wearing away. Some will have it that these were once at the Landing (8 Miles lower) & thro the length of Time have wore away the Rock thus far; others believe it was from the beginning where it now is. I have two reasons for believing them Originally here, 1st) because the lower end of the Island, which is one solid Rock (only being 12 or 15 feet higher than the 2 sides over which the Water falls) ranges with both these sides exactly. & secondly, because I cannot comprehend what should become of such a body of Rocks as must have tumbled down for 8 Miles in length from a quarter to half a Miles in breadth, & where on both sides the River for this distance the Rocky Mountains stand erect from 150 to 200 feet.

The fabulous Story the Massasagues & other Indians give, that a Monster of a Snake, a Number of Years ago passed out of Lake Superior thro Huron, St. Clair, & Erie, & so over the Falls of Niagara, where in going down he made that great notch (the Angles) & from thence dashing with his Tail in every direction to the Landing: had knocked the Rocks which had cram'd up the River, in little pieces & so opened a passage for the Water: can have no weight here.

From time to time Lives are lost at these Falls, & but a few Years ago a Serjeant & 4 Privates of the 26th Regiment, who in a Canow had mistaken their way, went over the same & Perished; & it frequently happens that Drunken Indians crossing the River above, fall into the suction & Perish. Yea at the time the Vessels from Detroit used to go to Fort Schlosser [opposite the north west end of Navy Island], one being under way above, & the Wind dying away suddenly, she was expected to go down, & every Person on Board lost in a few Minutes, but fortunately the Captn. having new Cables to his

To Detroit: 1793

Anchors, & these sunk in the cavity of the Rocks, which bore the Vessel untill next Day, when a very high Wind sprung up in his favour & he got off. But this he did not attempt untill he had made an experiment by making additional Sails of every piece of Canvas he had on hand, & crowding all Sails at once, found the Cables to slacken, when he immediately cut Cables & got off.

The People living above the Falls, for several Years together lost all their Geese & Ducks, these by swimming out, being taken off by the suction, but now they have got into a method of saving them, Viz.^{t} by plucking the feathers out of the Breast about the size of a Dollar, which naked spot, when they go into the Water, chills them, so that they return to Land again.

June 5th we embarked on Board the Dunmore Captn Ford, & left Fort Erie at 2 in the Afternoon with a light Breeze. We were in all 12 Cabbin Passengers, & on Deck were 50 Indians of the Mohock, Massasage & Mohicon Tribes, among the former was Captain Johny, head Warrior from the Bay of Canty [Quinte] in Canada, & among the latter Captain Hendricks from the Oneidas Country. At 5 we passed Point Ebone [Abino?]; in the Evening the Sugar Loaf; & in the course of the Night long Point on the North & Presque-Isle [Erie] on the South Side, but the Wind changing, we had to beat about & stand on a Tack the 3 succeedings Days, crossing the Lake from side to side, & were in this last Night not a little alarmed, when during the sharp claps of Thunder & Lightening, our Captain informed Us that one third of the Cargo was Gun Powder for the Indian Department. However this Night passed over, without an accident & the Wind turning in our favour were June 9th early in the Morning in sight of the Islands which lay off Sandusky, & some hours after passed the dangerous Rocks & Shoals off Point a plair [Pelee], where according to the soundings, the sudden changes in the depth of Water, was from 6 to 2 fathom, & our Vessel drew full 9 feet water. We next hove in Sight of the 3 Sisters, (3 Islands lying in the course from Detroit River to Miami [Maumee] Bay, & Bass Islands) A Calm for a few Hours prevented our proceeding, untill in the Afternoon a fresh Breeze springing up we ran by 10 at Night into the Mouth of Detroit River, & Anchored close by the Ground where our Indian Congregation had dwelt a Year ago, & early next morning run up with a very high Wind to Detroit, 18 Miles. We Breakfasted with our Captn on Board, & after paying him 3 Guineas & 7/6 a piece for our Passage, took Lodging in the Town at Mr Dolsons Tavern, from whence I visited in the following Days my friends & old Acquaintances, & in particular Mr John Askin. Lieut.^{t} Colonel England, whom I visited several times, spoke very favourable of our Mission on River Thames, yet observing that the Indians were very poor, & surrounded with poverty, but he hoped they would do well in a Year or two, as they were industrious, & lived on a rich spot of Land. He observed that they had Petitioned the Councill (Assembly) for a whole Township of Land, which in his Opinion was *too* much. I gave him my reasons why I thought it not too much, & he agreed with me afterwards. As I was determined to go & see them myself, I began to look out for an Opportunity to go thither, but as there is no passable Road by Land, & the Wind blowing for several Days past very hard, & right ahead, I had to wait untill the 13th when the Wind changing favourable, & Mr Dolson furnishing me with a Boat & hands, I sat off, briskly passing up the River & thro Lake St Clair, about 40 Miles, & then entered the River La Trenche (or Thames as it is now called) where after passing 6 Miles up thro 1,000^{ds} of Acres of natural Meadows, viewing in some places various curious groves of Trees bordering on the same, & passing by an Antient Battle ground where a Number of Graves are to be seen, in some of which (as I was told) upwards of 100 Bodies were burried: called to see an Acquaintance of mine, from hence we proceeded yet 6 Miles higher up the River, passing all the Way by Farms on its Banks, & at Evening put up at Mr Daniel Dolsons, where I met with several of our Indian B.^{rn} in Canows, who were out to purchase Provision. Finding upon enquiry, that the distance to our Indian Settlement was nearly twice as far by Water as by Land, & that I might easily reach them in one Day on Horseback, I hired one, & took one of the Indian B.^{rn} with me as a Pilot. In the first 20 Miles we often touched on new Farms on the River, the Country being pretty generally Rich, & in many places covered with black Walnut Timber; but the last 15 Miles we had to pass thro a Wilderness, attacked in every direction by Swarms of Musquetos, untill at 6 oClock in the Evening I arrived at this place, finding all our white & Ind.ⁿ B^{rn} & Sisters buisy at Work in their Corn fields, & other Clearings— The report of my arrival soon spread arround, & both Surprise & Joy bespoke the Countenances of all among whom I now arrived a *second* time unexpectedly; & having recieved no Letters from Beth.^m this 12 Months, believed that a stop must have been put to the Correspondence between the United States & Canada, moreover as Govr Simcoe of Upper Canada had signified to them last Winter, that it was the Kings Will & Pleasure, that all Correspondence between these Countries should cease; & that actually an Act of Parliament had been passed some time ago, forbidding the Bishops & Clergy of Canada, to correspond with any Person of the same denomination in the United States. I had fortunately come across 2 Packets of Letters for them, by the Way, & these with the few Articles of Cloathing I brought them; was very Acceptable. I had my Lodging in the Single B.^{rs} House which was the most spacious & recognoitered.

June 17th with the B.^{rn} Senseman, Mich^l Young & Edwards, all the Corn fields, some of the Sugar Camps, & the adjoining Lands; & returned thro the high Lands home again.

June 18th at evening 2 White Men from New England whom I had seen at Niagara, & who were in search of Land arrived here. They seemed to be tollerably well pleased with this Country with regard to the Soil & Timber; but were apprehensive of early & late Frosts, & thought Mill seats very scarce, if any at all; It seems the Governor has promised them 3 Townships of Land

To Detroit: 1793

(each Township 10 Miles square) provided they bring Settlers on this Fall. By what I can learn of our Ind.ⁿ Bʳⁿ who are Hunters; or Travellers, & what I have seen myself, I find the Country for a small distance from the River (say several 100 Yards) very rich & fertile, but back of this wet & Swampy, chiefly covered with Beech, Sugar Maple, black Ash &.ᶜ & here the Swarms of Musquetos are incredible. The River, which is here from 20 to 30 Yards wide, is confined by Banks from 20 to 70, or 80 feet high. The Soil of the Bottoms or low Grounds, is a deep black Sand, covered with black Walnut, Cherry, Linden, Elm, White Ash, Oak & white Hickory; under which Nettles & weeds spring up & grow thrifty. The Uplands where they join the River are here a Sandy Soil, covered with a thin black Loam. About 30 Miles higher up, I am informed they are Clay. The River throughout is very winding, muddy & pretty Deep, & rises sometimes in a fresh from 15 to 18 feet. The Moravian Town, (as it is called here) is situate on the Bank of the River, on a level & pleasant Spot. The Bank which is at least 60 feet high falls away gradually to the River, & affords several small Springs of good Water. The Houses, which are about 30 in Number are principally of Log's, some of which are hewed & well built. The Corn fields are on both sides the River, & according to my Judgement they had about 90 Acres of as promising & forward Corn, as ever I have seen at this Season of the Year, besides Vegetables; but few of them had any thing to live upon, except what they pick up daily in the Woods, their last Years Crop being entirely killed by a Frost which fell in August. The Weather while I was there was exceeding hot, so that on the 17.ᵗʰ the Mercury was up to 85, on the 18ᵗʰ to 86, & on the 19ᵗʰ to 87, but on Thursday the 20ᵗʰ it fell down again to 76, & next day the 21.ˢᵗ to 72 when it rained all day very hard.

June 22ᵈ we heard by an Indian, immediately from Sandusky, that a party of Wyondot Warriors were returned with the Scalps of 20 Women & Children, which (they say) they murdered while the Men were out at Work. A Number of Cajugas from Buffaloe Creek passed also this Day by here in 3 Canows for the Indian Treaty. The Mercury was this Day down to 62. As neither Bʳ Senseman nor I, had any time to loose; his Buissness being with the Council at Niagara now sitting, unto whom he was to present a Petition for Land, & I to go to the Indian Treaty, we sat out

June 23 in a Canow & some Indian Bʳⁿ for Detroit. In passing down the River we called to see some friends & Acquaintances, & after taking some refreshment at Mʳ Surpluss'es at Sun set, resolved to take the advantage of the bright Moonshine & calmness of the Weather, proceeded down to the Lake, 6 Miles, & from thence thro the same by 6 oClock next Morning, when we breakfasted on Shore, & arrived at Detroit by 10, where I found all my Travelling friends well, yet almost out of Patience at the delay of the Treaty; moreover as it had been signified this Day to them: that we should not leave this place this 3 Weeks yet; & the Commissioners, who were expected here before this, were neither arrived. The Quakers were however rejoiced to see some of our Ind:n B:rn, & finding upon enquiry of me, that they were in a starving Condition, they immediately resolved to give 100 Dollars to their relief, which was accordingly laid out in Provision, & sent them, & the Indian Congregation afterwards thanked their Benefacters in a Letter written by B:r Zeisberger ——

June 26:th B:r Senseman embarked on the Chippuwa, Capt:n Harra for Fort Erie & Niagara, touching by the Way at the Tawa, or Miami [Maumee] River, in order to land Provision & Amunition there for the Indians— The Quakers, M:r Wilson & I, dined at M:r Askins, who signified sincere wishes, that a Peace between the Indian Nations & the United States might take place this ensuing Treaty. He had however his Doubts whether this would be accomplished, & thought we run a very great risk in going out. The conversation afterwards turning on the Northwest Trade, carried on by a Comp:y of Merchants in Montreal, M:r Askin as well as Capt:n Drake, (the former a partner, the latter a Capt:n in this Service) gave us a minute discription of this Bussiness & that Country &:c by which it appears that at least 1,500 Persons, are from Year to Year, employed as hands in this service— That according to the Route they take, the distance is 3,000 Miles from Montreal, or 2,500 from S:t Mary's, (Mouth of Lake Superior) That at a place far beyond this Lake, called the grand Portage, or (great Carrying place) the hands meet each other & here exchanging Goods & Pottery, return back again— That to perform the whole Journey, would require 2 Sommers Travelling— That a M:r M:cKinsey, who has followed that course the farthest, gives an account of his meeting in the Month of July, with extensive frozen Waters or Seas, which were Salt. Likewise large Mountains of Salt, & banks of Virgin Copper, some of which he brought in with him, and that he is now sent out by Government with 10 Men, to explore that Country & make discoveries, & is expected back again in 3 Years ——

Note. Some Gentlemen suppose these frozen Seas to be the same that Capt:n Cook met with, when in search of a North West Passage.

June 30:th I took a Walk 9 Miles up Lake S:t Clair, to a M:r Nathan William's, an old Acquaintance of mine, & after spending this, & part of the next day very agreeable with the Family returned again.

July 2:d Our Landlord took us in his Boat 6 Miles down the River, & on the opposite side, to his Farm, where we had an Opportunity of seeing that part of the Country, & spending this exceeding hot day in a cool & agreeable place— Various accounts of intelligent Persons, communicated to Us in these Days, run to this: That unless the Commissioners agree at the Treaty, to the demands of the Indian Nations, which will be: that the Ohio River be declared the Boundary Line between the United States & them, there will be no Peace; yea they & all with them may be knocked in the head.

July 3:d we were informed that about 1,000 Indians were now assembled at the Rapids of Miami to Council among themselves; & that they agreed to send a Deputation to the Commissioners at Niagara to enquire first of them:

what the meaning of Genl. Wayne's movements were &c. & secondly whether they had Power to make a new boundary Line. The Mercury was this day up to 96, &

July 4th at 100 in the Shade. About 20 of the Oneidas, who had come up from Brother Town with an Intention to go to the Treaty, & urge the Nations to Peace, but were not permitted by the Brittish Ind. Agents to go there visited Us this Day; and a Shawnese Man, who visited Us in full Dress, had to the Number of 1,600 Silver Broaches in his Shirt.

July 5th we were visited by 2 Shawnese Indians directly from the great Council, who informed Us: that the 2 Indn. Chiefs from each Nation, accompanyed by Buttler, Brandt, & Simon Girty, were actually gone as a Deputation to the Commissioners at Niagara, to enquire of them whether they had Power to give up the Country to the Ohio, &c. That it was determined: should a Treaty take place, & the Commissioners would even only make proposals, short of what *they* demanded, they would instantly knock them in the head. This day the Mercury was at 102.

July 8 in the forenoon we had a hard Gust with large hail stones, which however did not cool the Air. Daily accounts of the Indians intentions to murder Us all at the Treaty, were circulating here, both among Indians & Whites.

July 9. we were visited by the noted Shawnese Warrior, Wawiapieschenwà (signifies a Whirlpool) otherwise called by the White People, Blue-Jacket; who tho seemingly friendly, was very reserved towards us.

July 10th. arrived the Sloop Detroit from Fort Erie; by which we were informed that the Commissioners had been on board the Dunmore 12 Days already, waiting for a fair Wind to take them out of the Current—& that the Chippuwa with the Deputation of Indians had not arrived then, neither was seen by the Detroit on her Passage.

July 12th our Landlord took us again in a Boat to his Farm, where we spent the Day in visiting Neighbours. In the Evening we were informed by a Sloop arrived from Fort Erie: that the Deputation of Inds. had arrived there, & that the Commissioners were returned with them to Navy-hall, where in the presence of the Governor they wished to transact their Business.

July 13 Mr. Wilson & I, who were alone at home to day, invited the great War Chieff Blue Jacket to dine with us. The conversation being of course on Indian affairs, we wished to hear his Sentiments, & whether there was a prospect of bringing about a Peace; but he conducted himself with that reservedness, so peculiar to Inds. & especially on such occasions. In the Afternoon of this day we had the Satisfaction to recieve by the Schooner Speedwell, Letters from our friends at home, as also from the Commissioners, informing us of their detention, but hopes of coming on soon. but fresh accounts from Miami, left us little hopes of a Treaty, & Peace this time; but rather evinced, that the Nations were assembling for War, there being already 1,100 Men on the Spot, & scarcely a Woman to be seen among them, whereas otherwise, when Indians go to Treaties, they are careful in bringing their Women & Children on, in order to obtain more Presents. And further: that a Deputation from the Cherokee & Creek Nations were arrived on the Miami, with a Brittish leader at their head, & that their Bussiness was: to encourage these Nations to continue the War, & to make known the great successes *they* had had to the Southward against the People of the United States of late, all which was confirmed by succeeding accounts, so that in our Opinion there was not any prospect of Peace.

July 15 the People of this Country began their Wheat Harvest, which is this Season about a fortnight earlier than for common. Tho to all appearance one should suppose that an Acre would produce 30 Bushels, yet the Farmer is well sattisfied if he has after all 10 or 12 Bushels of clean Wheat. For 16 Bush. is the highest per Acre, & often he has no more than 5 or 6, the greatest part generally turning into Smut, the cause of which is ascribed by some to early sowing in the Fall, & by others to much Rain & hot weather when in Blossom. The Smut Ear is not easily discovered, & looks as full as the other, but on squeezing or rubbing the grain, is found filled with a black substance like Chimney Sut. The Wheat therefore after it is Thrashed must be put into large Tubs, & there washed 4 or 5 times over in fresh water; well rubbed all the time. The Smut is rubbed up, & turns the Water Black; & the Wheat when clean must be dried again. The general Complaint of the People of Niagara is: that their Wheat turns into Cheat; which they ascribe to sowing successively on one Spot. But this cheat certainly cannot come out of the Wheat.

July 17. arrived Mr. Wilbank (formerly a Printer with Mr. Rivington of New-York; but now the Conductor of those Inimical Indians from the Southward) from Miami; & was furnished immediately with a Vessel for Niagara to the Governor. The above Deputation sent from Miami, pieces of Painted Tobacco for Smoking to all these Nations. *Note.* This is a general Custom among the Indians, & is to strengthen them to War. The consequence was: that parties sat off immediately.

July 21st. arrived at length the Dunmore with the Commissioners, who were landed at the Mouth of the River 18 Miles below this, & had taken Quarters at Mr. Elliots, according to—Orders, (for they were not permitted to go to Detroit) The Oneidas rejoiced, sat out & encamped near them, & the Dunmore having come up to Discharge her Cargo, & take in Provisions; being ready, we went down with her, & encamped in Tents on the pleasant Green fronting the House where the Commissioners were. Every Person engaged in the Treaty Buisness, was now on the Spot, (except Mr. Parish who was gone Express to Philadelphia) and their Names are as follows: Vizt: Genl. Lincoln from Massachusetts, Governor Randolph from Virginia, & Timothy Pickering from Pensylvania, (Commissioners). Charles Storer from the Province of Main, Secretary to the same. General Chaping Indn. Agent under Congress, from Buffaloe Creek as assistant, Doctor McCoskry from Carlisle, as Docter. Willm Scott from Connecticut, as Commissary. William Wilson & Sylvester Ash, as Interpreters for the Delaware & Shawnese Nations from Fort Pitt. Mr Jones Interpreter to the Senecas &.^c from Ginnessee. Mr Dean temporary Interpreter to the Oneidas &.^c from Mohawk River. The 6 Quakers: William Savory, John Parish, John Elliot, Jacob Lindly, Joseph Moore & William Hartshorne: The 4 first mentioned from Pensylv.^a & the 2 latter from Jersey; & I from Beth.^m Govr Simcoe had on his part sent 2 Officers, (Captn Bombary of the Regulars, & Lieut^t Gibbins of the Queens Rangers) to accompany the Commissioners, & Protect them during the Bussiness. A Cook, & of course several Domestics were in the Family; and the Dunmore at our Service, lay at Anchor in the River, opposite our Camp. There was nothing wanting now, & more wished for by Us, but a speedy meeting with the assembled Indian Nations, & a Peace; but tho' the Commissioners were in great hopes that this end would be obtained, moreover as the late Deputation at Navy Hall had told them: that now there was a Prospect of Peace, & hoped soon to have the pleasure of taking them by the hand, & leading them to the Treaty: yet some of Us, being better acquainted with the manner the Bussiness was carried on, doubted very much, whether we should ever see the Treaty Ground & expected rather a Message to return home again, & so it turned out as will be seen by the Sequel.

During our stay here B.^r Senseman on his return from Niagara visited us on the 26th & several Indian B.^rn from River Thames brought me a Letter from Mr Zeisberger. These together with B.^r Senseman returned home again next Day. Captn Brandt who was a Cabbin Passenger with the latter, & being alone one Day, had much Conversation with Senseman; in which he gave his full approbation to the Conduct of the Commissioners, saying they certainly would effect a Peace with the Indians, were they left to act for themselves &.^c

July 28 we were visited by several Merchants from Detroit, friends to the United States, but who gave it as their Opinion that there would be no Treaty. That most of the Indians would be glad of a Peace, but that they durst not Act as they wished; but as they were told &.^c The Oneidas had this evening a Dance at their Quarters.

July 29th in the Afternoon a Deputation of about 30 Indians arrived here from the Council on Miami, among whoom were Pachkantschihillas, head Warrior of the Delawares; Captn Johny a principle War Chief of the Shawnese; & also a head Warrior of the Wyondotts. With these came also Matthew Elliot, deputy Indian Agent; James McKee, Son of Col.^l McKee, principle Agent in this Quarter, & Thomas Smith an assistant to the latter. The Indians did not land even on this Side, but encamped on the Island in the River, where they remained this Day. But of the 3 British Officers we soon learnt the Errand they were come upon, & which was to undo all which had been done by the first Deputation with the Commissioners at Navy Hall, accusing these of having got Drunk there, & not attended to the Bussiness as they were directed— This agreed with what the Indians had told us at diferent times already at Detroit, only with this alteration: That Capt.ⁿ McKee, Elliot & others had in order to undo what had been done there: dictated this Language to them &c.

In order to throw Light on the Deputation referred to, & to justify both Parties on what was done at Navy-Hall; I will relate the principle parts thereof. Vizt: This Deputation was sent off from the general Councill of the Indian Nations at the Rapids on Miami assembled, to ask the Commissioners there 2 Questions: "What means the movement of Gen! Wayne's Army? Is it intended to destroy us while assembled at the Treaty? Or to destroy our Woemen & Children at home while we are absent?" &c

secondly. Have you Power to make a new Boundary Line between Us & You?

To the first Question the Commissioners assured them, that not only no harm was intended them untill the event of the Treaty should be known, but also produced the two Proclamations of the President & General Wayne himself, forbidding evry Person, or any body of People to injure, or carry on any secret Expeditions against any Indians &c. & that there certainly was no Deciet in the Matter &c.

To the second Question they Answered: *That they were empowered to make a new Boundary Line between them & the United States.* But that it was generally the case; that where two Persons or Parties were at variance with each other, they were apt to act hastily, not attending to right nor Reason. This was exactly the case here; & therefore the only way to settle the Dispute would be: that both parties make some Concessions— This matter was further explained to Capt.ⁿ Brandt by the Commissioners, & the reason assigned why the Ohio could *not* be made the boundary line Vizt: Because the Land was sold, & in part settled.

After all these Conferences the Indians appearing well sattisfied told the Commissioners: that now there was a Prospect of Peace; & that they expected they would soon be taken by the hand & led to the Treaty— The present Deputation after crossing the River,

July 30th. & seating themselves, began with the usual ceremony of thanking the great Spirit for the Opportunity of meeting this Day; & then with a few Words made to naught all the Bussiness which had been transacted at the last Deputation, & said: In Order that no such mistakes may be made again, we deliver you our Sentiments in Writing, (handing a piece of Paper on which nearly these Words were written) Vizt. At a Treaty held at Fort Stanwix 25 Years ago, it was agreed that the Land on the North side of the Ohio River should ever remain our Property, & *that* River be the boundary Line between the White People & us— Will You now henceforth continue this the boundary Line, & remove all White People settled on these Lands to the other Side of the Ohio? The Commissioners told them they would give them an Answer tomorrow.

Among these Indians were several whom I well knew, & especially one, a particular friend of mine, whoom I asked to my Tent, & had some Conversation with him on the subject of a Peace; but he told me his Mouth was stop'd, & he durst not venture to disclose any of their Secrets. He however lamented that there were so many bad Advisers among them; and feared the Labour of the Commissioners would be in vain.

July 31st the Deputation came across at 9 oClock, in order to hear the Commissioners Answer to their Speech; but these not yet being ready, the 4 Dellawares present paid me & Mr Wilson a Visit— It seemed upon the whole, that they meant to stand to what they had said, & not suffer any Settlements on this side of the Ohio. They found much fault with the United-States in sending Armies into their Country, whereas (said they) *they* had never marched in a Body yet out against them. It was true, that some of their foolish young People had killed the Whites on & over the Ohio, but not all had turned out &.^c

Note going out in small parties, signifies nothing now a Days with the Ind.^s & Horse Stealing is never looked upon by them, as a Crime.

In the Afternoon the Deputation Assembled, & the Commissioners returned them a plain, generous, but determined Answer, explaining all Bussiness hitherto transacted between the U. States & them, referring to Treaties, which they had Voluntaryly signed, & producing Speeches likewise Voluntarily sent from them to Congress, in which they signify their Satisfaction at what *had* been done— That in consequence of all these Treaties & Speeches: & the Goods they had recieved for the Bargain; Congress, having no more the least Doubt, but that the Indian claim was extinguished; had sold *some* of these Lands, & principally those bordering on the Ohio River; & that it therefore was out of their Power to turn People off of their Improvements, &.^c But that they, the Commissioners, wishing to do them Justice in evry respect—for the sake of Peace—& to convince them of the good disposition of the United States towards them: were willing to give them in addition to what they had already got at former Treaties, a greater sum either in Money or goods, than ever was given at any Treaty heretofore, from the first settling of this Country— And besides this: they would give them yearly Presents for ever— They also observed: that former Commissioners had laid a false Construction on the Country ceded at the Treaty of Peace between the U. States, & Great Brittain; & that the King *did* not, nor *could* even give to the United States any Land belonging to the Indians, & that all the right the U. States had within the Line in their Country, was a *preemption right* of Purchasing Land, whenever they had any for Sale— But that they never would urge them to sell their Lands— They well knew that they must have Lands to live on— All they now wished, was to meet them in Councill at the appointed place, where they hoped evry thing would go well; & *there* they will be willing to make such concessions, as will be found Necessary, & satisfactory to all parties— That the only way to settle Disputes between People at Variance; was to meet face to face; & not to keep at a distance and speak by Deputations; for in this case they remained Strangers— They hoped this Speech would convince the Nations of the sincerity of the United States; & they (the Commissioners) expected soon to be taken by the hand to the Treaty &c.

The Deputation replied: that they would return an Answer in the Morning. accordingly

Aug.st 1.st they assembled in the Morning, & said there Words were but few— That the Commissioners had told them Yesterday that they could *not* give up the Land on the Ohio— That they (the Nations) were all Brethren & United, *not* to give up these Lands—& that the Commissioners might now go home again, & tell this to Washington— However, Capt.n Elliot, who unguarded had said "*No, No, they was not to have said (the last Words)*" got them to amend the Speech by saying: "*We will take Your Speech to the great Councill, from whence You shall recieve an Answer; & we desire You not to go, but to wait for our Answer*"

A Number of British Officers from Detroit attended at each Meeting, & Simon Girty the Indians Interpreter cut a shocking figure. The Deputation sat off immediately, & several Officers besides those who had come with them conducted them to the Miami.

Aug.st 2.d several Wyondotts from the Neighbouring Villages visited Us, & were kindly treated. These People have a Number of Prisoners among themselves.

Aug. 3.d A Prisoner gave us a most shocking Account of the manner such Prisoners are treated, who are condemned to Die. And that there are a Number of Canibals among them, is well known by the People of this Country. They frequently while torturing a Prisoner, cut pieces out of his flesh, roast & eat it before his face; yea often offer the Prisoner his own flesh to eat &c. I could not learn that the Dellawares, Wyondotts & Shawnese had adopted this horrid act: but with the Twichtwees (or Miamis) Potawattemes, Chippuwas & Massasagues it is now a days customary.

Sunday Aug. 4. passed by this place the Ottawa from the Miami River, where she had landed a Number of Indians brought on from Niagara. A Sloop from Michilimackinac, with 20,000 weight of Beaver Furr on board, anchored beside the Dunmore, & next day proceeded further to Fort Erie.

Aug. 6 we were again visited by Neighbouring Wyondotts, who apeared friendly; yet their addresses to the Commissioners were in the Language they have adopted to all the People of the United States Vizt. Brothers the big Knife! &c.

Aug. 8. Several Merchants from Detroit who had visited Us here, returned chearfully home again. In the Evening 2 Mohican Messengers from Capt.n Hendricks at Miami, arrived with Letters from the latter to the Commissioners, by which it appeared that the assembled Ind.n Nations were nearly agreed to a Treaty; & that we should be sent for in a few Days. This Information was confirmed next Day by 13 Ind.s from thenc, of the Monsey, &

Chippuwa Tribes; who further related that great disputes had arisen among the assembled Nations, on the cause of the War, & the impropriety of continueing it longer— And that the combined Nations had charged both the Brittish & the 5 Nations as the cause of these Troubles; they having put the Tomhawk into their hands. At evening a set of Drunken Ind[s] from Detroit arrived here, & having brought Liquor with them, they got soon our visiters also Drunk. These then became so troublesome, that we had to keep a Watch all Night, & especially as one of the Monsy's would be among our Tents, & was continually bawling out: "I am called a Devil. A Devil I am, & as a Devil I will behave; & I neither fear the big Knifes, nor the English."— And on the Morning when he asked Us for Rum which was refused him: he said, all I told you yesterday in favour of Peace, was Lies. The War must continue &c.

Sunday Aug[st] 11 Arrived M[r] Jasper Parrish, whom the Commissioners had sent Express to Philadelphia. M[r] Wilbank who is mentioned above, came in the same Vessel, & took now lodging at Capt[n] Caldwels a Mile above this, untill an Opportunity offers for the Miami River. We were all cherrished anew, by Letters from our friends at home. We were also visited by friends from Detroit. By daily accounts from Miami we learn, that a distemper prevails there among the Indians, which carries them off on the 2[d] or 3[d] Days, & that several principle Chieffs of the Chippuwas Nation had died of the disorder. With Jacob (Shebosch Son in Law) who had heard of my being here, & had come across the Lake to see me, I had a good deal of Conversation, & endeavored to put him in the right path again. The incredible swarms of Musquettoes by this sultry Weather we have, leave us no rest at Nights, tho our Tents are filled with Smoke. This Evening the Commissioners sent off 2 Oneida Indians, with Letters to Capt[n] Brandt & Hendricks, in order to learn why no Answer was returned to their Speech, & whether they might expect one. They also sent a written Speech to be read by these Persons in general Councill. At Night a very heavy Rain set in, preceeded by heavy Thunders, which kept us allert untill Morning, the Water being up to our Ancles in the Tents.

Aug. 14 several Wyondotts came to tell us some good News, which they pretended to have heard from Miami but all they wanted was a Dram, & which they got—so their News turned into Smoke.

Aug. 16 arrived here from the Councill 2 Young Wyondotts, with a written Speech to the Commissioners as an Answer to their former Speech, delivered on this Ground; which Speech was both Impertinent & Insolent, & intended to put an end to Treaty Bussiness. The Language in the Speech was such, that no Person having knowledge of Indians, would believe it an Indian Speech, but be that now as it will: there were assembled at Miami by this time 1,500 Warriors, & anxious for Mischief, they threw off the Mask. The Messengers, who agreeable to Simon Girty's orders, had gone off after they had delivered there Message were sent after by the Commissioners, &

desired to take an Answer to the Councill back again, which they agreed to. This Speech was to remind them of the Pains the United States had taken to bring about a Peace with them—& as they had been inattentive to their Welfare, & disappointed the United States; they must abide by the Consequences, & only blame *themselves* & *their advisers* for future events &c.

We now prepared for our return, & sent our Baggage this afternoon yet on board the Dunmore, & next Morning Augst 17th embarked and made our way (tho a head Wind) by morning, to the Bass Islands, where we cast Anchor, close by the Christ^n Ind^n Encampment in 1786. In the afternoon of the 18th we got under way again, passing Middle Island, & cruising 4 days, under the difficulty of contrary Winds of & on, sometimes near the North, & at other times near the South Shores viewing the Country at a distance —observing the difference of the Country on the sides of the Lake, it being on the North-side low & flat, but on the otherhand on the South side high, Ridgey & delightful; all this time being much diverted by 2 little Birds, which probably had been blown off the Islands as we passed them, & continued with us all the Voyage—untill in the Night of the 22^d the Wind changed in our favour; & blowing very fresh run at the rate of 8 Miles an hour, in which time we passed long Point & Presque Isle, *60* Miles above Fort Erie, & afterwards the Grand River *40* Miles from F. Erie, & at length came to Anchor at this place by 1 oClock in the Morning.

Aug. 23 we were confined to our Vessel all Day on account of the Wind blowing so Violent; but the Day following being pretty calm, our Company parted, those who had Horses, sat out by Land to their respective Homes; the Commissioners Randolph & Pickering by way of Albany & NYork, & others by way of the Chinessee Country for Pittsburg, & other places; but Gen! Lincoln, the Secretary, Docter, Commissary, 2 Quakers & myself had no alternative, but to proceed by Water: either by way of Oswego, Wood Creek, Mohock River & Hudsons, or by way of Cattarakway [Cataraqui, i.e., Kingston], Montreal, Lake Champlain, & so down the Hudson to NYork (home again).

A Number of Cochnowaga [Caughnawaga] Indians who were come on with their Interpreter Mr Lorimier from La Chiene [Lachine] above Montreal, in order to attend at the Treaty at Sandusky; visited Us on Board; & afterwards gave us an invitation to visit them this Evening on Shore, which we complied with; They had prepared seats for Us on the one Side, & for some other Gentlemen of this place on the other; their Intention being to honor & divert Us with a Dance. The performer apeared in a Dress, far Superior to any I had seen before; which consisting of a kind of Jacket with a Number of Bells hanging to it, a Cap, Leggins, Mokosins, Garters, Neck-Laces or Belts, alltogether most curiously worked with Died Porcupine Quills on Leather; and all done by themselves; which together, (I suppose) could not be procured for less than 100 Dollars. After the Ceremony, which was conducted with Decorum, & during which, their Countenances denoted a sensibility, & much of Gratitude; that an American General (Gen¹ Lincoln) &ᶜ had complied with their requests; & they having had the pleasure of conferring in some measure, marks of esteem on him, & the People of the United-States: the General made them a Present of—& each of the Company followed his Example—Mʳ Lorimier related to Us a remarkable fact, which happened 2 Months ago at the Indian Village at La chiene; & which on account of its singularity, deserves a place here. Vizt. There were in this Village 2 remarkable Men, (Indˢ) the one for Stateliness, being 6 feet 4 Inches high; & the other for Srength & activity. These happening to meet together one Day in the Street (a third being present) some Language proceeded from the Mouth of the former, which the latter could not put up with, especially as it consisted of Boasts tending to prove his inferiority— The latter replied: You have insulted me this time, but henceforth You shall do it no more; & stabbing him in that Instant thro the Body with his Knife so that he fell Dead at his feet. The alarm being immediately spread thro the Village, a Crowd of People assembled, & the Murderer having seated himself on the Ground beside the Dead Body, coolly submitted to his fate, which he could not well expect to be any other, than immediate Death, moreover as the cry of the People was: Kill him, Kill him. But tho he bent his Body & head forward to receive the Tomhawk, (Ax) no Person would lay hands on him; & removing the Dead Body soon after, left him alone. After some time he rose from this place, for a more publick part of the Village, & there lay down in hopes of being the sooner dispatched; but, the Spectators only viewing him, & then retiring again; & he wishing to have the Bussiness settled took the resolution to go to the Mother of the Deceased (an aged Woman) whom he addressed in these Words: "Woman! I have killed thy Son, who had insulted me. But altho this was the case, yet he was thine, & Valuable with *thee*. I therefore now surrender myself up unto thee. Direct as thou wilt have it, & release me speedily from Misery"— The Woman replied: "Thou hast indeed killed my Son, who was dear to me & my only supporter in my old Age. *One* life is now lost already, that is true; but to take *thine* on that account, cannot be of any service to me, nor better my situation— thou has however a Son Wilt thou therefore give me *thy* Son in *his* stead, so shall all be wiped away!— He answered, Mother! my Son is but yet a Child, (10 Years old) & can be of no service to you, but only be a Trouble & charge on thee! but here am *I*, truly capable of Supporting & maintaining thee! If thou wilt accept of *me* as *thy* Son, nothing shall be wanting in me to make life comfortable unto thee while thou livest!" The Woman instantly agreed, adopted him together with the whole family; & took them to her house.

Sunday Aug. 25ᵗʰ after parting with most of the Baggage & settling with the Captⁿ & others; we went down in Boats to Chippuwa; where after Dining, some proceeded in a Waggon to the Landing; other remained here with the Baggage untill next Day, and Willᵐ Hartshorne & I went once more to take a View of the Falls; where after spending 5 hours in contemplating with astonishment the Works of Nature: & he having returned from the Bottom of the Falls, from whence he appeared to me, (standing on the Rock above) no bigger than a Child of 5 Years old: we walked 4 Miles further on, towards the Landing, & took Lodging at Mr Rouch's Tavern; but not being accustomed to rest nigh such a Report as the Falls make; moreover as it sounded as if these were but at the back of the House: I slept but little.

Aug. 26 after Breakfast we proceeded to the Landing, & took lodging at a Mr Phelps's. Numbers of People in this Country, are Sick & Dying on a Billious Fever, which setts in, in this flat wet Country, regularly towards the Fall, but proves this Season particularly fatal, & especially to the poorer People, who live chiefly on Vegetables, & have no other drink but Water.

Aug. 28 we proceeded in a Boat down the River to Navy Hall, & were lodged in the Gov.^{rs} House; he & his family being gone across Lake Ontario to Toronto, 70 Miles; which place is intended for the Seat of Government of upper Canada. Here we were to remain untill Captn Bombary (who had gone on our arrival at Fort Erie, immediately off in a Vessel for that place to the Governor) should return again with the Governors pleasure, or per- mission for us to proceed on our Journey. But a Vessel arriving here on the

29th directly from Toronto, having had a fair Wind & but a few Hours Passage, which knew nor saw any thing of the above Vessel, & the Captn assuring us that the Govr on his departure had not heard any thing yet of our arrival; it was supposed the Vessel was lost & all on Board: moreover, as it had been predicted by some at her setting out: she being overladen; & a Violent Storm springing up soon after she sat out; we could not wait any longer, but embarked on the Sloop Caldwell, Captn Paxton for Kingston at 4 oClock in the Morning of the

30.th & with a favorable strong Breze, run at an amazing rate, even so, that had it not been for some Islands in this Lake (called the Ducks) where there are Shoals, & on which account we were obliged to stand off during the Night: we should have been at Kingston by Day break, a distance of 160 Miles, but so we did not get in untill 9 oClock that morning. Lake Ontario is very deep, some say they find no Bottom by soundings; others will have found Bottom at 120 Fathom. The Seas ran amazing high, & our little Sloop Danced properly up & down. Within a few Miles of Kingston we passed the Bay of Canty on the North side, which Bay is said to be Navigable upwards, into the Country for 70 Miles. Here a Number of the Mohocks live, with Captn Johny at their head; They have also a Minister & Schoolmaster; the latter a Mr John Beninger, Son to Abraham Beninger Senr

Kingston is a new Town situate on the same Point of Land on which the French Fort Frontinac stood, & adjoining a British Fort on the same spot. It contains nearly 100 Houses, mostly new, & settled by People from the United States; some of which visiting Us, called themselves of those un- fortunate People who had taken the wrong Side last War &.^{c} This Point appears to be altogether a Limestone Rock, thinly covered with Earth. A Number of Islands, curiously ranged & well covered with White Pine Timber lay off in the River. The River, Bays & coves affoard a great plenty of Fish, & principally the Salmon Trout. About 30 Miles in a Southern Direction is Carlton [Carleton] Island, also Fortified. Numbers of the Massasage Indians live up & down this River, & on some Islands, but whose love for Liquor, causes them to spend much of their time at this Place. Our Captain landed those of this Tribe he had brought here from the Treaty; & who could not part with Us without a farewel Dram.

A Boat being procured for Us, with 4 French Canadians to work the same, we embarked down the River St Larence, from 2 to 4 Miles wide, & thro a Number of big & small Rocky Islands, where the Channels were often very narrow. At Night we arrived at the 1,000 Islands, & passing thro these during the whole Night, found ourselves clear by 5 in the Morning, & in a most beautiful River about one Mile wide, the Banks of which on the North side was lined with fine Farms. At 7 we put to Shore to Breakfast, where our Landlord, a West India Gentleman, charged Government with the improper steps they had taken in prohibiting Grain & any Produce to be exported to any other place than Great Brittain; that therefore the Grain lay on the Farmers hands, who must either keep it, or sell it at a very low Price. Wheat for 2/ Hallifax (3/ Pensylv^a) per Bush. & for this they must take Merchandize. He also disclosed matters of Consequence respecting the failure of the Indian Treaty &^{c} We were now opposite Swigatschi Fort [Oswegatchie, Ogdensburg], 70 Miles below Kingston, from this 4 Miles lower down the Rapids begin, in which are several Rocky Islands, & Fort Levi, (built by the French.) Below the Rapids on the South side we saw 15 well built houses of hewn Log's, & were told that Government had built those for the Indians. half after 10 we passed the Galloo Falls, & below these a Number of Islands inhabited by Cochnowaga Indians, having a well built Church with a Steeple & Bell in their Village. At half after 3 we arrived at the long Sue [Sault], a most dangerous Rapid to pass thro, & 6 Miles long, where our Boatsmen showed us a second Cross, to which they took off their Hatts, bowed down, & muttered something in French, the reason of which upon enquiry, were told: that many of their People, (Catholiks) following the Water, had been Drowned from time to time—that whereever such an accident happened, they put up a Cross, & evry time passing by the same, prayed to some Saint & the Virgin Mary to have them released from Purgatory. They also shewed us a small Leather Bag, which they have hanging round their Necks, in which there is consecrated Bread given them by the Priests, to keep them from Drowning. The Country below these Falls has again a fine appearance, & much like that on the Mohock River. At 5 oClock we stop'd at Cornwell [Cornwall] a small Town of 35 Houses.

From hence downwards we passed Islands again inhabited by Cochnowaga Indians; and at Sunset we approached Lake St Francois, a Lake of 21 Miles in length, & 6 in breadth, & in which we were nigh being burried that Night; owing to the imprudent conduct of the Boatsmen. These had namely at Night, after we had laid down in the Boat to rest, put out into the middle of the Lake in order to make a short cut to a Point they intended to go to, & put up for that Night. About 10 oClock they cried out, *a Storm! a Storm. down* with the Sail. In an Instant we were alert, & got the Sail down, tho with difficulty. But the Storm had come on so of a Sudden, & the Wind blew with such Violence, that it seemed as if the Boat would be carried off, if not overset instantly; which was what evry one of us expected evry moment. The Sky was at the same time entirely overcast with a black Cloud, even so, that not one of us were able to see the other. We wished to work for the Land, but nobody knew which way that lay, untill a flash of Lightening, (followed by a sharp clap of Thunder) discovered this to us at a great distance. Evry exertion was made to run as much as possible before the Wind, & yet make towards the Shore, which we only could see when it Lightened; but twice we got Broadside between the Swells, which by this time ran amazingly high, & we were on the point of filling. But even after the Boat was righted, she was in such motion that little could be effected with the Oars, & the Men frequently cast from their Seats. One of these now cried out, We *must* Perish, We *must* Perish, & it does not signify to Labour any more! Some of the Passengers had stripped for Swimming, but *where* to, they did not know themselves. However William Hartshorne, a Quaker from Shrewsbery (an old Sailor) with *great* presence of mind, addressed the Crew to take Courage, & do their duty—that he *yet* believed we might make the Land by exerting ourselves; brought them *once more* to Work; he assisting all that lay in his Power. The Lightning served by this time rather to frighten, than do us any good, for tho we observed we were drawing nigh to Land, we did not know where, & were under apprehension of being dashed against the Rocks; some of these Shores being lined with the same. At length we were blown into a little Cove, & aground a few Rods from the Land. By this time the Gust was fairly up, one flash of Lightening, & one Clap of Thunder succeeding the other, & the Rain pouring down upon Us, at an amazing rate. We had to fasten our Boat to the trunk of a large Tree Sunk in the Sand, but the Motion of the Water caused us to look for a more secure place, which was soon found a little higher up where she lay secure & close to Shore. We were now out of all danger of drowning here, but our Sufferings were not at an end. A fresh Gust had sprung up, & the heavy Rain we had to sustain now a second time so *compleatly* soaked Us; that *we* were not only wet to the Skin, but all our Blankets we had to cover Us. The Rains being over, & a very Cold Wind blowing, Fire was much wished for, & indeed wanted, for one of the Company declared: that he absolutely must Perish before Day break, if he must remain in the Condition, he now was in. The Point under which we lay was an open, barren, & swampy ground, full of stinking Pools of Water, which we could not discover, untill we were in. At length however we found a small Spot of dry ground, from whence we went in search of Wood (tho in the Dark) & fortunately hitting on an old Tree, in the hollow of which was a quantity of dry rotten Wood, I struck up a Fire with my Fireworks, which I had carefully put up in my Tobacco Box when the Rain came on. We now could see where we were, & soon found a quantity of Drift Wood; but tho we kept up 2 large Fires, we could scarcely dry ourselves during the Night; & durst not lay down to Sleep, on account of the high Wind & wet ground. Day approaching at length, we took a warm Breakfast of Chocolate; gratefully acknowledging our deliverance; for now we saw what according to appearance our lot would have been, had we not just struck at *this* Place; for but a few Rods both above & below this little Cove, the Rocks lay out from the Shores into the Lake.* The Wind abating in a great measure, & blowing now right down the Lake (the course we had to go) we sat out at 8, soon passing Point Bordet [Baudet], where on the Opposite Side of the Lake the Land Line between the United States & lower Canada commences; & which is also the corner of the division Line between the 2 Canadas. At 10 we put in for refreshment at Mr Makintires, where again on a Point our Boatsmen bowed to a Cross, sat up in remembrance of drowned Persons. At 11 we sat out again passing Point Diable (Devils Point) at the upper end of the Cedar Rapids; & where the current is so swift in *one* place, that (as the saying goes) no Passenger has yet been able to make out the Number of Cedar Trees standing on a Bank, without being told before; & tho their Number is but *8*. The whole 9 Miles to the French Church, we made in 33 Minutes. At 1 we passed the Grand Portage River; a River which runs up into the Country towards Lake Huron, & up which all the goods are taken for the North West Company Trade &^{c} from hence for 16 Miles the St Laurence River is full 3 Miles wide; & here downwards the high Banks on its sides are lined with Farms, small Villages, & a Number of Churches, which give a Beautiful appearance from the River. We next passed Nuns Island (a Beautiful Island belonging to one Class of Nuns at Montreal, & on which 2 remarkable high Mounds are) & passing by several more Islands, arrived at 4 in the Afternoon at La Shiene [Lachine] 9 Miles above Montreal, where we put up at Mr Grants Tavern for this Night. We had now made 451 Miles in 4 Days & 3 Nights. Vizt. from Aug. 30th at 4 in the Morning to 9 oClock next Morning thro Lake Ontario 160 Miles, & from Noon that Day to 4 this Afternoon down the River St Laurence 291 Miles. La Chine on the opposite side of the River is a large Cochnowaga Indian Town, consisting of near an 100 well built Houses & a fine Church. These Indians are all Civilized after the manner of the Canadians, to the Catholick Religion; & I am informed there were 1,500 Souls in this Village, in which the above mentioned Mr Loremer acts as a kind of Governor. The Country on this

---

* 4 of our Company were taken with a Fever this Day in consequence of last Night. —Heckewelder's note.

side (namely the North) is closely Inhabited; & here on this spot are large Store Houses for Goods & Peltry, the Navigation from hence downwards to Montreal being too rapid & dangerous; wherefore all Goods &c. are transported by Land. The French had indeed at the time of the French War between 50 & 1760 done much Labour in cutting a Canal in part from hence across to Montreal; but that Country falling to the Brittish, nothing has been done since.

Sept.r 3.d We sat out in the Morning in 4 Colashes [*calèches*] (a clumsy king of Chair) & with 2 Carts to carry our Baggage, for Montreal. The 4 first Miles were a horrid Road, consisting of Mud holes & Rocks, but the next 5 were dry & level. Our poor Ignorant Drivers had many Compliments to pay at the different *Crosses* put up by the Way. At 10 we arrived here, & after taking Breakfast took a View of the Town, in the course of which I paid a Visit to an acquaintance of mine (M.r Jacob Sheffelin Merch.t formerly Clerk to the Governor of Detroit) The Town of Montreal (as is well known) is situate on the North side of the River S.t Laurence, at the extremity of Navigation for Vessels; & on an Island occasioned by large Rivers which encircle the Town at some distance. The Buildings are principally of stone & adjoining each other. The Streets are Narrow, paved & clean. The Market takes up a Square, & is well served with good & cheap Articles, as for instance: Beaf 6 Coppers a lb. a Couple of Fowls from 10 to 11.d a good fat Turkey 1/6.d & in the Winter 2/6 the Couple &c. The poor People bring their Vegetables, Poultry &c. to Market in small Waggons (each holding about as much as a common Wheelbarrow) & drawn by one or more large Dogs, & in the Winter Season many poor People make a living by drawing Water on light Sleighs from the River in same manner, each Dog being capable of drawing 15 or 16 Gallons at a time. There are 6 or 7 different Churches & Meeting houses, & as many Nunneries in this place; the former are crouded beside the Walls in the inside with Paintings, Pictures & Immages, (namely such as belong to the Catholicks) & the latter consist of different descriptions & classes, some being appropriated for the benifit of Sick Persons of all Denominations; & others to attend the Blind, the Lame, & any Person meeting with an accident, or recieving hurt, where they are taken care of & cured, if curable, gratis; & if dying while under their care, decently burried, or if of any other Persuasion, & burried by the same; yet the charges borne by themselves. We were also told of a Class of Men here called the Recollées [*Récollets*], or *poor Brotherhood,* who are to live poor in this World & Die so; & when Dead are sunk down into a Deep Cell or Pit, dug & Wall'd out for this purpose. These have a Priest of their own, & who must be on a level with them, both while living & Dead. The whole of these are a set of Beggars, & live entirely by that, but dare take no Money, nor Goods; Nourishment & Raiment being all they may recieve. The cause of this Institution (as I was informed upon enquiry) is to give the Rich an Opportunity, of bestowing Charity unto the poor, & thereby merit the Favour of our Saviour who has commanded this—& to give an Example to the World, that Mankind *can* live, *be* happy & contented, *without* Riches; & with food & Raiment *only*. The Inhabitants of this place consist of French, English, Irish, Scotch, some few Germans & People from the United States; principally from N^w England. There sole object is Trade, & when they have made Money enough, they go to their former homes; (for to live in such a remote Country; where the communication with Europe is but a few Months in the Year; & where the Winters are long, & the Snows deep: moreover as it is found, that the Sun shine on the frozen Snow is hurtful to the Eyes, so that many People turn Blind) is not consistent with their wishes. The Merchants however in order to pass time in the Winter: ride either out in their Carryawls, (Sleighs) or are improving Roads, & cutting Canals in the Coffee house; but when the time, (Spring) arrives that this Buisness *really should* be done; Trade opens, & all their Plans & schemes blow off; especially as their is no Money to be made by this Bussiness. Since the last Fire in Montreal which destroyed so much of the Town; they have adopted the method of covering their Houses with sheet Tin instead of Shingles, & all Steeples on Churches throughout the Country, are done in like manner. The Town which consists of near 1,000 Houses is Fortified by a strong Stone Wall, about 15 feet high, round the same; & tho to all appearance one should imagine it were not possible that Vessels could come up a River, which is generally Rapid, & appears here to be very Shallow; yet there is a safe Channel for Merchantmen to come up & lay close under the Town, & between this & an Island; but it requires a good Breeze to bring up a Vessel to this place. There arrive some Seasons from 20 to 30 Vessels from England & Ireland at this place, but this Year there were but few & these a Month later than usual. At the back of the City is a very high Hill or Mountain, yet no more than about 2 Miles in length, from whence there is a most beautiful Prospect over the Country, & both up & down the River St Laurence, even for half way to Quebec, tho the distance be 160 Miles; but our hurry in getting along speedily, deprived me of many Pleasures, among which was this.

At Evening we crossed the River, here 2 Miles wide, & lodged at the Ferry house, from whence we had a very Beautiful Prospect of the whole City, this lying on the Side of the Hill fronting the River & just opposite Us. We had also in full view 4 different Parrish Churches above & below the City, & on both sides of the River, among which that of the Town of La prairie [La Prairie] 9 Miles above gave the best appearance. Colashes for us to ride in, & Carts to carry our Baggage being procured by Order of the Commanding Officer of this Post, we sat out

Septr 4th at 6 in the Morning for St Johns at the upper end of the River Sorell. After passing Longare [Longueuil] (a Parish Village & Church) we had a causeway thro a wet sunken Country for 10 Miles, yet Inhabited all the Way; and Crosses put up at certain distances, on some of which were such Implements as mentioned in Scripture that had been made Use of at the

Crucifying of our Saviour; all which was particularly taken notice of (as above mentioned) by our Canadian drivers. From here we had a tolerable good Road 4 Miles to Chamblee [Chambly], a remarkable strong French Fort on Sorrell River, & the fine Farms & small Villages on this River delighted Us much. Our course from hence was 13 Miles up the River on an excellent Turnpike Road to S:t Johns. At S:t Johns where there is besides the Fortification a considerable Village we Dined, & afterwards embarked in a small Vessel for Skeensborough [Skenesborough, now Whitehall]. We had now to pass thro Lake Champlain 160 Miles in length, & dangerous on account of Rocks, Shoals, & its being crouded up in some places between the Mountains. The Wind being ahead, we made but 4 Miles this Afternoon, when we put up at dirty Widdow Chesters, where I chose the hay loft for my Bed.

Sept:r 5th still the same Wind we made but 8 Miles in the course of the Day, & put up at Watsons, a tolerable house.

Sept:r 6 We sat out with a favourable gentle Wind, passing the Illinore [Isle aux Noix] at 7, (an Island on which extensive Fortifications & a Number of Brittish Troops are stationed; & where all Boats & Vessels passing & repassing must come to for examination, the same as is done at S:t Johns). At 12 oC. we crossed the Line between Canada & the United States; & had now the Settlements in NYork State on our right, & those of Vermont State on our left, the Lake being here no more than 1½ Miles wide. 6 Miles higher up, & within the American Lines, we had to come to, to the Brittish Ship of War Maria, for Examination; which lay at Anchor in the Channel of this Lake, off Point a Fair [Pointe au Fer]. From here the Lake begins to widen, & soon measures 16 Miles across. The Wind rising high but fair, we sailed briskly, but had to put in at the Custom House of the United States for Examination. Here we left the Capt:n of the Boat, who had sat out Sick on the Fev. & Ago [fever and ague], & would go no further. His Boatswain, a Boy of about 14 Years of Age was to be our Pilot, & *we* to steer the Boat, which we easily could do, having some good Watermen with Us. Our intention also was to put into a Creek, which was a good Harbour, but dark coming on, & the Boy mistaking the place, we got aground, the Wind blowing very high. It was very fortunate for us, that the Bottom was Sand & not Stony or Rocky, for tho it was a full half-hour before we got the Boat off, & out where we could Anchor her, in which time She was continually thumping on the ground, she recieved no damage. Here we had to pass a dark cold Night very uncomfortable, tho near the Shore on which we could see the lights in the Houses. But all our calls for help, & that we were in distress availed nothing, untill Morning when the Wind ceased blowing so hard; then they came to apologize for not coming out. They assisted us however in wrighting our Sails & rigging, & directed Us how to Steer to Bason [Basin] Harbour in Vermont, 12 Miles distance, & which we reached by 7. After taking a warm Breakfast, (which was the first warm bit these 2 Days) we sat out again, the Wind encreasing in our favour; but now our Pilot (the Boy) was taken Sick on the Fev. & Agoe & he was the only one on Board who knew the Channel. However, we got better along than we expected, for at 11 oClock we passed Crown Point, a strong Fortification formerly, built by the French, with a Ditch of a Mile in Circumference cut round the same thro the Rocks. We next passed some Brittish built Fortifications, & at 1 passed Putnams Point; at 6 Ticonderoga, Mount Independant, & Rattle Snake hill, where General Abercrombie was defeated by the French & Indians in 1759. Here 2 Rocky Points run from both Shores towards each other; on these were the above Fortifications & a Chevaux de Frize sunk across the River. Just above Ticonderoga Point, Lake George emptieth itself into this Lake thro which General Burgoyne took his Artilery, Baggage &c across to the Hudson River. We proceeded this Evening yet 10 Miles up the Lake or River, where it is very Narrow, & cram'd up between the Mountains, & took lodging at Mr Noles in Vermont, & where our Captn overtook us in the Night in a Boat.

Septr 8th there being no Wind we had to row our Boat 8 Miles to Skeensburought, passing by the way that place, where Genl Putnam was way laid & cut off by the French Indians, in the French War. Just above this the Line between the 2 States NYork & Vermont strike the River, so that now we passed the last mile to Skeensborough, where arrived at 12, entirely in the State of NYork. Here we rested this Day, only taking a View of the Iron Works, & a canal cut thro the Rocks accross the Falls, &

Septr 9th sat out in the Stage for Albany, 72 Miles from here. The first 11 Miles to Fort Ann were very bad indeed, but from thence to Kingsburough [Kingsbury] good. Here I saw in the Burying Ground White Marbel of the first Quality, which is in great abundance 16 Miles from here in Vermont. We next passed thro a small Village, named Sandy hill, where we were on the North River [Hudson]. at Fort Edward, 7 Miles further, we viewed the Falls, where a Canal is also cutting, & after passing 11 Miles farther to Mr Neals, took lodging. Here I met with Col! Connoly from Canada, who was come for the benefit of the Saratoga Springs

Septr 10th we continued our Route down the North River, passing by Fort Miller; the Ground where Gen! Burgoyne had his Encampment, & a Number of Entrenchments & Fortifications on nob's of hills, occupied at that time, both by Gen! Burgoynes Army & the Americans, untill we came to Saratoga & Still Water where on Gen! Schylers Seat, we passed the Meadow where Gen! Burgoyne's Army laid down their Arms; exactly 30 Miles above Albany, & took Breakfast at Ensigns Inn. We next passed a Gentlemans Seat, on which were excellent Buildings, but all shut up & not occupied this 3 Years, on account of its being haunted (as we were told) for (tis said) a Negro Wench without a head, & chained by her Leg to a Block, makes her appearance at Night. We were further told that 100 Dollars had been offered by the owner to any Person that would stay 2 Nights in the House, but altho attempts have been made, they have failed. (Note *Perhaps a guilty Con-*

science haunts the mind.) 6 Miles farther at Stillwater Meeting House, we took a View of the Locks, now nearly compleated here, for from hence in order to avoid a 13 Miles Rapid, a Canal is cutting that distance & indeed nearly finished. We next passed Scatticok River, tho on the opposite Side, & at half Moon, a little Town; & the end of the Canal, we crossed the North River a second time, & proceeding one mile down the River on the East Side, arrived & took Dinner at the New City or Lansingburgh, where Industry is observed at first View, & in every direction. We then continued our Route 3 Miles further down to the City Troy, (the Extent of Tide Water), where the Banks were lined with Lumber ready for Shipping to NYork. here we cros'd the North River the third time, & saw the last branch of Mohock emptying in this River; which River dividing in 4 Branches below the Cahoos [Cohoes] or Falls, puts in between this & half Moon. These last 6 Miles to Albany were close on the Bank of the River, & thro excellent Low Land, principally belonging to the Patroon (Lord of the Manor) Mr Ranselær. We had now passed near 60 Miles on the banks of this River & thro a Number of fine Farms; yet scarcely observing any Oarchards, which caused me to enquire by the way into the Reason of this. The Tenants informed me: that as it was principally Manor Land, & Leased at a high rate; they could not attend to these matters, but must make as much as they could out of the Land while they were on; but conversing at Albany with a Gentleman concerned, he would not admit of this excuse, but gave this as the reason: that Oarchards had been neglected from the first Settlement of this Country; & the general rule of the Farmers here was: to do as their Fathers had done, & no otherwise. Much Land is sold up this River where the quit-rent is yearly one Shilling per Acre, for ever.

At Albany, where we remained untill the 12th I had the Satisfaction to be an Eye Witness, of the consolation & Blessing conferred on a Dying Young Gentleman (19 Years of Age) (Brother to one of the Misses (Bleecher) who had recieved her Education at the boarding School in Bethlehem) by means of religious Instruction usually imparted in the Brethren Church— The Young man assuring me: that nothing now could induce him to wish to remain longer in this transitory World, having found Grace, & being fully assured that after departing this Life, he should be with his Redeemer, &^{c}.

Septr 12th at 10 in the forenoon, we embarked on Board the Sloop Fly of Albany, Captn Marselles for NYork. The Wind blowing down the River & fresh, we were in hopes of being at N York next Day, but our Vessel being to heavy laden with Lumber & Peas, we ran aground on the Overslaw, (Bar) 2 Miles below the City, where being disappointed in getting off with the next Tide, we had to remain here 24 Hours, & then were obliged to unload part of the Lumber, & Raft it down the River 5 Miles which alltogether taking up so much time, we lost the Wind, & of course must expect a long

Passage, for now we could make no way, except at the return of the Tide, & therefore during the intervals lay at Anchor.

Sept.br 14th we anchored at Mr Reads Wharf at Red hook, where I went on Shore & passed the Afternoon agreeable with this family, during which time several of the Livingston family, & relations of Mrs Reads, came on a Visit, where much was related in favor of Beth.m & the boarding School at that place.

Sunday 15th we anchored at Night at Pogepsie; & on the 16th opposite West Point.

Sept.r 17th a favourable Breeze springing up in the morning we sailed briskly, & arrived at NYork by 1 oClock in the Afternoon, where being unwell of the Influenza, which all the Passengers had caught during this passage, I resolved to stay some Days. Here I took leave of my fellow Travellers, & in particular of my good friend Gen.l Lincoln, with whoom I had Travelled this Journey upwards of 2,200 Miles. Those 4 who had fell Sick in consequence of that dreadful Night above mentioned on Lake St Francois, were not yet recovered, & the Comisary being one of them, was so ill that we had to leave him behind at Skeensborough. William Savory, a Quaker Preacher from Philadelphia, thought on our arrival at this place, he felt himself some thing better.

After taking leave on the 23d of Br & Sister Birkbys with whoom I lodged, Br Tenbrook & family & other friends I sat out for Beth.m where I arrived on the 25th —

As the different Nations or Tribes of Indians on this Continent are not universally known: I shall conclude with giving an account of the same, & their Numbers; as published in the last Years Calender of Quebec.

The Names of all the different Indian Nations in North America (hitherto discovered) the situation of their Countries— With the Number of their fighting Men.

The Choctaw or Flatheads ⎤ on the Mobile, ...	4,500
The Natches, ... ⎬ and	150
The Chickesaws, ... ⎦ Missisippi	750
The Cherokees, South Carolina	2,500
The Catawbas, between North & S. Carolina	150
The Piantias, a wandering Tribe on both sides the Missisippi .	800
The Kasgreasquias, or Illinois in general on the Illinois River, & between the Ouabache & the Missisippi	600
The Piankishaws, . ⎤	250
The Ouachtenons, ⎬ on the Oubache (Wabash)	400
The Kikapous, . ⎦	300
The Shawnese on Sciota	500

The Dellawares on the West of Ohio	300
The Miamis, on the Miamis River falling into Lake Erie & the Miamis	350
The upper Creeks, back of Georgia ⎫ The middle Creeks, behind West Florida ⎬ The Lower Creeks in East Florida ⎭	4,000
The Caouitas, on the East of the River Alibamous	700
The Alibamous, West of the Alibamous	600
The Akansawas, on the Akansaw River, falling into the Missippi on the West Side	2,000
The Anjoues, North of the Missouri	1,000
The Padelonians, West of the Missisippi	500
The White Panis ⎫ South of the	2,000
The Freckled, or Prickled Panis ⎭ Missisippi	2,000
The Canses, ⎫	1,600
The Osayes ⎬ South of the Missouri	600
The Grand Eaux ⎭	1,000
The Missouri, upon the River Missouri	3,000
The Sioux of the Woods ⎫ towards the heads	1,800
The Sioux of the Meadows ⎭ of the Missisippi	2,500
The Blanks, Barbus or White Indians with Beards	1,500
The Assiniboils ⎫ far North near the	1,500
The Christaneaux ⎭ Lakes of the same	3,000
The Ouisconsins, on a River of that Name that falls into the Missisippi, on the East Side	550
The Mascoutens ⎫ South of	500
The Sakis ⎬ Puans	400
The Mechecouakis ⎭ Bay	250
Folle Avoine, or the Wild-Oat Indians ⎫	350
The Puans . . . near Puans Bay ⎭	700
The Potawatamis, near St Joseph & Detroit	350
The Messesagues, or River Indians, being wandering Tribes on the Lakes Huron & Superior	2,000
Ottawhas, ⎫ near Lake Superior	900
The Chipewas, ⎭ & Michigan	5,000
The Wiandots, near Lake Erie	300
The Six Nations, or as the French call them Iroquois, on the Frontiers of New York &.^{c}	1,500
The Round headed Indians, near the head of the Ottahwa River (Canada)	2,500
The Algonkins, near the above	300
The Nepissins, near the above also	400

To Detroit: 1793

The Chalas . .	⎫ Sᵗ Laurence Indians	130
The Amelistes .	⎪ on the back	550
The Mickmacks	⎬ of	700
The Abenaquis .	⎭ Nova Scotia &ᶜ	350
The Conawaybrunas, near the Falls of Sᵗ Lewis		200
	Total amount	58,780

This being the whole Number of Men fit for bearing Arms, from hence we may be enabled to form some Idea of the Number of all the Indian Inhabitants, Men, Women & Children, on the Continent of North America; which calculation however, we are ready to confess; can be but a Vague Conjecture.

There being 58,780 Warriors, it may be computed that about one third of the same Number more are old Men, unfit for bearing Arms, which makes the Number of Males come to Maturity, amount to 78,373; & multiplied by Six will produce 470,238; which we consider as the whole Number of Souls Vizt. Men, Women & Children of all the Indian Nations that are come in any degree within our knowledge, throughout the Continent of North America.

NB. There were many Milions of the Natives, when first discovered by the Whites; a rapid depopulation!

The Numbers on this side the Missisippi, are considerable from the Gulph of Mexico, to the Lakes of Canada inclusive. it is computed there may be about 35,000 Warriors— Beyond the Missisippi, they are much more Numerous, are very open, and hospitable. ———

NB The above enumeration, or calculation was made between the Years 1770 & 1780 ———

XXXI

Gnadenhütten Revisited: 1797

BOTH AMERICAN AND BRITISH authorities tried to compensate the Moravians for the injuries they had suffered during the Revolutionary War. In 1785 Congress reserved for them the sites of their three towns on the Tuscarawas (as this branch of the Muskingum was now called), with as much of the adjoining land as the Surveyor General might think proper. In 1791 the legislature of Pennsylvania made them a grant of new tracts on French and Conneaut Creeks. In 1792 the British granted the Moravians a tract of land north of Lake Erie on the Thames River in Upper Canada.

Jacob Eyerly managed, at some risk, to survey the French and Conneaut Creek lands in 1794; but it was not until three years later that the Moravians succeeded in surveying the lands on the Tuscarawas.

In 1788, as we have already seen, John Heckewelder called on Thomas Hutchins, Surveyor General, at Pittsburgh, and had traveled with that gentleman down the Ohio to attend a projected treaty with the Indians, who, it was hoped, would approve the surveying of these lands for the Christian Indians. As it turned out, the Indians let it be known that they would resist the survey of lands granted by Congress until such time as they recognized that Congress had the right to grant them.

It was not until the Treaty of Greenville in 1795, following Anthony Wayne's victory of the preceding year at Fallen Timbers on the Maumee, that ownership of the territory concerned passed to the United States.

Two years later, John Heckewelder was sent to the Muskingum (Tuskarawas) to supervise the surveying of the Moravian lands there. His account of this journey, entitled, "Report on the Muskingum Business with Notes, etc.," is scarcely a travel journal. For a description of the familiar route through Shippensburg, Strasburg, Fannettsburg, Fort Littleton, Raystown (Bedford), Fort Ligonier, and Greensburg to Pittsburgh, we have the journal of William Henry * who accompanied him. But since Heckewelder's journal contains, nevertheless, some new material that supplements his earlier narratives of the Indian mission, it is summarized here and some extracts from it are given.

Heckewelder in company with William Henry, John Rothrock, Christian Clewell, and a Mr. Kamp of Graceham in Maryland who had joined them in Pittsburgh, reached Gnadenhütten on the Muskingum, May 11, 1797. Before anything could be done, they had to find the Surveyor General, who was then at Marietta. John Heckewelder, accordingly, set out once more for the site of Fort Harmar at the mouth of the Muskingum. Realizing how important it was that the Indians of the neighborhood should have their minds at rest about the purpose of the survey and know that it was being made for their good friends, the Moravians, he went first to White Eyes Town, where he found Captain Joseph White Eyes (son of the chief who had died in 1778) and "Peemaholand." He requested them to spread the word, and invited White Eyes to visit the Moravians at Gnadenhütten.

The further journey, which he made by way of the Salt Spring, was not without its difficulties, chief among which was the scarcity of provisions. There were days when he had nothing to eat. There was game in the forest, but he and his companion got none of it, and the wild turkey eggs which might have helped them were found to have already been hatched. At Marietta there was a tedious wait of two weeks, but at last on the 2nd of June two heavily laden canoes set out up the river. The company consisted of Heckewelder, General Rufus Putnam (recently appointed Surveyor General of the United States), his son William Rufus Putnam as "the real surveyor," two chain bearers, two axeman, a cook, a hunter, and a young tenderfoot surveyor from Philadelphia who wanted to supplement his theoretical training with a little practical experience. They camped at Salem on the 8th. Next day they

---
* *Pennsylvania Magazine of History and Biography,* Vol. X (1886), pp. 125-157

went on to Gnadenhütten and commenced the surveying of this tract, which they completed on the 17th. Another week was spent surveying the Salem tract, and by June 30 they had also surveyed the Schönbrunn tract. Then, as Heckewelder writes, "the General requested me to go with him to Tuscorawas, to show him the Foarding Place above Fort Lawrence (the north-east corner from which the Territorial Line between the Indians and the United States' land to Lorimer's Store on the Miami was to be run)."

They returned to Gnadenhütten on July 3, and from there set out by water for Marietta, which they reached on the evening of July 8.

During my journeys by land & water and during my stay in Marietta, I have seen and talked with many Indians, some of whom I knew while others were strangers to me, and they all seemed peacefully disposed; indeed, some of them have moved back from the Miami to the Wahlhanding, where they have built cabins for themselves and planted Indian corn, as White Eyes & Peemaholand (his father-in-law) have done, they having settled ten miles below Salem, built good houses, cleared land, and ploughed and cultivated it on shares with a white man. Tetepachkschi, the present Delaware chief, also plans to remove in the spring to Kinhanschican (an old Delaware town at the head of the Scioto not far from Wahlhanding).

Different Indians asked me why the Christian Indians did not come back, now that there is peace? I answered them: You have driven them away with your war! And what should they do in your neighborhood; you don't want to become Christians. Some said: If the Christian Indians lived on this side of the Lake, they would like to try and see if they could not be Christians, too, but they never wanted to go to the Chippewa country. I believe that if a part of the Indian congregation accompanied by a teacher settled on this side of the Lake, many would join them. The warlike part of the Delawares have moved to the Wabach, whence their chiefs send message after message bidding those who have stayed behind to follow them. I was often told by these latter: Our chiefs have run away, consequently they can no longer give orders to us; we want to stay here, hunt diligently, and sell our peltries to the Americans.

The 3 towns, Gnadenhütten, Salem and Schönbrunn are now surveyed; each tract consists of 4000 acres of land. The river, which runs through the tracts, has been deducted.

Gnadenhütten consists of good, level land, enough for 18 or 20 farms, each of them more than 100 acres. The tract includes also quite a bit of hilly land, but from what Surveyor Putnam says, not an acre too much. I tried to have included a splendid Bottom, some 100 acres in extent, which lies at the lower end on the east side; but it could not be done, and we got only a corner of it. And on the upper end I should have liked to see our land run up to the Foarding Place, but we did not get within half a mile of it. The old townsite is pretty much overgrown with schumeck [sumac], wild plums, honey locust, and hazel bushes; and the rest of the woodland, which used to be clear of underbrush, is thickly grown up with briars and shrubs. The fields in the bottoms can be brought back into condition without too much labor.

Salem contains a lot of good, level building land. It has a good deal, too, of hilly land, but between the hills some good plantations can be laid out. A long village could be very nicely laid out here, and one would not have to go more than 15 or 20 feet deep for water. The river here is much wider than at the other two towns, and flows by a beautiful plain, where, however, all is so densely overgrown with hedges and thorns that one hates to go into it. . . .

With the Schöenbrunn Tract I am not at all satisfied. The level land on the east side is cut up too much, and on the west side a good three quarters of it is hills. If we could have excluded New Schönbrunn [across the river] (at least the upper field), we could have got in more of the good land down stream, and avoided the hills; but (according to the Ordinance) all improvements had to be included in the tracts. Here I approached the Surveyor General to see if a stop could not be made and a new line started. But he replied: No! I have already exceeded my instructions, and expect to be reprimanded for it.

Old and New Schönbrunn have gone back to the wilderness: but the fields in the bottoms can be restored with a little labor.

. . . There are no good and reliable millstreams on our lands. There are, however, "runs" like that at Christiansbrunn but larger which could be used for sawmills and probably also for grinding six months in the year. The New Englanders on the Ohio and Muskingum build a kind of mills on the river, which they call Floating-Mills; the whole work costs little, and they can grind the whole year through.

. . . There are sugar trees, more in some places than in others.

The great consumption of sugar with the increase of settlements has made the people in the west much concerned about the preservation of this tree. Landlords bind the tenants not to cut down any sugar trees. On the Ohio it is quite common to see sugar-tree lands fenced off. In Washington County, large stretches of country are kept out of cultivation simply to protect the sugar trees and yet they yield a profit: the trees are rented at 6^d apiece to neighbors & townsmen. The renter binds himself under penalties not to drill more than 2 holes a year in a tree, and he must not touch the tree with an axe.

Nota: There are sometimes as many as 100 trees on *one* acre, but 50 is usual.

There certainly is no lack of good timber of many kinds. At the present time there are plenty of bears, wolves, deer, foxes, turkeys, hares, and snakes on our lands on the Muskingum. Partridges and mocking birds are frequently heard.

When I went to Marietta I forgot to take along the History of the Mission * which the President of the Society had sent to the General. So it was not presented to him until my return to Gnadenhütten. He thanked me for the gift, and said, "I will tackle it at once and read it through." He could be seen reading every day, from morning till night, until he had finished it. What impressed him particularly was that he was reading it in the very country and indeed on the very spot where an Indian congregation had lived and where the captivity had taken place. As soon as we arrived here he had had me show him the desolate place, and when he saw it many a tear rolled down his cheek.

At Gnadenhütten, I dug by the upright stones at the corners where the meeting house had been, and also at the front corners of Daniel's house, where the rest of the Brethren and Sisters had been burned. I have almost cleared the burial place of brush and put posts on all 4 corners. [Marginal note: I also marked Beaver's grave.] †—Heckewelder's "Report on the Muskingum Business, with Notes, etc." Translated from the German.

---

* George Henry Loskiel, *History of the Mission of the United Brethren Among the Indians in North America*. Translated from the German by Christian Ignatius Latrobe (London, 1794).

† Captain Beaver had died and been buried at Gnadenhütten.

XXXII

To Fairfield (Moraviantown) in Upper Canada: 1798

THE THREE TRACTS on the Muskingum, amounting to twelve thousand acres, which Heckewelder had seen surveyed in 1797, were patented by the United States Government to the Moravians in trust for their Indian Brethren on February 24, 1798.* No time was lost in taking possession of these recovered lands. On April 20 John Heckewelder left Bethlehem for the purpose of escorting members of the so-called "Wandering Congregation" from the new mission town of Fairfield on the Thames River in Upper Canada to their old home on the Muskingum.

He was accompanied by an enthusiastic young missionary, Benjamin Mortimer, who was going north to serve as Zeisberger's assistant at Fairfield. Heckewelder kept no diary of this trip, but Mortimer kept an excellent one. Since Heckewelder was the leader of the expedition, chose the route, showed Mortimer what was worth seeing, and caused a stream of Heckewelder reminiscences to punctuate the younger man's writing, it is fitting that Mortimer's English-language journal be included in this collection.

---

* Leslie R. Gray, "From Fairfield to Schönbrun—1798": *Ontario History*, 1957, Vol. XLIX, No. 2.

*Diary of the brethren John Heckewelder and Benjamin Mortimer, on their journey from Bethlehem in Pennsylvania to Fairfield in Upper Canada, from the 30th April to the 22^{d} May 1798.**

Having been recommended, in the most affectionate manner, by Br. Klingsohr, in the evening meeting on Sunday the 29th April, to the remembrance of the brethren and sisters in Bethlehem, in their prayers before our Saviour; and having taken special leave of many friends, particularly of the dear brethren of the Helpers Conference, and the other Directors of the Society for propagating the gospel among the heathen; we set off on our journey on the 30th in the afternoon. We felt very sensibly that the spirit of the congregation attended us, which, with the sense we had of our Saviour's nearness, were inexpressibly comfortable to us. A considerable number of Bethlehem Brethren went with us for a few miles on the way. In the evening we stopped at Nazareth, to receive the blessing of the brethren and sisters there, which we were assured of, through Br. Reichel, in the evening meeting.

To bid a last adieu to dear friends is always a trying stroke to human nature; but when in these friends we recognize fellow participants of the same grace in our Saviour, though the tie is on that account so much the stronger, yet there is something in the nature of the wound, which makes it the more easily heal itself. We cannot be separated, because we are united in spirit, in Jesus our common Saviour; we are members of the same body, of which he is the head; and where he is, there we know we shall be with him for ever. In none of the vicissitudes of life is the comfort of these truths perhaps more powerfully realized, than when we are conscious, that our bodily separation is a voluntary act of obedience on our part, to the ever blessed will of our Saviour, with an humble but sincere view to the promotion of his cause in the world. Then "his ways" always become "ways of pleasantness, & his paths, paths of peace."

This consolation was experienced in particular by Brother Mortimer, at his farewell with the brethren and boys living in the pedagogium at Nazareth, who with the brethren Reichel and Zeisberger, and many other kind friends, accompanied us the next morning as far as Michler's tavern, 4 miles from Nazareth. It was affecting to him to take leave of the dear brethren, with whom he had for years very agreeably drawn in the same yoke, and of those beloved pupils who had been the objects of their joint care. For a few moments he could not but give way to his feelings. But the thoughts of our common bond of union in Christ, and of our destination and privilege, through grace, to spend our lives in his service, outweighed and banished every other reflection, and produced the most pleasing sensations, in the prospect of the joys of eternity!

---

* This journal, with full annotations by Leslie R. Gray, has been published in *Ontario History*, Vol. XLVI (1954).

To Fairfield: 1798

In Schöneck we took leave of Br. & Sr. Molther, and other brethren and sisters of that congregation.

The brethren Reichel, Höber, Schmick, Kremser & Steuben of Nazareth, Levering & Kreiter of Bethlehem, and Christ.ⁿ Heckewelder of Emmaus, accompanied us 7½ miles beyond Nazareth to Heller's tavern [Windgap], where we breakfasted; after which we bid farewell to all this dear company, except the brethren Höber, Schmick & Christ.ⁿ Heckewelder, who very kindly proposed to attend us still further on our journey. We are much obliged to B.^r Reichel, and all the above mentioned brethren, for the friendly escort they afforded us thus far on our way into the wilderness. It was a token of their love to the Indian congregation, & to us, which will remain unforgotten by us.

At Sichel's tavern [McIlhaney] we joined company with Mr Jacob Schäfer of Sacona [Saucon, Pa.], who had been last year to Niagara, and could, thus far at least, be a guide to us. We refreshed ourselves at Springgarden, the estate of B.^r Christ.ⁿ Heckewelder, of whom we took leave at the foot of the Broad mountain, formerly called Wolf's mountain, and arrived at ½ past 8 o'clock at Sax's tavern [Stoddartsville], 35 miles from Nazareth. It lies in the midst of a considerable pine swamp, near a place which was rendered remarkable to the brethren Gregor & Lorez, on their way [in 1771] to the Indian congregation at Friedenshütten, on account of the immense number of young pigeons they saw there.

As we proceeded the next morning, B.^r Heckewelder shewed us the places where the Indian brethren and sisters, and the missionaries, used formerly to encamp on their journies to and from Friedenshütten, and the other congregation places on the Susquehanna. One of these encamping grounds was opposite to Sichel's tavern, near the Lehigh falls. From the Wioming hills we had a pleasing view of the Susquehanna hills & river, and could not but observe how much more forward vegetation was here, than we had left it two days before on the banks of the Lehigh at Bethlehem.

We arrived at Wilkesbarre, at 5 o'clock in the evening. It has a well-chosen situation, contains about 70 houses, and is the capital of the county of Lucerne. This town is built on the very spot where Count Zinzendorf encamped in the year 1742, on a visit to the Shawanoes, and where he and his company were in the greatest danger of being murdered by them. Their escape was a very remarkable instance of the interposition of God, for the deliverance of his servants in time of danger. Neither the Count nor any of his company suspected any mischief, and there was no interpreter present, who could be the means of finding out the horrid plot that had been laid against them, which the savages were on the eve of putting into execution; when Conrad Weisser, who had been absent on business in another part of the country, and was become at once so uneasy, that he hastened with all speed to Wioming, himself not knowing for what reason, on his arrival immediately discovered & disconcerted it.*

Wilkesbarre, and all the country up the Susquehanna, is at present settled chiefly by New-Englanders. Their claim to the land is disputed by the State of Pennsylvania, which prevents their improving it, as they otherwise would do. There are no churches, and but few schools; the children living out of the town are ragged and dirty; we found however in every instance that they could give a becoming answer to every question that was put to them. We saw here no such large stone barns, or neatly fenced gardens, as grace the premises of the German settlers in Pennsylvania.

At the recommendation of B^r Horsfield of Bethlehem, we put up at Dr Covell's tavern, where we were well entertained. We visited sundry gentlemen in the town, who seemed desirous to shew us any civility that lay in their power. As Wilkesbarre is only 69 miles from Bethlehem, many of the inhabitants have some knowledge of the Brethren, and speak of them with respect. They remember with pleasure a sermon which B^r Reichel preached in the court-house there about 8 years ago, when Mr Timothy Pickering, the present Secretary of State, took the lead among the singers.

The 3^d early in the morning we took leave of our dear brethren Höber and Schmick, in whose company we had been very happy, and they set off on their return to Nazareth. Parting seemed hard on both sides.

Our brethren, in their journies up the Susquehanna, used formerly to travel altogether on the E. side of it. Now there is a ferry here, and a road on the W. side, which is much shorter than the old road. We crossed the river therefore in a flat. For the first 9 miles the road was good, the country thickly settled, and the lands of the best quality. As a proof of the forwardness of vegetation in this district, it may not be amiss to observe, that the leaves of the lime, maple, and beech trees were then fully out. We breakfasted at the extremity of the settlement, at the house of a Mr Scovell [West Pittston], 9 miles from Wilkesbarre. The country now assumed a new & less pleasing appearance. We exchanged the fine, thickly settled bottoms of Wioming, for barren uninhabited hills. Our open, level road, which was equal to any that we had seen in other parts of Pennsylvania, dwindled into a mere horse-path, sometimes winding along the edges of precipices, then ascending or descending steep hills, never straight, and but in a few places passable for carriages. The soil however was such, that it would in most places, reward the industry of the laborer, and produce him good wheat. But as long as there are rich lands to be procured in other parts of the country, at low prices, the Susquehanna hills will never be full of inhabitants. The bottoms only, and the borders of the creeks, are well peopled. We lodged tonight at the house of a farmer of the name of Harding.

---

* Conrad Weiser's account of this incident is less dramatic. See Wallace, *Conrad Weiser: Friend of Colonist and Mohawk* (Philadelphia, 1945), pp. 140 ff.

To Fairfield: 1798

The 4 th we crossed the Susquehanna at Hunt's ferry [Falls, Pa.]. Here is a grist-mill, turned by a very small run of water, conveyed at least 60 feet in wooden gutters [from Buttermilk Falls] to the mill. Such contrivances do credit to the ingenuity of the New Englanders. Their ferries also are safe, as their flats are constructed in the best manner, and carefully managed. We breakfasted at Mr. Hunt's house. The people were very civil to us, but we cannot praise them for their industry or cleanliness. Though Mr. Hunt is a miller, yet there was no bread in the house; and we did not see that preparation was made to bake any. Very fortunately Br. Heckewelder examined the teapot before our tea was put into it, or its flavor would have been much injured, for want of washing out the old leaves &c. There is a custom prevailing in many families in the country, which our palates had in former places reminded us of: When it is proposed to bake bread, the dough is prepared early in the morning, and put in the bed to rise, as soon as the children are taken out of it.

After breakfast we proceeded along the E. side of the Susquehanna. Br. Heckewelder soon recollected the road, and the general appearance of the country, which was familiar to him from his frequent visits in Friedenshütten and Tschechschequannink [Sheshequin], when the Indian congregation resided there. He shewed us a very cold spring, where he drank freely in the year 1769, when much heated, which had nearly cost him his life. By the blessing of God on the means made use of by Sr. Schmick, he was perfectly cured. To day we crossed the Meshopping creek, near the place where Br. Ettwein once experienced a remarkable preservation. He had been directed to cross the creek at a fording-place near its mouth, where the banks on both sides were low, & where the passage was said to be perfectly safe. The creek was at that time unusually high, which he had not been apprized of. Had he plunged into it, the rapid stream would have hurried him down into the Susquehanna, where his life would have been in the most imminent danger. At the moment when he came to the bank of the creek, two Indian brethren, who had run 30 miles that day without intermission, themselves not knowing why, called out to him, and warned him of his danger. Thus our dear Saviour watches over, and preserves his servants! Though their deliverance may not be as miraculous as that of Daniel in the den of lions, or of Jonah in the belly of the whale, yet it is as signal. The hand of God was as wonderfully displayed in the leading of Joseph, where events, though extraordinary, seemed naturally to follow upon each other, as in all the more splendid miracles performed by the hand of Moses.

The learned feel a kind of extacy when they think themselves on classic ground; we were now happy to find ourselves on missionary ground; on ground which had been frequently trodden by a Spangenberg, a Cammerhof and a Zeisberger on their way to and from Onondago, and which many other of our brethren and sisters, now resting from their labors, had gone over before us. May we, and all our brethren who cross these hills, be animated by the same zeal for the enlargement of our Saviour's kingdom, and the same devotedness to his service, which glowed in the bosoms of our forefathers! They traversed this country when still a perfect wilderness; now it affords the necessary comforts of life. There are houses of entertainment to be met with all the way up the Susquehanna.

To day we passed a rock, under which there is a spacious room, where our brethren who travelled this way used formerly to pass the nights. As a place of shelter, it is as serviceable as a house. B^r Heckewelder shewed us a place on the W. side of the river, where 30 years ago, after riding three days without seeing any human being, he had the pleasure to espy a German, who on seeing him, with an elevated voice sung the hymn: "To God on high all glory be &c." in his native language. Had our voices been musical, we would like him, have made the woods ring with the same song of praise!

We lodged on the Wialusing land, at the house of a Mr Brown. We had intended to pass the night on the very spot where Friedenshütten formerly stood, but were prevented by a thunder storm. The land where the settlement was, is at present occupied by two farmers of the name of Pauling and Stevens. It is a fine, open place. The name Friedenshütten is quite out of use. The whole settlement bears the Indian name of Wialusing.

Thence we proceeded 6 miles to breakfast, to a tavern [at Standing Stone] kept by [Anthony] Le Fevre, a frenchman. Before arriving at it, we had to descend a very steep hill, where certainly no kind of carriage could travel. The late B^r Rothe, in one of his diaries, declared himself obliged to go down it on his knees. From the summit of this eminence there is a fine prospect of the town of Asylum [Azilum], or, as it is called in this neighborhood, Frenchtown, because inhabited alone by French people. It is situated on a pleasant spot, but the soil, it is said, is not of the best quality. The houses, about 50 in number, were chiefly built by men of property, who were attached to the royal cause, & fled from France on account of the revolution. Many of the first settlers have quitted the place again, on account of the want of company & amusements, and their houses stand empty. The present inhabitants are principally traders, who by their industry and obliging behaviour have engrossed a considerable traffic up and down the river. It is not true that the Duke de Noallies [General Louis de Noailles], late ambassador of France to the court of Vienna, had any concern in this settlement. The person who gave himself out for the Duke, was an impostor. The town is built on the W. side of the river. We remained on the E. side, and so had only a distant view of it. LeFevre's tavern is a small log hut, without any kind of plaster. It is not however totally destitute of French finery. Opposite to the door is a large pier looking-glass, with a gilded frame, around which hang many small portraits of distinguished characters in France, who were famous at the commencement of the revolution. Not far from the looking-glass hangs also a fiddle.

To Fairfield: 1798

In the course of this day, we passed along the side of a very steep hill, which has acquired the name of Breakneck-hill, from the following circumstance. An Indian brother, going to Tschechschequannink, drove a horse before him, which was loaded with a bed. The path being narrow, the horse slipped, fell down the precipice and broke his neck long before he reached the bottom of it. Uncommon pains have been taken to make this part of the road good; and it is now perfectly safe for horses to carry beds, or any other baggage along. The gentleman under whose direction this has been done, deserves the thanks of the public.

We lodged at the house of Obadiah Gore Esqr of Tschechschequannink, where we had excellent accomodations. The house stands on the E. side of the river; the former Indian town was on the W. side. This extensive settlement seems to be in every respect, superior to Wialusing.

The 6th we passed over a high and steep mountain, and the river Susquehanna, to Tioga point. The road along this mountain, in its present state, is really dangerous to travel over. It should be widened, & made level, like that at Breakneck-hill. It is remarkable that all the hills on the Susquehanna are steeper on the N. than on the S. side. From Tioga point [Athens] we sent a letter to Bethlehem, by a private post, which goes every week to Wilkesbarre. There is no public post W. of Tioga point, on the route we went. It goes N. by way of Albany, Whitestown, Geneva & Canandagua to Niagara.

It is but 10 years since the Seneka Indians had a town at Tioga point, and only 3 years since they totally removed from these parts. The white people have now built a town here, which promises to become a place of considerable trade, as it lies at the conflux of the Susquehanna & Tioga rivers, both which are navigable for small craft to a great distance up the country. The trade down these rivers principally consists in boards, shingles, scantling &c. This spring they have begun to send down floats of ship timber to Baltimore. On the Susquehanna mountains there is abundance of pine timber, & some places abound in good pit-coal. The trade up these rivers is merely to furnish the inhabitants with the necessary store-goods, which are Scarce and dear. It is 90 miles from Wilkesbarre to Tioga-point, in which distance the Susquehanna retains nearly one uniform width, and has no falls. It contains a great variety and abundance of fish. This was the season for catching shad: in one place they informed us that they had taken five thousand at one haul.

At Tioga point we breakfasted. As we pursued our course in a N. W. direction, 20 miles to Newton [Elmira], the mountains to our right & left diminished in size. The country at times appeared open and pleasant, and the lands near the banks of the Tioga fertile. Upon the whole however we perceived that we had advanced into a colder climate. The leaves of the trees in most places had hardly made their appearance, and we were informed that the harvests in these parts are generally three weeks later than in the more southerly parts of Pennsylvania. We had to pass some very swampy places, and sometimes on account of the steepness of the hills and their vicinity to the river, to ride along the edges of rocks, or in the water. Such places are called "narrows." Had the Tioga been as high as it has been known to be at this season, we cannot conceive how we could have proceeded on our journey on this route. Three miles from Tioga point we crossed the Pennsylvania line, and entered into New York state. During a thunder storm, we stopped at a M͡r McDowel's, eight miles from the Point. He formerly lived near the Blue mountains, and was well known in Nazareth. His farm now belongs to a M͡r Shaw. It was Sunday, and his family were employed in reading religious books, which is the only way in which that day can be celebrated in these parts, as there is no regular public worship here.

At Newton, where we lodged, we found some reputable people, who were very polite to us. Among them was a M͡r Kuncle, of German extraction, who formerly lived near the Hope, and was well acquainted with B͡r Leinbach there. He is one of the judges of the court. The town of Newton is the capital of the county of Tioga. It contains upwards of 30 houses, and lies on a branch of the Tioga, called the Schamung, which signifies, in the Mohawk language "long horn," because an uncommon long horn of some creature was found there.

The 7th we breakfasted, 6 miles from Newton, with an honest German of the name of Mennier. Here we heard that the country had been covered with snow but two weeks before, and that they could keep no sheep on account of the many wolves on the neighboring hills.— It may be well to observe here, that a tract of land like that which we were now travelling over, is called: "a new country"; because newly settled by the white people. A piece of land lately cleared, if belonging to an old farm, is called: "new land"; if detached and solitary: "an improvement." It is necessary to understand these terms when travelling in North America, in order to enter into the ideas and common conversation of the people.

Eighteen miles from Newton we came to a small town called the Painted Post, so named because the Indians when going to war, used to assemble at a painted post, which was fixed in this place, where they painted themselves in their usual frightful manner, were equipped, and arranged into companies, and regulated all their warlike enterprizes. Here also, after an encounter, they brought their prisoners, to kill, or otherwise dispose of, according to their customs. In the Indian country there are many such painted posts. We proceeded to day over swampy, narrow roads, within 6 miles of Bath, to the house of a M͡r Dolson.

The 8th we breakfasted at Metcalf's tavern in Bath. This flourishing town, the capital of the county of Steuben, was begun to be built about five years since, and contains at present above 40 houses, some of which are built in an unusual style of elegance for a country place. The history of the origin of this town is somewhat singular. Some years ago a company of married men in London [the Pulteney Association] purchased several millions of acres of land in these parts, and appointed a Capt. Williamson of Scotland to be their agent. This gentleman in consequence moved to this country with his family. Most of the lands he disposed of again on terms, at once advantageous to the company, and alluring to settlers. He required no ready money for any purchases made of him, but only an engagement, to pay the whole principal due, in a certain stipulated time, with interest at 6 per cent.: and for the security of the company, he took a deed of mortgage from every purchaser. His good lands soon obtained settlers, or were grasped at by greedy speculators. Perceiving that a considerable body of poor lands were likely to remain on his hands, he built himself an elegant mansion, on a choice spot, in the center of them, for a town residence; to which he gave the name of Bath. Through his influence, on the erection of the county of Steuben, he procured this place to be made the capital of it. Here he erected mills of different kinds, a printing office, and houses for his clerks. In the neighborhood he built good farm houses, which he allowed to be tenanted on the most easy terms. By these means, and by others, his poorest lands obtained a new value; and Bath has acquired a genteel and elegant appearance, which is surprising, considering how lately it was begun to be built, and the swampy, unpromising appearance of the surrounding country.—Capt. Williamson, by his public spirit, which he has particularly evinced in useful buildings in the towns of Geneva, Canandagua & Bath; by his lenity to poor settlers, none of whom he has ever distressed; by his attention to business, obliging manners and affable behaviour, has entirely won the hearts of the people of this country. No individual has perhaps been the means of the settlement and cultivation of so much land in America as he has been. We were credibly informed that the interest accruing to him on lands sold, and not paid for, was upwards of 50,000 dollars per annum.

In Bath we drank the first cup of coffee we had tasted since we left Wilkesbarre. In some places they had furnished us with a beverage of that name, made of burnt rye, peas or crust of bread. Coffee and tea are scarce articles in most of the back parts of America. Sugar is procured in great abundance, and of excellent quality, from the juice of the maple tree.

We met to day with a Capt. Fawkener of Easton, and a Mr Colhoun of Northumberland, who afterwards joined company with us. By the former gentleman we wrote the day following to B^r Ettwein. Eight miles from Bath, we stopped at McWhorter's, and took up our lodging 12 miles farther on at Hooker's [near North Cohocton]. In this part of the country the roads are so bad, that it is necessary to stop frequently, and go but few miles in a day, if the horses, though fed in the best manner, are to hold out on long journies. It would be a great advantage to travellers, if the roads were cut wider, as by that means, they would become dry more early in the spring, and after rainy weather. But the country is as yet too new for this.

We were now on the Allegheny mountain, which is 18 miles across in this place. In order to avoid the steep ascent, and roads which were represented to us as almost impassable, we went over it by a circuit of 27 miles. It is covered here chiefly by tall pines of different kinds, interspersed, in some places with maple, beech &c. The broad base and vast extent of this mountain, the high timber with which it is covered, and the natural barrier which it occasions between the eastern and western parts of the United States, render it conspicuous, and distinguished among all the other mountains, to the east or the west of it. It has been called the backbone of the United States; and considered as such it bears some proportion in size to the country through which it runs.

The 9th we took our morning meal at Bivins's [Biven's, North Cohocton], two miles from Hooker's. Here we were told that they had frosts every month in the year. Cucumber plants were killed last year by frost in the month of July. There are many bears and racoons in this neighborhood, and beavers in the creeks. The Indians, who hunt in these parts, sell their skins to the traders. After riding about 10 miles, we arrived at the steep descent of the Allegheny on the W. side, and had the pleasure to see the rapid creeks, on both sides of us, run to the westward, to add their streams to the river Genesee (called by the Indians Tschenésheo), which has given its name to all the adjacent country. A little below the foot of the Allegheny, we came to the small town of Caniseraga, now called Danville [Dansville]. It was begun to be built about 3 years since, is pleasantly situated, & contains 11 houses. The country around us now displayed an appearance, very different from what we had been accustomed to on the other side of the Alleghany. It was no longer that broken, irregular, stony land, which only here and there invites the abode of man. Here it was universally habitable and enticing. The highest hills appeared fruitful to their summits, and the valleys exhibited the most abundant luxuriance of verdure. Our road, if not always as good as we could wish, was pleasant, because all the surrounding country seemed to smile on us.

> *It is content of heart*
> *Gives nature pow'r to please;*
> *The mind that feels no smart*
> *Enlivens all its sees.*

In the evening we supped at the house of a Mr. McGee, who removed about two years since from the neighborhood of Nazareth.

The 10th early we arrived at Williamsburg, so called after Capt. Williamson. This poor, little, dirty town, in its present state certainly does him no honor. His endeavors for the settlement of the surrounding country have been ill requited; and in this instance he has been very unfortunate in the means he has made use of. From the high character of the German farmers in many parts of the United States for industry, sobriety, honesty and thriftiness, he was induced to wish to make a German settlement on his estates. With this in view, through his agents he entered into an engagement with 40 families of that nation, to leave their native country, and settle here. He was to discharge their travelling expences, build them houses & barns, furnish them with horses & cattle, and with provisions for a year: and they were to pay him a fixed rent for the same. The contract was punctually performed on his part, agreeable to the stipulated terms, and the settlers took possession of their tenements. They were treated by him in the most liberal manner, and received every kind of encouragement desirable within the bounds of reason. But they proved themselves unworthy of such a generous patron, repaying his kindness with more than savage brutality. Before the expiration of the first year, these base wretches entered into a combination, from which none of them were permitted to recede under pain of death, to dispose of their livestock & other movables, and emigrate into the Niagara settlement. They even threatened Capt. Williamson's life, if he should dare to oppose or molest them. Some of their no less villainous neighbors were accessory to their conspiracy by encouraging and assisting them in the sale of the property entrusted to their care, which was mostly effected at very reduced prices. They all got safe to Canada with their booty, and to the scandal of the British government there, were well received by General Simcoe. We were afterwards informed that they told the governor a plausible story. By this whole procedure, Capt. Williamson has sustained a loss of above £ 13,000 N. York Curr.^{y} [Currency].— A few of their abettors have been brought to justice. The high opinion entertained in these parts of German honesty, has not been injured by this shameful conduct, as the settlers have all been branded with the name of Hessians.

At Williamsburg we met with Mr Jones, a well-known Indian interpreter, who travelled with B.^{r} Heckewelder and the American commissioners to Detroit in the year 1793. Three miles from thence we passed through the Indian town of Big-tree [Geneseo]. Here a Mr Wadsworth has built a very elegant house, which commands the most beautiful prospect which we had as yet witnessed on our journey. It is however exceeded by that from the steeple of Nazareth-hall. In front are the Genesee river and flats or meadow grounds; and in the background very extensive ridges of beautiful hills, on which the eye of the spectator, wrapt into futurity, fancies that he sees rise before his view, towns and villas, with all the embellishments and decorations, produced by the hand of taste, aided by time. If in travelling in the interior of America, we have frequent occasion to observe its present rude state, we have at same time the pleasure to think, that it is in every respect in a state of amelioration and improvement. The gentlemen who have settled in these parts seem desirous of introducing the European taste for genteel country seats, of which Mr Wadsworth's mansion is only one example among many that might be mentioned. We do not recollect having seen such buildings in the eastern part of the States, except in the neighborhood of great cities.

Fourteen miles from Williamsburg we came to the ferry over the Genesee, at the little town of Conewage [Avon], which signifies in the Mohawk language, "a stinking-place." We saw many Indians on the road. At the ferry there is a tavern, where between 30 and 40 of them were assembled to a frolic. Most of them were drunk; some had fought till they were bloody, and they altogether exhibited a most deplorable spectacle. Excessive drinking is the grand cause of the ruin of the Indians. Could not some means be devised of controuling this evil? Or, would all civil regulations be ineffective for this purpose? And is it the gospel alone that can herein effect a reformation? Say, ye despisers of the word of Jesus! Try your best, and shew the world for once what wonders you can do! All the good you shall effect, you shall receive the credit of.

The river Genesee in this place is deep, but not broad. The banks, though very high, are sometimes overflowed. The ferry is safe, and well attended.

The tract of land which we now entered, extending to the river St Laurence on the W., goes by the name of the "new purchase," because lately purchased of the Indians by the State of New York. The Indians have reserved for themselves 200,000 acres, in three several lots, where their towns are. For the remainder they received 100,000 dollars, which they had the prudence in consequence of good advice given to them, to place in the Bank of the United States, as a fund for their use for ever. They receive the interest annually, and divide it among them.

We lodged tonight at the house of a Dane of the name of Laurence Petersen, 8 miles from the ferry. Here is a remarkably fine spring, sufficiently copious to supply a large city with water. Capt. Williamson intends to build a town here next year, to be called Caledonia. We had met with a gentleman on the road, who was commissioned by him to engage German settlers, from the counties of York and Lancaster in Pennsylvania, to move next spring to this quarter.

The country W. of the river Genesee appeared to us to be on the whole more inviting than what we had seen of the eastern Genesee country. It has been observed in Pennsylvania, that the few singing birds there are seldom heard in the woods, but more frequently near the habitations of man. Here, when in the most literal sense, in the midst of the wilderness, where there are but few human dwellings, we were charmed with the singing of birds, unknown on the eastern shores of America, whose pleasing and varied notes shortened the passing hours, and reminded us of the still superior strains of the feathered songsters in European groves. We remarked that where the land had the most fertile appearance, and vegetation was the rankest, the singing birds were the most numerous and entertaining, as if to say to the traveller who seeks a settlement: "here take up thy residence." How delightful their strains! And chiefly so, because they chaunt forth the praises of their Creator!

Here too the ground is at this season every where strewed with flowers, which to an American who had never before crossed the Alleghany, would

To Fairfield: 1798

be an engaging novelty. To a lover of nature, the sight of flowers is always a fruitful source of innocent amusement; while the botanist finds in them the means of enlarging the bounds of useful science.

The 11th we rode 7 miles, and then stopped to breakfast at the second and last house we should meet with between the Genesee river and Lake Erie.* Thence we proceeded 20 miles to the so called "plains." These are extensive tracts, where the timber has been from time to time destroyed by fires, or by high winds, or more probably by both. They have the appearance of fallow fields. To day we proceeded in all about 32 miles, and then took up our lodging in a cabin or hut near the Taniwandi [Tonawanda] creek, about 5 or 6 miles from the Indian town of that name. As the road we were on is much travelled, both to Niagara & Buffaloe, and whoever goes it, must lie out in the woods at least one night, a great many cabins have been erected along the road from time to time, both by the white people and the Indians. Their construction is very simple, as their object is merely to afford a shelter against the rain, and to guard against the dampness of the ground. They are of an oblong form, generally about 9 feet by 6. In front they are about 5 feet high, and behind about 3½ feet, that the roof may have a descent. The four corners are supported by as many stakes, which are joined together at top by cross pieces. The roof is made of the bark of trees, which is laid across in strips of equal length. The ground below is also covered with strips of bark, as large as can be procured. The sides are generally left open. In case of rain, they are sometimes enclosed with branches of trees. The lodging in such a cabin, or indeed wherever there is no house, is called "encamping." The places chosen to encamp on are, open spots, where there is no danger from the fall of trees, or branches of them, in case of storm; where there is grass for the horses, dry wood to make a fire of, and a creek or spring not far distant. The first thing to be attended to in taking possession of a hut (if one does not build one for oneself) is to turn over all the pieces of bark which lie on the ground, to see if there be any snakes under them. Then a large fire is made in front; after which preparation is made to go to rest. B^r Heckewelder, through his great experience in travelling in the woods, knew how to manage every thing in the best manner. We enjoyed a comfortable cup of tea to our supper, and then wrapping ourselves up in our blankets, committed ourselves to the protection of the ever faithful watchman of Israel, who neither slumbers nor sleeps. The weather was cool, and it rained a little in the night, from which however we perceived no inconvenience. We arose early in the morning, and after taking another refreshing draught of tea, proceeded on our journey.

---

* Ganson's log tavern, the best known inn between Albany and Buffalo, just east of the present village of Le Roy (home of Jell-O), built by Charles Wilbur in 1793, was conducted in 1798 by Captain John Ganson, a Revolutionary soldier who fought at Bunker Hill.—Leslie R. Gray.

This was the 12th May, which we called to mind as a memorial-day * in that division of the church of Christ, to which we have the happiness through grace to belong, though far separated in body from any of our congregations.— In some place we saw Indians, lying in their huts, by fires. They were every where very friendly. We passed many creeks, all of which have stony bottoms, and a rapid fall towards lake Ontario. This lake lay about 30 miles to the N. of us; its vicinity was evident by the streaked appearance of the sky near that part of the horizon. In the evening we had the pleasure to find ourselves at the settlement called Buffaloe, at the mouth of Buffaloe creek. Though one may pass the night very comfortably in fine weather in a hut, yet it is hardly necessary to say, that it is much more desirable to enjoy a warm supper, and a good bed, where one can get it, in a tavern. At Buffaloe we derived much information, concerning our future route, from Mr Johnson the Indn interpreter, to whom the settlement belongs, and who intends to lay out a town here. From here we learnt, that the best road to Fairfield was by way of the Falls of Niagara; and that the country was so much settled, that we should not have occasion to lie out more than one or two nights. This is the same Mr Johnson who delivered the war-speech to the chiefs of the western Indians, a few years since, when it was apprehended that hostilities would commence between Britain and the United States of America.

The 13th we went 3 miles along the banks of lake Erie, to the ferry above the fort of the same name, where we crossed over the St Laurence [Niagara] into the province of Upper Canada, at a place where the river is about half a mile wide. This ferry is held by an Irishman, who ought to be dismissed from his office, for his inattention to his business, his careless discharge of it, and the abusive language which he makes use of. Lake Erie, which we passed the N. W. corner of, is an immense body of fresh water, very dangerous to navigate in. It abounds with fish of various kinds, and the most delicious flavors, whose names are not generally known, being undescribed by any naturalist. This lake is connected with lake Ontario, and the other great lakes of N. America, by means of the river St Laurence, which runs through them all into the Atlantic Ocean. Opposite to fort Erie were two British vessels from Detroit, lying at anchor.

We had now proceeded 352 miles on our journey; and as from the badness of the roads, and the heavy loads our horses had to carry, both we and they were much fatigued, we resolved to rest a day, that we might be enabled with fresh vigor, to pursue and go through the remainder of it. The place we chose for that purpose was a private house, near the Falls of Niagara, belonging to a German farmer of the name of Bender. Afterwards, on the

---

* May 12, 1724, five men destined to be leaders of the Renewed Moravian Church arrived at Herrnhut, Saxony; May 12, 1727, with the adoption of the Brotherly Agreement, the modern Moravian Church came into being; May 12, 1749, the British Parliament, recognizing the Moravian Church as "an ancient Protestant Episcopal Church," gave it full church privileges in all British lands.

representation of our fellow traveller M:̣ Schaefer, who had business in these parts, and wished to continue the journey in our company, we resolved to stay there two days. Accordingly we rode only 20 miles slowly to day along the banks of the S:ṭ Laurence, which from half a mile, soon opened to be 3 or 4 miles wide, and containing many considerable islands. The river is deep, and appears of a green color, much resembling that of salt water. On the American side we saw only one farm, viz:ṭ Stedman's, where formerly stood fort Schlosser. The Canada side, where the land does not appear to be so good, is closely settled all the way down the river. What has invited people into Canada, is the free gift of 200 acres, which is made by government to every actual settler. The climate is cold, and the spring very backward. There had been frost here every night for the last 3 weeks. The May-apples we saw, were killed; and the peach and cherry-trees were just beginning to put forth their blossoms.

Most of the inhabitants of Canada are emigrants from the United States; but no sooner did we enter the country, than we perceived that some difference exists between their national characters. In the States, the principal subject of conversation in most public companies which we entered, was the quality of lands. From Tioga to Buffaloe every traveller is supposed to be in quest of them; and little else is cared about, if bargains of that kind can only be made or disposed of to advantage. In Canada, the settlers are more humble in their views. They are mostly poor people, who are chiefly concerned to manage, in the best manner, the farms which have been given them by government. They are distinguished by an eagerness for news. We have hardly entered a house, or enquired the road of any person on the highway throughout the whole province, without being asked what was the latest news from the States; while in the States, in parts of the country where they have no public papers, nobody asked us a question on the subject. If some of the people of Canada have their complaints to make against the government, there seems upon the whole to be more loyalty and attachment to it, than we have been able to discover among the inhabitants of the States. At same time they rejoice every where that the two nations are now connected in the most amicable manner.

The day we entered Canada was Sunday. In the course of the morning we met a gentleman dressed in black on horseback, whom we afterwards heard was a clergyman, and that he was going to preach in a neighboring church. This was something quite new to us, as we had not seen, or been able to hear of any church or meeting-place, all the way we had travelled, since we left Nazareth and Schöneck. The people we had been among, were chiefly from New England. Many were from New Jersey, Pennsylvania & the eastern parts of New York. It is not true therefore, what has been asserted in print, that the New Englanders, when they form a new settlement, generally take a minister along with them.* We have seen many of their settlements while on this journey, and in none of them have they a minister. Hence has arisen the common saying, that—"the New Englanders, when they leave their country, leave their religion behind them." In most places however they have schools. This proves that they are more concerned for the temporal, than for the eternal welfare of their children. The one they ought to do, & not to leave the other undone.— The above is, thank God, not a picture of the general state of religion in America. In many, and perhaps most of the old settlements, the case is very different. One of our brethren a few years since made a circuit of about 200 miles, through the counties of Northampton, Berkshire, Daughiny [Dauphin] and Lancaster in Pennsylvania, which are inhabited chiefly by Germans, and had the pleasure to count nearly 40 edifices, erected by the free subscriptions of the people, and dedicated to divine worship. And to the credit of that nation, the settlement we were now travelling through, was composed almost entirely of Germans.

In the evening we passed the fort at Chippewa, the commander of which was very civil to us. We were no where asked for a pass, had any duties to pay, or were officially interrogated. At Mr Bender's, which is the nearest house to Niagara Falls, we were courteously received. Hereabouts the people are almost entirely from the Jersies. They have built a small church not far from the Falls [at Lundy's Lane], which is free for ministers of all denominations.

During the two next days, we were chiefly employed in contemplating the falls of Niagara, which are universally allowed to be one of the most astonishing curiosities of nature, which America, or any other part of the world affords. They are formed by a general descent of the country between lake Erie and lake Ontario of about 300 feet, the slope of which is generally very steep, and in many places almost perpendicular. This general descent of the country is observable for about 100 miles to the E., and above 200 miles to the W. or rather N. W. of the Falls. The slope is formed by horizontal strata of stone, great part of which is lime-stone. At fort Erie, which is 20 miles above the cataract, the current is sometimes so strong, that it is impossible to cross the river in a ferry-boat. Proceeding downwards, the rapidity of the stream increases. It may however generally be crossed by hard rowing in a boat opposite to the mouth of Chippewa creek. As we rode along the St Laurence, we heard the sound of the Falls at the distance of 10 miles. The wind was N. E., and the air clear; had it been N. W., or the atmosphere dense, we should have heard it at a much greater distance. In heavy weather, and with a fair wind, the sound is sometimes heard 40 or 50 miles. The rapids, or first falls, begin about half a miles above the great

---

* Footnote in the MS., but in a different hand: "a Settlement by Government, and a Settlement by Straglers and Emigrants from the State, are different Institutions."

cataract. In one instance has a man been saved, who had been carried down to them. His canoe was overturned, he retained fast hold of it, and it very providentially fastened itself to the uppermost rock. Some people on shore seeing this, ventured to his assistance, and saved his life at the risk of their own. As we approached the Falls the first time, the sun was low in the W., which gave us an opportunity of viewing the beautiful rainbow which is occasioned by the reflection of his rays on the cloud or fog which is perpetually ascending from below. We found afterwards that the whole phenomenon is never viewed so much to advantage on the Canada side, as in a clear evening. The vast fog, ascending from the grand cataract, being in constant agitation, appears like the steam of an immense, boiling cauldron. In summer it moistens the neighboring meadows, and in winter, falling upon the trees, it congeals, and produces a most beautiful crystaline appearance. The view of this fog at a distance, which when the cause of it is known is in itself a singular phenomenon, fills the mind with awful expectation of something pleasing and great, which on a nearer approach, can never end in disappointment. The first sight of the Falls arrests the senses in silent admiration! Their various hues, arising from the depth, descent & agitation of the water, and the reflection of the sun beams on them; their great height; their position between lofty rocks; and their roaring noise, altogether render them an unparalleled display of nature's grandeur. But what chiefly distinguishes them, and gives them a majesty incomparably superior to any thing of the kind in the known world, is the immense body of water which they precipitate into an immense abyss. The St Laurence is one of the greatest rivers of America, it is very deep, and about 742 yards wide at the Falls. The perpendicular descent there is about 140 feet, down to the level of the water below. How far the water rushes down into the chasm below, is uncertain. It falls 58 feet within the last half mile immediately above the Falls, which adds to the force and velocity of the cataract. The sound occasioned by the great and precipitate fall of such a vast body of water has the most grand effect that can be conceived. It far exceeds in solemnity any other sound produced by the operations of nature. It is only at the Niagara falls, that the force of that figure made use of in the book of Revelation, can be fully felt: "I heard a voice as the voice of many waters." And what did that voice say? It proclaimed aloud: "Hallelujah: for the Lord God omnipotent reigneth!" This is the language that has been thundered for ages from the Falls of Niagara!

Every hour of the day, and every change of the weather varies the scenery at this romantic—this magnificent exhibition of wonders, compared with which every attempt of art to produce the sublime, sinks into nothingness. The first day that we spent there, the weather was clear; the next day, it became cloudy and rained a little. As we were desirous to enjoy the prospect before us from every possible point of view, we went down the high bank below the cataract, into the immense chasm below, and thence walked, or rather climbed along the rocks, so near to the cataract, till it appeared ready to overwhelm us. The descent, though steep, is not dangerous. General Simcoe, the late governor of the province, caused a ladder to be fixed in the most perpendicular part of it, which is so safe, that his lady ventured to go down it. Below, the air is in some places strongly tainted with the smell of dead fish, which lie in great numbers on the beach. Every creature that swims down the rapids is instantly hurried to destruction. We saw a loon a little above them, who was unknowingly approaching swift ruin. Even birds who fly above them, are frequently impelled downwards by the strong current of the air, as their shattered fragments among the rocks bear witness.

When the river is low, it is easy to walk up to the foot of the Falls; but when high, one has to climb over rocks, and piles of large loose stones for near half a mile. This last was the case when we were there. In many places the impending masses of stone appeared ready to fall on us.

It is known that the Falls are divided into the great and lesser Falls, by means of a lofty island between them. At the place of descent we were nearly opposite to the lesser Falls, which rush down in a direction nearly parallel with the beach we walked along. They are again divided into two very unequal Falls, the least of which probably discharges more water than the great fall of the Rhine in Switzerland, which is accounted the most famous water-fall in Europe. Below these lesser Falls, among the rocks, lay huge masses of ice.

We now approached the great Fall, which discharges at least four times as much water, as the two lesser ones together. It is nearly in the form of a horse-shoe. We observed below, what is imperceptible above, that this fall has not throughout the same pitch. In the hollow of it, where the greatest body of water descends, the rocks seem to be considerably worn away. We cannot however subscribe to the opinion, that the cataract was formerly at the northern side of the slope near the landing, and that from the great length of time, the quantity of water, and the distance which it falls, the solid stone is worn away for about 9 miles up towards lake Erie. This notion seems extravagant. The island which separates the Falls is a solid rock, and so high, that the river can never have run over it. Its bank towards the Falls runs in the same direction with them, and at the same time does not project beyond them, which would surely be the case, if the whole body of rocks from which the water descends, was fast wearing away. The situation and appearance of the Falls is exactly the same as described & delineated by French artists 160 years ago. Besides, according to the laws of motion, the principal pressure of the water here, must be in the direction in which it moves, and consequently not against the rocks it merely flows over, and where it meets with no opposition; for the stronger the current, the less is the pressure downwards. There is therefore less probability of the bottom wearing away here, than in any other river of equal depth, where there are no such Falls. If the solid stone at the Falls was wearing away at the rate of a mile in a thousand or more years, it might be expected that the Rapids would in length of time become smooth, or vary their appearance, which has not been observed to be the case. That the perpendicular descent of such a vast body of water has produced a vast chasm below, is more than probable; and that where the greatest quantity of it falls, the surface of the rocks may in great length of time have become more hollow, is very credible. But it appears very difficult for us to conceive that in any known period, however long, an immense bed of rocks should have been so completely worn away for nine miles, that no vestige should be left of them; and the Falls exhibit at length their present appearance. An old Indian told us, that many years since a grey-headed Chippewa had said to him: "the white people believe that the Falls were once down at the landing. It is not true. They were always where they are now. So we have heard from our forefathers." We are led therefore to conclude, that the Niagara falls received their present singular position at the command of Omnipotence at the creation, that the children of men should admire, wonder, and sink in silent adoration!

It is generally supposed, because it has frequently appeared in print, that it is possible to go behind the descending column of water at the Falls, and remain there in perfect safety. Conversation, it has been said, may be held there without interruption from the noise, which is less here than at a considerable distance. People who live near the spot, have daily to contradict these fables. They have themselves been repeatedly as far as possible under the Falls, and are in the habit of conducting strangers. Their information is therefore to be relied on. Under the so called Table rock, from a part of which the water descends, there is, 'tis true space sufficient to contain a great number of people in perfect safety. But how shall they get there? Were they to attempt to enter the cavity behind the Fall, the very current of the air, say the guides, were the stream of water not to touch them, would deprive them of life. The truth is, it is possible to go under, that is, below the Falls, as we did, but not to go behind them.

The motion of the water below the cataract, is, as may easily be supposed, extremely wild and irregular; and it remains so for several miles below the landing. As far as the fog extends, it is impossible to judge of the state of the atmosphere with respect to heat or cold. In summer it cools it, & in winter renders it milder. Below, on the beach there are no petrifications, and nothing worth notice, but a soft white stone, which, when reduced to powder, is taken inwardly as an emetic. The surrounding country on the Canada side is very delightful, affording charming situations for pleasure-grounds, from whence the Falls might be viewed to advantage. On this account the land here will probably once sell for a very high price. It is at present valued at £ 10 an acre. The banks round the Falls are lined with white pines and cedars.

We have been the more particular in our account of the Falls of Niagara, as they are well worthy the attention of travellers, and few of our brethren ever have had, or probably ever will have, an opportunity of viewing them. Many of the printed descriptions are erroneous.

The 15th in the evening Mr. Schaefer came to us at our lodging, according to appointment, and we prepared to proceed on our course the next morning. Much of the country we had passed through was never travelled by any brother before us, which with the progressive state of improvement, and future importance of the present state of things in the so called new countries considered as well in a religious as civil view; has led us to be more particular than we otherwise should have been, in the description of them. We were now going to pursue a route which a few years since was trodden by none but savages, and which according to all the maps that have as yet been published, would appear to be leading through land unknown or uninhabited.

May 16th we took leave of our worthy host Mr. Bender, and entered a road thirty-three feet wide, which led us, in a N. W. course, through a country full of farms & cottages. There was not a field to be seen, but was full of the stumps of trees, which shewed that the land had been but newly settled. Almost all the people we spoke to to-day, were from Sussex county in New Jersey. As we had to cross from the road we were in, in order to enter the great Newark or New Niagara road leading to York [Toronto] & Detroit, we had often occasion to enquire for the way; but the eagerness of the people for news sometimes made it difficult to obtain the desired information as readily as we could have wished.* Thirteen miles from the Falls, we descended the Niagara hill to Hamilton's mills, and 5 miles from thence arrived by bye-paths at Renchey's tavern on the main road. We had now an open highway before us, mostly over lands of excellent quality. The country bordering on lake Ontario, (near which we were), is esteemed on the whole superior to that round lake Erie. At the house of a Mr. James Henry [about two miles west of Jordan], we stopped to bait our horses. It may not be amiss to mention for once the general drift of the questions put by tavernkeepers to travellers, and by travellers to each other, both in Canada and the States, according to our experience and observation. A traveller after asking for refreshment for himself & his horse, naturally makes enquiry about the state of the roads, the turns to the right and to the left, the marks by which he may discover the course he has to pursue, and the best houses of entertainment to call at. Questions of this kind are very obligingly answered. You are then perhaps asked about the news; or your host tells you how long he has occupied his farm, what kind of soil it is, or what land sells for in that neighborhood &c. All this is very suitable conversation for a public house. But your new friend generally proceeds some steps further; he wishes to become more intimately acquainted with you. If your saddle-bags are bulky, you are supposed to be a speculator in lands. You are asked where you come from, and where you are going to. Are you communicative on these heads, your name, business and condition of life are then asked after. It is not supposed that there is any

---

*This may be accounted for from the general expectation then prevailing, that war would soon break out between the United States and France.—Mortimer's note.

impertinence in all this; it is the custom of the country. The tavern-keeper, from the time you enter under his roof, seems to consider you as belonging to his family. But you must understand him aright; he is curious to hear your story, only that he may be able to tell it again, while at the same time his curiosity has so much of the semblance of true friendship, and he is really so well disposed towards you, that he will not be displeased, if you take upon yourself to be as inquisitive as he has been, and enter very minutely into the circumstances of himself and family. This, by the bye, is not a bad mode of defence, if his questions come too close upon you. The best general rule is, like D.̱ Franklin, to tell a plain, open story to every enquirer. So we have done, and have in consequence been blessed with the good wishes of the whole country we have passed through, confirmed by many a hearty shake of our hands.

In the course of this day we passed by one of the heads of lake Ontario, near which we saw a rattlesnake lying dead in the road. B.̱ Heckewelder pronounced it to be the largest he had ever beheld. It was 4 feet 8 inches long, & had 10 rattles. In Canada the rattlesnakes are less numerous, but of a different and far more poisonous species than they are to the southward. Their bite is said to occasion a very speedy death, if recourse is not had to the proper remedies.

We put up tonight at the house of M.̱ Charles Anderson [Grimsby, Ont.], on the 40 mile creek, so called because about 40 miles distant from Newark, the present seat of government. He has a distillery, good plantation, and accomodations for travellers, equal to what is to be met with in any tavern on the road between Bethlehem & Philadelphia.

In Canada, a well improved plantation bespeaks, not only an industrious, but a hard-working owner. Money will effect but little, as it is difficult for any consideration, to hire laborers, in a country where every one may have land for himself, by only asking for it. The whole expense of surveying, obtaining a deed, &c. is only 9d per acre. The policy of the British government is principally directed to the obtaining settlers. By this means the government is strengthened, and a more extensive vent is obtained for their home manufactures. Should the Canadians ever throw off their allegiance to the mother country, (which is improbable), the commercial connexion, which is what chiefly renders the province valuable to her, would not be diminished, as appears in the case of the United States.— How admirable are the ways of God in the government of the world! It is his command to mankind, given above 4000 years ago: "Increase, multiply & replenish the earth." He has purposed that this ordinance should be brought into fulfilment in America as well as in the other quarters of the globe. Men therefore in their national & individual capacities, are instrumental in furthering his views. They are allured thereto by the prospect of outward advantages; while every exterior cause combines to produce the effects designed by infinite wisdom.— So also will it be before the knowledge of the glory of the Lord shall cover the earth. Events not to be controuled, least expected, and but calculated to answer the purpose, shall tend to the propagation of the gospel. The command to "go & teach all nations" is not of 2000 years standing, yet much has been effected. As the time when the gospel is to be universally made known approaches, every obstacle will recede, vanish or be overcome, and both friends and enemies to the cause, will lend their aid, to "prepare the ways of the Lord, & make his paths straight before him."

This was one of the pleasantest days rides we had had on our whole journey. The weather was delightful, the road good, and the prospects pleasingly varied between hill and dale. We began now to count the days when we might expect to be with our brethren and sisters in Fairfield. Our joy was heightened by the surprize at finding ourselves in so beautiful a country, so far to the Northward. We were also in a fertile country, which is a point of some importance to the traveller; for, in addition to the gratification it affords, to see nature all around blooming and vigorous, we had observed that where the land was good, the entertainment to be had was in every respect so much the better for it.

The 17th we breakfasted at Pettit's [Winona], 5 miles from Anderson's. Though the country continued to be full of farms, yet we saw no towns. There are no Capt. Williamsons here, to lay them out and build them. When however a tract of land is thickly settled, there is no doubt but towns will arise in consequence. Near this place, the principal road turns off to the N. to the new city of York, formerly called Toiondo [Toronto], which is designed to be the capital of Upper Canada. It lies on lake Ontario. From the top of Niagara-hill, which we ascended again today, we had a very extensive view of the great western head of the Lake, and a vast range of country to the N. & E. On the W. this hill quite encompasses the Lake. We passed over much new land, where all the timber was in flames, or burnt to ashes. This is very troublesome to travellers. They have to suffer from the smoke & heat; the hot ashes may scorch the feet of their horses, and make them start; and above all, burning trees or branches may fall upon them. In one place, a large limb of a tree that was yet standing, dropped down very near to us.

Twenty miles from Pettit's, we came to a house and mill belonging to a Mr. St. John [Jean Baptiste Rousseau of Ancaster]. He was not at home. We would fain have bought some grain for our horses, but it was absolutely denied to us by his morose wife, who said she had it, could spare it, but would not part with any. Wherever we have been, we have been treated civilly, till we came to this place. Mr. St. John used formerly to keep tavern, but the unhappy disposition of his wife obliged him to give it up. She has sometimes positively refused to let travellers have any thing to eat, upon any consideration whatever. This woman deserves to be most sincerely pitied and prayed for, by all who pass by her house, as her ill-temper undoubtedly causes her much more uneasiness, than it can do to them, how much soever they may

To Fairfield: 1798

suffer by it. Her countenance, by nature agreeable, exhibits at present a shocking picture of a mind tortured with malicious ill-nature, and all the baser passions. The sun was still pretty high, and we rode on 12 miles further, to the house of a poor but honest New Englander of the name of Dexter, who willingly accomodated us in the best manner he could. He gave us a supper of bacon and eggs, and a corner of his cottage to lie down in.

Fourteen miles of our road today were over swamps. The weather had long been remarkably dry, or we should have found it difficult to pass them so speedily and successfully as we did, without any accident. The bridges were also very troublesome to us, as many of them were ill-constructed, or out of repair. Bridges over swampy places should always be covered with earth, which would make them last the longer, and be the more safe for travellers. Those over creeks should at least be well braced together at the sides, to prevent the round, and sometimes crooked stems of trees, which form their surface, from rolling asunder. When broken or decayed, they should be repaired without delay. We have crossed thousands of bridges in the course of this journey, many of which, though intended for the accomodation of passengers, we found more dangerous than swamps in which the horses sunk up to their bellies.

The farther we penetrated into the country, the dearer we found every article we had occasion for. In some places we had to pay 5d a quart for oats, and 8d for Indian corn. We could not complain of this: Settlers in a new country must take high prices for every article they have to dispose of, as they themselves must purchase most of the necessaries of life at very high rates, and fetch them from great distances.—

The 18th early we arrived at the Mohawk village, or castle [on the outskirts of modern Brantford], commonly called Brandt's town, from Colonel Brandt, the principal person in the settlement. It lies on the Grand river, which flows into lake Erie. When the six nations were subdued by the Americans, in their revolutionary war, and their towns on the Mohawk river burnt, the British, on account of their attachment to them, made them a grant of all the territory, on both sides of the Grand river, for 6 miles inland. Thither most of them retreated, and have ever since remained, in alliance with, and under the protection of the British government. They are in no respect subject to their laws, as the following anecdote will sufficiently testify. Two years ago a white man was murdered by Colonel Brandt's son [Isaac], merely because he had not made him a saddle in the promised time. The young Indian found him at a frolic, and after exchanging some words with him on the subject, dispatched him with his tomahawk. The affair happened on the Indian territory, and the culprit remained unpunished by any human tribunal. But divine justice did not permit him to escape. Shortly after, he raised up his polluted hand against his father, with an intention to murder him also; but the experienced warrior adroitly warded off the blow,

& gave him such a cut in the head with his long knife, that he instantly dropped down at his feet. He died in two days after.*

Colonel Joseph Brandt, whose name has frequently occurred in the public papers, and in the diaries of our Indian congregation, is one of those extraordinary characters, who by dint of superior genius, know how to avail themselves of circumstances, so as to raise themselves into eminence, among an uncivilized or unwary people. He had the advantage of a liberal education in Dartmouth college, and of the patronage of Sir Willm Johnson, through whom he was made a captain in the British service. Though no chief among his nation, and incapable of becoming one, on account of the meanness of his descent, yet he possesses a vast ascendency in it. He is their efficient chief, both in the council and in the field. Nothing of moment is resolved on, or undertaken, among all the six nations in Canada, contrary to, or without his consent. His authority is supreme, and they all pay him uncommon respect. He sells land to the white people, or permits them to settle on it, at his discretion, and on the terms which he is pleased to prescribe; and all the settlers are in a kind of vassalage to him. None of them may sell spirituous liquors, either to the Indians or white people. He has lately forbid it, on account of the disorders which it has occasioned; and no one dares to transgress his mandate. In his own house, he is said to keep every kind of wine and spirits which is to be procured for money, which he makes a free use of; but when he invites other Indians to his table, he knows well how to keep them within the bounds of temperance. He is styled general of the Indian army, and on muster days, the white people living on his territory, must also arrange themselves under his banners. When in England, some years since, and presented to his Britannic Majesty at court, he refused to kiss his hand, alledging that he also was a king in his own country. But he had no objection to pay that mark of high respect to the Queen.

The Mohawk village we passed through is large, irregularly built & scattered. The houses, like all Indian dwellings, are small, having only one room, of a square form. Colonel Brandt has a handsome two story house, built after the manner of the white people. Compared with the other houses, it may be called a palace. Near it stands the great council-house of the nation, which is not quite finished. A church, with a handsome steeple, has lately been erected here by order of the British government. Here the service of the English church is read every Sunday, by an Indian, in the Mohawk language, and an English sermon, interpreted into Mohawk, is preached twice a year, by a minister from Newark, who afterwards administers the sacraments. The Indian church is well attended, both by the Indians and white people, and the greatest order is preserved. The book of common prayer of the English church, the gospel according to St Mark, and other well-selected portions of scripture, have lately been printed in London, in the Mohawk and English languages, under the direction of the Society for the propagation of the gospel

---

* The wound was slight, but it became infected.

in foreign parts, and at the expence of the British government, expressly for the use of these people. St Mark's gospel was translated by Colonel Brandt. The whole is bound together in one volume, which is embellished with copper-plates, representing the principal scenes of our Saviour's life. Colonel Brandt some time since, on his way through Fairfield, presented B.^r Senseman with a copy of this performance.

We stopped in the village to purchase Indian corn for our horses, which afforded an opportunity to enquire who we were, and where we were going to. When going away, Colonel Brandt ran after us, and gave B.^r Mortimer a letter to Mr Allen at the Delaware township. He is very polite, has a dignified & pleasing aspect, dresses well after the Indian manner, and speaks the English language with great fluency.

Two miles from the Mohawk village, at the house of a Mr Douglass, we stopped again to breakfast. He lives on Indian land, and of course is not permitted to sell liquors: but no objection is made to his entertaining travellers. Mr Douglass at our desire very civilly rode through the Grand river with us, in order to shew us the best place of fording. It is a deep and rapid stream, and in this place about 150 feet wide.

In the course of today we had to suffer much from the musquitoes, who were particularly troublesome in low, swampy grounds. They seemed to be of a larger size than those we had seen in the States. Their bite often drew blood, both from us and our horses. In the latter end of the month of May, as soon as the frosty nights cease, they make their appearance, and continue to be a great plague both to man & beast for about 6 weeks, when they begin gradually to disappear. Excessive heat debilitates them, and night frosts put a period to their existence. During the period of their greatest activity, there is no standing still out of doors for a moment, except in the night or during rain, without being covered with them. Smoke alone will drive them away. Where a great body of land is cleared, and there are no morassy grounds, they are fewer in number; but this is the case in few places in the new countries.

From Grand river we proceeded 10 miles over plains to Fowler's [west of Burford], where we entered thick woodlands. Here they informed us that there was plenty of game. The settlements now became rarer, and consisted of single farms. Towards Niagara, as observed above, the inhabitants are altogether from Pennsylvania & New Jersey. Here we heard of none but New Englanders, whose lusty arms are best fitted to clear heavy-timbered forests. Where they design to make an improvement, they first build a hut, and then in a short time cut down & destroy the timber all around them. Their perseverance is astonishing. After having made a tedious journey of many hundred miles, from a well-settled country into the wilderness, they patiently endure all the difficulties they have there to contend with, esteeming the cheapness of their new purchase a compensation for every inconvenience. They farm here chiefly with oxen, and as the winters are long, and they are mostly poor, use sleighs instead of waggons, throughout the whole year. In one place, speaking with them of the badness of the roads, and the apparent impossibility that oxen could travel over them with sleighs, on account of the heaps of fallen timber lying in all directions, which as it were block them up; they told us that—"that was all nothing, when one was used to it. If the oxen could but put their *noses* over the trees, they must jump over them, and then the sleighs must follow."

From the time that we entered Canada, we found every where that the inhabitants had some knowledge of the Indian congregation at Fairfield. Some call them, by way of distinction, "the Christian Indians"; but their most general name is that of "Moravian Indians." We had the pleasure to hear that they bear universally an excellent character. They were described to us as more civil, friendly & industrious than other Indians, and as not given like them to drinking. Many spoke of the hospitality and kindness they had experienced from them, and praised in particular the good order prevailing in their town, for which they gave their ministers much credit. "One would not have thought it possible," said some, "that Indians could be so far civilized. They live in a great measure like the white people, only they are better than they." This was the testimony given of them in some places, before it was known that we were bound to their settlement, which it may easily be conceived, was highly gratifying and encouraging to us. This is just as the case should be. Wherever there is a living congregation of Jesus, whether gathered from among nominal Christians, or real heathens, it ought to be, and if faithful to its call of God, it will be, a light to the surrounding country. Men will see their good works, and in consequence, whether they intend it or not, be induced to glorify their Father which is in heaven.— We can truly say that additional respect has always been paid to us, when it was known that we came from Bethlehem; and that respect increased, the nearer we approached to Fairfield. Who then that has a right to these names, need be ashamed of them? But might all be careful not to sully them!

We supped and took our night's lodging at Campfield's, 14 miles from Fowler's. The people here were poor, and had not much to set before us; but their zeal to serve us was so great, that our hostess, in her haste to prepare our supper, made so great a fire, that the flame caught hold of the roof of the house, and all hands had to exert themselves, to extinguish it. What a contrast was this to the reception at St Johns! This good woman is a child of sorrow. The house wherein she lived in New Hampshire before she moved here, was burnt to the ground, with her two daughters of the ages of 12 & 10 years, and all the property she had. She has now a son who is an idiot, and a most moving spectacle. All these tribulations she seems to bear with more than philosophical composure, even with Christian resignation, which her edifying expressions, and the humble serenity of her countenance bespeak. If she does not enjoy the good things of this life, it is perhaps in mercy to her; at least it is for some good reason, best known to her Saviour. When all her troubles are at an end, she will once, like Lazarus, be conveyed by angels to Abraham's bosom.

The next morning we breakfasted with a very talkative man of the name of Hoskins. He afterwards rode with us to the last house in the settlement, belonging to a M.^r [Seth] Putnam, who is a distant relation of General Putnam, surveyor-general to the United States, who was so friendly & serviceable to the Brethren last year on the Muskingum. Mr Putnam's house lies on the N. E. branch of the river Retrenche or Thames, about 8 miles above where it is joined by the N. W. branch, and at the distance of 43 miles from the Mohawk town on Grand river. To this place the settlements may be said to extend Westwards from Niagara. Those between Grand River and the Thames have altogether been made within the last year. The land on the Thames is tempting, being generally of the best quality. Messrs Hoskins & Putnam live in a township which was taken up by a Major Ingerson [Ingersoll] from New England, who engaged in a certain stipulated time, to bring 50 families to settle on it. All the emigrants are said to have been on the road, but as they did not appear at the time agreed on, the contract has been declared void. The Major has, by the forfeit of his land to government, sustained a loss of above £ 1,000, but the poor people will each receive the free grant of 200 acres.

There are no stores or shops in the whole province of Upper Canada, except in the towns of Newark and York, and in the neighborhood of Detroit. The most common articles, to be had in every village in the eastern parts of the United States, can hardly be procured here for any money. B.^r Heckewelder for instance was in want of tobacco, and could get none. He began at length to day to smoke dried leaves of trees. Tradesmen, who follow their professions, are also few in number. There is not a saddler to be met with in the whole province.

The situation of the settlers with respect to religious instruction & schools, is much to be deplored. In all the inland parts both are totally wanting. In one place they remarked to us: "The Indians in Moravian town and Brandt's town have churches and schools. The white people have neither. Our children will become heathen, and theirs Christians." *

At Ingerson's intended settlement the river Thames is the boundary between the British and Indian territories. The land to the N. of it belongs to the Chippeways and Massasaugies. Lower down on the river the British line extends farther Northward.

The 20th we rode 36 miles through woodlands, without seeing a house, to the so called Delaware township. When we stopped any where, we made a fire to keep off the musquitoes. It is not the heat, or the flame, but the smoke chiefly that drives away these unwelcome guests: and if to breathe the sooty

---

* The people in Brandt's town bear however but a poor character. They are said to differ but very little from other heathen.—Mortimer's note.

exhalation, be at all disagreeable, it is in this case only submitting to the least of two evils. Our path was a "newly opened road," in some places hardly discernible, were it not for the "blazes" or marks made by cuts in the bark of the trees, on both sides of them.

We saw, and passed over, immense tracts of land, which had lately been set fire to by Indian hunters, and were in part still burning. In some places the sun was obscured, and the musquitoes were expelled, by the clouds of smoke ascending from the wide-extended conflagration. By this means the country is made more open to hunt in, and produces greater abundance of grass for the deer to feed on. This burning of the woods in the western countries, is probably the sole cause of that peculiar kind of haziness, which is frequently observed, throughout the Eastern part of the continent, to follow a Westerly wind, in the spring and fall of the year. It seems to have a great influence on the weather. The burning generally takes place during the first dry weather in the spring; perhaps the smoke for a time absorbs the moisture of the atmosphere, preventing the union of the watery particles, that would otherwise float together; at length they become too ponderous, and then follow those torrents of rain which generally fall in the month of May. When the woods are set fire to before winter, it is followed with similar effects. Hence the Indians, when they see any body set the woods a burning, commonly say: "So, you intend to have much rain soon!"

The Delaware township was begun to be settled about three years since by Mr. Ebenezer Allen, from the Genesee country. It contains at present 30 families. They have good land, excellent timber, fine creeks for mill-seats, and springs of the best water. All these advantages are rarely to be met with in one district. Their trade is with Detroit. We lodged at Mr. Kilburn's [Kilbourn], who has built a grist & saw mill [on Dingman Creek]. According to Mr. Allen's contract with government, he is bound to build a church here next year, & the settlers are to choose a minister. Both Mr. Allen & Mr. Kilburn informed us, that from the acquaintance of the people there with the brethren in Fairfield, they were desirous to obtain a minister of our church. They said they had conversed with Mr. Senseman and Mr. Young on the subject, and would be glad to receive either of them. They would also be willing to submit to the tenets and discipline of our church. We told them that it was not so much a disposition to receive our doctrine & church constitution, as a sincere desire after salvation, that was looked for in persons who wished to join our fellowship. On their desire to know to whom they should make their request regularly, we directed them to write to the Revd John Ettwein, Bethlehem, at same time giving them little encouragement to expect that their wish would be complied with. They have upon the whole the character of serious, orderly people, though a principal person there, does not set the brightest example with respect to morals.

So far we had been able to proceed on our journey without a guide; but now it was necessary to take one, on account of the pathless course we had to

To Fairfield: 1798

pursue, and the great difficulty of proceeding at all, if not well acquainted with the country. Guides are here, by a perversion of language, universally called "pilots." At Monsy town, 10 miles from Allen's & 45 from Fairfield, we crossed to the N. side of the Thames. This town is pleasantly situated, on a high bank near the river; but the Indians there have a black & dirty appearance. In their houses & persons, they did not appear to us to be so decent as the Indians of Brandt's town. They are all heathen, and because they have a bad character among the white people, when from home, sometimes call themselves "Moravian Indians." Here we bought milk for our breakfast, and Indian corn for our horses.

The Monsys are a tribe of Delawares: B^r Heckewelder could therefore speak with them. He entered into conversation with a friendly old man, who had been in Bethlehem above 40 years ago, and remembered the names of some of the brethren there. He asked in particular after the late B^r Kliest, of whom he said he bought the best gun he had ever had in his life. He had heard that Bethlehem was destroyed during the war, for which he was very sorry, as the people there were always very kind to the Indians. It was to his no small joy that B^r Heckewelder assured him that Bethlehem was still standing, and that the inhabitants loved the Indians as much as ever. "In particular," said he, "an old chief, whose hair is more gray than yours," (meaning B^r Ettwein), "has a great affection for all the Indians, and prays for them every day to the great Spirit."&c

Here, as usual in the neighborhood of congregations of the brethren, there are individuals who have left our fellowship. We saw two women of this description, who knew us to be brethren. Their countenances, before B^r Heckewelder could recollect them, seemed to us to betray that characteristic consciousness of a something that condemned them, which is as discernible in the copper-colored face of the Indian, as in the more delicate skin of the European. Hence the expression: "he looks like a runaway Moravian."

This was the most fatiguing day we had experienced throughout our whole journey. The weather was warm, the musquitoes troublesome, our road uncertain, & in many places swampy or intersected by gullies and steep precipices, and we had mostly to fight our way through thick bushes. Add to this, we hastened in order to get forward. We comforted ourselves with the thoughts, that these inconveniences, not to say hardships, which we had expected, would soon have an end, at least for the present. Missionaries to the Indians should not be discouraged at trifles, but always be in expectation of greater trials, because very great ones may come upon them. What we have endured was nothing, compared with the sufferings of our brethren and sisters when taken prisoners by the Wiondats, and unmercifully driven before them like beasts of burden.

At night we made a fire, and laid ourselves down to rest on the bank of the Thames. We were too much tired to build a cabin; and the favorable weather rendered it unnecessary. The night was made pleasant by a refreshing breeze that sprung up, so that we could sleep soundly. Had we reclined, on beds of down, in the most commodious chamber, we could not have felt ourselves more refreshed than we did the next morning. A few sausages that we had taken with us from Bethlehem, were at this very time very acceptable with our tea, furnishing us with a relishing and substantial supper and breakfast.

The 22^d What impeded our progress considerably, both yesterday & to-day, was the vast quantity of timber that had been blown down by two great storms, which raged in these parts last year. This obliged us to go many miles round about. We heard of one man who had missed his way here for 14 days, & of another who found it again at the end of 16, both almost famished to death. Our inexperienced guide also lost it more than once, and would probably not have easily found it again, had he not been directed by the superior judgment of B^r Heckewelder, confirmed by an appeal to a small pocket compass, which we had along with us. The weather was cloudy, threatening rain, and he was leading us N. E. instead of S. W. We parted with him when within 6 miles of Fairfield, thankful for the services he had rendered us, notwithstanding his blunders. His pay was a dollar a day. Soon after, the paths became wider & more numerous, and we saw frequent tracks of cattle and horses. Approaching still nearer to the place of our destination, we observed trees peeled, sugar huts, and other marks of the vicinity of an Indian town. At length, quitting the woods, our gladdened eyes discovered *Fairfield*, finely presenting itself on a regular and beautiful eminence, on the northern bank of the Thames, and surrounded by fruitful fields and gardens, enclosed with neat fences. We hastened over the well-constructed bridge at the northern entrance of the town, towards the church, where we alighted at the house of B^r & Sr Zeisberger, by whom we were most heartily welcomed, as also immediately after by B^r & Sr Senseman, B^r Edward, B^r Young, and by all the Indian brethren and sisters. Our joy was great at finding ourselves so happily arrived at the end of our journey, or at least at a place where we could refresh ourselves for a time among our white and Indian brethren & Sisters. And we were above all filled with humble thanks to our Saviour, for his gracious preservation amidst all the dangers which had surrounded and sometimes threatened us, and of which it is not too much to say, that those only who have made *such* journies, can have adequate conceptions. We have travelled in all 583 miles, through a tract of country, which though not altogether a wilderness, in its present rude state, is in many respects as perilous as if it were so. The angel of the Lord has watched over us by day and by night, and preserved us from all evil.

This journal has been written off thus extensively, at the desire of some brethren and sisters in Bethlehem and Nazareth, our particular friends. If they * think that the perusal of it would be acceptable to our brethren and

---

* The Society for the propagation of the gospel which meets in Bethlehem, or the Directors of the same.—Note in manuscript.

To Fairfield: 1798

sisters generally, and other lovers of Zion, they are at liberty to give it a wider circulation, either in its present form, or curtailed. In addition to the effort to entertain Christian friends, our objects have been, to display "the ways of God to man," and give useful and interesting information. We call upon and intreat all who may read or hear what we have written, to unite with us in praises to God our Saviour, for the mercies conferred on us, in that we have been counted worthy to be employed in the propagation of his gospel among the heathen, and been brought safe thus far on our journies. and we request their fervent prayers: that the blessing which has hitherto rested on the missions of the Brethren in America, may be continued & enlarged; and that all heathen nations may be brought to the saving knowledge of the gospel; that Jesus, who alone is worthy, may see of the travail of his soul & be satisfied. To him be all honor & glory, both now and ever. Amen.

Explanation of some Indian names of rivers and places, collected on a journey to Canada, in May 1798.

N. B. The spelling is after the German, as better calculated than the English to shew accurately the true Indian pronunciation. When words have two accentuated syllables, the stress laid on the second is always the greatest.

Wèh-to-pi-jàh-neck, a Delaware word, signifies "Alder river"; called at present To-pi-haǹ-na; a creek in the great pine swamp, which empties itself into the Lehigh or Lecha.

Teǹk-han-neck, Delaware, signifies "Small river," now called Tuǹk-han-na; another creek in the pine swamp which empties itself into the Lehigh.

Meèch-han-neek, Delaware, signifies "Large river." This creek forms the chief branch of the Lehigh.

Lèh-cha-weèk, the Delaware name for the little Lehigh at Allenstown. This word has no particular signification.

Lèh-cha-wì-tank, the Delaware name for the forks of the Delaware, where Easton now stands.

Mŏch-è-woam-ing, Delaware, signifies "where water runs through large clear flats"; called at present Wi-ò-ming.

Sëes-quèh-han-neek, Delaware, signifies "Muddy river." Why this river is so named, is uncertain, as the stream is clear. Called by the white people, Sùs-que-haǹ-na.

Lèh-cha-wà-hen-neek, Delaware, signifies "the forks." The name of a creek, 9 miles above Wilkes-barre, on the Susquehanna.

Kŭi-lù-ta-men, Delaware, signifies "place of surprize." The name of a flat 16 miles above Wilkesbarre, where a party of Indians was once surprized.

Maàsch-pink, Delaware, signifies "Wonderfull water"; the name of a creek, running into the Susquehanna, whose water is in many respects singular. It is pronounced erroneously by most Indians "Ma-schà-pink," which signifies "on the beads"; by the white people it is called Meshòpping.

Whi-a-lù-sis. Delaware, signifies "an old man." The name Whialùsing,* which the Indians gave to the creek and district which are still so called, was derived from the circumstance of an old man's living there for many years.

Schih-schì-quan-nink. † This is the Delaware name of a rattle, made by enclosing pebbles, or other small, hard substances within a tortoise shell. It is used at their heathen sacrifices. How the place on the Susquehanna, which is so called, obtained that appellation, is uncertain; probably such rattles were once made there.

Ti-a-ò-ga, the Mohawk word for "the forks." It is now written Tiòga.

Scha-mùng, Delaware, signifies "horn." So that branch of the Tioga river is called, which flows by Newton. The Indian tradition is, that on the destruction of a large nest of rattle-snakes near this river, one extraordinary large one was found with a horn.

Ko-hòk-ton, Mohawk, "long timber." This is the name of a creek flowing eastwards from the Alleghany towards Bath, on which the timber is remarkably high.

Ka-nis-krà-ga, Mohawk, "slippery elm"; which tree is found in that neighborhood.

Tsche-ne-schè-o, Seneca, "a handsome (or fine) valley"; descriptive of the adjacent country; at present spelt Geneseè or Genesseè.

Ta-ne-wàn-di, Seneca, "rapid stream"; a creek flowing from the Genesee country into the St Laurence.

From Fairfield Heckewelder returned, as he tells us in a brief summary, "in company of William Edwards and 2 Indians, by way of Detroit, Brownstown, River Raison, Miami old Fort, The Rapids, Upper Sandusky, Owl Creek, Walhondi, to Gnadenhütten. Then from Gnadenhütten to Pittsburg to escort Eldridge, and thence back again. In the autumn, in company with Bro. Mortimer (who with Mr. and Mrs. Zeisberger had led a number of Indians from Fairfield to Gnadenhütten) to Bethlehem." ‡

Two years later, when the Moravian Mission Board was preparing to send an assistant missionary to Fairfield in Canada, Heckewelder was asked to prepare an itinerary. He submitted two. They make such good reading that they are here reproduced in full.

---

* By mistake spelt Wialusing in the diary.—Note in manuscript.

† This mode of spelling this name is more agreeable to the Indian pronunciation, than that made use of in Loskiel's mission history.—Note in manuscript.

‡ "John Heckewelder's Travels from 1754 to 1814": Archives of the Moravian Church, Bethlehem, Pa.

To Fairfield: 1798

Route No. I

100	miles	from Bethlehem to New York by land.
160	"	from New York to Albany, by vessel.
16	"	to Schenectady, by Land with wagon.
140	"	to Fort Schuyler, by open boat up the Mohawk River.
2	"	across the Carrying Place to Wood Creek.
140	"	down Wood Creek, through Oneida Lake to Fort Ontario, by boat.
160	"	up Lake Ontario to Newark and Fort Niagara, by boat.
7	"	up Niagara River to the landing, by boat.
10½	"	over the Great Carrying Place to Chippewa River, in wagon.
18	"	to Fort Erie, where passengers take shipping for Detroit in British vessels or in open boats.
250	"	to Detroit, cabin passage, two to three guineas.
80	"	to Fairfield direct; 15 miles farther, if all the way by water.

1083½ "   from Bethlehem to Fairfield.

Remarks: Making allowances for delays occasioned by vessels not being ready, contrary winds, etc., the journey will be performed in 55 days. Granting 8 days delay on the whole, it may be performed in from 35 to 40 days. I have travelled it in less time.

Inconveniences attending this route:—Some danger in stormy weather in open boats on these lakes, and no going on shore when one has occasion for it. While the wind is fair no boat will put in shore through the whole day, and even frequently run all night,—yet on such occasions will put in towards evening, cook, and then go on again.

Conveniences attending this route:—No jogging of wagons, no danger of over-setting them, children and all ride easy, baggage convenient to hand, expenses less. Best manner of going safe in boats on the lakes, is to be civil and friendly to the boatman always, and to have some liquor along so as to serve out to them after a fatiguing spell, and to promise them that you will furnish them with a couple of gallons on their return home.

If this route should be decided upon, I should, for the sake of safety and to be sure of meeting with no disappointments, advise the following preparatory steps to be taken, viz: Write to Henry Tenbrook on the subject, and desire him to make inquiry whether the Schenectady boats carry passengers and baggage as usual between this place and Niagara? What a family would have to pay from Schenectady to the landing above Niagara Fort? Whether, if these boats only go to Fort Ontario, there be vessels there that sail backwards and forwards between these places; and next, to write to his correspondent at Schenectady, to make choice of a good, trusty boatman, and upon the whole to furnish the missionary with letters of introduction, as far as his connections reached, but above all at Schenectady.

Route No. II

310 miles to Pittsburgh by land.
68½ "   Franklin   "
39 "   LeBoeuff   "
13½ "   Presque Isle   "
200 "   Presque Isle to Detroit in vessel thro' Lake Erie.
80 "   to Fairfield, 40 by water & 40 by land.

---

711 miles from Bethlehem to Fairfield.

Remarks: Were it practicable that loaded wagons could go through in the Spring of the year, it should take them at least five weeks to perform the journey to Presque Isle. But from what I have seen and heard, I do not believe that even a five-horse team could go through at any rate, and with any kind of a load, without losing more or less horses, there being near 40 miles of road through an entire swamp, where the horses are continually up to their knees in the mud. To go by water in a boat from Pittsburgh to LeBoeuff takes 30 days, then there remains 13½ miles of the worst road.

Next is to be considered delays at Presque Isle, which may happen to be two, three, four or five weeks. Boarding and lodging very dear, 3 shillings per meal.

Inconveniences attending this route: Too numerous to enumerate.
Conveniences: None. Journey long; expenses great.*

---

* *PHMB,* IX (1885), 356-57.

XXXIII

To French Creek: 1800

IN 1799 JOHN HECKEWELDER, accompanied by Jacob Bush, journeyed from Bethlehem to see the Indian community which Zeisberger had re-established on the Muskingum. The new town was called Goshen. It is seven miles northeast of Gnadenhütten, near Schönbrunn, though on the opposite side of the river, in Goshen Township, Tuscarawas County, Ohio. The graveyard, containing David Zeisberger's remains, may still be seen.

Heckewelder's "Diary of the Journey of the Brethren J. Heckewelder and Jacob Bush to Gnadenhütten on the Muskingum . . ." is not a travel journal but a mission diary concerning itself with the internal affairs of the little community. We shall, therefore, not pause over it longer than to note Heckewelder's description of the Pittsburgh Road:

"The 26th [May, 1799] in the morning we reached Pittsburg. Though I had made the journey between Bethlehem and Pittsburg some twenty-odd times, and at all seasons of the year: I do not remember ever having found it drier and better. What bothered us most was the dust, which lay fully an inch deep on the ground."

He returned to Bethlehem, December 3.

The next year, 1800, saw him once more in Western Pennsylvania. He accompanied Christian Frederic Dencke to Gnadenhütten, where they arrived May 14. In the Fall of the same year he journeyed to Pittsburgh and from there north, on a commission from the Society for

Propagating the Gospel, to view the Moravian lands in the neighborhood of French Creek.

The Legislature of Pennsylvania in 1791 made a grant to the Moravians of two tracts of land near lake Erie, each of 2,500 acres. One was on French Creek, between the present Waterford and Union City; the other, on Conneaut Creek a few miles to the west. Hopefully, the Moravians named the first tract "Good Luck," the second "Hospitality"; but the disturbed condition of the Pennsylvania border, under the constant threat of Indian war, made the Christian Indians, who remembered only too well the massacre at Gnadenhütten, unwilling to risk themselves in as close proximity as these places now were to irresponsible white settlers. The Indians never settled here.

In 1800 John Heckewelder made a journey to look these lands over and report on them to Bethlehem.

A Journey from Pittsburgh to Le Beauff on the far Side of French Creek, in which all Roads, Tracts, and Places are Truthfully described.*

Nov. 1, 1800. Early in the morning I was ferried across the Allegheny River, and rode 9 miles to Willeby's [Perryville], where I fed. Here I saw an odd thing: the landlord had hung his sign, the picture of a deer, from a pole resting in the crotches of two trees that grew side by side. At Samuel Duncan's (an acquaintance) where I stopped again for a short time, I examined a new horse-mill which he had built. A woman who was going my way for five miles or so from here told me, when we came to Breakneck Hill, that a few years ago a drunken man, as he was going down the hill, fell off his horse and broke his neck, and so the place got its name. On the far side of the run, where there is a plantation, I met another acquaintance, who would not let me go by without stopping. During the short time I was here, I learned that it was true what we heard at the Muskingum, namely that on the 19th of August all the Indian corn and garden stuff had been frozen. That is about what I had expected from what I had seen of the country since I left the first inn, it was all so bare of trees, and where any were still standing they were mostly white oak and these were all stunted. The country continued like this for a few miles more till I came to the Ganachquenesink [Conoquenessing] Creek, where one Amberson lives, with whom I stayed overnight. Here I met 3 wagons and a cart with draymen who were on their way to Cassawaga [Meadville] and had a lot of cattle and hogs with them.

The 2nd. After I had gone about 5 or 6 miles, the road going up hill and down dale almost continuously as it did yesterday, though the land was much better today, an entirely different countryside came into sight. The timber was heavier and the soil richer and not so clayey. In short, the country became

---

* Translated from the German.

To French Creek: 1800

flat, and one did not see a hill for 15 miles. The many fine plantations showed clearly enough that one could make a living here. This country seemed to me very much like that at Lebanon, though not nearly so well built up. A beautiful river [marginal note in manuscript: (Slippery Rock)] about one sixth as wide as the Lecha [Lehigh] flows through this region, and discharges itself, after first uniting with the Ganachquenesink, into the Big Beaver Creek. During the morning I stopped for a while at Barthel Lauffer's (a brother-in-law of Henrich Strauss in the Settlement) who by his own admission had through card-playing fallen from his former prosperity into poverty. In the afternoon I fed at Reed's, the best plantation I have seen in this whole journey. This same Reed had to pay $4 an acre for the mere improvement-right. In the evening I came to one Adams, where I stayed overnight. By this time I had got out of the country I have just been describing. The land had become hilly and stony again. In the morning I found that Adams did not lag behind the other innkeepers on this road (of which there are many) in his charges. Here again there were many wagons and drivers.

The 3rd. I set off as usual by daybreak, and found these 14 miles to Fort Franklin the hilliest and stoniest road I have had so far, But the timber indicated a rich soil. After I had breakfasted here, I crossed French Creek and took the Indian path to Cassawaga, or Meadville. For the first 9 miles to Johnson's, the country was much like what I have just been describing. While feeding my horse here, I learned that the frost already noted as of August 19, had hit many places hard and *completely* missed others. There were some people on their way to the mill here. I asked them how far they had to go. They answered, 18 miles. Immediately behind Johnson's fence is a little hill and a run, and here the country changed for the better, and I found it similar in many respects to our Muskingum upland. But there were three things I didn't like: 1. There were so many ferns on the land, which indicates a *hard, cold soil.* 2. Too much moss on the branches and treetops, which is a sure sign of an area of *cold.* 3. the tops of all the trees were blunted except those that those that had been growing for a year or two from the stumps, which plainly shows that every now and then exceptionally *early or late frosts* occur, which kill the tips of the branches. By this time I had come 10 miles on this path without meeting a soul from whom I could have made inquiries about the road or anything else. Night, or at least twilight, had descended, and where I was there was no grass in the woods for my horse. So I decided to go back a quarter of a mile and camp by a run. Just as I turned, a dog approached me, and as I looked, an Indian appeared carrying a deer on his back. I first asked him in English where he was camping, and if there were a house nearby. But he did not understand me. I tried him then in Delaware. This he understood, and answered me, in Monsy, that a little more than a mile ahead of us was a blacksmith, that this blacksmith was now mending a gun for him, and he was bringing this meat for payment. Though the man was neither a Delaware nor a Monsy, but belonged to the Senneca nation, he was glad to meet someone with whom he could talk, and afterwards, when we stopped at the blacksmith's, I was his interpreter. The meat was *à propos*, and I received good entertainment at a reasonable price.

The 4th. I set out early again and found the country much better than the day before. I rode past many fine plantations. I was told, however, that this was nothing in comparison with the land towards the south as far as French Creek. This much I could have seen for myself, that the hills on the south side of French Creek form a barrier, and that consequently no good land was to be found on the far side. After I had ridden 9 miles, Cassawaga or Meadville came into view from a beautiful hill. In this little town I lodged with a German, named Reigart. After breakfast I went, on Eyerly and Huber's business, to see Major Alden, agent of the Holland Company, who lives here, and by whom I was well received. He even called on me at my lodging that night and gave me a friendly letter of introduction to his deputy, Mr. [William] Miles, who lives close to the Moravian lands. Other acquaintances also called on me, and I had opportunity to see and talk to many persons from the vicinity of Coneaught. They all agreed on this: that the finest country and the best soil in the northwestern part of the State *lay around Coneaught Lake*. Meadville (of which Col. Meade is the Proprietor) consists of about 40 houses, most of them well built and a few outstanding, in particular Mead's and Alden's, for their size and excellent workmanship. There are several good stores and also some good taverns, which have the usual signs hanging out in front. There is a mill on the bank of French Creek, which here makes a turn in shape of a bottle. The gardens are for the most part enclosed with good board fences, and the inhabitants seemed to me to be much quieter than I have usually found them in these frontier towns. The situation, on the high bank of French Creek, affords a fine view. Now that the place has become a county town—the courts actually sat here in October—it is likely to have a rapid development. The only thing I have to say against it is that the lots are too small [Note in manuscript: 50 foot frontage], and consequently the houses are too close together. I suppose, however, that Mr. Mead had good reason for having it laid out this way, no doubt with an Indian war in mind. In the evening I met a poor old negro in the kitchen, who had something I could not have found a name for if he had not told me. He called it a fiddle. It was a round closed box with an exceptionally long neck and 4 strings. I would well imagine what kind of a night I was going to have if he started in scraping here in the tavern. So I asked him how much he earned by it. "Oh," he said, "good people give poor negro sometimes pennys, sometimes something to eat & drink." I came to an agreement with him for a small price not to play here tonight, whereupon he went off to another tavern.

The 5th. I continued my journey in company with 4 New Englanders who live not far from Le Beauff [Le Boeuf, now Waterford]. For the first 6 or 7 miles the woods were pleasant, and the roads good, but now we got into a beech swamp where not only was there a deep marsh but the many roots of

To French Creek: 1800

these trees, roots which, as is well known, lie for the most part on or above the ground, made it dangerous for the horses, which often got a leg stuck. I asked my companions how long this would continue. They answered: "Most of the way until you reach your destination." After 18 miles we came to one of Major Alden's sawmills, in charge of a German named Fetterman, but this person was not then at home. Here was a stand of the finest white pine I had ever seen, and beside the mill were well over a 100 thousand feet of boards. It was now evening, and we still had 7½ miles to go. Since we had to go through white and spruce pine swamps almost the whole way, and it was getting darker and darker, I chose to ride behind someone who had a white horse, but the air being thick with smoke made the darkness so heavy that soon I could neither see the white horse nor my hands when I held them up before my eyes. The path continued to be swampy and there were often deep holes in which first one and then another got stuck. Every now and again the leader, who was usually the first to spot such places, called to us to look out, but nobody knew where, because we could not see a thing. We frequently lost our way, and at last a branch took the hat off my head. There was a long search before it was found, because it could only be found by groping around for it, and it turned out that my horse was standing on it with one foot. During this search (they would not let me get off) one of their horses got away. I asked if it would not be better to stay where we were until daylight. But it began to snow, and a wind came up: we could hear trees falling here and there. The darkness was so great that you could see no more than in a closed barrel. Every moment I feared an accident, but there was nothing else to be done, we *had* to go on, and anyway, unless these people were wrong, we should reach a house in less than a mile. Oh, but this mile seemed long to me. Finally, however, we saw a light ahead of us, and at last reached it. My companions, who knew the place, called to me at once: "Dont alight, Daddy. The muck is middle-leg deep, uel [we'll] lay some rails for you to walk on." * (I was traveling without being able to wear a shoe or boot on the one foot because it had been rather badly crushed by my horse's stepping on it and was very much swollen). These good people looked after me so well that they made a causeway from the fence (where I had to alight) to the house door. The people in the house were just about to go to bed, but they made a big fire and my companions made some torches of dry linden bark. On one side of the fire sat a little old man who had on a reddish wig, and on the other side were 3 good looking young women, who picked up their work again as soon as we entered the house. I wondered how such a genteel family as this one seemed to be could have got into this wild gloomy place, so I sounded the man out, and this is the story he told me. "My name is Kerr. I left my country (Ireland) 4 years ago with my wife and 9 children in

---

* These words were written in English, with spelling and phrasing a German reader would understand."

order to escape the disturbances there and arrived early in August at Wilmington. But I had been only a few days in the country when my wife died, and before the month was up 3 of my children. The fame of this French Creek country even in Ireland, was known to me and I was strongly advised, on my arrival in America, to go out there. Accordingly I bought a wagon, 2 oxen and 2 horses, and started out. The hardships of that journey—the winter there, and food not to be had even for money, made my situation very unpleasant and precarious. I sent my son to Pittsburg to buy flour and have it sent here, which was done, but out of 6 barrels I got only 1½ and that had to be fetched from 37 miles away. My two horses died and one of my oxen became ill and I felt obliged to butcher it to keep us alive. For over 2 years I have had to buy my flour from the Holland Comp^y, and at 18 $ a barrel, likewise for every lb. of meat I have had to pay 2/6 per lb. and for potatoes 15/ to 25/ per bushel, and in addition have had to haul them 27 miles. Now, (said he) I have got over the worst of it." I answered, "I wonder you got so far." "Ah (said he) it was the *Crowns* I had in my Pocket that did the business, had I not had them, we either must have perished, or be Slaves all our Life time." I asked him if he was now satisfied with his situation. He answered "Yes!" However, he would be better satisfied if these 400 acres he owns here were within half a mile of Dublin. One of my companions asked him if there were Moravians in Ireland, too? "Plenty (he replied) and they are very fine people, a credit to their country, and I have often wished a body of them would come over and settle the good land belonging to the Moravians here; it is a pity it should be lying idle like this." "Yes," said one of the daughters (with great modesty), "I, too, wish the Moravians would make a settlement on their land, I would often visit them!" Each of the others chimed in, "Me, too." I said, "There are many Moravians in this country. Have you never seen any?" Ans. "Not one!"

Then my companions told them the secret. "There is one sitting right in front of you," they said. "He has been talking to you all this while." They were delighted, and went on talking about the Brethrens' land (a corner of which touches theirs) and the proposed settlement. By this time my companions were ready to go on, and I could not desert so loyal a company, and, besides, I wanted to see the end of my journey. We took our leave—the torches were lighted—and we went on. We were not more than a few hundred steps from the house, however, when the hindmost rider missed the one-pole bridge which led over a boggy place, and sank so deep into the mud, that it was only with difficulty his horse was pulled out again. But a little further on we came out on to high, dry land, and somebody shouted: "We've made it! We are on the Moravian Line." Along this line we rode another 1½ miles to Robert King's where we arrived at 11:30, and found everybody in bed. The Kings were wakened—we had refreshments—I acquainted him with the object of my journey, and we retired about 2 o'clock. What an inexpressible contrast it seemed to me in the morning, after such a long, dirty,

To French Creek: 1800

dark ride, to find myself now in such nice, dry, open country on the banks of lovely French Creek, and in a fine two-story house. From 3 sides of this house one looks out across half a mile of beautiful flats (dry clear meadow-like plains). Right after breakfast on the 6th Mr. King rode with me over to the Moravian land, and where possible we followed the line. He seemed to be well acquainted with the place and spared no effort to show me all its advantages. Soon he took me to those fine flats, where there were large haystacks, then to the site of a projected town, after that to a waterfall where a mill could be installed, and finally to the Forks [the junction of LeBoeuf and French Creeks], where Mr. Miles has a storehouse standing on the Brethren's land, where a few acres of land have been cleared, and where he has put a family to superintend it. We had hardly sat down in the house when the man (a Prussian by birth) berated Mr. Miles most violently in my presence, and explained to me in a pitiful manner what would happen to him if he and his wife and children were now driven out of the house with winter at the door as Mr. Miles threatened. I promised to talk to Mr. Miles about this, and did so when I next saw him, but afterwards I had to tell the man, as Miles told me, that he had brought it upon himself—that he did not bear a good name and was unfaithful. Nevertheless at my request Mr. Miles was willing to give him another chance. By this time we had come to the great road which runs from Capt. King's through the Moravian lands to Mr. Miles' mills. We were going to take it, but Capt. King asked me to make a little detour with him to see some poor people whom I perhaps might help with a little good advice, as he very much hoped. I was the more ready to do so as I saw in him a loving heart and sympathy for the poor. The woman was alone in the house with the children, and poverty looked out of their eyes. This is the story: The woman is a daughter of Henry Singer of Reading. But she, in an unlucky hour 11 years ago when the troops were in Reading, attached herself to a corporal and eloped with him against all advice from her parents, whereupon her father (who was well-to-do) was so enraged that he disinherited her. Now she wished that, when I came to Reading, I would intercede for her and try to appease her father. She knew she had acted badly, and she was sorry for it. She was living quietly with her husband, and they had 5 children. But they were very poor, and very much in debt. They owed the Holland Comp^y alone between 5 and 600 dollars for provisions for the last few years. I advised her to write to her parents through me and to send the letter to my lodging by tomorrow evening. *Note.* On my arrival in Reading I found that both her parents had died this very year. [Note in author's manuscript: Her father stuck by his decision and disinherited her.] I have, however, brought her circumstances to the attention of her brothers and sisters and hope it will have some effect. The oldest son of the family mentioned above now went with us to show us a corner of the Moravian line, which was only a few hundred steps from their house. From this point on we went by the great road, and rode up the branch another 2 miles to Mr. Miles' mills, where I found the men I mentioned, and handed him the letter of recommendation I had got from Major Alden, and was well received. Here (when we were alone) Mr. Miles opened a large book and showed me how deeply the people of the neighborhood were in debt to the Holland Comp^y. On each sheet, under where the debt was added up, was the signed acknowledgment of the debtor. For most of them this was between 2 and 800 $, and this was all for groceries and tools. It is so hard for many poor people to get started in this country. And what will they have in the end if they cannot pay their debts? Nothing. On the contrary, they have sacrificed their labor for the benefit of the speculators and satisfied the law only to *those* persons' advantage. What I mean by that is this: The Assembly 8—9 years ago, when the law for selling and settling the northwest part of this state was made, added this clause: That likewise all lands in this district (Donation Lands excepted) located by or with bought warrants are subject to settlement, as the act reads—and this says: 2 years after the conclusion of a peace with the Indians, for every 400 acres an improvement shall be begun, and this shall consist of one dwelling house and 8 acres of land cleared and well fenced; and on this improvement the improver and his family must have lived 5 years before he can get a deed from the state for this land, etc. Now the Comp^y speculators hunted up poor people who would improve *their* lands for a certain share. Some promised the improver 100 acres, some 150 and some even more. So these people came on to the land, but they had nothing to live on and no money, either. The speculators gave them on credit *at top price* what they needed. Now the improvements are ready, and next year is the time when the original holder by warrant first, & now by settlement, can get his deeds. As long, however, as the improver has not paid off his debt, he gets no deed, or if he did get a deed, his improvement would be put under mortgage. Consequently he has nothing in the end because he will never be able to pay the debt.

Now we set off again on our return; we took, however, a different route across the Brethrens' land, and reached King's house just as it got dark.

The 7th early we rode again over the Moravian lands, partly to look at the north side of the tract, partly to see an elevated place for a possible town site. From this place we rode along the line to King, Jr., who has a plantation here. Afterwards we cut through the woods to the Le Beauff road and followed it till we reached that place. There we stayed for about 2 hours, because an officer there whom I had known at Detroit would not let me pass unless I dined with him. Bethlehem and the boarding school there, the Moravian tract, and the wish that the Moravians would soon settle on it,—this was the whole substance of our talk at the table, in which King joined. Then we rode off together to look over this place, of which I already had a pretty good idea. I did not find, however, what I expected, at least not in all respects. The town location, where the fort is, is on a dry, level rise with well over 100 acres of cleared land covered with tame grass. There are, besides a few small houses, some larger ones which serve as stores and inns. The place

To French Creek: 1800

has this further advantage that everything can be brought here by water from Pittsburg so that from here to Presque Isle there remains only 13½ miles of land transport, which is certainly a great help to trade. There were some things here, however, I did not like. The surrounding marshes and the swampy land—a lake of over 100 acres in extent within a quarter of a mile of the town, unapproachable for 100 yards *from every side* because of the swamps that surround it. And somebody told me that 10 of the 13½ miles to Presque Isle are so swampy as to be almost impassable; for which reason I was glad enough to give up my plan to go there. I liked very well *that* part of the reservation which touches the Moravian lands on the one side and Kings or French Creek on the other, a good 100 acres of which have been cleared (it looks like the flats at Wyoming), and which is for the most part dry and grown over with oak trees. This is the highest-priced part of the reservation, at 4 dollars per acre. King, who was anxious that I should carry a good impression of the land back to Bethlehem, took me on our return over the Moravian land again to show me the wild hops growing there, and from here we rode home. As I had now seen everything and attended to all necessary business, I was ready to return. I was afraid, however, of the road I had come by, through Meadville. But they gave me reason to hope that, if I took the new road laid out from Bald Eagle [Milesburg] on the West Branch of the Susquehanna [actually on Bald Eagle Creek, which flows into the West Branch at Lock Haven] to Le Beauff, which this past week had been graded for the first 15-16 miles to where it crosses the Franklin Road, I should have pretty good going for at least so much of the way because it is not yet all cut up. From there on there would be some bad road before I reached Fort Franklin, to which place I would in this way go directly. They told me about the contract under which this new road had been made: cutting down trees for a road 2 rods wide and hauling them away at 20 $ a mile, and for grading and making wooden bridges 14/6 a rod.

On the 8th I set off early over the new road and found fairly dry going until I came to the first saw mill, at the place mentioned above where this road crosses the Meadville Road, except for one section, about half a mile long so that I was able to ride without interruption, because the road keeps to the higher land. At the sawmill the Irishman there advised me to take some oats along because he said I would not find another house for 15 miles and there was no feed to be had at that house. I was glad of the advice and rode on, keeping on fairly high ground and sometimes in pleasant woods where there were white, black, and *Spann* [Spanish?] oaks, chestnuts, cherries, poplar and Cumcumer trees [cucumber trees, belonging to the magnolia family]. Here and there, however, were little pine and beech swamps, where the ground was all soft and soggy. At last, a tree on which the miles were engraved (a custom in this country) the Franklin road appeared, and with it deep mud, the road being badly cut up. From this point on I had to wade almost continuously through the mud for a full 8 miles. On this road I met 5 heavy freight wagons which carry freight for the United States all summer from Franklin to Presque Isle and back. To each of these wagons 6 of the largest, strongest oxen were hitched. Man and beast looked quite exhausted. I asked the men how far they could go in a day on such a road. They replied, 5 or 6 miles. That certainly takes courage and patience, I thought. At last I came suddenly out of the darkness into the light, that is to say I emerged from a gloomy pine swamp into dry oak country at Luce's. He used to live near Hope in Jersey, and remembered the Brethren there kindly—he knew them all— and asked me to remember him to them when I could, especially his friend, Linebach. He wanted to entertain me overnight as his guest, if I would stay. However, I could not afford to lose an hour of this fine weather, for I still had a long way to go. But now I saw how people lie for the sake of making money. After what the man at the sawmill had said about there being no fodder here, I paid him 4 pence a quart for oats and on his advice took 8 quarts along with me; and here I could have had all I wanted for 3 pence. From here I rode 6 miles over good dry oak country to Plummer's, where I put up. I had been there only a few minutes when a drunken Seneca Indian came in, followed soon by several others, who were not, however, the worse for liquor. The innkeper showed them into an adjoining building, where on towards midnight they held a dance, to which their women folk sang an accompaniment. I cannot say they bothered me much, for where I lay I could *not* hear the dancing, and the singing being somewhat muted served rather as a slumber song. From asking a lot of questions everywhere about who owned the land, I learned that John Field, a Quaker in Philadelphia, owns most of the Landed Property in this part of the country.

The 9th By daybreak I was on my way again. For these last 9 miles to Fort Franklin, I found the road dry and the country covered with good oak timber, with this change only, that the last 3 or 4 miles were more hilly and stony than the first. In Franklin (or as the town should properly be called) Waterford,* I went down to the fort after breakfast in company with an acquaintance, Marcus Huling, who is a nephew of old Mrs. Jones near Bethlehem, in order to see the mouth of French Creek where it empties into the Allegheny River. This sight is worth seeing, and to my taste is better than that at West Point on the Hudson. These two rivers look, from the fort, like an English T upside down. French Creek here is nearly as wide as the Lecha, and the Allegheny about 3 times as wide. A long narrow plain on the lower or south side of French Creek and the west side of the Allegheny, over which houses are scattered here and there for a quarter of a mile, is picturesquely hemmed in with high steep hills, so that no other gaps are visible but the inlet and outlet of these streams. There were large boats here which, as I was told, carry 14 tons from here to LeBeauff. I counted about 20 houses, but most of them, like the gardens and some of the fields, are under water at flood time.

---

* Waterford was the new name, not of Franklin (formerly Venango), but of LeBoeuf.

The Commanding Officer, Captain Fowler, tried to persuade me to spend the day with him and his wife, so I could tell them all about Bethlehem, where they have now a grandchild (Miss Butler) in the boarding school. I had to promise, if ever I came here again, to stay with no one else but him. I still had 68½ miles to Pittsburg. Just as I was about to start 2 Mennonites named Showalter (former neighbors at Bethlehem) joined me and kept me company until we came to the pleasant country I described before, where they were engaged in land purchase, they being as much attracted to *these* parts as they were repelled by the lands lying farther north. We spent the night at Funk's.

The 10th at noon I stopped again at an acquaintance's, and in the evening took lodging at Sam! Duncan's.

By the afternoon of the 11th I was back again in Pittsburg. This was the 16th day that I had been unable to wear either boot or shoe, my foot being badly swollen after my horse had stepped on it and I had to go round with nothing but a sock on it. The day before yesterday a woman bound it in a strip of linen covered with tar, and from that hour the swelling went down and the pain was eased, and today I could get a boot on again. I mention this for the benefit of others who may be in the same fix. The woman said this plaster *really* should have been made of wagon-grease as it runs off the axle, which is supposed to be far better for bruises. Another good remedy is this for ear-ache and headache: red schumeck or shumack berries, boiled in water, and bring the steam to the ear through a funnel.

XXXIV

Thirty Thousand Miles with John Heckewelder: 1754-1813

AFTER THE TRIP to Le Boeuf in 1800, John Heckewelder's journal-writing days were over, though not his journeyings. In 1801 he moved with his family from Bethlehem to Gnadenhütten on the Tuscarawas, and remained there as agent of the Society for Propagating the Gospel until 1810. During these years, with Gnadenhütten as his headquarters, he travelled much: frequently to Zanesville, occasionally to Marietta, twice to Bethlehem. In 1809 (Ohio having become a state in 1803) he was appointed by the Assembly, as he notes, with other commissioners to locate two new County seats, visiting Canton, Wooster, Richland, &c. . . .* He negotiated successfully with the Ohio legislature for the incorporation of the Society of which he was a representative.

Heckewelder concludes his autobiography with the words, "In 1810, I returned again to Bethlehem with my family, in order to spend the remainder of my days in retirement."

To John Heckewelder, retirement did not mean oblivion. In 1813 he visited again the scene of his most dramatic adventures: "For the last time to the Western Country," he notes, "travelling by way of Pittsburg, Harmony, Beaver Town, Tuscarawas to New Philadelphia and

---
* "John Heckewelder's Reisen zwischen 1754 und 1814": Archives of the Moravian Church, Bethlehem, Pa.

Gnadenhütten— From there to Zanesville and back to Gnadenhütten then home again"—in all a journey of 955 miles.*

Even after he had finally given over these long trips to the frontier, his spirit continued to roam over the scenes and incidents of his early travels. Through letters and books he put his knowledge of early America into lasting form. As early as 1816, at the request of Caspar Wistar of Philadelphia, he had begun to write pieces about the Indians as he had known them. These sketches grew into the well-known book from which Fenimore Cooper drew for his *Leatherstocking Tales.* Heckewelder's book appeared under the title, *An Account of the History, Manners, and Customs of the Indian Nations Who Once Inhabited Pennsylvania and the Neighbouring States* (Philadelphia, 1819). This was followed by *A Narrative of the Mission of the United Brethren Among the Delaware and Mohegan Indians, from Its Commencement, in the Year 1740, to the Close of the Year 1808* . . . (Philadelphia, 1820). His last work, completed a few months before his death, did not appear in print until ten years later.: *Names which the Lenni Lenape or Delaware Indians, who once inhabited this country, had given to Rivers, Streams, Places, &c. &c. within the now States of Pennsylvania, New Jersey, Maryland and Virginia: and also Names of Chieftains and distinguished Men of that Nation; with the Significations of those Names, and Biographical Sketches of some of those Men. By the late Rev. John Heckewelder of Bethlehem, Pennsylvania. Communicated to the American Philosophical Society April 5, 1822, and now published by their order; revised and prepared for the press by Peter S. Du Ponceau* (Philadelphia, 1833).

The eagerness which had carried him through so many adventures in his youth now brought him distinctions of another kind. People came from far and near to hear him talk. They called at his home on Heckewelder Alley (now Heckewelder Place), where his house may still be seen, exchanged flowers and plants with him, discussed Indian affairs, and listened to his stories, of which he had a considerable fund. "Pappy Heckewelder's Ghost Story" at one time had a vogue among the young people of Bethlehem.

In his eightieth year, he found himself in failing health. The last night of his life he was heard repeating to himself the words he had once seen inscribed by Indians on a peeled tree at Pettquotting: "The Savior's blood and righteousness . . ."

---

* *Ibid.*

He died at six o'clock in the morning of January 31, 1823.

His wife, Sara, had died before him, June 20, 1815. His three daughters—Polly (Johanna Maria), Sally (Anna Salome, now Mrs. Joseph Rice), and Susanna (Mrs. John Christian Luckenbach)—survived him for many years.

On his gravestone in the Moravian Cemetery at Bethlehem these words are inscribed:

In Memory
of
JOHN
HECKEWELDER
who was born
March 12th 1743
in Bedford England
and departed this Life
January 31
1823

But a more fitting memorial is the list he made—evidently with relish, for he revised it several times—of his 30,156 miles (as he calculated it) in the service of the Indians he loved.

John Heckewelder's Travels Between 1754 & 1814 *

Year	Description	Miles
1754	Jan. From Fulneck to London (11 years old)	200
	ditto from London to New-York	3,000
	From New-York to Bethlehem by way of Braunschweig [Brunswick]	100
1762	From Bethlehem with Christ.ⁿ F. Post to Muskingum	420
	returned in Nov. of the same year	420
1763	To New-York and back	200
1765	To David Zeisberger at Friedenshutten for a short stay, and then back again	300
1767	To Wayomick with D. Zeisberger and back alone	160
1768	To Wayomick with Zeisberger, Ettwein, Senseman and Angerman (the Brother who was careless with the light)	80
	Back with Angerman	80
1769	To Friedenshütten by myself, as messenger, & back	160
1770	To Friedenshutten and Scheschequon as a messenger	180
	Return with Br. Rothe and some Indians	180

* Translated from the German.

Thirty Thousand Miles: 1754-1813

1771	To Friedenshütten with Dav. Zeisberger & return	300
	Then with Dav. Zeisberger to Langundowi-Otenink on Beaver Creek, Ohio............	380
	dito from there to Pittsburg, & return.........	120
1772	From Langundowi-Oteney to the Allegheny to meet the Friedenshütten congregation & Br. Ettwein & Rothe....	180
	Then with D. Zeisberger, Ettwein, and Indians to Schönbrunn on the Muskingum...........	80
	Return with Dav. Zeisberger and Shebosh to Langundowi Otenink, and back to Schönbrun..........	160
1773	To Langundowi Otennink with Indians by land.....	80
	From there by water with a part of the Indian congregation in 23 canoes down the Beaver Creek and Ohio to the mouth of the Muskingum............	180
	Then up the Muskingum to Schönbrun........	160
1774	With 4 Indian Brethren from Schönbrun straight through the woods to the Great Island, and Gnadenhütten on the Mahony, to Bethlehem, and back the same way....	800
1775	With Schebosch and Indians by way of Sikheunk, Mahonink, Shenango, Langundowi Otenink after stolen horses...	200
1776	With David Zeisberger and 8 families of Indians to Lichtenau (Apr. 11) by water 70, by land.........	42
	and back again in the fall in order to teach school....	42
1777	To Bethlehem alone...............	420
1778	Beginning of March by way of Lancaster & Yorktown with Shebosch to Pittsburg, Gnadenhütten, and Lichtenau, meeting many dangers because of the warriors......	450
	ditto in the fall, journey to Tuscorawas and back with Indians	110
1779	There and back again with Indians.........	110
1780	Went with Indians to Salem by water.........	45
1781	Taken to Upper Sandusky as a prisoner.......	100
	ditto with Dav. Zeisberger, Edwards, Senseman and 4 Indians to Detroit, on the Commandant's orders......	110
	Return from Detroit to Upper Sandusky.......	110
1782	Back to Detroit—with all the missionaries......	110
	ditto to the Huron River, and return to Detroit by water	80
	Back again [to the Huron River] with Senseman, this time to stay	40
1783	May. From the Huron River to Detroit and back in a batteau with Mich. Young and Edwards.........	80
	Oct. With Senseman by water in a canoe to Detroit. On the way we were nearly wrecked..........	80
1784	Again by water to Detroit and back.........	80
1785	Twice back and forth during the year........	160

1786	April. Left Huron River and went by vessel to Detroit and Rocky Point—then in a bark canoe to Cayahaga River . .	160
	ditto in Oct. with family to Bethlehem	420
1787	With Mich. Jung and Wygand to Pitsburg & back	640
1788	June. With Br. Ettwein by way of Staten Island to N. York .	100
	Back with him by a detour, and through Hope	130
	August, to New York again by myself and return	200
	Sept. With Matth. Blickensdorffer to Pittsburg, and from there with Capt. Thos. Hutchins, Surveyor General of the United States, by water to Marietta, and, after a stay of 9 weeks, return with Blickensdorffer. Altogether	940
1789	With Br. Abraham Steiner to Petquottink and back . . .	980
	With Charles Colver to Carlisle and back	230
1792	At request of Gen. Washington through the Secretary of War, Gen. Knox, took a 9 months journey with Gen. Putnam to try to make peace with the Indian nations:	

From Bethlehem to Pittsburg (at that time it was still this far)	320	miles
From Pittsburg to the Wabash (according to Hutchins)	1022	
Up the Wabash by water to Vincennes	160	
From Vincennes by land to Falls of the Ohio	150	
From Falls of the Ohio to Pittsburg .	705	
From Pittsburg to Philadelphia by way of Bethlehem	370	
Total	2727	. . . 2,727

1793 Again at the request of the government I went on April 8th to Philadelphia to join the 3 commissioners, General Lincoln from Boston, Col. Timothy Pickering from Philadelphia, and the former Governor of Virginia, Beverly Randolph, and some other gentlemen, on a journey to Detroit and the Miami, to hold a treaty with the hostile Indians. The journey from here by way of Philadelphia, New York, Albany, Schenectady, Fort Stanwix, Oneida Lake, Fort Oswego, Lake Ontario, Fort Niagara, Newark, Queenstown, Niagara Falls, and Lake Erie to Detroit, total   800

ditto from Detroit by myself to Fairfield and back to Detroit   140

Return trip. Aug. 18th from Detroit through Lake Erie to Niagara—through Lake Ontario to Kingston (formerly

	called Fort Frontenac)— From Kingston down the St. Lawrence River to Montreal— From Montreal by land to St. Johns—then by boat down Lake Champlain to Skeensborough (also called Whitehall), then overland by stage down the North River to Albany—then by ship to New York, and overland to Bethlehem	1,310
1794	With Jacob Eyerly to Pittsburg (he was on his way to survey the French Creek lands) and return	620
1797	With William Henry Esq. and others to Gnadenhütten on Muskingum, for the survey	410
	ditto. From there I travelled through the woods to Marietta, part of the way alone, the rest with an Indian	125
	From Marietta with Gen. Putnam and his surveyor west to Gnadenhütten for the survey—and then west with him to the Tuscarawas foarding place—then back by water to Marietta, and from there to Bethlehem	840
1798	From Bethlehem with Benjamin Mortimer through the Genessee Country to Buffaloe, Black Rock, Niagara Falls, Queenstown, New-Ark, the head of Lake Ontario, Burlington Heights, Grand River or Brandts-Town, the Pinery, Monsey Town, to Fairfield, Upper Canada	530
	Then from Fairfield with William Edwards, and 2 Indians by way of Detroit, Brownstown, River Raison, Rapids of Miami, Upper Sandusky, Owl Creek, Walhandi, to Gnadenhütten	270
	From Gnadenhütten to Pittsburg to escort Mr. Eldrige—and back	200
	Then in the fall with Benj. Mortimer (who had come down with D. Zeisberger and some Indian families) to Bethlehem	410
1799	To Muskingum and back to Bethlehem	820
1800	With Christ. Fr. Dencke to Gnadenhütten	410
	In the fall from Gnadenhütten to Pittsburg, and from there by way of Fort Franklin and Meadville to Le Beauf on a commission from the Directors of the Heathen Society [Society for Propagating the Gospel among the Heathen] to view the lands on French Creek belonging to them—then back again by way of Pittsburg to Bethlehem—total . . .	660
1801	Moved with my family to Muskingum	410
	Also travelled to Marietta and back	220
1802	From Gnadenhütten to Marietta and back	220
	ditto in the fall at my own expense to Bethlehem and back again	820

1803	To Marietta and back	220
	ditto in the fall with the Loskiels from Gnadenhütten to Pittsburg and back	200
1804	On official business, as an associate appraiser of houses to Zanesville and other places	140
1805	To Zanesville, and back	120
1806	To Zanesville to pay taxes, and back	120
	Then to Bethlehem at my own expense and back by way of Philadelphia	860
1807	To Zanesville and back	120
1808	To Zanesville and back, to pay taxes	120
1809	August. To Zanesville and back	120
	And in the month of April at the request of the Assembly with 2 other commissioners to locate two "Seats of Justice" in new counties, travelled to Canton, Wooster, Richland etc., and then back again	190
	ditto in December by way of Zanesville & New Lancaster to the Assembly in Chilocothe, with a petition for an Act of Incorporation for the Heathen Society, and in Jan. 1810 back with them	245
1810	To Zanesville and back to pay taxes	120
	In Oct. went with my family to Bethlehem	410
1811	Then in January I went to Lancaster with a petition from William Henry Killbuck to the Assembly, and back home by way of Philadelphia	190
1813	For the last time to the Western Country, by way of Pittsburg, the Harmonie, Beaver Town, Tuscorawas, to New Philadelphia, Goshen and Gnadenhütten, and from there by way of Coshocton, Waketemeki to Zanesville and back home, in all	955

Total Miles 30,156

Note Besides the journeys listed above, I have made many shorter trips, as for instance 5 times
to the Hope . . . . (30) . . . 150
Seven times to Gnadenhütten on the Mahony (27) . . . 189
At least 15 times to Philadelphia . . . . (50) . . . 750
Twice to Reading & beyond, & back, say . . (40) . . . 160
Once in the year 1777 for Henry V. Vleck to Morristown in Jersey, and thereabouts and home by way of Hope . . . . . . (160) . . . 160
Once to the Dutch Valley in Jersey . . . (40) . . . 80
Several times to Wechquetank . . . . . (27)

Very often to Nazareth, Christianbrunn etc. (9-10)
often as a messenger, both by day and by night
And in the last 10 years of my sojourn on the
  Muskingum, I have been about 200 times
  to Goshen or New Philadelphia . . . . (7-10)
And a number of shorter trips on horseback—
(I have crossed the Allegheny Mountains exactly 30 times) & in 3 separate places. . . .

Note. As for the mileage, I have informed myself carefully, consulting experts living in those places, printed books, calendars, and route maps, and I have often deducted something from the estimated mileage, especially if the numbers were uneven.

Similarly I have omitted those of my many travels which were less than 40 miles, as, for example, some visits I made to Gnadenhütten on the Mahony—to Wechquetank where our Indians used to live—to the Hope, where I have been several times; and the many times I travelled in former years between Bethlehem & Nazareth—and Christiansbrun, as also in the Indian country between one Indian mission place and another—and particularly in the last 10 years of my residence on the Muskingum, when seldom a week passed that I did not go once or twice to Goshen etc.

I have not once mentioned my frequent journeys from Bethlehem to Philadelphia, and sometimes from there to Burlington, and home again, except a few times when I went to some other place *by way of* Philadelphia. There were many such journeys which I have omitted.

If we counted in all these—which of course is not possible—we should have to add many more thousands of miles.

Turning all these travels over in my mind, I have often asked myself the question whether, supposing I had had uninterrupted good health for 10 years, I could have done so much traveling in that space of time, taking all the attendant difficulties into account. Take the round number, 30,000 miles, and divide it into 10 years—or 3650 days: that would mean doing 8 miles a day. A good deal of time, besides, would have to be deducted for the obstacles that kept cropping up and often made travel impossible for days on end.

Epilogue

AFTER THE GNADENHÜTTEN MASSACRE, writes Ilse Loges in *Irokesen und Delawaren im Spiegel des Herrnhuter Mission*,* the Moravian mission among the Delawares came to an end of its effectiveness. Without visible fruits it trickled away into the sand. But, she adds abruptly, without answering the question, "Were there really no fruits?"

When David Zeisberger died at Goshen in 1808, he was oppressed with a sense of failure. The Indian congregation to which he had devoted his life, and to which Heckewelder had devoted the years of his prime, had travelled far in search of a peace and security which seemed only to elude them. They were caught between opposing fires of fanaticism, as we see in the misfortunes of Joshua, the Mahican, and his family. His two daughters were murdered by white men at Gnadenhütten, and he himself was burned to death by the followers of the Shawnee Prophet on the White River in 1806. A "Trail of Tears" led Zeisberger's "Wandering Congregation" from Friedenshütten on the Susquehanna through Friedensstadt on the Beaver, Schönbrunn and Gnadenhütten on the Muskingum, Captives Town at Upper Sandusky, New Gnadenhütten above Detroit, Pilgerruh (Pilgrims' Rest) on the Cuyahoga, and Pettquotting on the Huron River, to Fairfield on the Thames River in Upper Canada. But here again, after twenty years, the cruelty of war caught up with them. In 1813 their town once more

---
* Göttingen, 1956, p. 239.

found itself in the path of armies. It was plundered and burned—though all its inhabitants escaped without harm—by General Harrison's army after the Battle of the Thames.

The destruction of Fairfield was not, however, the end for them. They came back and founded New Fairfield just across the river, where you will find their descendants living to this day. This Delaware community (the Mahicans among them have long since been absorbed), established in the quiet countryside of Kent County, Ontario, is a living monument to heroic men like Glickhikan, Captain White Eyes, and Killbuck who joined David Zeisberger and John Heckewelder in an experiment in race relations of which the two peoples concerned in it may be proud.

The example of these steadfast men and of many others, even those who, like Anton, were beaten down ("In great attempts," wrote Longinus, "it is glorious even to fail"),—are these not visible fruits? And what about the living? The names of persons who appear in Heckewelder's journals still may be found among these Kent County Delawares, names such as Shebosh, Snake, and Newalike. The holders of these names are educated citizens, a few of them farmers, most of them commuters who drive to work in neighboring towns and return at night to their homes in the vicinity of the New Fairfield Church.

We cannot think the words inscribed on the monument at Gnadenhütten are mere rhetoric: "Here triumphed in death ninety Christian Indians."

The death of these brave people shocked men, even among the killers themselves, to a realization of the meaning of the Moravian work and to a horror of race bigotry.

"Must then a Christ perish in torment in every age to save those that have no imagination?"—Bernard Shaw, *St. Joan.*

Biographical and Geographical Glossary

Containing the names of most of the persons and places mentioned in this book, with the exception of such as are well known and easily identifiable.

A.

ABEL—d. 1782: Moravian Indian, son of Magdalene and husband of Johannetta; died in the massacre at Gnadenhütten.

ABRAHAM—d. 1782: A Mahican Indian, son of Jonathan and Anne, two early Moravian converts; baptized, 1749, at Gnadenhütten on the Mahoning; accompanied Heckewelder from the Muskingum to Bethlehem, 1774; died in the massacre at Gnadenhütten, Ohio.

ADAM (WULALOWECHEN)—d. 1782: Moravian Indian, baptized, 1780, at Lichtenau; appointed guard over Heckewelder's house in Salem, May 6, 1781; died with his wife, Cornelia, in the massacre at Gnadenhütten.

ADAMS: Innkeeper on the Franklin road near present Mechanicsburg (Wesley P. O.), Irwin Twp., Venango County, Pa. Heckewelder stopped here for the night, November 2, 1800.

ALDEN, MAJOR ROGER: Revolutionary soldier, deputy secretary to Congress. In 1795 he took post as agent for the Holland Land Co. at Mead's settlement on French Creek, where Heckewelder met him in November, 1800. He erected a saw mill on Kelly's Run about 1799.

ALLAN, EBENEZER: Soldier, trader, Indian agent; served with Butler's Rangers during the Revolution; later went to Upper Canada, where he promoted settlement in what is now Delaware Twp., Middlesex County, Ont.

ALLEN, FORT: At what is now Weissport, Pa.; built, 1756, by Benjamin Franklin to command the Nescopeck Indian Path and protect the settlers south of the Lehigh Gap.

ALLISON, DR. RICHARD: Army surgeon; saw service on the frontier under Brodhead, Harmar, St. Clair, Wilkinson, and Wayne; with St. Clair in the defeat at Fort Recovery, 1791, and with Anthony Wayne in the victory at Fallen Timbers, 1794. After 1789 his home was at Cincinnati.

ANCRUM, MAJOR WILLIAM: British officer who succeeded De Peyster in command at Detroit, 1784.

ANDERSON, CHARLES: Owner of a two-story frame house on what is now the main street of Grimsby, Ont. Here Heckewelder spent the night of May 16-17, 1798.

ANDREAS: Moravian Indian, baptized, 1779, at Schönbrunn. Later he left the Moravians, went to war, and fought against Anthony Wayne in the Battle of Fallen Timbers.

ANGERMAN, REV. JOHN—d. 1775: Moravian missionary; came to America, 1761; visited Friedenshütten with John Heckewelder; went to Barbados, 1773, where he died.

ANNA BENIGNA—d. 1782: Wife of the Munsee chief, Glickhikan (Isaac); died in the massacre at Gnadenhütten.

ANTON—d. 1782: Son of the Moravian Indian, John Martin; brought letters to Lichtenau, December 2, 1779; died in the massacre at Gnadenhütten.

ANTON (WELOCHALENT, alias LUKE HOLLAND): Son of Jo Peepe and his wife, Juliana; baptized, 1771, at Friedenshütten; helped James O'Hara escape hostile Indians, 1777. In 1782, embittered by the murder of his wife and three children at Gnadenhütten, he went to war against the "Long Knives."

ANTON, MARCUS—d. 1782: Son of Anton, Welochalent; baptized at Gnadenhütten, 1774; died with his mother and two sisters in the Gnadenhütten massacre.

ARBO, REV. JOHN—1713-1772: Moravian deacon, came to America, 1760; served as steward for the Single Brethren at Bethlehem and as mission agent.

ARUNDLE: Trader at Lower Sandusky (now Fremont, Ohio); entertained the Moravian missionaries on their way to Detroit in the spring of 1782; at his house Zeisberger read the burial service for the Indians killed in the massacre at Gnadenhütten.

ASH, SYLVESTER: Interpreter for the Delawares and Shawnees at the Detroit conference, 1793.

Glossary

Askin, John: Merchant of Detroit, partner in the North West Co., friend of the Moravians. In 1786 his ships, the *Mackinac* and the *Beaver*, transported the Moravian congregation from Detroit to the Cuyahoga.

Asylum (Azilum): On the west bank of the Susquehanna in Asylum Twp., Bradford County, Pa.; established, 1793, by French refugees. A house was prepared here for Marie Antoinette in the hope of rescuing her from the guillotine.

B.

Baasman: See Bausman.

Bâby, Jacques Duperon: British Indian agent and commissary; one of the interpreters at the trial of the Moravian missionaries at Detroit, November 9, 1781.

Bagge, Rev. Nicholas Lawrence—1732–1789: Moravian minister at Bethabara, the first Moravian settlement in North Carolina, 1773–1784; at Emmaus, Pa., 1785; at Hebron, 1786.

Baker's Fort: At Baker's Bottom on the Ohio, opposite the mouth of Yellow Creek. Here the murder of Logan's family occurred, April 30, 1774: the final incident precipitating Lord Dunmore's (the Shawnee) War.

Bald Eagle: Former Indian settlement (now Milesburg, Center County, Pa.) on Bald Eagle Creek; named for the Munsee chief, Woapalanne, "Bald Eagle."

Bausman, Jacob—d. 1797: Kept a ferry across the Monongahela at Pittsburgh from the foot of Wood Street to the foot of Coal Hill.

Bawby. See Bâby.

Beaver (Tamaqua), "King"—d. 1769: Brother of Shingas and Pisquetomen. "He was for many years a head chief of the Delawares in the western country, and had his residence while I was out in 1762, at Tuscorawas on the Muskingum. At the request of the governor of Pennsylvania, he went in that year with Christian Frederick Post to the treaty at Lancaster. He was admired and befriended by all who knew him. I considered him as my particular friend, and indeed he acted that part; for when he found that the Indian nations had resolved on a war with the British, he immediately apprised me of it, requesting me in a fatherly manner to go out of the country to a place of safety. He died about the year 1770 [1769], on the spot where, two years afterwards, the Christian Indians from the Wyalusing, on Susquehanna, built the town called Gnadenhütten."—Heckewelder.

Beaver Falls: The rapids on the Beaver River, about five miles from its mouth, at present Beaver Falls, Pa.

Beaver Town: Beaver, Pa., at the mouth of the Beaver River; named for the Delaware chief, "King" Beaver, who at one time lived here.

Belpre: A settlement on the Ohio, opposite the mouth of the Little Kanawha, Washington County, Ohio.

BENDER, GEORGE PHILIP: First settler (about 1777) at what is now Niagara Falls, Ont. His home, directly opposite the American Falls, was near the site of the present General Brock Hotel.

BENINGER (BÜNINGER, BININGER), REV. ABRAHAM: An itinerant Moravian missionary (ordained 1756), who preached at Tulpehocken and other settlements in Pa., and among the Indians at Pachgatgoch and Wechquadnach, Conn.

BENINGER, JOHN: Son of Rev. Abraham Beninger; schoolmaster among the Mohawks on the Bay of Quinte.

BENJAMIN (CUWES)—d. 1789: Moravian Indian, son of Elisabeth; baptized, 1787, at Cayahaga; died at Pettquotting.

BENNINGTON, FORT. See BREWERTON, FORT.

BETHEL, PA.: The Berks-Lebanon county line bisects the old township of Bethel, which was formerly in Lancaster County. It lies on Little Swatara Creek. The present town of Bethel is in Berks County.

BIG BONE LICK: Big Bone, Boone County, Ky.

BIG BOTTOM: A settlement founded, 1790, about thirty miles up the Muskingum.

BIG COVE: Settlements in the valley of Big Cove Creek, south of present McConnellsburg, Pa., which were devastated by war parties under "King" Shingas in the French and Indian War.

BIG TREE: A Seneca chief who accompanied Cornplanter to Philadelphia, 1790, and to Detroit, 1793.

BIG TREE, N. Y.: Now Geneseo; formerly an important Seneca town; destroyed by Sullivan, 1779.

BININGER. See BENINGER.

BIRD, CAPT. See BURD.

BIRKBY, REV. JAMES: Moravian minister living on Fair St. in New York City, with whom Heckewelder lodged, 1793, on his way to and from the Detroit Indian conference.

BIVEN, JOSEPH: In 1794 he established a tavern at what is now North Cohocton, N. Y.

BLENNERHASSET'S ISLAND: In the Ohio River, near Belpre, Washington County, Ohio; named for Harman Blennerhasset, who bought it in 1797, built a mansion and retired here with his books, chemical apparatus, and music. He entertained Aaron Burr here in 1805. During the winter of 1806–1807, militia men destroyed the mansion.

BLOODY RUN: Enters the Raystown Branch of the Juniata River at Everett, Bedford County, Pa.

BLUE JACKET (WAWIAPIESCHENWA, "WHIRLPOOL")—d. c. 1805: Shawnee warrior; leader of the Indian forces opposed to Anthony Wayne at Fallen Timbers, 1794.

Glossary

Boas: Probably the Munsee Delaware, baptized, 1771, at Friedenshütten, who came to live at Schönbrunn, and during the Revolutionary War saved Zeisberger's life from an assassin.

Böhler, Rev. Peter—1712–1774: Moravian bishop, next to Zinzendorf and Spangenberg the most important leader in the early years of the Renewed Moravian Church; came to Georgia, 1738, and to Pennsylvania, 1740; brought the first "Sea Congregation" to America in 1742, remaining here till 1745; active in Bethlehem again, 1753–64.

Bombary, Capt. See Bunbury.

Bömper, Abraham—1705–1793: Moravian silversmith in Bethlehem; assisted in founding a mission in Surinam.

Bonnet, John, Sr.: An innkeeper, four miles west of Bedford, at the parting of two roads to Pittsburgh: the Forbes Road by way of Ligonier, and the Burd Road by way of the Glades (Berlin and vicinity).

Bouquet, Col. Henry—1719–1765: British officer, second in command to Gen. Forbes in the capture of Fort Duquesne, 1758. During Pontiac's War, he won the Battle of Bushy Run, 1763, and raised the siege of Pittsburgh. His march to Tuscarawas the following year forced the Indians to sue for peace.

Bousman. See Bausman, Jacob.

Braddock's Field: Now Braddock and North Braddock, Pa.; site of Braddock's defeat, 1755, near the Monongahela, about nine miles from Fort Duquesne.

Brant, Capt. Isaac—1767–1795: A Mohawk, eldest son of Col. Joseph Brant. He frequently travelled with Capt. David (Hill) on embassies for the Six Nations, and was present with him at Marietta, 1788.

Brant, Joseph (Thayendenegea)—1742–1807: Mohawk chief, leader of the Six Nations during the late eighteenth century; born in the Ohio Valley; educated at Eleazer Wheelock's Indian school (now Dartmouth College); fought for the British in the French and Indian War, Pontiac's War, and the Revolutionary War. A strong defender of the white man's religion and culture, he translated the Gospel of Mark and other religious works into Mohawk.

Brant's Town: A Six Nations settlement on the outskirts of the present Brantford, Ont., named for Col. Joseph Brant. Brant's Town, containing a population of about seven hundred, was abandoned by the Indians during the nineteenth century when they moved a few miles south to the present reservation. The population is now about seven thousand.

Breakneck Hill, Bradford County: On the road beside the Susquehanna south of the present town of Rummerfield.

Brethren's Garden (Brüder Garten): A Moravian station, founded 1760, on the mainland of India at Tranquebar, Madras.

BREWERTON (BENNINGTON) FORT: At the west end of Oneida Lake; now Brewerton, N. Y.

BRODHEAD, GEN. DANIEL—1736–1809: Sent to Fort Pitt in 1778, he took command there, 1779–1781. He invaded the Seneca country from the west, 1779; destroyed the Delaware capital of Goschachgunk on the Muskingum, April 19, 1781; was appointed Surveyor-General, 1789.

BROTHERTON ("BROTHER TOWN"): An Indian reservation in Oneida Township, N. Y.

BROWNSTOWN, Michigan: At the mouth of the Detroit River, where on August 5, 1812, Tecumseh's Indians cut General William Hull's communications with Ohio, thus hastening the surrender of Detroit.

BUCKONGEJELAS: See PACHGANTSCHIHILAS.

BUFFALO, W. Va.: Now Wellsburg, Brooke County; also known as Charleston.

BUFFALO CREEK: A stream that flows into the Ohio at Wellsburg, W. Va.

BUFFALO SALT LICK: On the Buffalo Trace, between Louisville, Ky., and Vincennes, Ind., at what is now French Lick, Orange County, Ind.

BULL, FORT: A British fort on Wood Creek, N. Y., protecting the portage between the Mohawk River and Oneida Lake. Its capture by the French in 1756 opened the Mohawk Valley to invasion.

BULL, JOHN JOSEPH (SHEBOSH, "RUNNING WATER")—1721–1788: Moravian lay missionary. Journeyed with Conrad Weiser, David Zeisberger, and Bishop Spangenberg to Onondaga, 1745; married Christiana, a Mahican from Esopus, 1746. In 1755, after the massacre of missionaries at Gnadenhütten on the Mahoning, he remained alone in the village to collect the fugitives. He was Heckewelder's companion to Goschochking with the message that withheld the Delawares from immediately declaring war on the United States. His son, Joseph, was killed in the massacre at Gnadenhütten on the Muskingum, March 8, 1782.

BUNBURY, CAPT.: Of the British Fifth Regiment; assigned by Governor Simcoe of Canada to escort the United States commissioners attending the Indian conference at Detroit, 1793.

BÜNINGER: See BENINGER.

BURD, CAPTAIN: Landed proprietor at Fort Littleton, Pa., which was sometimes known as "Burd's." He visited Heckewelder at Burnt Cabins, November 1, 1786.

BURLINGTON HEIGHTS: At the west end of Lake Ontario, overlooking the present city of Hamilton, Ont.

BURNT CABINS ("BURNING CABINS"): In Dublin Township, Fulton County, Pa. The town was so named because in 1750 Pennsylvania government agents burned the cabins of settlers trespassing here on Indian lands.

BUSH, JACOB: One of the first white men to accept the invitation of the

Glossary

Society for Propagating the Gospel to settle beside the Christian Indians on their Muskingum lands.

BUSHY RUN: The Battle of Bushy Run was fought a mile and a half east of the present Harrison City, Westmoreland County, Pa. Colonel Bouquet's victory here in 1763, during Pontiac's War, enabled him to raise the siege of Pittsburgh.

BUTLER, COL. JOHN—1728–1796: During the French and Indian War, he led the Indians in the capture of Fort Niagara. A Loyalist during the Revolutionary War, he headed Butler's Rangers; defeated Zebulon Butler in the Battle of Wyoming, 1778; was himself defeated by General Sullivan at Newtown (Elmira), 1779.

BUTLER, GENERAL RICHARD—1743–1791: Soldier in the Revolutionary War, Lt. Col. of Morgan's Rifles. As Indian Commissioner, he negotiated the Shawnee Treaty at the mouth of the Great Miami, 1786. In the same year he was appointed Superintendent of Indian Affairs for the Northern District. Second in command to General Arthur St. Clair, he was killed in the defeat of November 4, 1791, at Fort Recovery.

C.

CACHNAWAGA: See CAUGHNAWAGA.

CALDWELL, COL. WILLIAM—d. *c.* 1820: Captain in Butler's Rangers, 1776–1784; assisted the Indians at Crawford's defeat, 1782; Lt. Col. of the Essex County Militia; present with his corps (in the British Fort) at the Battle of Fallen Timbers, 1794; O. C. Captain Caldwell's Rangers, 1812–1814; succeeded Matthew Elliot as Deputy Superintendent of the Indian Department, 1814; died at Amherstburg, which he had founded, near the mouth of the Detroit River.

CALHOUN, THOMAS: Indian trader, friend of the Moravians. His trading post on the Tuscarawas River was just above the site of Bolivar, Ohio. He helped Heckewelder to escape from the Muskingum, November, 1762, before the outbreak of Pontiac's War.

CAMMERHOFF, REV. JOHN CHRISTOPH FREDERIC—1721–1751: Moravian bishop; came to America, 1747; visited the Indians at Shamokin (Sunbury, Pa.), 1748, and at Onondaga (near Syracuse, N. Y.), 1750.

CAMPBELL, JOHN: Indian trader and surveyor; one of the founders of Louisville, Ky.

CAMPFIELD: See CANFIELD.

CAMPUS MARTIUS: A stockade and blockhouse built, 1788, by General Rufus Putnam on the east side of the Muskingum at Marietta, Ohio.

CANFIELD ("CAMPFIELD"), SAMUEL, SR.: Owner of a property fourteen miles west of present Burford, Ont., where Heckewelder spent a night, May 19, 1798, on the Indian path to Fairfield and Detroit.

CANISERAGA: DANSVILLE, N. Y.

CANONSBURG: The early academy to which Heckewelder refers in his 1792 journal became Jefferson College, which later merged with Washington College to form the present Washington and Jefferson College at Washington, Pa.

CANTY, BAY OF: See QUINTE.

CAPTIVES' TOWN: See UPPER SANDUSKY, No. 4.

CARVER, JONATHAN—1710–1780: American explorer; travelled among the Indians of the northern Mississippi Valley; published *Travels through the Interior Parts of North America in the Years 1766, 1767 and 1768* (London, 1778), the originality of which has been questioned.

CASCASKI (CASCASKUNG, CUSHCUSHKE): See KUSKUSKY.

CASSAWAGA: See CUSSEWAGO.

CAT, BIG: See MACHINGWE PUSHIS.

CATARAQUI: The present Kingston, Ont., at the eastern end of Lake Ontario and at the mouth of the Cataraqui River. First named Kataracui but soon renamed Fort Frontenac; it was founded by the French to protect the St. Lawrence route from the Iroquois. In 1758 it was captured and destroyed by Gen. John Bradstreet; refounded by United Empire Loyalists, it became the capital of Canada, 1841–1844.

CATFISH: Washington, Pa. A former Indian village, Catfish Camp. Although renamed Washington in 1781, the old name persisted for many years. Heckewelder visited it, 1788.

CAUGHNAWAGA, N. Y.: Before its destruction by the French in 1693, this Mohawk "castle" was situated on the north bank of the Mohawk River half a mile west of what is now Fonda. After 1693 the Indians reëstablished the village at the eastern end of present Fonda, where the name survives although the Indians have long since departed.

CAUGHNAWAGA INDIANS: The "Praying Indians," Mohawk and Oneida converts to Roman Catholicism who in 1668 left their homes in the Mohawk Valley and settled on the St. Lawrence near Montreal. In 1755 a colony of these Caughnawagas settled at St. Regis, N. Y., where their descendants live today.

CAYAHAGA: In Heckewelder's day the word had four distinct meanings:
  1. The Cuyahoga River, which enters Lake Erie at Cleveland, Ohio.;
  2. An Indian village and trading place, "Cayahaga Old Town," situated on the northeast side of the Cuyahoga near what is now Akron, Ohio;
  3. "Pilgerruh," a Moravian settlement on the site of an old Ottawa Indian town about twelve miles up the Cuyahoga at the mouth of Tinker's Creek (near Bedford, Ohio);
  4. The general area, including the mouth of the river and sev-

eral Indian settlements above it. In 1774 Wyandot chiefs from Cayahaga visited the Moravian mission on the Muskingum, and in 1777 Cayahaga was represented at the Delawares' Great Council at Goschachgunk.

CHAMBERSTOWN: Chambersburg, Pa.

CHAMBER'S FERRY: Crossed the Susquehanna River from a point just south of what is now Steelton, Pa., to a wharf half a mile below the mouth of Yellow Breeches Creek.

CHAPIN, GEN. ISRAEL: Revolutionary soldier; appointed General Agent for Indian Affairs of the United States, 1791.

CHARLESTOWN, KY.: Now Wellsburg, Bracken County, Ky.; on the Ohio, at the mouth of Locust Creek.

CHARLESTOWN, W. VA.: Now Wellsburg, Brooke County, W. Va.; at the mouth of Buffalo Creek.

CHELLOWAY: See CHILLOWAY.

CHILLOWAY, BILL (WILHELM)—d. 1791: A Delaware Indian, baptized, 1771, at Friedenshütten. During the Revolutionary War, he exerted a steadying influence within the mission and represented it in the councils of the Delawares at Gekelemuchpekink and Goschachgunk. He travelled frequently with Zeisberger and Heckewelder.

CHEMUNG RIVER: Formerly known as the Tioga; enters the Susquehanna at Tioga Point (Athens, Pa.). Its valley offered an entrance, by canoe or Indian trail (the "Forbidden Path," *q. v.*) to the Seneca country.

CHIBBAWAYS (CHIPPUES): See CHIPPEWA.

CHINESEE: See GENESEE.

CHIPPEWA, OJIBWAY: A numerous Algonquian people, formerly living on the shores of Lake Superior, Lake Huron, and the Georgian Bay. During the eighteenth century they moved westward across Minnesota to North Dakota and southward to Lake Erie and Detroit. In the latter movement, they forced the Iroquois out of southern Ontario. The Missisauga are a sub-tribe of the Chippewa.

CHRISTIAN—d. 1782: Delaware Indian, baptized, 1750; charter member of Lichtenau, 1776; trustee at Salem, 1780. During the Revolutionary War, he undertook dangerous diplomatic errands beneficial to the United States. Died in the massacre at Gnadenhütten.

CHRISTIANSBRUNN ("CHRISTIAN SPRING"): Former Moravian settlement two miles southwest of Nazareth; named in honor of Count Zinzendorf's son, Christian Renatus.

CINCINNATI, OHIO: First settlement, 1788; named Cincinnati, 1790, by Gen. St. Clair, who had recently been made president of the Society of the Cincinnati. Visited by Heckewelder, 1792.

CLARK, REV. DANIEL—d. 1834: Early Baptist minister at Columbia (now part of Cincinnati, Ohio). His ordination here, September, 1792, at which the Rev. Dr. John Gano assisted Elder John Smith, is said to have been the first ordination of a minister in the Northwest Territory.

CLARK, GEN. GEORGE ROGERS—1752–1818: Revolutionary soldier and Indian fighter. In 1778, from a rendezvous at the Falls of the Ohio (Louisville, Ky.), he surprised and captured the British post at Vincennes. He destroyed the Shawnee villages at Chillicothe, 1782, and led an attack on the Wabash Indians, 1786.

CLARKSVILLE: At the Falls of the Ohio, opposite Louisville, Ky.; named for Gen. George Rogers Clark.

COLUMBIA, OHIO: Founded, November 18, 1788, by Benjamin Stites at the mouth of the Little Miami; now part of Cincinnati.

CONESTOGA: An Indian village, three miles southeast of Washington Borough, Lancaster County, Pa., where a remnant of the Susquehannock (Conestoga) Indians survived until 1763, when the "Paxton Boys" murdered them.

CONEWAGO (CONEWAGUS, CONEWAGARUS): Former Seneca town on the Genesee River, now Avon, Livingston County, N. Y. As early as 1789 there was a tavern (Gilbert's) and a ferry here.

CONOCOCHEAGUE: A creek flowing southward through Franklin County, Pa., to enter the Potomac at Williamsport, Md. Settlements in the valley were destroyed by war parties under Shingas during the early months of the French and Indian War.

COOCHOCKING: See GOSCHACHGUNK.

COON, ABRAHAM: See KUHN.

CORNPLANTER (GYANTWAHIA)—1740–1836: Seneca chief, brother of the prophet, Handsome Lake. He fought for the British during the Revolutionary War, but later kept his people from joining in the war for the Northwest Territory. For this friendly attitude Pennsylvania gave him the Cornplanter Tract on the Allegheny River near the New York State border.

COVELL, DR. MATTHEW: Innkeeper, physician, and Justice of the Peace at Wilkes-Barre (formerly Wyoming), Pa. Heckewelder and Mortimer put up at his tavern, May 2, 1798.

CRAWFORD, COL. WILLIAM—1732–1782: An officer under Gen. Hand in the Squaw Campaign, 1778; in command of the militia attacking Upper Sandusky, June, 1782. Taken prisoner by Capt. Pipe, he was put to death in retaliation for the Squaw Campaign (in which Capt. Pipe's brother was killed and his mother wounded) and for Col. Williamson's massacre of ninety Christian Indians at Gnadenhütten, March 8, 1782.

CREVER, JACOB: Innkeeper at Carlisle, licensed 1781–1805. There is evidence that in 1786, when Heckewelder stopped at his place, he was proprietor of the Indian Queen at what is now 133 East High Street.

Glossary 405

>After 1800 he kept the President Jefferson near the northeast corner of the Public Square.

CROSSING, THE: See JUNIATA CROSSING.

CROWSTOWN: A Mingo town near the present Conway, Beaver County, Pa. It was named for the Crow, an Iroquois Indian (or Mingo, as the Iroquois of the Ohio Valley were often called), who died in 1761.

CUHN, ABRAHAM: See KUHN.

CUSSEWAGO: Now Meadville, Crawford County, Pa.

CUYAHOGA: See CAYAHAGA.

D.

DANIEL (TSCHITQUIECHEN): A Munsee Delaware, nephew of Glickhikan; baptized at Lichtenau, 1778. He was not on the Muskingum in March, 1782, but it was in his house at Gnadenhütten that many of the Christian Indians were confined and killed by Col. Wilkinson's militia.

DAVID: See ZEISBERGER, DAVID.

DAVID, CAPTAIN: See HILL, CAPT. DAVID.

DAVID (MAMSOCHALET)—d. 1797: Delaware Indian; baptized, 1755, at Gnadenhütten on the Mahoning. In 1765 he guided Zeisberger and his party to Wyoming by a route later followed by the Wilkes-Barre Turnpike.

DAVIS: See NATHANAEL DAVIS.

DEFIANCE, FORT: Established by Anthony Wayne, August, 1794, at the junction of the Maumee River and the Auglaize.

DELAWARE: An Indian nation, properly known as the Lenni Lenape or Original People, whom most other Indians of eastern North America honored with the title, "Grandfather." Their home territory was in the Delaware River basin (from which they received their name) until pressure from the white man forced them out. Some moved north to take refuge in the Six Nations country, while a greater number moved west to set up new councils in the Ohio Country.

DENCKE, REV. CHRISTIAN FREDERICK—d. 1838: Moravian missionary, at one time a teacher of Latin and botany at Nazareth Hall. He succeeded Senseman in the mission at Fairfield, Upper Canada.

DE PEYSTER, MAJOR (Later COL.) ARENT SCHUYLER: Grandson of Abraham De Peyster, Chief Justice of New York; British commandant at Michilimackinac, 1774–1779, and at Detroit, 1779–1784. He removed the Moravians from the Muskingum, 1781, but afterwards proved to be their friend. After the Revolutionary War, he retired to Dumfries, Scotland, where he became a friend of Robert Burns. Author of a volume of verses, *Miscellanies* (N.Y., 1788).

DE SCHWEINITZ, JOHN CHRISTIAN—1740–1802: Administrator of the estates of the Moravian Church in America, 1770–1797.

DESERONTO, Ont.: Named for a Mohawk chief, Deserontyou, who after the Revolutionary War settled on the Bay of Quinte with Mohawks from New York State, to whom this vicinity has long been sacred. Deganawidah, founder of the Five Nations (Iroquois) Confederacy, is said to have been born here, and it was from here that he is reputed to have set out on his missionary journey to create a League of Nations designed to bring peace to mankind. There is a legend that here the Seven Dancers left the earth and danced into the sky to become what we call the Pleiades.

DESERONTYOU, CAPT. JOHN: In 1784 this chief, with Aaron and Isaac Hill, led the Mohawks to a settlement on the Bay of Quinte, now known as Deseronto. The Thendinaga Mohawk Reserve is near the modern town.

DICKINSON COLLEGE: At Carlisle, Pa.; chartered 1783, and named for John Dickinson.

DOLSON, DANIEL: Canadian settler (brother of Matthew Dolson of Detroit) who lived twelve miles up the Thames River near what is now Chatham, Ont.

DOLSON, JOHN: At Savona, Bath Twp., Steuben County, N. Y.

DOLSON, MATTHEW: A Loyalist from Pennsylvania who escaped to Canada, joined Butler's Rangers, and in 1781 settled at Detroit, where he became a successful merchant and innkeeper, owner of Dolson's Tavern. He was a warm friend of the Moravians.

DONEGAL: Early Scotch-Irish settlement, established about 1720, in the vicinity of present Mt. Joy, Lancaster County, Pa. The Moravians had a small settlement at Mt. Joy before the Revolution.

DOUGHTY, MAJOR JOHN—1757–1826: Officer commanding U. S. troops which erected Fort Harmar, 1788, at Marietta, and Fort Washington at present Cincinnati, 1789. He designed both forts.

DOUGLAS, WHEELER—b. 1750: At one time a storekeeper at Albany, N. Y.; in 1798 he was living at Brantford, Ont.

DRAKE, CAPT.: In the service of the Northwest Company. Heckewelder met him at Detroit, 1793.

DRUM, SIMON—1751 (c.)–1822: One of the first residents of Greensburg (incorporated 1799), and proprietor of the Drum House, a tavern of the better class.

DUER, WILLIAM—1747–1799: Delegate from New York to the Continental Congress, 1777; secretary to the Board of the Treasury, 1786. Engaging in large land speculations (e.g., on the Scioto, 1787), he went bankrupt and in 1792 was imprisoned for debt.

DUNCAN, DAVID: Partner in the firm of Duncan and Wilson of Pittsburgh.

Glossary

DUNLAP'S (DUNLOPE'S) STATION: A stockade built in 1790 around John Dunlap's settlement (now Colerain, Ohio) on the east side of the Great Miami River, twelve miles above its mouth. It was the northwest outpost of Cincinnati's early defenses. It was attacked by Indians, January, 1791, relieved by a detachment from Fort Washington, but soon afterwards abandoned.

DUTCH VALLEY: Now German Valley, in Schooley's Mountains, Washington Twp., Warren County, N. J.

E.

EBONE: See POINT ABINO.

ECHPALAWEHUND, PETER—d. 1782: A Delaware chief, member of the Grand Council at Gekelemuchpekink; baptized, 1774, and named Petrus. In 1772 he helped Zeisberger's Indians move from Friedensstadt on the Beaver to the Tuscarawas branch of the Muskingum. He was a distinguished Christian statesman who maintained his position on the Delaware Grand Council. Died in the massacre at Gnadenhütten.

EDMOND'S SWAMP: About two miles north of present Buckstown, Somerset County, Pa. Here the forest of white pine was so dense that it was known as the Shades of Death.

EDWARDS, REV. WILLIAM—1724–1801: Moravian missionary. From 1776, when he came to Lichtenau as Zeisberger's assistant, he remained with the Christian Indians in all their wanderings until his death at Goshen, Ohio.

EEL RIVER INDIANS: A Miami tribe living on the Eel River, a tributary of the Wabash, at the time of General Scott's invasion, 1791. Whether they were emancipated descendants of Wea Indians centered at Ouiatenon on the Upper Wabash, or a group with an independent heritage, is not known.

EISENHART FAMILY: Prominent in the Moravian congregation at Emmaus, near Bethlehem, during the eighteenth century.

ELLIOT, JOHN: Probably the John Elliot, Quaker, who is known to have died in Philadelphia, 1810, at the age of seventy.

ELLIOT, CAPT. MATTHEW—d. 1814: Trader and Indian agent. A Loyalist during the Revolutionary War, he had much to do with the removal of the Moravians, 1781, to Upper Sandusky. In later years he befriended them. British Superintendent of the Western Indians, 1796–1798 and 1808–1814.

EMMAUS: A town west of Allentown, Pa.

ENGLAND, LT. COL. RICHARD: Commandant at Detroit, where Heckewelder visited him in 1793.

ERVIN, GENERAL: See IRVINE.

Esopus: Kingston, Ulster County, N. Y.

Ettwein, Rev. John—1721–1801: Moravian bishop; came to Pennsylvania with Heckewelder, 1754; president of the Provincial Elders Conference, 1783–1806. He was the moving spirit of the Moravian Church in America during the greater part of Heckewelder's career. He encouraged the establishment of schools for Indian children, and urged the missionaries to undertake ethnological studies.

Evan, Abraham: Wyandot captain from Lower Sandusky.

Everlasting Gospel: "Wellings Everlasting Gospel," which John Bonnet showed Heckewelder in 1786, is not known under that title in the Library of Congress; but both that Library and the British Museum have a copy of the book Heckewelder very likely had in mind; *The Everlasting Gospel*, by Georg Klein-Nicolai (pseudonym, Paul Siegvolck), translated by "John S." (in the British Museum copy the name "Sechla" has been supplied in manuscript on the title page), printed by Christopher Sower, 1753, at Germantown. The full title is here given from the card in the Library of Congress: "The everlasting gospel, commanded to be preached by Jesus Christ, judge of the living and the dead, unto all creatures, Mark xvi. 15. concerning the eternal redemption found out by Him, whereby devil, sin, hell and death, shall at last be abolished, and the whole creation restored to its primitive purity; being a testimony against the present anti-Christian world."

Eyerly, John Jacob—1757–1800: Moravian, elected to the Pennsylvania Assembly, 1789. He selected and surveyed the lands on French and Conneaut Creeks which had been granted by the Assembly to the Moravians.

F.

Fairfield: Moravian Indian town established, 1792, by David Zeisberger on the Retrenche (now Thames) River, near present Thamesville, Oxford Twp., Kent County, Ont. Here in 1813 was fought the Battle of the Thames, known in Canada as the Battle of Moraviantown.

Fallen Timbers: See Maumee Rapids.

Falls of the Beaver: At Beaver Falls, Pa., about five miles above the mouth of the Beaver River.

Falls of the Muskingum: At Duncan Falls, a few miles below Zanesville.

Falls of the Ohio: At Louisville, Ky.

Fetterman, George: Early settler in Crawford County, Pa., engaged by Major Alden to run the Holland Land Co. sawmill on Kelly's Run.

Field, John—d. 1826: Member of Philadelphia Monthly Meeting, having been received on certificate from Chesterfield Monthly Meeting (near Trenton), 1764. Married Elizabeth Wilson at Philadelphia, 1770. Their son, John Field, Jr., was born in 1771.

Fonda, John: Owner of the tavern at which Heckewelder breakfasted, May 11, 1793; now Fonda, Montgomery County, N. Y.

Glossary

Forbidden Path: An Indian trail that ran from the Susquehanna at Tioga (Athens, Pa.) to Oswayo Creek, a tributary of the upper Allegheny. For military protection the Senecas, whose lands it crossed, forbade its use by white men. C. F. Post was turned back from it in 1760; David Zeisberger followed it on his way to Goschgoschink in 1767. Gen. Sullivan used the opening sketches of it, 1779, to invade the Seneca country.

Ford, Capt. Joseph: Captain of the *Dunmore*, on which Heckewelder sailed from Fort Erie to Detroit, 1793.

Forres Ferry: At what is now Steelton, on the Susquehanna, about three miles below Harrisburg. Forres and Chambers Ferries were on the main route from Lancaster to Carlisle and west.

Fowler, Capt.: Commanding officer at Fort Franklin, Pa., in 1800.

Fowler, John: Owner of a place, 1798, near Burford, Brant County, Ont.

Freeman, ———: Messenger sent by Gen. Wilkinson to the Indians on the Maumee, 1792. Taken prisoner, he was released after the Battle of Fallen Timbers, 1794.

Frey, Hendrick: A Palatine, living on the south side of the Mohawk River about two miles west of present Canajoharie.

Friedenshütten ("Tents of Peace"): Moravian Indian village on the Susquehanna near Wyalusing (Papunhank's town), Bradford County, Pa.; established, 1765, abandoned, 1772.

Friedensstadt ("Peace Village"): Moravian settlement near present Moravia on Beaver Creek below New Castle, Pa.; established by Zeisberger, 1770, to receive the Moravian Indians from the Upper Allegheny.

Friedensthal ("Valley of Peace"): Early Moravian settlement about two miles east of Nazareth.

Frontenac, Fort: Near the outlet of Lake Ontario, on the site of modern Kingston, Ont. The original French fort was La Salle's base, 1674–1689. Count Frontenac restored it, 1696. Its capture, 1758, by the British gave them control of the lake. See also Cataraqui.

Fry's: See Frey, Hendrick.

Fulnek: A town in Yorkshire, England, named for Fulnek in Moravia, which had once been a center of the *Unitas Fratrum*.

Funday's: See Fonda, John.

G.

Gajahaga: See Cayahaga.

Gallipolis, Ohio: Settled by French people, 1790, on the Ohio River in what is now Gallia County, Ohio. Visited by Heckewelder, 1792.

Ganaquenising (Ganachquenesink): Connoquenessing Creek in Beaver and Butler Counties, Pa.

GANO ("GUNNO"), MAJOR GENERAL JOHN STITES—1766–1822: Son of the Rev. Dr. John Gano of Columbia, Ohio; married Mary Goforth, daughter of Judge William Goforth. See Gano Papers, Historical and Philosophical Society of Ohio, Cincinnati.

GANSON, CAPT. JOHN: Revolutionary soldier who, in 1798, was proprietor of a tavern on the Niagara Road just east of the present Le Roy, N. Y.

GAWIAHÄTTE ("HEDGEHOG"): A Wea Indian, adoptive father of the interpreter, William Wells.

GEKELEMUKPECHINK (NEWCOMER'S TOWN): On the north bank of the Tuscarawas and the eastern outskirts of what is now Newcomerstown, Oxford Twp., Tuscarawas County, Ohio. This first capital of the Delaware nation in Ohio was founded, 1770, by Netawatwees (Newcomer).

GELELEMEND: See KILLBUCK, JOHN, JR.

GENESEO SENECAS: The western division of the Seneca nation.

GIBBINS, LT.: Of the Queen's Rangers, part of the escort provided by Gov. Simcoe for the U. S. Commissioners at Detroit, 1793.

GIBSON, COL. JOHN—1740–1822: After taking part in the expedition against Fort Duquesne, 1758, he settled at Fort Pitt as an Indian trader; was captured by Indians, 1763, and released, 1764. During the Shawnee War, 1774, he acted as intermediary, and it was through him that Logan sent his message, now known as "Logan's Lament," to Lord Dunmore. He served as commandant at Fort Laurens (formerly the Indian town of Tuscarawas, now Bolivar, Ohio), 1778–1779, and at Fort Pitt, 1781–1782. Secretary of the Indian Territory, 1800–1816.

GIRTY, SIMON—1741–1818: Employed as interpreter and scout around Fort Pitt, he deserted in 1778 and participated in Indian raids against the American settlements. A hard-drinking, violent partisan; friend of the Indians (he had been brought up among the Senecas) and hostile to those whom he suspected of injuring them.

GLADES: The "Stony Creek Glades" were a region of natural meadows—tall grass and swamp—embracing many townships at the head of Stony Creek, Somerset County, Pa.

GLICKHIKAN ("GUN SIGHT," alias ISAAC)—d. 1782: A famous Munsee warrior, statesman, and orator, chief counsellor of Chief Pakanke of Kuskusky. Baptized by Zeisberger at Friedensstadt, he became a powerful advocate of Christianity among his people. Died in the massacre at Gnadenhütten.

GNADENHÜTTEN on the Mahoning: A prosperous Moravian Indian village (now Lehighton, Pa.), established in 1746 on Mahoning Creek near its junction with the Lehigh. It was destroyed by a Munsee-led war party, November 24, 1755, when eleven Moravian mission workers were killed.

Glossary

GNADENHÜTTEN, Ohio: The second Moravian town on the Tuscarawas, Schönbrunn being the first; founded, 1772, about eleven miles south of the present New Philadelphia; abandoned, 1778; reoccupied, 1779. On March 8, 1782, ninety Christian Indians were murdered here by militia under Col. David Williamson.

GNADENHÜTTEN, NEW, Michigan: The third Moravian settlement by that name, the first having been destroyed by Indians, the second by white men. Established, 1782, on the Huron (now Clinton) River at what is now a western suburb of Mt. Clemens, Mich.; abandoned, 1786.

GNADENTHAL ("VALLEY OF GRACE"): Early Moravian settlement about a mile east of Nazareth, Pa. One of the old Moravian buildings here is now part of the Northampton County Home.

GOFORTH, JUDGE WILLIAM: Early resident of Columbia (now part of Cincinnati), Ohio. His daughter, Mary, married John Stites Gano.

GOKHOSING: See KOKOSING.

GOODALE, MAJOR NATHAN—1743–1793 (c.).: Minute-man and later officer during the Revolution; settled at Belpre, Ohio, 1789; appointed captain of a company of militia at Marietta, 1789; commanded garrison of the Farmer's Castle near Belpre; was captured by Indians, 1793, and died among them.

GOODAL'S STATION: A military post on the Ohio, opposite the mouth of the Little Kanawha, fourteen miles below Marietta, at what is now Belpre, Ohio.

GOOSE ISLE: Grosse Isle, in the Detroit River.

GORE, JUDGE OBADIAH: From Connecticut; settled at Sheshequin (now Ulster, Bradford County, Pa.), 1784.

GOSCHGOSCHINK: A Munsee Delaware settlement, established 1765. It consisted of three small villages on the west bank of the Allegheny above and below the present West Hickory, Forest County, Pa. Zeisberger first visited Goschgoschink, 1767; returning, 1768, he established a mission here, which he withdrew, 1770, to Friedenstadt.

GOSCHOCHKING (GOSCHACHGUNK): This, the second capital of the Delaware nation in Ohio, was established at the confluence of the Tuscarawas and the Walhonding. Destroyed by Brodhead, 1781.

GOSHEN, Ohio: Near Schönbrunn on the Tuscarawas River; founded, 1798, by David Zeisberger with thirty-three Indians from Fairfield. Here Zeisberger died, 1808, and is buried.

GRACEHAM: In Frederick County, Md.; founded by the Moravians, 1758.

GRACEHILL: A Moravian settlement near Ballymena, County Antrim, Ireland.

GRAHAM, COL.: A gentleman from Virginia, head of a settlement below the mouth of the Scioto, with whom Heckewelder had supper, Nov. 5, 1792.

GRAND PORTAGE: A nine-mile portage in northeastern Minnesota, between Lake Superior and Pigeon River, connecting the Great Lakes with the waterways of Western Canada.

GRAND PORTAGE RIVER: The Ottawa River, which enters the St. Lawrence by way of the Lake of Two Mountains above Montreal. It was the route used by the *voyageurs* in going to Lake Superior and the far west.

GRAVE CREEK: Enters the Ohio at Moundsville, W. Va., where the Grave Creek Mound still stands, approximately eighty feet high.

GREAT ISLAND, THE: In the Susquehanna at present Lock Haven; an Indian settlement and important trail and waterways junction.

GREATHOUSE, DANIEL: Leader of the massacre, April, 1774, at the mouth of Yellow Creek on the Ohio, when many members of Logan's family were killed.

GREBER: See CREVER.

GREENLAND, HISTORY OF: English edition (London, 1767) of a German book originally published at Barby and Leipzig, 1765: *The History of Greenland: Containing a Description of the Country, and Its Inhabitants: and Particularly, A Relation of the Mission, carried on for above these Thirty Years by the* Unitas Fratrum, *at* New Herrnhuth *and* Lichtenfels, *in that Country*. By David Crantz ...

GREENSBURG ("GREENSBOROUGH"): County town of Westmoreland County, Pa., since 1787.

GREENVILLE, FORT: Established, 1793, by Anthony Wayne at present Greenville, Darke County, Ohio. By the Treaty of Greenville, signed here, 1795, the Indians ceded large territories to the United States.

GREGOR, REV. CHRISTIAN—1723–1801: Moravian bishop, member of the Governing Board of the Church, Herrnhut, Germany. In 1771 he visited the Indian mission at Friedenshütten (Wyalusing) on the Susquehanna.

GREY, SAMUEL: Delaware warrior who took part in the removal of the Moravians, 1781, from the Muskingum.

GRUBE, REV. BERNARD ADAM—1715–1808: Moravian missionary, stationed at Wechquetank from 1760 till it was abandoned in 1763. He accompanied the Moravian Indian refugees to Philadelphia and Province Island, 1763–1765; visited the Muskingum, 1780, where on July 4 he officiated at the marriage of John Heckewelder and Sara Ohneberg.

GUNNO, MAJOR: See GANO.

H.

HALFTOWN: A Seneca chief who helped to keep his people at peace with the United States after the Revolutionary War. In 1790 he visited Philadelphia with Chiefs Cornplanter and Big Tree.

HAMILTON, FORT: Erected, 1791, by Gen. St. Clair on the Great Miami River at the present Hamilton, Butler County, Ohio.

Glossary 413

HAMILTON, ROBERT: Operated mills, 1787–1800, near the present village of Power Glen, Grantham Twp., Welland County, Ont.

HAMTRAMCK, COL. JOHN FRANCIS: Commander of troops from Vincennes sent as convoy for Gen. Putnam on his journey to the Wabash, 1792. At the Battle of Fallen Timbers, 1794, he commanded the left wing of Wayne's army.

HAND, GEN. EDWARD—1744–1802: Commandant at Fort Pitt, 1777–1778. In March, 1778, he sent Heckewelder and Shebosh with a message to the Grand Council of the Delawares at Goschachgunk.

HANNASTOWN: The county seat of Westmoreland County, Pa., 1773–1787.

HARDIN, COL. JOHN: One of three messengers who were taken prisoner by the Indians in 1792, and released in 1794 after Wayne's victory at Fallen Timbers.

HARDING: The Harding with whom Heckewelder and Mortimer lodged, May 3, 1798, was either John Harding (1763–1826) or Captain Stephen Harding (1748–1816), who lived near what is now the village of Harding on the west bank of the Susquehanna, opposite Campbell's Ledge, about two miles north of Pittston.

HARMAR, GEN. JOSIAH—1753–1813: Soldier in the Revolutionary War. In 1785 he was given command of the forces on the Ohio River. He invaded the Shawnee and Miami Indian country, 1790, without success.

HARMAR, FORT: Erected, 1785, on the west bank of the Muskingum River at its mouth. An Indian treaty was held here in the winter of 1788–1789.

HARMONY: Founded on the Connoquenessing, 1803, by George Rapp; the headquarters of the Harmony Society. In 1815 the Harmonites moved to Indiana, founding New Harmony on the Wabash. Returning to Pennsylvania in 1825, they set up a colony at Economy, Beaver County.

HARRIS'S FERRY: Now Harrisburg, Pa.; formerly an Indian settlement, known as Peshtank, Paxtang, or Paxton. This was a trail junction, and here the Allegheny Path—from the Atlantic coast to the Forks of the Ohio (now Pittsburgh) forded the Susquehanna.

HARRODSBURG ("HARRETSBURG"): Near the head of Salt River, Mercer County, Ky.

HARTSHORN, WILLIAM—d. 1833: Quaker preacher of Shrewsbury, N. J.

HASCALL, CAPTAIN: Commandant at Marietta, who entertained Heckewelder and the Indians, November 20, 1792.

HAY, JOHN—d. 1785: Soldier, Indian agent, governor. Lieutenant at Detroit, 1762; appointed Indian Commissary, 1766, and major of Detroit militia, 1776. Taken prisoner with Hamilton at Vincennes and sent to Virginia, he was exchanged, 1781, and became Lt. Gov. of Detroit, 1782.

HEBRON: An early Moravian settlement on the eastern outskirts of what is now Lebanon, Pa.

HECKEWELDER, ANNA SALOME ("SALLY")—1784–1857: John Heckewelder's second child; born at New Gnadenhütten (Mt. Clemens, Michigan); died at Bethlehem, Pa.

HECKEWELDER, CHRISTIAN RENATUS—1750–1801: John Heckewelder's younger brother; storekeeper at Emmaus, Pa., and later at Hope, N. J.

HECKEWELDER, REV. JOHN GOTTLIEB ERNESTUS—1743–1823: Born, Bedford, England, March 12, 1743; came to America, 1754; with Post on the Muskingum, 1762; missionary among the Indians in Pennsylvania, Ohio, Michigan, 1772–1786; ordained a deacon at Lititz, 1778; agent in Ohio for the Society for the Propagation of the Gospel, 1788–1810; assistant peace commissioner for the U. S. at Vincennes, 1792, and at Detroit, 1793; died January 31, 1823.

HECKEWELDER, JOHANNA MARIA ("POLLY")—1781–1868; John Heckewelder's eldest child; born at Salem on the Muskingum; the same year taken prisoner with her parents and moved to Upper Sandusky. From New Gnadenhütten above Detroit, her parents sent her to Bethlehem, Pa., for her education. She was appointed, 1801, a teacher in the Ladies' Boarding-School at Lititz, Pa.

HECKEWELDER, SARA (OHNEBERG)—1746–1815: John Heckewelder's wife; married, July 4, 1780, at Salem, Ohio.

HECKEWELDER, SUSANNA—1786–1867: John Heckewelder's youngest daughter, born at Bethlehem; wife of John Christian Luckenbach.

HELLER'S TAVERN: At Windgap, Plainfield Twp., Northampton County, Pa. Heckewelder and Mortimer breakfasted here, May 1, 1798.

HELLTOWN: An Indian settlement on one of the branches of the Walhonding River in Ohio, on the route between Coshocton and Upper Sandusky. It received its name from the fact that here several traders had been murdered.

HELPERS CONFERENCE: Forerunner of the present Provincial Elders Conference, the governing board of each province of the Moravian Church.

HENDRICKS, CAPT.: A Mahican Indian who served as General Putnam's messenger in 1792.

HENDRICKS, CAPT.: An Oneida Indian; delegate from the Oneida country to the conference at Detroit, 1793.

HENDRICKS, FORT: On the south side of the Mohawk, a short distance east of Little Falls. Heckewelder visited it May 12, 1793.

HENRY—d. 1782: A Moravian Indian. March 7, 1782, he guided Williamson's militia, not suspecting their intention, to Salem on the Tuscarawas. He was murdered by them next day at Gnadenhütten.

HENRY, JAMES: A watchmaker at Pittsburgh, son of William Henry of Lancaster. In 1792 Heckewelder met him at Pittsburgh; by 1798 he had moved to Detroit.

HENRY, CAPT. JAMES—1757–1827: Early settler, about two miles west of Jordan, Lincoln County, Ont.

HENRY, JOHN JOSEPH—1758–1811: The "John Henry" who called on Heckewelder and Steiner at Harrisburg, June 19, 1789, was probably John Joseph Henry (son of William Henry of Lancaster), a lawyer who later became President Judge of the Second Judicial District of Pennsylvania. He was a member, 1775–1776, of Capt. Matthew Smith's company from Paxtang on the Canada expedition under Arnold. He is buried in the Moravian graveyard at Lancaster.

HENRY, WILLIAM—1729–1786: A Moravian of Lancaster, Pa.; inventor, manufacturer, patriot. From 1750 on, he manufactured firearms and was one of the early makers of the Pennsylvania ("Kentucky") rifle. Armorer to Braddock, 1755, and to Forbes, 1758; one of the commissioners to survey a canal route between the Lehigh and the Susquehanna Rivers; member of Congress, 1784.

HENRY, WILLLIAM, JR.—1757–1821: Son of William Henry (1729–1786) of Lancaster; Justice of the Courts of Northampton County and a manufacturer of firearms. He established the Boulton Gun Works on Bushkill Creek, 1813; was one of the Presidential Electors from Pennsylvania, 1792.

HERRNHUTERS: A popular name for the early Moravians in America, given them because the renewed life of their church had begun at Herrnhut, Saxony, where in 1722 Count Zinzendorf had received them as refugees from Moravia.

HILL, CAPT. DAVID (KARONGROTE, KAROWYONTE—"FLYING CLOUD")—d. 1790: A Mohawk, brother of Capt. Isaac Hill; frequently sent on embassies for the Six Nations; with Captain Isaac Brant at Marietta, 1788.

HOCKHOCKING, FORT: Probably Fort Gower, built in 1774 by Lord Dunmore at the mouth of the Hocking River on the site of present Hockingport.

HOCKHOCKING (FRENCH MARGARET'S TOWN): A Delaware Indian town at what is now Lancaster, Ohio, on the headwaters of the Hocking River.

HODGDON, COL. SAMUEL: Appointed Quartermaster of the Army, March 4, 1791; superseded, April 19, 1792.

HOLLAND LAND COMPANY: A group of Dutch bankers who acquired large tracts in New York and northwestern Pennsylvania, where they built roads, established towns, and sold land directly to settlers.

HOOKER, RICHARD: Innkeeper near present North Cohocton, Steuben County, N. Y.

HOPE, N. J.: A Moravian settlement in Hope Twp., Warren County, N. J., ten miles northeast of present Belvidere.

HOPE'S COVE: A deep harbor in Bass Island, Lake Erie, which sheltered the vessels transporting the Moravians from Detroit to the Cuyahoga, 1786.

HORSFIELD, JOSEPH: A Moravian, postmaster at Bethlehem, 1798.

HUBER, GEORGE—1760–1813: Blacksmith at Bethlehem; appointed postmaster, 1801.

HÜBNER, REV. JOHN ANDREW—1737–1809: Pastor at Bethlehem, 1780; at Lititz, 1790; consecrated bishop, 1790.

HUNT'S FERRY: Now Falls, Wyoming County, Pa., named for the Buttermilk Falls of Buttermilk Creek, which here enters the Susquehanna.

HURON RIVER, Mich.: Now the Clinton River, which flows through Macomb County to enter Lake St. Clair.

HURON RIVER, Ohio: Enters Lake Erie at Huron, Erie County. On its bank near present Milan, was the Moravian Indian village of Pettquotting.

HUTCHINS, THOMAS—1730–1789: Soldier, frontiersman, surveyor. In 1781 he became Geographer to the United States, and in 1785 was given charge of the survey of the Northwest Territory.

I.

IDEA FIDEA FRATRUM oder Kurze Begrif der Christlichen Lehre in dem evangelischen Brüdergemeinen, dargelegt von August Gottlieb Spangenberg (Barby and Leipzig, 1779). Barby, Saxony, was at that time the Moravian headquarters. English editions of this book were published in 1784 and 1796: *An Exposition of Christian Doctrine as taught in the Protestant Church of the United Brethren or Unitas Fratrum.*

INGERSOLL ("INGERSON"), MAJOR THOMAS: Founder of a settlement in Ontario. The town of Ingersoll (formerly called Oxford), Ont., at the head of the portage between Lake Erie and the Thames River, was named for him.

IRONDEQUOIT (THIRUNDIGAT, GE RUNDEGUT) BAY: Four miles east of the mouth of the Genesee River, at what is now Rochester, N. Y. It was the northern end of the Allegheny-Genesee Trail and of the portage from Genesee Falls to Lake Ontario.

IROQUOIS: See SIX NATIONS.

IRVINE, GEN. WILLIAM—1741–1804: Physician at Carlisle, Pa.; Commandant at Fort Pitt, 1781–1783; delegate to the Continental Congress, 1786–1788; commanding officer of state troops employed to put down the Whiskey Rebellion, 1794.

ISRAEL (WELAPACHTSCHIECHEN, alias CAPTAIN JOHNNY)—d. 1782: Delaware chief; baptized, 1777, at Lichtenau; died in the massacre at Gnadenhütten.

Glossary

J.

JACOB: Moravian Indian. After the massacre at Gnadenhütten, March 8, 1782, he left the mission with his wife, Louisa, and their children.

JACOB—d. 1821: Son of Israel (Welapachtschiechen) and son-in-law of Shebosh (John Bull) whose daughter, Christiana, he married. Baptized at Lichtenau, 1778; narrowly escaped being killed in the massacre at Gnadenhütten; later went to Fairfield in Upper Canada; met Heckewelder at Detroit, 1793. It was probably this Jacob (there were several Moravian Indians of that name) who accompanied Heckewelder on his journey from Cayahaga to Pittsburgh, 1786.

JACOBS, CAPT.—d. 1756: A famous Delaware war chief, brother of Shingas and King Beaver; killed at Kittanning, September 8, 1756, in Col. John Armstrong's attack.

JAMESON'S: An inn at Burnt Cabins, Fulton County, Pa., at which Heckewelder stopped, November 1, 1786.

JEFFERSON, FORT: Erected, October, 1791, by Gen. Arthur St. Clair on the Green River, about six miles south of present Greenville, Darke County, Ohio.

JEMISSON, JENNESON: See JAMESON.

JOHANAN: A Delaware Indian, son of Mariane; baptized, 1749, at Bethlehem, Pa.; visited Gekelemukpechink, 1771; met Heckewelder at Marietta, 1788.

JOHANNES (CAPT. JOHN DOUGHTY): Moravian Indian; came with horses to help Heckewelder and his party at the Falls of the Beaver, April 13, 1773.

JOHNNY, CAPT. (Delaware): See ISRAEL.

JOHNNY, CAPT. (Mohawk): See DESERONTYOU.

JOHNNY, CAPT. (Shawnee): A leading war chief of the Shawnee; arrived at Detroit from the Indian council on the Maumee, July 9, 1793.

JOHNSON, SIR JOHN: A Tory leader in northern New York State; son of Sir William Johnson. With St. Leger, he defeated Gen. Herkimer at Fort Stanwix. In 1791 he was appointed by the British Superintendent General of the Six Nations of Indians and their Confederates.

JOHNSTON, HUGH: Settled east of Utica, Canal Twp., Venango County, Pa., about 1797.

JOHNSTON, CAPT. WILLIAM—d. 1807: Indian interpreter; first permanent settler at what is now Buffalo, N. Y.

JONAS—d. 1782: Son of Jo Peepe and brother of Anton; baptized, 1775, at Gnadenhütten; appointed a National Helper at Salem, 1780, where he conducted the children's service. May 6, 1781, he was one of the guards at Heckewelder's house, and next day attended the parley with Chief Pachgantschihilas. Died in the massacre at Gnadenhütten.

JONES, CAPT. HORATIO—1763– ? : Born in Chester County, Pa.; captured by the Senecas, 1781, and adopted by them; released, 1784. At the Detroit Conference, 1793, he was interpreter for the Genesee Senecas. In 1798 Heckewelder met him at Williamsburg, Livingston County, N. Y.

JONES, MRS.: The old Jones house still stands on the eastern outskirts of Bethlehem, Pa.

JONES, REV. DAVID: Baptist minister who travelled with George Rogers Clark down the Ohio from Pittsburgh to visit the Indian country. Author of *A Journal of Two Visits Made to Some Nations of Indians on the West Side of the River Ohio in the Years 1772 and 1773* (N. Y., 1865). Heckewelder met him at Marietta, 1788.

JOSHUA—1742–1806: Mahican Indian, son of Joshua (Nanhun); baptized at Bethlehem, 1749. He was the mission's foremost musician, playing the spinet and leading the choir. His daughters, Anna and Bathsaba, died in the massacre at Gnadenhütten, March 8, 1782. He himself was burned to death by followers of the Shawnee Prophet on the White River, 1806.

JOUNG: See YOUNG.

JUDITH: A Moravian Indian; baptized, 1774, at Schönbrunn; member of Heckewelder's congregation at Salem, Ohio; died in the massacre at Gnadenhütten.

JUNG: See YOUNG.

JUNGMAN: See YOUNGMAN.

JUNIATA CROSSING: Where travellers on the Pittsburgh Road crossed the Raystown Branch of the Juniata; six miles east of the present Everett, Pa.

K.

KASKASKIES: See KUSKUSKY.

KASKASKIA: An Algonquian tribe settled, during the eighteenth century, west of the Weas, about the mouth of the Kaskaskia River.

KENNY, JAMES: Indian trader, clerk to Josiah Davenport in the Indian Commissioners' store at Fort Pitt, 1762.

KERR: An Irish settler near Le Boeuf (Waterford), Erie County, Pa.; visited by Heckewelder, November 5, 1800.

KICKAPOO: An Algonquian tribe dependent on the Wea. In 1791 they had a town across the Wabash from Ouiatenon.

KIEFER'S: An inn near Upper Strasburg, Franklin County, Pa.

KILBOURN, TIMOTHY and AARON: Owners, 1798, of a mill on Dingman Creek, Middlesex County, Ont.

KILLBUCK, JOHN, JR. (GELELEMEND, alias WILLIAM HENRY)—1737–1811:

Glossary 419

A Delaware Indian, grandson of Netawatwees. During the Revolutionary War, his sympathies were with the Americans. Baptized under the name of William Henry (after William Henry of Lancaster), 1789, at Pettquotting; declined to accept position of head chief of the Delaware nation; became a National Helper and the leader of the Moravian Indians.

KILLBUCK, JOHN, SR.: A Delaware chief, interested in but suspicious of the Moravians. Heckewelder met him on the Muskingum, 1773. Father of Gelelemend.

KILLBUCK CREEK: Flows through Wayne, Holmes, and Coshocton Counties to enter the Walhonding near Coshocton, Ohio.

KING, CAPT. ROBERT—d. 1826: Revolutionary soldier, friend of Lafayette, whom he attended when wounded at Brandywine; first settler (1794) in Erie County; visited by Heckewelder on French Creek, 1800; lived to greet Lafayette at Waterford, 1825.

KING, THOMAS: An innkeeper, eighteen miles east of Pittsburgh on the road to Bedford. Here Heckewelder spent an unquiet night, October 23, 1786.

KINHANSCHICAN: A Delaware Indian town on the eastern headwaters of the Scioto; home of the war chief, Wingenund.

KIRKLAND, REV. SAMUEL—1741–1808: Missionary to the Oneida Indians for forty years. During the Revolutionary War he persuaded the Oneidas to support the colonies; after the war, he helped to bring the Six Nations as a whole to take a friendly attitude toward the United States.

KITTANNING: The present Kittanning, Armstrong County, Pa., is on the site of a Delaware Indian town which in 1756 was the home of Shingas, the Beaver, and Capt. Jacobs. Though destroyed by Col. Armstrong in 1756, it remained for many years an important Indian trail junction. Here Col. Brodhead erected Fort Armstrong, 1778–1779.

KLIEST, DANIEL—d. 1792: A locksmith at Bethlehem.

KLINGSOHR, REV. JOHN AUGUSTUS—1746–1798: Moravian minister at Lititz, Pa., 1783; at Bethlehem, 1790, where he was Head Pastor and President of the Elders Conference.

KNOX, FORT: At Vincennes, Indiana, where Gen. Putnam held his treaty, 1792, with the Indians.

KOKOSING ("HABITATION OF OWLS"): Delaware Indian town on the Kokosing River, not far from Mt. Vernon, Knox County, Ohio, about halfway between Coshocton and Upper Sandusky. Heckewelder and the Moravian captives reached it September 25, 1781.

KOKOSING RIVER ("OWL CREEK"): A branch of the Walhonding River, on the canoe route between Coshocton and Upper Sandusky, Ohio.

KONKLE, JOHN—1757–1828: One of the earliest settlers at what is now

Elmira (formerly Newtown), N. Y. He surveyed most of the early town lots; was town clerk for a term, and became in 1801 the town's first postmaster.

KOQUETHAGACHTON: See WHITE EYES.

KREMSER, JOHN—1758–1823: Shoemaker by trade; landlord of the Inn at Nazareth. Accompanied Heckewelder and Mortimer from Nazareth to Windgap, May 1, 1798.

KUHN, ABRAHAM: A Wyandot chief from Lower Sandusky; assisted in the removal of the Moravians from the Muskingum, 1781.

KUNKLE, JOHN: See KONKLE.

KUSKUSKY: There were at different times several Indian towns, known as the Kuskuskies, in the vicinity of present New Castle, Lawrence County, Pa. Pakanke's town was probably at New Castle. The "Cascaskung" through which Heckewelder passed, October 15, 1786, on his way from Cayahaga to Pittsburgh, was at the present Edinburg.

L.

LACHINE: A city on Montreal Island, Quebec, at the head of Lachine Rapids; founded by La Salle, 1668; named in mockery of La Salle's hope to find a way to China.

LANCELEGRASSE: "A Village in Louisiana, on the Mississippi, below St. Louis." —Morse, *American Gazetteer* (Boston, 1804).

LANDING, THE: Queenston, Ont., and Lewiston, N. Y., at the mouth of the Niagara Gorge, where boats used to land for the old Niagara Portage.

LANGUNDOWI-OTENINK (LANGUNDO-UTENINK): Moravian Indian village, better known as Friedenstadt ("City of Peace") at what is now Moravia, on the west bank of Beaver Creek below New Castle, Pa.; founded by Zeisberger, 1770, with Indians from Goschgoschink.

LANS LE GRESS: See LANCELEGRASSE.

LANSING, CAPT. ABRAHAM: Captain of the sloop *Schenectady*, which took Heckewelder up the Hudson River from New York to Albany, 1793.

LA SHIENE: See LACHINE.

LA TRANCHE: See THAMES RIVER, Ont.

LAUREL HILL: The highest ridge of the Alleghenies between Harrisburg and Pittsburgh. The road crosses it between Jennertown and Ligonier.

LAURENS, FORT: Built, 1778, by Gen. McIntosh at Tuscarawas, about half a mile below present Bolivar, Ohio.

LAWUNAKHANNEK: Moravian Indian village, founded by Zeisberger in 1769 on the east bank of the Allegheny about three miles above Goschgoschink, in Forest County, Pa.

Glossary

LEATH, JOHN: A white man, married to a white woman who had been taken captive and adopted by the Indians when she was six months old. After marriage, she refused to leave her adoptive people. The couple lived for a time at the Moravian town of Salem on the Tuscarawas, but, after the massacre at Gnadenhütten in 1782, they left the mission and lived among the Indians.

LE BOEUF: Now Waterford, Erie County, Pa. Here, at the head of navigation on French Creek and at the end of a portage from Presque Isle on Lake Erie, the French built a fort, 1753. It was evacuated, 1759. The English fort at this place, built in 1760, was burned by Indians during Pontiac's War. The United States built a fort here in 1794.

LECHA: The Lehigh River (once known as the West Branch of the Delaware), which flows past Bethlehem to enter the Delaware at Easton, Pa. The territory within the angle made by the two rivers was formerly known as the Forks.

LeFEVER, ANTHONY: One of the Frenchmen who, during the French Revolution, escaped to America and founded Asylum (Azilum) on the Susquehanna. Moving to nearby Standing Stone (named for a glacier stone in the Susquehanna), he kept a well-known tavern, licensed in 1794.

LEINBACH, FREDERICK: Storekeeper at Hope, N. J.

LEVALLIE (LEVELLIE), FRANCIS: A French Canadian who in 1782 escorted the Moravian missionaries as prisoners to Detroit.

LEVERING, ABRAHAM: Landlord of the Sun Inn (established 1760) at Bethlehem. He accompanied Heckewelder and Mortimer from Nazareth to Windgap, May 1, 1798.

LEWIS, GEN. ANDREW—1720–1781: In 1754 he was with Washington at the surrender of Fort Necessity; in 1768 he helped to frame the Fort Stanwix Treaty, which set new Indian boundaries. His defeat of the Shawnees in the Battle of Point Pleasant, at the mouth of the Kanawha, 1774, determined the outcome of the Shawnee War (Lord Dunmore's War).

LICHTENAU ("MEADOW OF LIGHT"): Moravian town in Ohio, established, 1776, at the request of Netawatwees. It was situated on the east side of the Muskingum, two miles below Goschochking (Coshocton), the new Delaware capital. When Gnadenhütten was abandoned in 1778, Lichtenau received its members. Lichtenau itself was evacuated, 1780.

LIMESTONE: Now Maysville, Ky. This was the transfer point, during the period of early settlement, from river to land transportation. In 1796 it became the terminal point of Zane's Trace, which started at Wheeling and passed through Zanesville and Chillicothe.

LINCOLN, GEN. BENJAMIN—1733–1810: Field commander at Saratoga, 1777; received Cornwallis' sword at Yorktown, 1781; Secretary of War, 1781–1783; elected Lt. Gov. of Massachusetts, 1787; commissioner from Massachusetts to the Indian conference at Detroit, 1793.

LINDLEY, JACOB—1744–1814: Quaker preached of New Garden, Pa.; attended the Indian conference at Detroit, 1793; wrote a description of Niagara Falls quoted by Benjamin Mortimer in his 1798 journal.

LITITZ: A Moravian town established, 1757, about eight miles north of Lancaster, Pa. Named for Lititz in Bohemia where, in 1457 some followers of John Hus formed the *Unitas Fratrum*, now known as the Moravian Church.

LITTLETON, FORT: Erected, 1756, at what is still known as Fort Littleton, Fulton County, Pa.

LOGAN, JOHN (TACHNECHDORUS, "SPREADING OAK"): A son of Shickellamy (Iroquois viceregent in Pennsylvania, 1728–1748). John, Shickellamy's son, came to be known as "John Logan," through false analogy with his younger brother's name, "James Logan," and in his later years was known simply as "Logan." Like his father, he was a friend of the English; but the murder of thirteen of his relatives at Yellow Creek on the Ohio destroyed his faith in the white man. He took an active part in the Shawnee War. His message to Lord Dunmore at the close of the war, which Thomas Jefferson transmitted to the public, has become famous as "Logan's Lament."

LOGSTOWN: An important Indian settlement, originally inhabited chiefly by the Shawnee but later by Iroquois and others; situated on the east bank of the Ohio about eighteen miles below Pittsburgh at present Legionville, just north of Ambridge, Pa. From here Washington took the trail to Fort LeBoeuf, 1753. Logstown was abandoned by the Indians in 1758.

LORAMIE'S STORE ("LORIMER'S"): Present Loramie (Fort Loramie), McLean Twp., Shelby County, Ohio; situated at the southern end of the portage between St. Mary's River and Laramie Creek, which thus connects the Maumee with the Miami waterways.

LORETZ, REV. JOHN—d. 1798: Member of the Governing Board of the Moravian Church, Herrnhut, Saxony; visited Pennsylvania, 1771, when he made a journey with Christian Gregor to Friedenshütten on the North Branch of the Susquehanna.

LOUISA: There were two Moravian Indians of this name in Heckewelder's time. The one to whom he most likely refers in his journal was a Delaware, daughter of Samuel and Helena Moor, baptized by Zeisberger at Schönbrunn, 1774.

LOWER SANDUSKY: Wyandot town and trading post situated at the head of navigation on the Sandusky River, at what is now Fremont, the county seat of Sandusky County, Ohio.

LUDLOW, ISRAEL: A surveyor, appointed in 1787 to survey the land of the New Jersey Company. He became part proprietor in 1789 of the land on which Cincinnati stands, and he laid out the streets. In 1795 he ran the Indian boundary line as established by the treaty of Greenville.

Glossary

LUNDY'S LANE: West of the old Portage Road, on the Canadian side at Niagara Falls. The Log church to which Heckewelder refers in his 1798 journal was built in 1795. It was damaged during the Battle of Lundy's Lane, 1812, and replaced by a larger building, 1821. This latter was succeeded by Drummond Hill Presbyterian Church.

M.

McCORMICK, ALEXANDER: A trader at Upper Sandusky, friendly to the Moravians, although in 1781 he took part with Capt. Elliot in removing them from the Muskingum. He sent food to them during their starving winter at Captives Town.

McCOSKRY, DR. WILLIAM A.: Army surgeon from Carlisle, Pa., who attended the Indian conference at Detroit, 1793. On retirement from the army in 1803, he settled at Detroit, where he practiced until his death.

McDOWEL, ROBERT: Brother-in-law of Col. Jacob Stroud. Captured by Indians in 1778 and taken to Niagara by way of the "Forbidden Path"; after the war he settled in the Chemung Valley on land which he had first seen as a captive.

McGEE, HENRY: In 1795 he sold his property near Nazareth and went north. Heckewelder and Mortimer were entertained by him at Dansville, N. Y., 1798.

McINTOSH, FORT: Built, 1778, by Gen. Lachlan McIntosh at the mouth of the Beaver River, Pa.

McINTOSH, GEN. LACHLAN—1725–1806: Appointed brigadier general in the Continental Army, 1776. In 1778 he was sent to command at Fort Pitt, and in the same year he built Fort McIntosh at the mouth of the Beaver and Fort Laurens at Tuscarawas (near Bolivar, Ohio). He was replaced, 1779, at Fort Pitt by Brodhead. Taken prisoner at Charleston, 1780.

McKEE, JAMES: Son of Col. Alexander McKee.

McKEE, COL. ALEXANDER—d. 1798: Trader and Indian agent. In 1778, with Matthew Elliot and Simon Girty he fled to Detroit and joined the British. After the war he became Superintendent of Indian Affairs for Upper Canada. He befriended the Moravians, entertaining them on his plantation at the mouth of the Detroit River.

McKINNEY: See KENNY.

MACKENZIE, SIR ALEXANDER—1764–1820: Fur trader and explorer, member of the North West Company. He built Fort Chippewyan on Lake Athabasca in 1788; followed the Mackenzie River to its mouth in the Arctic Ocean, 1789; and in 1792–1793 crossed the continental divide from the Peace River to the Fraser and reached the Pacific Ocean.

McKINZIE: See MACKENZIE.

McMAHAN, MAJOR WILLIAM: A major in the 2nd Legion, whom Heckewelder met at Wheeling, W. Va., 1792.

McWHORTER, THOMAS: In 1795 he purchased from Capt. Williamson 169 acres of land at present Avoca, N. Y.

MACHINGWE PUSHIS (BIG CAT): Delaware Chief. On the death of Netawatwees, he served with Gelelemend and Tetepachksi as regent during the minority of the hereditary head chief.

MAHICAN: An Algonquian nation formerly occupying both banks of the Hudson River. After 1673, at the end of a long war with the Iroquois, they were dispersed, some moving to Massachusetts, some north to find protection under the Iroquois, and some west to the Delawares by whom they were soon absorbed. The first Moravian Indian mission was among the Mahicans at Shekomeko and Wechquadnach on the New York-Connecticut border.

MAHONING CREEK, Pa.: Enters the Lehigh River from the west at Lehighton, Pa. At its mouth was the Moravian Indian town of Gnadenhütten, established in 1746.

MAHONING OLD TOWN: On the Mahoning River, near Newton Falls, Trumbull County, Ohio. Visited by Heckewelder, October 11, 1786.

MAHONING RIVER, Ohio and Pa.: Flows through Youngstown, Ohio, and unites with the Shenango near New Castle, Pa., to form the Beaver River. The Mahoning was at one time known as the Big Beaver.

MARCUS (MARK)—d. 1783: A Mahican, one of the foremost National Helpers in the Moravian Indian mission. In 1782 he led a body of Christian Indians from Captives Town (near present Upper Sandusky) to the Shawnees on the Scioto, among whom he died.

MARIETTA: The first white settlement in Ohio; founded, April 7, 1788, at the mouth of the Muskingum River by a colony from Massachusetts led by Gen. Rufus Putnam. Named in honor of Queen Marie Antoinette.

MARTIN: Early innkeeper at Cincinnati, with whom Heckewelder stayed, July 2, 1792.

MARTIN, JOHN—d. 1782: Moravian Indian, a National Helper in the Muskingum mission; died in the massacre at Gnadenhütten.

MARTIN'S STATION: New Martinsville, at the confluence of Fishing Creek and the Ohio, Wetzel County, W. Va.

MASCOUTEN: An Algonquian tribe closely related to the Wea. During the latter part of the eighteenth century, a considerable number of the Mascoutens were living on the Wabash.

MASSASAGA: See MISSISAUGA.

MASSIE'S STATION: Now Manchester, Ohio; on the north side of the Ohio River, about twelve miles above Limestone (Maysville), Ky.

MAUMEE RAPIDS: Near Waterville, Lucas County, Ohio. Here was McKee's trading post and the British Fort Miami. In 1793 the Indians held a conference at the Maumee Rapids, at which it was decided not to

Glossary

negotiate with the United States Commissioners at Detroit. Anthony Wayne defeated the Indians here in the Battle of Fallen Timbers, 1794.

MEAD, DAVID: Made settlement at Meadville, Crawford County, Pa., in 1788.

MEADVILLE: Formerly the Indian town of Cussewago. Laid out, 1793, by David Mead, it was for some years a military supply depot, furnishing supplies for troops between Fort Franklin and Fort Le Boeuf.

MENNIER: See MYNEER.

MERCER'S STATION: See MASSIE'S STATION.

MESHOPPEN CREEK: A creek on the east side of the Susquehanna in Wyoming County, Pa. The Great Warriors Path and the pioneer road forded it at its mouth, where the present town of Meshoppen stands.

METCALF, JOHN: In 1798 he had a log tavern at Bath, N. Y., on Morris Street, west of the square.

MIAMI: See MAUMEE RAPIDS.

MIAMI RIVER: Three rivers with the name Miami appear in Heckewelder's journals: The Great Miami, which enters the Ohio some fifteen miles west of Cincinnati; the Little Miami, which enters the Ohio in the eastern outskirts of Cincinnati; and the Miami of the Lake (now the Maumee), which enters Lake Erie at Toledo, Ohio.

MICHAEL—d. 1758: A Munsee Delaware warrior, baptized at Shekomeko, 1742. The Moravian missionaries called him "the crown of the congregation."

MICHLER'S TAVERN: Nathaniel, son of Bishop Michler, was host at Jacobsburg Tavern, Bushkill Twp., Northampton County. He later taught at Nazareth Hall.

MILES, WILLIAM: Agent of the Holland Land Company; served as Roger Alden's deputy on French Creek, where Heckewelder met him in 1800.

MILLERSTOWN: Now Annville, Lebanon County, Pa. It was laid out by Abraham Miller, 1762.

MINGO BOTTOM } Now Mingo Junction, Jefferson County, Ohio. In 1768
MINGO TOWN   } some sixty Iroquois families were living here.

MINGO: There has been much confusion in the use of this name. It is an Algonquian word, *mengwe*, meaning "stealthy," applied by the Delawares to the Iroquois and cognate tribes. More particularly, according to James Mooney, it was used by Americans during the late colonial period to designate those Iroquois who had left the homeland in upstate New York to live in the Ohio country, where they associated with the Delawares and Shawnees.

MINISINKS: "Place of the Minsi (or Munsee)," a name given to a populous settlement, centering in Minisink Island, on the Delaware River three miles below Milford, Pike County, Pa. The term, "the Minisinks," was extended to cover the river flats all the way from what is now Port Jervis to Stroudsburg.

MISSISAUGA: A sub-tribe of the Chippewa. In historic times they were wanderers, coming from the shores of Lake Superior, Lake Huron, and the Georgian Bay. In the eighteenth century, many of the Missisauga were living in the vicinity of Detroit and in southern Ontario.

MOHICAN: See MAHICAN.

MOLTHER, REV. JOHN: Moravian minister at Hebron, 1793; Schöneck, 1796; York, Pa., 1798; Emmaus, 1802; New York, N. Y., 1805; Schöneck, 1813.

MONSEY: See MUNSEE.

MONSEY TOWN: See MUNCEY, Ont.

MONTGOMERY, FORT: On the west bank of the Hudson, six miles south of West Point.

MOORE: See SAMUEL MOORE, an Indian.

MOORE, JOSEPH—1732–1793: A Quaker farmer living near Flemington, N. J.; member of Kingwood Meeting. His journal of the journey to the Indian conference at Detroit, 1793, has been published in the *Friends Miscellany*, IV (1835), 289–343.

MORGAN, COL. GEORGE—1743–1810: Fur trader, Indian agent, coloniser. In 1776 he was appointed land officer of the Indiana Company. In 1789 he founded New Madrid in what was then Spanish territory and is now the State of Missouri. When Heckewelder met him, December 11, 1788, in Pittsburgh, Morgan was about to set out on this colonising expedition to the mouth of the Ohio.

MORTIMER, REV. BENJAMIN—1767–1834: A teacher in Nazareth Hall. In 1798 he accepted a call to be Zeisberger's assistant, and, in company with Heckewelder, travelled to Fairfield in Upper Canada to join him. After Zeisberger's death in 1808, Mortimer became pastor of the First Moravian Church in New York City.

MUNCEY (MONSEYTOWN): A village on the Thames River, Middlesex County, Ont., settled in the eighteenth century by Munsee Delawares.

MUNSEE (MONSEY, MINSI): The northern and most warlike division of the Delawares, sometimes called the Wolf Tribe. Displaced by the Walking Purchase from their Minisink lands on the Delaware, many of them moved west to the Allegheny and Muskingum.

MUSKINGUM (ELK'S EYE) RIVER: Provided a good canoe route from the Ohio at present Marietta, with a mile-long portage between the Tuscarawas branch and the Cuyahoga, to Lake Erie. See also FALLS OF THE MUSKINGUM.

MUSQUETONS: See MASCOUTEN.

MYNHEER, CHRISTIAN: In 1787 he built the first house and planted the first orchard at Big Flats, about five miles west of Elmira, N. Y.

Glossary

N.

NAIN: A Moravian Indian village, about two miles north of Bethlehem on the west side of Monocacy Creek; established, 1757, for the Mahicans; abandoned, 1763, during Pontiac's War.

NANTICOKE: An Algonquian people from the Eastern Shore of Maryland who, under pressure from the whites, left their native country and moved north to the protection of the Six Nations. In 1766 a body of them on this journey stopped for three weeks at the Moravian town of Friedenshütten (Wyalusing) on the Susquehanna.

NANTICOKE, SAMUEL: See SAMUEL NANTICOKE.

NATHANAEL DAVIS (GUTTENAMEQUIN, "A YEARLING FISH"): Delaware Indian, baptized, 1769, at Friedenshütten; moved to Schönbrunn on the Muskingum; was sent, 1772, on a diplomatic errand to Gekelemukpechink, the Delaware capital. In 1789 he moved to the Maumee River.

NATIONAL HELPERS: The official term applied to Indian assistants (Elders) in the Moravian mission towns. The word "national" was used to avoid such belittling terms as "native" and "tribal."

NAVY HALL: Gov. John Graves Simcoe's headquarters in Newark, 1791–1792, opposite Fort Niagara.

NAZARETH: In 1740, on the site of an Indian village some ten miles north of what is now Bethlehem, George Whitefield began the construction (with the assistance of a number of Moravians) of a school and orphanage for negroes. Next year the Moravians bought the tract, named it Nazareth, and established what in time became one of their principal centers in America. It is now the headquarters of the Moravian Historical Society, which preserves the Whitefield House as a museum.

NEES HAWS: Mahican warrior. In 1780 he led a raid against the American settlements in the Ohio country.

NESBITT, DR.: See NISBET.

NESCOPECK: An Indian town on the North Branch of the Susquehanna, below Wyoming (Wilkes-Barre). During the French and Indian War it was a rendezvous for Indians hostile to Pennsylvania. A good Indian path led from Nescopeck to Bethlehem.

NETAWATWEES (NEAWATWHELEMEN, KING NEWCOMER)—1678 (c.)–1776: Head chief of the Delawares in the Ohio country; founded Gekelemukpechink (also called Newcomer's Town), 1770; invited the Christian Indians to settle nearby on the Muskingum, 1771; founded a new capital, Goschochking, 1776. "Chief Netawatwees died 31st Octob. in Pittsburg."—The Bethlehem Diary, "Memorabilien," 1776.

NEWALIKE (NEWOLIKE, "THE FOUR STEPS"): Delaware chief of the Unami tribe. At one time he lived at Wechpakak on Tunkhannock Creek, Wyoming County, Pa. He visited Friedenshütten, 1766, to arrange assistance for Tuscaroras and Nanticokes travelling north. He was baptized, 1774, at Schönbrunn, but left the mission, 1777.

NEWARK: Now Niagara-on-the-Lake, at the mouth of the Niagara River, opposite Fort Niagara. John Graves Simcoe, Gov. of Upper Canada, made it his headquarters, 1791–1792.

NEWCOMER, KING: See NETAWATWEES.

NEWCOMER'S TOWN: See GEKELEMUKPECHINK.

NEW FURNACE: Probably Elizabeth Furnace, near Brickerville, Elizabeth Twp., Lancaster County, Pa.

NEW GNADENHÜTTEN: See GNADENHÜTTEN, Michigan.

NEW MADRID: A settlement on the Mississippi below the mouth of the Ohio, founded by George Morgan, 1789. Today the town is the county seat of New Madrid County, Missouri.

NEWOLIKE: See NEWALIKE.

NEW SCHÖNBRUNN: A Moravian Indian town, established, 1779, on the west bank of the Tuscarawas, almost opposite Schönbrunn (near the present New Philadelphia).

NEW SPAIN: Mexico.

NEWTOWN: Indian settlement at what is now Elmira, N. Y.; destroyed by Gen. Sullivan, 1779.

NISBET, DR. CHARLES—1736–1804: First Principal of Dickinson College, Carlisle, Pa., 1795–1804.

NITSCHMANN, DAVID ("THE CARPENTER")—1696–1772: The first bishop of the Renewed Moravian Church. He accompanied the second group of Moravian missionaries to go to Georgia, 1736, meeting John Wesley on the voyage and greatly influencing him. He travelled in Germany, England, Denmark, Norway, Sweden, Pennsylvania, Maryland, New York, North Carolina. In 1754 he came in the Moravian ship, *Irene*, from London to Philadelphia with John Heckewelder and brought him to Bethlehem.

NIXON, WILLIAM: By profession a cedar cooper in the early "Economy" at Bethlehem.

NOAILLES, GEN. LOUIS MARIE ANTOINE, VICOMTE DE—1756–1804: French soldier and statesman, younger brother to the fourth Duc de Noailles. He served under Lafayette in the American Revolution and concluded the capitulation at Yorktown. Elected a member of the Estates General in France, he proposed that titles be abolished; but, the French Revolution going too far for him, he escaped to the United States, where he took a leading part in the establishment of Asylum, on the Susquehanna, for French refugees.

NORTH BEND: Town a few miles below Cincinnati, established by John Cleves Symmes, 1787.

Glossary

North River: The Hudson River.

North West Company: Created, 1787, by Montreal traders in order to compete with the Hudson's Bay Company in the fur trade of the West.

O.

O'Hara, Gen. James—1752–1819: Revolutionary soldier, Indian trader, government contractor, manufacturer. Pittsburgh in large measure owed her early commercial prominence to him. In 1777 Heckewelder and the Indian, Anton, saved him from hostile warriors.

Ohio Company of Associates: Founded at Boston, 1787, by a group of New Englanders for the settlement of lands on the Ohio (not to be confused with the Ohio Company—of Virginia—chartered, May 19, 1749). The company hastened passage of the Northwest Ordinance, 1787. On October 27, 1787, the company contracted for 1,500,000 acres at the confluence of the Muskingum and the Ohio, where in April, 1788, Gen. Rufus Putnam founded the town of Marietta.

Ohneberg, Sara: See Heckewelder, Sara.

Ojibway: See Chippewa.

Oneida: One of the Six Nations, closely associated with the Mohawks and occupying lands between the latter and the Onondagas. The Oneidas sided with the colonies during the Revolutionary War.

Onondaga: The Onondaga nation provided the geographical as well as the administrative center of the Iroquois League (the Six Nations). The chiefs of the Onondaga nation were the "Fire Keepers," serving as the steering committee of the Onondaga Council. Their head chief, Otatarho, was the head chief of the League, and each nation sent delegates to the Great Council, which met at Onondaga.

Oriskany: Near Utica, N. Y., site of the battle fought, August 6, 1777, between the Americans under Gen. Herkimer and the British under Col. St. Leger and Col. Joseph Brant. Herkimer died of wounds received here.

Oswegatchie, Fort: On the St. Lawrence, at the mouth of the Oswegatchie River, present Ogdensburg, N. Y.

Ottawas ("Traders"): An Algonquian nation; for many years the middleman in the fur trade between the western tribes and the French. Closely related politically to the Chippewas and the Potawatamis, they were also allies of the Hurons or Wyandots, to whom they gave shelter after their dispersal by the Iroquois in 1649. Originally from Manitoulin Island and the shores of the Georgian Bay, they spread north, west, and south. In Heckewelder's day some of their towns were found among the Wyandots east of Detroit along the south shore of Lake Erie.

Ouiatenon: Chief village of the Weas, situated on the Wabash below the mouth of Wea Creek, a few miles south of Lafayette, Tippecanoe County, Indiana. General Scott destroyed this town in 1791.

OVERSLAW: The Castleton Bar (known by Hudson River pilots as the "Overslaugh"), a well-known bar below Albany, extending from Van Wies's Point opposite to Castleton about two miles up the Hudson River.

OWL CREEK: See KOKOSING RIVER.

P.

PACHGANTSCHIHILAS: Head war chief of the Delaware nation; a wise statesman, exercising a moderating influence. May 6, 1781, he advised the Moravians to withdraw from their villages on the Muskingum.

PAINTED POST: An Indian settlement at the junction of the Tioga and Cohocton Rivers in New York, and at the fork of important trails connecting the Susquehanna with the Allegheny and Niagara. Indian paintings here celebrated the exploits of war parties.

PAKANKE: A Munsee Delaware chief living at Kuskusky (near New Castle, Pa.). After the conversion to Christianity in 1770 of his chief counselor, Glickhican, he invited the Moravian Indians to take up residence among his people. In response they established Friedenstadt.

PAPUNHANK—d. 1775: A Munsee prophet and social reformer who settled at Wyalusing in 1758. He was visited there by the Moravian, Christian Frederick Post, in 1760, and baptized by Zeisberger, 1763. During Pontiac's War he conducted twenty-one Moravian Indians to Philadelphia for safety. In 1765 he invited the Moravians to settle their Indians at Wyalusing, and he helped to lay out Friedenshütten for them there. He accompanied Zeisberger, 1767, over the Forbidden Path to Goschgoschink. Later he became warden of the congregation at Schönbrunn.

PARRISH, JOHN—1729–1807: Philadelphia carpenter and builder, active member of Philadelphia Monthly Meeting; visited the Indians at Newcomers Town with Brigadier General John Lacey, 1773; accompanied Heckewelder to the Indian conference at Detroit, 1793.

PATH VALLEY: Originally known as the Tuscarora Path because it was used during the eighteenth century by parties of Tuscarora refugees from North Carolina coming north to put themselves under the Iroquois aegis.

PAULUS (WANSPACHECH)—d. (c.) 1758: A Wampanoag Indian; baptized, 1749, at Wechquadnach by Pezold.

PAULUS (SESAPIT)—d. 1782: Baptized, January 16, at Schönbrunn. In June 1780, he went to Pittsburgh with horses to bring out the missionary, Grube, who was to officiate at Heckewelder's marriage in July. In October of the same year Paulus went again to Pittsburgh to meet Shebosh (John Bull). He died in the massacre at Gnadenhütten.

PAWLING, HENRY: Purchased the Moravian lands at Wyalusing from Job Chillaway, former resident of the Moravian village of Friedenshütten who had remained behind when the congregation left in 1772 for

Glossary

western Pennsylvania and the Muskingum country. The site of Friedenshütten is still known as the Chillaway Farms.

PAXTON (PAXTANG): Now Harrisburg, Pa. Heckewelder informs us that the name Paxton is "corrupted from PEETSTANK, signifying *where the waters stand*." Paxton was an Indian settlement at an important ford of the Susquehanna River, where Harris's Ferry was later established. The name Paxton or Paxtang was applied to a wide area including the early Scotch-Irish settlement in the vicinity of John Elder's Paxtang Presbyterian Church.

PAXTON BOYS: A body of settlers from Paxton (now Harrisburg) who, in 1763 murdered a small remnant of the Conestoga Indians near Lancaster. They were prevented from doing the same to the Moravian Indians who had taken refuge in Philadelphia, by the armed intervention of the citizens.

PEMAHOLAND, JACOB—d. 1806: Baptized, 1799, at Zeisberger's newly established town of Goshen (near Schönbrunn) on the Tuscarawas. He later joined the Moravian mission on the White River.

PETERS, REV. CHRISTOPHER: Minister at the Moravian Church at Hebron, a mile east of Lebanon, Pa., 1792–1793.

PETERSEN, LAURENCE: Early tavernkeeper, of Danish extraction, on the Niagara Road some eight miles west of Avon, N. Y.

PETIT, DR.: One of the original property owners at Gallipolis, Ohio. Heckewelder dined with him, June 28, 1792.

PETTIT, CHARLES: Owner of a property at what is now Winona, Saltfleet Twp., Wentworth County, Ont.

PETTQUOTTING: A Moravian Indian town, sometimes called New Salem; founded, 1787, on the east side of the Pettquotting (Huron) River, near present Milan, Erie County, Ohio.

PEZOLD, REV. JOHANN GOTTLIEB—1720–1762: Moravian minister, a pursemaker by trade, ordained, 1748; spiritual adviser of the Single Brethren at Bethlehem, 1754–1762; built the Single Brethren's House at Lititz, 1759.

PIANKASHAW: An Algonquian tribe (closely related to the Wea), who at one time had a settlement at what is now Vincennes on the Wabash.

PICKERING, TIMOTHY—1745–1829: Revolutionary soldier and statesman. After the war, he was assigned many missions to the Indians, whom he endeavored to protect from outrage and exploitation. He was Commissioner from Pennsylvania to the Indian conference at Detroit, 1793; Secretary of War, 1795; U. S. Senator, 1803–1811; Congressman, 1813–1817.

PICKS KILL: Peekskill.

PILGERRUH: See CAYAHAGA. 3.

PINE SWAMP: A heavily-wooded forest in the Pocono Mountains of Monroe and Carbon Counties, Pa., so dark that it was sometimes called the "Shades of Death." William Scull in his map of 1770 calls it the Great Swamp.

PINERY, THE: Near Burford, Ont.

PIPE, CAPT. (HOPOCAN, "TOBACCO PIPE")—d. 1794: A Munsee chief, the designated successor to Pakanke. After 1763 he was called by his own people, Konieschquanoheel, "Maker of Daylight," but the whites continued to call him Capt. Pipe. During the American Revolution, his brother was killed and his mother wounded in the Squaw Campaign. Pipe led the pro-British party among his people. He removed the Moravian missionaries from the Muskingum, 1781, but defended them during their subsequent trial at Detroit.

PITT, FORT: Built, 1758, in place of Fort Duquesne at the Forks of the Ohio (Pittsburgh); came into possession of the Americans, 1777. These were the commanders during the Revolution: Gen. Edward Hand, 1777–1778; Gen. Lachlan McIntosh, 1778–1779; Col. Daniel Brodhead, 1779–1781; Gen. William Irvine, 1781–1783.

PLATT, COL. RICHARD—1754–1830: Revolutionary soldier; Quarter-Master General, 1780; Paymaster, U. S. Army, 1817–1820. In 1787 he was appointed Treasurer of the Ohio Company of Associates.

POGEPSIE: Poughkeepsie.

POINT ABINO ("EBONE"): On Lake Erie, eleven miles west of Fort Erie, Ont.

POINT A PLAIR: Point Pelee, on the north shore of Lake Erie, near Leamington, Ont.

POLLIPAS ISLAND: Polopels (Polliples) Island, a small, rocky island in the Hudson River, at the northern entrance to the Highlands; "remarkable only as the place where sailors require a treat of persons who have never before passed the river."—Jedidiah Morse, *The American Gazetteer* (1797).

POMOACAN—d. 1788: The Half King of the Wyandots at Sandusky. He protected Zeisberger's life, 1777. In 1781 he headed the expedition which removed the Moravians from the Muskingum.

PONTIAC—1720 (c.)–1769: Ottawa chief, a leader in what is now known as Pontiac's War, during which an Indian force composed of Ottawas, Senecas, Delawares, Chippewas, Shawnees, Wyandots, and others captured (1763) all British posts west of the Alleghenies except Detroit and Pittsburgh.

POPUNHANK: See PAPUNHANK.

POST, CHRISTIAN FREDERICK—1710–1785: Moravian missionary: to the Indians of New York and Connecticut, 1743–1749; among the Eskimo, 1752; at Wyoming, 1754–1755; to the Delawares on the Tuscarawas, 1761 and again in 1762 (with John Heckewelder). He attempted unsuccessfully to establish a mission on the Mosquito Coast of Honduras, 1764, 1767. Adventurous and fearless, he undertook for the Pennsylvania government in 1758 dangerous journeys carrying peace belts to the Ohio Indians.

POTAWATOMI: An Algonquian tribe south of Lake Michigan, closely related to the Chippewa and Ottawa.

PRESQUE ISLE: Now Erie, Pa. The French built a fort here in 1753; the British, in 1760. The latter was surrendered to the Wyandots, Ottawas, Chippewas, and Senecas, June 22, 1763.

PRIOR, CAPT.: Officer in charge of the detachment that accompanied Heckewelder and the Indians, 1792, from Vincennes overland by way of the Buffalo Trace to Louisville, Ky.

PUTIWATIMA: See POTAWATOMI.

PUTNAM, GEN. RUFUS—1738–1834: During the French and Indian War, saw service in the Lake Champlain region; brigadier general, 1783; one of the founders of the Ohio Company of Associates, 1787. He reached the site of Marietta, Ohio, on April 7, 1788, and began to lay out the town. In 1792 he made a treaty at Vincennes with the Indians on the lower Wabash. He was Surveyor General of the United States, 1796–1803.

PUTNAM, SETH: A settler living near the present Ingersoll, Ont. In 1798 his was the last house west of Niagara on the way to Fairfield.

Q.

QUINTE, BAY OF: West of Kingston, Ont., on the north shore of Lake Ontario. This region belonged at one time to the Huron Indians; after the American Revolution Mohawks under Deserontyou settled here.

R.

RAISIN RIVER: Enters the west end of Lake Erie at Monroe, Mich.

RANDOLPH, BEVERLEY: Member of the Virginia Assembly during the American Revolution; Governor of Virginia, 1788–1791; Commissioner from Virginia to the Indian conference at Detroit, 1793.

RAPIDS, THE: See MAUMEE RAPIDS.

RED BANKS: Now Henderson, Henderson County, Ky.

REED, ROBERT: A Robert Reed settled about 1797 on the Franklin Road in the vicinity of present Harrisonville, Mercer Twp., Venango County, Pa.

REED'S TAVERN: Situated on Nine Mile Run, Unity Twp., Westmoreland County, Pa.; the first house in the vicinity of present Youngstown. Heckewelder stopped here, 1789. Soldiers camped round it at the time of the Whiskey Rebellion, 1794.

REICHEL, REV. CARL GOTTHOLD—1751–1825: Minister at Nazareth, Pa., and principal of Nazareth Hall; later a bishop of the Moravian Church.

REIZENBACH, REV. PHILIP JACOB—1725–1802: Moravian minister at Heidelberg and later at Bethel, Pa., 1779; at Hebron, 1790; at Schöneck, 1791.

RENATUS (SCHONQUEH)—d. 1795: A Mahican, baptized by the Moravians, 1749, and named for Christian Renatus, son of Count Zinzendorf. At Nain in 1763 he was wrongly accused of murder. Imprisoned at Philadelphia, he was tried and acquitted. He left the Moravians for a time, but in 1783 he returned to them at New Gnadenhütten, north of Detroit.

RENCHEY'S TAVERN: See RUNCHEY, ROBERT.

RETRENCHE: See THAMES RIVER.

REYMER, FREDERICK: An innkeeper at Chambersburg, Pa., with whom Heckewelder breakfasted, September 14, 1788.

RIED: See REED.

RIVINGTON, JAMES—1724–1802: Printer and bookseller in New York City; publisher of *The Royal Gazette*, etc.

ROBBINS, OBEDIAH: A trader at Lower Sandusky, who in March, 1782, assisted the Moravian missionaries on their way to Detroit. He visited the Christian Indians at Captives Town and sent them food.

ROCKY ISLAND: In Lake Erie, near Scott Point, Ottawa County, Ohio.

ROCKY POINT: A promontory south of the Bass Islands, Lake Erie.

ROTHE, REV. JOHN—1726–1791: Moravian missionary at Friedenshütten, 1765–1769; at Sheshequin, 1769–1772. In 1772 he and Bishop Ettwein escorted some two hundred Indians from these two missions, by way of the Great Island and Kittanning, to Friedenstadt near the Kuskuskies on the Beaver. He moved to Gnadenhütten and Schönbrunn on the Muskingum in 1773.

ROUGH, SERGEANT: British non-commissioned officer at Detroit; accompanied Moravian missionaries with an escort of Rangers from Upper Sandusky to Detroit, 1782.

RUDOLPH, MAJOR MICHAEL: Captain in the Maryland Line during the Revolutionary War; Major of Cavalry, 1792; Adjutant and Inspector of the Army, 1793.

RUNCHEY, ROBERT: Owner of a tavern on what is now Highway 8, in Louth Twp., Welland County, Ont., about a mile east of Jordan.

RYAN'S: Probably "The Lyon," shown on Reading Howell's map of Pennsylvania (1792) in the vicinity of present Schellsburg.

Glossary

S.

St. Clair, Gen. Arthur—1734–1818: Revolutionary soldier; President of the Continental Congress, 1787; first Governor of the Northwest Territory, 1789; Commander-in-Chief of the forces invading the Miami country, 1791. On November 4, 1791, his army was defeated by Indian forces under command of Little Turtle.

St. Clair, Fort: Near what is now Eaton, Preble County, Ohio; erected during the winter of 1791–1792. This was the first fort to be erected above Fort Hamilton in the line of defense extending from Cincinnati to the mouth of the Maumee on Lake Erie.

St. John: A popular name for John Baptiste Rousseau, miller, tavernkeeper, and Indian interpreter of Ancaster, Wentworth County, Ont. His wife, Margaret Kleine, had been a ward of Joseph Brant after her family was killed, 1760, in the Mohawk Valley.

St. Mary's: Sault Ste. Marie.

St. Vincent, Post: See Vincennes.

Salem: Founded by Heckewelder, 1780, when Lichtenau was evacuated; situated on the Tuscarawas River six miles below Gnadenhütten and a mile and a half southwest of what is now Port Washington.

Salt Spring, Muskingum County, Ohio: At what is now Chandlersville, Salt Creek Twp. Visited by Heckewelder, 1773. "Such a quantity of water flows as to keep 1000 gallons constantly boiling."—Jedidiah Morse, *The American Gazetteer* (Boston, 1797), under "Muskingum."

Salt Spring, Trumbull County, Ohio: In Weatherfield Twp., half a mile south of the Mahoning River and about a mile southwest of what is now Niles, Ohio, on the Indian path between Cayahaga and Pittsburgh. Heckewelder visited it, October 13, 1786.

Samuel Moore—d. 1782: A Jersey Indian, grandson of Papunhank; baptized at Friedenshütten, 1771; interpreter and National Helper in the Muskingum mission; died in the massacre at Gnadenhütten.

Samuel Nanticoke—d. 1805: A Nanticoke Indian; baptized at Friedenshütten, 1766; became a National Helper. He accompanied Zeisberger to Onondaga, 1766; travelled with Heckewelder to Pittsburgh, 1773; was a delegate from Captives Town to the Shawnee towns, seeking relief, 1781; attended the treaty at Fort Harmar, 1788. Heckewelder found him in 1789 at Pettquotting.

Sandusky: See Upper Sandusky and Lower Sandusky.

Sandy Hill: Now Hudson Falls, Washington County, N. Y.

Sarepta: On the Volga River, Russia; destroyed, June 2, 1775.

Sargent, Major Winthrop—1753–1820: Surveyor of the Seven Ranges in Ohio, 1786; secretary of the Ohio Company of Associates, arriving at

Marietta in July, 1788; land contractor for both the Ohio Company and the Scioto Company (see Gallipolis); secretary of the Territory Northwest of the River Ohio, 1787; St. Clair's adjutant general; wounded in the engagement of November 4, 1791, at Fort Recovery; first Governor of Mississippi Territory, 1798.

SAVERY, WILLIAM—1750–1804: A tanner in Philadelphia and prominent Quaker preacher. His reports on the treaty at Canandaigua helped the movement to establish missions among the Seneca Indians. He left a journal of his trip to the Indian conference at Detroit. See *The Friends Library*, I, 325–429; and Francis R. Taylor, *Life of William Savery* (New York, 1925), 67–118.

SAX: This may have been George Sox (Sax, Socks), who by 1800 was known as proprietor of an inn at or near what is now Stoddartsville, Tobyhanna Twp., Monroe County, Pa.

SCHÄFFER'S TAVERN: Nicholas Schäffer had a tavern (thought to be the old Cross Keys Inn) beside the Schuylkill five miles north of Reading.

SCHÄFFER, JACOB: Of Lower Saucon Twp., near Bethlehem, Pa.

SCHAMUNG: See CHEMUNG.

SCHLÄGEL, REV. FREDERICK—d. 1805: Moravian minister at Warwick, Pa., 1754; at Bethlehem, Pa., 1755; at York, Pa., 1757. He later became a missionary in Jamaica.

SCHLOSSER, FORT: On the American side of the Niagara River, opposite Navy Island, at the head of the Upper Rapids and at the southern end of the Niagara Portage.

SCHMICK, REV. JOHN JACOB—1714–1778: A Moravian missionary who served at various stations. At Friedenshütten (Wyalusing) he began his philological work, "Miscellanea Linguae Nationis Indicae Mahikan dictae . . . ." (manuscript in the American Philosophical Society, Philadelphia). His wife, by her medicinal care, saved Heckewelder's life in 1769.

SCHMICK, JOHN JACOB, JR.: Son of the above; friend of Benjamin Mortimer. In 1798 he was living at Nazareth, Pa.

SCHÖNBRUNN ("BEAUTIFUL SPRING"): The first Christian town in Ohio, established by the Moravians, 1772, on the east bank of the Tuscarawas branch of the Muskingum, about two miles southeast of what is now New Philadelphia.

SCHÖNECK: An early Moravian village about a mile north of Nazareth, Pa.

SCHUYLER, GEN. JOHN PHILIP—1733–1804: Served in the French and Indian War; major general, 1775; member of the Continental Congress, 1779–1781, and of the U. S. Senate, 1789–1791, 1797–1798.

SCHUYLER, FORT (OLD FORT SCHUYLER): At what is now Utica, N. Y. During the Revolution, Fort Stanwix (Rome) was sometimes known as Fort Schuyler.

Glossary 437

SCHWEINITZ: See DE SCHWEINITZ.

SCOTT, GEN. CHARLES—1739 (*c.*)–1813: Revolutionary soldier; Governor of Kentucky; took part in Gen. Harmar's abortive attack on the Indians of the Scioto, 1790; destroyed the Wea villages on the Wabash, May and June, 1791, taking women and children prisoners; shared Gen. St. Clair's disastrous defeat at Fort Recovery, November 4, 1791.

SCOVELL, JAMES—d. 1810: His first tavern, licensed in 1798, was situated a few miles above Wilkes-Barre at what is now West Pittston.

SEMPLE'S: An inn at Mount Rock, Cumberland County, Pa., popular with wagoners before the railroad was opened in 1837. It was situated on the Mount Rock branch of the Pittsburgh Road, at the well-known Mount Rock Spring.

SENSEMAN, REV. GOTTLOB—1745–1800: Moravian missionary, son of Joachim Senseman. His mother was killed, 1755, by Indians at Gnadenhütten on the Mahoning. In 1768 he accompanied Zeisberger over the Forbidden Path to Goschgoschink on the Allegheny. For a time he was stationed at Schönbrunn. He died at Fairfield, Upper Canada.

SHÄFERS: See SCHÄFFER'S TAVERN.

SHAWANO TOWN: See WAKETAMEKI.

SHAWNEE: A warlike Algonquian people some bands of whom, during the first part of the eighteenth century, lived in scattered settlements in eastern Pennsylvania, and later were found on the Muskingum, Scioto, and Miami Rivers.

SHEBOSH: See BULL, JOHN JOSEPH.

SHEBOSH, JOSEPH—d. 1782: Son of John Joseph Bull and his Mahican wife; baptized at Christiansbrunn, 1758; died in the massacre at Gnadenhütten.

SHENANGO: An Indian town on the Shenango River at what is now West Middlesex, Mercer County, Pa.

SHERMAN ("SHEARMAN'S") VALLEY: Sherman Creek flows east through Perry County, Pa., to enter the Susquehanna at Duncannon. A branch of the Allegheny Path traversed the upper part of this valley.

SHESHEQUIN (SCHECHSCHQUANÜNK): A Munsee Delaware village on the Susquehanna (home of Queen Esther, about 1772) at what is now Ulster, Bradford County, Pa. In 1769 John Rothe established a mission here. It was abandoned in 1772 when the Moravian Indians moved to Friedenstadt on the Beaver.

SHINGAS—d. winter of 1763–1764: Delaware war chief, nephew of Olumapies (d. 1747). During the early months of the French and Indian War he devastated the Cove and other western settlements in Pennsylvania. June 11, 1752, he was named "King" (i.e., accredited spokesman) of the Delawares on the Ohio. He held that position until 1758 when, his hostility having made him *personna non grata* with the English, his brother, the Beaver, became King in his place.

SHOWALTERS: Jacob, John, Christian, and Peter Showalter, Mennonites, came to America on the ship *Brotherhood* in 1750 and settled in the vicinity of the present town of Northampton, near Bethlehem, Pa. Descendants moved into the Shenandoah Valley and into Western Pennsylvania. In 1800 Heckewelder met two of them at Franklin, prospecting for land.

SICKEUNCK (SIKEUNK): See SALT SPRING.

SILVER HEELS: A Shawnee Indian living at Waketameki.

SIMCOE, JOHN GRAVES—1752–1806: British soldier, statesman, administrator. During the Revolutionary War, he trained the Queen's Rangers. In 1791 he was appointed first Governor of Upper Canada.

SIMON: Probably the "Simon" who had been baptized March 8, 1789, at Pettquotting and whose wife was Jacobina (d. 1797).

SINCLAIR: See ST. CLAIR.

SIX NATIONS: The United Nations of the Iroquois: Mohawk, Oneida, Onondaga, Cayuga, Seneca, Tuscarora. Their home territory in Heckewelder's day lay between the Hudson and Niagara Rivers in northern New York, but they claimed ownership of lands far outside those bounds in Pennsylvania, the Ohio Valley, and elsewhere.

SKEENESBOROUGH: Now Whitehall, Washington County, N. Y.

SKINNER: The Reading Howell map of Pennsylvania (1792) shows "Skinner's" on Conodoguinet Creek in Horse Valley about four miles west of Strasburg (now Upper Strasburg).

SMITH, HON. JOHN: "The first pastor of the first Baptist Church in Ohio, organized at Columbia, near Cincinnati, in 1790. . . . Elected United States Senator during the administration of Jefferson."—*Baptist Encyclopaedia* (Philadelphia, 1881), p. 1068.

SMITH, THOMAS: British soldier during the Revolutionary War; later a surveyor and prominent merchant of Detroit.

SNAKE, JOHN and THOMAS: Two Shawnee war chiefs on the expedition that removed the Moravians from the Muskingum to Upper Sandusky.

SNAKE SPRING: On the Pittsburgh Road, about three and a half miles east of Bedford, Pa.

SOCK, WILL—d. 1763: An Indian of Conestoga, near Lancaster, Pa. It was rumored that he secretly gave assistance to Indians in the French interest. He was murdered by the "Paxton Boys," 1763.

SODUS, GREAT ("BIG SORES"): A bay on the south shore of Lake Ontario, about twenty-four miles southwest of Oswego.

SOLOMON: Son of the Delaware Indian, Nathanael Davis. Solomon left the Moravians after the massacre at Gnadenhütten. Heckewelder met him, October 27, 1788, at Marietta, Ohio.

Glossary

Sores, Big: See Sodus.

Sorrel River: Now the Richelieu River, which drains Lake Champlain into the St. Lawrence.

South Bend: A settlement established by John Cleves Symmes, 1789, several miles up the Ohio River from North Bend, Ohio, in the outskirts of present Cincinnati.

Spangenberg, Rev. Augustus Gottlieb—1704–1792: Moravian bishop; a great organizer and, next to Count Zinzendorf, the most influential member of the Renewed Moravian Church. On his fourth visit to Pennsylvania, he remained for eight years, 1754–1762.

Spangenberg, Rev. Cyriacus—d. 1795: Pastor of Trinity Reformed Church, Berlin, Somerset County, Pa., 1788–1794. Trinity was one of the earliest Reformed congregations west of the Alleghenies. In 1777 Reformed and Lutherans of Brothers Valley (in the vicinity of Berlin) joined in building a log church to serve both congregations.

Squaw Campaign: A body of Pennsylvania militia under Gen. Edward Hand went out, February, 1778, against Sandusky, where the British were reported to have a supply depot. Failing to reach their objective, the troops instead attacked and plundered peaceful Delaware camps at Sickeunk (the Salt Spring) and one of the Kuskuskies. They killed one man (Capt. Pipe's brother) and a number of women and children, and wounded Capt. Pipe's mother. Four years later, when Col. William Crawford, who had been on the Squaw Campaign, was captured at the Battle of Upper Sandusky, Capt. Pipe declined to save him from death by torture.

Standing Stone, Ohio: Former landmark in the Cuyahoga River, a short distance above Kent, Franklin Twp., Portage County, Ohio, where the Indian path to the Kuskuskies and Pittsburgh forded the river.

Stanwix, Fort: Built, 1758, by Gen. John Stanwix at what is now Rome, N. Y. It commanded the eastern end of the portage between the Mohawk River and Oneida Lake. At a treaty with the Six Nations here in 1768, the Indian boundary was established. In 1784 the United States signed another treaty here with the Six Nations.

Steg, Rev. John Michael: Lutheran pastor at Berlin, Somerset County, Pa., 1788–1792.

Stedman, Philip: A farmer living at the site of Fort Schlosser (Niagara Twp., Niagara County, N. Y.), which had formerly guarded the southern end of the Niagara Portage.

Steiner, Rev. Abraham: Moravian missionary. In 1789 he accompanied Heckewelder to Pettquotting on the Huron River in Ohio. After exploratory tours of the Cherokee country in 1799 and 1800, he established a mission at Spring Place, Murray County, Georgia, 1801.

Steitz, Major: See Stites.

Stephanus (Weskhattees): Five Indians named Stephanus appear in the early Moravian records. The one who accompanied Heckewelder from Cayahaga to Pittsburgh and who was bitten by a spider, October 13, 1786, was probably No. 740 in the Baptismal Register. This was Weskhattees, baptized, 1774, at Schönbrunn; later resident at New Gnadenhütten, Michigan; a National Assistant.

STEUBEN, DR.: A physician at Nazareth who lived at John Kremser's inn.

STEUBEN, FORT: 1. At Steubenville, Ohio; built 1786.
   2. At Jeffersonville, Ind., opposite Louisville, Ky.; at one time known as Fort Finney (Fenny).

STEVENS: Farmer at Wyalusing, son-in-law of Henry Pawling.

STITES, BENJAMIN: Fur trader from New Jersey; founded Columbia (now a part of Cincinnati), 1788, at the mouth of the Little Miami.

STONE'S STATION: On the Ohio, near Belpre, Washington County, Ohio.

STONY CREEK: Crossed by the Pittsburgh Road near present Kantner, Somerset County, Pa.

STORER, CHARLES: Justice of the Peace, 1792, at Passamaquoddy, Washington County, Maine. In 1793 he was secretary to the commissioners—Benjamin Lincoln, Beverley Randolph, Timothy Pickering—sent "to negotiate a peace with the Western Indians" at Detroit.

STRASBURG: See UPPER STRASBURG.

SUGAR CREEK: A tributary of the Tuscarawas River, Ohio; known as late as 1795 as a good place to hunt beaver and bear.

SUGARLOAF: A large sand hill, 120 feet high, northwest of Sugarloaf Point, which is at the west point of Gravelly Bay, outer harbor of Port Colbourne, Ont., about ten miles west of Point Abino.

SWIGATSCHI: See OSWEGATCHIE.

SYMMES, JOHN CLEVES—1742–1814: Member of the Continental Congress. Interested in western colonization, he made a journey down the Ohio, 1787, to what is now Louisville, Ky.; was appointed judge of the Northwest Territory, 1788; bought land (the "Miami Purchase") between the two Miamis; founded North Bend, Ohio, 1789.

SYMONS: See SYMMES.

T.

TANIWANDI CREEK: See TONAWANDA.

TANNER'S STATION: A military post on the Ohio River in Boone County, Ky., opposite the present Lawrenceburg, Ind.

TAWA: See OTTAWA.

TAWA RIVER: Now known as the Maumee River; formerly called the Tawa, Miami, or Miami of the Lake.

TEEDYUSCUNG—1700 (c.)–1763: A Delaware from New Jersey; baptized by the Moravians at Gnadenhütten on the Mahoning, 1750. In 1753

Glossary

he left the mission, and soon after took a prominent part against Pennsylvania in the French and Indian War. After the conclusion of peace, the Six Nations appointed him their spokesman ("king") and guardian of the Wyoming Valley. He was murdered at what is now Wilkes-Barre in 1763.

TENBROOK, HENRY: A prominent merchant of New York City during the late eighteenth century, and trustee of the First Moravian Church there. He gave two acres of land in the Bowery to the Moravians.

TETEPACHKSI (TEDPACHXIT, alias WEAPICAMIKUNK, alias GLAIZE KING)— d. 1806: Head chief of the Delawares in 1797; friend of Moravians. In 1802 he visited President Jefferson. Accused of witchcraft by Delawares on the White River during the nativist frenzy raised by Tecumseh and the Shawnee Prophet, he was in 1806 deposed from his chieftainship. The same year under torture he accused Joshua, the Moravian, of practising magic; when he recanted, he was burned alive.

THAMES RIVER, Ontario: Formerly known as La Tranche; flows through London and Chatham, Ont., to Lake St. Clair. On its northern bank, between what are now Thamesville and Bothwell, Zeisberger in 1792 established the Moravian town of Fairfield.

THIRUNDIGAT: See IRONDEQUOIT.

THOMAS—d. 1786: A Mahican Indian; baptized, 1769, at Friedenshütten. During the massacre at Gnadenhütten, March 8, 1782, he was knocked down and scalped, but he survived. In 1786 he was drowned in the Cuyahoga River.

THOMAS (GUTKIGAMEN)—d. 1792: A grandson of Netawatwees; baptized, 1774, at Schönbrunn; a National Helper and an important figure in negotiations with the outside world. Died at Fairfield, Upper Canada.

THREE RIVERS: A point in Clay Township, Onondaga County, N. Y., where the Seneca River and Oneida River unite to form the Oswego River.

TILL, REV. JACOB: Moravian minister at Warwick, Pa., 1758; at Gnadenthal, 1759; at "Bethel on Swatara," 1765–1783.

TIOGA ("WHERE IT FORKS"): The point of land between the Chemung (formerly the Tioga) River and the Susquehanna at their junction; now Athens, Pa. Once an important Indian town, a southern gateway to the Six Nations country. Gen. Sullivan brought his army this way in 1779.

TOBIAS (MELIMIAS)—d. 1782: Moravian Indian, baptized at Friedenstadt, 1773 (the last baptism at this place); appointed a member of the National Helpers Conference at Schönbrunn, 1776; saved Heckewelder's life from hostile warriors, May 3, 1781; died in the massacre at Gnadenhütten.

TOIONDO: Toronto, Canada.

TONAWANDA: A Seneca settlement and reservation on Tonawanda Creek, Niagara County, N. Y.

TRUEMAN, MAJOR ALEXANDER: Of the First United States Regiment; one of the three messengers (Trueman, Freeman, Hardin) who were taken prisoner by the Indians in 1792 and released in 1794 after the Battle of Fallen Timbers.

TRUM, SIMON: See DRUM.

TSCHESCHEQUANNINK: See SHESHEQUIN.

TUPPER, GEN. BENJAMIN—1738–1792: Revolutionary soldier from Massachusetts; a leader in the westward movement. One of the organizers of the Ohio Company of Associates, he accompanied the first settlers to Marietta, 1788; as a judge, he conducted the first court in Marietta, September, 1788.

TUSCARAWAS (TUSKERAWY): Delaware Indian town on the west bank of the Tuscarawas River (formerly known as the Muskingum) at the fording place near what is now Bolivar, Ohio. In 1762 it was the home of Shingas and his brother, King Beaver. Here in 1778 Gen. McIntosh built Fort Laurens.

TUSCARORA: The sixth nation of the Iroquois League. Driven out of North Carolina, they moved north in a series of migrations through Pennsylvania to the Six Nations country, where they were accepted "on the cradleboard," as members of the Confederacy. First the Oneidas and later the Senecas gave them domicile. They have a reservation today near Lewiston, N. Y.

TYGART'S ("TYGER") CREEK: A Kentucky stream, entering the Ohio at Sciotoville, Greenup County, opposite the mouth of the Scioto at what is now Portsmouth.

U.

UPPER SANDUSKY: In the general area that went by this name, four towns are to be distinguished:

1. The present Upper Sandusky, county seat of Wyandot County, Ohio.

2. Upper Sandusky, the Wyandot Half King's town during the Revolutionary War, three miles southeast of the present Upper Sandusky.

3. Upper Sandusky Old Town, the deserted Indian village which Zeisberger, Heckewelder, and the other Moravian prisoners reached October 1, 1781. This was at the junction (in Antrim Twp., Wyandot County) of Broken Sword Creek with the Sandusky River, halfway between modern upper Sandusky and Bucyrus.

4. Captives Town (as later historians have called it, the Moravians at the time having given it no special name), a mile up the river from Upper Sandusky Old Town.

UPPER STRASBURG: A town in Letterkenny Twp., Franklin County, Pa.; at the foot of the Blue Mountain, on a short cut—over three mountains to Burnt Cabins—used by travellers to Pittsburgh.

Glossary 443

V.

VANDERBURG, HENRY: Merchant and Judge of Probate at Vincennes, 1792. He travelled with Heckewelder from Louisville to Vincennes.

VAN VLECK, ISAAC: Early resident of Three Rivers, Onondaga County, N. Y. His son, Abraham, is said to have been the first male white child born in Onondaga County.

VENANGO: An Indian town at what is now Franklin, Pa., at the junction of French Creek with the Allegheny River. Here the French built Fort Machault, 1755; the English, Fort Venango, 1760. The latter was captured and burned by Indians during Pontiac's War, June, 1763.

VINCENNES (ST. VINCENT), Indiana: On the Wabash, in the country of the Wea Indians. Here the French established a mission, 1702, and built a fort, c. 1730. In 1763 it was occupied by the British. George Rogers Clark captured it for the Americans, 1779. After the defeat by Little Turtle of Gen. Harmar in 1790 and of Gen. St. Clair in 1791, Gen. Putnam, accompanied by Heckewelder, met the Indians here in a peace conference, 1792.

W.

WADSWORTH, JAMES: Land promoter who developed the Genesee region in New York State; built a handsome residence at the Indian town of Big Tree (Geneseo).

WAKETAMEKI: A Shawnee town on the Muskingum near Dresden, just below the mouth of Waketameki Creek, Jefferson Twp., Muskingum County, Ohio. It was destroyed, 1774, during Lord Dunmore's War. A later Shawnee town on the Mad River below Zanesfield, Ohio, was given the same name.

WALDHAUER'S (WALTHOUR'S): Walthour's Fort, twelve miles east of Pittsburgh, a refuge for local settlers during the Revolutionary War, was for some time a stopping place on the Harrisburg-Pittsburgh Road.

WALHONDING ("WALHONDI") RIVER: Joins the Tuscarawas at Coshocton, Ohio, to form the Muskingum River.

WALLACE, WILLIAM: Of West Virginia. Indians from Sandusky, early in 1782, killed his wife and five children. This was one of the causes of Col. David Williamson's expedition, which resulted in the massacre, March 8, 1782, of ninety Moravian Indians at Gnadenhütten.

WANGOMEN: A Munsee prophet, said to be a brother of Glickhican. He preached that there were two ways to God, the Indian's and the white man's. He came to Goschgoschink in 1768 to counteract Zeisberger's work.

WASHINGTON, Pa.: See CATFISH.

WASHINGTON, FORT: On the north bank of the Ohio, opposite the mouth of

Licking Creek, at what is now Cincinnati. At this point the Indians had a much-used crossing of the river.

WAWIACHTENO: See WEA.

WAWIAPIESCHENWA: See BLUE JACKET.

WAYOMICK: See WYOMING.

WEA (WAWIACHTENO): An Indian nation within the Miami confederacy, with headquarters at Ouiatenon on the Upper Wabash. Gen. Scott destroyed their villages in 1791.

WEBER, REV. JOHN WILLIAM: Pastor of the Evangelical Reformed Church; served a union congregation of Reformed and Lutherans at Pittsburgh, 1782–1794. First services were held "in a small blockhouse at the corner of present Wood and Diamond Streets." In 1791–1792 a log church was built at Sixth and Smithfield, forerunner of the present Evangelical Protestant Church in the same block. See Mulkearn and Pugh, *Traveler's Guide to Historic Western Pennsylvania* (Pittsburgh, 1954).

WECHQUETANK: A Moravian Indian town on Pohopoco Creek, Polk Twp., Monroe County, near present Gilbert, Pa. Established, 1760, by Gottlob Senseman and Indians from Gnadenhütten on the Mahoning; abandoned, October 11, 1763.

WEISER, CONRAD—1696–1760: German by birth, naturalized British citizen, Mohawk by adoption; for many years Pennsylvania's ambassador to the Six Nations. In 1742 he was with Count Zinzendorf in the Wyoming Valley.

WELHIK-TUPPEEK: See SCHÖNBRUNN.

WELLBANK, CAPT.: Trader, Indian agent. Having lived among the Creeks and Cherokees, he conducted deputations from these tribes to the Indian conference at Maumee Rapids, 1793.

WELLING: See EVERLASTING GOSPEL.

WELLS, WILLIAM: An Indian interpreter who in boyhood had been captured by the Eel River Weas; travelled with Heckewelder, 1792, from Louisville to Vincennes.

WELOCHALENT: See ANTON (WELOCHALENT).

WEQUETANK: See WECHQUETANK.

WEYGAND (WYGAND), JOHN: A Moravian messenger who made several journeys from Bethlehem to the Ohio; in 1781, after the removal of the missionaries from the Muskingum; in 1782, to take letters for them to Detroit; in 1787, with Heckewelder to Pittsburgh and back.

WHITE EYES (KOQUETHAGACHTON)—d. 1778: Head chief of the Delawares (succeeding Netawatwees), 1776–1778. Originally from eastern Pennsylvania, he settled for some years at the mouth of the Beaver River, where Post and Heckewelder visited him in 1762. He moved to

Glossary 445

>Gekelemukpechink in 1770. A strong supporter of Moravian work among his people, and a friend of the Americans. He became a colonel in the U. S. Army shortly before his death.

White Eyes' Town: On the Tuscarawas, Oxford Twp., Coshocton County, Ohio, six miles west of Gekelemukpechink (Newcomer's Town). Site of Col. Brodhead's camp, April, 1781.

White Woman's Creek: The Walhonding River.

Wialusing: See Wyalusing.

Wilbank: See Wellbank.

Wilhelm: See Chilloway.

Wiling: Wheeling, W. Va.

Wilkes-Barre: Site of the Indian town of Wyoming, headquarters of Teedyuscung in his attempt, as an accredited agent of the Six Nations, to save this part of the country for the people of his race; subsequently the center of the struggle between Pennsylvania and Connecticut for possession of the Wyoming Valley.

Wilkinson, Gen. James—1757–1825: Soldier, trader, politician. During his spectacular career he was implicated in the Conway Cabal, the Spanish Conspiracy, and Aaron Burr's scheme for a southwestern empire. In 1791 he led a force of volunteers against the Indians beyond the Ohio. He became Governor of Louisiana, 1805.

William Henry (Gelelemend): See Gelelemend.

Williams, Isaac: An Indian from Sandusky; Heckewelder's guide from Pittsburgh to Pettquotting on the Huron River, 1789.

Williams, Nathan—d. 1798: Of Detroit; carpenter, merchant, and (after 1796) Judge of the Court of Common Pleas.

Williamsburg, N. Y.: Former town on Canaseraga Creek, near present Mount Morris, Livingston County, N. Y.

Williamson, Capt. Charles—1757–1808: Appointed agent, 1791, of the Pulteney Association in America. His ten years in that position, opening up land to settlers and laying out turnpikes, did much to develop western New York State.

Williamson, Col. David: A colonel of volunteer militia from Washington County, Pa., in command at the Gnadenhütten massacre, March 8, 1782; second in command to Col. William Crawford in the defeat at Upper Sandusky a few months later; elected sheriff of Washington County; failed in business and died in poverty.

Wills Mountain: The name now given to the mountain broached by the Juniata west of Everett is not Wills (as in Heckewelder's journal) but Tussey.

Wilson, James—d. 1792: The earliest innkeeper at what is now Washington (formerly Catfish), Pa. He received license, October, 1781, "for keeping a Public house of entertainment at Catfish Camp." Heckewelder stayed at his log tavern, December 9, 1788.

WIOMING: See WYOMING.

WINGENUND—d. (c.) 1791: A Delaware war captain from Kinhaschican on the Scioto; met Heckewelder at Tuscarawas, 1762; was at Goschochking, 1776; accompanied the expeditionary force that removed the Moravians from the Muskingum, 1781.

WYALUSING: Indian settlement on the North Branch of the Susquehanna at the mouth of Wyalusing Creek, Bradford County, Pa.; home of Papunhank, Munsee religious reformer. Nearby, on invitation from Papunhank, the Moravians established the mission village of Friedenshütten, 1765. They evacuated it, 1772, and moved to Friedenstadt on the Beaver River.

WYANDOT (HURON): An Iroquoian people, formerly inhabiting lands south of the Georgian Bay. Defeated by the Five Nations (the Iroquois Confederacy) in 1649, they abandoned their homelands. After a long migration, they were found in Heckewelder's day settled around Detroit and Sandusky. At a council held at the mouth of the Scioto, 1750–1751, Ohio lands were allotted to the Wyandots by the Six Nations. When, on invitation from the Delawares, the Moravians settled in the Muskingum Valley, they sent wampum to the Wyandot chiefs, "the acknowledged owners of the Muskingum lands," for confirmation of the Delaware grant.

WYGAND: See WEYGAND.

WYOMING: A rich and beautiful valley on the North Branch of the Susquehanna, of which the center was the Indian town of Wyoming (now Wilkes-Barre). Here Teedyuscung was murdered in 1763. In revenge, his son Captain Bull emptied the valley of its white inhabitants.

WYOMING HILLS: Now known as Wilkes-Barre Mountain, overlooking the former Indian town of Wyoming and the Wyoming Valley from the southeast.

Y.

YORK, Ont.: Founded, 1793, on the site of the French Fort Toronto. In 1797 it became the capital of Upper Canada. The name was later changed to Toronto.

YORKTOWN: York, Pa.

YOUNG (JUNG), REV. MICHAEL—1743–1826: Moravian missionary. Sent to the Muskingum, 1780, he remained for some years thereafter with the Indian mission in its wanderings. Heckewelder met him at Pettquotting, 1789.

YOUNGMAN (JUNGMAN), REV. JOHN GEORGE—1720–1808: Entered Moravian missionary service, 1770, as assistant to Zeisberger at Friedenstadt on the Beaver; went to Schönbrunn, 1772; taken captive and brought to Upper Sandusky, 1781.

Glossary

Z.

ZACHARY—d. 1763: An Indian, formerly of the Moravian community at Wechquetank. He was murdered, along with other members of his family, by soldiers under Capt. Jacob Wetterholt at the Lehigh Water Gap.

ZANE, EBENEZER—1747 (*c.*)–1812: With his brothers, Silas and Jonathan, he founded Wheeling, W. Va., 1770, and became the town's leading citizen. Receiving permission from Congress to blaze a trail from Wheeling to Limestone (Maysville), Ky., he opened a road—Zane's Trace—by way of Zanesville and Chillicothe.

ZEENEY (ZEENER): See ZANE.

ZEISBERGER, REV. DAVID—1721–1808: Born at Zauchtenthal, Moravia; came to America, 1737. For sixty-five years (1743–1808) he headed the Moravian mission work among the Indians. He spoke Onondaga, Delaware, Mahican, Ojibway. Author of *A Delaware and English Spelling Book*, etc., etc.

ZEISBERGER, REV. DAVID, JR.: A cousin of David Zeisberger, the missionary.

ZINZENDORF, NIKOLAUS LUDWIG, COUNT VON—1700–1760: Founder and patron of the Renewed Moravian Church. In 1722 he received refugees from Moravia, members of the ancient Unitas Fratrum. On his estate of Berthelsdorf, they built the town of Herrnhut, which became the headquarters of the church and its world-wide missions. Zinzendorf was consecrated a bishop of the Moravian Church without losing his status as a Lutheran clergyman, his aim being not to create a new church but to develop a "heart religion" in the churches already established.

Index

Names in the Foreword and Introduction are not included in this index.
Italicized numbers refer to pages in the Glossary.

Abel (Moravian Indian), 195, *395*
Abercrombie, Gen. James, 329, *395*
Abnaki Indians, 333
Abraham (Mahican), 194, 198, *395*
────── Kuhn. *See* Kuhn, Abraham.
Adam (Wulalowechan), 192, *395*
Adams, ──────, 375, *395*
Adamstown, Pa., 234
Akansawas. *See* Quapaw Indians.
Akron, Ohio, 253, 402
Albany, N. Y., 70, 295, 298, 320, 329 f., 345, 351, 371, 388 f.; description of (1793), 297
Alden, Major Rogers, 376 f., *395*
Alexander, Major, 236, 256, 260, 293
Algonkin Indians, 332
Allan, Ebenezer, 363, 366 f., *395*
Allegheny Mt. (New York), description of, 347 f.
────── Mt. (Pennsylvania), 39, 216, 221, 239, 241, 256; description of the ascent, 240
────── Mts., 64, 391
────── River, 40, 95, 98, 197, 222, 244, 255 f., 260, 387; at Pittsburgh, 243; at Franklin, Pa., 382
Allen, Fort, 83, 89, *396*
Allentown, Pa., 369, 407
Allison, Dr. Richard, 270, *396*
Alte Herrnhuter Familien, 164 n.

Amboy, N. J., 79
Ambridge, Pa., 223, 422
Amelistes. *See* Malecite Indians.
American Philosophical Society, 385; *Transactions,* 396
American Pioneer, 118 f.
Amherst, Lord Jeffrey, 63
Amsterdam, N. Y., 299 n.
Ancaster, Ont., 360, 435
Ancrum, Major William, 206, *396*
Anderson, ──────, 233
──────, Charles, 359 f., *396*
Anderson's, 239
Andreas, 253 f., *396*
Angerman, Rev. John, 386, *396*; careless with a candle in the gunpowder shed, 90
Anjoues. *See* Iowa Indians.
Anna (Joshua's daughter), 418
────── Benigna (wife of Glickhikan), 198, *396*
Annville, Pa. *See* Millerstown.
Anthony's Nose, 299 n.
Anthony. *See* Anton (Welochalent).
Anton (John Martin's son), 194 and n., *396*
──────, Marcus, 199, *396*
────── (Welochalent), 106, 135 f., *394*, *396*, 417; the murder of his family, 198 f.; how this affected him, 245

449

Apple Tree Harbour, 303
Arbo, Rev. John, 102 f., *396*
Archives of the Moravian Church, 259 n.
Armstrong, ———, 279
———, Col. John, 57
Arundle, ———, 162 f., 201 f., *396*
Ash, Sylvester, 315, *396*
Askin, John, 206, 309, 312, *397*
Assiniboin Indians, 332
Asylum (Azilum, Frenchtown), *397*, *421*; description of (1798), 344
Athens, Pa. See Tioga.
Auglaize River, 294, 405
Avoca, N. Y., 424
Avon, N. Y., 349 f., 404, 431

Baasman. See Bausman.
Bâby, Jacques Duperon, 134, 185 and n., 186 and n., 187, *397*
Bagge, Rev. Nicholas Lawrence, *397*
Baker's Fort, 223, *397*
Bald Eagle, Chief, *397*
——— ———, Pa., 381, *397*
——— ——— Creek, 249
Baltimore, Md., 343; peltries sent to, from Pittsburgh, 243
Barbus. See White Indians.
Barnard, ———, 301
Baron, Widow, 215
Bass Islands, Lake Erie, 309, 320, 416, 434
Bath, N. Y., 370, 425; history of, 346 f.
Bathsaba, 418
Bausman, Jacob, 214, 222, *397*
Bausman, Joseph H., *History of Beaver County, Pa.*, 58, 151
Bawby. See Bâby.
Beard, ———, 269
Beaver (Tamaqua), King, 64, 67, 88, 98, *397*; his grave at Gnadenhütten, Ohio, 338 and n.
———, Pa., 162, n., 223, 384, 390, *397*; remains of French fort at, 105
——— Falls, Pa., 408. See also Falls of the Beaver.
——— River, 41, 67, 87, 94 ff., 105 f., 134, 136, 147, 214, 223, 245, 254 f., 375, 387
Beaver, the, *397*
Bedford, Eng., 34
———, Ohio, 402
———, Pa., 39, 221, 238, 335, 438; description of (1789), 256
Belcher, Friedrich, 279

Bellepreé. See Belpre.
Belleville, W. Va., 265
Belpre, Ohio, 262, 290, 397, 442; description of (1792), 265
Bender, George Philip, 352, 354, 368, *398*
Beninger, Rev. Abraham, 322, *398*
———, John, 322, *398*
Benjamin (son of Nathanael Davis), 222
——— (Cuwes), *398*; funeral of, 251
Bennington, Fort. See Brewerton, Fort.
Berlin, Pa., 239 f., 439; description of (1789), 237
Bethabara, N. C., *397*
Bethel, Pa., 271, *398*
Bethlehem, Pa., 34, 36 f., 50, 63, 67, 70 f., 73 ff., 83, 85, 96, 111, 145 f., 217 ff., 230 f., 244, 256, 266, 270, 293, 297, 331, 340 f., 367 f., 380, 382 ff.; family economy at, 88 f.; mileages, Bethlehem to Fairfield, 371 ff.
Bethlehem Diary, 89, 173
Big Bone Lick, Ky., 135, *398*
——— ——— ——— Creek, 287
Big Bottom, Ohio, 259, *398*
Big Cat (Machingwe Pushis), 152, *424*
Big Cove, Pa., 58, *398*
Big Mahony, 254
Big Sandy River, 267, 289
Big Tree, Chief, 306, *398*
——— ——— (Geneseo), N. Y., 349, *398*
Bininger. See Beninger.
Bird, Capt. See Burd.
Birkby, Rev. James, 232, 296, 331, *398*
Biven, Joseph, 348, *398*
Black Lion Inn, on the Pittsburgh Road, 239
Black Rock, 389
Blackwater Creek, 247, 253
Blanks. See White Indians.
Blennerhasset's Island, 265, *398*
Blickensderfer, Matthew, 220, 388
Bloody Run, Pa., 238, *398*
Blue Jacket (Wawiapieschenwa), 313, *398*
Blue Mt., 37, 83, 217, 234, 236 f., 256, 260, 346
Boas (a Munsee), 106, *399*
Bohanan. See Buchanan.
Bohemian Brethren. See Moravian Church.
Böhler, Rev. Peter, 75, *399*
Bolivar, Ohio, 37, 41
Bombary, Capt. See Bunbury.
Bömpers, Abraham, 233, *399*

Index

Bonnet, John, 216, 221, 260, *399;* description of the country round his inn, near Bedford, Pa., 239
———, John, Jr., 215 f.
Boone, Daniel, arrives from Kentucky with a cargo of ginseng, 227
Boston, Mass., 388
Bouquet, Col. Henry, 37, 43, 152, *399,* 401
Bousman. *See* Bausman.
Boyd, ———, a printer, 222
Braddock, Gen. Edward, 57 f.
———, Pa., 399
Braddock's Bay, 303
——— Field, 37, 40, *399*
Brant, Capt. Isaac, 228, *399;* death of, 361 f.
———, Col. Joseph, 250, 298, 313, 315 f., 319, *399;* is reported to be for war (1788), 227; his letter to Gen. Harmar, 230; character and appearance, 361 ff.
Brant's Town, 361 f., 365, 367, 389, *399*
Brantford, Ont., 399
Breakneck Hill, 345, 374, *399*
Brethren's Garden, 293, *399*
Brewerton, Fort, 302, *400*
Brickerville, Pa., 428
Broad Mt., 83, 341
Brodhead, Col. Daniel, 133 f., 152, 165 f., 177, 193, *400*
Brokaw, 108 ff.
Broken Sword Creek, 442
Brotherton, 313, *400*
Brown, ———, of Wyalusing, 344
———, Col., 223
———, Dr., 230
Brownstown, 370, 389, *400*
Brunswick, N. J., 295, 386
Buchanan, ———, at Carlisle, Pa., 218
Buckongejelas. *See* Pachgantschihilas.
Buckstown, Pa., 407
Buffalo, N. Y., 351 f., 389
———, W. Va., *400. See also* Charleston.
——— Creek, W. Va., 223 f., 231, 261, 292, 311, 314, 352, *400,* 403
——— Salt Lick, 284, *400*
——— Trace, 284
Bühler's, 231
Bull, John Joseph, *400. See also* Shebosh.
———, Fort, 301, *400.*
Bunbury, Capt., 315, 322, *400*
Büninger. *See* Beninger.
Burd, Capt., 216, *400*

Burford, Samuel, 401
———, Ont., 363, 409, 431
Burgoyne, Gen. John, 149, 297, 329
Burlington, N. J., 295, 391
——— Heights, Ont., 389, *400*
Burning Spring (Kanawha Valley), 265 and n.
Burnt Cabins, 37, 216, *400,* 417
Bush, Jacob, 373, *400*
Bushy Run, 37, 40, 221, 256, 399, *401*
Butler, Miss, 383
———, Col. John, 298, 301, 313, *401*
———, Gen. Richard, 222, 226, 230, 233, 236, 260, *401;* visited by Heckewelder at Carlisle (1786), 217 f.
Buttermere, Essex, England, 34
Buttermilk Falls, Pa., 343

Cachnawaga. *See* Caughnawaga Indians.
Cahokia, 283
Caldwell, Capt. William, 319, *401*
Caldwell, the, 322
Caledonia, N. Y., 350
Calhoun, Thomas, 41, 59, 62, 64 ff., *401*
Cammerhof, Rev. John Christoph Frederic, 343
Campbell, John, 278, *401*
Campfield. *See* Canfield.
Campus Martius (Marietta), 225 ff., 228, 230, 263, 270, 290, *401;* description of (1792), 262
Canada, 250, 281, 298 f.; national characteristics, 353 f.; land settlement policy, 359
——— Creek, N. Y., 301
Canagotshik. *See* Conococheague.
Canajoharie, N. Y., 299, 409
Canandaigua, N. Y., 345, 347
Canestoga. *See* Conestoga.
Canfield, Samuel, 364, *401*
Canhawa River. *See* Kanawha River.
Caniseraga, 348, *402*
Canonsburg, Pa., 293, *402*
Canses. *See* Kansas Indians.
Canton, Ohio, 384, 390
Canty, Bay of. *See* Quinte.
Caouitas. *See* Kawita Indians.
Captives Town, 199, 393, 442. *See also* Upper Sandusky.
Carleton Island, 323
Carlisle, Pa., 38, 215, 243, 256, 260, 293, 295, 314, 388; visited by Heckewelder, 217; description of (1789), 235

Carver, Jonathan, 47 f., *402*
Cascaski, Cascaskung. *See* Kuskusky.
Cassawaga. *See* Cussewago and Meadville.
Cataraqui, 320, *402*. *See also* Kingston, Ont.
Catawba Indians, 331
Catfish, Pa., 220, 231, *402*. *See also* Washington, Pa.
Caughnawaga, 299 and n., *402*
Caughnawaga Indians, 302, 320, 323, 325, 333, *402*
Cayahaga, 206 f., 213, 253, *402*; *see also* Pilgerruh.
——— River, 67, 209 f., 253, 255, 388
Cayuga Indians, 87, 118; claim the Susquehanna lands, 85; attend treaty at Detroit, 311
Cayuga Lake, 86, 302
Cedar Rapids, 325
Chala Indians, 333
Chambers Ferry, 235, *403*, *409*
Chambersburg, Pa., 221, *403*, *434*
Chambly, Que., 328
Champlain, Lake, 320, 389; Heckewelder's journey on, 328
Chandlersville, Ohio, 123, 435
Chapin, Gen. Israel, 314, *403*
Charlestown, W. Va., 292, *403*. *See also* Wellsburg, W. Va.
———, Ky., 288, *403*
Chatham, Ont., 406
Chelloway. *See* Chilloway.
Chelsea, England, 34
Chemung (Tioga) River, 345 f., 370, *403*
Chenos, rainmaker, 128 f.
Cherokee Indians, 68, 214, 314, 331; condole for the death of Capt. White Eyes, 153 ff.
Chester, Widow, 328
Chestnut Ridge, 40, 241
Chibbaways. *See* Chippewa Indians.
Chickasaw Indians, 331
Chillicothe, Ohio, 390, *404*
Chilloway, Bill, 249 f., *403*
———, Job, 430
Chinesee. *See* Genesee.
Chippewa, Ont., 305 f.
——— Creek, 354, 371
——— Indians, 68, 168, 172, 220, 307, 318 f., 321, 332, 336, 354, 365; impatient for the Moravians to leave their country, 205 f.; invoke the manitos of the wind and the water, 209; escape from prison, 226; a band living south of Lake Erie, 250 ff.; tradition that the Falls of Niagara are where they always were, 357
Chippewa, the, 312 f.
Choctaw Indians, 331
"Choirs" (Moravian), 23 f., 38
Christian (a Delaware), 193, *403*
Christiana (a Mahican), 400, 417
Christiansbrunn, Pa., 35, 241, 301, 337, 391, *403*
Christineaux. *See* Cree Indians.
Cincinnati, Ohio, 286 f., *403*, *444*; description of (1792), 267 ff.; funerals of Wawiachteno chiefs at, 272, 288
Clark, Rev. Daniel, 268, 273, *403*
Clarke, Gen. George Rogers, 277, 281, *404*
Clarksville, Ind., 277, *404*
Cleveland, Ohio, 207, *402*
Clewell, Christian, 335
Clinch River, 270
Clinton, Fort, 296
——— River, 411, 416
Clymer, George, 142
Cohocton River, 370
Cohoes, N. Y., 329
Colerain, Ohio, 407
Colhoun, ———, of Northumberland, 347
Collins, Capt., 274, 276
Columbia, Ohio, 272 ff., 288, *404*, *440*; description of (1792), 267
——— River, 270
Colver, Charles, 288
Comanche Indians, 332
Conawaybrunas. *See* Caughnawaga Indians.
Conestoga, Pa., 76 ff., 132, 165, 225, *404*
Conewago (Avon), N. Y., 349, *404*
United States Congress, sends commissioners to explain the Revolutionary War to the western Indians, 130; offers protection to the Delawares, 131; considers the admission to the Union of an Indian state, 151; grants lands on the Muskingum to the Moravians, 206; grants lands to the Ohio Company of Associates, 220 ff.; gift to the Indians, 233
Conhawa. *See* Kanawha.
Conneaut Creek, 334, 374, 376
——— Lake, 376
Connelly, ———, 242, 255
Connolly, Col., from Canada, 329
Connoquenessing Creek, 255, 374 f., *409*. *See also* Ganaquenising.

Index

Conococheague Creek, 58, 237, *404*
Conodoguinet Creek, 237, 438
Conrad Weiser, Friend of Colonist and Mohawk (Wallace), 73, n., 342, n.
Conway, Pa., 245, *405*
Coochocking. *See* Goschochking.
Cook, Capt. James, 312
———, John, 213, 228 f.
———, Julius, 31
Coon, Abraham. *See* Kuhn.
Cooper, James Fenimore, 385
Cooperstown, N. Y., 299
Coquehagechton. *See* White Eyes.
Cornelia (Moravian Indian), 395
Cornplanter, Chief, 260, 306, 398, *404;* at Fort Harmar (1788), 227
Cornwall, Ont., 323
Coshocton, Ohio, 129, 156, 182, 390, 421. *See also* Goschochking.
Covell, Dr. Matthew, 342, *404*
Crantz, David, *History of Greenland,* 239, *412*
Crawford, Col. William, 175, *404,* 439; captured at Upper Sandusky, 199
Cree Indians, 332
Creek Indians, 314, 332
Cresap, Col. Michael, 119, 225
Crever, Jacob, 217, *404*
Crossing, the. *See* Juniata Crossing.
Crow (a Mingo), *405*
———, Chief (Cherokee), 153
Crown Point, N. Y., 329
Crowstown, 247, *405*
Cuhn, Abraham. *See* Kuhn.
Cuscuskee, Cushcushke. *See* Kuskusky.
Cussewago. *See* Meadville.
Cuyahoga. *See* Cayahaga.

Daniel (Tschitquieschen), 338, *405*
Dansville, N. Y., 348
Dartmouth College, Joseph Brant attends, 362
Davenport, Josiah, 40, *405,* 418
David. *See* Zeisberger, David.
———, Capt. *See* Hill, Capt. David.
——— (Mamsochalet), 83 f., *405*
———, Christian, helps Moravian members of the *Unitas Fratrum* to escape to Herrnhut, 19 ff., 26, 29, 34
Davis. *See* Nathanael Davis.
Day, ———, at Red Banks, Ky., 279
Dean, ———, interpreter for Oneidas at Detroit, 315

Deep River, 250
Defiance, Fort, 294, *405*
Delaware Indians (Lenni Lenape), 27, 30, 45 f., 55 ff., 70, 315, 317 f., 332, 375, 394, 397, *405,* 410; at Tuscarawas, 37 ff.; in the West, 64; during Pontiac's War, 67 f.; refugee Indians well treated by the soldiers, 81; the Delaware prophet, Wangomen, 94; the great Delaware Council at Gekelemukpechink decides to accept Christianity, 95 ff.; position of Moravian Indians in the Delaware nation, 102; policy of neutrality during the early months of the Revolutionary War, 131; wampum records, 132; war parties (1780), 134 f.; dissuaded by Heckewelder from declaring war on the Americans, 145 ff.; save Zeisberger from death, 158 ff.; not properly represented at Fort Harmar (1789), 220, 228; advise the Mingos to mend their ways, 246; writing on a peeled tree at Pettquotting, 248; migration of part of the nation to the Wabash, 336. *See also* Munsee Indians.
———   ———, *forms of address* among, 96 ff., 136, 154
———   ———, *status* of, as "Women," 86 f., 131
———   ———, *three tribes of*, Turtle, Turkey, Wolf, 51, 94, 152, 198
——— River, 27, 128, 299, *405*
Demler, ———, 266
Dencke, Rev. Christian Frederick, 373, 389, *405*
Denison, ———, 66
Denning's Creek. *See* Dunning Creek.
De Peyster, Major Arent Schuyler, 196, 201 ff., *405;* conducts trial of Moravian missionaries at Detroit, 175; releases Moravian prisoners, 187; leaves Detroit for Niagara, 205
De Schweinitz, Edmund, *Life and Times of David Zeisberger,* 136
———, John Christian, 232, *406*
Deseronto, Ont., *406*
Deserontyou, Capt. Johnny, a Mohawk, 309, 322, *406*
De Shae Creek, 382
Detroit, 42 f., 66, 68, 110, 120 f., 158, 162, n., 163, 170, 173, 183, 195 f., 202 ff., 241 f., 250, 253, 258, 294, 297, 303 ff., 311, 319, 332, 358, 365 f., 370 ff., 380,

454   *Index*

387 ff., 393, 405; Heckewelder arrives at (1781), 184; trial of Moravian missionaries, 185 ff.; agriculture in this vicinity, 314 f.; Indian conference at (1793), 316 ff.
Detroit, the, 313
Detroit River, 208, 309, 400
Devil's Point, 325
Dexter's, 361
Dickinson College, *406*, *428*; description of (1789), 236
Diefenbach's, 238
Dingman's Creek, 366
Dodge, Lieut., 73 and n., 74
Dolson, Daniel, 310, *406*
———, John, 346
———, Matthew, 309 f., *406*
Donaw, Count, 216
Donegal, Pa., 235, *406*
Doughty, Major John, 222, 224, *406*
Douglas, Wheeler, 363, *406*
Doyle, Capt., 276, 280, 285 f.
Drake, Capt., 312, *406*
Dresden, Ohio, 111, 443
Drum, Simon, 406
Dublin, Ireland, 378
Duer, William, 289 f., *406*
Dui, ———, 217
Duncan, David, *406*
———, Samuel, 383
Duncan Falls, Ohio, 111, n., *408*
Dunkard Creek, Pa., murders at, 244
Dunkers (German Baptists), 6, n., 306
Dunlap, John, 407
Dunlap's Station, 274, *407*
Dunmore, John Murray, Earl of, 119, 122
Dunmore, the, 305, 309, 313 ff., 318, 320, *409*
Dunning Creek, 238 f.
Du Ponceau, Peter S., 385
Duquesne, Fort, 37, 57, 104
Dutch Valley, N. J., 390, *407*

Easton, Pa., 84, n., 347, 369; Treaty of (1758), 70
———, Ohio, 435
Ebone. *See* Point Abino.
Echpalawehund, Chief (Petrus), 198, *407*; conversion of, 202 ff.
Edinburg, Pa., 255, 420
Edmond's Swamp, 37, 39, 221, 240, *407*
Edward, Fort, 329
Edwards, Rev. William, 157, 167, 179, 183, 204, 248, 250, 252 f., 310, 368, 370, 387, 389, *407*
Eel River Indians, 271, 282 f., *407*. *See also* Wea Indians.
Eighteen Mile Island, 276, 286
Eis, George, 216
Eisenhart family, 266, *407*
Eldridge, ———, 370, 389
Elisabeth (daughter of Anton Welochalent), 199
——— (mother of Benjamin Cuwes), 398
Elizabeth Furnace, *428*
Elizabethtown, Pa., 235
Elliot, John, 295, 307, 315, *407*
———, Capt. Matthew, 133, 146, 158, 167, 169 f., 172 f., 175, 182 ff., 204, 314 ff., 318, *407*
Elmira, N. Y. *See* Newtown.
Emmaus, Pa., 234, 341, 397, *407*
England, Lt. Col. Richard, 309, *407*
Ensign's Inn, Saratoga, N. Y., 329
Ephrata, Pa., 235
Epty, ———, 79, 83
Erie, Fort, 304 f., 307, 309, 312 f., 318, 320, 322, 371
———, Lake, 234, 247, 249, 332, 334, 351, 358, 361, 372, 374, 388; cycle of high and low water, 250; quality of the water in, 251; Heckewelder's voyage on (1793), 309, 320; description of (1798), 352
Ernst, Lt., in command at Fort Pitt (1788), 222, 233
Ervin. *See* Irvine.
Esopus, N. Y., 296, *408*
Ettwein, Rev. John, Bishop of the Moravian Church, 9, 90, 98, 104, 230 ff., 343, 347, 366 f., 386 ff., *408*
Evan, Capt. Abraham (Wyandot), 170, *408*
Everett, Pa., 418
Everlasting Gospel, The (Welling), 216, *408*
Eyerly, John Jacob, 334, 389, *408*

Fairfield, Upper Canada, 258, 339 and n., 352, 360, 363 f., 366 f., 370 ff., 389, 393, *408*, 441; description of (1793), 310 f.; Mortimer's journal, Bethlehem to Fairfield (1798), 340-72; Heckewelder visits (1798), 368 f.; destroyed after the Battle of the Thames, 394
Fallen Timbers, Ohio, 334. *See also* Maumee Rapids.

Index

Falls, Pa., 343, 416
——— of the Beaver, 95, 98, 105, *408*; military post at, 223, 245
——— of the Muskingum, 111, n., 229, *408*
——— of the Ohio, 388, *408*
Fannettsburg, Pa., 335
Faulkner, Capt. Peter, 347
Federal Indian Relations (Mahr), 151
Fetterman, 377, *408*
Field, John, 382, *408*
Finney, Fort, 440
Fish Creek, 302
Five Nations (Iroquois), 98, 406. See also Six Nations.
Flathead Indians, 331
Fly, the, 330
Folk, George, 244, 247 f.
———, William, 244
Folle Avoine. See Menominee Indians.
Fonda, John, 298 f., *408*
———, N. Y., 402, *408*
Forbes, Gen. John, 37, 104
Ford, Capt. Joseph, 305, 309, *409*
Forks of the Delaware, 369
——— of the Ohio, 37. See also Pittsburgh.
——— of the Road (Bonnet's), 221, 239
Forres Ferry, 235, *409*
Forty Mile Creek, 359
Four Mile Creek, 241
Fowler, Capt., 383, *409*
Fowler, John, 363, *409*
Fox, ———, 78, 83
Fox Indians, 332
Franklin, Benjamin, 359, 396
———, Pa., 230, 375, 443; description of site, 382
———, Fort, 375, 381 f., 389, *409*
Freeman, ———, 269 and n., 272, *409*
Freemasonry, 292; funeral of Gen. Tupper at Marietta, 263 f.
Freemont, Ohio, 162, n., 396, 422
French Creek, 334, 375 ff., 382, 389
——— Lick, Ind. See Buffalo Salt Lick.
Frenchtown, 344
Frey, Hendrick, 299, *409*
Friedenshütten, 69, 92 f., 96, 98, 101, 104, 135, 218, 343 f., 386 f., 393, *409*; development of the town, 87 ff.
Friedensstadt, 87, 95, 104, 118, 393, *409*, 420; description of (1771), 97
Friedensthal, *409*

Friedrich, Abraham, 235
Friends, Society of (Quakers), 76, 80, 306, 315; members take up arms to defend Moravian Indians from the mob, 79 f.; attend Indian treaty at Detroit (1793), 295
Friends Library, The, 295, n.
Friends Miscellany, The, 295, n.
Frontenac, Fort, 322, 389, 402, *409*
Frueauff, Clara, 259, n.
Fry, ———, officer at Detroit, 203
Fry's. See Frey, Hendrick.
Fulneck, 17, 20, 386, *409*
Funday's. See Fonda, John.
Funk's, 383
Fur trade, 86, 222, 245, 250 f.; in Pittsburgh (1789), 243; North West Company, 312; in the far west, 336

Gage, Gen. Thomas, 79
Gajahaga River. See Cayahaga.
Gallipolis, Ohio, 265, 292, *409*, 431; description of (1792), 266; history of, 289 f.
Galops (Galloo) Rapids, 323
Ganaquenising Creek, *409*. See also Connoquenessing.
Gano, Major Gen. John Stites, 288, *410*
Ganson, Capt. John, 351, *410*
Garrison, Capt., of the *Irene*, 34
Gawiahätte (Wea), 271, *410*
Gayahaga. See Cayahaga.
Gekelemukpechink (Newcomerstown), 95 f., 98, 102 f., 111, 261, 407, *410*
Gelelemend. See Killbuck.
General Schuyler, the (Hudson River sloop), 296
Genesee country, 320, 370, 389; description of (1798), 350 f.; extensive settlement expected here, 349
——— River, 303, 348, 351
——— Senecas, 68, 315, *410*, 418
Geneseo, N. Y. See Big Three, N. Y.
Geneva, N. Y., 345, 347
George, Capt. Robin, 285
———, Lake, 329
German Flats, N. Y., 300
——— Valley, N. J., 407
Gibbins, Lt., 315, *410*
Gibson, Col. John, 146 f., 215, 222, 242 f., 245, *410*
Gilbert, Pa., 71, 444
Girty (Girdi), Mrs., 244, 247 f.

Girty, Simon, 133, 146, 158 f., 167, 244, 272, 313, 318 f., *410;* accuses the Moravians of corresponding with the Americans at Pittsburgh, 196; threatens to kill the missionaries, 201 f.
Glades, the, 239, *410*
Glaize King, the. See Tetepachksi.
Glickhican, 104, 138 f., 141, 158, 167, 177, n., 178 and n., 193, 394, 396, *410;* conversion of, 94 ff.; death of, 198, 200
Gnadenhütten on the Mahoning, 70, 198, 387, 390 f., 400, *410*
——— on the Muskingum, 3, 30 f., 98, 101, 104, 107, 113, 121 f., 132, 136, 146 ff., 150, 157, 159, 164 ff., 171, 174, 176 ff., 185, 206, 212, 232, 261, 335, 338 and n., 370, 373 f., 384 f., 389 f., 393, 397, *411;* massacre of Christian Indians at, 189 ff., 261; its effect on the survivors, 245; description of the site (1792), 292; survey of, 1797
———, Michigan (New Gnadenhütten), 109, n., 393, *411;* Moravian Indians at, 204 ff.
Gnadenthal, *411*
Goforth, William, 268, 410, *411*
Goguethagechton. See White Eyes.
Gokosing. See Kokosing.
Goodal's Station, 290, *411*
Goodale, Major Nathan, 265, *411*
Goose Isle. See Grosse Isle.
Gore, Obadiah, Esq., 345, *411*
Goschochking (Goschachgunk), 129, 136, 142, 148, 150, 153, 158 ff., 165, 172, 400, *411*. See also Coshocton, Ohio.
Goschgoschink, 90, 94 f., 226, 409, *411*
Goshen, Ohio, 373, 390 f., 393, *411*
Gower, Fort, 415
Graceham, Md., 335, *411*
Gracehill, Ireland, 216, *411*
Graham, ———, 216
———, Col., 289, *411*
Grand Eaux. See Pahatsi Indians.
Grand Portage (Great Carrying Place), 312, 371, *412*
——— Portage River, 325, 332, *412*
——— River, Upper Canada, 320, 361, 363, 365, 389
Grant's Tavern, 325
Grassman, Very Rev. Thomas, 299, n.
Grave Creek, 231, *412*
Gray, Leslie R., 340, n.
Great Carrying Place. See Grand Portage.

Great Island, 387, *412*
Great Warriors Mt., 238
Greathouse, Daniel, 119, n., *412*
Greber. See Crever.
Green Bay (Puans Bay), 332
——— River, 279
Greencastle, Pa., 260
Greensburg, Pa., 221, 241, 335, 406, *412*
Greenville, Fort, 412
———, Treaty of, 334
Gregor, Rev. Christian, 341, *412*
Grey, Samuel (a Delaware), 175, *412*
Grimsby, Ont., 359, 396
Grosse Isle, 204, 411
Grube, Rev. Bernhard, 74, 83, 164, n., *412*
Gunno, Major. See Gano.
Gutkigamen. See Thomas (Gutkigamen).
Guyondot River, 266 f., 289

Hagerstown, Md., 260
Half Moon, N. Y., 330
Half King, the (Six Nations). See Tanacharisson.
——— ——— (Wyandot). See Pomoacan.
Halftown, Chief, *412;* at Fort Harmar (1788), 227
Halle, Germany, 259
Hamilton, Henry, Lt. Gov. of Detroit, 205, 281
———, Rt. Rev. Kenneth G., *John Ettwein,* 38, 145
———, Robert, Hamilton's mills, 358
———, Ohio, 412
———, Ont., 400
———, Fort, 273 f., 287, *412*
Hamtramck, Col. John Francis, 279, 281, 413
Hand, Gen. Edward, 133, 146 f., 274, 404, 413, 439
Handbook of the American Indians (Hodge), 152
Handsome Lake (Seneca prophet), 404
Hannah, wife of Jo Peepe, 135, 198
Hannastown, Pa., 221, 256, *413*
Hardin, Col. John, 269 and n., *413*
Harding, John or Stephen, 342, *413*
———, Pa., 413
Hare, Robert, 260
Harmar, Gen. Josiah, 224 f., 230, 259, 272, *413*
———, Fort, 222, 224, 227 ff., 335, 406; Indian treaty at (1788-89), 219 ff., 242
Harmony, Pa., 384, 390, *413*

Index

Harra, Capt., 305, 312
Harris's Ferry, 38, *413*
Harrisburg, Pa., 235, 431; description of (1789), 256
Harrison, Gen., 394
———— City, Pa., 37, 401
Harrisonville, Pa., 433
Harrodsburg, Ky., 271, *413*
Hartshorn, William, 295, 315, 321, 324, *413*
Hascall, Capt., 290 f., *413*
Hay, John, Gov. of Detroit, 215 f., *413*
"Heathen Society." *See* Society for Propagating the Gospel Among the Heathen.
Hebron, Pa., 260, 397, *414*
Heckewelder, Anna Salome (Sally), 212, 386, *414*
————, Christian Renatus, 341, *414*
————, David, 33 f.
————, George, 33 f.
————, Johanna Maria (Polly), 386, *414;* taken prisoner by the Indians (1781), 176; returns to Bethlehem (1785), 212
————, Rev. John Gottlieb Ernestus, *414;* his character, 2, 88; use of the lot in his marriage, 10; early life, 33; awakening of missionary impulse, 34; first sight of Indians, 35; journey to Tuscarawas (1762), 37 ff.; passes a night in Edmond's Swamp, 39 f.; endures famine at Tuscarawas, 43, 65 f.; attends the funeral of Shingas's wife, 59 ff.; is warned by friendly Indians to leave, 66; returns to Bethlehem, 67 f.; at Wyalusing, 69; helps to save the lives of Indians at Wechquetank (1763), 70; resolves to return to England, 87; apprenticed to a cedar cooper, 88; illness at Cold Spring, 91; to the Beaver River as Zeisberger's assistant (1771), 97; makes his home at Schönbrunn (1772), 100; teaches in an Indian school, 101; makes good progress in language study, 102; finds an Indian remedy for sciatica, 103; travels by canoe from the Beaver River to the Tuscarawas (1773), 105 ff.; meets John Logan, the Indian, 118; aids the Americans during the Revolutionary War, 133 f.; helps to save the life of James O'Hara, 135; is saved himself by an Indian, 144; submits the question of marriage to the lot, 145; dissuades the Delawares from declaring war on the Americans, 145 ff.; moves to Salem on the Tuscarawas (1780), 159 f.; further progress in the Delaware language, 163; marriage (1780), 164; saved from death by a friendly Indian, 168; visited at Salem by the Wyandot Half King and his warriors (1781), 171; summoned by hostile Indians to a conference at Gnadenhütten, 174; made a prisoner by the Wyandots, 175; his first hours of captivity, 177 ff.; journey as a prisoner to Upper Sandusky, 182 f.; further journey to Detroit, 183 f.; tried for treason but acquitted, 185; learns of the massacre of Christian Indians by Col. Williamson's militia at Gnadenhütten (1782), 189 ff.; is summoned again to Detroit, 196; meets Anton, 199; goes to Detroit, 202; travels with Indians to New Gnadenhütten in the Chippewa country, 204; travels from Detroit to Cayahaga (1785), 208 ff.; leaves the Indian mission and returns with his family to Bethlehem (1786), 212; visits Pittsburgh 215; visits Carlisle, Pa., 217; journey to Marietta, Ohio (1788), 219 ff.; meets Col. David Williamson, 220; visits Wheeling, W. Va., 224; helps to lay out a tree nursery there, 230; discusses the Gnadenhütten massacre, 232; returns to Bethlehem, 233; makes a journey to Pettquotting (1789), 234 ff.; conducts the funeral of Thomas Hutchins, U. S. Geographer, 243; visits the site of his early mission at Tuscarawas, 246; reaches Pettquotting, 248; visits old Indian forts, 251; leaves Pettquotting, 252; examines a peeled tree with elaborate Indian pictographs, 253-54; visits Pittsburgh, 255; visits Carlisle, 256; returns to Bethlehem, 257; is invited by the U. S. government to accompany Gen. Rufus Putnam to Vincennes (1792), 260; reaches Marietta, 261; passes the dangerous mouth of the Scioto, 267; visits Cincinnati, 267 ff.; witnesses the funeral of a Wawiachteno chief at Cincinnati, 272 f.; visits the Falls of the Ohio at Louisville, Ky, 276-77; ascends the Wabash to Vincennes, 279 f.; describes Vincennes, 280 ff.; describes the Indian treaty at (1792), 282 ff.; travels with Indians over the Buffalo Trace to

Louisville, 284 f.; gets lost at the Buffalo Salt Lick, 284 f.; witnesses the funeral of another Wawiachteno chief at Cincinnati, 288; returns to Bethlehem (1792), 293; sets out for the Indian conference at Detroit (1793), 294; journey up the Hudson by sloop, 296 f.; visits Albany, 297; visits Niagara Falls, 306 ff.; reaches Detroit, 309; visits Fairfield in Upper Canada, 310 f.; bad news from the Indians assembled at Miami Rapids, 312 ff.; failure of the peace conference at Detroit, 315 ff.; leaves Detroit, 320; sails down Lake Ontario, 322; descending the St. Lawrence, is nearly wrecked during a storm on Lake St. Francis, 323 ff.; visits Montreal, 326 f.; returns to Bethlehem (1793), 331; travels to the Tuscarawas River to survey Moravian lands there (1797), 335 ff.; marks King Beaver's grave, 338; accompanies Mortimer to Fairfield, Upper Canada (1798), 339 ff.; visits Niagara Fall, 354 ff.; reaches Fairfield, 368; returns to Bethlehem (1798), 370; travels to see the Moravian lands near Presque Isle (1800), 374 ff.; meets a Seneca Indian on the trail, 375; visits Meadville, 376; returns to Pittsburgh and records some popular medicinal remedies, 383; pays a last visit to the western country (1813); itemizes his travels, 386 ff. For Heckewelder's writings, see Journals and other accounts.
———, Polly. See Johanna Maria Heckewelder.
———, Sara (Ohneberg), 10, *414*; her marriage to John Heckewelder referred to the lot and postponed, 145; the marriage takes place, 164 and n.; is taken prisoner by the Wyandots (1781), 176
———, Susanna, 386, *414*
Heckewelder Place (Alley), 385
Hedgehog. See Gawiahätte.
Hehl, Rev. Matthew, 145
Heidelberg, Pa., 256
Helena Moore (Jersey Indian), 422
Heller's Tavern, 341, *414*
Helltown, 247, *414*
Henderson, Ky., 279, 433
Hendricks, Capt. (Mahican), 268, *414*
———, Capt. (Oneida), 309, 318 f., *414*
———, Fort, 299, *414*

Henry (Moravian Indian), 192, *414*
———, James, 293, *414*
———, Capt. James, 358, *415*
———, John Joseph, 256, *415*
———, William, 77, n., 293, 419, *415*
———, William, Jr., 335, 389, *415*
———, William (a Delaware). See Killbuck.
Herkimer, Gen. Nicholas, 301
———, N. Y., 300
———, Fort, 300
Hermit's Field, the, 92
Herrnhut, Saxony, 33 f., 352, n.
Hessians, 349
Heymachers, 214
Hilary, Robert, 295
Hill, Aaron (Mohawk), 406
———, Capt. David (Karongrote), 244, 399, *415*; arrives at Fort Harmar (1788), 228
———, Isaac, 406
Historical Society of Pennsylvania, 294
History of Beaver County (Bausman), 58, 151
History of Greenland (Crantz), 239, 412
History of the Mission of the United Brethren among the Indians in North America (Loskiel), 69
Höber, of Nazareth, 341 f.
Hockhocking, 226, *415*
———, Fort, 226, *415*
———, River, 265
Hockingport, *415*
Hodgdon, Col. Samuel, 264, *415*
Hodge, Frederick, Webb, *Handbook of the American Indians North of Mexico*, 152
Holland Land Company, 376, 378, 395, *415*
Hooker, Richard, 347 f., *415*
Hope, N. J., 346, 382, 388, 390 f., *415*
Hope's Cove, 208, *416*
Hopson family, 276
Horse Valley, 237, 438
Horsfield, Joseph, 342, *416*
Hoskins, Elisha, 165
Huber, George, *416*
Hübner, Rev. John Andrew, 271, *416*
Hudson, N. Y., 296 f.
——— Falls, N. Y., 435. See also Sandy Hill.
——— River, 320, 329, 389, 429; Heckewelder's journey in a sloop from New York to Albany (1793), 296 ff.

Index

Hufnagel, ———, 241
Hughes, Capt., 231
Huling, Marcus, 382
Hummelstown, Pa., 218, 256
Hunt, ———, 343
Hunt's Ferry, Pa., 343
Hunter, Fort, N. Y., 298
Huntington, Frank, 152, n.
Huntsecker, Lt., 83
Huron, Ohio, 416
———, Lake, 332
——— Indians. See Wyandot Indians.
——— (Clinton) River, Mich., 87, 109, n., 110, 204, 206, 387, 411, *416*
——— River, Ohio, 234, 348 ff., 393, *416*
Huss, John, 33
Hutchins, Thomas, 221 ff., 228, 232, 334, 388, *416*; promises to survey the Moravian lands on the Muskingum, 233; death of, 242; his funeral conducted by Heckewelder, 243

Idea Fidei Fratrum (Spangenberg), 221, 239, *416*
Illinois Indians, 331
——— River, 283, 331
Independence, Mt., 329
Indian Council of 1793 (Shipman), 220
Indian *agriculture*, 255
——— *amusements*, "frolics," 53
——— *archives*, 132
——— *cannibalism*, 318
——— *canoes*: birch bark, 208; elm bark, 209
——— *dances*: at Vincennes (1792), 283 f.; among Caughnawaga Indians, 320
——— *death and burial*: burial rites among the Delawares seen in the funeral of Shingas's wife (1762), 58 ff.; condoling for the death of White Eyes (1778), 153 ff.
——— *dress and ornament*, 51, blankets, moccasins, the dressing of hides, 52; face painting, 53; beards, 53; tattooing, 54; ear cutting, 55; woman's dress, 59 f.; feathers, the eagle plume, 148; scalp lock, 194; silver brooches, 313; decoration, bells and porcupine quills, 320
——— *education*, 31; the interpretation of wampum belts, 132
——— *food and cooking*: burial feast, 60; taboo against eating wildcat, 99 f.; maple sugar, 103, 255, 368; the Three Sisters, corn, beans, and squash, 115; Indian meals, 116; different methods of preparing corn, 116; Indian bread, 117; food carried on the warpath, 137
——— *hermit*, 92
——— *housing*: Chippewa and Delaware houses compared, 250; wayside cabins, 351 f.
——— *hunting*: methods, 116; setting fire to the woods, 366
——— *language,* copiousness of expression, 44 ff.
——— *love and marriage,* 56
——— *medicine,* 58; poultices, 103; sweat oven, 108 ff.; emetics, 121; sorcerers, 125 ff.; a treatment for spider bite, 213
——— *mounds*: at Grave Creek (Moundsville) W. Va., 231; at Gallipolis, Ohio, 266
——— *patriotism,* 211, 280
——— *personality traits*: courage, endurance, 99; loyalty to friends, 123 ff.; the passion of revenge, 123 f.; friendship not to be purchased by presents, 125 f.; friendliness, 225; hospitality, 113 ff.; independence and abhorrence of tyranny, 113, 252; powers of observation, 214; "high-mindedness," pride, 160 ff.; punctuality, 47 f.; respect for elders, 84; fear of the occult, 125 ff.; love of the marvellous, 47
——— *pictographs*: painted posts, 61, 261; rock painting on the Mohawk River described, 299; peeled trees, 247, 368; elaborate Indian painting described and interpreted, 254
——— *punishment*: for murder, 321
——— *rainmakers,* 128 f.
——— *religion and mythology*: the Great Spirit, 51; the after-life, 62; prayer, thanks to the Creator, 112; the brotherhood of man, 113 f.; invocation of the manitos of the air and of the water, 209; the world on the Turtle's back, 227; the Missisauga account of the origin of Niagara Falls, 308
——— *taboos*: eating rabbit or ground hog, 50; eating wildcat, 98 ff.; killing rattlesnakes, 50 f.
——— *totems,* Turtle, Wolf, and Turkey, 51
——— *trails*: Allegheny Path, 413; Alle-

gheny-Genesee Path, 416; Buffalo Trace (Indiana), 284 ff.; Cayahaga Path, 253, 435, 438; Forbidden Path, 94, 430, 403, 409; Great Warriors Path, 425; to Kentucky, 267; Nescopeck Path, 396, 427; Tuscarora Path, 430; Wyandot warpath from Kokosing, 157; Wyoming Path (David's Path), 83 f.; Wyoming to Tioga, 342; trail obliterated by fallen timbers, 368; trails through the swamps in what is now Erie County, 377; constructing bark shelters for the night, 351. *See also* Portages.

——— *tribes*: census of, 1770-80, 331 ff.

——— *wampum*, 59, 78, 102, 192, 204; black belt, 95; archival belts, 132; in condolence ceremony, 153 f.; as a voucher, 168; "a Bunch of black Wampum," 196; peace belts, 283

——— *warfare*: discipline in war parties, 138; Fear Halloo (Alarm Yell), 183, n., 197 and n.; forage, 136 f.; runners, 183; Scalp Halloo (Death Halloo), 175 and n., 176, 179, 186; scalp lock and eagle plume, 148, 194; seasons for the warpath, 156

——— *-white relationships*: Indian distrust of the white man based on land-grabbing, 42, 64; on false interpreters, 86; on the liquor traffic, 97; on thievery, 97; on violence and murder, 120

——— *witchcraft*, 95, 126

Ingersoll, Major Thomas, 365, *416*
———, Ont., 365, *416*, 433
Iowa Indians, 332
Irene, the (Moravian ship), 34, 89
Irish, Justice, 256
Irish Settlement, Pa., 71
Irokesen und Delawaren im Spiegel des Herrnhuter Mission (Loges), 393
Irondequoit Bay, 303, *416*
Iroquois. *See* Six Nations, Five Nations.
Irvine, Gen. William, 217, *416*
Isaac. *See* Glickhican.
Isle aux Noix, 328
Israel (Welapachtschiechen, alias Capt. Johnny), 192 f., 198, *416*

Jacob (son-in-law of Shebosh), 191, 214, 319, *417*
———, 227, *417*
Jacobs, 57, *417*
Jacobson, Capt. of the *Irene*, 89

Jameson's, 216 f., 237, *417*
Jansen, Just, 279
Jeffers, Lt., 260
Jefferson, Thomas, *Notes on Virginia*, 119
———, Thomas, *Writings of*, 119
——— Fort, 268, 272, *417*
——— College, 402
Jeffersonville, Ind., 276, 440
Jemisson's, Jennison's. *See* Jameson's.
Jennerstown, Pa., 221
Jennings, John, Esq., 75
Johanan (a Delaware), 226, *417*
Johannes (Capt. John Doughty), 105, 229, *417*
Johanneta, 395
John, Teedyuscung's son, 70 f.
John Ettwein and the Moravian Church During the Revolutionary Period (Hamilton), 38
John Doughty. *See* Johannes.
John Heckewelder's Indians and the Fenimore Cooper Tradition (Wallace), 168 n.
Johnes. *See* Jones.
Johnny, Capt. (Delaware). *See* Israel.
———, Capt. (Mohawk). *See* Deserontyou.
———, Capt. (Shawnee), 315, *417*
Johnson, Sir John, 205, 298, *417*
———, Sir William, 78, 81, 298, 362
Johnson's. *See* Johnston, Hugh.
——— Creek, N. Y., 304
——— Hall (Johnstown, N. Y.), 298
Johnston, Hugh, 375, *417*
———, Capt. William, 352, *417*
Jonas (Jo Peepe's son), 192, 198, *417*
Jonathan, 395
Jones, Mrs., 382, *418*
———, Rev. David, 107 f., 230, *418*
———, Capt. Horatio, 315, 349, *418*
Jordan, Ont., 358, 434
Joseph (son of Anton Welochalent), 199
——— (son of Shebosh), 400
Joshua (Mahican), 195, n., 393, *418*, 441; shows Heckewelder two old Indian forts, 251
——— (Nanhun), *418*
Joung, Michael. *See* Young.
Journals and other accounts:
  1762—To the Muskingum (Heckewelder), 37-44, 63-68
  1773—From Langunto Utenink to Welhik Tuppeek (Heckewelder), 105-112
  1786—From the Cayahaga River to Bethlehem (Heckewelder), 213-18

Index

1788—To Marietta, Ohio (Heckewelder), 210-33
1789—To Pettquotting (Steiner), 234-57
1792—To Vincennes on the Wabash River (Heckewelder), 250-93
1793—To Detroit (Heckewelder), 294-333
1797—To the Muskingum (Heckewelder), 336-38
1798—To Fairfield (Mortimer), 340-72
1799—To Gnadenhütten, Ohio (Heckewelder), 373
1800—To Le Boeuf (Heckewelder), 374-83
"Captivity and Murder" (Heckewelder), 98, 100, 143, 170-76, 177-81, 182-98, 201-207
History, Manners, and Customs of the Indians (Heckewelder), 44-49, 50-56, 58-62, 73, n., 83-84, 92, 98-100, 103, 109-110, 112-17, 120-21, 123-29, 151, 160-63
Memoir of the Life of Brother John Gottlieb Heckewelder (autobiography), 35, 89, 96
Narrative of the Mission of the United Brethren among the Delaware and Mohegan Indians (Heckewelder), 31, 64-65, 69, 71-83, 85-87, 94-97, 118-20, 130-42, 144-50, 152-60, 165-69, 208-211
Travels Between 1754 and 1814 (Heckewelder), 71, 386-91
Judith, 195, *418*
Juliana (wife of Anton Welochalent), 136, 198, 396
Jung, Michael. *See* Young.
Jungman. John George. *See* Youngman.
Juniata Crossing, 39, 238, 256, *418*
——— River (Raystown Branch), 216; description of, 238 f.

Kain, ———, 300
Kamp, ———, 335
Kanawha River, 119, 265 f.
Kansa Indians, 332
Kantner, Pa., 440
Kapp, ———, 256
Karongrote. *See* Hill, Capt. David.
Kaskaskia (Kasgreasquia) Indians, 283
Kaskaskies. *See* Kuskuskies.
Kawita Indians, 332
Kelly's Run, 395

Kenny, James, 40, *418*
Kent, Ohio, 439
Kentucky boats, 226, 229 ff., 271, 276, 288; description of, 244; attacked by Indians, 267; useless for upstream work, 279; thousands of emigrants pass Marietta in Kentucky boats (1792), 290 ff.; destroyed by ice in the Ohio River, 292
——— River, 244, 287
Kerr, ——— *418*; journey from Wilmington, Del., to French Creek, Pa., 377 f.
Kickapoo Indians, 283, 331, *418*
Kiefer's, 236, 256, *418*
Kilbourn, Aaron and Timothy, 366, *418*
Killbuck, John Jr. (Gelelemend, alias William Henry), 134, 151 f., 390, 394, *419*; condoles for the death of White Eyes, 154; sends a son to college at Princeton, 252
———, John, Sr., 111, *419*
——— Creek, 253, *419*; difficulty in crossing, 246
Killbuck's Island, 243
King, Robert, 378, *419*
———, Thomas, unquiet night at his tavern, 215
———, Capt., 379
Kingsbury, Capt., 227
Kingston, N. Y., 296, 320
———, Ont., 388, 402, 409; description of (1793), 322 f. *See also* Cataraqui.
Kinhanschican, 336, *419*
Kirkland, Rev. Samuel, 300, 302, *419*
Kittanning, Pa., 57, 98, *419*
Kittatinny, Mt., 37
Klein-Nicolai, Georg, 408
Kliest, Daniel, 367, *419*
Klingsohr, Rev. John Augustus, 216, 218, 340, *419*
Knox, Gen. Henry, Secretary of War, 287, 294, 388
———, Fort, 282, 284, *419*
Kokosing, 157, 182, 292, *419*
——— River, 182, *419*
Konieschquanoheel. *See* Pipe, Capt.
Konkle, John, 346, *419*
Koquethagachton. *See* White Eyes.
Kreiter, ——— (of Bethlehem), 341
Kremser, John, 341, *420*
Krug, Jacob, 276
Kuhn, Abraham (Wyandot), 175 f., 178 f., *420*
Kuilutamen. *See* Wyolutimunk.

Kuncle, John. *See* Konkle.
Kuskuskies, the, 94 ff., 104, 118, 214, 255, *420*

Lachine, Que., 320, 325, *420*
Lackawanna River, 369
Lafayette, Ind., 429
Lakesang, ———— (L'Estaing?), 278, 286
Lancaster, Ohio, 415
————, Pa., 38, 63 f., 67, 76 f., 221, 243, 274, 276, 387, 390, 397
Lancelegresse, 290, *420*
Land grants to the Moravians, 210, 224, 293, 334, 446; grant by Congress of lands on the Muskingum, 206; proposal to survey these, 219; plans for the survey, 226; the survey interrupted, 228 ff., 242 ff., 249 f., 256; legislative grants, American and British, 374; lands on French and Conneaut Creeks, 374 ff.
Land settlement: New England settlements in the Ohio Valley, 262 f.; New England settlements in the Wyoming Valley of Pennsylvania, 342 f.; New England settlements in Canada, 363 f.; British land policy in Canada, 359; Pennsylvania policy, 380
Land speculation: in the Ohio country, 119; at Gallipolis, Ohio, 289 f.; travellers in quest of land, 353; in the French Creek country of Pennsylvania, 378 ff.
Landing, the (Queenston, Ont.), 304, 306, 308, 321 f., 356 f., 388 f., *420*
Lang, Ensign, 286
————, Augustus de, 300
Langundo-Utenink, 95 and n., 104 f., 123, 387, *420*
Lans le Gress. *See* Lancelegresse.
Lansing, Capt. Abraham, 296 f., *420*
Lansingburgh, N. Y., 297, 330
La Prairie, 327
La Shiene. *See* Lachine.
La Tranche River, 304 f., 310. *See also* Thames River, Ont.
Latrobe, Christian Ignatius, 338
Lauffer, Bartel, 375
Laurel Hill, 40, 215, 221, 256, 260, *420*; description of the road that crosses it, 240
Laurens, Henry, 146
————, Fort, 152, 246, 336, 410, *420*
Lawrenceburg, Ind., 440
————, Ky., 276

Lawunakhannek, 94 f., *420*
Leach Island, 78
Leath, John, 213, *421*
Leatherstocking Tales, 385
Lebanon, Pa., 256, 260, 375, 414
Le Boeuf, Pa., 68, 372, 374, 376, 384, 389, 418, *421*; description of the site, 380 f.
Lecha River. *See* Lehigh River.
LeFever, Anthony, 344, *421*
Legionville, Pa., 223, 422
Lehigh (Lecha) River, 27 f., 36, 70, 101, 265, 369, *421*
———— Falls, 341
Lehighton, Pa., 410
Leinbach, Friedrick, 346, 382, *421*
Lenni Lenape. *See* Delaware Indians.
Le Roy, N. Y., 351, 410
Levallie, Francis, 198, 201 f., *421*
Levering, Abraham, 341, *421*
Lewis, Col. 290, *421*; defeats the Shawnees (1774), 265
Lexington, Ky., 267, 271, 278
Lichtenau, 136, 138, 141 f., 148, 150, 152 f., 156 ff., 163 f., 198, 226, 387, 396, *421*
Licking Creek, 230
———— River, 230, 270
Life and Times of David Zeisberger (De Schweinitz), 136
Ligonier, Pa., 221, 233, 239, 241, 256, 335
Limestone (Maysville), Ky., 227, 231, 288, *421*; description of (1792), 267
Linch, ————, 301
Lincoln, Gen. Benjamin, 295, 297, 299, n., 302, 314, 320, 331, 388, *421*
Lindley, Jacob, 295, 299, n., 315, *422*; his description of Niagara Falls (1793), 307 f.
Linebach. *See* Leinbach.
Lititz, Pa., 37 f., 145, 164, n., 217, 220, 233, 235, 293, *422*
Little Beaver Creek, 223
———— Falls, N. Y., 301, 414; description of, 299 f.
———— Guyondot River, 266 f.
———— Kanawha River, 265, 397
———— Miami River, 268, 404, 425
———— Muskingum River, 224, 231
———— Nose, 299, n.
Littleton, Fort, 237, 335, *422*
Livingston family, 331
Lock Haven, Pa., 381
Locust Creek, 403

Index

Logan, ———, of Philadelphia, 78
Logan, John (Tachnechdorus, son of Shickellamy), 118 ff., 225, n., 397, 410, 422; murder of his family at Yellow Creek, 118 f.; "Logan's Lament," 120
Logans, Sons of Shickellamy (Swanger), 119, n.
Loges, Ilse, *Irokesen und Delawaren im Spiegel des Herrnhuter Mission*, 393
Logstown, 223, 422; description of (1789), 244 f.
London, England, 346, 362, 386
Long Point, Ont., 309
Long Reach, Ohio River, 108, 224
Long Sault, the, 323
Longueuil, Que., 327
Loramie's Store, 336, 422
Lord Dunmore's War. *See* Shawnee War.
Loremer, ———. *See* Lorimier.
Loretz, Rev. John, 341, 422
Lorimier, ———, 320 f., 325
Loskiel, George Henry, *History of the Mission of the United Brethren among the Indians of North America*, 69, 122, n., 152, 338 and n., 370, n.; visits the Muskingum country, 390
Louise, wife of Jacob, 227, 417, 422
Lot, the, settling questions by, 7 ff.; examples of its use, 26; an appeal to, causes postponement of Heckewelder's marriage, 145; finally sanctions the marriage, 164
Louisville, Ky., 271 f., 274, 276, 279, 286, 388, 408; description of (1792), 277 f.
Love Feast, 39; origin of, 23; at Pettquotting (1789), 252
Lovelace, ———, 228, 230
Lower Sandusky, 56, 162, 196, 294, 396, 422, 434
Loyalhanna, 104. *See also* Ligonier.
Luce's, 382
Luckenbach, Mrs. John Christian. *See* Heckewelder, Susanna.
Ludlow, Israel, 246, 422
Luke Holland. *See* Anton Welochalent.
Lundy's Lane, Ont., 354, 423
Lyon Inn. *See* Ryan's.

McCaskry, Dr. *See* McCoskry.
McConnellsburg, Pa., 398
McCormick, Alexander, 158, 169, 174, 423;
Moravian missionaries meet at his house at Upper Sandusky, 196
McCoskry, Dr. William A., 295, 304, 314, 423
McDowel, Robert, 346, 423
McGee, Henry, 348, 423
McIlhaney, Pa., 341
MacIntire, Capt., 293
MacIntire's, 325
McIntosh, Gen. Lachlan, 151 f., 162, n., 423
———, Fort, 162, 173, 223, 423
McIntosh's Tavern, Marietta, Ohio, 290
McKee, Col. Alexander, 67 f., 133, 146, 148, 158, 167, 179, 315, 423
McKee, James, 315 f., 423
McKinney. *See* Kenny.
Mackenzie, Alexander, 312, 423
McMahan, Major William, 223, 261, 292, 423
McMechan, Dr. James, 107
McWhorter, Thomas, 347, 424
Machingwe Pushis. *See* Big Cat.
Magdalene (Moravian Indian), 395
Mahican Indians, 27, 29 f., 87, 98, 104, 170, 297, 309, 318, 393 f., 424
Mahoning, Ohio, 387
——— (Mahony) Creek, Carbon County, Pa., 30, 101, 387, 424
——— Old Town, 213, 254, 424
——— River, Ohio, 123, 213, 254, 424
Mahr, August C., 102, 105, n.; *Federal Indian Relations, 1774-1788*, 151
Malecite (Amelistes) Indians, 333
Mamasu, 244
Manchester Island, 267
Manheim, Pa., 235
Mannittohaliechk, 226
Marcus (son of Anton Welochalent), 199, 424
Maria, H. M. S., 328
Mariane, 417
Marietta, Ohio, 222, 242, 261, 270, 284, 335 f., 338, 384, 388 ff., 399, 413, 424; fear of Indian attack at (1788), 225; description of (1792), 262 ff.; public dinner for the chiefs at (1792), 290 f. *See also* Campus Martius and Harmar, Fort.
Marselles, Capt., 330
Martin, ———, 268, 424
———, John, 148, 150, 191 f., 194, 396, 424

Martin's (Juniata Crossing), 256
———— Station, 261, *424*
Martyrs of the Oblong and Little Nine (Smith), 195, n., 199, n.
Mascouten Indians, 283, 332, *424*
Massasaga, Massasaugies, Massesagues. *See* Missisauga Indians.
Massie's (Mercer's) Station, 267, *424*
Mau, Rev. ————, 271
Maumee Rapids, 370, 389, *424;* Indian council at (1793), 315 ff.
———— River (Miami of the Lake, Tawa), 183, 294, 309, 312, 314 f., 319, 332, 334, 388, 405, *440;* Indian council at (1788), 222, 227; delegates from Indian council at (1788), 229 f.
May, ————, 221, 239
Maybee's, 298
Maysville, Ky. *See* Limestone, Ky.
Mead, Col. David, 376, *425*
Meadville, Pa., 374 f., 381, 389, 395, 405, *425;* description of (1800), 376
Mechanicsburg, Venango County, Pa., 395
Mechecouaki Indians. *See* Fox Indians.
Meechhanneck, 369
Melimius. *See* Tobias (Melimias).
Mennier. *See* Myneer.
Menominee Indians, 332
Menzius (Menzies), Col., 269
Mercer's Station. *See* Massie's Station.
Meshoppen, Pa., *425*
———— Creek, 343, 369, *425*
Messesagues. *See* Missisauga Indians.
Metcalf, John, 346, *425*
Meyerstown. *See* Myerstown.
Miami Indians, 259, 285, 318, 332
————, Rapids of the. *See* Maumee Rapids.
———— River, 120, 166, n., 244, 269, 274, 276, 287, 305, 336, *425, 440.* See also Maumee River.
———— of the Lake. *See* Maumee River.
———— Old Fort, 370
Michael (Munsee), 55, 214, *425*
Michigan, Lake, 283, 332
Michilimackinac, 318
Michler's Tavern, 340, *425*
Micmac Indians, 333
Middletown, Pa., 38; description of (1789) 235
Milan, Ohio, 222, 248, *416*
Miles, William, 376, 379, *425*
Milesburg, Pa., 381, 397
Mill Creek, 223

Miller, Jack (Edmond's Swamp), 39
————, Fort, 329
Millerstown, Pa., 256, *425*
Mingo Bottom (Mingo Town, Mingo Junction), 105, 223, *245*
Mingos (Iroquois), 105, 158, 163, 170, 172, 179, n., 186, 222, 246 f., 253, *425*
Minisinks, 71, 168, n., *425*
Missisauga Indians, 305, 308 f., 323, 332, 365, *426*
Mississippi River, 98, 232, 242, 271, 281, 331
Missouri River, 242
———— Indians, 332
Mobile River, 331
Mohawk Indians, 87, 298, 305, 309, 406; arrive at Fort Harmar (1788), 228; on the Bay of Quinte, 322; village at Brantford, 361 f.
———— River, 297, 315, 320, 330, 361, 371, 400; description of (1793), 298 ff.
Mohawk-Caughnawaga Museum, 299, n.
Mohican, Mohegan. *See* Mahican Indians.
Molther, Rev. John, 341, *426*
Monocacy Creek, Pa., 231
Monongahela Ferry, 232
———— River, 40, 58, 214, 222, 242 ff.
Monsey. *See* Munsee.
Monsy Town. *See* Muncey, Ont.
Muncey, Ont., 367, 389, *426*
Montgomery, Fort, 296, *426*
Montreal, Que., 303, 312, 320, 325, 389; description of (1793), 326 f.
Monture, John, 222
Moore, ————, 83
————, Joseph, 295, 307, 315, *426*
Moravia, Pa., 95, 409, 420
Moravian Church: history of, 1-32. *See also* "Choirs," Land Grants to the Moravians, Lot, Love Feast, Moravian Indians, Moravian Missions.
———— Indians: their independent position within the Delaware nation, 102; their services at Pettquotting described, 250 ff.; character of, 364
———— missions: significance of, 2; extent of, 27; methods and practices described, 31, 105 f.; assistance given by the missionaries in interpreting documents for Delaware councils, 132 f.; final estimate of the mission, 393 f.
Moraviantown. *See* Fairfield.
Morgan, Col. George, 143, 152, *426*, 428;

Index

invites the Moravians to settle at the mouth of the Ohio, 232 f.
Morrison, ———, 255
Morristown, N. J., 390
Mortimer, Rev. Benjamin, 389, *426*; his journey to Fairfield in Upper Canada (1798), 339-72; describes Niagara Falls, 354 ff.; offers advice to travellers, 358 f.
Moundsville, W. Va., 231, 412
Mt. Clemens, Mich., 204, 411
Mt. Joy, Pa., 235, 406
Mt. Morris, N. Y., 445
Mt. Rock, Pa., 38, 437; the spring, 236
Muddy Run, 255
Munsee Indians, 51, 55, 94, 99, n., 104, 150, 170, 318 f., 367, 375, *426*
Murrysville, Pa., 37
Muskingum, Falls of, *426*; proposed site of Indian treaty (1788), 219
——— River, 37 ff., 41 f., 64 ff., 87, 96 ff., 100, 105, 134, 136, 146, 148, 157, 183, 197, 220 f., 246, 250, 334 f., 337, 339, 373 f., 386 ff., 391, *426*, 443; Heckewelder's ascent of by canoe (1773), 108 ff.; Moravian Indians return to for food (1782), 188
Musquetons. *See* Mascouten Indians.
Myers' Tavern, 256
Myerstown, Pa., 256
Myneer, Christian, 346, *426*

Nagel, Peter, 305
Nain, 71 ff., 83, *427*
Names of Delaware Chiefs . . . (Heckewelder), 58
Names which the Lenni Lenape or Delaware Indians had given to Rivers, Streams, Places &c (Heckewelder), 385
Nanticoke Indians, 87, *427*
Narrative of the Mission of the United Brethren . . . (Heckewelder), 385
Narrows, the (Mohawk River), 299
Natchez, 331
Nathanael Davis (Guttenamequin), 192
Navy Hall, Upper Canada, 304, 306, 315 f., 322, *427*
Navy Island, 308
Nazareth, Pa., 71, 74, 83, 96, 164, n., 276, 340 f., 346, 348, 368, 391, *427*
Neal's, 329
Nees Haws, 135, *427*
Nellis, John Christian, 299
Nepissins. *See* Nipissing Indians.

Nesbitt, Dr. *See* Nisbet.
Nescopeck, Pa., 83, *427*
Netawatwees (Newcomer), 88, 96, 98, 102 ff., 111, 152, 198, 410, *427*
New Castle, Pa., 94 f., 214, 255, 409, 420
New Fairfield, 394
New Furnace, 218, *428*
New Gnadenhütten. *See* Gnadenhütten, Mich.
New Lancaster, Ohio, 390
New Madrid, Mo., 232, 290, *428*
New Martinsville, W. Va., 424
New Orleans, La., 266
New Philadelphia, Ohio, 98, 101, 384, 390 f., *428*, 436
New River. *See* Kanawha.
New Salem, 258, 431; description of (1789), 248 ff. *See also* Pettquotting.
New Schönbrunn, 337, *428*
New Spain, 271, *428*
New Windsor, 296
New York, N. Y., 34, 78 f., 88 f., 295, 297, 331, 371, 386, 389
Newalike, 131, 141, 394, *427*
Newark, N. J., 88
———, Upper Canada, 304, 306, 362, 365, 371, 388 f., *428*
Newcomer, King. *See* Netawatwees.
Newcomerstown. *See* Gekelemukpechink.
Newport, Ky., 271
Newtown (Elmira), N. Y., 345, 370, *428*
——— Falls, Ohio, 424
Niagara, 227, 250, 295, 297 f., 311, 313, 345, 349, 351; settlements west of, 365
———, Fort, 163, 205, 303 f., 312, 371, 388, 401, *428*; description of, 306
——— Falls, 322, 352, 388 f.; description of, by Lindley and Heckewelder (1793), 304 ff.; description of, by Mortimer (1798), 354 ff.
——— Hill, 358, 360
——— Portage, 420, 423, 436
——— River, 306, 352 f., 371
——— Road, 358
Niagara-on-the-Lake, 427
Nicholson, ———, Indian interpreter, 243
Nicolson, Jacob, 227
Niles, Ohio, 213, 435
Nine Mile Island, 279
——— ——— Run, 241
Nipissing Indians, 332
Nisbet, Dr. Charles, 236, *428*
Nixon, William, 37, 88, *428*

Noailles, Gen. Louis Marie Antoine, Vicomte de, 344, *428*
North Bend, Ohio, 269, 287, *428*; description of (1792), 275
North Braddock, Pa., 399
North Cohocton, N. Y., 347 f., 398, 415
North River. *See* Hudson River.
North West Company, 312, 325, 397, 406, 423, *429*
Northumberland, Pa., 347
Northwest Passage, 312
Noses, the, 299, n.
Nuns Island, 325

Oak Orchard Harbour, 303
Ogden, ———, 90
Ogdensburg, N. Y., 323, *429*
O'Hara, James, 141, 198, 243, 396, *429*; his life saved by Heckewelder and Anton, 135 f.
Ohio, Falls of the, 267, 284; description of (1792), 276 ff.
——— Company of Associates, 220, 225, 228, 231, 259, 263, 290, *429*
——— River, 72, 95, 98, 103 f., 118 f., 135, 138, 157, 220, 242 ff., 332, 337; canoe journey on, from Beaver River to the Muskingum, 105 ff.; Heckewelder's river journey from Pittsburgh to Marietta (1788), 222 ff.; Heckewelder's journey from Pittsburgh to Louisville, Ky. (1792), 261-80; return, 286-92
Ohio State Archaeological and Historical Quarterly, 102, n.
Ohneberg, George, 164, n.
———, Sara. *See* Heckewelder, Sara (Ohneberg).
———, Susanna, 164, n.
Ojibway. *See* Chippewa Indians.
Olumapies (Sassoonan), 64
Oneida Indians, 227, 297, 302, 314 f., 319, *429*; come to Detroit for treaty, 313
——— Lake, 302, 371, 388, 400
——— River, 302
Onondaga (Syracuse), N. Y., 302, 343, 400
——— Indians, 86 f., 302, *429*
——— Lake, 302
Ontario, Fort, 371
———, Lake, 303, 306, 352, 358 ff., 371, 388 f., 400; description of (1793), 322
Ontario History, 340, n.
Origins of Iroquois Neutrality (Wallace), 63

Oriskany, N. Y., 301, *429*
Osage Indians, 332
Oswegatschie, Fort, 323, *429*
Oswego, Fort, 303, 320, 388
——— Falls, description of (1793), 302 f.
——— River, 441
Ottawa Indians, 68, 168, 172, 179 f., 220, 332, *429*
——— River, Canada, 325, 332, 412. *See also* Grand Portage River.
Ouabache. *See* Wabash.
Ouachtenons. *See* Wea Indians.
Ouiatenon, 418, *429*
Ouisconsins. *See* Wisconsin Indians.
Overslaugh, Albany, N. Y., 330
Owen, Daniel, 285
Owl Creek, 370, 389

Pachgantschihilas, 200, 220, 315, 417, *430*; urges the Moravians to come away from the Muskingum for safety, 165 f.
Padelonians. *See* Comanche Indians.
Pahatsi Indians, 332
Paint Creek, 253
Painted Post, N. Y., *430*; supposed origin of name, 346
Pakanke, Chief, 94 f., 198, 410, 420, *430*, 432
Panis. *See* Pawnee Indians.
Papunhank, John, 76 f., 81, 99 and n., *430*
Parish, John, 295, 314 f., 319, *430*
Path Valley, 237, *430*
Patton, ———, 215
Paulus (Sesapit), 194 and n., *430*
——— (Wanspachech), 194 and n., *430*
Pawling, Henry, 344, *430*
Pawnee Indians, 332
Paxton, Capt. (of the sloop *Caldwell*), 322
Paxton, Pa., 76, *431*
——— Boys, 76 ff., 86, 131 f., *431*; repulsed by armed Philadelphians, 80
Peace Village. *See* Langundo-Utenink.
Pecks Tavern, 256
Peekskill, 296
Peepe, Jo (a Delaware), 135, 198, 396, 417
Pemaholand, Jacob, 335 f., *431*
Penn, William, 76, 100
Pennamite Wars, 93
Pennsylvania Archives, 135
Pennsylvania Boundary Line, 223, 255, 293; carved through the forest, 245

Index

Pennsylvania Magazine of History and Biography, 259, n., 335, n.
Pennsylvania Road, 239
Peoria Indians, 331
Periodical Accounts, 34 f., 89
Perrysville, Pa., 374
Peters, Capt., 274, 276, 279
———, Rev. Christopher, 260, *431*
Peterson, Lawrence, 350, *431*
Petit, Dr., 266, *431*
Petrus. *See* Echpalawehund.
Pettit, Charles, 360, *431*
Pettquotting, 222, 228 ff., 242, 244, 247, 258, 305, 385, 388, 393, 398, *431*; description of Moravian mission at (1789), 248 ff. *See also* New Salem.
Pezold, Rev. Johann Gottlieb, 38, *431*
Phelps's (Queenston), 322
Philadelphia, Pa., 57, 107, 132, 173, 227 f., 284, 287, 295, 390 f.; citizens give protection to Indian refugees, 74-83; peltries sent to, from Pittsburgh, 243
Piankashaw Indians, 283, *431*
Piantias. *See* Peoria Indians.
Pickel, ———, 271
Pickering, Timothy, 314, 320, 342, 388, *431*; views on the treaty at Fort Harmar, 219
——— Papers, 220, n., 294
Pilgerruh, 212, 393, 402. *See also* Cayahaga.
Pine Swamp, Great (Monroe County, Pa.), 83, 92, 341, 369, *431*
Pinery, the (Upper Canada), 389, *432*
Pipe, Capt., 43, 88, 148, 150 ff., 159, 167, 170, 182 ff., 228, *432*, 404, 439; declares for the British, 131 f.; his horse is stolen, 177 f.; character of, 185 f.; defends the Moravian prisoners on trial at Detroit, 187; defeats Crawford and Williamson at Upper Sandusky, 199; present at Fort Harmar (1789), 220
Pisquetomen, 397
Pitt, Fort, 37, 40, 43, 94, 151, 243, 315, 400, 413, *432*
Pittsburgh, Pa., 40 f., 67 f., 95, 104, 120, 133, 136, 142, 144 ff., 148, 151 f., 165, 172 f., 177 ff., 196 f., 199, 218, 222, 231, 242, 253 ff., 271, 274, 278, 334 f., 370, 374, 378, 384, 387 ff., 401; Heckewelder visits (1786), 215; Heckewelder visits (1788), 221 f.; Heckewelder returns to from Marietta (1788), 232; description of (1789), 243 f.; Heckewelder visits (1792), 260; Heckewelder returns to, 293; mileages, Pittsburgh to Detroit, 372
Platt, Capt., 306
———, Col. Richard, 263, *432*
Plummer's, 382
Pocono Mts., 84, n., 431
Point Abino, 309, *432*
——— a Plair. *See* Point Pelee
——— Baudet, 325
——— Breeze, 304
——— Ebone. *See* Point Abino.
——— Pelee, 309, 432
——— Pleasant, W. Va., 265, 290 f.
Pointe au Fer, 328
Polopels Island, 296, *432*
Pomoacan (Wyandot Half King), 134, 136, 162, 167, 182 f., 196, *432*, 442; arrives with warriors at Salem, 169; urges Moravians to come away from the Muskingum for their own safety, 170
Pontiac, 68, *432*
Pontiac's War, 43, 66, 68 f., 71, 94, *432*
Poor, ———, 279
Popunhank. *See* Papunhank.
Port Colbourne, Ont., 440
Port Washington, 159
Porteus, ———, 300
Portages: from the Genesee Falls to Lake Ontario, 416; from Lake Erie to the Thames River, 416; from Presque Isle to French Creek, 421; from St. Mary's River to Laramie Creek, 422; from the Tuscarawas to the Cuyahoga, 426; from the Mohawk River to Oneida Lake, 439 f. *See also* Niagara Portage.
Post, Christian Frederick, 36 ff., 58, 63, 66 ff., 217, 246, 386, 397, *432*; speaks before the Indian council at Tuscarawas (1762), 42 f.; leaves Tuscarawas (1762), 64
———, John, 300
Post Vincent. *See* Vincennes.
Potawatomi Indians, 68, 272, 283, 318, 332, *433*; at Fort Harmar (1789), 220
Poughkeepsie, N. Y., 296, 331, *432*
Power Glen, Ont., 413
Presque Isle, Pa., 68, 253, 309, 320, 372, 381 f., *433*
Prior, Capt., 279 f., 284 ff., 288 ff., *433*
Proceedings of the Northumberland County Historical Society, 119, n.

Province Island, 76 f.
Puans. *See* Winnebago Indians.
Puans Bay. *See* Green Bay.
Put-in-Bay, 208
Pulteney, Sir William: the Pulteney Association, 346
Putiwatima. *See* Potawatomi Indians.
Putnam, Gen. Rufus, 220, 230, 265 f., 268, 273, 279 f., 282 ff., 287, 290 ff., 329, 335 ff., 365, 388 f., 401, *433*; travels to Vincennes to make peace with the Indians (1792), 259-93; surveyor at Schönbrunn (1797), 337 f.
———, Seth, 365, *433*
———, William Rufus, 335
———, Fort, 296
Putnam's Point, 329
Pyrlaeus, John Christopher, 51, *433*

Quakers. *See* Friends, Society of.
Quapaw Indians, 332
Quebec, Que., 327
——— Calendar, 331 ff.
Queen's Rangers, the, 306, 315, 410
Queenston, Ont. *See* Landing, the.
Quinte, Bay of, 309, 398, 406, *433*
Quisohackin, 227

Raccoon Creek, 147
Raisin, River, 370, 389, *433*
Rankin, ———, 228
Randolph, Beverley, 295, 314, 320, 388, *433*
Ranselaer. *See* Rensellaer.
Rapids, the. *See* Maumee Rapids.
Rapp, George, 413
Rattlesnake Hill, 329
Rauch, Rev. Christian Henry, 29 f., 104
Raystown. *See* Bedford, Fort.
Read, ———, 296
Read's Wharf (Red Hook), 331
Reading, Pa., 234, 379, 390
Reamstown, Pa., 235
Recovery, Fort, 401
Red Banks, Ky., 279, *433*
Red Hook, N. Y., 296
Reed, Henry, 278
———, Robert, 375, *433*
Reed's Tavern, 241, *433*
Reichel, Rev. Carl Gotthold, 340 ff., *434*
———, William C., 55, n., 84, n., 99, n., 109, n., 152, n., 162, n.
Reigart, ———, 376

Reizenbach, Rev. Philip Jacob, 271, *434*
Renatus (Schonqueh), 75, 81, *434*
Renchey's Tavern. *See* Runchey, Robert.
Rensellaer, ———, 297
Retrenche (La Tranche) River. *See* Thames River, Ont.
Reymer, Frederick, 221, *434*
Rhinebeck, N. Y., 296
Rice, Mrs. Joseph. *See* Heckewelder, Anna Salome.
Richelieu River, 439
Richland, Ohio, 384, 390
Ried. *See* Reed's Tavern.
River Indians. *See* Missisauga Indians.
Rivington, ———, 314, *434*
Robertson, Capt., 78 f.
Robins, ———, 222
———, Obediah, 162, 201, 253 f., *434*
Robinson, ———, 214
Rocky Island, 208, *434*
Rocky Point, 208, 388, *434*
Rome, N. Y., 300, 436, 439
Rondthaler, Rev. Edward, *Life of John Heckewelder*, 37-44, 63-68, 90-91, 212, n.
Roscommon, Pa., 84, n.
Rothe, Rev. John Andrew, 98, 104, 218, 344, 386 f., *434*
Rothrock, John, 335
Rouch's Tavern, 322
Rough, Sergeant, 202, *434*
Round Heads. *See* Têtes de Boule.
Rousseau, John Baptiste, 360, 364, *435* (St. John)
Ruchline, Sheriff, 83
Rudolph, Major, 289, *434*
Rummerfield, Pa., 399
Runchey, Robert, 358, *434*
Ryan's Inn, 239, *434*

St. Clair, Gen., 219, 233, 241 f., 403, *435*; discusses the Moravian Indian mission with Heckewelder, 225; discusses Indian mythology, 227; insists on holding the Indian treaty at Fort Harmar, 229; is ill with the gout, 230 f.; is defeated, Nov. 4, 1791, by Little Turtle, 259
———, Fort, 274, *435*
———, Lake, 310, 312
St. Croix, 27, 274
St. François, Lake, 331; Heckewelder is caught in a storm on, 323 ff.
St. John. *See* Rousseau, John Baptiste.

Index 469

St. John's, Que., 328, 389
St. John's Day, 264, 292
St. Joseph, Mich., 332
St. Joseph, Lake, 283
St. Lawrence River, 333, 350, 352 ff., 370, 389; Heckewelder's descent of, from Kingston to Montreal, 323 ff.
St. Lewis, Falls of. *See* Sault St. Louis.
St. Mary's, 312, *435*
St. Regis, N. Y., 402
St. Vincent. *See* Vincennes.
Sakis. *See* Sauk Indians.
Salem, Ohio, 164 and n., 165, 167 f., 173, 176 ff., 196, 206, 213, 230, 335 f., 387, 395, *435*; the mission town of Salem established on the Muskingum, 159 f.; visited by the Wyandot Half King (1781), 169 ff.; the site is surveyed (1797), 337
Salomons, the, 228
Salt Spring (Chandlersville, Ohio), 110, 123, *435*
——— (Trumbull County, Ohio), 335, 387, *435*, *439*; murder at (1786), 213 f.; salt-boiling at, 254
Samuel Moore, 193, 422, *435*
——— Nanticoke, 229 f., 249 f., 252, 255, *435*
Sandusky, 67 f., 142, 144, 147, 152, 156, 158 f., 162, n., 168, 171, 187, 196 ff., 201 f., 213, 242, 244, 248, 253, 295, 309, 311, 320. *See also* Lower Sandusky, Upper Sandusky.
——— River, 182, 247
Sandy Creek Harbour, 303
——— Hill, N. Y., 329, *435*
——— Islands, 267
Saratoga, N. Y., 297, 329
Sarepta, 226, *435*
Sargent, Major William, 227 f., 273, *435*; gives a public dinner in honor of the Indians (1792), 287
Saucon, Pa., 341
Sauk Indians, 332
Sault St. Louis, 333
Savery, William, 295, 315, 331, *436*
Savona, N. Y., 406
Sax's Tavern, 341, *436*
Scaticook River, 330
Schäfer, ———, 272
Schaefer, ———, at Niagara, 358
———, Rev. ———, at Carlisle, 217
Schäffer, Jacob, 341, *436*

Schäffer, Nicholas, 234, *436*
Schamung. *See* Chemung.
Schebosch. *See* Shebosh.
Schellsburg, Pa., 434
Schenectady, N. Y., 297 f., 371, 388
Schenectady, the, 296, 420
Schenk, Martin, 37
Scheschequon. *See* Sheshequin.
Schlägel, Rev. Frederick, 271, *436*
Schlosser, Capt., 79 and n.
———, Fort, 308, *436*
Schmick, Rev. John Jacob, 83, *436*
———, John Jacob, Jr., 341 ff., *436*
Schmidt, Melchior, 215
Schohary, N. Y., 298
Schönbrunn (Welhik-Tuppeek), 98, 103 ff., 120 ff., 132, 135, 141 f., 150, 157 ff., 164, 167, 176, 195 f., 261, 336, 339, n., 373, 387, 393, *436*; description of, 101; site surveyed (1797), 337. *See also* New Schönbrunn.
——— Diary, 136
Schöneck, 341, *436*
Schuyler, Gen. John Philip, 297, 329
———, Fort, 300, 371, *436*
Scioto River, 141, 150, 159, 228, 244, 289, 331, 336, 446; Indian attacks at the mouth of, 267, 271
Sciotoville, Ohio, 442
Scott, Capt., 295
———, Gen. Charles, 259, 268, 407, *437*
———, Dr. William, 315
——— Point, Ohio, 434
Scovell, James, 342, *437*
Sebastian, 286
Semple's, 236, *437*
Seneca Indians, 87, 118, 151, 227, 276, 315, 375, 382; influence the Delawares against the English (1762), 67; conduct an expedition against the Cherokees, 68; guard the Forbidden Path, 94; retaliate for the murder of Logan's family, 120; join a scouting party from Pittsburgh, 260; leave Tioga (1795), 345. *See also* Genesee Senecas.
——— Lake, 302
Senseman, Rev. Gottlob, 90, 176, 179, 183, 204, 256, 304, 310 ff., 315, 363, 366, 368, 386 f., *437*
Seylers, ———, 224
Shaw, ———, 346
Shawnee Indians, 68, 70, 102, 118, 120 ff., 141, 150, 159, 315, 318, 331, *437*;

"noted for much talk," 161; not represented at Fort Harmar Treaty (1789), 220; discuss the U. S. coat-of-arms, 275; at Detroit, 313
———— Prophet, the, 393, 418
———— Towns, 122, 182, 203 f., 213 f. *See also* Waketameki.
———— War, the (Lord Dunmore's War), 225, 397; causes of, 118 ff.
Shebosh, 105, 145 f., 183, 188, n., 191, 196, 204, 319, 387, 394; death of, 230. *See also*, Bull, John Joseph.
————, Joseph, 196, 437
Shekomeko, N. Y., 104, 424, 437
Shenango, 387, 437
Sherman's Valley, 58, 437
Sheshequin, 96, 135, 218, 343, 345, 370, 386, 437
Shickellamy, 118
Shingas, 57 ff., 64, 88, 397 f., 404, 437
Shipman, Fred Waldo, *The Indian Council of 1793*, 220
Shippensburg, Pa., 37 f., 217, 256, 260, 335; description of (1789), 236
Showalter, ————, 383, *438*
Shrewsbury, 324
Sichel's Tavern, 341
Sickeunk. *See* Salt Spring.
Sideling Hill, 216, 221, 256; description of the mountain road, 237
Siegvolck, Paul, 408
Silver Heels, *438*
Simcoe, Gov. John Graves, 304, 306, 310, 313, 315, 322, 349, 356, *438*
Simon, 248, *438*
Sinclair. *See* St. Clair.
Singer, Henry, 379
Sioux, 332
Six Mile Island, 276
Six Nations, 63 f., 70, 78, 96, 136, 332, 399, 405, *438*; bring Pontiac's war to an end, 82; claim "lordship" over lands on the Susquehanna, 85; Zeisberger's influence with, 86 f.; at the Treaty of Fort Stanwix (1768), 93 f.; called Mingos, 158; offer the Moravian Indians to the Chippewas and Ottawas "to make broth of," 168; indecision in their councils (1788), 227; given territory on the Grand River in Upper Canada, 361. *See also* Five Nations.
Skeenesborough (Whitehall), N. Y., 328 f., 331, 389, *438*

Skinner, ————, 237, *438*
Slippery Rock Creek, 255, 375
Smith, ———— (of Detroit), 253
Smith, ———— (of Cincinnati), 269
————, DeCost, *Martyrs of the Oblong and Little Nine*, 195, n., 199, n.
————, James, 66
————, Rev. John, 268, *438*
————, Thomas, 315, *438*
Snake (Mannittohaliechk, a Munsee), 226, 260, *438*
————, John (a Shawnee), 170, *438*
————, Thomas (a Shawnee), 170, *438*
———— Spring, Pa., 221, 238
Snip (a Mingo), 179 and n.
Society for Propagating the Gospel Among the Heathen (Moravian), 340, 362 f., 373, 384, 389
Society for the Propagation of the Gospel (English), 26
Sock, Will, 77, *438*
Sodus, Great, 303, *438*
Solomon, 227, *438*
Sorrel River, 327, *439*
South Bend, Ohio, 275, *439*
Spangenberg, Rev. Augustus Gottlieb, 37, 88, 215, 343, 400, *439*
————, Rev., Cyriacus, 237, *439*
Spear, Lt. (at Beaver Falls), 245
Sprenkel, Michael, 279
Spring Garden, 341
Squaw Campaign, the, 31, 131, 432, *439*
"Squirrel" (a French-Canadian), 250
Stadler's, 240
Standing Stone (Cayahaga River), 253, *439*
———— (Susquehanna River), 344, 421
Stanwix, Fort, 298, 300 f., 388, 436, *439*
————, Fort, Treaty of, (1768) 93, (1768) 96, n., (1784) 258
Staten Island, 388, *439*
Stedman, Philip, 353
Steelton, Pa., 235, 403, 409
Steg, Rev. John Michael, 237, *439*
Steiner, Abraham, 388, *439*; Journal, Bethlehem to Pettquotting (1789), 234-57
Steinmetz, ————, 241
Stites (Steitz), Major Banjamin, 268, 273, 288, 404, *440*
Stephanus (Weskhattees), 196, 252, *439*; cured of a spider bite, 213

Index

Stephanus, 228 f.
Steuben, Dr., 341, *440*
———, Fort, Indiana, 276 f., 280, 285, *440*
———, Fort, Ohio, 223, *440*
Steubenville, Ohio, 223, 440
Stevens, ———, 344, *440*
Stillwater Creek, 261, 330
Stinton, John, 73
Stoddartsville, Pa., 341, *436*
Stone's Station, 265, *440*
Stony Creek, 40, 410, *440*; the crossing of (1789), 240; a new ford discovered, 256
Storer, Charles, 295, 297, 314, *440*
Stoyestown, Pa., 256
Strasburg, Pa. *See* Upper Strasburg.
Strauss, Heinrich, 375
Stroudsburg, Pa., 71
Sugar Creek, 246, *440*
Sugar Loaves, Indiana, 182
Sugarloaf, Ont., 306, 309, *440*
Superior, Lake, 312, 332
Surinam, 89
Surpluss, ———, 311
Susquehanna River, 38, 70 f., 85, 256, 299, 300, 369; Heckewelder encounters drift ice in, 233; Steiner's description of the crossing below Harrisburg (1789), 235; Mortimer's description of the North Branch Valley (1798); West Branch, 381
Swanger, Harry E., *The Logans, Sons of Shikellamy*, 119, n.
Sweat ovens, 108 ff.
Sweet House. *See* Pomoacan.
Swigatschi. *See* Oswegatchie.
Symmes, John Cleves, 227, 268, 275, 287, 428, 439, *440*

Table Rock, Niagara, 357
Tamanend, 143
Tamaqua. *See* Beaver, King
Tanacharisson, 64
Taniwandi Creek. *See* Tonawanda.
Tanner, Rev. ———, 287
Tanner's Station, 276, 287, *440*
Tapan Bay, 296
Tarrytown, N. Y., 296
Tawa (Ottawa) River. *See* Maumee.
Tedpachxit. *See* Tetepachksi.
Teedyuscung, King, 64, 70, *440*, 445
Tenbrook, Henry, 303, 331, 371, *441*

Ten Mile Reach, 268
Têtes de Boule, 332
Tetepachksi, 152, 336, *441*
Thames, Battle of the, 258, 394
——— (La Tranche) River, Ont., 87, 258, 304 f., 309 f., 315, 334, 339, 365, 367, 393, *441*
Thirundigat. *See* Irondequoit.
Thomas (a Mahican), *441*; scalped at Gnadenhütten but alive, 195; death by drowning, 212
——— (Gutkigamen), 229, 252, 254, *441*
Thousand Islands, 323
Three Rivers, N. Y., 302, *441*
Three Sisters (Lake Erie), 309
Ticonderoga, N. Y., 329
Till, Rev. Jacob, 271, *441*
Tinker's Creek, 402
Tioga, Pa., 94, 370, 403, 409, *441*; description of (1798), 345 f.
——— (Chemung) River, 345 f., 403
Toads Town, 110
Tobias (Melimias), 193, 198, 229, 253, *441*; escapes from the "slaughter house at Gnadenhütten," 195
Tobyhanna Creek, 369
Toiondo. *See* Toronto.
Tonawanda, 351, *441*
——— Creek, 351, 370, *441*
Toronto (York), Ont., 322, 358, 360, 365, *441*, 446
Travels through the Interior Parts of North America (Carver), 47 and n., 402
Trenton, N. J., 78
Troy, N. Y., 330
Trueman, Major Alexander, 269 and n., 272, *442*
Trum, Simon, 241, *442*
Tscheschequannink. *See* Sheshequin.
Tschoop (Job). *See* Wassamapah.
Tsquallutene (Toads Town), 110
Tucker, ———, 206
Tunkhannock Creek, 369
Tupper, Gen. Benjamin, *442*; funeral of, at Marietta, Ohio, 263 f.
Turtle Creek, Pa., 242, 293
Tuscarawas, Indian town of, 37, 41, 50, 57, 66, 98, 101, 152, 164, 167, 336, 384, 387, 389 f., 397, 399, *442*
——— Plains, 246
——— River, 246, 253, 334, 384. *See also* Muskingum River.
Tuscarora Indians. 87, 305, *442*

Tuscarora Mt., 37
Tussey Mt., 238
Tutelo Indians, 87
Twakachshawsu, 54
Twelve Mile Island, 276
Twichtwee Indians, 318
Two Mile Run, 241
Tybout, ———, 186 and n.
Tygart's Creek, 289, *442*

Ulster, Pa., 96
Unami dialect, 44
Union City, Pa., 374
Unitas Fratrum. See Moravian Church.
United Brethren's Missionary Intelligencer, 90 f.
Upper Sandusky, 158, 162 and n., 170, 175, 196, 199, 201, 370, 387, 389, 393, 404, *442*; journey to (1781), 182 f.
——— ———, Battle of, 199
Upper Strasburg, Pa., 260, 335, 418, 438, *442*
Utica, 300, 436, 429

Vanango. *See* Venango.
Vanderburg, Henry, 269, 274, 278 f., *443*
Van den Benden, 292
Van Sweringen, ———, 261
Van Vleck, Henry, 302
——— ———, Isaac, 302
Venango, 68, 222, 230, 253, *443*
Vermilion River, 253
Vigo, ———, 269
Vincennes, 158, 222, 259, 269, 271 f., 274, 279, 290 f., 388, 419, *443*; Indian treaty at (1792), 280 ff.
Virgin Bottom, 227 f.
Vocabularium Barbaro-Virgineorum, 44
Volga River, 226

Wabash Indians, 135
——— Island, 279
——— River, 222, 258 f., 273, 279 f., 282 ff., 294, 336, 388
Wadsworth, James, 349, *443*
Wajomick. *See* Wyoming.
Waketameki, 111, 121, 390, 438, *443*
Waldhauer, ———, 241, *443*
Walhandi, 389
Walhonding River (White Woman's Creek), 182, 247, 292, 336, 370, 445
Walker, Col., 142
Walker brothers, 276

Walking Purchase ("the long walk"), 168
Wallace, A. F. C., *Origins of Iroquois Neutrality*, 63, n.
———, Paul A. W., *Conrad Weiser*, 73, n., 168, n., 342, n.
———, William, 190, *443*
Walthour's Fort. *See* Waldhauer.
Wampano Indians, 87
Wangomen, 94 ff., *443*
Wapanachki, name given to Heckewelder, 291
Washington, George, 149, 265, n., 287, 388; instructions to troops after the massacre at Gnadenhütten, 199
Washington, Ky., 267
———, Pa., 220, 231, 244, 402, *445*; description of (1792), 261. *See also* Catfish.
———, Fort, 264, 268, 270, 273, 286, 288, 291 f., 406, *443*
——— Borough, Pa., 76
Washington and Jefferson College, 293, 402
Waterford (Le Boeuf), Pa., 374, 376, 382 and n.
Watson's, 328
Wawiachteno. *See also* Wea, Eel River Indians.
Wawiapiechenwa. *See* Blue Jacket.
Wawundochwalend, 54
Wayne, Gen. Anthony, 292, 294, 313, 316, 334, 405
Wayomick. *See* Wyoming.
Wea (Wawiachteno) Indians, 259, 269, 283, 331, 429, 443, *444*; funeral of a Wea chief at Cincinnati, 272; massacre of, at Vincennes, 281; funeral of another Wea chief at Cincinnati, 288; name given to Capt. Prior, 290. *See also* Eel River Indians.
Weapicamikunk. *See* Tetapachksi.
Weber, Rev. ———, 215, *444*
Websters, 256
Wechnas, 254 f.
Wechquetank, 76, 390 f., 412, *444*; Moravian Indians escape from, 71 ff.
Weiser, ———, 270
———, Conrad, 36, 400, *444*; with Zinzendorf in the Wyoming Valley, 341
Weiss, Jacob, 78, 81
———, Lewis, 78
Weissport, Pa., 83, 396
Welhick-Tuppeek. *See* Schönbrunn.

Index

Wellbank, Capt., 314, 319, *444*
Welling. *See Everlasting Gospel.*
Wells, Squire ———, 221
———, Charles, 293
———, William, 271, 274, 278, 284, 410, *444*
Wellsburg, Ky., 403
———, W. Va., 400; description of (1792), 261
Welochalent. *See* Anton (Welochalent).
Weskhattees, 440
Wesley, P. O., Pa., 395
West Hickory, Pa., 226, 411
West Middlesex, Pa., 437
West Pittston, Pa., 437
West Point, 331, 382; description of (1793), 296
Wetterhold, Capt. John Jacob, 73 f.
Weygand, John, 204, 388, *444*
Wheeling, W. Va., 135 f., 157, 222, 227, 231, 244, 292, 447; description of (1788), 224; description of (1792), 261
——— Creek, 231
White, Judge, 301
White Eyes, Capt. Joseph, 335 f.
——— ——— (Koquethagachton), 41, 43, 104, 142, 144 f., 148 ff., 156, 159, 394, *444*; declares for the Americans, 131 f.; keeps the Delawares in line with American policy, 151 f.
——— ——— Town, 335, *445*
White Indians, 332
——— River, Indiana, 87, 284, 393
——— Woman's Creek, 247, *445*. *See also* Walhonding Creek.
Whitehall. *See* Skeenesborough.
Whitestown, N. Y., 300 f.
Wiachteno. *See* Wea.
Wialusing. *See* Wyalusing.
Wiandot. *See* Wyandot.
Wickham, Capt., 303
Wilbank. *See* Wellbank.
Wild Oats Indians. *See* Menominee.
Wilhelm. *See* Chilloway, Bill.
Wiling. *See* Wheeling.
Wilkes-Barre, Pa., 70, 84, n., 341 f., 345, 369, 404, *445*, *446*. *See also* Wyoming.
Wilkinson, Gen. James, 259, 264, 268, 270, 272 ff., 287, 409, *445*
Willeby's, 374
William Henry. *See* Killbuck (Gelelemend).
Williams, ———, 264

Williams, Isaac, 242, *445*; guides Heckewelder from Pittsburgh to Pettquotting (1789), 244 ff.
———, Nathan, 312, *445*
Williamsburg, N. Y., 348 f., 418, *445*
Williamson, Col. David, 152, 185, *445*; escapes after the Battle of Upper Sandusky, 199; meets Heckewelder (1788), 220
———, Capt. Charles, 360, *445*; develops a large settlement in the vicinity of Bath, N. Y., 346 f.; founds Williamsburg, N. Y., 348 ff.
Williamstown (Williamsburg), W. Va., 264, 281
Wills Mt., Pa., 238, *445*
Wilmington, Del., 378
Wenternute's Tavern, 305
Wilson, James, 231, *445*
———, William, 228, 230, 305 f., 312 f., 315, 317
Winchester, Va., 229
Windgap, Pa., 341, 414
Wingenund, 144, 170, 182 f., *446*
Winnebago Indians, 332
Winona, Ont., 360, 431
Wioming. *See* Wyoming.
Wisconsin Indians, 332
Wistar, Caspar, 385
Wisthof, ———, 243
Wolf's Creek, 262
——— Mt., (Broad Mt.), 341
Wolfsburg, Pa., 256
Womelsdorf, Pa., 256
Wood Creek, 301 f., 320, 371, 400
Wooster, Ohio, 384, 390
Wulalowechan. *See* Adam.
Wyalusing, 72, 76, 83, 85, 89, 93, 96, 101, 344 f., 370, 409, *446*
——— Creek, 85
Wyandot Indians, 98, 136, 138, 147, 170, 311, 315, 318 f., 332, 367, *446*; invite the Moravians to settle in the Muskingum country, 96; war parties (1780), 134; an example of "high-mindedness," 161 ff.; take Heckewelder prisoner, 175; bring complaints against the Moravians, 196
Wygand. *See* Weygand, John.
Wyolutimunk (Kuilutamen), 369
Wyoming, 74, 83 f., 89 f., 92 f., 369, 405, *445*, *446*; massacre of (1763), 70. *See also* Wilkes-Barre.

Wyoming Hills, 341, *446*

Yellow Creek, 225, 397
Yellow Breeches Creek, 235, 403
York, Ont. *See* Toronto.
York (Yorktown), Pa., 146, 173, 220 f., 358, 387, *446*
Youghiogheny River, 242
Young, Rev. Michael, 167, 176, 183, 204, 248, 252, 304, 310, 368, 387 f., *446*
Youngman, Rev. John George, 176, 183, 204, *446*
Youngstown, Pa., 433

Zachary, *447*; murder of (1763), 72 f.
Zane, Ebenezer, 224, 231, 261, *447*
———, Jonathan, *447*
———, Silas, *447*

Zane's Trace, 421, 447
Zanesville, Ohio, 111, n., 384 f., 390, 408
Zeeney. *See* Zane.
Zeisberger, Rev. David, 72, 83 f., 90, 94 ff., 101, 105, 111, 142, 150, 157, 165, 176, 178, 182 f., 196, 201, 204, 215, 222, 230, 248 ff., 258, 312, 315, 339, 343, 368, 370, 373, 386 f., 389, 393 f., 396, 399, 400, 409, 411, *447*; adopted by an Onondaga chief, 86; a plot against his life, 158 ff.; conducts Indian school, 252
———, Rev. David, Jr., 340, *447*
———, Melchior, 28
Zimmerman, Michael, 240
Zinzendorf, Christian Renatus, 403, 434
———, Nikolaus Ludwig, Count von, 9, 21 ff., 28, 33 f., 214, *447*; visits the Shawnees in the Wyoming Valley, 341